ation

SEVENTH EDITION

WORLD POLITICS
Trend and Transformation

SEVENTH EDITION

Charles W. Kegley, Jr.
University of South Carolina

Eugene R. Wittkopf
Louisiana State University

Bedford/St. Martin's   Boston ♏ New York

World Politics:
Trend and Transformation, Seventh Edition

Library of Congress Catalog Card Number: 98-84989

Manufactured in the United States of America.

ISBN: 0-312-16657-5

Printing: 2   3   4   5   02   01   00   99

Executive Editor: James R. Headley
Project Director: Scott E. Hitchcock
Editorial Assistant: Brian Nobile
Design Director: Jennie R. Nichols
Production Editor: Douglas Bell
Production Manager: Barbara Anne Seixas
Project Coordination: Ruttle, Shaw & Wetherill, Inc.
Text Design: Joan Greenfield
Picture Editor: Joyce Deyo
Cover Design: Lucy Krikorian
Cover Art: Copyright © Terry Hoff/Jerry Leff Associates, Inc.
Cover Printer: Phoenix Color Corporation
Composition: Ruttle, Shaw & Wetherill, Inc.
Printing and Binding: R. R. Donnelley & Sons, Inc.

Published and distributed outside North America by:
MACMILLAN PRESS LTD
Houndmills, Basingstoke, Hampshire RG21 6XS and London.
Companies and representatives throughout the World.

ISBN: 0-333-75238-4

A catalogue record for this book is available from the British Library.

For information, write: Bedford/St. Martin's, 75 Arlington Street, Boston, MA 02116
(617-426-7440)

Acknowledgments

Acknowledgments and copyrights appear at the back of the book on pages 603–605, which constitute an extension of the copyright page.

About the Authors

CHARLES W. KEGLEY, JR. received his doctorate from Syracuse University. Currently, he is Pearce Professor of International Relations at the University of South Carolina. A past president of the International Studies Association (1993–1994), Kegley has held appointments at Georgetown University, the University of Texas, Rutgers University, and the People's University of China. He is the editor of *Controversies in International Relations Theory: Realism and the Neoliberal Challenge* (St. Martin's Press, 1995) and *The Long Postwar Peace* (HarperCollins, 1991), and has published extensively in scholarly journals. With Gregory A. Raymond, Kegley is the coauthor of *How Nations Make Peace* (St. Martin's/Worth, 1999), *A Multipolar Peace? Great-Power Politics in the Twenty-First Century* (St. Martin's Press, 1994), and *When Trust Breaks Down: Alliance Norms and World Politics* (University of South Carolina Press, 1990).

EUGENE R. WITTKOPF received his doctorate from Syracuse University. He is currently R. Downs Poindexter Distinguished Professor of Political Science at Louisiana State University. He has also held appointments at the University of Florida and the University of North Carolina at Chapel Hill. Wittkopf is author of *Faces of Internationalism: Public Opinion and American Foreign Policy* (Duke University Press, 1990), coeditor of the third editions of *The Future of American Foreign Policy* (St. Martin's/Worth, 1999) and *Domestic Sources of American Foreign Policy: Insights and Evidence* (Roman & Littlefield, 1999). He has also published extensively in professional journal literature. In 1997 he received the highest award given by Louisiana State University in recognition of faculty contributions to research and scholarship when he was named the LSU Distinguished Research Master of Arts, Humanities, and Social Sciences.

Together, Kegley and Wittkopf have coauthored and edited several texts and readers for St. Martin's Press, including *American Foreign Policy: Pattern and Process,* Fifth Edition (1996); *The Future of American Foreign Policy* (1992); *The Nuclear Reader: Strategy, Weapons, War,* Second Edition (1989); and *The Domestic Sources of American Foreign Policy* (1988). They are also the coeditors of *The Global Agenda: Issues and Perspectives,* Fifth Edition (McGraw-Hill, 1998).

For Jeannie—CWK

For Debra and Jonathan—ERW

Summary Table of Contents

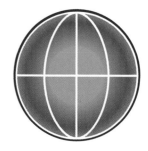

Contents

PART I: TREND AND TRANSFORMATION IN WORLD POLITICS

PART II: THE ACTORS AND THEIR RELATIONS

PART IV: GLOBAL CONFLICT AND ITS MANAGEMENT

Focus Boxes and Maps

LIST OF MAPS

Preface

The rapid changes in world politics in the brief period since the Cold War pose an enormous challenge to students, scholars, and policymakers alike. Without a single, overriding global issue to frame inquiry and understanding, there is little agreement about which dimensions of world politics are most important and the probable characteristics of the approaching century. This uncertainty necessitates thinking critically and theoretically about the forces of global change and continuity that increasingly influence our lives. That is our purpose in *World Politics: Trend and Transformation*. The book seeks to comprehensively cover evidence that describes how the world works and theories that explain what is unfolding. Its goal is to inform your understanding of relations among global actors, the historical developments and issues that underlie them, and the ways in which today's trends are likely to alter the global future.

In this, the seventh edition of *World Politics: Trend and Transformation*, we attempt to keep pace with the dramatic march of events and the reconstructed concepts and theories newly advanced to interpret contemporary international relations. This edition also introduces a number of stylistic revisions and a more user-friendly design—all in an effort to make our message more accessible to undergraduate students.

● ● ●

OVERVIEW OF THE SEVENTH EDITION

Part I: Trend and Transformation in World Politics

Part I explains the global, multilevel, multi-issue approach that frames the book's analyses. Chapters 1 and 2 focus on the major tools of analysis and the realist and liberal theoretical traditions that most scholars and policymakers use to comprehend and discuss emerging trends and transformations in world politics. The terminology and theories introduced here are drawn on throughout the rest of the book to characterize, clarify, and conceptualize contemporary world politics.

Part II: The Actors and Their Relations

Part II investigates the principal actors on the world stage. Because states command particular attention, we concentrate on their foreign policy decision-making processes and the rational choice and other theories that seek to account for how states conduct their foreign relations. Great-power rivalries, as played out in three global conflicts of the twentieth century, are emphasized in this section, as is an updated discussion of the changing place of the Global South and its struggle to close the gap between rich and poor countries. We also examine the expanding role of nonstate actors on the global stage—intergovernmental organizations (IGOs) as well as nongovernmental organizations (NGOs) such as ethnopolitical groups, religious movements, terrorists, and multinational corporations—and the ways in which their activities are accelerating the globalization of international relations and eroding the sovereign power of governments.

Part III: The Politics of Global Welfare

Part III analyzes issues related to material welfare. States' changing positions in the world political economy are given special attention, with trade and monetary issues featured. The globalization of the international political economy through the integration of national economies, trade, information, production, and labor, and the challenge globalization poses to states' autonomy, are put into perspective. So, too, are the dynamics of demographic changes and their effects on international politics, and the controversies surrounding preservation of the earth's ecological system.

Part IV: Global Conflict and Its Management

Part IV explores the perennial issues regarding the search for peace and security. Threats caused by recent trends in armed conflicts within states, the factors spurring preparations for national defense, the changing national security strategies of the great powers, the exercise of coercive diplomacy, and the management of crises are some of the problems covered. This section also compares the various paths to peace prescribed by the realist and liberal theoretical traditions.

Part V: Toward the Twenty-First Century

We conclude with a discussion of how underlying trajectories in world politics might influence future trends. We discuss how today's world will affect tomorrow's, asking questions about the ways contemporary trends will shape the policy problems and issues that today's students—the policymakers and citizens of tomorrow—will face in the twenty-first century.

● ● ●

CHANGES IN THE SEVENTH EDITION

Many global changes have taken place in the thirty months since the publication of the sixth edition. They required us to revisit every passage in the book and integrate the latest developments with the most current information available as this edition went to press. In addition, we sought to expand the coverage by including, where appropriate, the rise of new issues on the global agenda and new departures in theory that attempt to interpret the transformed setting. In addition to capturing the texture of global politics on the eve of the twenty-first century, the seventh edition has been rewritten to help readers better understand a complex subject; to make the intellectual journey easier, you will now find:

- **Chapter topics and themes.** We begin each chapter with an organizational outline that lists the major ideas discussed, in the order in which they are presented, and in language that is more descriptive of the contents than the chapter headings and subheadings.

- **Abridged chapter titles.** To better describe the contents of each chapter, the titles have been condensed and put in phraseology that the reader can immediately comprehend. Running heads on the top of consecutive pages further assist locating the topics addressed in the text.

- **Dramatic full-color design.** New maps, photographs, illustrations, and tables have been added to heighten interest and to help students interpret and remember the latest information and key concepts.

- **Marginal glossary terms and definitions.** To aid readers' comprehension, selected key terms are defined directly in the margins on the pages where they appear. This new aid is intended to elaborate and explain, in alternate language, the terminology discussed in the text itself, so that the reader can readily understand, or be reminded of, a phrase or word that might otherwise be unfamiliar.

- **Captions.** All maps, figures, and photos now have informative captions to instruct readers about their meaning and importance.

- **Comprehensive glossary terms.** Key terms that are part and parcel of the vocabulary of world politics are highlighted in **bold face,** listed at the end of each chapter in the order in which they appear, and reassembled *with definitions* in a glossary at the end of the book for easy cross-referencing.

- **Footnotes.** To make the text material as easy to follow as possible, footnotes have been eliminated and the critical information formerly introduced in footnotes has now been integrated directly into the text.

- **Suggested reading.** At the end of each chapter, students are provided with a select list of authoritative and current books and articles to consult for further information or to use as a starting place for conducting further research on the topics and themes discussed in each chapter.

- **Where on the World Wide Web?** This new feature lists major Internet web sites on which readers can locate additional late-breaking information on the topics discussed in each chapter. Many site references also include suggested activities for further learning and research.

Beyond changes in design and pedagogy, substantial changes have been made in the organization and contents of the book.

- Chapter 1: Our introductory chapter, "Exploring Twenty-First-Century World Politics," opens with a provocative story to show readers why they should explore the topics introduced. (Similarly, many other chapters now begin with a message to stimulate interest.) The chapter has been reorganized to integrate a discussion of the ways peoples' perceptions of international affairs color their often inaccurate images of international realities. The chapter has also been rewritten to more sharply define the multi-level, multi-issue approach of the book; it includes an explicit definition of the three levels of analysis (individuals, states, and the global system) that is relied on to organize much of the interpretation of particular aspects of world affairs. The chapter concludes with a select list of questions that identifies some of the major issues that are discussed throughout the remainder of the text.

- Chapter 2: "Rival Theoretical Interpretations of World Politics" has been reorganized to highlight the two major theoretical interpretations of world politics: the realist and liberal traditions, including their recent neorealist and neoliberal variants. The presentation ties rival theories to concrete global issues more closely, and links particular issues and trends to the other theoretical schools that directly address them.

- Chapter 4: "Great-Power Rivalries and Relations" has been revised to summarize, in the context of the great powers' long-term evolving relationships, forecasts about the likely twenty-first-century character of these relations as the ratio of power and resources among them undergoes a transition.

- Chapter 5: "The Plight and Policy of the Less Developed Global South" brings to bear greater coverage of the rapid economic development of the rising new industrial economies and formerly communist countries in transition. It also extends the indications of the widening gap between the rich and poor *within* the Global South by elaborating on how the globalization of trade, investment, and information is altering conditions within, and the policies of, Global South winners and losers.

- Chapter 6: "Universal and Regional Intergovernmental Organizations (IGOs)" presents the profound changes in the growth, structure, and goals of intergovernmental organizations, concentrating on the reorganized United Nations and European Union as examples.

- Chapter 7: "Nongovernmental Actors on the World Stage" greatly expands and updates the activities of ethnopolitical groups and indigenous peoples, and sharpens the discussion of the impact of nonstate actors such as religions, terrorists, and multinational corporations on the globalization of world politics and the devolution of states' sovereign authority and power.

- Chapter 8: "Trade and Monetary Issues in a Globalized Political Economy" has been completely reorganized to accentuate how the growth of international trade is transforming the globalized market at the same time that it is undercutting monetary stability. The prospects for sustained prosperity, free trade, and the control of currency and banking crises are now evaluated in light of recent institutional changes (such as the European Union's new "euro" common currency) by comparing the perspectives of commercial liberalism, mercantilism, and hegemonic stability theory on the probable ways politics and markets will intersect in the twenty-first-century international political economy.

- Chapter 9: "Globalization and the Impact of Vanishing Borders" has been reconfigured and expanded to capture the heated debate about the costs and benefits of globalization. To frame the presentation, new material portraying the death of distance and integration of a borderless global village has been added. Contrasting evaluations of the globalization of information, investments, currencies, production, and labor have been sharpened to illustrate the ways in which different members of the international community gain and lose from the rise of an interdependent global marketplace.

- Chapter 11: "Ecological Security and the Preservation of the Global Commons" has been revised to capture the latest information regarding global challenges to environmental preservation and the problems and possibilities of balancing competing demands in a world poorly organized to address transnational issues. Coverage includes institutional efforts, such as the 1997 Kyoto Protocol on global warming, to manage the common ecological problems facing humanity.

- Chapters 12 and 13: "Armed Conflict between and within States" and "The Changing Character of Military Power and National Security" have both benefited from the revisions of the analysis of different types of warfare and of the preparations for war by states to increase their military capabilities. To give the rise of civil wars and the demise of wars *between* states in recent years their just due, for example, the coverage of the causes of internal rebellions within fragile and failing states has been expanded. Likewise, the revolution in military technology and the proliferation of new ways of waging warfare, as well as their consequences for states' national security, is emphasized. In addition, the comparative analysis of the great powers' new national security strategies has been thoroughly revised to take account of their new doctrines and policies on the eve of the twenty-first century.

- Chapter 14: "The Use of Coercive Diplomacy for Defense, Deterrence, and Bargaining" has been expanded to include how states exercise influence with weapons and by methods short of war. New sections better cover the use of military intervention for humanitarian and peacekeeping purposes, states' growing use of economic sanctions as a method of coercion, and diplomatic negotiation as a substitute method for conflict and crisis management.

- Chapters 15 and 16: "The Realist Road to Security through Alliances, the Balance of Power, and Arms Control" and "The Liberal Institutional Paths to Peace through Law, Integration, and Democratization" have been recast to give greater attention to the place of human rights, ethics, war crimes, and the threat of failed and failing states in the equation that determines the preservation of peace or its collapse. New material also brings up to date recent developments within the United Nations and the "enlargement" of the European Union and NATO, the wave of recently reached disarmament agreements, and the shifting geostrategic balance of power as a result of the new alignments among the great powers and the threat of nuclear proliferation following nuclear tests by India and Pakistan.

● ● ●

MULTIMEDIA COMPANION

World Politics: Trend and Transformation is accompanied for the first time by an interactive Web site <www.worthpublishers.com/kegley7>. This learning component for instructors and students includes chapter outlines, summaries, learning objectives, teaching suggestions, Internet applications, and suggested materials for inclusion, such as transparency masters of the major maps and figures that appear in the book or that are available elsewhere to supplement the text. For students, the Web site offers Web links, interactive activities, and chapter quizzes.

● ● ●

INSTRUCTOR'S RESOURCE MANUAL AND TEST BANK

The seventh edition of *World Politics* is also supported by an extensive *Instructor's Resource Manual and Test Bank*. The manual includes chapter outlines, lecture guides, and a test bank containing over five hundred essay and multiple-choice questions. A computerized version of the test-bank portion of the manual is also available in formats for DOS, MAC, and Windows.

• • •

ACKNOWLEDGMENTS

Many people have contributed to the goal of making the seventh edition the most timely and useful version of *World Politics* since the book was first published in 1981. In addition to the many people named in previous editions, we wish to acknowledge the special assistance and advice provided by those who have helped to make this, a leading text, even better.

We greatly appreciate the constructive and supportive comments and suggestions that were offered by the reviewers of the seventh edition. In particular, we single out for providing expert evaluations of the treatment in their areas of specialization: David P. Forsythe, University of Nebraska; Ted Robert Gurr, University of Maryland; and Neil R. Richardson, University of Wisconsin. We thank the following individuals for their constructive critiques of the manuscript: Khalil Dokhanchi, University of Wisconsin-Superior; Manochehr Dorraj, Texas Christian University; S. Maggie Hanson, Northwestern University; Lynn Kuzma, North Dakota State University; Juliet Kaarbo, University of Kansas; Kelechi A. Kalu, University of Northern Colorado; Larry Martinez, California State University-Long Beach; Clark D. Mueller, University of North Alabama; Jeffrey Pickering, Kansas State University; Maria Sampanis, University of California-Davis; Bob Switky, State University of New York-Brockport; and Nina Tannenwald, Brown University.

We also express our gratitude to Lynn Kuzma at North Dakota State University and Greg Raymond at Boise State University who collected sites for the "Where on the World Wide Web?" chapter feature. Lynn Kuzma also contributed her talents to the development of *World Politics PLUS*⊕.

At St. Martin's/Worth, our new Political Science Editor James Headley, President Susan M. Driscoll, and Director of Production Michael Weinstein are to be thanked for applying their own talents and their staff's to so professionally produce a redesigned publication with many new stylistic features. Doug Bell, our production editor, exercised professionalism throughout the production process that brought this edition into print. In addition, Tom Conville and the staff at Ruttle, Shaw & Wetherill, Inc., as well as Susan McIntyre, our copy editor, contributed significantly to the preparation, polish, and production of the book.

Beyond the St. Martin's/Worth staff and their associates, we are pleased to acknowledge the following individuals for their contributions: Leann Brown, Sarah Buchanan, Sallie Buice, Steven Campbell, Roger Coate, Ruth Cooper, Jonathan Davidson, Margaret Hermann, Fernando Jimenez, Christopher Kautz, John Kinnas, Christina Payne, Don Puchala, Gregory Raymond, Joseph Reap, Alpo Rusi, Sten Rynning, Zerik Smith, Harvey Starr, Homer Steedley, Rodney Tomlinson, Jeannie Weingarth, Franke Wilmer, Jonathan Wilkenfeld, and Zhiqun Zhu.

Charles W. Kegley, Jr.
Eugene R. Wittkopf

WORLD POLITICS
Trend and Transformation

SEVENTH EDITION

CHAPTER 1

Exploring Twenty-First-Century World Politics

•••
Great things are achieved by guessing the direction of one's century.

—GIUSEPPE MAZZINI,
Italian political leader,
1848

•••
We refer, awkwardly, to the "post-Cold War era," as if our brave new world could be defined by the era that preceded it. Our new world has no name, for it is still in a state of becoming, not yet being. History will record the mid–1990s not as a post-revolutionary period but as the mid-point of an era of revolutionary upheaval in the wake of the Cold War.

—ROBERT L. HUTCHINS,
Director, *Woodrow Wilson International Center for Scholars, 1996*

CHAPTER TOPICS AND THEMES

■ The challenge of investigating international affairs

■ How perceptions influence images of reality

■ Organizing images to conduct inquiry: Actors, issues, and their interactions

■ Investigating world politics from different levels of analysis: Individuals, states, and the global system

■ Pathways to discovery: The book's approach

■ Facing the future: Key questions to confront

Picture yourself returning home from a week's vacation on an island where you had no access to the news. You enjoyed the peace and quiet, but now you are curious about what happened while you were away. As you pick up the newspapers piled outside your door, headlines catch your eye. They tell you that in the short time you were gone, leaders of the Group of Seven (G-7) major industrial democracies concluded a historic summit, at which they included Russia as a full participant for the first time. They also squabbled over global warming, prodded Middle East countries to resume peace negotiations, denounced human cloning, and celebrated the trade cooperation that had accelerated economic growth. The following day's headlines report that the French president, Jacques Chirac, attacked the United States as "one of the world's largest polluters" and criticized the U.S. resistance to meeting targets for reducing greenhouse gases. The next day's headlines proclaim that seventy heads of state gathered at the United Nations to discuss the lack of progress on environmental issues in the five years since the Earth Summit in Rio de Janeiro.

Turning to CNN, you then hear that the Dow Jones industrial average tumbled nearly 200 points the previous day—its worst point loss since the 1987 crash—as a perceived threat by Japan to dump U.S. bonds spurred a crush of profit taking. Surfing to another channel, you view images of Chinese troops marching in preparation for a symbolic show of force on the eve of the British transfer of Hong Kong to the sovereign control of the People's Republic of China, with the nervous announcer questioning whether democracy and civil liberties would survive in that prosperous city-state. Perplexed, you turn off the television and connect to the Internet where you learn that another terrorist bombing incident just occurred in Northern Ireland, that weapons proliferation continues to expand through the vigorous growth of exports of advanced weapons and technologies, and that new civil wars erupted in Albania, Cambodia, and Zaire. You also read that the international community's response to stop the flood of refugees seeking to flee the starvation and genocide was once again limited and feeble.

Suddenly, the temptation to wish that the world—this kind of chaotic and changing world—would just "go away" is overwhelming. If only the world would stand still long enough for a sense of predictability and order to prevail. But alas, that does not appear likely. You cannot escape the world or control its turbulence, and you cannot single-handedly shape its direction.

The scenario just described is not hypothetical. The events reported actually occurred in July 1997 within a single week. Undoubtedly, many individuals experienced dismay, fear, and confusion. We are all a part of the world, and the world is an integral part of each of us. Hence, if we are to live adaptively amidst the fierce winds of global change, we must face the challenge of discovering the dynamic properties of world politics. Because every person is influenced increasingly by world events, all must confront the challenge of investigating how the global system works, how it influences how (and if) we will survive and, optimistically, prosper. Only through learning how our own decisions and behavior, as well as those of powerful governments and transnational actors, contribute to the global condition and how they all are in turn heavily conditioned by it will we, and all the globe's six billion residents, address what U.S. President Bill Clinton in 1993 defined as "the question of our time—whether we can make change our friend and not our enemy."

THE INVESTIGATIVE CHALLENGE

How can we best understand the political convulsions in the world that confront us almost daily? How can we anticipate their future significance? And how can we understand the factors and forces that most influence them? On the eve of the twenty-first century, we are being engulfed in futurist talk. We are forced to use unfamiliar language—"new century," "new millennium," "new world"—and to speculate, "what will the new world be like?" Will it be different? As global conditions change, will the human victims and beneficiaries change in the process? Or will the patterns of the past endure?

How can we visualize our probable human destiny and see beyond the confines of our immediate time? For beginners, it is important to appreciate the interaction of previous ideas and events with current realities. As philosopher George Santayana cautioned, "Those who cannot remember the past are condemned to repeat it." Similarly, British Prime Minister Winston Churchill advised, "The farther backward you look, the farther forward you are likely to see." Thus, to understand the dramatic changes in world politics today and to predict how they will shape the future, we will view them in the context of a long-term perspective that examines how the **international political system**— the patterns of interaction among world political actors—has changed and how some of its fundamental characteristics have resisted change. What do evolving diplomatic practices suggest about the current state of world politics? Are the dramatic changes that often have recently sent shock waves throughout the world clearing the way for a truly new twenty-first century world order? Or will these dramatic developments ultimately prove temporary, mere spikes on the seismograph of history?

We invite you to explore these questions with us. To begin our search, we introduce three concepts that can help us orient our effort.

Continuity, Change, and Cycles in World Politics

Every historical period is marked to some extent by change. Now, however, the pace of change seems more rapid and its consequences more profound than ever. To many observers, the cascade of events on the eve of the twenty-first century implies a revolutionary restructuring of world politics. Numerous integrative trends point to that possibility. The countries of the world are drawing closer together in communications, ideas, and trade, as the integration of national economies has produced a globalized market, forming interdependent bonds between countries and cultures. Globalization is changing the way the world works. Likewise, disintegrative trends are shaking the globe and restructuring the way it operates. The end of stability imposed by the **bipolar distribution of power** between the United States and the Soviet Union and their respective allies, the proliferation of conventional and unconventional weapons, global-environmental deterioration, and the resurgence of nationalism and ethnic conflict all portend a restructuring marked by disorder. The opposing forces of integration and disintegration point toward a transformation in world politics as extensive and important as the system-disrupting convulsions following World Wars I and II.

bipolar distribution of power
the division of the balance of power into two coalitions headed by rival military powers, each seeking to contain the other's expansion.

New global systems sometimes emerge quickly, when a single, global-shattering development alters prevailing conditions. That happened overnight when the nuclear age began on August 6, 1945, with the U.S. atomic bombing of Hiroshima. More recently, the dismantling of the Berlin Wall in November 1989 signaled the end of the Cold War system. As exuberant citizens chipped away at the last vestiges of a divided nation, Germany moved toward reunification for the first time in over forty years, and the post-Cold War era began.

transformation a change in the characteristic pattern of interaction among the most active participants in world politics of such magnitude that it appears that one "global system" has replaced another.

Distinguishing meaningful **transformations** (true historical watersheds) from ephemeral changes (those that gradually unfold with the passage of time but sometimes fail to last) is difficult. Transformations do not fall neatly into easily defined periods, signaling that one system has truly ended and a new one has begun. Still, major turning points in world politics usually have occurred at the end of major wars, which typically disrupt or destroy preexisting international arrangements. In this century, World Wars I and II stimulated fundamental breaks with the past, as each set in motion major transformations. The end of the Cold War was a historical breakpoint of no less epic significance. As U.S. President George Bush put it in 1992, the changes stimulated by the end of the Cold War were "of biblical proportions," providing countries an opportunity, for the first time since 1945, to rethink the premises underlying their interests, purposes, and priorities.

Despite all that is radically different in world politics, much remains the same. Indeed, "history usually makes a mockery of our hopes and expectations." Thus leaders must "question . . . the ways and areas in which the future is likely to resemble the past" (Jervis 1991–92).

How can we determine when an existing pattern of relationships gives way to a new international system? Following Stanley Hoffmann (1961), we will proceed by assuming that we have a new international system when we have a new answer to one of three questions: (1) *What are the system's basic units?* (e.g., states or transnational religious movements); (2) *What are the predominant foreign policy goals that these units seek with respect to one another?* (e.g., territorial conquest or material gain through trade); and (3) *What can these units do to one another with their military and economic capabilities?*

These criteria might lead us to conclude that a new system *has* emerged. First, new trade partnerships have been forged in Europe, North America, and the Pacific Rim, and these trading blocs may behave as unitary, or independent, actors as they compete with one another. Moreover, international organizations, such as the World Trade Organization and the European Union, now sometimes flex their political muscles in contests with individual states; and transnational religious movements, such as Islamic fundamentalism, challenge the **global system** itself (a system of **state** and/or national actors, autonomous political units whose people perceive themselves as unified by a common language, culture, or ethnic identity). At the same time, some states have disintegrated into smaller units. The Soviet Union has fragmented into fractious political entities searching for national identity and autonomy. Other national units could disintegrate as well—peacefully, like the former Czechoslovakia, or violently, like the former Yugoslavia.

> **state** an independent, territorially defined community in the global system administered by a sovereign government.

Second, territorial conquest is no longer the predominant goal of many states' foreign policies. Instead, their emphasis has shifted from traditional military methods of exercising influence to economic means. Meanwhile, the ideological contest between the democratic capitalism of the United States and the Marxist-Leninist communism of the Cold War-era Soviet Union no longer comprises the primary cleavage in international politics.

Third, the proliferation of weapons technology has profoundly altered the damage that states can inflict on one another. Great powers alone no longer control the world's most lethal weapons. Their economic well-being, however, is sometimes dependent on those with an increasing capacity to destroy.

The profound changes in units, goals, and capabilities of recent years have dramatically altered the ranking of states in the pecking orders that define the structure of international politics. Still, the hierarchies themselves endure. The *economic hierarchy* that divides the rich from the poor, the *political hierarchy* that separates the rulers from the ruled, the *resource hierarchy* that makes some suppliers and others dependents, and the *military asymmetries* that pit the strong against the weak all still shape the relations among states, as they have in the past. Similarly, the perpetuation of international **anarchy** in the absence of institutions to govern the globe, and chronic national insecurity continue to encourage preparations for war and the use of force without international mandate. Thus change and continuity coexist, with both forces simultaneously shaping contemporary world politics.

The interaction of constancy and change makes it difficult to predict whether the twenty-first century will bring a wholly new and different international system. What is clear is that this interaction will determine future relations among global actors. This, perhaps, explains why **cycles** so often appear to characterize world politics: Periodic sequences of events occur that resemble patterns in earlier periods. Because the emergent international system shares many characteristics with earlier periods, historically minded observers may experience *déjà vu*–the illusion of having already experienced something actually being experienced for the first time.

The challenge, then, is to observe unfolding global realities objectively in order to describe and explain them accurately, and hence to understand their future impact. This requires that we understand how images of reality shape our expectations. It also requires a set of tools for analyzing the forces of constancy and change that affect our world and that of the future. Thus, the remainder of this chapter will briefly examine the role that images of reality play in our understanding of world politics, and then will describe the theoretical orientation of the book. Chapter 2 will examine the theoretical perspectives we will use in this book to interpret trends and transformations in world politics.

• • •

HOW PERCEPTIONS INFLUENCE IMAGES OF REALITY

We all carry mental images of world politics—explicit or implicit, conscious or subconscious. But whatever our level of awareness, our images simplify "reality" by exaggerating some features of the real world while ignoring others. Thus we live in a world defined by our expectations and images.

These mental pictures, or perceptions, are inevitably distortions, as they cannot fully capture the complexity and configurations of even physical objects, such as the world itself (see Focus 1.1, pages 8 and 9). Thus many of our images of the world's political realities may be built on illusions and misconceptions. Even images that are now accurate can easily become obsolete if we fail to recognize changes in the world. Indeed, the world's future will be determined not only by changes in the "objective" facts of world politics but also by the meaning that people ascribe to those facts, the assumptions on which they base their interpretations, and the actions that flow from these assumptions and interpretations—however accurate or inaccurate they might be.

The Nature and Sources of Images

There is nothing harmful about simplifying views of the world. Just as cartographers' projections simplify complex geophysical space so we can better understand the world, each of us inevitably creates a "mental map"—a habitual way of organizing information—to make sense of a confusing abundance of information. Although mental maps are neither inherently right nor wrong, they are important because we tend to react according to the way the world appears to us rather than the way it is. How we *view* the world (not what it is really like) determines our attitudes, beliefs, and perhaps our behavior. Political leaders, too, are captives of this tendency. As political scientist Richard Ned Lebow (1981) warns, "Policymakers are prone to distort reality in accord with their needs even in situations that appear . . . relatively unambiguous."

Most of us—policymakers included—look for information that reinforces our preexisting beliefs about the world, assimilate new data into familiar images, mistakenly equate what we believe with what we know, and deny information that contradicts our expectations. We process information using *schematic reasoning*; that is, we rely on learned ways of psychologically perceiving new information and we interpret it in light of our memories (Rosenberg 1988). We use information shortcuts both to make political judgments and to help orient our attitudes and beliefs toward specific events and policy issues. A **schema** thus aids in the organization of information and shapes our perceptions of the world.

We organize information about the world to help us simplify it. Our goal is "to cope with an extraordinarily confusing world by structuring views about specific foreign policies according to [our] more general and abstract beliefs"

(Hurwitz and Peffley 1987). Our preexisting values and beliefs encourage us to accept some images as accurate while rejecting from consciousness others that are incongruent with our prior beliefs, a psychological conflict known as **cognitive dissonance** (see Festinger 1957). Thus our view of world politics depends not only on what happens in the world but also on how we interpret and internalize those events; our mental maps inevitably help to shape our dispositions toward world affairs.

People's perceptions of and reactions to conflicting or inconsistent information often differ because the act of viewing is not passive. The mind selects, screens, and filters what it perceives. Several factors influence our perceptions of politics:

- Our psychological needs, drives, and dispositions (e.g., trust or mistrust), which are ingrained in our personalities as a result of early childhood experiences.
- Our views of international affairs (e.g., tolerance or fear of cultural diversity) as filtered through the socialization or learning we receive as children.
- Our images of world history as shaped by the teachers and books to which we are exposed.
- Opinions about world affairs articulated by our frequent associates, such as close friends.
- Attitudes expressed by policymakers, political pundits, and others whose expertise we respect.
- Positions we occupy and roles we perform (student, parent, bureaucrat, policymaker, diplomat, etc.).

Tolerance of ambiguity and receptivity to new ways of organizing thinking vary among individuals and personality types. Some people are receptive to diversity and therefore better able than others to revise perceptual habits to accommodate new realities. Nevertheless, to some extent, we are all prisoners of the perceptual predispositions that have shaped us and that in turn shape our attitudes, beliefs, and images of world politics. This is why political **ideologies** tend to develop and attract adherents who gather to express their common beliefs.

The Role of Images in World Politics

We must be careful not to assume automatically that what applies to individuals applies to entire countries. Still, leaders' images of historical circumstances often predispose them to behave in particular ways toward others, regardless of "objective" facts. For instance, the loss of 26 million Soviet lives in the "Great Patriotic War" (as the Russians refer to World War II) created an exaggerated fear of foreign invasion, which caused a generation of Soviet policymakers to perceive U.S. defensive moves with considerable suspicion and often alarm. Similarly, the founders of the United States viewed eighteenth-century European power politics as "dirty," contributing to two seemingly contradictory tendencies later evident in U.S. foreign policy: (1) America's isolationist impulse (its disposition to withdraw from world affairs), and (2) its determination to reform the world in its own image. The former led the country to reject membership in the League of Nations after World War I; the latter gave rise to the U.S.

The Cartography of World Politics
Projections of Reality

These four maps depict the distribution of the earth's land surfaces and territory, but each portrays a different image. Each is a model of reality, an abstraction that highlights some features of the world while ignoring others, but all distort reality in one way or another. One distortion they all share is their depiction of the world, which is a sphere, as a flat surface. The difficulty cartographers face can be appreciated by trying to flatten an orange peel.

MAP 1.1

Orthographic Projection

The orthographic projection, centering on the mid-Atlantic, conveys some sense of the curvature of the earth by using rounded edges. The relationships among sizes and shapes are inevitably inaccurate in some places, but the distortions are less than in other representations.

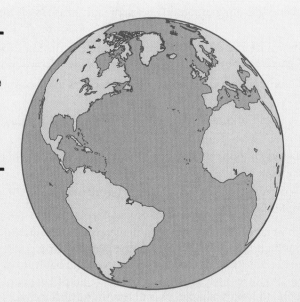

MAP 1.2

Mercator Projection

This Mercator projection, popular in sixteenth-century Europe, is a classic Eurocentric view of the world. It placed Europe at the center of the world and exaggerated the continent's importance relative to other land masses. Europe appears larger than South America, which is twice Europe's size, and two-thirds of the map is used to represent the northern half of the world and only one-third the southern half.

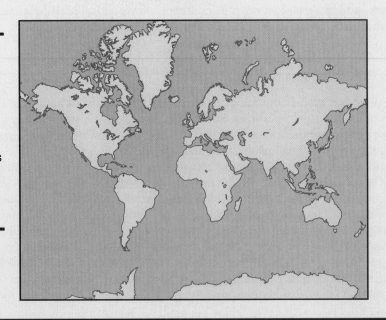

MAP 1.3

Peter's Projection

In the Peter's projection, each land mass appears in correct proportion and in its correct position in relation to all others. In contrast with most geographic representations, it draws attention to the less-developed countries of the Global South where more than three-quarters of the world's population lives today.

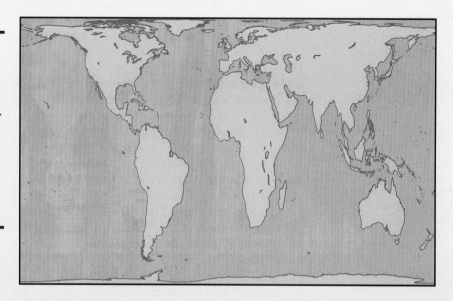

MAP 1.4

World Time View

This map is a modified south pole projection portraying the world's twenty-four standard time zones. Note that these zones often follow state borders rather than straight latitude lines. Knowledge of time-zone differences is critical in today's economically interdependent world.

SOURCE: IVN Communications, Inc.

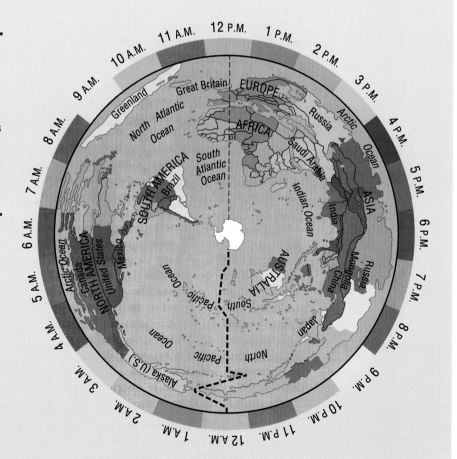

9

mirror images the tendency of
states and peoples in
competitive interaction to
perceive each other
similarly—to see others the
same way they see us.

globalist foreign policy after World War II, which committed the country to active involvement nearly everywhere on nearly every issue. Most Americans failed to recognize that others might regard such a far-reaching international policy position as arrogant or threatening; they saw only good intentions. As President Jimmy Carter once lamented, "The hardest thing for Americans to understand is that they are not better than other people."

Because leaders and citizens are prone to ignore or reinterpret information that runs counter to their beliefs and values, mutual misperceptions often fuel discord in world politics, especially when relations between countries are hostile. Distrust and suspicion arise as conflicting parties view each other in the same negative light—that is, as **mirror images** develop. This occurred in Moscow and Washington during the Cold War. Self-righteousness often leads one party to view its own actions as constructive but its adversary's responses as negative and hostile. When this occurs, conflict resolution is extraordinarily difficult, as the Cold War and the recurrent ethnic conflicts since illustrate. Thus fostering peace is not simply a matter of expanding trade and other forms of transnational contact, or even of bringing political leaders together in international summits. Rather, it is a matter of changing deeply entrenched beliefs.

Although our mental maps of world politics are resistant to change, change is possible. Overcoming old thinking habits sometimes occurs when we experience punishment or discomfort as a result of clinging to false assumptions. As Benjamin Franklin once observed, "The things that hurt, instruct." Dramatic events in particular can alter international images, sometimes drastically. The Vietnam War caused many Americans to adjust their previous images about the use of force in contemporary world politics. The defeat of the Third Reich and revelations of atrocities committed before and during World War II caused the German people to confront their past as they prepared for a democratic future imposed by the victorious allies. The use of atomic bombs against Japan in the waning days of World War II caused many to confront the horrors of modern warfare and the immorality of weapons of mass destruction. More recently, the unexpected collapse of communist rule in the Soviet Union and Eastern Europe prompted policymakers and political commentators alike to reexamine their assumptions about foreign policy priorities in a new, post-Cold War system. Often such jolting experiences encourage us to create new mental maps, perceptual filters, and criteria through which we may interpret later events and define situations.

As we shape and reshape our images of world politics and its future, we need to think critically about the foundations on which our perceptions rest. Are they accurate? Are they informed? Might they be adjusted to gain greater understanding and empathy? This rethinking is one of the challenges we face in confronting the world politics of the twenty-first century.

• • •

ORGANIZING IMAGES TO CONDUCT INQUIRY: ACTORS, ISSUES, AND THEIR INTERACTIONS

To predict which forces will dominate the future, we must think in multicausal terms. No trend or trouble stands alone; all interact simultaneously. The future is influenced by many determinants, each connected to the rest in a complex web of linkages. Collectively, these may produce stability by limiting the impact

When the world first read that in September 1996 the Taliban militia had taken control of the city of Kabul in Afghanistan, reactions were positive. A sort of peace—any peace—seemed preferable to a continuation of the genocidal butchery, forced migration, and fighting that had been going on for sixteen years. However, this view soon seemed quixotic as the Talibans decreed Islamic law, forced men to be bearded and women veiled from head to toe, and burned films and broke up television sets to prevent the spread of non-Islamic values. This kind of backlash against cultural diversity and globalization has become frequent across the globe.

of any single disruptive force. If interacting forces converge, however, their combined effects could accelerate the pace of change in world politics, moving it in directions not possible otherwise.

A Multilevel Perspective

Because world politics is complex and our images of it are often discordant, scholars differ in their approaches to understanding the contemporary world. In this book, we adopt a multilevel, multi-issue perspective, which frames the investigation by looking at: (1) the characteristics, capabilities, and interests of the principal "actors" in world politics (states and various nonstate participants in international affairs); (2) the principal welfare and security issues that populate the **global agenda;** and (3) the patterns of cooperation and contention that influence the interactions between and among actors and issues. As we probe these interactions, we will discover why **politics**—the exercise of influence to affect the distribution of particular values, such as power, prestige, or wealth— is the most pervasive and controversial aspect of international affairs.

We believe that a multi-level, multi-issue perspective is needed because the changing global political scene cannot be reduced to a simple vision focusing on a single set of issues. Because international affairs includes many types of actors and activities, a comprehensive worldview that takes all of them and

global agenda the primary issues, problems, and controversies on which states and humanity concentrate their attention and allocate resources to address.

politics to Harold Lasswell, "who gets what, when, how and why?"

their interactions into account is required. Such a perspective is useful, further-more, because it not only takes into account the interaction of constancy and change on the eve of the new millennium, but it also avoids dwelling on any particular events, countries, individuals, or other transitory phenomena whose long-term significance is likely to diminish. Instead, the perspective seeks to identify behaviors that cohere into general global patterns—trends and trans-formations that measurably affect global living conditions. Thus we explore the nature of world politics from a perspective that places general patterns into a larger, lasting theoretical context, providing the conceptual tools and theories that will enable us to interpret subsequent developments.

• • •

INVESTIGATING WORLD POLITICS FROM DIFFERENT LEVELS OF ANALYSIS

Our dynamic, multilayered perspective fits well with a distinction commonly used to understand world politics. Many international-relations scholars agree that world politics can best be understood by focusing on one (or more) of three levels. Known as **levels of analysis,** this classification distinguishes: (1) individ-uals, (2) states or other world political actors, and (3) the entire global system.

The **individual level of analysis** refers to the personal characteristics of humans, including average citizens whose behavior has important political consequences and those responsible for making important decisions on behalf of state and nonstate actors. Here, for example, we may properly locate the im-pact of individuals' images on their political attitudes, beliefs, and behavior, and explore the question of why each human being is a crucial part of the global drama, and why the study of world politics is relevant to our lives and fu-ture (see Focus 1.2).

The **state level of analysis** consists of the authoritative decision-making units that govern states' foreign policy processes and the internal attributes of those states (e.g., their type of government, level of economic and military power, and number of nationality groups), which both shape and constrain leaders' foreign policy choices. The processes by which states make decisions regarding war and peace and their capabilities for carrying out their decisions, for instance, fall within the state level of analysis.

The **global level of analysis** refers to interactions of states and nonstate global actors whose behaviors ultimately shape the international political sys-tem and the levels of conflict and cooperation that characterize world politics. The capacity of rich states to dictate the choices of poor states properly falls within the global level of analysis. So does the capacity (or incapacity) of the United Nations to maintain peace.

Examples abound of the diverse ways in which global trends and issues are the product of influences that originate at each level of analysis. Protectionist trade policies by an importing country, to make one illustration, increase the costs to consumers of clothing and cars and reduce the standard of living of cit-izens in the manufacturing states. Such policies are initiated by a *state* govern-ment (national level), but diminish the quality of life of *people* living both within the protectionist country and those living abroad (individual level), and reduce the level of *global* trade while threatening to precipitate retaliatory trade wars. Similarly, many international events need to take account of factors at each level if their causes and consequences are to be adequately understood. Of course, for some developments and issues, factors and forces emanating pri-

levels of analysis the different aspects of and agents in international affairs that may be stressed in interpreting world politics, depending on whether the analyst chooses to focus on "wholes" (the complete global system and large collectivities) or on "parts" (individual states or people) in explaining global phenomena.

Why You Matter to the Globe's Future and How You Can Make a Difference

Many people feel powerless, and question whether they can influence the ways events and developments in world politics affect their lives. That questioning itself can, and must, also be questioned. The world depends on how we act, and our actions can contribute positively to global welfare, providing we recognize our responsibilities and our true place in the overall scheme of things.

In the overall scheme, many philosophers have sought to explain why everyone matters, and why each decision and action matters in influencing the course of history. Part of the reason is because the whole world is composed of each of its parts, and each individual plays a part in shaping the globe's consensus about basic human values in the worldwide community. Alexander Pope expressed how we learn to see beyond our immediate selfish needs, to accept our moral obligations not only to ourselves and those closest to us but also to conceptions of justice that apply to everyone, when he wrote in *An Essay on Man:*

> God loves from Whole to Parts: but human soul
> Must rise from Individual to the Whole.
> Self-love but serves the virtuous mind to wake,
> As the small pebble stirs the peaceful lake;
> The center mov'd, a circle strait succeeds,
> Another still, and still another spreads,
> Friend, parent, neighbour, first it will embrace,
> His country next, and next all human race. . . .

"If you're not part of the solution, you're part of the problem" is an adage that speaks to our involvement in the making of a more just or unjust world. How, then, should we proceed? Passivity is not an alternative because, as the British author Edmund Burke reminds us, "The only thing necessary for the triumph of evil is that good men do nothing." To make a positive contribution, and set standards for a better world, *everyone* must take a stand. Dr. Tony Evans, an African American theologian, explains wisely why and how we should accept moral responsibilities to one another as global citizens if we want a more just world order.

The fact is that if you're a messed-up person and you have a family, you are going to contribute to a messed-up family. And if you're a messed-up person contributing to a messed-up family, and your family goes to church, then your messed-up family will contribute to a messed-up church.

And if you're a messed-up person contributing to a messed-up family contributing to a messed-up church, and your church is in a neighborhood, then your messed-up church will lead to a messed-up neighborhood.

And if you're a messed-up person contributing to a messed-up family contributing to a messed-up church leading to a messed-up neighborhood, and your neighborhood resides in a city, then your messed-up neighborhood will result in a messed-up city.

Now if you're a messed-up person contributing to a messed-up family contributing to a messed up church leading to a messed-up neighborhood resulting in a messed-up city, and your city resides in a county, then your messed-up city will cause a messed-up county.

And if you're a messed-up person contributing to a messed-up family, contributing to a messed-up church leading to a messed-up neighborhood resulting in a messed-up city residing in a messed-up county, and your county is part of a state, then your county will help create a messed-up state.

But that's not all. . . . If you're a messed-up person contributing to a messed-up family contributing to a messed-up church leading to a messed-up neighborhood resulting in a messed-up city residing in a messed-up county helping to create a messed-up state. . . . and your nation is part of the world, your messed-up country will leave us with a messed-up world!

So, if you want a better world composed of better countries, inhabited by better states, made up of better counties, composed of better cities inhabited by better neighborhoods, illuminated by better churches made up of better families, then we need to become better people. It all starts with personal responsibility! (Evans 1997, 2–3)

marily from one or two particular levels provide more analytical leverage than do those at the other(s). Accordingly, as we confront specific global issues in subsequent chapters, we will emphasize those levels of analysis that provide the best lens for viewing them. In the next section, we outline the path to discovery that *World Politics* will pursue.

• • •

PATHWAYS TO DISCOVERY: THE BOOK'S APPROACH AND ORGANIZATION

Our journey into the dynamics of world politics begins in Chapter 2 with an overview of the major realist and liberal theoretical traditions that scholars and leaders use most to interpret world politics. This provides the intellectual background for the description, explanation, and prediction of the issues and developments that are treated in the remaining chapters. Chapter 3 begins the analysis of actors, issues, and their interactions, with a close examination of foreign policy decision-making processes *within* states (which remain the principal actors in world politics). Chapter 3 also covers the individual level of analysis, as we consider the role of leaders in making foreign policy, but the bulk of the chapter addresses how other forces at the state or domestic level can constrain the impact of individuals.

We will then turn our attention to the actors in world politics and examine how their characteristics and capabilities affect their interests and influence in the world. **Great powers** (those wealthy countries with the biggest militaries) are the focus of attention in Chapter 4, "lesser powers" in Chapter 5; both inquiries fall primarily within the state level of analysis. In Chapters 6 and 7 we will extend this level to include **nonstate actors**—international organizations, multinational corporations, religious and enthnopolitical movements, and terrorist groups—that challenge the supremacy of states by either transcending or subverting states' sovereign control over their destinies.

The next group of chapters properly falls within the global system level of analysis. Here we shift attention to global issues and inquire into how the characteristics, capabilities, and interests of the principal actors in world politics affect interactions and outcomes of the principal welfare and security issues on the global agenda. Welfare issues—the so-called **low politics** of problems relating to economics, demography, and the environment—are the subjects of Chapters 8 through 11; Chapters 12 through 16 examine the so-called **high politics** of security issues—war and peace—that traditionally command attention on the global agenda.

great powers the most powerful countries, militarily and economically, in the global system.

nonstate actors all transnationally active groups other than states, such as organizations whose members are states and nongovernmental organizations whose members are individuals and private groups from more than one state.

low politics the category of global issues related to the economic, social, demographic and environmental aspects of relations between governments and people.

high politics those issues related to the military, security, and political relations of states.

• • •

FACING THE FUTURE: KEY QUESTIONS TO CONFRONT AT THE DAWN OF THE NEW MILLENNIUM

Chapter 17 concludes our inquiry into the trends and transformations comprising contemporary world politics. It draws on the ideas and information presented in earlier chapters in order to address ten questions regarding the global issues that will dominate political discourse during the next decade. We anticipate those questions here by posing several that will also inform our inquiry in the chapters that follow.

1. Are States Obsolete? The territorial state has been the primary actor in world politics for more than four centuries. The resurgence of nationalism throughout the world attests to the continuing quest by national independence movements for self-governance and statehood, as the principal drive of nationalistic enthnopolitical movements is to secure their own national existence within the (legally) impenetrable shell of state sovereignty. This motive explains why the United Nations had 166 member "states" in 1991 and 185 in 1997, and "because of ethnic divisions could one day end up with 400 or more," even if many of these "states" are likely to be fragile (Peirce 1997).

In some respects, the territorial state is flourishing because it is still needed to give people identity, raise taxes, provide safety nets for the needy, protect the environment, and provide military security. But in other aspects it is dying because "it can no longer fulfill some of the most important traditional functions" (Hassner 1968). In fact, many have proclaimed "the end" of **state sovereignty** (Guéhenno 1995) and its supreme authority in the face of growing challenges from home and abroad. To them, "A wide variety of forces has made it increasingly more difficult for any state to wield power over its people and address issues it once considered its sole prerogative. Among these forces are the communications revolution, the rise of transnational corporations, increasing migration, economic integration, and the global nature of economic and environmental problems" (Stanley Foundation 1993).

"While states may not be about to exit from the political stage, and while they may even continue to occupy center stage, they do seem likely to become vulnerable and impotent" (Rosenau 1995). Can the state cope with the challenges it now faces? Auguste Comte, a nineteenth-century French political philosopher, argued that societies create institutions to address problems and meet human needs. When they are no longer able to perform these functions, they disappear. Today, as the managerial capabilities of states fail to inspire confidence, their future seems increasingly in doubt.

2. Is Interdependent Globalization a Cure or a Curse? Global **interdependence**—the degree to which the quality of life within states is dependent on conditions in other states—lies at the heart of the external challenges states now face. As the range of global issues has expanded and the integration of national economies has created a globalized market, interdependence in a borderless world has reduced states' ability to govern their affairs. Mutual vulnerabilities reduce states' autonomy by curtailing their control of their own fates.

From one perspective, an awareness of the common destiny of all, alongside the declining ability of many sovereign states to cope with global problems through national means, may energize efforts to put aside interstate competition. Conflict, according to this reasoning, will recede, as humanity begins to better recognize how little protection national borders and oceans provide them against the multiple dangers arising from the global revolution in travel, communications, and trade. Consequently, states *must* cooperate, and therefore we should welcome the continued tightening of interstate linkages.

From another, more pessimistic perspective, interdependence will not lead to transnational collaboration. Regardless of how compelling the need or how rewarding the benefits, contact and mutual dependence will breed enmity, not amity. Intertwined economies will sour relations more often than sweeten them. Under conditions of fierce competition, scarcity, and resurgent nationalism, the temptation to seek isolation from foreign economic dependence by creating barriers to trade and other transactions may be irresistible. The temptation to achieve political benefits by military force will also continue. Thus the tightening web of global interdependence foretells danger as well as opportunity.

3. Is Technological Innovation a Blessing or a Burden? "The dynamics of globalization unleashed by technology," James N. Rosenau (1995) concludes, "are the dominant catalyst in world affairs." The consequences, however, are not cer-

state sovereignty under international law, the status of states as equals in that they are within their territory and subject to no higher external authority.

interdependence a situation arising when the behavior of international actors greatly affects others with whom they have contact, so that the parties to the exchange become mutually sensitive and vulnerable to the others' actions.

tain. Like interdependence, technological innovations solve some problems but cause others. Not only can technological innovations create new ways of preventing or treating disease, but they can also enhance the sophistication and destructiveness of weapons of war. As Meg Greenfield (1997) correctly reminds us, "Illness, ignorance and want have obviously not been eliminated. But millions upon millions of people living today, who not all that long ago would have been direly afflicted by all three, will never know them in anything like their once common form if they know them at all." Yet no generation but ours has faced the kind of random violence made possible and accessible by modern weapons technology.

Discoveries in microelectronics, information processing, transportation, energy, agriculture, communications, medicine, and biotechnology profoundly affect our lives and shape our future (Dyson 1997). They have united the globe into a single international market and common culture, while paradoxically breaking down people's sense of citizenship and community (Barber 1995). "There appears to be a fundamental lag between the current rate of technological change and the rate of adjustment to these changes among decision makers" (Blumenthal 1988). Technological change requires proper and constructive management, but is this possible in a selfish, disintegrative world in which science and technology are often exploited without serious consideration of their impact and ethical consequences?

4. Will Geo-Economics Supersede Geopolitics? Throughout modern history, states have competed with one another militarily for position and prominence in the hierarchy of international power. For more than three centuries, world politics has been largely a record of preparing, waging, and recovering from interstate war. Military might was equated with prestige and influence, and military conquest became the means to economic as well as political preeminence.

To some, the battlefield in world politics has shifted to economic issues. National destinies will be determined by commercial competition, not military conquest. If issues of **geo-economics** (the distribution of wealth) become more important than conventional issues of **geopolitics** (the distribution of political and military power), will states' foreign policies also change? If wealth is converted into political muscle, nationalistic pride can give rise to competition and self-assertiveness. But economic interdependence and tight commercial relationships can also collapse into trade disputes and political rivalry. Nevertheless, the apparent shift of priorities to the economic dimensions of world politics is certain to shape the distribution of twenty-first-century global power. This shift is also likely to increase the porousness of national borders.

5. What Constitutes Human Well-Being on an Ecologically Fragile Planet? The worldwide quest for **human rights** requires people and governments to define and distinguish the fundamental values to which they are entitled. Throughout history, many have placed money and prosperity as their first priority. However, that value preference has been challenged, and the once popular **limits-to-growth proposition**—the belief that the world cannot forever increase its productive capacity—has been replaced by the maxim of sustainability. Sustainability emphasizes "the growth of limits" in the global *ecology* (the total pattern of relations between organisms and their environment on earth). Thus **sustainable development** means learning to live off the earth's interest without encroaching on its capital, in order that the planet can continue to provide the means to life that makes the pursuit of other values such as political freedom and religious principles possible.

geo-economics the relationship between geography and the economic conditions and behavior of states that define their levels of production, trade, and consumption of goods and services.

geopolitics the relationship between geography and politics and their consequences for states' national interests and relative power.

limits-to-growth proposition the theory that the earth's capacity to support life has natural limits and that if important resources such as fresh water are depleted, many will perish.

As we consider the future, we must ask ourselves whether technological innovation is inevitably the answer to our concerns. Although we are now able to send satellites into space and receive photos from planets we will never visit, we remain unable to eliminate hatred or aggression, or to achieve peace on earth.

Gross national product (GNP)—the total monetary value of goods and services produced in a state during a specified period, usually a year—is the common measure of national economic well-being. It is an index of relative standards of living "closely bound up with human welfare. . . . Human welfare has dimensions other than the economic one. But it is widely held that the economic element is *very* important, and that the stronger the economy the greater the contribution to human welfare" (Daly and Cobb 1989). Indeed, many states' values are highly materialistic; money is perceived as a means to a secure and happy national existence—almost a human rights entitlement.

There are, of course, serious problems with this conception. Beyond the danger that conspicuous consumption and greed pose to other values, a state's increasing economic output has different consequences for poor societies than for rich ones. To the inhabitants of most Global South countries, growth in GNP may mean more food, better housing, improved education, and an increased standard of living. However, affluent people in the Global North already enjoy these basic amenities; therefore, additional income usually allows them to satisfy comparatively trivial needs.

The global impact of population growth, as well as the continued striving for economic growth, are great. Whereas people in poor countries make few demands on world resources, to maintain their high standard of living, people in rich countries contribute greatly to the depletion of the world's resources and the global pollution. In both cases, continued population growth is detrimental—for poor societies, because it inhibits increases in per-capita income and welfare; for rich societies, because it further burdens the earth's delicate ecological system. Unbridled exploitation and consumption, disregarding responsibility to others, are ultimately self-destructive. As Soviet President Mikhail Gorbachev warned in 1988, we must halt "humanity's aggression against nature."

These ideas challenge the core values of Western civilization. Although sustainable development is an attractive goal, even it will be hard to realize. Sustainable economic welfare requires economic growth managed to limit natural

17

resource depletion and environmental damage, while protecting people's rights of leisure and liberty. But can this kind of growth in a finite world proceed infinitely? How long can finite energy sources sustain uncontrolled consumption before automobiles sputter to a stop, industries grind to a halt, and lights go out? How many pollutants can the atmosphere absorb before irreparable environmental damage results? And how many people can a delicately balanced ecosystem support?

The Challenge of Understanding

Understanding today's world requires a willingness to confront complexity. A true but complicated idea always has less chance of success than a simple but false one, the French political sociologist Alexis de Tocqueville (1969) cautioned in 1835. The challenge is difficult but the rewards warrant the effort. Humankind's ability to chart a more rewarding future is contingent on its ability to entertain complex ideas, to free itself from the sometimes paralyzing grip of the past, and to develop a questioning attitude about rival perspectives on international realities. On that hopeful yet introspective note, we begin our exploration of world politics at the dawn of a new millennium.

KEY TERMS

international political system
bipolar distribution of power
transformation
global system
state
anarchy
cycles
schema
cognitive dissonance
ideologies

mirror images
global agenda
politics
levels of analysis
individual level of analysis
state level of analysis
global level of analysis
great powers
nonstate actors
low politics

high politics
state sovereignty
interdependence
geo-economics
geopolitics
human rights
limits-to-growth proposition
sustainable development
gross national product (GNP)

SUGGESTED READING

Diamond, Jared. *Guns, Germs, and Steel: The Fates of Human Societies*. New York: W. W. Norton, 1997.

Doctors Without Borders. *World in Crisis: The Politics of Survival at the End of the 20th Century*. New York: Routledge Press, 1996.

Holsti, Ole R., Randolph M. Siverson, and Alexander L. George, eds. *Change in the International System*. Boulder, Colo.: Westview Press, 1980.

Kaplan, Robert D. *The Ends of the Earth*. New York: Random House, 1996.

Kegley, Charles W., Jr., and Eugene R. Wittkopf, eds. *The Global Agenda: Issues and Perspectives*, 5th ed. New York: McGraw-Hill, 1998.

Lugo, Luis E., ed. *Sovereignty at the Crossroads? Morality and International Politics in the Post-Cold War Era*. New York: Cambridge University Press, 1996.

Morse, Edward L. *Modernization and the Transformation of International Relations*. New York: Free Press, 1976.

Rosenau, James N. *Along the Domestic-Foreign Frontier: Exploring Governance in a Turbulent World*. Cambridge, Eng.: Cambridge University Press, 1997.

Sandler, Todd. *Global Challenges: An Approach to Environmental, Political and Economic Problems*. New York: Cambridge University Press, 1997.

Vasquez, John A., and Richard W. Mansbach. "The Issue Cycle: Conceptualizing Long-Term Global Change," *International Organization* 37 (Spring 1983): 257–80.

Weaver, James H., Michael T. Rock, and Kenneth Kusterer. *Achieving Broad-Based Sustainable Development*. West Hartford, Conn.: Kumarian Press, 1997.

Worldwatch Institute, *State of the World 1998*. New York: W. W. Norton, 1998.

WHERE ON THE WORLD WIDE WEB?

As you begin your exploration of world politics, keep in mind that our conception of international relations has always been linked to the existing information technology of our time. One of the important technological innovations of the late twentieth century has been the Internet (see Chapter 9 for a discussion on the Internet's role in the globalization process). The Internet is a global network of computers that communicate with each other. This network allows stored computer information to be distributed to any linked computer in the world.

One of the features of the Internet is World Wide Web (WWW or Web). The Web provides the technology needed to offer a navigable, attractive interface for the Internet's vast sea of resources the same way that a toolbar on a word processor screen simplifies the intimidating codes that are the computer program. The Web is designed to distribute information across the Internet in a system known as *hypertext* (visible links to other documents) that you click onto using your mouse. The Web also has the ability to display images, videos, and sound. It has made the Internet a multi-media environment.

The Web's features make it a powerful tool for providing access to global information sources. Using the Web, students have instant access to documentation of important international events and agreements. Online information is current and often more complex than traditional sources. It also quickly reflects the changing nature of international events. The Web's international reach also permits users to locate opinions and perspectives from individuals across the United States and around the world. Many from the international community post their work on the Web. Everyday more sources become available online as individuals and institutions discover the wonders of the Web.

The "Where on the World Wide Web?" sections provide you with interesting Web links to explore. Through this investigation, you will become an active participant in the globalization of world information. You will also gain a greater understanding of concepts and terms discussed in *World Politics*.

As you begin to examine the trends and transformation of world politics, it is important that you understand the evolution of international events and keep abreast of the ever-changing world of international politics. The Web links listed here will help you analyze current events.

http://www.nytimes.com

New York Times on the Web "All the news that's fit to print" is online free of charge for those who take a moment to register. International news stories are easily accessed by clicking on the "International" news category. Keep in mind that the *Times* is a news source produced in the United States and may have American biases. While you read the news stories, think of ways in which they may have an "American slant."

http://www.newslink.org/news.html

American Journalism Review News Link If you are interested in "going to the source" for your news, check out the *American Journalism Review's* website. This site provides links to electronic newspapers from the United States or anywhere in the world. Even campus papers are accessible through this site. You can read the news in a foreign language or try to find an English version. You may want to compare the same news story found in different newspapers around the world to see how different countries interpret the same event.

(continued)

http://www.npr.org/
National Public Radio Online   If you are tired of reading the news, access National Public Radio Online. This site lets you listen to the top news stories and is updated every hour. Don't forget, however, that you will need to download the RealAudio player to listen to the news. You may also want to take a minute to cruise the discussion area and give your thoughts on the headline stories.

http://www.cnn.com/WORLD/
CNN Interactive World News   Surf the Web site of the news organization that changed the way world news is reported. CNN's World News main page is divided according to world region and reports the top stories in each area. Over the course of a week, compare and contrast the content of the top stories from each region. Do you see a pattern concerning what "type" of news stories are reported for each area?

http://www.lib.utexas.edu/Libs/PCL/
Map_collection/Map_collection.html
University of Texas Library Online Map Collection   Have you ever wondered "where in the world is Djibouti?" Well, wonder no more! The Perry-Castaneda Library Map Collection of the University of Texas at Austin is an extensive collection of electronic maps. It features regional as well as state maps according to political and shaded relief criteria. When reading about a specific country in *World Politics,* make sure you can locate the country and identify its neighbors. This allows greater understanding of international events. By the way, to find Djibouti, click on "Maps of Africa" when you arrive at the library's homepage.

CHAPTER 2

Rival Theoretical Interpretations of World Politics

> •••
> *It's important that we take a hard, clear look . . . not at some simple world, either of universal goodwill or of universal hostility, but the complex, changing, and sometimes dangerous world that really exists.*
>
> —JIMMY CARTER,
> *U.S. president, 1980*

> •••
> *For liberals, the configuration of state preferences [societal ideas, ideals, and institutions] matters most in world politics—not, as realists argue, the configuration of capabilities.*
>
> —ANDREW MORAVCSIK,
> *international theorist, 1997*

CHAPTER TOPICS AND THEMES

- Thinking theoretically to interpret global issues
- The evolution of theories and paradigms
- The liberal-idealist and neoliberal theoretical orientations
- The realist and neorealist theoretical orientations
- Behavioral science and theory testing
- Systems theory and structuralism
- Feminist theories of world politics
- "Complex interdependence" and transnational relations
- International regime theory
- Critical theory: Postmodern deconstructionism and social constructivism
- The quest for theoretical understanding of global complexity and change

Imagine yourself a newly elected president of the United States. You are scheduled to deliver a State of the Union Address on your views of the current world situation and your foreign policy to deal with it. You face the task of both defining those aspects of international affairs most worthy of attention and explaining the reasons for their priority. This challenge, in turn, requires that you identify the issues and concepts that best communicate how the global condition can be meaningfully understood. You must, in short, think *theoretically*. At the same time, you must be careful, because your interpretations will necessarily make assumptions about international realities that your citizens might find questionable. The effort to explain the world, predict new global problems, and sell a policy to deal with them is bound to result in controversy, because reasonable people often see realities differently.

When leaders face these kinds of intellectual challenges, they fortunately benefit from the existence of a body of theoretically informed ideas from which they can draw guidance. In this chapter we distinguish among the major theoretical perspectives policymakers and scholars use to interpret international relations. Since the perceived "realities" of international affairs that these theories seek to explain influence their content, we will examine how perceived changes in underlying international conditions have shaped various theories. In addition, our review of contending political theories will identify the intellectual heritage that informs this book.

● ● ●

UNDERSTANDING WORLD POLITICS: THE ELUSIVE QUEST FOR THEORY

paradigm derived from the Greek *paradeigma* meaning an example, a model, or an essential pattern, a paradigm structures thoughts about an area of inquiry.

Social scientists construct different theories to make international events understandable. Over time, **paradigms,** or dominant ways of looking at a particular subject, such as international relations, tend to arise to influence judgments regarding which of its characteristics are most important, what puzzles need to be solved, and what criteria should govern their investigation. These paradigms or "fundamental assumptions scholars make about the world they are studying" (Vasquez, 1997) tend eventually to be revised in order to explain new developments in world affairs. Thus, the paths to knowledge that guide the thinking both of policymakers and scholars in different historical circumstances tell us much about world politics itself.

Throughout history, paradigms have been revised or abandoned when their assertions have failed to mirror the prevailing patterns of international behavior. Major wars have been especially potent in bringing about significant changes in the theoretical interpretation of world affairs, and influencing "what ideas and values will predominate, thereby determining the ethos of succeeding ages" (Gilpin 1981). Three such system-transforming wars have dominated the twentieth century: World War I, World War II, and the Cold War. "Every war . . . has been followed in due course by skeptical reassessments of supposedly sacred assumptions" (Schlesinger 1986) and has reshaped policymakers' perceptions of world politics and the policy programs that would best preserve world order. Each struggle caused the dominant paradigm to be jettisoned and encouraged the search for new theoretical orientations.

This chapter will concentrate on the two core perspectives that have most influenced thinking about world politics throughout history: liberalism and realism and their neoliberal and neorealist variants that have commanded a large following in the last two decades. In highlighting these traditions, keep in mind that this coverage is very selective. At least six additional major schools of thought regarding particular aspects of world politics also deserve attention, and each will be introduced—along with still other theoretical subspecialties linked to them—in later chapters where they best help to interpret the topic covered. First, as explained in Chapter 3, *decision-making theory* accounts for the ways leaders and other actors seek to make policy choices rationally, and the limits to this aspiration. Second, as introduced in Chapter 4, *long-cycle theory* seeks to explain the historical ebb and flow of world politics, global leadership, and systemwide war (Goldstein 1988; Modelski and Thompson 1996). The rise and fall of the great powers and empires is its central concern. Third, *dependency theory*, first treated in Chapter 5, examines the pattern of dominance and dependence that characterizes the unequal relationship between the world's rich and poor states (Packenham 1992). Fourth, to understand how cooperation among states is encouraged to deal with problems primarily in the realm of "low politics" (Chapters 8–11), *hegemonic stability theory*, a hybrid of liberal/neorealist theory (Gill 1993b), examines what happens when a clearly predominant state, a "hegemon," exercises leadership and control of the international system by setting and enforcing the rules governing international trade, finance, investment, and other issues, such as environmental regulation (see Gilpin 1981; Levy 1991). Fifth, to expand this coverage and move to other topics dealing with global security, *world-system theory* looks at system dynamics from a long-term, structural perspective, emphasizing its economic underpinnings, to explain the Western capitalist societies' rise to dominance and the lack of economic development in many other geographic areas (Chapters 5–11) and their military repercussions (Chapter 11) (see Wallerstein 1980). Finally, to systematically organize inquiry about how states fit into international phenomena from diverse levels of analysis, advocates of the *comparative study of foreign policy* seek to probe the similarities and differences in states' international circumstances, national attributes and capabilities, foreign policy decision-making processes, and individual policymakers (see Hermann, Kegley, and Rosenau 1987). For now, though, we will concentrate on the two major theoretical traditions that have historically organized thinking about international affairs—the liberal and realist world views.

The Evolution of Theoretical Inquiry

When the formal study of international relations began at the dawn of the twentieth century, the world abounded with optimism. Many people believed that peace and prosperity had taken root and would persist. The Hague peace conferences in 1899 and 1907 had inspired hope of controlling arms and sparing Europe another series of wars like those between 1848 and 1870. Moreover, numerous individuals—including the Scottish-American industrialist Andrew Carnegie, who gave much of his fortune to the cause of world peace—assumed that as industrialization progressed and the costs and risks of war increased, the chance of protracted war among the great powers would decline dramatically (see also Angell 1910).

In those tranquil times, students of international relations studied history to glean insight on the events of the day. The study of international relations consisted mainly of commentary about personalities and events, past and present. Rarely did scholars seek to generalize theoretically about the "lessons" of history or about the principles or "laws" that might account for states' characteristic responses to similar stimuli or influences. Sir Halford Mackinder (1919) and Alfred Thayer Mahan (1890) were exceptions. Both sought to generate theoretical propositions pertaining to the influence of geographic factors on national power and international politics—efforts that laid the foundations for the study of political geography, which survives today as an important approach to world politics (see Demko and Wood 1994).

The large-scale death and destruction that World War I exacted from 1914 to 1918 destroyed the security that had made the **current history approach** popular. This catastrophic war was a painful lesson that stimulated the search for knowledge to address contemporary policy problems in a theoretical context. However interesting descriptions of recent or past wars might be, they were of dubious use to a world in search of ways to prevent wars of mass destruction. For those purposes, policymakers and scholars needed a **theory**—a statement attempting to account for general phenomena or patterns rather than explaining unique or individual instances of the general phenomenon of which it is part—that could reliably predict war and instruct leaders on the best policies to prevent it.

Liberalism

World War I initiated a paradigmatic revolution in the study of international relations, in which several perspectives competed for attention. While the current history approach continued to claim some disciples in the waning days of World War I, after Russia's Bolshevik Revolution, Marxist-Leninist thought became increasingly influential, with its critique of capitalism's creation of inequality, class conflict, and imperialistic war. In the 1930s, with the rise of Adolf Hitler in Germany, national socialism (or fascism) also challenged conventional European thinking about world politics. Nazism, the German variant of national socialism, was particularly provocative. Not only did Nazism glorify the role of the state (as opposed to that of the individual) in political life, it also championed war as an instrument of national policy. Emerging as dominant, however, was a perspective known as liberalism, which assumed that people were not by nature sinful or wicked but that harmful behavior was the result of structural arrangements motivating individuals to act in their own self-interest.

The Liberal Worldview. Because advocates of the liberal school of thought were inspired by their interest in ideals, they are sometimes referred to as **liberal idealists.** After World War I, they became known simply as "idealists," even if they were a diverse group within the larger liberal tradition. Post-World War I idealism, as advocated by such scholars and policymakers as Alfred Zimmern, Norman Angell, James T. Shotwell, and Woodrow Wilson, derived from ancient liberal philosophy and has been interpreted variously in different periods. These idealists knew their worldview from such liberal thinkers as Immanuel Kant, Thomas Jefferson, James Madison, John Stuart Mill, John Locke, David Hume, Jean Jacques Rosseau, and Adam Smith (see Doyle 1995, Howard 1978, and Zacher and Matthew 1995).

At the core of liberalism is an emphasis on the impact of ideas on behavior, the equality and liberty of the individual, and the need to protect people from

current history approach an approach focusing on the description of contemporary and particular historical events rather than theoretical explanations.

theory a set of hypotheses postulating the relationship between variables or conditions, advanced to describe, explain, or predict phenomena, and make prescriptions about how positive changes ought to be engineered to realize particular ethical principles.

liberal idealists advocates of a paradigm predicated on the hope that the application of reason and universal ethics to international relations can lead to a more orderly, just, and cooperative world, and that international anarchy and war can be policed by institutional reforms that empower international organizations and laws.

Influenced by David Hume and Jean Jacques Rousseau, Immanuel Kant (left) in *Perpetual Peace* (1795) helped to redefine modern liberal theory by advocating global (not state) citizenship, free trade, and a federation of democracies as a means to peace. Richard Cobden (right) primarily foresaw the possibility of peace across borders; in his view, if contact and communication among people could expand through free trade, so too would international friendship and peace, secured by prosperity that would create interdependence and eliminate the need for military forces to pursue rivalries.

excessive state regulation. From this comes a conceptualization of the individual as the seat of moral value and virtue and the belief that human beings should be treated as ends rather than means. Liberalism emphasizes ethical principle over the pursuit of power and institutions over interests as forces shaping inter-state relations.

Collectively, the post-World War I liberal idealists embraced a worldview based on the following beliefs:

1. Human nature is essentially "good" or altruistic, and people are therefore capable of mutual aid and collaboration through reason and ethically inspired education.

2. The fundamental human concern for others' welfare makes progress possible.

3. Bad human behavior, such as violence, is the product not of flawed people but of evil institutions that encourage people to act selfishly and to harm others.

4. War and international anarchy are not inevitable and war's frequency can be reduced by strengthening the institutional arrangements that encourage its disappearance.

5. War is a global problem requiring collective or multilateral, rather than national, efforts to control it.

6. Reforms must be inspired by a compassionate ethical concern for the welfare and security of all people, and this humanitarian motive requires the inclusion of morality in statecraft.

7. International society must reorganize itself in order to eliminate the institutions that make war likely, and states must reform their political systems so that self-determination and democratic governance within states can help pacify relations among states.

While not all liberal idealists subscribed to each of these tenets with equal conviction, they shared a moralistic, optimistic, and universalistic image of international affairs as taking place within a global community.

The Liberal Reform Program. Although liberal idealists differed significantly in their prescriptions for reforming the international political system (see Herz 1951), after World War I they generally fell into one of three groups. The first group advocated creating international institutions to replace the anarchical and war-prone balance-of-power system, characterized by coalitions of independent states formed to wage war or to defend a weaker coalition partner from attack. In place of this competitive unregulated system, idealists sought to create a new one based on **collective security.** This approach dealt with the problem of war by declaring any state's aggression an aggression against all, who would act in concert to thwart the aggressor. The League of Nations was the institutional embodiment of collective security through international organization, reflecting simultaneously the liberal idealists' emphasis on international institutions and the possibility of international cooperation for global problem solving.

A second group emphasized the use of legal processes such as mediation and arbitration to settle disputes and avoid armed conflict. This facet of the idealists' policy prescriptions was illustrated by the creation in 1921 of the Permanent Court of International Justice to litigate interstate conflicts and by the ratification of the Kellogg-Briand Pact of 1928, which "outlawed" war as an instrument of national policy.

A third group followed the biblical injunction that states should beat their swords into plowshares. This orientation was exemplified by efforts during the 1920s, such as those negotiated at the Washington and London naval conferences, to secure arms control and disarmament agreements.

Several corollary ideas gave definition to the idealists' emphasis on encouraging global cooperation through international institutions, law, and disarmament. These included:

- The need to substitute attitudes that stressed the unity of humankind for those that stressed parochial national loyalties to independent sovereign states.
- The use of the power of ideas through education to arouse world public opinion against warfare.
- The promotion of free international trade in place of economic nationalism.
- The replacement of secret diplomacy by a system of "open covenants, openly arrived at."
- The termination of interlocking bilateral alliances and the power balances they sought to achieve.

In seeking a more peaceful world, some idealists saw the principle of **self-determination**—giving nationalities the right through voting to become independent states—as a means to redraw the globe's political geography to make national borders conform to ethnic groupings. Related to this was U.S. presi-

self-determination the principle that the global community is obligated to give nationalities their own governments.

dent Woodrow Wilson's call for democratic domestic institutions. "Making the world safe for democracy," liberals believed, would also make it secure and free from war, because democracies do not fight one another. Wilson's celebrated Fourteen Points speech to Congress in 1918 proposed the creation of the League of Nations and, with it, the pursuit of other liberal idealists' aims such as free trade to create wealth and a global harmony of states' interests. This speech, perhaps better than any other statement, expressed the sentiments of the liberal world view and program.

Although a tone of idealism dominated policy rhetoric and academic discussions during the interwar period, with the exception of the League of Nations and the precedent-setting Washington Naval Disarmament Treaties, little of the liberal reform program was ever seriously attempted, and even less of it was achieved. When the winds of international change again shifted and the Axis Powers pursued world conquest, enthusiasm for liberal idealism as a worldview receded.

Realism

The drive for global conquest that led to World War II provoked strong criticism of the liberal idealist paradigm. Critics blamed the outbreak of war on what they believed to be the so-called idealists naive legalistic and moralistic assumptions about the possibility of peace and progress through human aspiration, and alleged that idealists were utopians who neglected the realities of power politics (see Carr 1939). The lessons the critics drew from the interwar period shaped a new set of perceptions and beliefs.

Advocates of the new, ascendant paradigm known as **realism,** or *realpolitik* as a general philosophy, emerged to frame an intellectual movement whose message reads like the antithesis of idealism. Among the principal prophets of this new worldview were E. H. Carr (1939), George F. Kennan (1951, 1954), Hans J. Morgenthau (1948), Reinhold Niebuhr (1947), and Kenneth W. Thompson (1960). Because it was compelling—and remains so today—realism deserves careful scrutiny.

realism a paradigm based on the premise that world politics is essentially and unchangeably a struggle among self-interested states for power and position under anarchy, with each competing state pursuing its own national interests.

The Realist Worldview. As a political theory, realism can trace its intellectual roots to the ancient Greek historian Thucydides and his account of the Peloponnesian War between Athens and Sparta (431–404 B.C.E.), the writings of Kautilya (minister to the Maurya emperor of India more than two thousand years ago), and especially the sixteenth-century political thought of the Italian theorist Niccoló Machiavelli and the English philosopher Thomas Hobbes.

Realism, as applied to twentieth-century world politics, views the state as the most important actor on the world stage since it answers to no higher political authority. Moreover, conflicts of interests among states are assumed to be inevitable. Realism also emphasizes the ways in which the anarchical nature of international politics dictates the choices that foreign policymakers, as rational problem solvers who must calculate their interest in terms of power, must make. (See Chapter 3 for discussion of the "rational" actor.)

Within the realist paradigm, the purpose of statecraft is national survival in a hostile environment. To this end, no means is more important than the acquisition of **power,** and no principle is more important than **self-help.** In this conception, **state sovereignty,** a cornerstone of international law, gives heads of

power the factors that enable one actor to manipulate another actor's behavior against its preferences.

self-help the principle that in anarchy actors must rely on themselves.

In *The Prince* (1532) and *The Leviathan* (1651) Niccoló Machiavelli and Thomas Hobbes, respectively, emphasized a political calculus based on interest, prudence, power, and expediency above all other considerations. This formed the foundation of what became a growing body of modern realist thinking that accepts the drive for power over others as necessary and wise statecraft.

state the freedom—and responsibility—to do whatever is necessary to advance the state's interests and survival.

According to this paradigm, respect for moral principles is a wasteful and dangerous interference in the rational pursuit of national power. To the hardcore realist, therefore, questions about the relative virtues of the values within this or that ideological system cannot be allowed to interfere with sound policy making. A state's philosophical or ethical preferences are neither good nor bad—what matters is whether they serve its self-interest. Thus, the game of international politics revolves around the pursuit of power: acquiring it, increasing it, projecting it, and using it to bend others to one's will. At the extreme, realism appears to accept war as normal and rejects morality as it pertains to relations between individuals.

At the risk of oversimplification, realism's message can be summarized in the form of ten assumptions and related propositions:

1. People are by nature narrowly selfish and ethically flawed, and cannot free themselves from the sinful fact that they are born to watch out for themselves.

2. Of all people's evil ways, none are more prevalent, inexorable, or dangerous than their instinctive lust for power and their desire to dominate others.

3. The possibility of eradicating the instinct for power is a utopian aspiration.

4. International politics is—as Thomas Hobbes put it—a struggle for power, "a war of all against all."

5. The primary obligation of every state—the goal to which all other national objectives should be subordinated—is to promote its **national interest,** and to acquire power for this purpose.

6. The nature of the international system dictates that states acquire sufficient military capabilities to deter attack by potential enemies.

7. Economics is less relevant to national security than is military might; economics is important primarily as a means of acquiring national power and prestige.

8. Allies might increase a state's ability to defend itself, but their loyalty and reliability should not be assumed.

9. States should never entrust the task of self-protection to international security organizations or international law and should resist efforts to regulate international conduct.

10. If all states seek to maximize power, stability will result from maintaining a balance of power, lubricated by fluid alliance systems.

national interest the goals that states pursue to maximize what is selfishly best for their country.

Realism in the Nuclear Age. The dour and pessimistic realist thinking that dominated policy making and academic discourse in the 1940s and 1950s fit the needs of a pessimistic age. World War II, the onset of rivalry between the United States and the Soviet Union, the expansion of the Cold War into a global struggle between East and West, the stockpiling of nuclear weapons, and the periodic crises that threatened to erupt into global violence all confirmed the realists' emphasis on the inevitability of conflict, the poor prospects for co-operation, and the divergence of national interests among incorrigibly selfish, power-seeking states.

The realists' interpretations appeared particularly persuasive, given the prevailing patterns of behavior. States and their incessant competition were accordingly seen as the defining elements of global reality; all other aspects of world politics became secondary. At the same time, the view that a threatening international environment demanded that foreign policy take precedence over domestic problems also appeared cogent. As the historical imperatives of "power politics" required unceasing attention to preserving peace, the logic of *realpolitik* asserted that military security was the essence of world politics.

The Limitations of Realism. However persuasive the realists' arguments about the essential properties of international politics, their contentions and conclusions were frequently at odds and even contradictory.

> Critics . . . noted a lack of precision and even contradiction in the way classical realists use such concepts as "power," "national interest," and "balance of power." They also see possible contradictions between the central descriptive and prescriptive elements of classical realism. On the one hand, as Hans Morgenthau put it, nations and their leaders "think and act in terms of interests defined as power," but, on the other, statesmen are urged to exercise prudence and restraint, as well as to recognize the legitimate national interests of other nations. Obviously, then, power plays a central role in classical realism. But the correlation between the

29

relative power balance and political outcomes is often less than compelling, suggesting the need to enrich analyses with other variables. (Holsti 1998, 135)

Thus, once analysis moved beyond the belief that people are wicked and the rhetoric requiring that foreign policy serve the national interest, important questions remained: What policies best serve the national interest? Do alliances encourage peace or instability? Do arms promote national security or provoke costly arms races and war? Are states more prone to act aggressively when they are strong or weak? Are the interests of states better served through competition or through cooperation? If humankind is unchanging, then how do we explain the observable evolution and transformation of the international system? Indeed, how do we explain the growth of collaborative multilateral institutions, economic expansion, and states' observable willingness to abide by ethical principles and agreements rather than to exploit others ruthlessly when the opportunity arises?

Because such questions are empirically verifiable and answering them satisfactorily requires real-world evidence and rigorous analysis, realism began to be questioned. Although it presented a distinctive perspective on international affairs by challenging the assumptions of liberal idealism, many of the assumptions of the realist paradigm were not testable, and realism did not have a methodology for resolving competing claims (Brooks 1997; Vasquez 1997). Realism offered no criteria for determining what data were significant and what rules to follow to interpret relevant information. Even the policy recommendations that purportedly flowed from its logic were often divergent. Realists themselves, for example, were sharply divided as to whether U.S. intervention in Vietnam served American national interests and whether nuclear weapons contributed to international security.

A growing number of critics also pointed out that realism did not account for significant new developments in world politics. For instance, it could not explain the construction of new liberal trade and political institutions in Western Europe in the 1950s and 1960s, where the cooperative pursuit of mutual advantage rather than narrow self-interest appeared to dominate (at least in economic, if not always in military, affairs). Other critics began to worry about realism's tendency to disregard ethical principles and about the material and social costs that some of its policy prescriptions seemed to impose, such as retarded economic growth resulting from unrestrained military expenditures. Consequently, by the end of the 1960s, realism found itself bombarded by criticism, especially by behavioral scientists who sought to replace realist thought and polemics with theories tested against evidence (see Focus 2.1).

Despite realism's shortcomings, much of the world continues to think about world politics in its terms, especially in times of global tension. This happened, for example, in the early 1980s when the Cold War competition between the United States and the Soviet Union entered an embittered new phase and their arms race accelerated. Because realism provides great insight into the drive for national security through military means, it tends to be used to explain such phenomena as the outbreak of bloody wars in the former Yugoslavia in the 1990s.

Although realism remains relevant in explaining many dimensions of national security affairs, a subset of realist theorists have recently reconstructed it as a general theory. This reformulated perspective, known primarily

A Behavioral Science of International Politics?

Realism prepared the way for serious theoretical thinking about global conditions and the empirical linkages among them. Nonetheless, dissatisfaction with its shortcomings mounted, and a counterreaction gained momentum in the 1960s and early 1970s to challenge the preexisting modes of studying human behavior, now called "traditionalism," as well as the ways in which traditionalists derived their truth claims. **Behavioralism,** as it came to be known, is better described as a methodology than as a theoretical perspective because it was defined largely by its application of scientific methods to the study of international relations. An often heated debate arose between the behavioralists and traditionalists as to the principles and procedures most appropriate for investigating international phenomena. Indeed, "theorizing about theory" (Singer 1960) rather than theorizing about international relations dominated this debate. The literature of this period tends to focus on methodological issues, not on the relative merits of propositions derived from either realist or liberal theories (see Knorr and Rosenau 1969; Knorr and Verba 1961).

Behavioralism sought generalizations or statements about international regularities that held across time and place. Science, the behavioralists claimed, is primarily a generalizing activity. From this perspective—a view incidentally consistent with that of many "traditional" realists and liberal idealists—a theory of international relations should be defined as a statement of the relationship between two or more variables that specifies the conditions under which the relationship(s) hold and explains why the relationship(s) should hold. To uncover such theories, behavioralists leaned toward using comparative cross-national analyses rather than case studies of particular countries at particular times. Behavioralists also stressed the need for data about the characteristics of countries and how they behave toward one another. Hence, the behavioral movement spawned and encouraged the comparative and quantitative study of international relations (see, for example, Rosenau 1980; Singer 1968).

What made behavioralism innovative was its attitude toward the purposes of inquiry: replacing subjective beliefs with verifiable knowledge, supplanting impressionism and intuition with testable evidence, and substituting data and reproducible information for mere opinion. In this sense, behavioralists embraced liberalism's "high regard for modern science" and its "attacks against superstition and authority" (Hall 1993). In

place of appeals to the "expert" opinion of authorities, behavioral scientists sought to acquire knowledge cumulatively by suspending judgments about truths or values until they had sufficient evidence to support them. They sought to avoid the tendency of previous scholarship to select facts and cases to fit preexisting hunches. Instead, *all* available data, those which contradicted as well as those which supported existing theoretical hypotheses, were to be examined. Knowledge, they argued, would advance best by assuming a cautious, skeptical attitude toward any empirical statement. The slogans "Let the data, not the armchair theorist, speak," and "Seek evidence, but distrust it" represented the behavioral posture toward the acquisition of knowledge.

As the behavioral movement progressed, however, some advocates began to question the approach and its suitability. One of the early proponents of behavioralism, David Easton (1969), asked if the field was not moving into a period of *postbehavioralism,* marked by increasing attention to the policy relevance of research. At the heart of this critical self-scrutiny was a common set of criticisms: (1) that some devotees of behavioralism had become preoccupied with method to the exclusion of addressing real-world problems; (2) that behavioralists often ignored policymakers' need for data-based knowledge about how to protect their state's security and make the world a better place; and (3) that behavioral methodology, which sought to ground theories in hard data, relied on past patterns of human experience that sometimes failed to apply to the rapidly changing world or the future. Hence the findings might be historically accurate but largely irrelevant to today's or tomorrow's world.

Although some behavioral research spoke directly to the moral issues that differentiated realism and liberal idealism, it was criticized nonetheless for neglecting the ethical aspects of poverty, hunger, violence, and other forms of malaise. Hence the **postbehavioral movement** arose, calling for a new research agenda that would focus on new issues and reexamine their underlying philosophical implications from a multidisciplinary perspective (see Easton 1969). However, these rarely recommended discarding scientific methods to test and reconstruct theories grounded in the realist and liberal traditions, despite the harsh criticism of behavioral science by "postmodern deconstructivists" (see Focus 2.4 on page 41).

neorealism a theoretical account of states' behavior that explains it as determined by differences in their relative power instead of by other factors, such as their values, types of government, or domestic circumstances.

as **neorealism,** emphasizes the anarchic nature of global society without governance rather than human nature and the unceasing lust for power in its explanation for why states interact as they do. For this reason, neorealism is sometimes referred to as **structural realism** theory because it emphasizes the influence of the structure of world power on the states within it.

The Neorealist or "Structural" Extension of Realism

In his influential book *Theory of International Politics* (1979), the pioneer of neorealism, Kenneth N. Waltz set out to convert the loose and disjointed body of realist "thought" into a formal "theory" (Waltz 1995). "To systematize political realism into a rigorous, deductive systemic theory of international politics" (Keohane 1986b), neorealism dismisses explanations developed at the individual and state levels of analysis and argues that explanations at the global system level are sufficient to account for the main trends in world politics. As Waltz (1995) expressed his neorealist conceptualization of the determinants of international behavior, "international structure emerges from the interaction of states and then constrains them from taking certain actions while propelling them toward others."

As in realism, in neorealism, anarchy or the absence of central institutions above states is the most important and enduring property of the structure of the system. States remain the primary actors, acting according to the principle of self-help and seeking to ensure their own survival. Thus, it is the neorealists' view that states do not differ in the tasks they face, only in their capabilities. Capabilities define the position of states in the system, and the distribution of capabilities defines the structure of the system and shapes the ways the units interact with one another.

Power also remains a central concept in neorealism. However, the quest for power is no longer considered an end in itself, as in realism; nor does it derive from human nature. Instead, states always pursue power as a means of survival. As Waltz (1979) explains, the "means fall into two categories: internal efforts (moves to increase economic capability, to increase military strength, to develop clever strategies) and external efforts (moves to strengthen and enlarge one's own alliance or to weaken and shrink an opposing one)." Furthermore, because the instinct for survival drives states, neorealism asserts that balances of power form automatically, regardless of whether "some or all states consciously aim to establish and maintain a balance, or whether some or all states aim for universal domination" (Waltz 1979). Once the global system is formed, its structure "becomes a force that the units may not be able to control; it constrains their behavior and interposes itself between their intentions and the outcomes of their actions" (Ruggie 1983).

Although neorealists recognize that states' goals sometimes "fluctuate with the changing currents of domestic politics, are prey to the vagaries of a shifting cast of political leaders, and are influenced by the outcomes of bureaucratic struggles," they contend that such factors as whether governments are democracies or dictatorships tell little about the process whereby states come to pursue the goal of balancing power with power. Instead, "structural constraints explain why the [same] methods are repeatedly used despite differences in the persons and states who use them" (Waltz 1979).

In its stress on the structure of the international system, that is, the state of anarchy among sovereign states, [neo]realism attaches little or no importance to what is going on inside states—what kind of regimes are in power, what kind of ideologies prevail, what kind of leadership is provided. According to [neo]realists, the foreign policies of all states are basically driven by the same systemic factors—they are like so many billiard balls, obeying the same laws of political geometry and physics. (Harries 1995, 13)

Neorealist theory also helps to explain why the prospects for international cooperation and change often appear so dim and why states are naturally wary of others and strive to compete. The anarchical structure of the system compels states to be sensitive to their *relative position* in the distribution of power.

When faced with the possibility of cooperating for mutual gain, states that feel insecure must ask how the gain will be divided. They are compelled to ask not "Will both of us gain?" but "Who will gain more?" If an expected gain is to be divided, say, in the ratio of two to one, one state may use its disproportionate gain to implement a policy intended to damage or destroy the other. Even the prospect of large absolute gains for both parties does not elicit their cooperation so long as each fears how the other will use its increased capabilities. (Waltz 1979, 105; see also Snidal 1993)

Impediments to global cooperation thus result not from the parties' attitudes toward potential collaborative efforts, but rather from the insecurity that the anarchical system breeds. "The condition of insecurity—at the least, the uncertainty of each about the other's future intentions and actions—works against their cooperation" (Waltz 1979), as does states' fear of dependence on others.

Not everyone, however, agrees that the prospects for international cooperation are so remote. Some liberals acknowledge that although conflict among states has been endemic throughout much of world history, so has international cooperation. They point out that the record suggests that patterns can change and that increased interdependence can lead to even higher levels of cooperation. This expectation lies behind the so-called neoliberal challenge to realism and neorealism (Doyle and Ikenberry 1997; Kegley 1995).

Neoliberalism

As the Cold War ended, dissatisfaction with realism and neorealism began to rise. Arguing that it was time for a new, more rigorous idealist alternative to realism, critics pointed to several shortcomings: (1) power-politics perspectives failed to predict the peaceful end of the Cold War and international social change in general; (2) research suggested that the "underlying theory of war and peace [of realism and neorealism was] flawed" (Vasquez 1993) because realists "oversimplified the concept of power and misunderstood the lessons of history" (Kober 1990); and (3) it appeared that realism's approach would "not be an adequate guide for the future of international politics" (Jervis 1992), because the broadened post-Cold War global agenda included many questions and problems that realist theory could not cover. The problems of AIDS, ecological deterioration, global warming, economic underdevelopment, and the globalization of trade and markets were among those for which the realistic approach was seen as deficient.

Asking "Is realism finished?" (Zakaria 1992–93), these critics also saw neorealism as "a research enterprise in crisis" (James 1993). But they went beyond

neoliberalism a perspective
that accounts for the way
international institutions
promote global change,
cooperation, peace, and
prosperity through collective
reform approaches.

the call to rethink and revise these theories by advocating that "the recovery of liberalism" (Little 1993) be treated as a theoretical goal in international relations. This view gained a following among policymakers. For example, in accord with Francis Fukuyama's conclusion (1992b) that there were "good reasons for examining aspects of the liberal international legacy once again," U.S. President Bill Clinton in 1995 maintained that "In a world where freedom, not tyranny, is on the march, the cynical calculus of pure power politics simply does not compute. It is ill-suited to the new era."

In light of this growing sentiment, in the early 1990s **neoliberalism,** a new approach to world politics that concentrates on the ways international organizations and other nonstate actors promote international cooperation, emerged. This analytic departure goes by several labels including "neoliberal institutionalism" (Grieco 1995), "neoidealism" (Kegley 1993), and "neo-Wilsonian idealism" (Fukuyama 1992a).

Neoliberalism seeks to build theories of international relations by giving the basic tenets of classical liberalism and post-World War I liberal idealism a fresh examination. Taking heart in the international prohibition, through community consensus, of such previously entrenched practices as slavery, piracy, dueling, colonialism, the slaughter of certain animals, and unrestrained exploitation of the planet's ecology, neoliberalism emphasizes the prospects for progress, peace, and prosperity. Studies of regional integration—processes whereby sovereign states might be politically unified—began to flourish in the 1950s and 1960s, paving the way for the new liberal theories that emerged in the 1990s. The expansion of trade, communication, information, technology, and immigrant labor propelled Europeans to sacrifice portions of their sovereign independence to create a new political community out of previously separate units. These developments were outside of realism's worldview, creating conditions that made the call for a theory grounded in the liberal tradition convincing to many who had previously been skeptical of realism.

Neoliberalism departs from neorealism on many assumptions (see Focus 2.2). In particular, neoliberalism focuses on the ways in which influences such as democratic governance, public opinion, mass education, free trade, liberal commercial enterprise, international law and organization, arms control and disarmament, collective security and multilateral diplomacy, and ethically inspired statecraft can improve life on our planet. Because they perceive change in global conditions as progressing through cooperative efforts, neoliberal theorists maintain that the ideas and ideals of the liberal legacy today can describe, explain, predict, and prescribe international conduct in ways that they could not during the conflict-ridden Cold War (see Moravcsik 1997).

Like realism and neorealism, neoliberalism does not represent a cohesive intellectual movement or school of thought. Neoliberals operate from different assumptions, examining different aspects of the processes through which international change and cooperation might be promoted. Some, like neorealists, embrace a structural theory that examines the characteristics of the international system. Others concentrate on the characteristics of the units and subunits that comprise it, such as the types of governments (democracies or dictatorships) and leaders who govern states. Still other neoliberals give primary attention to the influence of international institutions such as the United Nations and nonstate actors such as multinational corporations. All neoliberals,

Point-Counterpoint
The Debate between Neoliberalism and Neorealism

According to David Baldwin (1993, 4–8): six focal points characterize the current debate between neoliberalism and neorealism:

- *The Nature and Consequences of Anarchy.* Although no one denies that the international system is anarchical in some sense, there is disagreement as to what this means and why it matters. . . .
- *International Cooperation.* Although both sides agree that international cooperation is possible, they differ as to the ease and likelihood of its occurrence. . . .
- *Relative versus Absolute Gains.* Although it would be misleading to characterize one side as concerned with relative gains and the other as concerned only with absolute gains, neoliberals have stressed the absolute gains from international cooperation, while neorealists have emphasized relative gains [by assuming that actors will ask, "Who will gain more?"].

- *Priority of State Goals.* Neoliberals and neorealists agree that both national security and economic welfare are important, but they differ in relative emphasis on these goals [with neoliberals stressing the latter and neorealists the former].
- *Intentions versus Capabilities.* Contemporary neorealists . . . emphasize capabilities more than intentions [whereas neoliberals emphasize] intentions, interests, and information [instead of] the distribution of capabilities. . . .
- *Institutions and Regimes.* Both neorealists and neoliberals recognize the multitude of international regimes and institutions that have emerged since 1945. They differ, however, with respect to the significance of such arrangements. . . .

Looking at the world, which set of assumptions do you think is the most accurate for interpreting contemporary world politics?

however, share an interest in probing the conditions under which the convergent and overlapping interests among otherwise sovereign political entities may result in cooperation.

To illuminate these similarities and differences among neoliberals, we will examine two theoretical perspectives that paved the way for neoliberalism's acceptance and are a part of its orientation: complex interdependence and international regimes. For the sake of brevity, we have selected only these two examples from among the many other divergent stands within neoliberal theorizing (see Zacher and Matthew 1995), such as the feminist critique of conventional theories in general and realism in particular (see Focus 2.3).

Complex Interdependence as a Worldview. As an explicit analytical perspective, **complex interdependence** arose in the 1970s to challenge the key assumptions of realism. Questioning the prevailing assumption that states are the only important actors in world politics, it treated other actors, such as multinational corporations and transnational banks, as "important not only because of their activities in pursuit of their own interests, but also because they act as transmission belts, making government policies in various countries more sensitive to one another" (Keohane and Nye 1988). In this sense, complex interdependence is a holistic, globalistic conception that views world politics as the sum of its many interacting parts in a "global society" (see Holsti 1998).

complex interdependence a theory stressing the complex ways in which the growing ties among transnational actors makes them vulnerable to each other's actions and sensitive to each other's needs.

What's Wrong with International Relations Theory?
The Feminist Critique

Feminist theory, a body of scholarship that emphasizes gender in the study of world politics, arose in the 1960s in response to the pronounced disregard of females in discussions about public and international affairs and the injustice and inequality that this prejudice caused. The mainstream literature on world politics underestimated or ignored the plight and contributions of women, treating differences in men's and women's status, beliefs, and behaviors as unimportant. Gender roles were also ignored, along with the evidence that sexism is a pillar of the war system (Reardon 1985) and that a remedy for this problem might be to give women the prominence and power in policy making that traditional practices denied them (see Beckman and D'Amico 1994; Peterson and Runyan 1993).

As feminist theory crystallized, it moved away from focusing on a history of discrimination against women and began to direct much of its criticism at realism. In particular, many gender studies alleged that realism, formulated and dominated by males, ignored the human roots of global conditions and promoted an essentially masculine interpretation of international relations that was inattentive to human rights and rife with rationales for aggression.

Derived in part from liberal principles supportive of fair play, justice, and the philosophical acceptance of love over power, feminist theory moved beyond this initial critique of realism's bias to chart an independent theoretical course (Keohane 1989). This perspective has focused on the performance of women as leaders of government and as members of infantry combat units (Grant and Newland 1991), as well as on theoretical explorations of the plight of women in business and in the Global South.

Perhaps of greatest influence in the field of international relations, however, has been Feminist theory's rejection of the realist preoccupation with states' military strategies in favor of developing strategies for world security (see Tickner 1992). In this sense, feminist theory, like neoliberalism generally, is motivated by the quest for discovering paths to greater international cooperation. In liberating conventional theory from its narrow focus, can feminist theory open a window on the full range of international activity and point the way toward a fuller appreciation of the ways in which human beings influence the global condition?

The complex interdependence school also questioned whether national security issues were truly dominant in states' decision-making agendas. Under conditions of states' mutual vulnerability, it seemed that their foreign policy agendas had become "larger and more diverse," because a broader range of "governments' policies, even those previously considered merely domestic, impinged on one another" (Keohane and Nye 1988).

In addition, this perspective disputed the popular notion that military force is the only means of exercising influence in international politics, particularly among the industrialized democracies. "Intense relationships of mutual influence exist between these countries, but in most of them force is irrelevant or unimportant as an instrument of policy" (Keohane and Nye 1988).

Advocates of the complex interdependence perspective extended many of these insights to the issues concerning inter-state economic interdependence that arose during the 1970s and, later, to environmental protection. International institutions commanded a central place in many of these analyses, as demonstrated in Robert O. Keohane and Joseph S. Nye's (1977, 1989) *Power and Interdependence*, the definitive statement on the complex interdependence extension of liberalism. A careful reading of the work reveals that this perspective does not altogether reject realism. Rather, the initial concern of its adher-

ents was "the conditions under which the assumptions of realism were sufficient or needed to be supplemented by a more complex model of change" (Nye
1987; see also Keohane 1983). Keohane and Nye drew on realism, in part, to account for the willingness of states to see their interests served by the creation of
international regimes, or the norms for behavior that are created when cooperation becomes institutionalized and actors expect them to be followed, even
though this necessitates a sacrifice of sovereignty. Complex interdependence
eventually became a central component of the neoliberal perspective and has
been used widely in analyses of international politics that seek to understand
states' willingness to enter into cooperative agreements with one another under
conditions of anarchy and fears of dependence and exploitation (Nye 1988).

International Regimes. Although the international system is still characterized
by anarchy, its nature is more properly conceptualized as an ordered anarchy,
and the globe as a whole as an "anarchical society" (Bull 1977), because
cooperation, not conflict, is often the observable outcome of relations among
states.

Given this reality, the question arises: How can **international regimes**
based on coordinated cooperation be established and preserved? Interest in
this question derives from two goals: first, "a desire to understand the extent
to which mutually accepted constraints affect states' behaviors" (Zacher
1987), and second, a desire to devise strategies for creating a less disorderly
"world order."

Regimes are institutionalized or regularized patterns of cooperation in a
given issue area, as reflected by the rules that make a pattern predictable. Because the international regime perspective necessarily looks primarily at global
institutions and to the ways in which norms influence state behavior, as opposed simply to the pursuit of national interests, it is perhaps best viewed as an
attempt to reconcile the liberal and realist perspectives on world politics (Haggard and Simmons 1987).

The global trade and monetary rules created during and after World War
II are vivid examples of international regulatory regimes. These rules, as well
as particular sectors within the trade system, have been the focus of considerable inquiry from the regime perspective. Together, the trade and monetary
regimes comprised a *Liberal International Economic Order (LIEO)* that limited
government intervention in the world political economy and otherwise facilitated the free flow of goods and capital across national boundaries. The General Agreement on Tariffs and Trade (GATT) that preceded the World Trade
Organization (WTO) and the International Monetary Fund (IMF) played important institutional roles in the LIEO and reconfirmed the importance of international institutions in fostering transnational cooperation (see Chapter 8
for elaboration).

Most illustrations of the regime perspective appear in the "low politics"
arena of economic and humanitarian relationships (for an example, see Map
2.1); until recently, relatively few "security regimes" (Jervis 1982) had emerged
in the "high-politics" defense issue area. Early exceptions were the nuclear nonproliferation regime and the regime that the United States and the Soviet
Union used to manage their crises (see George 1986). But after the Cold War,
the pressures of globalization can be expected to foster creation of regimes in
widening areas of international conduct. This is likely to accelerate efforts to

international regimes a
perspective that explains the
benefits of actors supporting
particular rules to regulate a
specific international
activity, such as disposal of
toxic waste.

MAP 2.1

Regimes and the Transnational Management of Global Problems: Acid Rain

Acid rain is a transboundary pollutant that attacks countries differently. Because it knows no national boundaries and its sources often lie abroad, solutions to acid rain's corrosive effects require international cooperation. The rules of *international regimes* help to enforce such cooperation.

SOURCE: Adapted from Seager (1995), 48–49.

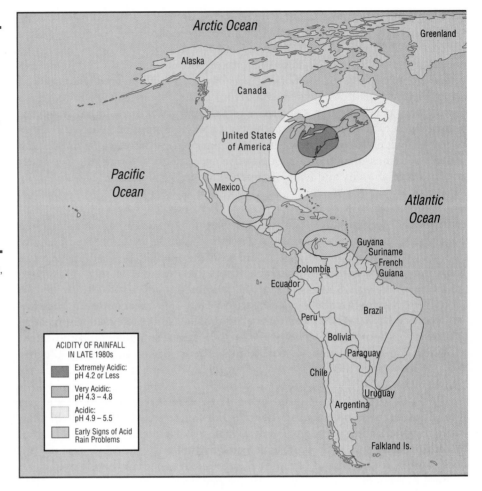

grapple theoretically with the causes and consequences of multilateral approaches to collective problem solving.

● ● ●

INTERNATIONAL POLITICS IN A WORLD OF CHANGE

To understand our changing world and to make reasonable prognoses about the future, we must begin by arming ourselves with an array of information and conceptual tools, entertaining rival interpretations of world politics, and questioning the assumptions on which these contending worldviews rest. Because there are a large (and growing) number of alternative, and sometimes incompatible, ways of organizing theoretical inquiry about world politics, the challenge of capturing the world's political problems cannot be reduced to any one simple yet compelling account, such as the four major theoretical traditions stressed here (see Table 2.1). Each paradigmatic effort to do so in the past, whether derived from liberalism or from realism, has ultimately been abandoned as developments in world affairs eroded its continuing relevance. Although grand theories fade with the passage of time, they often regain their attractiveness when global transformations make them useful once again. In fact, world politics is so resistant to clear, comprehensive, and convincing

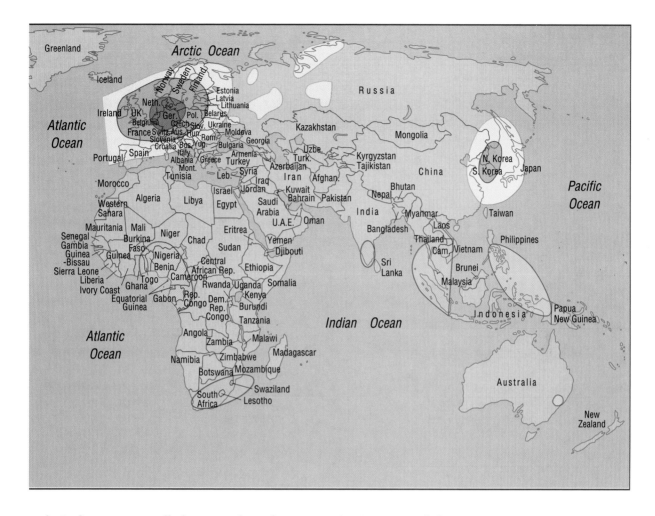

analysis that some so-called **postmodern deconstructionists** contend that international complexity defies description, explanation, and prediction (see Focus 2.4), while others working within the so-called **chaos theory** are struggling with discovering new methods of modeling this kind of turbulent global change. In addition, some theorists are persuaded that **social constructivism** can best interpret international relations by bridging the gap between neorealist and neoliberal theories; they see as necessary a reflective approach that inspects how state actors subjectively define and construct meanings as they acquire their interests and identities through their collective interactions (Wendt 1992; see also S. Smith 1997). Social constructivism is useful because it reminds us that how we think about the world matters, because all theories shape and construct our mental models of world politics.

The task of interpretation is complicated because the world is itself complex. As one scholar frames the challenge:

> Conceptually speaking, world affairs today can be likened to a disassembled jigsaw puzzle scattered on a table before us. Each piece shows a fragment of a broad picture that as yet remains indiscernible. Some pieces depict resurgent nationalism; others show spreading democracy; some picture genocide; others portray prosperity through trade and investment; some picture nuclear disarmament; others picture nuclear proliferation;

chaos theory the application of mathematical methods to identify underlying, episodically recurring patterns in rapidly changing and seemingly unconnected relationships (as many global phenomena appear) in order to better interpret complex reality.

social constructivism a liberal-realist theoretical approach advocated by Alexander Wendt that sees self-interested states as the key actors in world politics; their actions are determined not by anarchy but by the ways states socially "construct" and then respond to the meanings they give to power politics, so that as their definitions change, cooperative practices can evolve.

	Realism	Neorealism	Liberalism	Neoliberalism
Key units	Independent states	The international system's structure	Institutions transcending states	Individuals; "penetrated" states and nonstate transnational actors
Core concern	War and security	Struggle for position and power under anarchy	Institutionalizing peace	Fostering interstate cooperation on the globe's shared economic, social, and ecological problems
Major approach	Balance of power	Balance of terror, military preparedness, and deterrence	International law; international organization, democratization	Complex interdependence and regimes
Outlook on global prospects	Pessimistic/stability	Pessimistic	Optimistic/progress	Expectation of cooperation and creation of a global community
Motives of actors	National interests; zero-sum competition; security; power	Power, prestige, and advantage (relative gains) over other states	Collaboration; mutual aid; meeting human needs	Global interests (absolute gains); justice; peace and prosperity; liberty; morality
Central concepts	Structural anarchy; power; national interests; balance of power; polarity	Structural anarchy; rational choice; arms races	Collective security world order, law; integration; international organization	Transnational relations; law; free markets; interdependence; integration; liberal republican rule; human rights; gender
Prescriptions	Increase national power; resist reduction of national autonomy	Preserve nuclear deterrence; avoid disarmament and supernational organizations	Institutional reform	Develop regimes and promote democracy and international institutions to coordinate collective responses to global problems

some indicate a reinvigorated United Nations; others show the UN still enfeebled and ineffective; some describe cultural globalization; others predict clashing civilizations.

How do these pieces fit together, and what picture do they exhibit when they are appropriately fitted? (Puchala 1994, 17)

Theories can guide us in fitting the pieces together to form an accurate picture. However, in evaluating the usefulness of any theory to interpret global conditions, the historical overview in this chapter suggests that it would be wrong to oversimplify or to assume that a particular theory will remain useful in the future. All theories are maps of possible futures. Nonetheless, as the American poet Robert Frost observed in 1911, any belief we cling to long enough is likely to be true again someday, because "Most of the change we think we see in life is due to truths being in and out of favor." So in our theoretical exploration of world politics, we must critically assess the accuracy of our impressions, avoiding the temptation to embrace one worldview and abandon another without any assurance that their relative worth is permanently fixed.

Is Understanding International Complexity beyond the Analyst's Capability?

The Postmodern Critique of Contemporary Theoretical Interpretations

The most recent critique of behavioralism, **postmodernism** is an approach to the study of international relations since World War II that emphasizes the study of texts, hidden meanings, and discourse in the writings and speeches of policymakers and analysts who interpret world affairs. It represents what is often described as a "postpositivist" reaction. **Positivism** is a philosophical tradition underlying the scientific method and concerned with positive facts and phenomena, to the exclusion of speculation about ultimate causes or origins. Thus behavioralists and those committed to the scientific method as a way of understanding the social and political world are typically described as positivists. Postmodernists are postpositivistic because they call for a reexamination of the philosophical basis for making truth claims in international relations theory.

As with the earlier debate between traditionalists and behaviorists, postmodernism is part of a broader movement in the humanities, variously known as "critical social theory," "poststructuralism," or "deconstructionism." Those associated postmodern theorists interpret the particular meaning and intentions of particular texts and the cultural context in which they are communicated. Critical theories take the inherently subjective nature of images of world politics and the "social construction reality" as their point of departure (for example, see Ashley and Walker 1990, Der Derian 1995, Onuf

1989, Sjolander and Cox 1994, and Walker 1993; for a critique of the postmodern critique, see Rosenau 1992).

Postmodern critical introspection into the foundations of scientific methods of inquiry in general and international relations theory in particular is characterized by questioning whether it is possible to truly understand reality. Postmodernists believe that there is no objective international reality that we can discover—it is inherently intangible, and what we assume to be "true" masks the values on which we base our analyses. The purpose of inquiry, therefore, is to expose the fallacy of those who contend that they understand reality. To this end, postmodernists refuse to study international relations; instead, they study the texts, "subtexts" (hidden meanings), and language in the writings, speeches, and arguments of policymakers and analysts who interpret world affairs. Revealing the distortions and misrepresentations of these "shrewd deceivers" through the deconstruction of words and texts, deconstructionists aim to identify the coexisting "multiple realities" and the fictional basis within the "stories" of modern authorities that assert stable truths. In short, postmodernism is a skeptical attack on conventional approaches to the study of international relations that attempts to show how they create reality, rather than convey it, through literary constructions and the reader's preconceived assumptions.

KEY TERMS

paradigm
decision-making theory
long-cycle theory
dependency theory
hegemonic stability theory
world-system theory
comparative study of foreign
  policy
current history approach
theory
liberal idealists

collective security
self-determination
realism
realpolitik
power
self-help
state sovereignty
national interest
behavioralism
postbehavioral movement
neorealism

structural realism
neoliberalism
complex interdependence
feminist theory
international regimes
postmodern deconstructionists
chaos theory
social constructivism
postmodernism
positivism

Baylis, John and Steve Smith, eds. *The Globalization of World Politics*. New York: Oxford University Press, 1997.

Beer, Francis A., and Robert Hariman. *Post-Realism: The Rhetorical Turn in International Relations*. East Lansing, Mich.: Michigan State University Press, 1996.

Brooks, Stephen G. "Dueling Realisms," *International Organization* 51 (Summer 1997): 445–77.

Dougherty, James E., and Robert L. Pfaltzgraff, Jr. *Contending Theories of International Relations: A Comprehensive Survey*, 4th ed. New York: Longman, 1997.

Doyle, Michael W., and G. John Ikenberry, eds. *New Thinking in International Relations Theory*. Boulder, Colo.: Westview Press, 1997.

Ferguson, Yale H., and Richard W. Mansbach. *The Elusive Quest: Theory and International Politics*. Columbia: University of South Carolina Press, 1988.

Jarvis, Darryl. *International Relations and the Challenge of Postmodernism*. Columbia: University of South Carolina Press, 1999.

Kegley, Charles W., Jr., ed. *Controversies in International Relations Theory: Realism and the Neoliberal Challenge*. New York: St. Martin's Press, 1995.

Keohane, Robert O., and Joseph S. Nye, Jr. *Power and Interdependence: World Politics in Transition*, 2nd ed. Glenview, Ill.: Scott, Foresman/Little, Brown, 1989.

Neumann, Iver B., and Ole Weaver, eds. *The Future of International Relations: Masters in the Making?* London: Routledge, 1997.

Thompson, Kenneth W. *Schools of Thought in International Relations*. Baton Rouge: Louisiana State University Press, 1996.

Tickner, J. Ann. "You Just Don't Understand: Troubled Engagements Between Feminists and IR Theorists," *International Studies Quarterly* 41 (December 1997): 611–32.

WHERE ON THE WORLD WIDE WEB?

http://www.lib.byu.edu/~rdh/wwwi/1918/14points.html
President Woodrow Wilson's Fourteen Points   As Chapter 2 notes, Woodrow Wilson's celebrated Fourteen Points speech before a joint session of Congress on January 8, 1918 "expressed the sentiments of the liberal world view and program." The World War I Document Archive has made this famous speech available online. Take a moment to read the document. Can you draw any parallels between this speech and one that President Clinton might give in his State of the Union address?

http://www.sas.upenn.edu/~pgrose/mach/
Machiavelli Online   The writings of Nicolo Machiavelli (1469–1527) are often cited as the base of realist thinking in international relations. As this chapter specified, the realist worldview is often primarily concerned with a state's drive for power. Visit Machiavelli Online for a complete informational resource on Machiavelli's life and times. There is also a link to his famous book, *The Prince,* which you can read online.

http://odwin.ucsd.edu/idata/
Data on the Net   Try your hand at being a behavioral social scientist. The University of California at San Diego has made available a searchable Web site where you can browse the collection of 813 Internet sites of numerous social science statistical data. On the homepage, type a topic area that interests you and receive data that is relevant to your topic area.

http://www.cudenver.edu/~mryder/itc_data/postmodern.html
Contemporary Philosophy, Critical Theory, and Postmodern Thought   The University of Colorado at Denver's School of Education has created a Web site that helps students understand the ideas behind critical theory and postmodern thought. Read about the main authors of postmodern thought and then access their works.

http://csf.colorado.edu/isa/ftgs/
Feminist Theory and International Studies   This is the homepage of the Feminist Theory and Gender Studies Section (FTGSS) of the International Studies Association. Through this site you can access the archives of FEMISA, a moderated discussion list where individuals discuss issues related to gender and international studies. You can also subscribe to the FEMISA list and join the lively debate.

CHAPTER 3

How States Make Foreign Policy Decisions to Cope with International Circumstances

●●●
Foreign policy is the system of activities evolved by communities for changing the behavior of other states and for adjusting their own activities to the international environment.

—GEORGE MODELSKI, *political scientist, 1962*

●●●
*We will be known as the world-class ditherers who stood by while the seeds of renewed global conflict were sown, or as the generations that took strong measures to forge alliances, deter aggression and keep the peace. . . .
Ultimately, it is a matter of judgment, a question of choice.*

—MADELEINE ALBRIGHT, *U.S. Secretary of State, 1997*

CHAPTER TOPICS AND THEMES

■ The emergence of the modern state system

■ The international and internal determinants of states' foreign policy behavior

● Levels of analysis

● Factors influencing foreign policy choices

■ The unitary actor and rational decision making

■ The bureaucratic politics of foreign policy decision making

■ The role of leaders in foreign policy decision making

■ Constraints on foreign policy making: Problems and prospects

In studying world politics we typically use the term **actor** to refer to entities that are its primary performers. These entities include countries (e.g., the United States and Japan), international organizations (the United Nations), multinational corporations (General Motors and Sony), nongovernmental organizations (Green Peace), nonstate nations (the Kurds in Iran and Iraq), and terrorist groups (the Irish Republican Army). The image is that of a stage on which those most capable of capturing the drama of world politics act out the roles assigned to them. The leading actors dominate center stage, and the supporting players are less evident as they move along the periphery.

Although we will discuss each type of actor in later chapters, here we focus on countries, usually called "states." We particularly emphasize the processes states use to make foreign policy decisions designed to cope with challenges from abroad. States demand attention because international law gives them status as the principal holders of economic and military capabilities in world affairs, and assigns to them alone the legal right to use force.

● ● ●

THE EMERGENCE OF THE MODERN STATE SYSTEM

As a network of relationships among independent political units, the state system was born with the Peace of Westphalia in 1648, which ended the Thirty Years' War in Europe. Thereafter, European rulers refused to recognize the authority of the Roman Catholic church, replacing the previous system of papal governance with geographically and politically separate states that recognized no authority above them. The newly independent states were all given the same legal rights: territory under their sole control, the freedom to conduct foreign relations and negotiate treaties with other states, and the authority to establish whatever form of government they chose. The concept of **state sovereignty**—that no one is above the state—captures these legal rights.

state sovereignty a state's supreme authority to manage internal affairs and foreign relations.

The Westphalian system still colors every dimension of world politics, and provides the terminology used to describe the primary units in international affairs. Although the term "nation-state" is often confusingly used interchangeably with "state" and "nation," technically the three are different. A **state** is a legal entity that enjoys a permanent population, a well-defined territory, and a government capable of exercising sovereignty. A **nation** is a collection of people who, on the basis of ethnic, linguistic, or cultural affinity, perceive themselves to be members of the same group. Thus the term nation-state implies a convergence between territorial states and the psychological identification of people within them. However, in employing this familiar terminology, we should exercise caution because this condition is relatively rare; there are few independent states comprised of a single nationality. As we shall explain in Chapter 7, most states are populated by many nations, and some nations are not states. These "nonstate nations" are ethnic groups, such as Native American tribes in the United States, Sikhs in India, or Basques in Spain, composed of people without sovereign power over the territory in which they live.

foreign policy the decisions governing authorities make in the name of the state to realize international goals.

When we speak generically about **foreign policy** and the decision-making processes that produce it, we mean the goals that officials representing states seek abroad, the values that underlie those goals, and the means or instruments used to pursue them. To begin our inquiry into how states make foreign policy choices, we first consider the setting for their choices and the circumstances outside national borders that make such choices necessary. Next we look at decision making as a *rational* process before considering two ways of viewing national decision making: the bureaucratic politics and the hero-in-history models. We conclude by examining how states' national attributes influence their foreign policy behavior.

• • •

THE INTERNATIONAL AND INTERNAL DETERMINANTS OF STATES' FOREIGN POLICY BEHAVIOR

Geostrategic location, military might, economic prowess, and system of government are all variables that affect foreign policy choices. Still, due to the diversity of states, as well as their different locations and positions within the contemporary state system, it is difficult to generalize about the influence of any one factor or combination of factors.

To determine the relative impact of specific factors under different circumstances, we must first distinguish between the global and internal influences on policy choices. Note the levels-of-analysis distinction pictured in Figure 3.1. In classifying the determinants not only of states' foreign policies but also of trends in world politics generally, the levels-of-analysis concept (introduced in Chapter 1) helps to describe the influences on states' decision-making

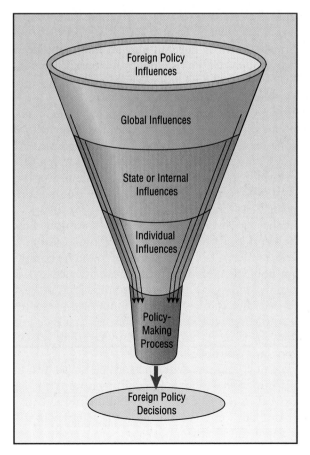

FIGURE 3.1

The Major Sources of States' Foreign Policy Decisions: Influences at Three Levels

The factors that shape states' foreign policies can be categorized at three basic levels. At the global level are those features of the international system such as the prevalence of civil wars and the extent of trade interdependence. At the state level are internal or domestic influences such as the state's type of political system or the opinions of its citizens. At the individual level are the characteristics of the leader—his or her personal beliefs, values, and personality. All three levels of influence simultaneously affect decisions, but their relative weight usually depends on the issues and circumstances at the time of decision.

processes. Recall that states and the global system make up two distinct levels, the "state" level, encompassing domestic characteristics, and the "global" or international system level, encompassing interstate relations and changes in these relations over time. Although these two traditionally discrete realms have become increasingly fused in what has become known as **intermestic politics,** highlighting the need for leaders to integrate their domestic and foreign policies, for purposes of analysis this categorical distinction is still useful.

intermestic politics those issues confronting a state that are simultaneously international and domestic.

International or "external" influences on foreign policy include all activities occurring beyond a state's borders that structure the choices its officials make. Such factors as the content of international law, the number of military alliances, deterioration of the global environment, and the changing levels of international trade sometimes profoundly affect the choices of decision makers.

Internal or "domestic" influences, on the other hand, are those that exist at the level of the state, not the system. Here attention focuses on variations in **states' attributes,** such as military capabilities, level of economic development, and types of government, that may influence different states' foreign policy behavior. Examples of both types of influences follow.

Geopolitics

One of the most important influences on a state's foreign policy behavior is its location and physical terrain. The presence of natural frontiers, for example, may profoundly guide policymakers' choices (see Map 3.1). Consider the United States, which has prospered because vast oceans separate it from Europe and Asia. This advantage, combined with the absence of militarily powerful neighbors permitted the United States to develop into an industrial giant and at times to practice safely an isolationist foreign policy for over 150 years. Consider also mountainous Switzerland, whose topography and geostrategic position have made neutrality a compelling foreign policy posture.

Similarly, maintaining autonomy from continental politics has been an enduring theme in the foreign policy of Great Britain, an island country whose physical separation from Europe served historically as a buffer separating it from entanglement in major-power disputes on the continent. Preserving this protective shield has been a priority for Britain and helps to explain why the British government in the early 1990s resisted greater integration of its economy into the European Union (see Chapters 6 and 16).

Most countries are not insular, however; they have many states on their borders, denying them the option of noninvolvement in world affairs. Germany, which sits in the geographic center of Europe, historically has found its domestic political system and foreign policy preferences profoundly affected by its geostrategic position. In this century alone, even before the unification of East and West, Germany had "undergone five radical changes in political personality—from Wilhelm II's empire to the Weimar Republic, from Hitler's *Reich* of the Thousand Years to its two postwar successors, the Federal Republic of Germany . . . and the German Democratic Republic" (Joffe 1985).

In much the same way, extended frontiers with the former Soviet Union shaped the foreign policies of China and Finland. Finland's neutrality in the Cold War helped ensure its survival in the face of a powerful and threatening neighbor. China, on the other hand, has long regarded its relationship with the now defunct Soviet Union as unequal, and in the late 1960s the two communist

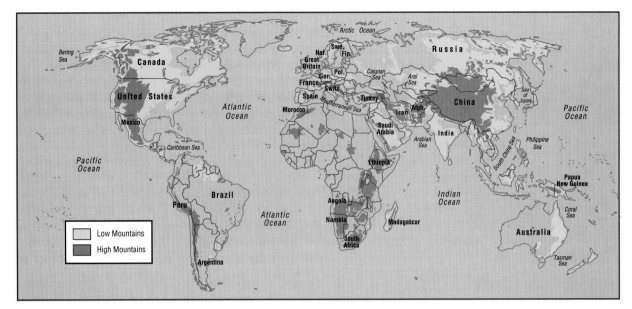

M A P   3 . 1

Geographic Influences on Foreign Policy

How countries act toward others is shaped by the number of neighboring states on their borders and whether they are protected from invasion by natural barriers such as mountains and oceans. This map suggests how the separation of the United States from Eurasia has encouraged an isolationist policy during many periods in America's history. Note also how topography, location, and other geopolitical factors may have influenced the foreign policy priorities of Great Britain, Germany, China, Finland, and states in South America—hypotheses advanced by the geopolitics approach to international politics.

giants clashed militarily as the Chinese sought to rectify past injustices. The "unequal treaties" between China and outside powers, which encapsulate these perceived injustices, resulted in part from China's size and location, which made it an easy target for the great powers that had carved it into spheres of influence in previous centuries.

Like China, the Latin American countries have found themselves geographically near a much stronger power, the United States, whose capabilities are in part a function of geophysical resources. Latin America has long been the object of studied interest and frequent intervention by the giant to the north. South America's economic dependence on the United States provoked a bitter response for many decades, because those countries felt they could not compete on an equal footing with the U.S. economic and military powerhouse. Their foreign policy of resistance to so-called Yankee imperialism was driven by their disadvantaged circumstances. Understandably, many other poor Global South countries without many resources also see that, given their geo-economic condition, their foreign policy goals should be geared to opposing **imperialism**—what Egypt's President Nasser defined as "the subjugation of small nations to the interests of the big ones."

History is replete with other examples of geography's influence on states' foreign policy goals, which is why geopolitical theories are useful (see Demko

geopolitics theory that states' foreign policies are determined by their location, natural resources, and physical environment.

and Wood 1994). The **geopolitics** school of realist thought and political geography generally stress the influence of geographic factors on state power and international conduct. Illustrative of early geopolitical thinking is Alfred Thayer Mahan's (1890) *The Influence of Sea Power in History*, which maintained that control of the seas shaped national power. Thus states with extensive coastlines and ports enjoyed a competitive advantage. Later geopoliticians, such as Sir Halford Mackinder (1919) and Nicholas Spykman (1944), stressed that not only location but also topography, size (territory and population), climate, and distance between states are powerful determinants of the foreign policies of individual countries. The underlying principle behind the geopolitical perspective is self-evident: Leaders' perceptions of available foreign policy options are influenced by the geopolitical circumstances that define their states' place on the world stage.

Geopolitics is only one aspect of the global environment that may influence foreign policy. In other chapters we will discuss additional global factors. Here, we comment briefly on three internal attributes of states that influence their foreign policies: military capabilities, economic characteristics, and type of government.

Military Capabilities

The proposition that states' internal capabilities shape their foreign policy priorities is supported by the demonstrable fact that states' preparations for war strongly influence their later use of force (see Levy 1989a; Vasquez 1993). Thus while all states may seek similar goals, their ability to realize them will vary according to their military capabilities.

Because military capabilities limit a state's range of prudent policy choices, they act as a mediating factor on leaders' national security decisions. For instance, in the 1980s Libyan leader Muammar Qaddafi repeatedly provoked the United States through anti-American and anti-Israeli rhetoric and by supporting various terrorist activities. Qaddafi was able to act as he did largely because neither bureaucratic organizations nor a mobilized public existed in Libya to constrain his personal whims and militaristic foreign policy preferences. However, Qaddafi was doubtlessly more highly constrained by the outside world than were the leaders in the more militarily capable countries toward whom his anger was directed. Limited military muscle compared with the United States precluded the kinds of bellicose behaviors he threatened to practice.

Conversely, Saddam Hussein, the Iraqi dictator, made strenuous efforts to build Iraq's military might (partly with the help of U.S. arms sales) and by 1990 had built the fourth-largest army in the world. Thus the invasion of Kuwait became a feasible foreign policy option. In the end, however, even Iraq's impressive military power proved ineffective against a vastly superior coalition of military forces, headed by the United States, which forced Saddam Hussein to capitulate and withdraw from the conquered territory. The conflict reignited in 1998 when Iraq resisted UN inspection of its weapons-production facilities.

Economic Characteristics

The level of economic and industrial development a state enjoys affects the foreign policy goals it can pursue. Generally, the more economically developed a state is, the more likely it is to play an activist role in the global political econ-

In 1990, Iraqi dictator Saddam Hussein used his country's formidable military capabilities to invade Kuwait. He was later repelled by the superior force of nearly forty states, led by the United States in Operation Desert Storm. The case suggests the lesson that the power to destroy does not necessarily give an aggressor the power to control.

omy. Rich states have interests that extend far beyond their borders and typically possess the means to pursue and protect them. Not coincidentally, states that enjoy industrial capabilities and extensive involvement in international trade also tend to be militarily powerful—in part because military might is a function of economic capabilities. Historically, only the world's most scientifically sophisticated industrial economies have produced nuclear weapons, which many regard as the ultimate expression of military prowess. In this sense nuclear weapons are the *result* of being powerful, not its cause.

For four decades after World War II, the United States and the Soviet Union stood out as superpowers precisely because they benefited from a combination of vast economic and military capabilities, including extensive nuclear weapons capabilities. This enabled both states to practice unrestrained globalism; their "imperial reach" and interventionist behavior were seemingly unconstrained by limited wealth or resources. In fact, historically major powers (rich states) have been involved in foreign conflict more frequently than minor powers (poor states). For this reason, gross national product (GNP) is often used in combination with other factors to identify great powers, and by itself is an important element in predicting the extensiveness of states' global interests and involvements.

Although economically advanced states are more active globally, this does not mean that their privileged circumstances dictate adventuresome policies. Rich states are often "satisfied" ones that have much to lose from the onset of revolutionary change or global instability and that usually perceive the status quo as best serving their interests (Wolfers 1962). As a result, they often forge international economic policies to protect and expand their envied position at the pinnacle of the global hierarchy.

Levels of productivity and prosperity also affect the foreign policies of the poor states at the bottom of the hierarchy. Some dependent states respond to their economic weakness by complying subserviently with the wishes of the rich on whom they depend. Others rebel defiantly, sometimes succeeding (despite their disadvantaged bargaining position) in resisting the efforts by great powers to control their international behavior.

Thus generalizations about the economic foundations of states' international political behavior often prove inaccurate. Although levels of economic development vary widely among states in the international system, they alone do not determine foreign policies. Instead, leaders' *perceptions* of the opportunities and constraints that their states' economic resources provide may more powerfully influence their foreign policy choices.

Type of Government

A third important attribute affecting states' international behavior is their political system. Although neorealism would predict otherwise, type of government demonstrably constrains important choices, including whether the use of force is threatened and whether the threat is carried out. Here the important distinction is between **constitutional democracy** (representative government) on one end of the spectrum and **autocratic rule** (authoritarian or totalitarian) on the other.

constitutional democracy
government processes that
allow people or their elected
representatives to exercise
power and influence the
state's policies.

In neither democratic (sometimes called "open") nor autocratic ("closed") political systems can political leaders survive long without the support of organized domestic political interests (and sometimes the mass citizenry). But in democratic systems those interests are likely to be politically potent, dispersed beyond the government itself, and active in their pressure on the government to make policy choices that benefit them. Public opinion, interest groups, and the mass media are a more visible part of the policy-making process in democratic systems. Similarly, the electoral process in democratic societies more meaningfully frames choices and produces results about who will lead than typically occurs in authoritarian regimes, where the real choices are made by a few elites behind closed doors. In short, in a democracy, public opinions and preferences may matter and, therefore, differences in who is allowed to participate and how much they exercise their right to participate are critical determinants of foreign policy choices (see Ray 1995; Russett 1993).

Compare, for example, the foreign policy of Saudi Arabia, controlled by a king and royal family, with that of Switzerland, governed by a multiparty democratic process. In the former, foreign policy decisions have sometimes been bold and unexpected, as exemplified by the Saudi royal family's revolutionary policies in summoning U.S. military forces to its territory during the 1991 Persian Gulf War, in contravention of long-standing Arab policies designed to prevent Western encroachments against Muslim lands. In Switzerland, where voting and mass political participation heavily influence decisions about Switzerland's international activities, the policy of neutrality has been pursued without deviation since 1815.

elitism argument that
because a "power elite"
really controls democratic
governments for their own
interests, ordinary citizens
are given participation
without power, involvement
without influence.

Although public preferences help shape democratic societies' foreign policies, so too does **elitism** (Mills 1956). Often, even in democratic governments, decisions are made by a small ruling elite; this is especially true when international crises erupt. Military-industrial complexes, obtrusively evident in many countries, are examples of elite groups sometimes believed to exercise disproportionate control over defense policy making, in both turbulent and calm times. Elitism's rival model, known as **pluralism,** sees policy making as an upward-flowing process in which competitive domestic groups pressure the

gression during times of economic and domestic crisis (Morgan and Campbell 1991), and some important exceptions to the general rule that democratic regimes are less bellicose can be found in history (Wright 1942). In addition, the record of democratic states' active participation in colonial wars undermines liberalism's expectation that democratic rule is an antidote to imperialism (see Chan 1984 and 1997). So, too, does democratic states' frequent practice of military intervention short of war (Kegley and Hermann 1997). Indeed, critics note that the longest surviving democracy, the United States, initiated or supported military or paramilitary actions against elected governments in Chile, Grenada, Nicaragua, and Panama, and that Hitler came to power through the ballot, only to wage the most destructive war in history. Consequently, we must suspend judgment on the question of whether a world of democracies will necessarily be a more peaceful world.

These observations about the ways in which states' attributes relate to their foreign policy-making processes highlight the extent to which internal conditions influence the foreign policy choices of even great powers. Contrary to realism's premise, the record shows that the type of government, and more specifically whether leaders are accountable to opposition groups through multiparty elections, strongly influences the kinds of goals these states pursue abroad (see Snyder 1991). Citizens' freedom clearly constrains their leaders choices and influences liberal democracies' patterns of international interactions. Many developments in world politics examined in later chapters will draw further attention to the internal roots of external behavior.

Having described the international settings to which policymakers respond and the internal factors that influence their decisions, we now turn to *how* foreign policy decisions are reached. We begin with the rational model of decision making.

• • •

THE UNITARY ACTOR AND RATIONAL DECISION MAKING

According to realist theorizing, the primary goal of states' foreign policies is to ensure their survival. From this viewpoint, strategic calculations about national security are the primary determinants of policymakers' choices. Domestic politics and the process of policy making itself are of secondary concern.

States as Unitary Actors

Realism, in both its classical and neorealist forms, emphasizes that the international environment determines state action. It assumes that foreign policy making consists primarily of adjusting the state to the pressures of an anarchical world system whose essential properties will not vary. Accordingly, it presumes that all states and the individuals responsible for their foreign policies confront the problem of national survival in similar ways. Thus all decision makers are essentially alike in their approach to foreign policy making:

> If they follow the [decision] rules, we need know nothing more about them. In essence, if the decision maker behaves rationally, the observer, knowing the rules of rationality, can rehearse the decisional process in his own

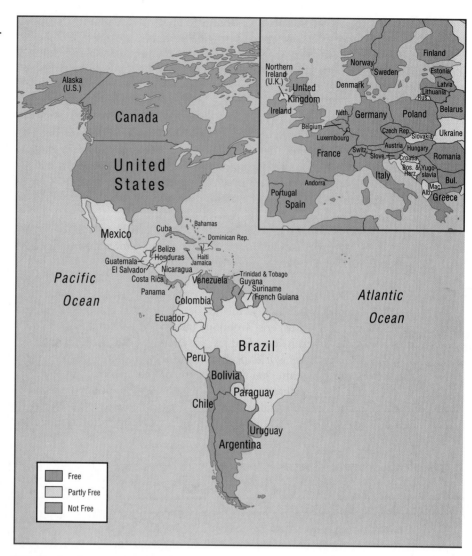

MAP 3.2

The Flow of Freedom: The Spread of Democratic Liberty throughout the World

Throughout most of modern history the majority of states were ruled autocratically and the people living in them were not free. However, since the mid–1950s, an increasing number of states undertook political reforms leading to transitions toward democratic governance and civil liberties. This map shows the location of 81 "free" countries as of 1997 whose governments provide their citizens with a high degree of political and economic freedom and safeguard basic civil liberties, 54 "partly free" electoral democracies whose citizens enjoy limited political rights amidst corruption and flawed justice, and 53 "not free" states where citizens' human rights and liberties are systematically abused or denied. Liberal democratic peace theory predicts that the spread of liberty, if it continues, will produce peaceful relations among the growing community of liberal democracies whose leaders are accountable to the public for their election and for approval of their policies.

SOURCE: Freedom House, an international organization dedicated to strengthening democratic institutions (see also Karatnycky and Cashdan 1997).

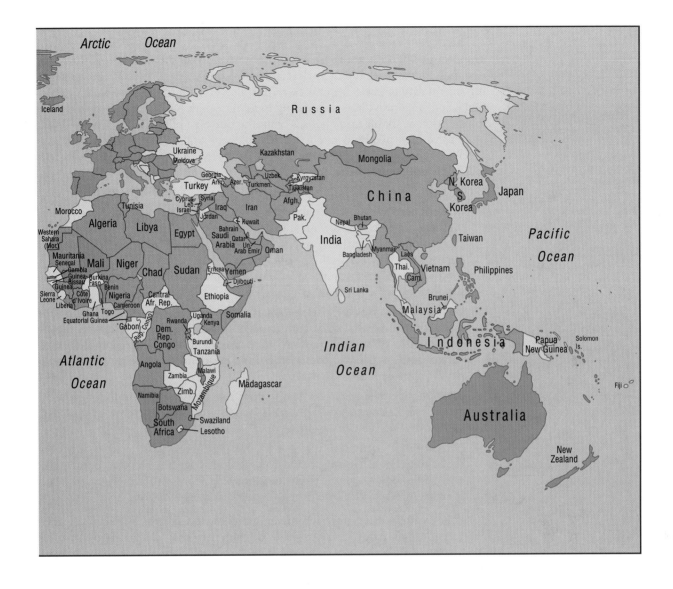

mind, and, if he knows the decision maker's goals, can both predict the decision and understand why that particular decision was made. (Verba 1969, 225)

Because realists believe that leaders' goals and their corresponding approach to foreign policy choices are the same, the decision-making processes of each state can be studied as though it were a **unitary actor**—a homogenous or monolithic unit with few or no important internal differences that affect its choices. One way to picture this assumption is to think of states as billiard balls and the table on which they interact as the state system. The balls (states) continuously clash and collide with one another, and the actions of each are determined by its interactions with the others, not by what occurs inside it. According to this realist view, the leaders who make foreign policy, the types of governments they head, the characteristics of their societies, and the internal economic and political conditions of the states they lead are unimportant.

unitary actor a transnational actor whose internal differences do not influence its international behavior.

55

Policy Making as Rational Choice

The decision-making processes of unitary actors that determine definitions of national interests are typically described as rational. We proceed here by defining **rationality** or **rational choice** as purposeful, goal-directed behavior exhibited when "the individual responding to an international event . . . uses the best information available and chooses from the universe of possible responses that alternative most likely to maximize his [or her] goals" (Verba 1969). Scholars describe rationality as a sequence of decision-making activities involving the following intellectual steps:

1. *Problem recognition and definition.* The need to decide begins when policymakers perceive an external problem and attempt to define objectively its distinguishing characteristics. Objectivity requires full information about the actions, motivations, and capabilities of other actors as well as the character of the international environment and trends within it. The search for the information must be exhaustive, and all the facts relevant to the problem must be gathered.

2. *Goal selection.* Next, those responsible for making foreign policy choices must determine what they want to accomplish. This disarmingly simple requirement is often difficult. It requires the identification and ranking of *all* values (such as security, democracy, and economic well-being) in a hierarchy from most to least preferred.

3. *Identification of alternatives.* Rationality also requires the compilation of an exhaustive list of *all* available policy options and an estimate of the costs associated with each alternative.

4. *Choice.* Finally, rationality requires selecting the single alternative with the best chance of achieving the desired goal(s). For this purpose, policymakers must conduct a rigorous means-ends, cost-benefit analysis guided by an accurate prediction of the probable success of each option.

Policymakers often describe their own behavior as resulting from a rational decision-making process designed to reach the "best" decision possible. Indeed, some past foreign policy decisions do reveal elements of this idealized process.

The 1962 Cuban missile crisis, for example, illustrates several ways in which the deliberations of key U.S. policymakers conformed to a rational process (Allison 1971; for a reassessment, see May and Zelikow 1997). Once Washington discovered the presence of Soviet missiles in Cuba, President John F. Kennedy formed a crisis decision-making group and charged it to "set aside all other tasks to make a prompt and intensive survey of the dangers and all possible courses of action." Six options were ultimately identified: Do nothing; exert diplomatic pressure; make a secret approach to the Cuban leader Fidel Castro; invade Cuba; launch a surgical air strike against the missiles; or blockade Cuba. Before the group could choose among these six, it had to prioritize goals. Was removal of the Soviet missiles, retaliation against Castro, or maintaining the balance of power the objective? Or did the missiles pose little threat to vital U.S. interests? Until it was determined that the missiles posed a serious threat to national security, "do nothing" could not be eliminated as an option.

Once the advisers agreed that their goal was removing the missiles, their discussion turned to evaluating the options of a surgical air strike or a blockade. They eventually chose the latter because of its presumed advantages, in-

Israeli Prime Minister Yitzhak Rabin, Egyptian President Hosni Mubarak, Jordan's King Hussein, U.S. President Bill Clinton, and the Palestine Liberation Organization's Yasser Arafat made history by signing an accord in September 1995 to expand Palestinian self-rule on the West Bank. The agreement was reached through step-by-step bargaining, to realize common objectives presumably carefully decided on by rational choice. Fateful diplomatic ties (like the neck ties they instinctively adjusted at the same time for the photo), can sometimes go off course, despite the best intentions. Five months later, the celebratory mood of the moment vanished when Rabin was assassinated by a terrorist as punishment for his act of courage.

cluding the demonstration of firmness it permitted the United States and the flexibility about further choices it allowed both parties.

President George Bush's decision to send a military force to the Middle East following Iraq's invasion of Kuwait on August 2, 1990, is another example of crisis decision making that conforms in part to the model of rational choice. As in the Cuban case, the "do nothing" option was quickly dismissed by the president and his advisers. Instead, "much of the initial debate among senior government officials on August 2 and 3 focused on diplomatic and economic retaliation against Iraq, and possible covert action to destabilize and topple Saddam Hussein" (Woodward and Atkinson 1990). By August 4, Bush decided to mount a military response. Two days later, after vowing that Iraq's invasion of Kuwait "will not stand," he ordered the dispatch of U.S. troops to pursue three missions: to deter further Iraqi aggression, to defend Saudi Arabia, and to "improve the overall defense capabilities of the Saudi peninsula" (Woodward and Atkinson 1990). Eventually, those defensive missions gave way to an offensive one designed to force Iraq out of Kuwait.

Impediments to Rational Choice

Despite the apparent application of rationality in these crises, rational choice is often more an idealized standard than an accurate description of real-world behavior. Theodore Sorenson—one of President Kennedy's closest advisers and speechwriters and a participant in the Cuban missile deliberations—has written not only about the steps policymakers in the Kennedy administration followed as they sought to emulate the process of rational choice but also of how actual decision making often departed from it. He described an eight-step process for policy making that is consistent with the model we have described: (1) agreeing on the facts; (2) agreeing on the overall policy objective; (3) precisely defining the problems; (4) canvassing all possible solutions; (5) listing the possible consequences that flow from each solution; (6) recommending one option; (7) communicating the option selected; and (8) providing for its execution. But he explained how difficult it is to follow these steps, because:

> [e]ach step cannot be taken in order. The facts may be in doubt or dispute. Several policies, all good, may conflict. Several means, all bad, may be all that are open. Value judgments may differ. Stated goals may be imprecise. There may be many interpretations of what is right, what is possible, and what is in the national interest. (Sorensen 1963, 19–20)

Despite the virtues rational choice promises, the impediments to its realization are substantial. Some are human, deriving from deficiencies in the intelligence, capability, and psychological needs and aspirations of foreign policy decision makers. Others are organizational, since most decisions require group agreement about the national interest and the wisest course of action. Reaching agreement is not easy, however, as reasonable people with different values often disagree about goals, preferences, and the probable results of alternative options. Thus the impediments to sound (rational) policy making are not to be underestimated.

Scrutiny of the actual process of decision making reveals other hindrances. Available information is often insufficient to recognize emergent problems accurately, resulting in decisions made on the basis of incomplete information. In fact, **bounded rationality** is typical (Simon 1982). Moreover, the available information is often inaccurate, because the bureaucratic organizations political leaders depend on for advice screen, sort, and rearrange it.

bounded rationality concept that decision makers' capacity to choose the best option is often constrained by many human and organizational factors.

In addition, determining what goals best serve national interest is difficult: "Decision making often takes place within an atmosphere marked by value-complexity and uncertainty. The existence of competing values about a single issue forces value trade-offs; uncertainty refers to the absence of complete and well-organized information on which to base a confident policy choice" (Walker 1991).

Furthermore, decision makers' inability to rapidly gather and digest large quantities of information constrains their capacity to make informed choices. Because policymakers work with overloaded **policy agendas** and short deadlines, the search for policy options is seldom exhaustive. "There is little time for leaders to reflect," observes former U.S. Secretary of State Henry Kissinger (1979). "They are locked in an endless battle in which the urgent constantly gains on the important. The public life of every political figure is a continual struggle to rescue an element of choice from the pressure of circumstance." In the choice phase, then, decision makers rarely make value-maximizing choices. Instead of selecting the option with the best chance of success, they typically end their evaluation as soon as an alternative appears that seems superior to those already considered. Herbert Simon (1957) describes this as **satisficing behavior.** Rather than "optimizing" by seeking the best alternative, decision makers are routinely content to choose the first option that meets minimally acceptable standards. Because they frequently face "unresolvable" choices that preclude satisfaction across competing preferences, often only "admissible" ones appear available (see Levi 1990).

policy agenda the changing list of problems or issues to which governments pay special attention at any given moment.

satisficing behavior the tendency for decision makers to choose the first available alternative that meets minimum acceptable standards.

The ability to make decisions is hindered by individuals' difficulties in abandoning formed opinions and their tendency to overreact in crises. **Prospect**

Linking State and System
How Leaders Play Two-Level Games When Making Policy Decisions

It is customary to differentiate foreign policy and domestic policy as formulated by sovereign state governments. *Foreign policy* traditionally is defined as a state's goals in its relations with other actors beyond its borders, the values that shape those goals, and the means or practices used to realize them. **Domestic policy** refers to governmental decisions affecting people's behavior *within* the state's borders. However, in an age of globalization and state interdependence, it is often difficult to know where foreign policy ends and domestic policy begins. Policies at home often have many consequences abroad. Similarly, foreign activities usually heavily influence a state's internal condition. This is why many leaders are likely to fuse the two sectors in their thinking when making policy decisions. Still, many leaders continue to try to separate the two areas in making choices. As the U.S. Department of State (1993, 79) observes, today "the assertion that all foreign policy is ultimately local is closer to the mark than many in government admit."

To better capture the way most leaders proceed as they make policy decisions, Robert D. Putnam coined the phrase "two-level games." He maintains that leaders are required to formulate policies simultaneously in both the diplomatic and domestic arenas, and this drives them to perform in accordance with the decision rules dictated by this "game." He writes:

> At the national level, domestic groups pursue their interests by pressuring the government to adopt favorable policies, and politicians seek power by constructing coalitions among these groups. At the international level, national governments seek to maximize their own ability to satisfy domestic pressures, while minimizing the adverse consequences of foreign developments. Neither of the two games can be ignored by central decision-makers so long as their countries remain interdependent, yet sovereign. (Putnam 1988, 434)

As the links between territorially bounded states become increasingly tighter, we can expect leaders of states to struggle to master this game as they make policy decisions.

---

theory informs us further that when estimating potential gains and losses, people are "risk acceptant" with respect to gains but even more stubbornly "loss averse" in their refusal to admit and correct costly mistakes. Like investors who take big risks in the hope of making big profits but hold losing investments too long, policymakers view the prospects of new policies hopefully but cling to failed policies long after their deficiencies have become apparent. This—along with the "sunk-cost fallacy" that having paid for something, people are unwilling to waste it no matter what the consequences, as well as people's tendency to select the option that looks preferable to some past reference point rather than one with better prospects for future gains—may account for leaders' reluctance to make and implement corrective policy decisions for fear of public criticism (Bostdorff 1993; also Levy 1992; Stein and Pauly 1993).

The assumption that states are unitary actors partially explains the discrepancy between the theory and practice of rational decision making. Most leaders must play **two-level games** by meeting the often incompatible demands of domestic politics and external diplomacy, and it is seldom possible to make policy decisions that respond rationally to both sets of goals (see Focus 3.2). In addition, states are administered by individuals with varying beliefs, values, preferences, and psychological needs, and such differences generate disagreements about goals and alternatives that are seldom resolved through tidy, orderly, rational processes. These procedures may be better described as **muddling through,** or making incremental policy changes through small steps (Lindblom 1979). As one former U.S. policymaker put it, "Rather than through grand decisions or grand alternatives, policy changes seem to come through a series of slight modifications of existing policy, with new policy emerging slowly and haltingly by small and usually tentative steps, a process of trial and error in which policy zigs and zags, reverses itself, and then moves forward" (Hilsman 1967).

Despite the image that policymakers seek to project, the actual practice of foreign policy decision making is an exercise that lends itself to miscalculations, errors, and fiascoes. Policymakers tend "to avoid new interpretations of the environment, to select and act upon traditional goals, to limit the search for alternatives to a small number of moderate ones, and finally to take risks which involve low costs" (Coplin 1971). Thus, although policymakers can sometimes absorb new information quickly under great pressure and take calculated risks through deliberate planning, more often the degree of rationality "bears little relationship to the world in which officials conduct their deliberations" (Rosenau 1980; see Table 3.1.)

Although rational foreign policy making is more an ideal than a reality, we can still assume that policymakers aspire to rational decision-making behavior, which they may occasionally approximate. Indeed, as a working proposition, it is useful to accept rationality as a picture of how the decision process *should* work as well as a description of key elements of how it *does* work (see Table 3.1).

• • •

THE BUREAUCRATIC POLITICS OF FOREIGN POLICY DECISION MAKING

Picture yourself as a head of state charged with managing your nation's relations with the rest of the world. To make the right choices, you must seek information and advice, and you must see that the actions your decisions generate

TABLE 3.1 Foreign Policy Decision Making in Theory and Practice

Ideal Rational Process	Actual Common Practice
Accurate, comprehensive information	Distorted, incomplete information
Clear definition of national interests and goals	Personal motivations and organizational interests bias national goals
Exhaustive analysis of all options	Limited number of options considered, none thoroughly analyzed
Selection of optimal course of action most capable of producing desired results	Course of action selected by political bargaining and compromise
Effective statement of decision and its rationale to mobilize domestic support	Confusing and contradictory statements of decision, often framed for media consumption
Careful monitoring of the decision's implementation by foreign affairs bureaucracies	Neglect of the tedious task of managing the decision's implementation by foreign affairs bureaucracies
Instantaneous evaluation of consequences followed by correction of errors	Superficial policy evaluation, uncertain responsibility, poor follow-through, and delayed correction

are carried out properly. Who can aid you in these tasks? Out of necessity, you must turn to those with the expertise you lack.

In today's world, states' extensive political, military, and economic relations require dependence on large-scale organizations. Leaders turn to these organizations for information and advice as they face critical foreign policy choices. Although this is more true of major powers than of small states, even those without large budgets and complex foreign policy bureaucracies make most of their decisions in an organizational context (Korany 1986). The reasons are found in the vital services that organizations perform, enhancing the state's capacity to cope with changing global circumstances.

Foreign Policy-Making Organizations

Making and executing a state's foreign policy generally involves many different governmental organizations. In the United States, for instance, the State Department, Defense Department, and Central Intelligence Agency are all key participants in the foreign policy machinery. Other agencies also bear responsibility for specialized aspects of U.S. foreign relations, such as the Treasury, Commerce, and Agriculture departments. Multiple agencies with similar responsibilities also characterize the foreign affairs machinery of most other major powers, whose governments face many of the same foreign policy management problems as the United States.

Bureaucracy, Efficiency, and Rationality

Bureaucratic management of foreign relations is not new. However, with the internationalization of domestic politics in this century, the growth of large-scale organizations to manage foreign relations has spread. Bureaucratic procedures based on the theoretical work of the German social scientist Max Weber are commonplace, primarily because they are perceived to enhance rational decision making and efficient administration.

Bureaucracies increase efficiency and rationality by assigning responsibility for different tasks to different people. They define rules and standard operating procedures that specify how tasks are to be performed; they rely on systems of records to gather and store information; and they divide authority among different organizations to avoid duplication of effort. Bureaucracies also permit the luxury of engaging in forward planning designed to determine long-term needs and the means to attain them. Unlike heads of state, whose roles require attention to the crisis of the moment, bureaucrats are able to consider the future as well as the present.

bureaucracies the agencies, regulatory commissions, and departments that conduct the functions of a central government.

Even the existence of many organizations may sometimes be a virtue. The presence of several organizations can result in "multiple advocacy" of rival choices (George 1972), thus improving the chance that all possible policy options will be considered.

The Limits of Bureaucratic Organization. What emerges from our description of bureaucracy is another idealized picture of the policy-making process. Before jumping to the conclusion that bureaucratic decision making is a modern blessing, however, we should emphasize that the foregoing propositions tell us how bureaucratic decision making *should* occur; they do not tell us how it *does*

bureaucratic politics model
a description of decision
making that sees foreign
policy choices based on
bargaining and
compromises among
government agencies.

policy networks leaders and
organized interests (such as
lobbies) that form temporary
alliances to influence a
particular policy decision.

caucuses informal groups
that individuals in
government join to promote
their common interests.

occur. The actual practice and the foreign policy choices that result depict a reality of burdens as well as benefits.

Consider again the 1962 Cuban missile crisis, probably the single most threatening crisis in the post-World War II era. The method that U.S. policymakers used in orchestrating a response is often viewed as having nearly approximated the ideal of rational choice. From another decision-making perspective, however, the missile crisis reveals how decision making by and within organizational contexts sometimes compromises rather than facilitates rational choice.

In his well-known book on the missile crisis, *Essence of Decision* (1971), Harvard political scientist Graham Allison identified two elements in the **bureaucratic politics model** (see also Bendor and Hammond 1992; Caldwell 1977; C. Hermann 1988). One, which he calls "organizational process," reflects the constraints that organizations and coalitions of organizations in **policy networks** place on decision makers' choices. The other, "governmental politics," draws attention to the "pulling and hauling" that occurs among the key participants and **caucuses** of aligned bureaucracies in the decision process.

One way in which large-scale bureaucratic organizations contribute to the policy-making process is by devising **standard operating procedures (SOPs)**—established methods to be followed in the performance of designated tasks. For example, once the Kennedy administration opted for a naval quarantine of Cuba, the Navy could carry out the president's decision according to previously devised procedures. These routines, however, effectively limit the range of viable policy choices. Rather than expanding the number of policy alternatives in a manner consistent with the logic of rational decision making, what organizations are prepared to do shapes what is and is not considered possible. In the Cuban crisis, a surgical air strike was seen as preferable to the blockade, but when the Air Force confessed that it could not guarantee complete success in taking out the missiles, the alternative was dropped.

Governmental politics, the second element in the bureaucratic politics model, is related to the organizational character of foreign policy making in complex societies. Not surprisingly, participants in the deliberations that lead to policy choices often define issues and favor policy alternatives that reflect their organizational affiliations. "Where you stand depends on where you sit" is a favorite aphorism reflecting these bureaucratic imperatives. Consequently, many students of the subject suspect that professional diplomats typically favor diplomatic approaches to policy problems, while military officers routinely favor military solutions.

Because the players in the game of governmental politics are responsible for protecting the nation's security, they are "obliged to fight for what they are convinced is right." The consequence is that "different groups pulling in different directions produce a result, or better a resultant—a mixture of conflicting preferences and unequal power of various individuals—distinct from what any person or group intended" (Allison 1971). Rather than being a value-maximizing process, then, policy making is itself intensely political. Thus, one explanation of why states make the choices they do lies not in their behavior vis-à-vis one another but within their own governments. And rather than presupposing the existence of a unitary actor, "it is necessary to identify the games and players, to display the coalitions, bargains, and compromises, and to convey some feel for the confusion" (Allison 1971). From this perspective, the decision to blockade Cuba was as much a product of *who* favored the

During crises that threaten a country's national security, decisions are usually made by the head of state and a small group of advisers, *not* by large-scale bureaucracies. Pictured here are members of the ad hoc decision-making team that President John F. Kennedy assembled to respond to the Cuban missile crisis, which included Attorney General Robert Kennedy, presidential adviser Theodore Sorenson, and Secretary of Defense Robert McNamara.

choice as of any inherent logic that may have commended it. Once Robert Kennedy (the president's brother and the attorney general), Theodore Sorensen (the president's special counsel and "alter ego"), and Secretary of Defense Robert McNamara united behind the blockade, how could the president have chosen otherwise?

"Who favored what" also colored President Bush's decision in 1991 to dispatch troops to Saudi Arabia. Although key Pentagon officials might have been expected to favor the use of force, some—specifically Dick Cheney, Secretary of Defense, and Colin Powell, the four-star general who was Chairman of the Joint Chiefs of Staff—only reluctantly supported the military option. Instead, members of the president's White House staff, notably Brent Scowcroft (the president's national security adviser and a retired air force lieutenant general) and the president himself (a World War II navy pilot) were the principal advocates of a military response (Woodward 1991). Scowcroft continued to push a reluctant military as the crisis evolved, until in the fall, the strategic plan changed from defense to offense.

The disastrous Vietnam War, which the professional military regarded as a debacle in part because it lacked public support at home and a clear political objective abroad, helps to explain the Pentagon's nonaggressiveness on the military option. General Powell, who served President Reagan as national security adviser and believed that "There is no legitimate use of military force without a political objective," apparently gave so much political advice during the early days of the crisis over Kuwait that "Cheney firmly suggested that the president would be better served if Powell offered more military advice" (Woodward and Atkinson 1990).

In some sense, what the military could offer constrained the Bush administration in much the same way it did Kennedy. For many years the Pentagon had been preparing for "low-intensity" conflicts in jungle or forested terrain. Thus, its SOPs were ill suited to mechanized warfare in the flat, open, and featureless desert terrain of the Middle East.

Daunting logistical obstacles confronted the Pentagon as it contemplated a mission in a distant region without U.S. military bases, and the gut response of

Powell and others during the early hours of the crisis was despair about the absence of preparations. How, then, to proceed? As in Cuba, the choice was shaped by previous decisions. The United States relied on a plan first devised in the early 1980s. A massive air- and sealift of military personnel and equipment and ground deployment of heavy armor and antitank weapons (Woodward and Atkinson 1990) became the basis for Operation Desert Storm. Once the president had ordered troops to the Persian Gulf region, a process was under way that the professional military could support and execute, and it became their standard for operations.

Attributes of Bureaucratic Behavior. In addition to their influence on the policy choices of political leaders, bureaucratic organizations possess several other characteristics that affect the decision-making environment. One such characteristic derives from the proposition that bureaucratic agencies are parochial and that every administrative unit within a state's foreign policy-making bureaucracy seeks to promote its own purposes and power. Organizational needs (such as large staffs and budgets) come before the state's needs, sometimes encouraging the sacrifice of national interests to bureaucratic interests (not because bureaucrats selfishly put their own interests over the country they serve but, instead, because they often come to see their own interests as the state's). Bureaucracies fight for survival, even when their usefulness has vanished.

> Programs that don't concoct some new argument or other for their continuing indispensability also tend to survive. This is because of [an] immutable law of government: even the most anachronistic, abysmal, extravagant and counterproductive government program will do at least one thing that is hard to assault. (Greenfield 1995)

As a corollary, bureaucratic parochialism breeds competition among the agencies charged with foreign policy responsibilities. Far from being neutral or impartial managers, desiring only to carry out orders from the head of state, bureaucratic organizations frequently take policy positions designed to increase their own influence relative to that of other agencies. Characteristically, they are driven to enlarge their prerogatives and expand the conception of their mission, seeking to take on other units' responsibilities and powers.

To protect their own interests, bureaucratic organizations attempt to reduce interference from and penetration by political leaders to whom they report as well as from other government agencies. Because knowledge is power, a common device for promoting organizational exclusivity is to hide inner workings and policy activities from others. The "invisible government" operating within the U.S. National Security Council during the Reagan administration illustrates this syndrome. Lieutenant Colonel Oliver North used his authority as a staff member of the council to orchestrate a secret arms-for-hostages deal with the Iranian government, part of what became popularly known as the Iran-*contra* affair.

The natural inclination of professionals who work in large organizations is to adapt their outlook and beliefs to those prevailing where they work. Every bureaucracy develops a shared "mind-set" or dominant way of looking at reality akin to the **groupthink** characteristic of the cohesiveness and solidarity that small groups often develop (Janis 1982). An institutional mind-set discourages creativity, dissent, and independent thinking; it encourages reliance on standard operating procedures and deference to precedent rather than the explo-

groupthink the propensity for members of a group to accept and agree with the group's prevailing attitudes, rather than speaking out for what they believe.

ration of new options to meet new challenges. This results in policy decisions that rarely deviate from conventional preferences.

The Consequences of Bureaucratic Policy Making. A corollary of the notion that bureaucracies are often self-serving and guardians of the status quo is their willingness to defy directives by the political authorities they are supposed to serve. Bureaucratic unresponsiveness and inaction sometimes manifest themselves as lethargy. At other times, bureaucratic sabotage is direct and immediate, again as vividly illustrated by the Cuban missile crisis. While President Kennedy sought to orchestrate U.S. action and bargaining, his bureaucracy in general, and the navy in particular, were in fact controlling events by doing as they wished.

> [The bureaucracy chose] to obey the orders it liked and ignore or stretch others. Thus, after a tense argument with the navy, Kennedy ordered the blockade line moved closer to Cuba so that the Russians might have more time to draw back. Having lost the argument with the president, the navy simply ignored his order. Unbeknownst to Kennedy, the navy was also at work forcing Soviet submarines to surface long before Kennedy authorized any contact with Soviet ships. And despite the president's order to halt all provocative intelligence, an American U–2 plane entered Soviet airspace at the height of the crisis. When Kennedy began to realize that he was not in full control, he asked his secretary of defense to see if he could find out just what the navy was doing. McNamara then made his first visit to the navy command post in the Pentagon. In a heated exchange, the chief of naval operations suggested that McNamara return to his office and let the navy run the blockade. (Gelb and Halperin 1973, 256)

Bureaucratic stubbornness is not unique to democracies. The resistance of bureaucracies to change is one of the major problems that reformers in the Soviet Union and the other centralized communist countries of Eastern Europe encountered, impairing their efforts to chart new policy directions and to remain in power. The foreign policy process in China, also a centralized communist government, operates similarly. It is "subject to the same vicissitudes of subjective perception, organizational conflict, bureaucratic politics, and factional infighting that bedevil other governments, perhaps more so given its size" (Whiting 1985). And in the United States nearly all chief executives have complained at some time about how the bureaucracy has undercut their policies, as Ronald Reagan did when bemoaned that "You know, one of the hardest things in a government this size is to know that down there, underneath, is the permanent structure that's resisting everything you're doing." The implementation of foreign policy innovations thus poses a major challenge to most leaders (see Smith and Clarke 1985).

Bureaucratic resistance is not the only inertial force promoting status quo foreign policies. The dynamics of governmental politics, which reduce policy choices to the outcome of a political tug of war, also retard the prospects for change. From the perspective of the participants, decision making is a high-stakes political game in which differences are often settled at the least common denominator instead of by rational cost-benefit calculations. As former U.S. Secretary of State Henry Kissinger described the process:

> Each of the contending factions within the bureaucracy has a maximum incentive to state its case in its most extreme form because the ultimate

outcome depends, to a considerable extent, on a bargaining process. The premium placed on advocacy turns decision making into a series of adjustments among special interests—a process more suited to domestic than to foreign policy. . . . The outcome usually depends more on the pressure or the persuasiveness of the contending advocates than on a concept of overall purpose. (Kissinger 1969, 268)

Thus it is not surprising that bureaucracies throughout the world are frequently the object of criticism by both the political leaders they ostensibly serve and the citizens whose lives they so often affect.

● ● ●

THE ROLE OF LEADERS IN FOREIGN POLICY DECISION MAKING

The course of history is determined by the decisions of political elites. Leaders and the kind of leadership they exert shape the way in which foreign policies are made and the consequent behavior of states in world politics. "There is properly no history, only biography" is the way Ralph Waldo Emerson encapsulated the view that individual leaders move history.

Leaders as Makers and Movers of World History

This **history-making individuals model** of policy decision making equates states' actions with the preferences and initiatives of the highest government officials. We expect leaders to lead, and we assume new leaders will make a difference. We reinforce this image when we routinely attach the names of leaders to policies, as though the leaders were synonymous with the state itself, as well as when we ascribe most successes and failures in foreign affairs to the leaders in charge at the time they occur. The equation of U.S. foreign policy with the Nixon Doctrine in the 1970s, the Reagan Doctrine in the 1980s, and the Clinton Doctrine in the 1990s, are recent examples.

Citizens are not alone in thinking that leaders are the decisive determinants of states' foreign policies and, by extension, world history. Leaders themselves seek to create impressions of their own self-importance while attributing extraordinary powers to other leaders. The assumptions they make about the personalities of their counterparts, consciously or unconsciously, in turn influence their own behavior toward them (Wendzel 1980), as political psychologists who study the impact of leaders' perceptions and personalities on their foreign policy preferences demonstrate (see Kelman 1965).

One of the dilemmas that leader-driven explanations of foreign policy behavior pose is that the movers and shakers of history often pursue decidedly irrational policies. The classic example is Adolf Hitler, whose ruthless determination to seek military conquest of the entire European continent proved disastrous for Germany. How do we square this kind of behavior with the logic of realism, which says that survival is the paramount goal of all states and that all leaders engage in rational decision making? If the realists are correct, even defects in states' foreign policy processes cannot easily explain such wide divergences between the decisions leaders sometimes make and what cold cost-benefit calculations would predict.

We can explain this divergence in part by distinguishing between procedural rationality and instrumental rationality (Zagare 1990). **Procedural rationality** is the foundation of the realists' billiard-ball image of world politics. It views all states as acting similarly because all decision makers engage in the same "cool and clearheaded ends-means calculation" (Verba 1969) based on perfect information and a careful weighing of all possible alternative courses of action. **Instrumental rationality** is a more limited view that says simply that individuals have preferences and, when faced with two or more alternatives, they will choose the one they believe will yield the preferred outcome.

The implications of these seemingly semantic differences are important. They demonstrate that rationality does not "connote superhuman calculating ability, omniscience, or an Olympian view of the world," as is often assumed when the rational-actor model we have described is applied to real-world situations (Zagare 1990). They also suggest that an individual's actions may be rational even though the process of decision making and its product may appear decidedly irrational. Why did Libya's leader, the mercurial Muammar Qaddafi, repeatedly challenge the United States, almost goading President Ronald Reagan into a military strike in 1986? Because, we can postulate, Qaddafi's actions were consistent with his preferences, regardless of how "irrational" it was for a fourth-rate military power to take on the world's preeminent superpower. This and many other examples serve as a reminder of the importance of the human factor in understanding how decisions are made. Temptation, lack of self control, anger, fear of getting hurt, religious conviction, bad habits, overconfidence—all play a part in determining why people make the kinds of decisions they do (see Kegley and Raymond 1999).

Factors Affecting the Capacity to Lead

Despite the popularity of the history-making individuals model, we must be wary of ascribing too much importance to individual leaders. Their influence is likely to be subtler a probability summarized by U.S. President Bill Clinton in 1998 when he observed, "Great presidents don't do great things. Great presidents get a lot of other people to do great things." Henry Kissinger, once described as "the most powerful individual in the world in the 1970s" (Isaak 1975), in 1985 urged against placing too much reliance on personalities:

> [There is] a profound American temptation to believe that foreign policy is a subdivision of psychiatry and that relations among nations are like relations among people. But the problem [of easing protracted conflicts between states] is not so simple. Tensions . . . must have some objective causes, and unless we can remove these causes, no personal relationship can possibly deal with them. We are [not] doing . . . ourselves a favor by reducing the issues to a contest of personalities.

Most leaders operate under a variety of political, psychological, and circumstantial constraints that limit what they can accomplish and reduce their control over events. In this context, Emmet John Hughes (1972), an adviser to President Dwight D. Eisenhower, concluded that "all of [America's past presidents] from the most venturesome to the most reticent have shared one disconcerting experience: the discovery of the limits and restraints—decreed by law, by history, and by circumstances—that sometimes can blur their clearest designs or dull their sharpest purposes." Abraham Lincoln in 1864 summarized his presidential experience with the conclusion, "I have not controlled events, events have controlled me."

The question at issue is not whether political elites lead or whether they can make a difference. They clearly do both. But leaders are not in complete control, and their influence is severely constrained. Thus personality and personal political preferences do not determine foreign policy directly. The relevant question, then, is not whether leaders' personal characteristics make a difference, but rather under what conditions their characteristics are influential. As Margaret G. Hermann has observed, the impact of leaders is modified by at least six factors:

> (1) what their world view is, (2) what their political style is like, (3) what motivates them to have the position they do, (4) whether they are interested in and have any training in foreign affairs, (5) what the foreign policy climate was like when the leader was starting out his or her political career, and (6) how the leader was socialized into his or her present position. World view, political style, and motivation tell us something about the leader's personality; the other characteristics give information about the leader's previous experiences and background. (Hermann 1988, 268)

The impact of leaders' personal characteristics on their state's foreign policy generally increases when their authority and legitimacy are widely accepted by citizens or, in authoritarian or totalitarian regimes, when leaders are protected from broad public criticism. Moreover, certain kinds of circumstances enhance individuals' potential influence. Among them are new situations that free leaders from conventional approaches to defining the situation; complex situations involving many different factors; and situations without social sanctions, which permit freedom of choice because norms defining the range of permissible options are unclear (DiRenzo 1974).

A leader's **political efficacy** or self-image—that person's belief in his or her own ability to control events politically—will also influence the degree to which personal values and psychological needs govern decision making (DeRivera 1968). This linkage is not direct, however. The citizenry's desire for strong leadership will affect it as well. For example, when public opinion strongly favors a powerful leader, and when the head of state has an exceptional need for admiration, foreign policy will more likely reflect that leader's inner needs. Thus Kaiser Wilhelm II's narcissistic personality allegedly met the German people's desire for a symbolically powerful leader, and German public preferences in turn influenced the foreign policy that Germany pursued during Wilhelm's reign, ending in World War I (Baron and Pletsch 1985).

Other factors undoubtedly influence how much leaders can shape their states' choices. For instance, when leaders believe that their own interests and welfare are at stake, they tend to respond in terms of their private needs and psychological drives. When circumstances are stable, however, and when leaders' egos are not entangled with policy outcomes, the influence of their personal characteristics is less apparent.

The amount of information available about a particular situation is also important. Without pertinent information, policy is likely to be based on leaders' personal likes or dislikes. Conversely, "the more information an individual has about international affairs, the less likely is it that his behavior will be based upon nonlogical influences" (Verba 1969).

Similarly, the timing of a leader's assumption of power is significant. When an individual first assumes a leadership position, the formal requirements of that role are least likely to restrict what he or she can do. That is especially true during the "honeymoon" period routinely given to new heads of state, during which time they are relatively free of criticism and excessive pressure. Moreover, when a leader assumes office following a dramatic event (a landslide election, for example, or the assassination of a predecessor), he or she can institute policies almost with a free hand, as "constituency criticism is held in abeyance during this time" (Hermann 1976).

A national crisis is an especially potent circumstance that increases a leader's control over foreign policy making. Decision making during crises is typically centralized and handled exclusively by the top leadership. Crucial information is often unavailable, and leaders see themselves as responsible for outcomes. Not surprisingly, therefore, great leaders (e.g., Napoleon Bonaparte, Winston Churchill, and Franklin D. Roosevelt) customarily emerge during periods of extreme tumult. A crisis can liberate a leader from the constraints that normally would inhibit his or her capacity to control events or engineer foreign policy change.

History abounds with examples of the seminal importance of political leaders who emerge in different times and places and under different circumstances to play critical roles in shaping world history. Mikhail Gorbachev dramatically illustrates an individual's capacity to change the course of history. Many experts believe that the Cold War could not have been brought to an end, nor Communist Party rule in Moscow terminated and the Soviet state set on a path toward democracy and free enterprise, had it not been for Gorbachev's vision, courage, and commitment to engineering these revolutionary, system-transforming changes (see Bundy 1990). Ironically, those reforms led to his loss of power when the Soviet Union imploded in 1991.

Limits to the History-Making-Individuals Model

Having said that the history-making-individuals model may be compelling, we must be cautious and remember that leaders are not all-powerful determinants of states' foreign policy behavior. Rather, their personal influence varies with the context, and often the context is more influential than the leader (see Focus 3.3).

Thus, the utility of the history-making-individuals model of foreign policy is questionable. The "great person" versus **zeitgeist** (spirit of the times) debate is pertinent here. At the core of this enduring controversy is the question, perhaps unanswerable, of whether the times must be conducive to the emergence of leaders or whether important people would have become famous leaders whenever and wherever they lived (see Greenstein 1987). At the very least, the history-making-individuals model appears much too simple an explanation of how states react to challenges from abroad. Most world leaders follow the rules of the game of international politics, which suggests that how states cope with their external environments is often influenced less strongly by the types of people heading them than by other factors. Put differently, states respond to international circumstances in often similar ways, regardless of the predispositions of their leaders. This may account for the

Do Leaders Make a Difference?

Some theorists, such as neorealists, embrace the assumption of rationality and assume that any leader will respond to a choice in the same way: The situation structures the reaction to the existing costs and benefits of any choice. But does this assumption square with the facts? What do we know about the impact of people's perceptions and values on the way they view choices? Political psychology tells us that the same option is likely to have different value to different leaders. Does this mean that different leaders would respond differently to similar situations?

Consider the example of Richard Nixon. In 1971, Americans took to the streets outside the White House to protest the immorality of Nixon's bombing policies in Vietnam. His reaction to this perceived threat was to shield himself from the voice of the people, without success, as it happened. Nixon complained that "Nobody can know what it means for a president to be sitting in that White House working late at night and to have hundreds of thousands of demonstrators charging through the streets. Not even earplugs could block the noise."

Earlier, on a rainy afternoon in 1962, John F. Kennedy faced a similar citizen protest. Americans had gathered in front of the White House for a Ban the Bomb demonstration. His response was to send out urns of coffee and doughnuts and invite the leaders of the protest to come inside to state their case, believing that a democracy should encourage dissent and debate.

Nixon saw protesters as a threat; Kennedy saw them as an opportunity. This comparison suggests that the type of leader can make a difference in determining the kinds of choices likely to be made in response to similar situations.

striking uniformities in state practices in a world of diverse leaders, different political systems, and turbulent change. In this sense, realists' postulates about states' foreign policy goals deriving from the rational calculation of opportunities and constraints and, above all, stressing survival are not without foundation.

• • •

CONSTRAINTS ON FOREIGN POLICY MAKING: PROBLEMS AND PROSPECTS

Can states respond to the demands that external challenges and internal politics simultaneously place on their leaders? For many reasons, that capability is increasingly strained.

Foreign policy choice occurs in an environment of uncertainty and multiple, competing interests. On occasion, it is also made in situations when policymakers are caught by surprise and a quick decision is needed. The stress these conditions produce impairs leaders' cognitive abilities and may cause them—

preoccupied with sunk costs, short-run results, and postdecisional rationaliza-tion—to react emotionally rather than analytically.

Although a variety of impediments stand in the way of wise foreign policy choice, it is possible to design and manage policy-making machinery to reduce their impact. No design, however, can transform foreign policy making into a neat, orderly system. It is a turbulent political process, which involves complex problems, a chronic lack of information, and a multiplicity of conflicting actors.

The trends and transformations currently unfolding in world politics are the products of countless decisions made daily throughout the world. Some de-cisions are more consequential than others, and some actors are more impor-tant than others. Throughout history, great powers such as the United States have at times stood at the center of the world political stage, possessing the combination of natural resources, military might, and the means to project power worldwide that earned them great-power status. How such major pow-ers have responded to one another has had profound consequences for the en-tire drama of world politics. To better understand that, we turn our attention next to the dynamics of great-power rivalry on the world stage.

KEY TERMS

actor	pluralism	bureaucracies
sovereignty	diversionary theory of war	bureaucratic politics model
state	democratic peace	policy networks
nation	unitary actor	caucuses
foreign policy	rationality, rational choice	standard operating procedures
intermestic politics	bounded rationality	(SOPs)
states' attributes	policy agendas	groupthink
imperialism	satisficing behavior	history-making-individuals model
geopolitics	domestic policy	procedural rationality
constitutional democracy	prospect theory	instrumental rationality
autocratic rule	two-level games	political efficacy
elitism	muddling through	zeitgeist

SUGGESTED READING

Bendor, Jonathan, and Thomas H. Hammond. "Re-thinking Allison's Models," *American Political Science Review* 86 (June 1992): 301–22.

Cederman, Lars-Erik. *Emergent Actors in World Poli-tics*. New Jersey: Princeton University Press, 1997.

Ferguson, Yale H., and Richard W. Mansbach. *Poli-ties: Authority, Identities and Change*. Columbia: University of South Carolina Press, 1996.

George, Alexander L. *Bridging the Gap: Theory and Practice in Foreign Policy*. Washington, D.C.: United States Institute of Peace, 1993.

Hermann, Charles F., Charles W. Kegley, Jr., and James N. Rosenau, eds. *New Directions in the Study of Foreign Policy*. Boston: Allen & Unwin, 1987.

Hilsman, Roger. *The Politics of Policy Making in De-fense and Foreign Affairs: Conceptual Models and Bureaucratic Politics*, 2nd ed. Englewood Cliffs, N.J.: Prentice Hall, 1990.

Janis, Irving L. *Crucial Decisions: Leadership in Poli-cymaking and Crisis Management*. New York: Free Press, 1989.

Jensen, Lloyd. *Explaining Foreign Policy*. Englewood Cliffs, N.J.: Prentice Hall, 1982.

Korany, Bahgat. *How Foreign Policy Decisions Are Made in the Third World*. Boulder, Colo.: Westview Press, 1986.

Ray, James Lee. *Democracies and International Conflict*. Columbia: University of South Carolina Press, 1995.

Rosati, Jerel A., Joe D. Hagan, and Martin W. Sampson III, eds. *Foreign Policy Restructuring: How Governments Respond to Global Change*. Columbia: University of South Carolina Press, 1997.

t'Hart, Paul, Eric K. Stern and Bengt Sundelius, eds. *Beyond Groupthink: Political Group Dynamics and Foreign Policy-Making*. Ann Arbor: University of Michigan Press, 1997.

WHERE ON THE WORLD WIDE WEB?

http://www.pbs.org/newshour/bb/international/july-dec97/foreign_12-23.html
PBS Online Newshour PBS's Online Newshour reviews 1997 U.S. foreign policy. It discusses the success, failure, and future of U.S. foreign policy. You can also listen to the program using RealAudio. Listen and see if you agree with their assessments.

http://www.pbs.org/wgbh/pages/amex/presidents/frames/featured/featured.html
The Presidents: PBS's "The American Experience" Another excellent Web site from PBS. "The American Experience" presents feature sites on Theodore Roosevelt, Franklin Roosevelt, Dwight Eisenhower, Harry Truman, John Kennedy, Lyndon Johnson, Richard Nixon, and Ronald Reagan. Sections focus on the U.S. foreign policy achievements of each president. Choose your favorite president and read about their accomplishments.

http://hyperion.advanced.org/11046/
Cuban Missile Crisis The Cuban Missile Crisis is often sited as an event that brought the superpowers to the brink of nuclear war. This site provides an in-depth account and analysis of the crisis and the actors and issues involved. Read dossiers of the primary players, hear segments of the ExComm meeting, and see U–2 spy plane photos. At the end, take an online quiz to see how well you know the crisis.

http://www.whitehouse.gov/WH/EOP/nec/html/main.html
National Economic Council The National Economic Council was created by a Clinton presidential executive order released January 25, 1993. The principal function of the Council is to coordinate the economic policy-making process with respect to domestic and international economic issues. The creation of this Council is an example of how states can no longer separate international and domestic policy arenas. Was Clinton wise to create this Council?

Great-Power Rivalries and Relations

CHAPTER TOPICS AND THEMES

- The quest for great-power hegemony: World War I, World War II, and the Cold War

- Long-cycle theory and hegemonic stability theory

- Rational choice and great-power relations

- Power transitions and war

- The future of great-power politics: A cold peace?

- Multipolarity

Who's number one? Who's gaining on the leader? What does this mean for the future, if and when the strongest is seriously challenged for predominant position?

These are the kinds of questions sports fans often ask when the rankings of the top teams are adjusted after the preceding week's competition. World leaders also adopt what former U.S. Secretary of State Dean Rusk once called a "football stadium approach to diplomacy." And many people throughout the world also habitually make comparisons of countries, asking which states are the biggest, strongest, wealthiest, and most militarily powerful and evaluating which states are rising and which are falling relative to one another. When making such rankings, both groups are looking at world politics through the lens of realism. They see a globe of competitors, with winners and losers in an ancient contest for supremacy. And they look most closely at the shifting rankings at the very top of the international hierarchy of power—at the rivalry and struggle among the "great powers." Moreover, they picture this conflict as continual. As Arnold J. Toynbee's (1954) famous cyclical theory of history explains, "The most emphatic punctuation in a uniform series of events recurring in one repetitive cycle after another is the outbreak of a great war in which one power that has forged ahead of all its rivals makes so formidable a bid for world domination that it evokes an opposing coalition of all the other powers."

Toynbee's conclusion lies at the center of realism. The starting point for understanding world politics, maintains Hans J. Morgenthau (1985), the leading post-World War II classical realist theorist, is to recognize that "All history shows that nations active in international politics are continuously preparing for, actively involved in, or recovering from organized violence in the form of war." Cycles of war and peace have dominated twentieth-century world politics. World Wars I and II, which began in Europe and then spread, were fought by fire and blood. The Cold War was fought by different means but was no less intense. Each of these three global wars set in motion major transformations in world politics. In this chapter we explore the causes and consequences of these great-power rivalries. By examining their origins and impact, we can better anticipate the character of great-power relations in the twenty-first century.

● ● ●

THE QUEST FOR GREAT-POWER HEGEMONY

Great-power war is not unique to this century. Changes in the balance of power over the past five hundred years have regularly preceded war's outbreak. For this reason, the relationship between the great powers' rise and fall and global instability is a core concern in theories of world politics.

One viewpoint, **long-cycle theory,** seeks to explain why periods of war and peace are associated with shifts in the major states' relative power (see Levy 1998; Modelski and Thompson 1989, 1996), and why each global war witnesses the emergence of a victorious **hegemon,** a dominant global leader capable of dictating "the rules and arrangements by which international relations, political and economic, are conducted" (Goldstein 1988; compare Nye 1998). With its acquisition of unrivaled power, the hegemon reshapes the existing system by creating and enforcing rules to preserve not only world order but also its own dominant position.

hegemon a single, overwhelmingly powerful state that exercises predominate influence over other global actors.

Preponderant State(s) Seeking Hegemony	Other Powers Resisting Domination	Global War	New Order after Global War
Portugal	Spain, Valois, France, Burgundy, England, Venice	Wars of Italy and the Indian Ocean, 1494–1517	Treaty of Tordesillas, 1517
Spain	The Netherlands, France, England	Spanish-Dutch Wars, 1580–1608	Truce of 1609; Evangelical Union and the Catholic League formed
Holy Roman Empire (Habsburg Spain and Austria-Hungary)	Shifting ad hoc coalitions of mostly Protestant states (Sweden, Holland) and German principalities as well as Catholic France against remnants of papal rule	Thirty Years' War, 1618–1648	Peace of Westphalia, 1648
France (Louis XIV)	The United Provinces, England, the Habsburg Empire, Spain, major German states, Russia	Wars of the Grand Alliance, 1688–1713	Treaty of Utrecht, 1713
France (Napoleon)	Great Britain, Prussia, Austria, Russia	Napoleonic Wars, 1792–1815	Congress of Vienna and Concert of Europe, 1815
Germany, Austria-Hungary, Turkey	Great Britain, France, Russia, United States	World War I, 1914–1918	Treaty of Versailles creating League of Nations, 1919
Germany, Japan, Italy	Great Britain, France, Soviet Union, United States	World War II, 1939–1945	Bretton Woods, 1944; United Nations, 1945; Potsdam, 1945
United States, Soviet Union	Great Britain, France, China, Japan	Cold War, 1945–1991	NATO/Partnerships for Peace, 1995; World Trade Organization, 1995

Hegemony characteristically imposes an extraordinary tax on the world leader, which must bear the costs of maintaining economic and political order while protecting its position and preserving its empire. In time, as the weight of global responsibilities takes its toll, new rivals rise to challenge the increasingly vulnerable world leader. Historically, this struggle for power has set the stage for another global war, the demise of one hegemon, and the ascent of another.

Long-cycle theory also draws attention to the fact that "world politics has rarely been reordered without a major war" (Jervis 1991–1992). "Only after such a total breakdown has the international situation been sufficiently fluid to induce leaders and supporting publics of dominant nations to join seriously in the task of reorganizing international society to avoid a repetition of the terrible events just experienced" (Falk 1970). Table 4.1 summarizes the cyclical rise and fall of great powers, their global wars, and their subsequent efforts to restore order.

The central premise of long-cycle theory is disarmingly simple, and for this reason it is not without critics. Must great powers rise and fall as if by the law of gravity—what goes up must come down? There is something disturbingly deterministic in a proposition which implies that global destiny is beyond policymakers' control. Fundamental hypotheses drawn from long-cycle theory are difficult to confirm. Long-cycle theorists disagree on whether economic, military, or domestic factors produce these cycles, as well as about their comparative influence in different historical epochs (see Lundestad 1994). Still, long-cycle theory provides important insights into a fundamental continuity in world politics and provokes questions about whether this entrenched cycle can be broken. It also invites critical consideration of **hegemonic stability theory,** which assumes that a stable world order requires a single dominant leader to enforce peace and punish those who challenge the status quo. Thus it usefully orients us to a consideration of the three great-power wars of the twentieth-century and the lessons they suggest.

• • •

THE FIRST WORLD WAR

World War I tumbled onto the world stage when a Serbian nationalist seeking to free Slavs from Austrian rule assassinated Archduke Ferdinand, heir to the throne of Austria-Hungary, at Sarajevo in June 1914. In the two months that followed, this event sparked a series of moves and countermoves by states and empires distrustful of each other's intentions, shattering world peace.

Before the assassination, two hostile alliances had already formed, pitting Germany, Austria-Hungary, and the Ottoman Empire against France, Britain, and Russia. The strategic choices of the two alliances culminated in World War I. By the time the longest European war in a century had ended, nearly ten million people had died, empires had crumbled, new states had been born, and the world's geopolitical map had been redrawn.

The Causes of World War I

How can such a catastrophic war be explained? Although the answers are numerous, many converge around *structural* explanations, which hold that World War I was inadvertent, not the result of anyone's master plan. It was a war bred

The carnage of major wars sobers world leaders, and they design new institutions to keep the postwar peace. Global wars also topple governments. The First World War led to the Bolshevik revolution in 1916 that brought a communist government to power in the Soviet Union, for example. The end of the Cold War in 1991 was followed by the rejection of communist rule and the creation of a fledgling democracy in Russia. Pictured here is the statue of the KGB's founder—a symbol of communist power—which was moved from its prominent place to the "sculpture graveyard" where the Russian government keeps retired Soviet icons.

by uncertainty and circumstances beyond the control of those involved, one that none wanted or expected.

Structuralism. Many historians find a structural interpretation framed at the global level of analysis convincing because on the eve of World War I "the sort of military system that existed in Europe at the time—a system of interlocking mobilizations and of war plans that placed a great emphasis on rapid offensive action—directly led to a conflict that might otherwise have been avoided" (Trachtenberg 1990–1991).

Proponents of **structuralism** emphasize that the great powers' prior rearmament efforts as well as their alliances and counteralliances—The Triple Alliance of Germany, Austria-Hungary, and Italy, initiated in 1882 and renewed in 1902, and the *entente cordiale* between Britain and France, forged in 1904—created a momentum that, along with "the pull of military schedules," dragged European statesmen toward war (Tuchman 1962).

A related element in the structuralist explanation focuses on the nineteenth century, when Britain dominated world politics. An island country isolated by temperament, tradition, and geography from European affairs, Britain's sea power gave it command of the world's shipping lanes and control of a vast empire stretching from the Mediterranean to Southeast Asia. This dominance helped to deter aggression. However, Germany would mount a challenge to British power.

After becoming a unified country in 1871, Germany prospered and used its growing wealth to create a formidable army and navy. With strength came ambition and resentment of British preeminence. As the predominant military and industrial power on the European continent, Germany sought to compete for international position and status. As Kaiser William II proclaimed in 1898, Germany had "great tasks outside the narrow boundaries of old Europe." With Germany ascendant, the balance of power shifted as its rising power and global aspirations altered the European geopolitical landscape.

Germany was not the only newly emergent power at the turn of the century, however. Russia was also expanding and becoming a threat to Germany. The decline in power of the Austro-Hungarian Empire, Germany's only ally, heightened Germany's fear of Russia—thus its strong reaction to Archduke Ferdinand's assassination. Germany became convinced that a short, localized, and victorious war was possible, fearing an unfavorable shift in the balance of power in the event of a long war. Accordingly, while the advantages seemed clear-cut, Germany gave Austria-Hungary a "blank check" to crush Serbia, which proved to be a serious miscalculation.

To Germany's imperial rulers, the risk involved in the blank check made sense from the viewpoint of preserving the Austro-Hungarian Empire. The disintegration of the empire would have left Germany isolated, without an ally. Unfortunately for Germany, its guarantee provoked an unexpected reaction from France and Russia, as the two powers joined forces to defend the Slavs. Britain then abandoned its traditional "splendid isolation" and joined France and Russia in opposing Germany. Although the immediate objective was to defend Belgian neutrality, the war later expanded across the ocean when in April 1917 the United States, reacting to German submarine warfare, entered the conflict. For the first time ever, war became truly global in scope.

structuralism a neorealists theory that sees the changing distribution of power within the global system as the primary determinant of states' behavior and of whether coalitions will form and peace will prevail.

This chain reaction and the rapidity of escalation that led to World War I fit the interpretation that it was an "inadvertent war." Simply put, European leaders were not in full control of their own fate. Still, historians ask why they miscalculated so badly. Did they simply fail to recognize their primary interest in successfully managing the crisis? If so, was this because their alliances gave them a false sense of assurance, blinding them to danger and dragging them into a conflict that was not a part of anyone's design?

Rational Choice. Rational choice theory provides an alternate interpretation of World War I. From this perspective, framed at the individual level of analysis, the war's outbreak was a result of German elites' preference for a war with France and Russia in order to consolidate Germany's position on the continent, confirm its status as a world power, and divert domestic attention from its internal troubles (Kaiser 1990). "It was the men gathered at the Imperial Palace in Berlin," Volker R. Berghahn (1995) concludes, "who pushed Europe over the brink."

If this interpretation is correct, then World War I is best seen as the consequence of the quest for power, which realists believe is an "iron law of history." From this perspective, World War I can be interpreted as resulting from leaders' values and choices that led to "an attempt by Germany to secure its position before an increasingly powerful Russia had achieved a position of equality with Germany (which the latter expected to happen by 1917)" (Levy 1999).

As these alternative interpretations suggest, the causes of World War I remain in dispute. Controversies over motives and causes—the decisive forces behind historic events—are difficult to resolve. Structural explanations, which emphasize the global distribution of power, and rational choice explanations, which direct attention to the calculations and goals of particular leaders, undoubtedly help us to understand the sequences that produced the world's first truly global war. We must, however, consider additional factors that, in association with these underlying causes, led to the guns of August.

Other Explanations. At the state level of analysis, some historians also argue that domestic factors within countries were influential causes. In particular, many view the growth of **nationalism,** especially in southeastern Europe, as having created a climate of opinion that made war likely. As nationalistic feelings intensified, they aroused long-suppressed ethnic and national hatreds, culturally inhibiting European statesmen's ability to avoid war.

Domestic unrest also inflamed these nationalistic passions, as did the pressure for war applied by munitions makers who played on nationalistic sentiments (Blainey 1988). The Austro-Hungarian Empire's reaction to the assassination crisis suggests the potency of national passions, which fed Austria-Hungary's diabolic image of the enemy, its hypersensitivity about the preservation of the empire, and its overconfidence in its military capabilities.

Austria-Hungary was not the only player driven by nationalistic passions. The Germans and Russians were also driven by intense nationalism, which caused them to make serious miscalculations. In particular, Germany's lack of empathy prevented it from understanding "the strength of the Russians' pride, their fear of humiliation if they allowed the Germans and Austrians to destroy their little protégé, Serbia, and the intensity of Russian anger at the tricky, deceptive way the Germans and Austrians went about their aggression" (White 1990).

nationalism a mindset glorifying the nationalities of a people living in a state that assigns loyalty to the state's national interests as a supreme value.

Europe before 1914	
The Triple Entente and Their Allies	
The Central Powers and Their Allies	
Neutral Countries	

Europe after 1920		
Soviet Russia	Austria in 1919	Turkey
Russian Losses	Austrian Losses	
Germany in 1919	Bulgaria	
German Losses	Bulgarian Losses	

MAP 4.1

Territorial Changes in Europe following World War I

SOURCE: Maps adapted from *Strategic Atlas Comparative Geopolitics of the World's Powers*, 3rd Edition by Gérard Chaliand and Jean-Pierre Rageau. Copyright © 1993 by Gérard Chaliand and Jean-Pierre Rageau. Reprinted by permission of HarperCollins Perennial, Inc.

Despite these national passions, World War I would not likely have unfolded without Anglo-German commercial rivalry, the Franco-Russian alliance, Germany's blank check to Austria-Hungary, and—perhaps most important—the formation of two entangling alliances. "One cannot conceive of the onset of World War I without the presence of the Triple Entente, which existed as an alliance of ideologically dissimilar governments" uniting Britain, France, and Russia (Midlarsky 1988). Consequently, the division of the multipolar balance-of-power system that drew the growing number of great-power contenders into two bipolar coalitions—and the absence of a hegemon to maintain order—may have made war inevitable, even though "political leaders in each of the great powers . . . preferred a peaceful settlement" of their differences (Levy 1990–1991).

The Consequences of World War I

World War I destroyed both life and property and changed the face of Europe (see Map 4.1). In its wake, three empires—the Austro-Hungarian, Russian, and

Ottoman (Turkish)—crumbled, and in their place the independent states of Poland, Czechoslovakia, and Yugoslavia emerged. In addition, the countries of Finland, Estonia, Latvia, and Lithuania were born. The war also contributed to the overthrow of the Russian czar in 1917 by the Bolsheviks. The emergence of communism under the leadership of Vladimir I. Lenin produced a change in government and ideology that would have far-reaching consequences.

Despite its costs, the coalition consisting of Britain, France, Russia, and (later) the United States and Italy succeeded in defeating the threat of domination posed by the Central Powers (Germany, Austria-Hungary, Turkey, and their allies). Moreover, the war set the stage for a determined effort to build a new international system that could prevent another war.

> For most Europeans, the Great War had been a source of disillusionment. . . . When it was all over, few remained to be convinced that such a war must never happen again. Among vast populations there was a strong conviction that this time the parties had to plan a peace that could not just terminate a war, but a peace that could change attitudes and build a new type of international order. . . .
>
> For the first time in history, broad publics and the peacemakers shared a conviction that war was a central problem in international relations. Previously, hegemony, the aggressive activities of a particular state, or revolution had been the problem. In 1648, 1713, and 1815, the peacemakers had tried to resolve issues of the past and to construct orders that would preclude their reappearance. But in 1919 expectations ran higher. The sources of war were less important than the war itself. There was a necessity to look more to the future than to the past. The problem was not just to build a peace, but to construct a peaceful international order that would successfully manage all international conflicts of the future. (Holsti 1991, 175–76; 208–9)

World War I evoked revulsion for war and for the doctrine of realism that rationalized great-power rivalry, arms races, secret alliances, and balance-of-power politics. The experience led the policymakers gathered at the Versailles Palace in Paris to reevaluate assumptions about the rules of statecraft and to search for other principles on which to build a new world order. These deliberations led to policies rooted in liberal international relations theory.

The two decades following World War I were the high point of liberal idealism, as reflected in Woodrow Wilson's "Fourteen Points," creation of the League of Nations, the Washington Naval Conference, and the **Kellogg-Briand Pact** (see Chapter 2). Nevertheless, the liberal idealists' proposals failed to deter the resumption of great-power rivalry. Another system-transforming global war was on the horizon.

Kellogg-Briand Pact a multilateral treaty negotiated in 1928 that outlawed war as a method for settling interstate conflicts.

● ● ●

THE SECOND WORLD WAR

Although it lost World War I, Germany did not lose its hopes for global status and influence. On the contrary, they were intensified. Thus conditions were ripe for the second great-power war of the twentieth century, as Germany again pursued an aggressive course.

Global in scope, World War II was a struggle for power cast in the image of realism. It pitted a fascist coalition striving for world supremacy—the Axis trio of Germany, Japan, and Italy—against an unlikely "grand alliance" of four great powers who united despite their incompatible ideologies—communism in the case of the Soviet Union and democratic capitalism in the case of Britain, France, and the United States.

The world's fate hinged on the outcome of this massive effort to meet the Axis threat of world conquest and restore the balance of power. Success was achieved over a six-year ordeal, but at a terrible cost: Each day twenty-three thousand lives were lost, as the war resulted in the death of fifty-three million people worldwide (for an account of the campaigns that finally led to victory, see Weinberg 1994).

The Causes of World War II

Several factors propelled renewal of Germany's hegemonic ambitions. Domestically, German nationalism inflamed latent **irredentism** and rationalized the expansion of German borders, both to regain provinces ceded to others and to absorb Germans living in Austria, Czechoslovakia, and Poland. The rise of **fascism**—the Nazi regime's ideology championing racism, flag, fatherland, nationalism, and imperialism—animated this renewed imperialistic push. That set of beliefs glorified the "collective will" of the nation and preached the most extreme version of realism, *machtpolitik* (power politics), to justify the forceful expansion of the German state.

German aggression was fueled further by resentment of the punitive terms imposed by the victors of World War I (France, Great Britain, Italy, Japan, and the United States). Bending to French pressure, the Peace of Paris (the Versailles treaty) insisted on the destruction of Germany's armed forces, the loss of territory (such as Alsace-Lorraine, which Germany had absorbed following the Franco-Prussian war of 1870–1871), and the imposition of heavy reparations to compensate the Allies for the damage that German militarism had exacted. In addition, the Austro-Hungarian Empire was splintered into divided political units.

Not only was the Peace of Paris punitive; more significantly and painfully, it prevented Germany's reentry into the international system as a coequal member. (Germany was denied membership in the League of Nations until 1926.) As a result of its exclusion, Germany sought to recover its rightful status as a great power by force.

Proximate Causes. Why did the victorious great powers permit German rearmament? A key reason was the failure of the British hope for Anglo-American collaboration to maintain world order, which vanished when the United States repudiated the Versailles peace treaty and retreated to a policy of **isolationism,** withdrawing from active international involvements. As a result, Britain and France each fought for its own advantage in the treatment of Germany. While France wanted to deter Germany's reentry into the international system and prevent its revival, Britain, in contrast, preferred to preserve the new balance of power by encouraging German rearmament and recovery as a counterweight against the chance that France or the Soviet Union might dominate continental Europe.

Acquiescence to German rearmament and other militaristic maneuvers led to the policy of **appeasement** or pacifying potential aggressors with concessions. Adolf Hitler, the German dictator who by the mid-1930s controlled Germany's fate, pledged not to expand German territory by force. He betrayed that

irredentism movement by an ethnonational group to regain control of territory by force so that existing state boundaries will no longer separate the group.

appeasement strategy of making concessions to an aggressor state without retaliation in the hope that, satisfied, it will not make additional claims on the territory of its neighbors.

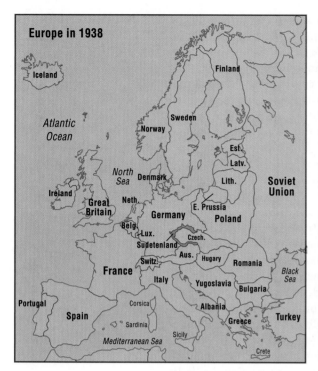

M A P   4 . 2

Territorial Changes in Europe following World War II

SOURCES: Based on Europe 1938 from Kegley and Raymond (1994), 118; Europe 1945 from Chaliand and Rageau (1993), 49.

promise in March 1938 when he forced Austria into union with Germany (the *Anschluss*). Shortly thereafter he demanded the annexation of the German-populated area of Sudetenland in Czechoslovakia (see Map 4.2). The fears that German expansionism provoked led to the September 1938 Munich Conference attended by Hitler, British Prime Minister Neville Chamberlain, and leaders from France and Italy (Czechoslovakia was not invited). Based on the erroneous conviction that appeasement would halt further German expansionism and lead to "peace in our time," Chamberlain and the others agreed to Hitler's demands.

Rather than satisfying Germany, appeasement whetted its appetite and that of the newly formed fascist coalition of Germany, Italy, and Japan, whose goal was to overthrow the international status quo. Disillusioned with Western liberalism and the Paris settlements, and suffering economically from the effects of the Great Depression of the 1930s, Japan embraced militarism. In the might-makes-right climate that Germany's imperialistic quest for national aggrandizement helped to create, Japanese nationalists led their country on the path to imperialism and colonialism. Japan's invasions of Manchuria in 1931 and China proper in 1937 were followed by Italy's absorption of Abyssinia in 1935 and Albania in 1939, and both Germany and Italy intervened in the 1936–1939

Spanish civil war on the side of the fascists, headed by General Francisco Franco, while the Soviet Union supported antifascist forces.

After Germany occupied the rest of Czechoslovakia in March 1939, Britain and France belatedly reacted by joining in an alliance to protect the next likely victim, Poland. They also opened negotiations with Moscow in hopes of enticing the Soviet Union to join the alliance, but failed. Then, on August 23, 1939, Hitler, a fascist, and the Soviet dictator Joseph Stalin, a communist, stunned the world with the news that they had signed a nonaggression pact. Now certain that Britain and France would not intervene, Hitler promptly invaded Poland on September 1, 1939. Britain and France, honoring their pledge to defend the Poles, declared war on Germany two days later. World War II had begun.

The war expanded rapidly as Hitler turned his forces to the Balkans, North Africa, and westward. The powerful, mechanized German troops invaded Norway and marched through Denmark, Belgium, Luxembourg, and the Netherlands. They swept around France's defensive barrier, the Maginot Line, and forced the British to evacuate a sizable expeditionary force from the French beaches at Dunkirk. Paris itself fell in June 1940, and in the months that followed, the German air force, the Luftwaffe, pounded Britain in an attempt to force it into submission as well. Instead of invading Britain, however, the Nazi troops launched a surprise attack on the Soviet Union, Hitler's former ally, in June 1941.

On December 7, 1941, Japan launched a surprise assault on the United States at Pearl Harbor. Almost immediately, Germany also declared war on the United States. The unprovoked Japanese assault and the German challenge pushed U.S. aloofness and isolationism aside, enabling President Franklin Roosevelt to forge a coalition with Britain and the Soviet Union to oppose the fascists.

Underlying Causes. Many historians regard the reemergence of a multipolar power distribution as a key factor in the onset and expansion of World War II. The post–World War I global system was placed "at risk when the sovereign states, which were its components, became too numerous and unequal in power and resources, particularly when (as happened after 1919) the great powers were reduced in number and new, lesser states proliferated" (Calvocoressi, Wint, and Pritchard 1989). In 1914, Europe had only twenty-two key states, but by 1921 the number nearly doubled. When combined with resentment over Versailles, the Russian Revolution, and the rise of fascism, the increased number of states and the resurgence of nationalistic revolts and crises made "the interwar years the most violent period in international relations since the Thirty Years' War and the wars of the French Revolution and Napoleon" (Holsti 1991).

The collapse of the international economic system during the 1930s also contributed to the war. Great Britain found itself unequal to the leadership and regulatory roles it had performed in the world political economy before World War I. Although the United States was the logical successor, its refusal to exercise leadership hastened the war. "The Depression of 1929–1931 was followed in 1933 by a world Monetary and Economic Conference whose failures—engineered by the United States—deepened the gloom, accelerated nationalist protectionism, and promoted revolution" (Calvocoressi, Wint, and

In the 1930s the nationalistic ideologies of national socialism and fascism—realist philosophies that regarded the state as supreme, accepted dictatorship, and called for expansion at the expense of neighboring countries—took root in Germany and Italy. Consistent with the realist view that states have an inherent right to expand, dramatic political rallies staged by Adolf Hitler's propaganda experts were organized to glorify the Führer (leader), persuade the German people of the need to persecute the Jews, and expand German borders by armament and aggression.

Pritchard 1989). In this depressed global environment, heightened by deteriorating economic circumstances at home, Germany and Japan sought solutions through imperialism abroad.

The League of Nations' failure to mount a collective response to the acts of aggression symbolized the weak institutional barriers to war. When Germany withdrew from the League of Nations in 1933, followed by Italy in 1937, war clouds gathered and the League was powerless to dispel them.

The Soviet Union's invasion of neutral Finland in 1939 provoked public indignation. In a final act of retaliation, the League of Nations expelled the Soviet Union. Nonetheless, characteristically, the burden of defense fell on the shoulders of the victim. Ninety thousand fiercely independent Finns gave their lives in the "Winter War" while the rest of the world watched in astonishment.

At the state level of analysis, psychological forces also led to World War II. These included "the domination of civilian discourse by military propaganda that primed the world for war," the "great wave of hypernationalism [that] swept over Europe" as "each state taught itself a mythical history while denigrating that of others," and the demise of democratic governance (Van Evera 1990–1991).

In the final analysis, however, the importance of leaders stands out. The war would not have been possible without Adolf Hitler and his plans to conquer the world by force. Hence "German responsibility for the Second World War is in a class of its own" (Calvocoressi, Wint, and Pritchard 1989). Under the mythical claim of German racial superiority as a "master race" and virulent anti-Semitism and anticommunism, Hitler waged war to create an empire that could resolve the historic competition and precarious coexistence of the great powers in Europe by eliminating Germany's rivals.

The broad vision of the Thousand-Year Reich was . . . of a vastly expanded—and continually expanding—German core, extending deep into Russia, with a number of vassal states and regions, including France, the Low Countries, Scandinavia, central Europe, and the Balkans, that would provide resources and labor for the core. There was to be no civilizing mission in German imperialism. On the contrary, the lesser peoples were to be taught only to do menial labor or, as Hitler once joked, educated sufficiently to read the road signs so they wouldn't get run over by German automobile traffic. The lowest of the low, the Poles and Jews, were to be exterminated. . . .

To Hitler . . . the purpose of policy was to destroy the system and to reconstitute it on racial lines, with a vastly expanded Germany running a distinctly hierarchical and exploitative order. Vestiges of sovereignty might remain, but they would be fig leaves covering a monolithic order. German occupation policies during the war, whereby conquered nations were reduced to satellites, satrapies, and reservoirs of slave labor, were the practical application of Hitler's conception of the new world order. They were not improvised or planned for reasons of military necessity. (Holsti 1991, 224–25)

The Consequences of World War II

Having faced ruinous losses in Russia and a massive allied bombing campaign at home, Germany's Thousand-Year Reich lay in ruins by May 1945. By August, Japan was devastated as well, as the U.S. atomic bombing of Hiroshima and Nagasaki destroyed Japan's receding hope of carrying on its war of conquest.

The Allied victory over the Axis redistributed power and reordered borders, resulting in a new geopolitical terrain. The Soviet Union absorbed nearly 600,000 square meters of territory from the Baltic states of Estonia, Latvia, and Lithuania, and from Finland, Czechoslovakia, Poland, and Romania—recovering what Russia had lost in the 1918 Treaty of Brest-Litovsk after World War I. Poland, a victim of Soviet expansionism, was compensated with land taken from Germany. Germany itself was divided into occupation zones that eventually provided the basis for its partition into East and West Germany. Finally, pro-Soviet regimes assumed power throughout Eastern Europe (see Map 4.2, p. 82). In the Far East, the Soviet Union took the four Kurile Islands—or the "Northern Territories," as Japan calls them—from Japan; and Korea was divided into Soviet and U.S. occupation zones at the thirty-eighth parallel.

The end of World War II also generated uncertainty and mistrust. The agreements governing goals, strategy, and obligations that had guided the Allied effort began to erode even as victory neared. Victory only magnified the great powers' growing distrust of one anothers' intentions in an environment of ill-defined borders, altered allegiances, power vacuums, and economic ruin.

The "Big Three" leaders—Winston Churchill, Franklin Roosevelt, and Joseph Stalin—met at the **Yalta Conference** in February 1945 to design a new world order, but the vague compromises they reached concealed the differences percolating below the surface. Following Roosevelt's death in April and Germany's unconditional surrender in May, the Big Three (with the United States now represented by Harry Truman) met again at Potsdam in July 1945. The meeting ended without agreement, and the facade of Allied unity began to fade.

World War II, like previous great-power wars, paved the way for a new global system. The Allies' plans for a new postwar structure of peace had begun even as the war raged, and as early as 1943 the Four Power Declaration advanced principles for allied collaboration in "the period following the end of

Yalta Conference 1945 summit meeting among Franklin D. Roosevelt, Joseph Stalin, and Winston Churchill to resolve postwar territorial issues and voting procedures in the United Nations.

hostilities." The product of the Allies' determination to create a new international organization to manage the postwar international order—the United Nations—was conceived in this and other wartime agreements. Consistent with the expectation that the great powers would cooperate to manage world affairs, China was promised a seat on the United Nations Security Council along with France and the Big Three. The purpose was to guarantee that all of the dominant states would share responsibility for keeping the global peace.

After the war, the United States and the Soviet Union were left standing tall, and their unrivaled power meant that they mattered more than all others, with the capacity to impose their will. The other major-power victors (especially Great Britain) had exhausted themselves and slid from the apex of the world-power hierarchy. The vanquished, Germany and Japan, also fell from the ranks of the great powers. Germany was partitioned into four occupation zones, which the victorious powers later used as the basis for creating the Federal Republic of Germany (West Germany) and the German Democratic Republic (East Germany). Japan, having been devastated by atomic bombs and then occupied by the United States, was also removed from the game of great-power politics. Thus, as the French political sociologist Alexis de Tocqueville had foreseen in 1835, the Americans and Russians now held in their hands the destinies of half of mankind. In comparison, all other states were dwarfs. In what eventually became known as the Cold War, Washington and Moscow used the fledgling United Nations not to keep the peace, but to pursue their competition with each other. As the most recent great-power war of the twentieth century, the Cold War still casts its shadow over the post-Cold War geostrategic landscape.

● ● ●

THE COLD WAR

As World War II drew to a close in 1945, it became increasingly clear that a new era of international politics was dawning. Unparalleled in scope and unprecedented in destructiveness, the second great war of the twentieth century not only had brought about a system dominated by two superstates, the United States and the Soviet Union; it had also hastened the disintegration of the great colonial empires assembled by imperialist states in previous centuries, thereby emancipating many peoples from foreign rule. The emergent international system, unlike earlier ones, featured a distribution of power consisting of many sovereign states outside the European core area that were dominated by the two most powerful. In addition, the advent of nuclear weapons radically changed the role that threats of warfare would play in world politics. Out of these circumstances grew the competition between the United States and the Soviet Union for hegemonic leadership.

The Causes of the Cold War

Determining the origins of the twentieth century's third hegemonic battle for domination is difficult because the historical evidence is open to different interpretations (see Gaddis 1997; Melanson 1983). Nonetheless, an evaluation of its postulated causes can help us to understand the sources of great-power rivalries and to explain why this one, unlike other twentieth-century conflicts, ended without recourse to great-power violence.

A Conflict of Interests. Realism provides one structural explanation of the Cold War's determinants: The preeminent status of the United States and the Soviet Union at the top of the international hierarchy made each naturally suspicious of the other and their rivalry inescapable. These circumstances gave each superpower reasons to fear and to struggle against the other's potential global leadership.

But was the competition truly necessary and predetermined? The United States and the Soviet Union each had demonstrated an ability to subordinate ideological differences and competition for power to larger purposes during World War II (Gaddis 1997). Neither had sought unilateral advantage relentlessly, while both had expressed their hope that cooperation would continue and had reached agreements toward that purpose. President Roosevelt, for example, advocated preserving accommodation through an informal accord to let each superpower enjoy dominant influence in its own **sphere of influence,** or specified area of the globe. Rules written into the United Nations charter, obligating the United States and Soviet Union to share (through the UN Security Council) responsibility for preserving global peace, further reflected the expectation of continued cooperation.

If cooperation was the superpowers' hope and aspiration when World War II ended, then why did they fail to achieve it? To answer that question, we must go beyond the logic of *realpolitik* and probe other explanations of the origins of the Cold War.

Ideological Incompatibilities. A second interpretation holds that the Cold War was simply an extension of the superpowers' mutual disdain for each other's political system and way of life. As U.S. Secretary of State James F. Byrnes argued at the conclusion of World War II, "there is too much difference in the ideologies of the U.S. and Russia to work out a long-term program of cooperation." To the extent that such assumptions were widely held in both Washington and Moscow, as they undoubtedly were, ideological differences made the Cold War a conflict "not only between two powerful states, but also between two different social systems" (Jervis 1991).

U.S. animosity was stimulated by the 1917 Bolshevik revolution, which brought to power a government that embraced the Marxist critique of capitalistic imperialism. Whether real or imagined, U.S. fears of Marxism stimulated the emergence of anticommunism as a counter-ideology (Commager 1983; Morgenthau 1983). Accordingly, the United States embarked on a missionary crusade of its own, to contain and ultimately remove the atheistic communist menace from the face of the earth.

American foreign policy was fueled by the fear that communism's appeal to Europeans and the world's less fortunate countries would make its continued spread likely. This prophecy was popularized in the 1960s as the **domino theory,** the view that one country's fall to communism would cause its neighbors to fall like a row of dominoes, thus bringing the entire world under communist domination unless checked by U.S. power.

Similarly, Soviet policy was fueled by the belief that capitalism could not coexist with communism. The purpose of Soviet policy, therefore, was to push the pace of the historical process in which communism eventually would prevail. However, Soviet planners did not believe that this historical outcome would occur automatically. They felt that the capitalist states, led by the United States, sought to encircle the Soviet Union and smother communism in its cra-

sphere of influence region dominated by the power of a foreign state.

Ideology as a Cause of International Friction
Was the East-West Conflict Irreconcilable?

Many scholars believe that all ideological systems of belief see other ideologies as a threat, and this competition breeds hatred and hostility in international affairs. Noting that many wars were actually struggles between religions (such as Christianity against Islam during the Crusades), they maintain that ideological contests over *ideas*, such as that between communism and capitalism, cause states to fight. A conflict driven by ideology "excludes the idea of coexistence. How can [one] compromise or coexist with evil? It holds out no pros-

pect but opposition with all might, war to the death. It summons the true believer to a *jihad*, a crusade of extermination against the infidel" (Schlesinger 1983). Lenin described the predicament—prophetically, it turned out—this way: "As long as capitalism and socialism exist, we cannot live in peace; in the end, either one or the other will triumph—a funeral dirge will be sung either over the Soviet Republic or over world capitalism."

dle, and that it was the Soviet obligation to resist. As a result, ideological incompatibility ruled out compromise as an option (see Focus 4.1). Although the adversaries may have viewed "ideology more as a justification for action than as a guide to action," once the interests that they shared disappeared, "ideology did become the chief means which differentiated friend from foe" (Gaddis 1983).

Misperceptions. A third explanation describes the Cold War as rooted in psychological factors, particularly in the superpowers' misperceptions of each other's motives, to which their conflicting interests and ideologies were secondary.

Mistrustful actors are prone to see only virtue in their own actions and only malice in those of their adversaries. When such **mirror images** exist, hostility is inevitable (Bronfenbrenner 1971). Moreover, when perceptions of an adversary's evil intentions become accepted as truth, **self-fulfilling prophecies** can develop. Prophecies are sometimes self-fulfilling because the future can be affected by the way it is anticipated. This tendency is illustrated by arms races: mistakenly anticipating that a rival is preparing for an offensive war, a potential victim then arms in defense, thereby provoking the rival to fulfill the prophecy by arming out of fear. The result is a classic illustration of the **security dilemma,** as each enemy's efforts to increase its own security by arming actually leads to a decline in security on both sides.

Both mirror images and self-fulfilling prophecies contributed heavily to the onset of the Cold War. The two countries' leaders imposed their definitions of reality on events and then became captives of those visions. As expectations shaped how leaders interpreted developments, what they saw influenced what they got. George F. Kennan, the American ambassador to the Soviet Union in 1952, noted that misread signals were common on both sides:

> The Marshall Plan, the preparations for the setting up of a West German government, and the first moves toward the establishment of NATO were taken in Moscow as the beginnings of a campaign to deprive the Soviet Union of the fruits of its victory over Germany. The Soviet crackdown on Czechoslovakia (1948) and the mounting of the Berlin blockade, both es-

sentially defensive . . . reactions to these Western moves, were then similarly misread on the Western side. Shortly thereafter there came the crisis of the Korean War, where the Soviet attempt to employ a satellite military force in civil combat to its own advantage, by way of reaction to the American decision to establish a permanent military presence in Japan, was read in Washington as the beginning of the final Soviet push for world conquest; whereas the active American military response, provoked by this move, appeared in Moscow . . . as a threat to the Soviet position in both Manchuria and in eastern Siberia. (Kennan 1976, 683–84)

Thus, in the Cold War's formative stage, U.S. leaders and their allies in the West saw the many crises that erupted as part of a Soviet plan for world domination. The Soviets saw these same crises altogether differently—as tests of their resolve and as Western efforts to encircle and destroy their socialist experiment. Mistrust led to misperceptions, which in turn bred conflict. And to the extent that the Cold War originated in conflicting images and in each superpower's insensitivity to the impact of its actions on the other's fears, it is difficult to assign blame for the deterioration of Soviet-American relations. Were both countries responsible because both were victims of their misperceptions? If so, then the Cold War was not simply a U.S. response to communist aggression (the orthodox American view), nor was it simply a product of postwar American assertiveness (the orthodox Soviet and revisionist historians' position; see Schlesinger 1986). Because each of the great powers felt threatened, and each had legitimate reasons to regard the other with suspicion, it is useful to view the Cold War as a conflict over reciprocal anxieties bred by the way policymakers on both sides interpreted the other's actions.

Additional factors beyond those rooted in divergent interests, ideologies, and images undoubtedly combined to produce this explosive Soviet-American hegemonic rivalry. Scholars have yet to sort out their relative causal influence. However, to grasp more completely the dynamics of this great-power rivalry in particular (and others in general), it is useful to move beyond its causes and examine its character.

The Characteristics of the Cold War

As the Cold War evolved, its character changed, in part because of the two rivals' policies and in part because of changing global circumstances. Several conspicuous patterns are observable, however, amidst the continual change:

- Periods of intense conflict alternated with periods of relative cooperation; reciprocal, action-reaction exchanges were also evident (friendly U.S. initiatives toward the Soviet Union were reciprocated in kind).

- Both rivals were willing to disregard their respective professed ideologies whenever their perceived national interests rationalized such inconsistencies; for example, each backed allies with political systems antithetical to its own when the necessities of power politics seemed to justify doing so.

- Both rivals consistently made avoidance of all-out war their highest priority. Through a gradual learning process involving push and shove, restraint and reward, tough bargaining and calm negotiation, the superpowers created a **security regime.**

security regime norms and rules for interaction agreed to by a set of states to increase their security.

These characteristics become visible when we inspect the evolution of the superpowers' relationship. For this, we divide the Cold War into three chronological phases, shown in Figure 4.1.

Confrontation, 1945–1962. A brief period of wary Soviet-American friendship soon gave way to mutual antagonism when the Cold War began. In this short period of **unipolarity**—one characterized by a single dominant power center in the international system—the United States alone possessed the capacity to devastate its adversaries with the atomic bomb.

Despite this restraining factor, all pretense of collaboration rapidly vanished as the superpowers' vital security interests collided in countries outside their clearly defined respective spheres of influence. At this critical juncture, George F. Kennan, then a diplomat in the American embassy in Moscow, sent to Washington his famous "long telegram" assessing the sources of Soviet

FIGURE 4.1

U.S.–Soviet Relations during the Cold War, 1948–1991

The evolution of U.S.–Soviet relations during the Cold War displays a series of shifts between periods of conflict and cooperation. As this figure shows, each superpower's behavior toward the other tended to be reciprocal, and, prior to the Cold War's end, confrontation prevailed over cooperation.

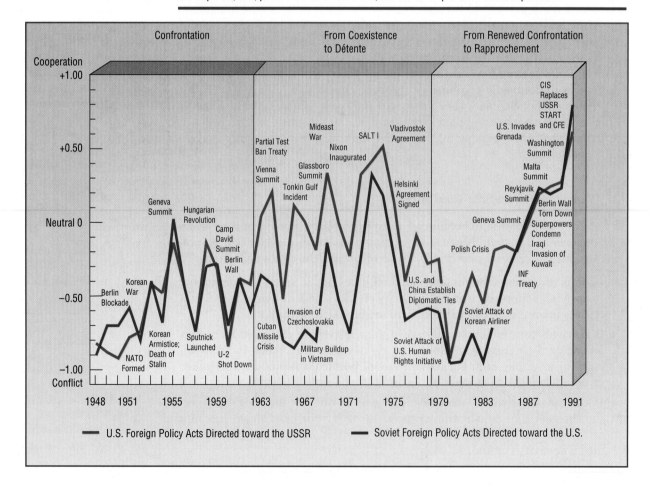

Was Military Containment Necessary?

Whether a military containment strategy was appropriate remains controversial. George F. Kennan thought that U.S. leaders misinterpreted his celebrated statement. He explained:

> I . . . went to great lengths to disclaim the view, imputed to me by implication . . . that containment was a matter of stationing military forces around the Soviet borders and preventing any outbreak of Soviet military aggressiveness. I protested . . . against the implication that the Russians were aspiring to invade other areas and that the task of American policy was to prevent them from doing so. "The Russians don't want," I insisted, "to invade anyone. It is not in their tradition. They tried it once in Finland and got their fingers burned. They don't want war of any kind. Above all, they don't want the open re-

sponsibility that official invasion brings with it." (Kennan 1967, 361)

As Kennan lamented, "the image of a Stalinist Russia poised and yearning to attack the West, and deterred only by [U.S.] possession of atomic weapons, was largely a creation of the Western imagination." Cautioning against "demonizing the adversary, overestimating enemy strength and overmilitarizing the Western response" (Talbott 1990), Kennan recommended a political rather than a military containment approach. It is worth considering whether, if Kennan's recommendations had been followed, the Cold War would have become so bitter or lasted so long.

conduct. Kennan's ideas were circulated widely in 1947, when the influential journal *Foreign Affairs* published his views in an article signed "X" instead of with his own name. In this article, Kennan argued that Soviet leaders forever would feel insecure about their political ability to maintain power against forces both within Soviet society and in the outside world. Their insecurity would lead to an activist—and perhaps aggressive—Soviet foreign policy. However, the United States had the power to increase the strains under which the Soviet leadership would have to operate, which could lead to a gradual mellowing or final end of Soviet power. Thus, Kennan concluded: "In these circumstances it is clear that the main element of any United States policy toward the Soviet Union must be that of a long-term, patient but firm and vigilant *containment* of Russian expansive tendencies" (Kennan 1947, emphasis added).

Soon thereafter, President Harry S Truman made Kennan's assessment the cornerstone of American postwar policy. Provoked in part by violence in Turkey and Greece, which he and others believed to be communist inspired, Truman declared, "I believe that it must be the policy of the United States to support free peoples who are resisting attempted subjugation by armed minorities or by outside pressures." Eventually known as the **Truman Doctrine,** this statement defined the strategy that the United States would pursue for the next forty years, over Kennan's objections (see Focus 4.2). This strategy, called **containment,** sought to prevent the expansion of Soviet influence by encircling the Soviet Union and intimidating it with the threat of a military attack.

A seemingly endless series of new Cold War crises soon followed. They included the Soviet refusal to withdraw troops from Iran in 1946; the communist coup d'état in Czechoslovakia in 1948; the Soviet blockade of West Berlin in

June of that year; the communist acquisition of power on the Chinese main-land in 1949; the outbreak of the Korean War in 1950; the Chinese invasion of Tibet in 1950; and the on-again, off-again Taiwan Straits crises that followed. The "war" was no longer merely "cold;" it had become an embittered worldwide quarrel that threatened to escalate into open conflict.

Nonetheless, superpower relations began to improve in the 1950s. After the Soviets broke the U.S. atomic monopoly in 1949, shifts in the balance of power prompted a movement away from confrontation. The risks of massive destruc-tion necessitated restraint and changed the terms of the struggle. In particular, both superpowers began to expend considerable resources recruiting allies. Their success produced a distribution of military power characterized by **bipo-larity,** with the United States and its allies at one pole and the Soviet Union and its allies at the other.

The focal point of the superpowers' jockeying for influence was Europe, where the Cold War first erupted. The principal European allies of the United States and the Soviet Union divided into the North Atlantic Treaty Organization (NATO) and the Warsaw Treaty Pact, respectively. These alliances became the cornerstones of the superpowers' external policies, as nearly all of the Euro-pean members of each alliance—grateful for protection and defense—yielded to their superpower patrons.

To a lesser extent, alliance formation outside of Europe involved other states in the two titans' contest. The United States in particular sought to con-tain Soviet (and Chinese) influence on the Eurasian landmass by building a ring of allies, including Iran and South Korea, on the very borders of the com-munist world. In return, the United States promised to protect these new client states from external attack through a strategy known as **extended deterrence.** Thus the Cold War expanded across the entire globe.

In the rigid two-bloc system of the 1950s, the superpowers often talked as if war were imminent, but they both acted cautiously (especially after the Ko-rean War). President Eisenhower and his Secretary of State, John Foster Dulles, pursued a strategy termed "rollback," which promised to move what was called the "Iron Curtain" separating East and West by "liberating" the "cap-tive nations" of Eastern Europe. They pledged to respond to communist aggres-sion with "massive retaliation," and criticized the allegedly "soft" and "re-strained" Truman Doctrine, claiming to reject containment in favor of an ambitious "winning" strategy that would finally end the confrontation with godless communism. However, containment was not replaced by a more as-sertive strategy. In 1956, for instance, the United States failed to respond to a call for assistance from Hungarian freedom fighters, who had revolted against Soviet control with armed resistance.

Because the Soviet Union remained strategically inferior to the United States, Nikita Khrushchev (who succeeded Stalin upon his death in 1953) pur-sued a policy of **peaceful coexistence** with capitalism. Nonetheless, the Soviet Union at times cautiously sought to increase its power in places where opportu-nities appeared to exist. As a result, the period following Stalin's death saw many Cold War confrontations, with Hungary, Cuba, Egypt, and Berlin becom-ing the flash points.

Despite the intensity and regularity of U.S.-Soviet confrontations, no threat to peace resulted in open warfare as both superpowers took accommodative steps toward improving relations. For example, the 1955 Geneva summit provided an important forum for the antagonists' meaningful dialogue about world problems,

bipolarity a condition in which power is concentrated in two competing centers so that the rest of the states define their allegiances in terms of their relationships with both.

peaceful coexistence Soviet leader Nikita Khruschev's 1956 doctrine that war between capitalist and communist states was not inevitable and that inter-bloc competition could be peaceful.

and in 1956 the Soviets dissolved the *Cominform* (the Communist Information Bureau, which coordinated the work of communist parties in other states).

From Coexistence to Détente, 1963–1978. Despite the Geneva conference, a dark shadow loomed over hopes for superpower peace. As the arms race accelerated, the threats to peace multiplied. In 1962 the surreptitious placement of Soviet missiles in Cuba set the stage for the greatest test of the superpowers' capacity to manage their disputes—the Cuban missile crisis. The superpowers stood eyeball to eyeball. Fortunately, one (the Soviet Union) blinked, and the crisis ended. This "catalytic" learning experience both reduced enthusiasm for waging the Cold War by military means and expanded awareness of the suicidal consequences of a nuclear war.

The growing threat of mutual destruction, in conjunction with the growing parity of American and Soviet military capabilities, made coexistence or nonexistence appear to be the only alternatives. Given this equation, finding ways to coexist became compelling. At The American University commencement exercises in 1963, U.S. President John F. Kennedy explained why tension reduction had become essential:

> Today, should total war ever break out again—no matter how—our two countries would become the primary targets. It is an ironical but accurate fact that the two strongest powers are the two in the most danger of devastation. . . . We are both caught up in a vicious and dangerous cycle in which suspicion on one side breeds suspicion on the other and new weapons beget counterweapons.
>
> In short, both the United States and its allies, and the Soviet Union and its allies, have a mutually deep interest in a just and genuine peace and in halting the arms race. . . .
>
> So let us not be blind to our differences, but let us also direct attention to our common interests and to the means by which those differences can be resolved. And if we cannot end now our differences, at least we can help make the world safe for diversity.

Kennedy signaled a shift in how the United States hoped thereafter to bargain with its adversary, and the Soviet Union reciprocally expressed its interest in more cooperative relations. Installation in 1963 of the "hot line," a direct communication system linking the White House and the Kremlin, followed. So did the 1967 Glassboro Summit and several negotiated agreements, including the 1963 Partial Test Ban Treaty, the 1967 Outer Space Treaty, and the 1968 Nuclear Nonproliferation Treaty. In addition, the superpowers agreed to accept the permanence of European borders, tacitly including those that divided Germany. Thus, in style and tone the United States and Soviet Union began to depart from past confrontational tactics, laying the foundation for "détente."

Soviet-American relations took a dramatic turn with Richard Nixon's election in 1968. Coached by his national security adviser, Henry A. Kissinger, President Nixon initiated a new approach to Soviet relations that in 1969 he officially labeled **détente.** The Soviets also adopted this term to describe their policies toward the United States.

In Kissinger's words, détente sought to create "a vested interest in cooperation and restraint," "an environment in which competitors can regulate and restrain their differences and ultimately move from competition to cooperation."

détente in general, a strategy seeking to relax tensions between adversaries.

As East-West tension waned, cooperation increased during the détente phase of U.S.-Soviet relations in the late 1960s. A considerable part of this departure from past confrontation was due to compromises at the bargaining table. Pictured here, President Richard Nixon, one of the architects of the U.S. "linkage" strategy along with Secretary of State Henry Kissinger, is toasting with Soviet Premier Leonid Brezhnev and fellow dignitaries their meeting to discuss approaches to relaxing tensions between the superpowers.

To engineer the relaxation of superpower tensions, Nixon and Kissinger pursued a **linkage strategy** to bind the two rivals in a common fate by making peaceful superpower relations dependent on the continuation of mutually rewarding exchanges (such as trade concessions). Furthermore, linkage made cooperation in one policy area contingent on acceptable conduct in other areas.

The shifts in policy produced results, as relations between the Soviets and Americans "normalized." As Figure 4.1 shows, cooperative interaction became more commonplace than hostile relations. Visits, cultural exchanges, trade agreements, and joint technological ventures replaced threats, warnings, and confrontations.

Arms control stood at the center of the dialogue surrounding détente. The **Strategic Arms Limitation Talks (SALT),** initiated in 1969, sought to restrain the threatening, expensive, and spiraling arms race by limiting the deployment of antiballistic missiles. The talks produced two agreements, the first in 1972 (SALT I) and the second in 1979 (SALT II); however, SALT II was signed but never ratified by the United States, due to opposition in Congress. This failure underscored the substantial differences that still separated the superpowers.

From Renewed Confrontation to Rapprochement, 1979–1991. Despite the careful nurturing of détente, its spirit did not endure. In many respects, the Soviet invasion of Afghanistan in 1979 catalyzed détente's demise. As President Jimmy Carter viewed it, "Soviet aggression in Afghanistan—unless checked— confronts all the world with the most serious strategic challenge since the Cold War began." In retaliation, he advanced the **Carter Doctrine** declaring America's willingness to use military force to protect its interests in the Persian Gulf. In addition, he attempted to organize a worldwide boycott of the 1980 Moscow Olympics and suspended U.S. grain exports to the Soviet Union.

Relations deteriorated dramatically thereafter. President Ronald Reagan and his Soviet counterparts (first Yuri Andropov and then Konstantin Chernenko) delivered a barrage of confrontational rhetoric. Reagan asserted that the Soviet Union "underlies all the unrest that is going on" and described the Soviet Union as "the focus of evil in the modern world." The atmosphere was punctuated by Reagan policy adviser Richard Pipes's bold challenge in 1981 that the Soviets would have to choose between "peacefully changing their Communist system . . . or going to war." Soviet rhetoric was equally unrestrained and alarmist.

As talk of war increased, preparations for it escalated. The arms race resumed feverishly, at the expense of addressing domestic economic problems. The superpowers also extended the confrontation to new territory, such as Central America, and renewed their public diplomacy (propaganda) efforts to extol the virtues of their respective systems throughout the world.

Dangerous events punctuated the renewal of conflict. The Soviets destroyed Korean Airlines flight 007 in 1983; the United States invaded Grenada soon thereafter. Arms control talks then ruptured, the Soviets boycotted the 1984 Olympic Games in Los Angeles, and the **Reagan Doctrine** pledged U.S. support for anticommunist insurgents who sought to overthrow Soviet-supported governments in Afghanistan, Angola, and Nicaragua. In addition, American leaders spoke loosely about the "winability" of a nuclear war through a "prevailing" military strategy that included the threat of a "first use" of nuclear weapons in the event of conventional war. Relations deteriorated as these moves and countermoves took their toll. The new Soviet leader, Mikhail Gorbachev, in 1985 summarized the alarming state of superpower relations by fretting that "The situation is very complex, very tense. I would even go so far as to say it is explosive."

However, the situation did not explode. Instead, prospects for a more constructive phase improved greatly following Gorbachev's advocacy of "new thinking" in order to achieve a **rapprochement** or reconciliation of the rival states' interests. He sought to settle the Soviet Union's differences with the capitalist West in order to halt the deterioration of his country's economy and international position. Shortly thereafter, Gorbachev embarked on domestic reforms to promote democratization and the transition to a market economy, and proclaimed his desire to end the Cold War contest. "We realize that we are divided by profound historical, ideological, socioeconomic, and cultural differences," he noted in 1987 during his first visit to the United States. "But the wisdom of politics today lies in not using those differences as a pretext for confrontation, enmity, and the arms race." Soviet spokesperson Georgi Arbatov elaborated, informing the United States that "we are going to do a terrible thing to you—we are going to deprive you of an enemy."

rapprochement in diplomacy, a policy seeking to reestablish normal relations between enemies.

Surprisingly, the Soviets did what they promised: They began to act like an ally instead of an enemy. Building on the momentum created by the **Intermediate-range Nuclear Forces (INF) disarmament agreement,** signed in 1987, the Soviet Union agreed to end its aid and support for Cuba, withdrew from Afghanistan and Eastern Europe, and announced unilateral reductions in military spending. Gorbachev also agreed to two new disarmament agreements, **Strategic Arms Reduction Talks (START)** for deep cuts in strategic arsenals, and the **Conventional Forces in Europe (CFE) Treaty** to reduce the Soviet presence in Europe (see Chapter 15 for a description of these agreements). In addition, the Soviet Union liberalized its emigration policies and permitted greater religious freedom.

The pace of steps to rapprochement then accelerated, and the "normalization" of Soviet-American relations moved rapidly. The Cold War—which began

Why Did the Cold War End Peacefully?

Opinions differ as to why the Cold War ended without mass destruction. The inferences drawn are important, because they will affect leaders' thinking about how to manage future great-power rivalries.

To some observers, the policies George Kennan recommended in his famous "X" article now appeared prophetic. In his version of nonmilitary containment, Kennan anticipated that this would "promote tendencies which must eventually find their outlet in either the breakup of or the gradual mellowing of Soviet power." Many believe that this was precisely what did happen, albeit more than forty years later!

Neorealists, in contrast, emphasize the contribution of nuclear weapons, the essential parity of military power, rigid bipolarity, and extended deterrence through alliances. In 1991, for example, an adviser to U.S. President Reagan, Richard Perle, articulated the realist view in his contention that "Those who argued for nuclear deterrence and serious military capabilities contributed mightily to the position of strength that eventually led the Soviet leadership to choose a less bellicose, less menacing approach to international politics."

Liberals and neoliberals cite other influences, as in political analyst Ted Galen Carpenter's (1991) observation that "Many of the demonstrators . . . who sought to reject communist rule looked to the American system for inspiration. But the source of that inspiration was America's reputation as a haven for the values of limited government, not Washington's $300-billion-a-year military budget and its network of global military bases."

Although no consensus has materialized about the ways in which these factors individually or in combination put an end to the Cold War, a fundamental question sits at the center of this postmortem speculation. Did *military* containment force the Soviet Union into submission, or did Soviet leaders succumb to the inherent *political* weaknesses of communism, which caused an internal economic malaise that left them unable to conduct an imperial policy abroad or retain communist control at home? In other words, was the end of Communist Party rule accepted because of the intimidation of U.S. military strength? Or was the outcome produced by other political and economic influences within the Soviet Union, as suggested in 1991 by Georgi Arbatov, Director of the U.S.S.R.'s Institute for the USA and Canada Studies, who argued that the realist theory "that President Reagan's 'tough' policy and intensified arms race . . . persuaded communists to 'give up' is sheer nonsense. Quite to the contrary, this policy made the life for reformers, for all who yearned for democratic changes in their life, much more difficult. . . . The conservatives and reactionaries were given predominant influence. . . . Reagan made it practically impossible to start reforms after Brezhnev's death (Andropov had such plans) and made things more difficult for Gorbachev to cut military expenditures."

Sorting out the contribution of different causes to ending the Cold War will doubtless intrigue historians for decades, just as determining the causes for its onset has done.

in Europe and centered on Europe for forty-five years—ended there in 1991, when the Soviet Union dissolved. All communist governments in the Soviet "bloc" in Eastern Europe, including even hardline Albania, permitted democratic elections in which Communist Party candidates routinely lost. In all instances, capitalist free market principles replaced socialism. To nearly everyone's astonishment, the Soviet Union acquiesced in these revolutionary changes (see Focus 4.3). Without resistance, the Berlin Wall came down, Germany reunited, and the Warsaw Pact dissolved.

The failed conservative coup against Gorbachev in August 1991 put the nail in the coffin of Communist Party control in Moscow, the very heartland of the international communist movement. As communism was repudiated in the Soviet Union, a new age began. Communism was in retreat, and as a result, massive changes swept world politics.

The abrupt end of the Cold War suggested something quite different from the lesson of the two World Wars, that great-power rivalries are doomed to end in armed conflict. The Cold War was different; it came to an end peacefully.

This suggests that great powers are capable of settling their struggles without bloodshed, and that it is sometimes possible for them to manage their competition and resolve their disputes.

The Consequences of the Cold War

The end of the Cold War has altered the face of world affairs in profound and diverse ways. It held out the promise of international peace but, at the same time, raised the specter of new kinds of global instability. As George Bush lamented in November 1991, "The collapse of communism has thrown open a Pandora's box of ancient ethnic hatreds, resentment, even revenge."

One consequence warrants particular attention: What does Russia's decline bode for the future? Can we expect another fifty years of great-power peace? Or will the transformed balance of power be a prelude to another great-power rivalry, and possibly war?

In the long run, Russia could again emerge as a superpower if it successfully addresses its long-neglected domestic problems. Lying in the heartland of Eurasia, a bridge between Europe and the Pacific Rim, with China and India to the south, Russia stands militarily tall—although it is surrounded by emerging great-power rivals (see Map 4.3). However, the immediate consequence of the Cold War's end is a transformed global hierarchy in which the former Soviet Union is no longer a challenger to U.S. hegemonic leadership. In accepting the devolution of its external empire, the Soviet Union has made the most dramatic peaceful retreat from power in history. The United States now sits alone at the top of the international hierarchy.

● ● ●

THE FUTURE OF GREAT-POWER POLITICS: A COLD PEACE?

The end of the Cold War liberated both the United States and the Soviet Union from a rivalry that had extracted enormous resources and reduced their economic strength relative to other ascending great powers, such as China, Germany, and Japan. In this sense, both "lost" (see Lebow and Stein 1994).

The collapse of the East-West contest left the world facing unfamiliar circumstances. No longer was there "a clear and present danger to delineate the purpose of power, and this basic shift invalidated the framework for much of the thought and action about international affairs in East and West since World War II" (Oberdorfer 1991).

Scenarios for the Twenty-First Century

The peaceful end of the Cold War does not ensure a peaceful future. On the contrary, the insights of long-cycle and realist theories predict pessimistically that prevailing trends in the diffusion of economic power will lead to renewed competition, conflict, and perhaps even warfare among the great powers, and that the range of new problems and potential threats will multiply. As political scientist Robert Jervis explains,

> Cyclical thinking suggests that, freed from the constraints of the Cold War, world politics will return to earlier patterns. Many of the basic generalizations of international politics remain unaltered: It is still anarchic in the

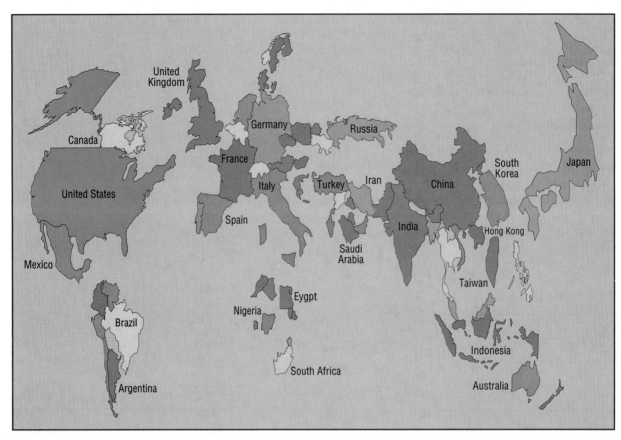

MAP 4.3

Emerging Centers of Power in a New International Hierarchy

Which countries are powerful and which are relatively weak can be estimated by different kinds of indicators. One common approach to predicting the power potential of states (i.e., their ability to project power and exercise influence in the world) is to measure and compare the size of their economies. This map pictures the distribution of power in 1996. The relative size of each country indicates proportional size of gross domestic product measured by purchasing power parities. In this estimate, the United States, Japan, China, Germany are the economic powerhouses, and Russia is a secondary power, ranking below Italy, India, and the United Kingdom, among others.

Note: Not all countries are identified, and many countries are not represented.

SOURCE: Map adapted from *Handbook of International Economic Statistics* (1997), 24.

sense that there is no international sovereign that can make and enforce laws and agreements. The security dilemma remains as well, with the problems it creates for states who would like to cooperate but whose security requirements do not mesh. Many specific causes of conflict also remain, including desires for greater prestige, economic rivalries, hostile nationalisms, divergent perspectives on and incompatible standards of legitimacy, religious animosities, and territorial ambitions. To put it more generally, both aggression and spirals of insecurity and tension can still disturb the peace. (Jervis 1991–1992, 46)

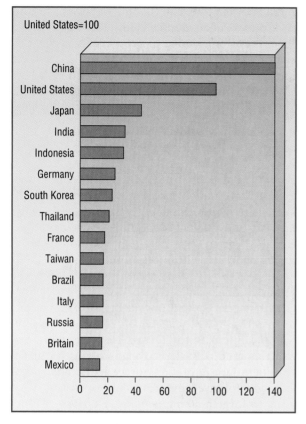

United States=100

China
United States
Japan
India
Indonesia
Germany
South Korea
Thailand
France
Taiwan
Brazil
Italy
Russia
Britain
Mexico

0   20   40   60   80   100   120   140

F I G U R E   4 . 2

Economic Projection of the Fifteen Largest Global Economies by 2020

Using purchasing power parities (PPPs) to account for differences in countries' price levels, the World Bank forecasts the probable size of the largest economies. The projections show that the rank order of the largest economic powerhouses by 2020 will be substantially different from today's. The political and military consequences are not predicted, but long-cycle theory postulates that the economic changes will breed political and even military conflict.

SOURCE: McGranahan (1995), 59.

To realists, great-power rivalry for power and position is likely to resume because the international anarchy that promotes it continues to shape the international conduct of states. Realists also foresee probable instability resulting from the changes unfolding in the international system's structure if U.S. hegemony continues to decay. As rivals rise to challenge U.S. leadership, a new structure will emerge.

A Twenty-First-Century Multipolar World

While the distribution of power in the Cold War system was bipolar, the post-Cold War world promises to be very different. Russia's demise produced a new unipolar structure, fleeting though it may be. In early 1991, when it victoriously fought the Persian Gulf War, the United States basked in a "unipolar moment." It was the "one first-rate power [with] no prospect in the immediate future of any power to rival it. . . . [It was] the only country with the military, diplomatic, political and economic assets to be a decisive player in any conflict in whatever part of the world it [chose] to involve itself" (Krauthammer 1991).

This condition is not likely to last into the next millennium, however. As Figure 4.2 shows, the long-term trajectories of history unmistakably point to the coming of a world in which China, and perhaps other great powers, will rapidly rise to challenge U.S. financial prominence and political clout, even if U.S. military supremacy remains unchallenged in the short run. China, Japan,

99

and others are growing in economic power relative to the United States, and this suggests that the pecking order of the world's countries is likely to look very different by the year 2020 than it does now (for a similar projection of "the next balance of power" to be by the year 2030, see *The Economist*, January 3, 1998). We call such a future world **multipolar** in order to contrast it with situations where either one (unipolar) or two (bipolar) countries possess overwhelming power.

The Challenge of Multipolarity. The character of a new multipolar structure may be very different from the stability that has characterized the unipolar and bipolar phases of international politics since World War II. In part this is because the emergence of a number of comparatively equal great powers will introduce more complexity and uncertainty about allegiances and alignments. This may also be the case because "international security issues will exhibit themselves in all their variety once again—issues of markets, resources, technology, ethnic animosities, political philosophy, and different conceptions of world order, as well as armies and nuclear weapons" (Carter 1990–1991). The multipolar global agenda will encompass continuing concerns with military security—the focus of realism—and mounting concerns about the great powers' economic relations—the focus of liberal international relations theory.

Many theorists point out the dangers inherent in multipolar distributions of power. Their warnings are inspired by the historical record, which suggests that if we look to the past to anticipate the future, we have many reasons to fear the reemergence of this kind of system. Today's hopes for great-power cooperation in the new millennium have many precedents. The end of every previous great-power war was followed by an initial hopeful burst of collaborative institution building to forge a stable new order among the victorious powers. But each of these great-power designs, constructed at the conclusion of a multipolar period's war, ultimately proved temporary when the postwar sense of urgency faded. Precedents include the Peace of Westphalia (1648), the Treaty of Utrecht (1713), the Concert of Europe (1815), the League of Nations (1919), and the United Nations (1945). In each case, as the great powers' relative strength changed, collaboration gave way to competition. Sooner or later, *every* previous multipolar system collapsed, as one or more of the major powers expressed dissatisfaction with the existing hierarchy, rejected the rules by which they had agreed to manage their relations, and attempted to overturn the status quo by force. Rivalry has routinely resulted in a hegemonic struggle for supremacy ending in a new catastrophic general war, each more destructive than the last. This invites the sobering conclusion that

> in a world of sovereign states a contest among them over the distribution of power is the normal condition and . . . such contests often lead to war. . . . The reasons for seeking more power are often not merely the search for security or material advantage. Among them are demands for greater prestige, respect, deference, in short, honor. Since such demands involve judgments even more subjective than those about material advantage, they are still harder to satisfy. Other reasons emerge from fear, often unclear and intangible, not always of immediate threats but also of more distant ones, against which reassurance may not be possible. The persistence of such thinking in a wide variety of states and systems over the space of millennia suggests the unwelcome conclusion that war is probably part of the human condition and likely to be with us for some time yet. (Kagan 1995, 569)

Multipolar politics looks especially menacing when we take into account the interplay of military and economic factors in the perceived rankings of the great powers. In such a system, differentiating friend from foe will be more difficult because allies in military security are likely to be rivals in trade relationships. In Lester Thurow's (1992) apt phrase, the United States, Europe, and Japan are likely to go "head to head" on the economic battlefield. In this arena we can expect China and perhaps a reascendant Russia, India, and Indonesia to join the fray. The U.S.-China and U.S.-Russia disputes in late-1997 about security issues and NATO enlargement at the very time they were also arguing about "fair trade" and the use of intervention to protect human rights within national borders illustrate the tensions that can easily escalate between powers at the pinnacle of the global hierarchy.

The diffusion of wealth predicts the likely intensification of great-power political competition. Throughout history, changes in comparative *economic* advantage have preceded *political* competition. When multipolarity has existed, economic rivals have struggled to protect their wealth and have competed politically for economic position, with military conflict usually following (Rusi 1997).

A "new Cold War" could emerge between any pair of great powers, such as the United States and China, if their competition escalates. However, this kind of armed rivalry need not develop; cooperation could increase instead. Quite different and inconsistent political types of great-power relations could emerge in the economic and military spheres. The probability of economic rivalry and conflict is generally high, whereas the likelihood of security cooperation for many of these same relationships is also high. For example, the United States, Japan, and China exhibit conflict in their commercial relations but have shown a capacity to manage their security relations collaboratively. Table 4.2 presents a projection of the kind of cross-cutting bilateral relationships that could develop among the great powers in the next century. It estimates the probability of military cooperation and economic conflict between any pair of the five major powers.

Awareness of these different possibilities may have been behind U.S. Secretary of State Lawrence Eagleburger's warning in 1989:

> The issue . . . is how well the United States accomplishes the transition from overwhelming predominance to a position more akin to a "first among equals" status, and how well America's partners—Japan and Western Europe—adapt to their newfound importance. The change will not be easy for any of the players, as such shifts in power relationships have never been easy.

TABLE 4.2   **The New Great-Power Chessboard: Economic Rivalry and Military Alliance Possibilities**

	Economic Rivalry						Military Alliance				
	United States	Japan	Germany	Russia	China		United States	Japan	Germany	Russia	China
United States	—					United States	—				
Japan	H	—				Japan	H	—			
Germany	H	H	—			Germany	M	L	—		
Russia	L	M	M	—		Russia	M	L	L	—	
China	H	H	L	M	—	China	L	L	L	M	—

Note: The symbols H = high, M = medium, and L = low signify the likelihood of bilateral relationships that may develop in the new millennium.

Few observers see advantages resulting from the emerging situation. As former U.S. Secretary of State Henry A. Kissinger surmised in 1993, this poses a serious challenge because "the United States has very little experience with a world that consists of many powers and which it can neither dominate nor from which it can simply withdraw in isolation."

Yet, we have no way of knowing whether the future will resemble the gloomy past history of multipolar systems. Patterns and practices can change, and it is possible for policymakers to learn from previous mistakes and avoid repeating them.

Responding to Multipolarity's Challenge. What, then, can the great powers do to prevent the resumption of their rivalry? What security policies should they pursue in order to avoid the dangers of shared power and rapid transitions in their position and strength in the great-power hierarchy?

The answers are highly uncertain. As we will discuss in Chapters 13–16, debate about the methods of guaranteeing international security in Washington, Moscow, Berlin, Beijing, and Tokyo today revolves around four basic options. Each is actively under consideration, and each will become more or less practical, prudent, or problematic for each great power depending on the circumstances that materialize in tomorrow's multipolar world.

A *unilateral* conception of a great power's role represents one possible option. Acting alone is especially attractive for a self-confident great power assured of its independent strength. With sufficient power, a potential hegemon can be self-reliant. Unilateralism can involve isolationism, an attempt to exert hegemonic leadership, or an effort to play the role of a "balancer" who skillfully backs one side or another in a great-power dispute, but only when necessary to maintain a military equilibrium between the disputants. Unilateralism can also invite the world leader to play the role of international bully, acting in the absence of limits put to it by others as if it has a blank check to run the world. Or unilateralism can lead to a power's decision to help itself first, as Japan announced it would in November 1997 by pulling back in leadership because it did not wish to pay the costs of acting as a locomotive for others.

Cultivation of a *specialized relationship* with another great power, similar to that between Great Britain and the United States in this century, illustrates a second approach that some pairs of great powers might pursue. The 1997 "Joint Declaration on the Multipolar World and a New World Order" signed in April 1997 between China and Russia suggests the kind of strategic bilateral partnership that can easily develop in a climate of fear in the future as well as the most probable reasons why such alliances may be forged between powers that have suffered from frosty relations in the recent past. Convinced that a dominant United States aimed to contain their influence, and asserting that "no country should claim hegemony for itself or pursue policy from positions of strength and monopolize international affairs," Moscow and Beijing announced their agreement to build warmer relations by joining in a common cause to counterbalance the United States as the world's lone superpower. That announcement led to a new agreement between the United States and Japan in July 1997 to strengthen their specialized defense relationship by working on a common military project. This in turn led China at the October 1997 summit meeting with President Clinton in Shanghai to seek "common ground despite differences," attempting to raise Chinese-American relations "to a new level by sharing responsibility for preserving world peace." Other types of specialized relations between pairs of great powers could follow, at various levels of mutual support and commitment. There are several variants of this strategic option, including informal understandings, cooperations (sometimes termed **ententes**), and formal alliances concretized by treaties.

A third strategy under consideration is construction of a **concert,** or a cooperative agreement among the great powers to manage the international system jointly and to prevent international disputes from escalating to war. The Concert of Europe, at its apex between 1815 and 1822, is the epitome of previous great-power efforts to pursue this path to peace.

Finally, some policymakers recommend that today's great powers unite with the lesser powers in constructing a true system of **collective security.** The principles rationalizing the formation of the League of Nations in 1919 exemplify this *multilateral* approach to peace under conditions of multipolarity, as did the December 1997 pledge by Russia and Nato to cooperate in building a twenty-first-century security partnership.

Whichever combination of approaches predominates in the strategies forged to prevent great-power rivalries from escalating to war in a multipolar future, the ultimate outcome will not depend on the great powers alone. The policy response of other, less powerful actors is likely to be increasingly important in shaping world politics, and their role must also be examined. We begin in Chapter 5 with a consideration of the history and characteristics of those states at the bottom of the international system's hierarchy, the Global South, and of the foreign policy interests and goals that motivate their behavior.

collective security a security regime agreed to by the great powers setting rules for keeping peace, guided by the principle that an act of aggression by any state will be met by a collective response from the rest.

K E Y   T E R M S

long-cycle theory
hegemon
hegemonic stability theory
structuralism
nationalism
Kellogg-Briand Pact
irredentism
fascism
machtpolitik
isolationism
appeasement
Yalta Conference
sphere of influence
domino theory
mirror images

self-fulfilling prophecies
security dilemma
security regime
unipolarity
Truman Doctrine
containment
bipolarity
extended deterrence
peaceful coexistence
Cominform
détente
linkage strategy
Strategic Arms Limitation Talks
  (SALT)
Carter Doctrine

Reagan Doctrine
rapprochement
Intermediate-range Nuclear
  Forces (INF) disarmament
  agreement
Strategic Arms Reduction Talks
  (START)
Conventional Forces in Europe
  (CFE) treaty
multipolar
entente
concert
collective security

S U G G E S T E D   R E A D I N G

Doran, Charles F. *Systems in Crisis: New Imperatives of High Politics at Century's End.* Cambridge, Mass.: Cambridge University Press, 1992.

Gaddis, John Lewis. *We Now Know: Rethinking Cold War History.* New York: Oxford University Press, 1997.

Garten, Jeffrey E. *A Cold Peace: America, Japan, Germany, and the Struggle for Supremacy*. New York: Random House, 1993.

Kegley, Charles W., Jr., and Gregory A. Raymond. *A Multipolar Peace? Great-Power Politics in the Twenty-First Century*. New York: St. Martin's Press, 1994.

Kennedy, Paul. *The Rise and Fall of the Great Powers*. New York: Random House, 1987.

Kissinger, Henry. *Diplomacy*. New York: Simon & Schuster, 1994.

Larson, Deborah Welch. *Anatomy of Mistrust: U.S.-Soviet Relations during the Cold War*. Ithaca, N.Y.: Cornell University Press, 1997.

Ruggie, John Gerald. *Winning the Peace*. New York: Columbia University Press, 1996.

Rusi, Alpo M. *Dangerous Peace: New Rivalry in World Politics*. Boulder, Colo.: Westview, 1997.

Stern, Geoffrey. *The Structure of International Society*. London: Pinter, 1995.

Thompson, William R. *Great Power Rivalries*. Columbia: University of South Carolina Press, 1999.

Vogel, Ezra, ed. *Living with China*. New York: W. W. Norton, 1997.

WHERE ON THE WORLD WIDE WEB?

http://www.lib.byu.edu~rdh/wwi/
The World War I Document Archive The World War I Military History List has assembled a group of primary documents from World War I. Read the treaties, scan personal reminiscences, see photos, and access links to other resources.

http://www.bunt.com/~mconrad/links.htm
World War II on the Web An all inclusive Web site on World War II divided according to "theater." Beside primary documents, visitors can access discussion groups, associations, and biographies. Extensive links to Holocaust Web sites are also available.

http://webcorp.com/mccarthy/
Senator Joe McCarthy: A Multimedia Celebration A multimedia site where students can see and hear the most famous speeches and hearings given by Joe McCarthy. This is an important site for contemporary students who have trouble believing "what all the fuss was about."

http://www.pbs.org/wgbh/pages/amex/u2/u2.html
Spy in the Sky This PBS series chronicles the U-2 spy plane. It has interviews with the original pilots, mechanics and engineers, historians and authors. The program provides an insider's view of the urgency, secrecy, and ingenuity surrounding the CIA's top-secret project during the Cold War.

http://sunsite.unc.edu/expo/soviet.exhibit/entrance.html
Soviet Exhibit This Web site is the Library of Congress's Soviet Archives exhibit. It is a virtual "walking tour." Go to the first floor to see the "Internal Workings of the Soviet System" or proceed directly to the second floor to see "The Soviet Union and the United States." Shuttle buses take you to other pavilions or let you visit the "Restaurant." You can leave messages for a current or future friend at the "Post Office."

CHAPTER 5

The Plight and Policy Posture of the Less Developed Global South

CHAPTER TOPICS AND THEMES

- The rise and fall of European empires and the birth of the Third World

- The Global South as a group: Commonalities and differences

- What is development?

- Why underdevelopment in the Global South?

- The foreign policies of the Global South

- The future of the Global South

The earth is divided into two hemispheres, north and south, at the equator. Life in the north is very different, in many ways, from life in the south. One American college student learned this lesson, painfully, during his first visit to South America. He found a reality far different from his own experience growing up in the United States. He was moved to write:

> I spent the first 24 years of my life in South Carolina. When I left . . . for Colombia [South America], I fully expected Bogota to be like any large U.S. city, only with citizens who spoke Spanish. When I arrived there I found my expectations were wrong. I was not in the U.S., I was on Mars! I was a victim of culture shock. As a personal experience this shock was occasionally funny and sometimes sad. But after all the laughing and the crying were over, it forced me to reevaluate both my life and the society in which I live.
>
> Colombia is a poor country by American standards. It has a per capita GNP of $550 and a very unequal distribution of income. These were the facts that I knew before I left.
>
> But to "know" these things intellectually is much different from experiencing first-hand how they affect people's lives. It is one thing to lecture in air conditioned classrooms about the problems of world poverty. It is quite another to see four-year-old children begging or sleeping in the streets.
>
> It tore me apart emotionally to see the reality of what I had studied for so long: "low per capita GNP and maldistribution of income." What this means in human terms is children with dirty faces who beg for bread money or turn into pickpockets because the principle of private property gets blurred by empty stomachs.
>
> It means other children whose minds and bodies will never develop fully because they were malnourished as infants. It means cripples who can't even turn to thievery and must beg to stay alive. It means street vendors who sell candy and cigarettes 14 hours a day in order to feed their families.
>
> It also means well-dressed businessmen and petty bureaucrats who indifferently pass this poverty every day as they seek asylum in their fortified houses to the north of the city.
>
> It means rich people who prefer not to see the poor, except for maids and security guards.
>
> It means foreigners like me who come to Colombia and spend more in one month than the average Colombian earns in a year.
>
> It means politicians across the ideological spectrum who are so full of abstract solutions or personal greed that they forget that it is real people they are dealing with.
>
> Somewhere within the polemics of the politicians and the "objectivity" of the social scientists, the human being has been lost. (Wallace 1978, 15–16)

What created these conditions that are characteristic of the countries in the south? To understand possible answers we need to begin by taking into consideration the legacy and impact of colonialism on the peoples who were colonized by European conquerors. The now independent sovereign states in the Southern Hemisphere were almost all former colonies.

The end of colonialism is one of the most remarkable developments in twentieth-century world politics. As U.S. Secretary of State George Shultz observed in 1983, "Since the Second World War, the world has undergone a vast transformation as more than 100 new states have come into being. An international system that had been centered on Europe for centuries, and that regarded all non-European areas as peripheral or as objects of rivalry, has become in an amazingly short span of time a truly global arena of sovereign states."

Despite their legal status as independent entities, sovereignty could not erase the colonial heritage and vulnerabilities that the former colonies faced. Indeed, the new poor states born after World War II were thrust into the international periphery; dominated by the rich great powers at the core of an international system they had no voice in shaping, the new states viewed the inherited rules and structures as barriers to their true independence and growth.

The term **Third World** was first used to distinguish the growing number of newly emerging, economically less developed states that tended to share a common colonial heritage from those identified with either the East or West in the Cold War struggle, but it soon took on largely economic connotations. Compared with the **First World** industrialized countries, the Third World had failed to advance toward levels of economic development comparable to Western Europe, North America, and Japan. The **Second World**—consisting of the Soviet Union, its allies, and other communist societies—was distinguished by a commitment to planned economic practices rather than reliance on market forces to determine the supply of and demand for goods and services. Today the states comprising the former Second World are commonly described as "countries in transition."

The term "Third World" carries Cold War baggage that makes it no longer useful. Today the terms **Global North,** which refers to what was previously known as the First World, and **Global South,** which refers to the rest of the world, are preferred. As always, placement of particular states within these categories is sometimes problematic. Many of the countries in transition, those formerly referred to as Second World, are particularly difficult to place. Generally, four dimensions distinguish the North and South: politics, technology, wealth, and demography.

States composing the Global North are democratic, technologically inventive, wealthy, and aging, as their societies tend toward zero population growth. Some states in the Global South share many of these characteristics, but none shares them all. Saudi Arabia is rich but not democratic; China is populous but only a fraction of its slow-growing population has recently become wealthy; India is democratic but burdened with an enormous and growing population; and Singapore is both wealthy and technologically innovative, with a comparatively modest population growth rate, but is not democratic. Beyond this are many states that are not democratic, technologically innovative, or wealthy, but who are experiencing rapid population growth that increasingly strains overtaxed social and ecological systems. These, the least developed of the less developed countries, are sometimes described today as the "Third World's Third World." Many, but not all, are in Africa, south of the Sahara.

The Global South is home to more than 80 percent of the world's people but commands less than 20 percent of its wealth. These disparities, illustrated in Figure 5.1, underlie the long festering "North-South conflict" dispute more than do political and technological differences. The contest between the wealthy North and the poor South has historically been "a politics of mutual suspicion and struggle" (Heilbroner 1991) because of the fears and resentments that differences in status and unequal opportunities to economically compete naturally arouse.

In this chapter we examine the roots and consequences of the often stark contrasts that set the Global South apart and the foreign policy postures that flow from them. Although considerable diversity exists within the countries of

Third World a Cold War term to describe the developing countries of Africa, Asia, the Caribbean, and Latin America.

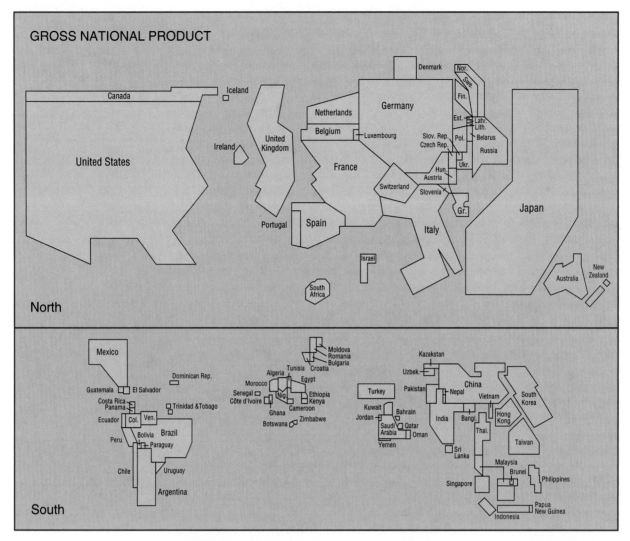

FIGURE 5.1

Differences in the Global North and South

If the countries of the world are redrawn to reflect the size of their economies and populations, the world appears lopsided indeed: Most of the wealth is in the North; most of the people are in the South.

the Global South, it is common to describe them as a united group quite distinct from the similarly diverse great powers. We begin with an examination of the colonial and imperial historical experiences of most developing countries that account for their subordinate international position, and the Global South's policy reaction to that circumstance.

• • •

THE RISE AND FALL OF EUROPEAN EMPIRES

The emergence of the Global South as an identifiable world actor is a distinctly contemporary phenomenon. Although most Latin American countries were in-

108

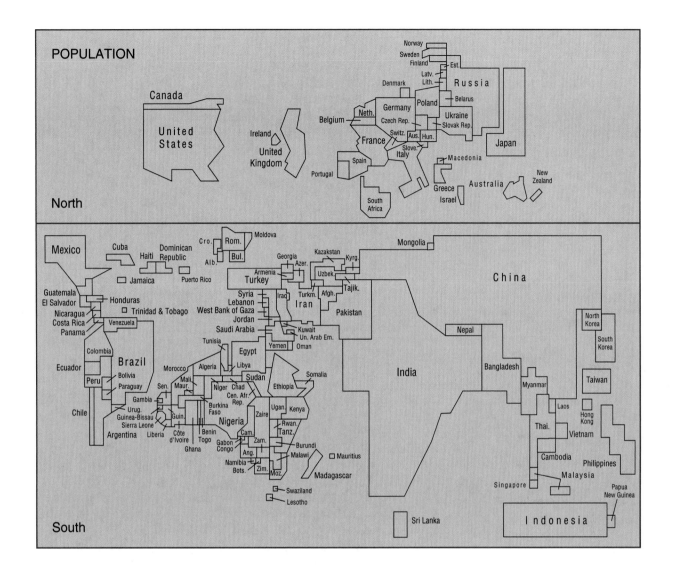

POPULATION

North

South

dependent before World War II, not until 1946 did the floodgates of decolonization first open. In the next five decades a profusion of new states joined the international community as sovereign entities, nearly all carved from British, French, Belgian, Spanish, and Portuguese empires built under **colonialism.**

Today, few colonies exist. Although the dozen or so remaining dependent territories may yet become independent members of the world community, most have populations of less than 100,000 and many have expressed a preference to retain their current political status. In short, the political process known as **decolonization**—the freeing of colonial peoples from their dependent status—is now complete.

colonialism the imperial policies by which the European great powers seized control of territories throughout much of the world, but especially in Africa, Asia, the Americas, and the Middle East.

Even after the decolonization process runs its complete course, more new countries can be expected because many existing states are fragmenting. When World War I broke out, only 62 independent countries existed; in 1998 there were 193. Many new sovereign states are very small. Pictured here is the "micro" state of Nauru, which has a president, Supreme Court, and the full apparatus of government to rule its tiny population. Half the globe's countries have populations smaller than the U.S. state of Massachusetts.

Most of the ethnic national conflicts now so prevalent have colonial roots, as the imperial powers drew borders within and between their domains with little regard for the national identities of the indigenous peoples. Similarly, the staggering poverty facing Global South countries may be a product of their imperial pasts, when the European powers exploited their overseas territories. Thus, as viewed through the eyes of nationalist leaders in many of the emerging states, the disparity between the rich North and the poor South is the consequence of **neocolonialism** or **neoimperialism**—unequal trade exchanges through which the advantaged exploit the disadvantaged by penetrating the latter's markets and by institutionalizing economic processes for this purpose.

neocolonialism the economic rather than military domination of foreign countries.

The First Wave of European Imperialism

The first wave of European empire building began during the fifteenth century, as the Dutch, English, French, Portuguese, and Spanish used their military power to conquer territories for commercial gain. As scientific innovations made the European explorers' adventures possible, merchants followed in their wake, "quickly seizing upon opportunities to increase their business and profits. In turn, Europe's governments perceived the possibilities for increasing their own power and wealth. Commercial companies were chartered and financed, with military and naval expeditions frequently sent out after them to ensure political control of overseas territories" (Cohen 1973).

The economic strategy underlying the relationship between colonies and colonizers during this era of "classical imperialism" is known as **mercantilism:** an economic philosophy advocating government regulation of economic life to increase state power and security. European rulers believed that power flowed from the possession of national wealth measured in terms of gold and silver,

mercantilism a government regulatory trade strategy for accumulating state wealth and power by encouraging exports and discouraging imports.

and that developing mining and industry to attain a favorable balance of trade (exporting more than they imported) was the best way to accumulate the desired bullion. "Colonies were desirable in this respect because they afforded an opportunity to shut out commercial competition; they guaranteed exclusive access to untapped markets and sources of cheap materials (as well as, in some instances, direct sources of the precious metals themselves). Each state was determined to monopolize as many of these overseas mercantile opportunities as possible" (Cohen 1973). To maximize national power and wealth, states saw the conquest of foreign territory as a natural byproduct of active government management of the economy.

By the end of the eighteenth century the European powers had spread themselves, although thinly, throughout virtually the entire world, but the colonial empires they had built now began to crumble. Britain's thirteen North American colonies declared their independence in 1776, and most of Spain's possessions in South America won their freedom in the early nineteenth century. Nearly one hundred colonial relationships worldwide were terminated in the half-century ending in 1825 (Bergesen and Schoenberg 1980, 236).

As Europe's colonial empires dissolved, belief in the mercantilist philosophy also waned. As the Scottish political economist Adam Smith argued in his 1776 treatise, *The Wealth of Nations*, national wealth grew not through the accumulation of precious metals but rather from the capital and goods they could buy. Smith's ideas about the benefits of the "invisible hand" of the unregulated domestic and international marketplace laid much of the intellectual foundation for **classical liberal economic theory.** Following the thinking of Smith and other liberal free-trade theorists, faith in the precepts of **laissez-faire economics** (minimal government interference in the market) gained widespread acceptance (see also Chapter 8). European powers continued to hold numerous colonies, but the prevailing sentiment was now more anti- than pro-imperial.

The Second Wave of European Imperialism

Beginning in the 1870s and extending until the outbreak of World War I, a second wave of imperialism washed over the world as Europe, joined later by the United States and Japan, aggressively colonized new territories. The portion of the globe that Europeans controlled was one-third in 1800, two-thirds by 1878, and four-fifths by 1914 (Fieldhouse 1973, 3). As illustrated in Map 5.1, nearly all of Africa was now under the control of seven European powers: Belgium, Britain, France, Germany, Italy, Portugal, and Spain. In all of the Far East and the Pacific, only China, Japan, and Siam (Thailand) remained outside the direct control of Europe or the United States. China, too, was divided into spheres of influence by foreign powers, and Japan itself also imperialistically occupied Korea and Formosa (Taiwan). Elsewhere, the United States expanded across its continent, acquired Puerto Rico and the Philippines in the 1898 Spanish-American War, extended its colonial reach westward to Hawaii, leased the Panama Canal Zone "in perpetuity" from the new state of Panama (an American creation), and exercised considerable control over several Caribbean islands, notably Cuba. The preeminent imperial power, Great Britain, in a single generation expanded its empire to engulf the entire world. By 1900 it covered one-fifth of the earth's land area and comprised perhaps one-fourth of its population (Cohen 1973, 30). As British imperialists were proud to proclaim, it was an empire on which the sun never set.

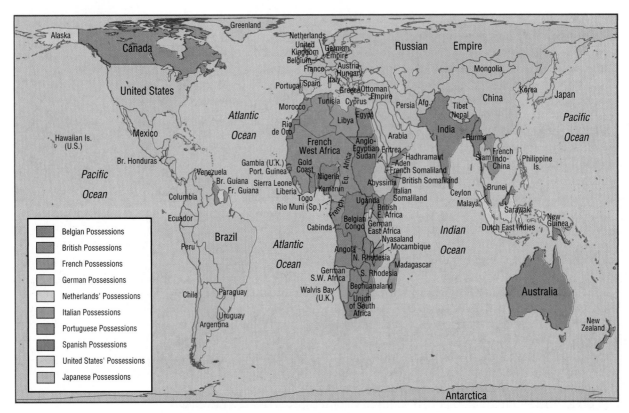

M A P   5 . 1

Global Imperialism, 1914

The ten major imperial powers competed for colonies throughout the globe, and on the eve of the First World War, their combined territories did indeed cover much of the world.

In contrast with classical imperialism, extraordinary competition among the imperial powers marked the late nineteenth century "new imperialism." The European-centered industrial revolution provided the military might and economic means to subjugate foreign territories, which became important symbols of national power and prestige. In the process, the local inhabitants of the conquered lands were often ruthlessly suppressed.

The imperial powers typically pursued their various interests overseas in a blatantly aggressive fashion. Bloody, one-sided wars with local inhabitants of contested territories were commonplace; "sporting wars," [Prussian leader Otto von] Bismarck once called them. The powers themselves rarely came into direct military conflict, but competition among them was keen, and they were perpetually involved in various diplomatic crises. In contrast to the preceding years of comparative political calm, the period after 1870 was one of unaccustomed hostility and tension. (Cohen 1973, 30)

Having abandoned their earlier acquired empires, why did most of the great powers—and those that aspired to great-power status—engage in this expensive and often vicious competition to control other peoples and territories?

Pictured on the left is the German philosopher Karl Marx (1818–1883), whose revolutionary economic theory argued that "the history of all hitherto existing society is the history of class struggle." Imperial conquest of colonial peoples could only be prevented, Marx warned, by humanity's shift from a capitalist to a socialist economy and society. Pictured on the right is the kind of imperialistic activity that provoked his wrath: ruthless, aggressive, and bent on acquiring property for profit, Britain's nineteenth-century imperial forces marched into battle to seize foreign territory.

What explains the new imperialism? The answers are rooted in economics and politics.

Economic Explanations for the New Imperialism. With the industrial revolution, capitalism grew, emphasizing the free market, private ownership of the means of production, and the accumulation of wealth. Theorists following Karl Marx saw imperialism's aggressive competition as the product of capitalists' need for profitable overseas outlets for their surplus ("finance") capital. Here is where the Soviet leader V. I. Lenin made one of his distinctive contributions to the communist thinking later described as **Marxism-Leninism.**

In his famous 1916 monograph *Imperialism, The Highest Stage of Capitalism*, Lenin argued that military expansion abroad was produced by the "monopoly stage of capitalism." Lenin concluded that the only way to end imperialism was to abolish capitalism. Classical or liberal economists, on the other hand, regarded the new imperialism not as a product of capitalism as such but rather as "a response to certain maladjustments within the contemporary capitalist system which, given the proper will, could be corrected" (Cohen 1973). What the two perspectives shared was the belief that economics explained the new imperialism: "The fundamental problem was in the presumed material needs of advanced capitalist societies—the need for cheap raw materials to feed

Marxism-Leninism communist theory as derived from the writings of Karl Marx, V. I. Lenin, and their successors, which criticizes capitalism as a cause of class struggle, the exploitation of workers, colonialism, and war.

113

their growing industrial complexes, for additional markets to consume their rising levels of production, and for investment outlets to absorb their rapidly accumulating capital" (Cohen 1973). Thus, from both the Marxist and classical (liberal) perspectives, the material needs of capitalist societies explained their imperial drive.

World-system analyses, like Marxist theories, also embrace an economic explanation. **World-system theory** postulates that a single capitalist world economy emerged during the "long 16th century" from 1450 to 1640, which created a world division of labor separating "core" (industrial) areas from those in the globe's (nonindustrial) "periphery" (Wallerstein 1974a; 1974b; 1980; 1988). Northwest Europe first emerged as the core. As the industrial revolution proceeded, the core states exchanged manufactured goods for primary agricultural and mineral products produced in the colonial territories at the periphery. From this perspective, colonization became the principal method for imperial control over foreign lands (Boswell 1989).

World-system theory interprets the new imperialism of the late eighteenth century quite differently from the previous colonial period. "The earliest colonies were usually coastal trading posts for merchants involved in long-distance preciosity exchange with the contact periphery, such as the spice trade. Following rivers upstream, these were later superseded by settler colonies involved in the production of necessities, primarily mining and cash-crop agriculture using coerced labor." In contrast, after 1870, colonies effectively became occupation zones in which a small number of European sojourners coerced an indigenous population into production for the global economy (Boswell 1989).

Political Explanations for the New Imperialism. Political factors also explain the new imperialism. J. A. Hobson argued in his influential 1902 book, *Imperialism*, that the jockeying for power and prestige between competitive empires had always characterized state behavior in the European balance-of-power system, and that imperialism through overseas expansion was simply an extension of this inter-European competition for dominance.

By the 1800s Britain emerged from Europe's perpetual conflict as the world's leading power. From this position it became the chief promoter of free international trade because a system with few legal barriers to exports and imports also promoted disproportionate economic growth in the core relative to the periphery (McGowan 1981). By 1870, however, Britain's superiority was on the wane. Germany emerged as a powerful industrial state, as did the United States. Understandably, Britain tried to protect its privileged position in the international division of labor in the face of growing competition from the newly emerging core states. Its efforts to maintain the status quo help to explain the second wave of imperial expansion—especially in Africa, whose partition served the imperial powers at the expense of local populations.

As Africa's ignominious fate illustrates, the European powers competed for power not in Europe itself, but in the peripheral areas of the capitalist world system, where competition for political preeminence led to economic domination and exploitation. As in the mercantile system of the past, Europe's colonies were integrated into the world political economy solely for the purpose of serving the interests of the colonial powers. "The political victors controlled investment and trade, regulated currency and production, and manipulated labor, thus establishing structures of economic dependency in their colonies which would endure far longer than their actual political authority" (Spero and Hart 1997).

world-system theory a theory that claims the perpetual and widening inequity among states is explained by capitalism's international division of labor and production, which over time allows the wealthy core countries to become richer while the peripheral states supplying raw materials and cheap labor become poorer.

114

The British-sponsored laissez-faire system of free trade promoted rapid economic growth in many colonial territories, but economic development elsewhere proceeded even more rapidly. Western Europe, North America, Australia, and New Zealand were able to complete their industrial revolutions during this period and to advance as industrial societies. Thus the gap between the world's rich and poor countries began to widen.

Colonialism and Self-Determination in the Interwar Period

The climate of opinion turned decidedly anti-imperial when the 1917 Versailles peace settlement that ended World War I embraced the principle of national **self-determination** advocated by U.S. President Woodrow Wilson. Self-determination meant that indigenous nationalities would have the right to decide which authority would represent and rule them. Wilson and others who shared his liberal convictions believed that freedom of choice would lead to the creation of states and governments content with their territorial boundaries and therefore less inclined to make war. In practice, however, the principle was applied almost exclusively to war-torn Europe, where six new states were created from the territory of the former Austro-Hungarian Empire (Austria, Czechoslovakia, Hungary, Poland, Romania, and Yugoslavia). Other territorial adjustments were also made in Europe, but the proposition that self-determination should be extended to Europe's overseas empires did not receive serious support.

Still, the colonial territories of the powers defeated in World War I were not simply parceled out among the victorious allies, as had typically happened in the past. Instead, the territories controlled by Germany and the Ottoman Empire were transferred under League of Nations auspices to countries that would govern them as "mandates" pending their eventual self-rule. In the Middle East, France assumed the mandate for Syria, and Britain assumed it for Iraq, Transjordan, and Palestine. In Africa, most of the German colony of Tanganyika went to Britain; the West African colonies of Cameroon and Togoland were divided between Britain and France; and the Union of South Africa gained responsibility for the mandate governing German South-West Africa. In the Pacific area, Australia, New Zealand, and Japan acquired jurisdiction over the former German colonies.

Many of these territorial decisions gave rise to political conflicts during the next half-century or more. The decisions relating to the Middle East and Africa were especially crucial, as the League of Nations called for the eventual creation of a Jewish national homeland in Palestine and arranged for the transfer of control over South-West Africa (now called Namibia) to what would become the white minority regime of South Africa.

The principle implicit in the League of Nations mandate system gave birth to the idea that "colonies were a trust rather than simply a property to be exploited and treated as if its peoples had no right of their own" (Easton 1964). This set an important precedent for the negotiations after World War II, when territories of the defeated powers placed under the United Nations trusteeship system were not absorbed by others but were promised eventual self-rule.

The End of Empire

Imperialism threatened the world again in the 1930s and early 1940s, as Germany, Japan, and Italy sought to expand their political control in Europe, Asia, and Africa. With their defeat in World War II, the threat of regional empire building receded and support for self-determination gained momentum. The decolonization process accelerated in 1947, when the British relinquished political control of the Indian subcontinent and India and Pakistan joined the international community as sovereign members. War eventually erupted between the new states as each sought to gain control over disputed territory in Kashmir. It ignited twice more, in 1965 and again in 1971, when East Pakistan broke away from West Pakistan to form the new state of Bangladesh. Violence also broke out in Indochina and Algeria in the 1950s and early 1960s as the French sought to regain control over colonial territories they had held before World War II. Similarly, bloodshed followed closely on the heels of independence in the Congo (now Zaire) when the Belgians granted their African colony independence in 1960, and it dogged the unsuccessful efforts of Portugal to battle the winds of decolonization that swept over Africa as the 1960s wore on.

Despite these political convulsions, decolonization for the most part was not only extraordinarily rapid but also remarkably peaceful. This may be explained by World War II having sapped the economic and military vitality of many of the colonial powers. World-system analysts contend that a growing appreciation of the costs of empire also eroded support for colonial empires (Strang 1990; 1991). Regardless of the underlying cause, colonialism became less acceptable in a world increasingly dominated by rivalry between East and West. The Cold War competition for political allies and the fear of large-scale warfare gave the superpowers incentives to lobby jointly for the liberation of overseas empires. Decolonization "triumphed," as Inis Claude (1967) explains, "largely because the West [gave] priority to the containment of communism over the perpetuation of colonialism."

The United Nations also contributed to the "collective delegitimization" of colonialism. With colonialism already in retreat, in 1960, Global South states took advantage of their growing numbers in the UN General Assembly to secure passage of the historic Declaration on the Granting of Independence to Colonial Countries and Peoples. "The General Assembly proclaimed that the subjection of any people to alien domination was a denial of fundamental human rights, contrary to the UN Charter, and an impediment to world peace and that all subject peoples had a right to immediate and complete independence. No country cast a vote against this anticolonial manifesto. . . . It was an ideological triumph" (Riggs and Plano 1994).

As the old order crumbled—and as the leaders in the newly emancipated territories discovered that freedom did not translate automatically into autonomy, economic independence, and domestic prosperity—the conflict between the rich Global North and the emerging states of the Global South began. And it continues today. While some see future international struggle as centered on a "clash of civilizations" (Huntington 1996), others argue that "'civilization clash' is not so much over Jesus Christ, Confucius, or the Prophet Muhammad as it is over the unequal distribution of world power, wealth, and influence, and the perceived historical lack of respect accorded to small states and peoples by larger ones" (Fuller 1995).

• • •

THE GLOBAL SOUTH: COMMONALITIES AND DIVERSITY

The Global South is sometimes described today as a "zone of turmoil" in large measure because, in contrast with the Global North where "peace, wealth, and democracy" prevail, most of the world's people live amidst "poverty, war, tyranny, and anarchy" (Singer and Wildavsky 1993). A particularly noteworthy difference is that the states in the Global North are democratic and rarely fight one another, whereas in the Global South, violent conflict remains rife both within and among many states.

Democracy has spread rapidly and widely since the end of the Cold War, becoming the preferred mode of governance throughout much of the Global South (China, Cuba, North Korea, and Vietnam being obvious exceptions). More than half of the countries in Africa are now pursuing democratic reforms, highlighted by the end of *apartheid* and the advent of majority rule in South Africa. However, the stable institutional arrangements common among the mature democracies in the Global North are not widespread in the Global South; furthermore, many Global South countries lack well-developed domestic market economies based on entrepreneurship and private enterprise. While history does not speak conclusively about the ability of democracy to survive in the absence of capitalism, the Global North pattern suggests that the existence of market economies and a large middle class are preconditions for democracy (Burkhart and Lewis-Beck 1994). Without the growth or development of market economies under capitalism, the continued enlargement of the liberal democratic community is not guaranteed.

Differences in technological capabilities also separate North and South. Typically, Global South countries have been unable to evolve an indigenous technology appropriate to their own resources and are dependent on powerful multinational corporations (MNCs) spawned in the North to transfer technical know-how. This means that research and development expenditures are directed toward solutions to the North's problems, with technological advances seldom meeting the needs of the South (Singer and Ansari 1988). And in the information age, the most striking developments are again taking place in the North. Information technology has not been distributed equally geographically: the highest density of computer connections to the global Internet is in the Global North, and the lowest is in Africa south of the Sahara, among the poorest countries in the world (see Chapter 9).

The fact that four-fifths of humanity is poor is both a reflection and cause of these unequally distributed resources. To measure the disparities, the World Bank differentiates **developing countries,** whose **gross national product (GNP)** in 1995 averaged less than $765 annually per person, from the **developed countries** above this level. This developed category includes several countries usually classified as members of the Global South that do not possess the political, technological, or demographic characteristics of the Global North. Among them are three oil exporting countries (Brunei, Kuwait, and the United Arab Emirates), as well as Singapore and Israel. In each case, either the United Nations or leaders in the countries themselves regard them as developing countries.

Among the developing countries, wide variations in economic performance are even more evident, which is why it is common to further divide them. Map 5.2 shows one estimate of the geographic distribution of the world's economies grouped as measured by GNP per capita.

Although GNP per capita is the most widely used measure of countries' economic performance, it is misleading to use it as a measure of individuals' economic well-being (see Focus 5.1). Because the geographic variations in the world's material (economic) well-being depicted in Map 5.2 are overlaid by other economic characteristics that further define the diversity of the Global

gross national product (GNP) and **gross domestic product (GDP)** measures of the production of goods and services within a given time period, which differ only in whether nationality (GNP) or residency (GDP) is used to delimit the geographic scope of production. GNP measures production by a state's citizens or companies, regardless of where the production occurs. GDP measures production occurring within the territory of a state, regardless of the national identity of the producers.

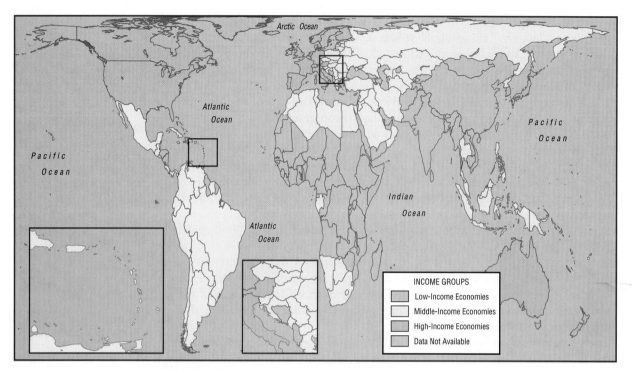

MAP 5.2

Groups of Economies: The Geographic Distribution of GNP per Capita, 1995

The people of the world are highly separated by levels of income, with the average person in some states living far below that of those living in the wealthy states. Another way to view the magnitude of the gap is by noting that 83 percent of global income goes to the richest fifth of the population, and 1 percent goes to the poorest fifth (*World Watch*, July/August 1996, 39).

SOURCE: *World Development Report 1997* (1997, 209).

South, it is useful to highlight four additional categories of development: the least developed of the less developed countries, exporters of oil and other fuels, the newly industrialized economies in Asia, and countries in transition.

Least Developed Countries

More than a half-billion people live in the forty-six countries classified by the International Monetary Fund as the **"least developed" of the less developed countries (LLDCs).** More than two-thirds are in Africa; most of the rest are in Asia.

Poverty is the most striking characteristic of the LLDCs, where the average annual GNP per person is only about *one U.S. dollar per year!* Clearly no one could live on such a meager sum if money were the only currency, and in fact much of the economic activity in the LLDCs takes place outside formal markets. Typically, **barter** exchanges of one agricultural good for another dominate economic transactions in the LLDCs, rather than the use of money to buy and sell goods.

The LLDCs are not participants in the global market: They have only 0.3 percent of world trade—half their share of a decade ago. Their exports are largely confined to inexpensive (nonfuel) primary products, including food-

Measuring Living Standards
GNP per Capita versus Purchasing Power Parity

The most widely used international yardstick of national wealth is gross national product (GNP) per capita. Much of this measure's popularity stems from its availability. GNP is the total of all goods and services produced by a country's economy in a given year—but that's all it is. The measure does not directly address how the average consumer in a country is faring. GNP per capita is a good indicator, however, for comparing large gaps in national wealth among countries. An African country with only $300 GNP per capita, for example, is obviously worse off than an industrialized country with a far higher value. But the measure's usefulness ends there.

GNP per capita is often mislabeled as "per-capita income," suggesting that it is the average money income for a person in a country. This mislabeling implies that GNP per capita can be used as a type of standard-of-living measure, but it really does not measure living standards in a meaningful way. For example, 1995 GNP per capita in Switzerland was $40,630. But per-capita money income was only $25,860—quite a difference. In Canada, 1995 GNP per capita was $19,380. Comparing the GNP of Switzerland and Canada suggests that the average person in Switzerland was about twice as well off as the average Canadian. Can the average Swiss citizen actually buy two times more goods and services of the same quantity and quality than the average Canadian?

Economists have worked for years to develop another internationally comparable measure of living standards called **purchasing power parity (PPP).** Although based on a complex econometric model, simply put, PPP compares the cost of goods in the purchasing power of each country's currency to what the same things might cost in the United States.

One major caveat is that the PPP cannot take into account the quality of such goods. The quality of a Russian Lada automobile compared with a Nissan Sentra or Ford Taurus is an obvious example. The comparative size of apartments in Europe with those in the United States is another.

While neither GNP nor PPP provides a perfect picture of a country's standard of living, these measures give an interesting snapshot of current economic conditions. What is more, the two measures provide some surprisingly different conclusions, as the table below illustrates.

Comparison of GNP per Capita and Purchasing Power Parity

Country	1995 GNP per Capita	1995 PPP
Japan	$39,640	$22,110
United States	26,980	26,980
United Kingdom	18,700	19,260
Greece	8,210	11,710
Brazil	3,640	5,400
Mexico	3,320	6,400
Russia	2,240	4,480
Indonesia	1,905	3,800
Egypt	790	3,820
China	620	2,920
India	340	1,400
Nigeria	260	1,220
Mozambique	80	810

Note: The U.S. dollar is used as the standard.

SOURCE: *World Development Report 1997* (1997, 214–15).

stuffs (e.g., cocoa, coffee, and tea), minerals (e.g., copper), hides, and timber. Because the LLDCs consume most of what they produce, theirs is typically a "subsistence economy," and the prospects for this changing are dim because "more than half of all developing countries have been bypassed by direct foreign investment, two-thirds of which has gone to only eight developing countries" (UNDP 1997, 9).

High rates of population growth in the LLDCs (2.8 percent in 1995, far in excess of the average worldwide rate of 1.5 percent) contribute to the widespread poverty, because it will take only twenty-five years for their population to double, compared with two and a half *centuries* for the Global North. LLDCs' economic growth rates in the recent past have averaged less than 0.1 percent per year. Growth rates elsewhere have almost uniformly been higher. Thus the rich minority gets richer while the poorest of the poor have remained stagnant.

Life for people in the LLDCs has changed little from that of their ancestors. Life expectancy at birth averages only fifty years (compared with seventy-four years in the Global North). Infant mortality rates are among the highest in the world. Less than half of the adult population is literate, a proportion even lower among women. And although industrialization has recently increased, agriculture remains the dominant form of productive activity. Similarly, four out of every five people live in rural areas even as the world is undergoing rapid urbanization. By contemporary standards, then, poverty and despair are everyday experiences for those on the bottom tier of the Global South.

Fuel-Exporting Countries

The poverty of the LLDCs contrasts starkly with the comparative wealth of the Global South states that have fossil fuels to consume and export. The sixteen developing-country exporters of oil and other fuels, and especially the twelve members of the Organization of Petroleum Exporting Countries (OPEC), have escaped the LLDCs' grim fate. Although many fall into the lower-middle or upper-middle income groups, some—notably OPEC members Kuwait, Qatar, and the United Arab Emirates—have risen to the high-income group, with standards of living rivaling those of Global North countries.

Given the importance of oil in the global market, exporters have had unusual opportunities to build a better life for their people. They seized this opportunity in the early 1970s when OPEC was able to drive up the price of global oil fourfold and realize huge financial gains, and the revenues were allocated to economic development (and military weapons). But global oil prices peaked in the mid-1980s and then plunged. Government programs for economic growth often fell victim to constraints imposed by declining export revenues. As a result, many oil-exporting countries are not dramatically better off today than they were twenty-five years ago.

The Newly Industrialized Economies in Asia

The **newly industrialized economies (NIEs)** in Asia have experienced greater success than the oil-exporting countries. Their success lies in moving beyond the export of primary products—characteristic of both the LLDCs and the oil exporters—to the export of manufactured goods. Today the NIEs are among the largest exporters of manufactured goods and the most prosperous members of the Global South.

Three states among the NIEs—the so-called **Asian Tigers:** South Korea, Singapore, and Taiwan—have, alongside Hong Kong prior to its 1997 reunification with China, taken extraordinary advantage of comparatively low wage rates to aggressively promote *export-led* economic growth. Pursuing strategies similar to the imperial powers of the past, the governments' neomercantilist practices include protecting so-called infant industries from foreign competition and providing financial incentives for manufacturing industries. Spectacular economic growth virtually unparalleled elsewhere followed, and by 1996 the NIEs commanded over 10 percent of world trade and 3.4 percent of world output (IMF 1997, 120). With their population growth generally in check, the

Given a competitive advantage by the availability of a large and compliant workforce used to long hours, tedious work, and low pay, newly industrialized countries in Asia have been able to promote aggressive export marketing strategies that capitalize on low manufacturing costs.

Asian Tigers have joined the ranks of the world's wealthiest states, and if the "fiscal flu" in securities and banking that swept Asia in late 1997 and 1998 are overcome, these states' futures look bright.

Countries in Transition

The **countries in transition,** the twenty-eight remnants of the former Second World in Central and Eastern Europe, lie economically somewhere between the Global North and South. Difficulties in placing a fair monetary value on the goods and services produced in centrally managed economies complicates their positioning. Furthermore, even though many of these countries developed significant manufacturing capabilities in heavy industry, in the emerging information age, most of these industries are dinosaurs. But the skills and educational levels of the people who built and operated them have prepared the countries in transition advantageously to undertake the structural adjustments necessary to compete in a capitalist global economy. At this point in time, however, the comparative economic performance of most countries in transition still resembles the low- and lower-middle income characteristics of the rural Global South.

• • •

THE GLOBAL SOUTH'S FEATURES AND FATE

As a group, despite wide differences, a daunting scale of poverty, misery, and marginalization are evident from which only a fraction of the Global South countries have begun to escape. For many people living there, the future is bleak, and the opportunities and choices most basic to human development are unavailable. "About a third—1.3 billion people—live on incomes of less than $1 a day," and in 1995, 161 countries had GNPs less than the amount spent world-wide at Wal-Mart (UNDP 1997, 3; *Harper's* October 1996, 13). Despite the ascent of many countries and the remarkable general reduction of poverty globally over the last half-century, the progress has been very uneven. For many, suffering is an everyday experience, without sufficient food, shelter, sanitation, safe water, or health care. Severely malnourished and often illiterate, many live in ecologically poisoned areas in which they will die at an early age unless they manage to join the millions of refugees who escape their impoverished home-lands each year.

However, this experience is not foreordained. Remarkable accomplishments have been made within some of the Global South's regions and countries, reducing the disparity between poor and rich, women and men, rural and urban. Coexisting with continuing poverty are pockets of impressive growth. Indeed, the term **emerging markets** has arisen to identify this subset of tweny-six countries that have started to shed the remnants of perpetual despair because their domestic political economies are particularly ripe for foreign investment. Neither geography nor current levels of comparative economic performance define the emerging markets, which are spread from South Africa and Zimbabwe in Africa, to India, Malaysia, and especially China in Asia, and to Brazil and Chile in South America. Instead, the Global South's emerging markets are identified by the potential for exceptionally high investment returns pending structural changes (not unlike those experienced by the countries in transition, some of which are also regarded as emerging markets). These countries are on the verge of economic revolution. Their governments and local elites have stabilized the value of their currencies, brought inflation under control, and "privatized" the businesses once owned by the government. While the emerging markets pose high risks, the payoff to foreign investors is high because local leaders have provided incentives to attract foreign investments to stimulate growth. The change in attitudes among the targets of foreign investment represents a fundamental shift in thinking about the causes of and cures for underdevelopment once prevalent throughout the Global South, and inspires hope that advances can be engineered to erase the conditions of underdevelopment.

The possibility of progress suggested by this mixed record of hope amidst unspeakable despair begs for an answer to the question of *why* development has been so rare and recent.

• • •

WHY UNDERDEVELOPMENT?

development the processes through which a country increases its capacity to meet its citizens' basic human needs and raise their standard of living.

Our discussion to this point implicitly equates **development** with a state's ability "to produce economic wealth, which in turn transforms society from a subsistence- or agricultural-based economy to one where most of society's wealth is derived from the production of manufactured goods and services" (Balaam and Veseth 1996). Urban populations, high literacy rates, well-fed people, and economies driven increasingly by the service sector mark today's developed economies. Why has the Global South lagged so far behind the Global North in its comparative level of well-being and development? And why have the development experiences even within the Global South differed so widely?

The diversity evident in the Global South invites the conclusion that under-development is explained by a combination of factors within developing countries and inherent in their relationships with the Global North—a plight for many, a promise for others. Some theorists explain the underdevelopment of most developing economies alongside the escape of others by looking primarily at differences *between* Global South states. Other theorists focus on the position of developing countries in the global political economy. We shall briefly discuss three variants on these interpretations, each of which has influenced policy thinking during the past half-century: classical economic development theory, structuralist theories of dominance and dependence, and neoclassical theory.

Classical Economic Development Theory

Based on the classical Western definition of development as increasing increments of per-capita GNP, liberal economic development theories of "modernization" first emerged in the early post-World War II era. They argued that the major barriers to development were posed by the Global South countries' own internal characteristics. To overcome these barriers, most classical theorists recommended that the wealthy countries supply various "missing components" of development, such as investment capital through foreign aid or private foreign direct investment (Todaro 1994).

Once sufficient capital was accumulated to promote economic growth, these liberal theorists predicted that its benefits would eventually "trickle down" to broad segments of society. In this way, everyone, not just a privileged few, would enjoy the benefits of rising affluence. Walt W. Rostow, an economic historian and U.S. policymaker, formalized this theory in his influential book *The Stages of Economic Growth* (1960). He predicted that traditional societies beginning the path to development would inevitably pass through various stages by means of the free market and would eventually "take off" to become similar to the mass-consumption societies of the capitalist Global North. That prognosis ultimately proved mistaken, as did other classical ideas about the route to economic development. Structural theorists who emphasize the links of developing countries to the global political economy purport to explain why the ideas (and ideals) of classical theorists failed.

Structural Theories

Two prongs of structuralism merit attention, as both locate the causes and potential cures of most developing countries' persistent underdevelopment in their positions of dominance and dependence in the global hierarchy. The first is dependency theory and its liberal variant, called "dualism." The second, which we have already introduced, is world-system theory.

Dependency Theory and Dualism. Dependency theory builds on Lenin's theory of imperialism, but it goes beyond it to account for changes that have occurred since Lenin first wrote his Marxist interpretation of capitalism as a cause of inequality and domination. Its central proposition is that the relationship between the advanced capitalist societies at the core of the world political

dependency theory a theory which maintains that less developed countries are exploited because global capitalism makes them dependent on the rich countries, who create rules for trade and production.

economy and the developing countries at the periphery is exploitative. Although the dependency theory literature is huge and many theoretical controversies surround the perspective (for a survey, see Packenham 1992), dependency theorists converge in their rejection of Rostow's stages-of-growth thesis, arguing that underdevelopment "is not a stalled stage of linear development, a question of precapitalism, retarded or backward development, but rather a [product of the less developed countries] structural position in a hierarchical world division of labor" (Shannon 1989). In short, the Global South's underdevelopment results from its subordinate position in a world political economy dominated by capitalistic industrialized countries.

Andre Gunder Frank (1969) wrote a definitive interpretation of chronic underdevelopment in Latin America that soon became a classic statement; he argued that "[t]he now-developed countries were never underdeveloped, though they may have been undeveloped." The reason, he argued, was colonialism—the historical expansion of the capitalist system that "effectively and entirely penetrated even the apparently most isolated sectors of the underdeveloped world."

Other theorists—frequently called *dependentistas*—shared Frank's concern about the "enslavement" of the South by the capitalist North. "The relation of interdependence between the two or more economies, and between these and world trade," Theotonio Dos Santos (1970) argued, "assumes the form of dependence when some countries (the dominant ones) can expand and can be self-sustaining, while others (the dependent ones) can do this only as a reflection of that expansion, which can have either a positive or a negative effect on their immediate development."

Dependent countries are vulnerable to penetration by outside forces. Dependency theorists argue that the overseas branches of giant multinational corporations (MNCs) headquartered in the North are the primary agents of neocolonial penetration because they transfer profits from the penetrated societies to the penetrators. Foreign investment—whether private or in the form of aid from other governments—is also an instrument of penetration. Technological dependence and "cultural imperialism," through which Global South societies become saturated with ideas and values alien to their indigenous cultures are among the consequences. Once penetration by advanced capitalist states has occurred, continues the dependency theory argument, the inherently unequal exchanges that bind the exploiters and the exploited are sustained by elites within the penetrated societies, who sacrifice their country's welfare for personal gain.

The argument that a privileged few benefit from dependency at the expense of their societies is logically similar to **dualism,** which even liberal theorists find persuasive. Dualism refers to the existence of two separate economic and social sectors operating side by side. Dual societies typically have a rural, impoverished, and neglected sector operating alongside an urban, developing, or advanced sector—but with little interaction between the two. Thus whatever growth occurs in the industrial sector in dual societies "neither initiates a corresponding growth process in the rural sector nor generates sufficient employment to prevent a growing population in the stagnant sectors" (Singer and Ansari 1988). MNCs contribute to dualism by promoting "the interests of the small number of well-paid modern-sector workers against the interests of the rest by widening wage differentials . . . and to worsen the imbalance between rural and urban economic opportunities by locating primarily in urban areas and contributing to the flow of rural-urban migration" (Todaro 1994).

In the 1990s Brazil, South America's largest country, has moved beyond its days of dictators and hyperdebt, and has become an emerging market seeking through its size, resources, and foreign investment in its privatized market to develop into an economic giant in the global economy. But like many developing countries, Brazil remains a dual economy, with a small advanced sector coexisting alongside an impoverished one, such as the Favela Rochina slum in Rio de Janeiro pictured here—in 1997 the largest continuous slum in South America. The World Bank cites Brazil as having the world's largest gap between rich and poor.

Like dependency theorists, those who emphasize Global South dualism reason that this economic condition stems from the colonial past, when the imperial powers regarded themselves as the best producers of manufactured goods and their colonies as the best suppliers of basic foodstuffs and raw materials. This relationship produced few "spread effects" in the colonial economies' secondary and tertiary sectors. Eventually, rapid population growth overwhelmed the ability of the colonies' rising incomes to generate continued economic growth (Higgins and Higgins 1979). Dependency theorists nonetheless reject the dualist argument as the most convincing explanation of the Global South countries' subordinate international position. Instead, they see the division into dual "modern" and "traditional" sectors as a consequence of a larger causal force—the impact of a "single international capitalist economy" that determines the destinies of states.

World-System Theory. World-system theorists, who also emphasize the structural level of analysis of the Global South's development difficulties, share dependency theorists' view that the world is divided into a core (the advanced capitalist states) and a periphery (the developing states). However, they take a longer-term perspective on the emergence of disparities between the two and the forces that determine where states are positioned in the global division of labor, treating the actors in world politics in terms of classes much as Karl Marx did.

For *world-system theory*, a critical issue is how states fit into the international division of labor. "Economic activities in each part of a true world-economy depend on and make possible the activities of the other parts. Each part or area has acquired a specialized role producing goods that it trades to others to obtain what it needs. Thus, the world-economy is tied together by a complex network of global economic exchanges" (Shannon 1989).

The core-periphery distinction is again particularly important. "Within the world division of labor, core states specialize in the production of the most 'advanced' goods, which involves the use of the most sophisticated technologies and highly mechanized methods of production ('capital-intensive' production). At least until recently, this meant that core states specialized in the production of sophisticated manufactured goods." Within the periphery, on the other hand, economic activities "are relatively less technologically sophisticated and more 'labor intensive'. . . . For most of the modern era, production for export was concentrated on raw materials and agricultural commodities" (Shannon 1989). Historically, states on the periphery have also been militarily inferior to core states and administratively less well organized, which limited their ability to compete with the capitalist states.

World-system theorists cannot easily explain the industrialization now taking place in the periphery's emerging markets. To account for this, they have coined the term *semiperiphery* to accommodate geographic areas or countries, such as the NIEs, that are not part of either the core or the periphery. Dependency theorists also have difficulty explaining these countries' growth. To interpret this anomaly, they sometimes use the term **dependent development** to describe the industrial development of peripheral areas in a system otherwise dominated by the Global North. The term suggests the possibility of growing prosperity, but not outside the confines of a continuing dominance-dependence relationship between North and South.

Neoclassical Development Theory

Structural theories, particularly popular during the 1970s, helped to galvanize leaders throughout the Global South to lobby for reforms of the global political economy and the multilateral institutions that help to run it, such as the World Bank and the International Monetary Fund. By the 1980s, however, these same institutions increasingly embraced neoclassical theorists who advocated reducing government interference in the economic life of the Global South.

> The [neoclassical theorists] argue that by permitting competitive free markets to flourish, privatizing state-owned enterprises, promoting free trade and export expansion, welcoming investors from developed countries, and eliminating the plethora of government regulations and price distortions in factor, product and financial markets, both economic efficiency and economic growth will be stimulated. . . . What is needed, therefore, is not a reform of the international economic system or a restructuring of dualistic developing economies or an increase in foreign aid or attempts to control population growth or a more effective central planning system. Rather, it is simply a matter of promoting free markets and laissez-faire economics within the context of permissive governments that allow the "magic of the

marketplace" and the "invisible hand" of market prices to guide resource allocation and stimulate economic development. (Todaro 1994, 85–86)

Neoclassical theorists could point to the success of the free-market practices Asian NIEs used to free themselves from the chains of poverty. Although the Asian Tiger governments routinely intervene in the marketplace, their export-led path to remarkable economic growth has encouraged others to emulate their strategies. In addition, the emerging markets have in some ways fulfilled the neoclassical predictions that market economies will thrive where government management of the market is minimal, and that entrepreneurial successes are more likely to occur where there is political freedom. Studies of the relationship between development and democracy tend to confirm the liberal argument (see, e.g., UNDP 1991; Moon and Dixon 1985).

The achievements of the NIEs and the emerging markets suggests that economic progress is within the grasp of Global South countries (see also Chapter 9). Still, neoclassical theory cannot explain one of the international economic system's most striking features: the gap between the world's rich and poor countries as a whole has continued to widen, not narrow. The ratio between incomes in industrializing western Europe and the rest of the world in 1900 is usually estimated to have been about 2 to 1. By 1950 the gap had opened to 10 to 1. "The ratio of the income of the top 20 percent to that of the poorest 20 percent rose from 30 to 1 in 1960, to 61 to 1 in 1991—and to a startling new high of 78 to 1 in 1994" (UNDP 1997, 9). Add to this the knowledge that nearly all of the world's population growth in the next century will occur in the Global South, and it is hard to see how the gap could close. Given the grim future of much of the Global South, "the greatest challenge global society faces today is preventing this fault line [separating the Global North and South] from erupting into a world-shaking crisis" (Kennedy 1994).

• • •

WHAT IS DEVELOPMENT?

If the economic chasm separating rich and poor states is unbridgeable—with potentially dire consequences for the future of world politics—does this mean that "development" is an impossible dream for 80 percent of humanity? Or do we need to broaden our understanding of development to move beyond the classical materialistic definition of it as accumulation of wealth?

The lot of many people in the Global South has in fact improved, thus narrowing the gap in *human* disparity between North and South even as the *economic* gap between them has widened. According to this definition, which sees poverty as much more than low income, it is easy to overlook the advances in human development realized globally. "In the past 50 years poverty has fallen more than in the previous 500. And it has been reduced in some respects in almost all countries" (UNDP 1997, 2). The Global South "has covered as much distance during [the past 30 years] as the industrial world did in a century. Life expectancy is now 17 years longer than it was in 1960. Infant mortality has been more than halved. . . . Even though the South has a per-capita GNP that is a mere six percent of the North's, it now has a life expectancy that is 85 percent, and nutritional levels and adult literacy that are 81 percent of those in the

North" (UNDP 1995, 15). Such evidence like this shows that the human dimension of development is often much brighter than the economic. However, this progress has not come without costs in both the North and South. The adverse side of wealth is also all too evident: high rates of violent crime; alcohol and drug abuse; the erosion of religious faith; heart disease; divorce; and HIV infection. Even among the "developed" countries, then, the *human dimension of development* warrants concern.

Basic Human Needs

The human dimension of development first gained attention in the 1970s, partly in response to the growing popularity of dependency theory. To address the root structural causes of underdevelopment by reducing the dominance-dependence relationship between rich and poor states, the World Bank and foreign-aid donors in the Global North sought ways for foreign-aid recipients to improve the lives of their own citizens. Advocates of a **basic human needs** approach argue that the trickle-down effects predicted by classical economic development theory have failed to materialize because of official corruption and other barriers to growth (many caused by Global South elites). Particularly disturbing is the fact that more than a quarter of the developing world's people are still living in **absolute poverty** without access to drinking water free of disease-carrying organisms and toxins, or adequate nutrition, sanitation, and health services (UNDP 1997, 3).

basic human needs adequate food intake (in terms of calories, proteins, and vitamins), safe drinking water, sufficient clothing and shelter, literacy, sanitation, health care, employment, and dignity.

Human Development

The basic human needs perspective required new ways to measure development beyond those focusing exclusively on economic indicators. Eventually the United Nations Development Programme (UNDP) constructed a **human development index (HDI)** to measure states' comparative ability to provide for citizens' well-being. Successive *Human Development Reports* have provoked fresh debate about the meaning of human development in national and international forums, including, for example, the 1992 UN Conference on Environment and Development, the 1994 UN Conference on Population and Development, and the 1995 World Summit for Social Development.

The UNDP's human development index (described in Focus 5.2) spreads broadly across not only economic factors but also the environment, politics, and social welfare in both the developing and developed worlds, to encompass the growing consensus that "the real purpose of development should be to enlarge people's choices." To capture this meaning, the index incorporates income within its calculation. The reason is simple: "Growth is not the end of development—but . . . the absence of growth often is" (UNDP 1995).

Human Development and Economic Growth. Table 5.1 records the HDI for thirty countries within three HDI categories and their rank among 175 polities. The table also includes each country's 1994 per-capita gross domestic product (GDP) rank as measured in terms of purchasing power parity as well as its position in the income and other economic categories introduced earlier.

The stratified groups' human development performance is correlated with their per-capita GDP level. Note, for example, that none of the high-income countries fall within the low human development category; similarly, none in

Measuring Development
GNP per Capita versus Human Development

Human development occurs when people's choices are expanded. At all levels of development, this occurs when people can live long with good health, acquire knowledge, and have access to the resources needed for a decent lifestyle. When people are denied these choices, no matter what their incomes are, many other opportunities vanish.

In 1990 the United Nations Development Program (UNDP) began to construct the *human development index (HDI)* under the conviction that adequate income, though certainly important, is not an all-consuming motive. The HDI index, as the UNDP defines it, seeks

> . . . to capture as many aspects of human development as possible in one simple, composite index and to produce a ranking of human development achievements.
>
> The concept of human development is much deeper and richer than what can be captured in any composite index or even by a detailed set of statistical indicators. Yet it is useful to simplify a complex reality—and that is what the HDI sets out to do. It is a composite index of achievements in basic human capabilities in three fundamental dimensions—a long and

healthy life, knowledge and a decent standard of living. Three variables have been chosen to represent these three dimensions—life expectancy, educational attainment and income.

The HDI value for each country indicates how far the country has to go to attain certain defined goals: an average life span of 85 years, access to education for all and a decent standard of living. The HDI reduces all three basic indicators to a common measuring rod by measuring achievement in each as the relative distance from the desirable goal. The maximum and minimum values for each variable are reduced to a scale between 0 and 1, with each country at some point on this scale. . . .

The HDI shows the distance a country has to travel to reach the maximum possible value of 1 and also allows intercountry comparisons. The difference between the maximum possible value of the HDI and the HDI value achieved by a country shows the country's shortfall in HDI. . . . HDI measures the overall progress of a country in human development.

SOURCE: UNDP (1997), 44.

the lowest income category falls within the high human development group. Clearly, the level of human development is highest in the Global North, where, on average, economic prosperity is also highest. Conversely, the quality of life is generally lower in the Global South, where per-capita economic output is substantially lower.

Some maintain that "redistributive" policies to meet basic human needs or otherwise enhance human welfare and growth-oriented policies through trickle-down effects work at cross purposes—the latter can only be attained at the expense of the former. Others question the trickle-down hypothesis while accepting the view that meeting basic human needs promotes long-term economic growth (e.g., Moon and Dixon 1992). Because the evidence shows remarkably wide variations in how people live within different countries, which are not determined exclusively by differences in income levels, most experts conclude that there is no automatic link between income and human development:

> High income poverty is associated with high human poverty, and low income poverty with low human poverty. But the two forms of poverty can move in different directions. High income poverty can coexist with low human poverty (Peru and Zimbabwe), and low income poverty can coexist with high human poverty (Côte d'Ivoire and Egypt).

TABLE 5.1 Level of Human Development and Other Economic Attributes Compared (selected countries)

	HDI Value	HDI Rank	Real Per-Capita GDP ($PPP) Rank	Income Group	Economic Group
High Human Development (HDI value .80 or higher): 64 of 175 countries, or 23 percent of world population					
Canada	.96	1	8	High	Developed
United States	.94	4	3	High	Developed
Singapore	.90	26	41	High	NIE
Costa Rica	.89	28	39	High	Developing
South Korea	.89	32	38	Upper-middle	NIE/EM
United Arab Emirates	.87	44	27	High	Oil exporter
Hungary	.86	48	43	Upper-Middle	CT
Poland	.83	58	72	Upper-middle	CT/EM
Thailand	.83	59	51	Lower-middle	EM
Belarus	.81	62	49		CT
Medium Human Development (HDI value .50 to .799): 66 of 175 countries, or 45 percent of world population					
Brazil	.78	68	68	Upper-middle	NIE/EM
Turkey	.78	74	69	Lower-middle	EM
Iran	.78	70	61	Lower-middle	Oil exporter
Saudi Arabia	.77	73	41	Upper-middle	Oil exporter
Jordan	.73	84	81	Lower-middle	EM
South Africa	.72	90	80	Upper-middle	EM
China	.63	108	105	Upper-middle	EM
Tajikistan	.58	115	80	Low	CT
Gabon	.56	120	95	Low	EM
Vanuatu	.55	124	114	Lower-middle	LLDC
Low Human Development (HDI value less than .50): 45 of 175 countries, or 32 percent of world population					
Zimbabwe	.49	129	119	Low	Developing
India	.45	138	133	Low	EM
Nigeria	.39	141	140	Low	Oil exp/EM
Yemen	.36	148	132	Low	LLDC
Madagascar	.35	152	136	Low	LLDC
Haiti	.34	156	151	Low	LLDC
Angola	.34	157	133	Lower-middle	Oil exp/LLDC
Senegal	.33	160	134	Lower-middle	Developing
Djibouti	.32	162	146	Lower-middle	LLDC
Niger	.21	173	165	Low	LLDC

Note: The following abbreviations are used: NIE—newly industrialized country; CT—country in transition; EM—emerging market; LLDC—least developed of the less developed countries; PPP—purchasing power parity.

SOURCE: Adapted from UNDP (1997), 44–48.

Analysis of different indicators of human poverty reveals more about the dynamics of income and human poverty. The relationship between income poverty and human poverty can change. During 1970–90 Malaysia and the Republic of Korea reduced income poverty and some aspects of human poverty by more than half. Colombia and Costa Rica also cut human poverty by half, but not income poverty. So income poverty and human poverty generally go hand in hand, but not automatically or always. (UNDP 1997, 37)

In short, income alone is not a good indicator of human development.

Inequalities. Neither GNP per capita nor HDI are able to measure inequalities *within* societies. Just as wealth is distributed unevenly at the international level, it is often concentrated in the hands of a few elites in the Global South. In Colombia, for example, the share of income enjoyed by the top 20 percent exceeded 55 percent in the early 1990s while the bottom 20 percent shared only 3.6 percent—a ratio of more than fifteen to one. In Japan, by contrast, the top 20 percent commanded 37.5 percent and the bottom 20 percent nearly 9 percent—or a ratio of about four to one (*World Development Report 1995* 1995, 220–21). Although income inequalities are difficult to measure precisely, the existing evidence suggests that the degree of income inequality is twice as great in the Global South as in the Global North (see Morley 1994).

Just as per-capita measures of economic production mask income inequalities, the HDI fails to reveal important regional, racial, and gender variations in human development within countries. In Brazil, for example, the HDI value for the northeastern region of the country is only two-thirds that in the south. Thus "south Brazil would rank alongside Luxembourg (number 27 in the global rankings), while [northeast] Brazil would rank between Bolivia (113) and Gabon (114)" (UNDP 1995, 22). Or consider South Africa, an emerging market country with an upper-middle income and a medium level of human development. Despite the end of apartheid and the election of President Nelson Mandela in 1994, the disparity between black and white income in South Africa is profound. The country's white minority—constituting only 13 percent of the population—still owns 75 percent of the land. "If white South Africa were a separate country, it would be among the highest-ranking countries in the world. Black South Africa would rank 128 (just after Cameroon). Not just two different communities, but two different worlds" (UNDP 1995, 22). Even in the United States wide disparities exist in the HDIs of White, African-American, and Hispanic populations.

Gender inequalities—differences in living standards between men and women—remain widespread both within and across states, despite the measurable improvement in the daily lot and future prospects of millions of women during the past several decades. Although many facets of human development are improving, the prevalent worldwide gender gap has been and remains especially wide throughout and within the Global South. For example, the 1990 literacy rate in Burundi was 47 percent among adult men but only 20 percent among adult women (UNDP 1995, 77). Worse still, women account for a much smaller proportion of the nonagricultural workforce than men, and their pay for the same work is routinely less. Females hold fewer teaching positions at all levels of education and fewer Ph.D.s, and their share of administrative and managerial jobs is minuscule. Much the same holds true in politics, where in 1994 women held only 10 percent of the seats in parliaments worldwide and only 6 percent of national cabinet posts. The reason: "the current institutional, legal, and socioeconomic constraints to [women's] access to opportunities" (UNDP 1995). Furthermore, gender differences continue at the most basic levels of human development: More girls than boys die at a young age; females' access to adequate health care is more restricted; and women face more barriers

gender inequalities
differences between men and women in opportunity and reward that are determined by the values that guide states' foreign and domestic policies.

to education at all levels. Thus it is easy to conclude that women remain victims of abuse and discrimination nearly everywhere (Arat 1995).

Human Development or Human Despair? The general record of HDI changes presents an arresting picture of unprecedented human progress and unspeakable human misery, of humanity's advance on several fronts juxtaposed with humanity's retreat on several others, of a breathtaking globalization of prosperity side by side with a depressing globalization of poverty (UNDP 1997). In many respects the gaps between the rich and poor continues to widen. However, in other respects, progress in human development has occurred and will likely persist (see Focus 5.3). Thus the future of world politics will not only be "a politics of mutual suspicion and struggle" between the Global North and South but also a contest between those who see global regress as inevitable and those who see global progress as possible.

• • •

THE GLOBAL SOUTH'S FOREIGN POLICY RESPONSE TO DOMINANCE AND DEPENDENCE

The vast political, economic, and social differences separating North and South indicate that the Global South is "weak, vulnerable, and insecure—with these traits being the function of both domestic and external factors" (Ayoob 1995). Coping with this insecurity has long been a primary foreign policy goal of Global South states, and efforts to overcome these insecurities have often brought the Global South into contention with the Global North. Ironically, the end of the Cold War magnified the challenge developing countries face, because the end of Soviet-American rivalry reduced the great powers' security interest in providing economic aid to Southern countries. Without foreign assistance, since 1990 the Global South experienced a burst of new armed conflicts. The globalization of finance and trade threatens to further expand the economic vulnerabilities of poor Global South states in the new millennium. "Globalization is not making the world less diverse and more equal. . . . The large majority of humankind is rapidly being left outside and far behind" (Heredia 1997).

As realists insist, power and wealth are states' core motives and are realized through military and economic prowess. Strategies designed to maximize power and prosperity continue to preoccupy foreign policy thinking in the Global South; here a "variety of political systems ranging from democracies to monarchies coexist side by side, and interdependence between peripheral states is subordinate to dependence on core states, [and] goals of wealth, population, and protection [against external and] internal instabilities" are predominate (Goldgeier and McFaul 1992). How are the Global South countries pursuing these objectives, particularly in their relationships with the Global North?

In Search of Power

The states emerging after World War II struggled on separate tracks to find a foreign policy approach that could provide them with the power and prosperity they lacked. The **nonaligned states** were determined to strike a neutral course in the Cold War contest, while a broader group (including, for example, many Latin American states allied with the United States whose independence had

A Balance Sheet on Human Development in the Global South

Progress

- Since 1960 the proportion of children in primary and secondary school has risen 1.5 times, from more than one-third to one-half.
- Since 1970 the gaps between women and men in adult literacy and school enrollment, were halved.
- Since 1960 the share of rural families with access to safe water has risen from 25 percent to 90 percent.
- Despite rapid population growth, per-capita food production rose by more than 20 percent during the past decade, and life expectancy in the Global South is now 85 percent that of the Global North.
- Since 1960, child death rates have been more than halved.
- Since 1960, malnutrition has declined by almost one-third.
- Developing countries' contribution to global emissions is less than one-fourth that of industrial countries, even though their population is 3.5 times higher.
- More than three-fourths of the human race lives under relatively pluralistic and democratic regimes.
- At the beginning of the twenty-first century some 3–4 billion of the world's people will have experienced substantial improvements in their standard of living, and about 4–5 billion will have access to basic education and health care.

Deprivation

- About one-third of the world (1.3 billion people) survives on less than the equivalent of $1 a day.
- In 1966 the poorest 20 percent of the world's people had 2.3 percent of the world's income but now have only 1.4 percent, while the richest 20 percent have increased their share from 70 percent to 85 percent.
- In the past fifteen to twenty years more than one hundred developing and transition countries have suffered disastrous failures in growth and deeper and more prolonged cuts in living standards than anything experienced in the industrial countries during the 1930s Great Depression. As a result of these setbacks, the incomes of more than 1 billion people have fallen below levels first reached ten, twenty, and sometimes thirty years ago.
- The ratio of global trade to GDP has been rising over the past decade, but it has been falling for forty-four developing countries, where more than 1 billion people reside. The least developed countries, with 10 percent of the world's people, have only 0.3 percent of world trade—half their share of two decades ago.
- By the start of the twenty-first century, 95 percent of the population growth will be in the Global South.
- By 2010, twenty-one of the world's most populous cities will be in the Global South; New York won't be in the top ten.
- Women are disproportionately poor, and 500,000 die each year in childbirth—at rates 10–100 times those in industrial countries.
- Among the world's nearly 1 billion illiterate people, women outnumber men two to one, and girls constitute the majority of the 130 million children without access to primary school.
- Nearly 840 million people go hungry each day, and about 600 million people are chronically undernourished.
- About 200 million people are severely affected by desertification; every year, some 20 million hectares of tropical forest are cleared outright or grossly degraded.
- In 1997, there were more than 40 million refugees and internally displaced people, and more than 500,000 poor people were living in ecologically fragile regions.
- One-third of the people in the least developed countries are not expected to survive to age 40.
- Well over a billion people lack safe water.

SOURCE: Adapted from UNDP (1997), 5, 7, 9, 15, 24; Edwards (1997), 14.

been secured in the nineteenth century) concentrated their efforts more directly on severing their economic dominance by and dependence on the North. (Few economic ties existed between the Second and Third Worlds.)

Nonalignment. The nonalignment movement began in 1955, when twenty-nine Asian and African countries met in Bandung, Indonesia, to devise a strategy to

Nonaligned Movement (NAM)
a group of more than one hundred newly independent, mostly less developed states that joined together as a group of neutrals to avoid entanglement with the superpowers' competing alliances and to advance the Third World's common interests in economic cooperation and growth.

combat colonialism. In 1961 leaders of the mostly former colonies met in Belgrade, Yugoslavia, where they created a lasting political coalition, the **Nonaligned Movement (NAM),** whose membership would later grow to more than one hundred countries.

Because the new states sought to avoid entrapment in the Cold War, they tried through nonalignment to maximize their own gains while minimizing their costs. The strategy energized both the United States and the Soviet Union to renew their efforts to woo the uncommitted "neutrals" to their own network of allies. Nonalignment in effect enabled developing states to play one superpower off against the other in order to gain advantage for themselves. The Cold War competitors became willing players in a bipolar **zero-sum** contest where one side's gains were the other's loss, often offering economic and military aid to win friends and influence allies.

The Cold War's end also ended much of the competitive rationale for providing foreign aid. It also eroded the bargaining leverage nonalignment had provided the Global South. As a strategy, nonalignment "died" with the Cold War. "More than that, the way the East-West rivalry ended, with the values and systems of the West vindicated and triumphant, undermined the very basis of the nonaligned movement, which had adopted as its foundation a moral neutrality between the two blocs" (Chubin 1998).

Although the original justification for nonalignment no longer exists, the passions behind it live on. As the Nonaligned Movement prepared for its second post-Cold War summit in late 1995, its leaders claimed that the ideals envisaged by its founders remained unchanged. "When the Nonaligned Movement began, it was inspired by one motive—that developing countries could take decisions and positions in international politics depending on their own interests and not according to one or the other of the superpowers," the hosts for the eleventh summit in Colombia announced at the opening ceremonies, adding "This continues to be valid."

The challenge facing the nonaligned states today is how to promote their interests in a world where few listen to their voices. The nonaligned Global South can complain, but its bargaining power to engineer institutional reforms is limited. This weakness is displayed in the United Nations, where the most influence the Global South has mustered has symbolically been to delay serious proposals to make Germany and Japan permanent members of the Security Council by insisting that a nonaligned state or one of the larger developing countries (such as Brazil, Indonesia, Mexico, or South Africa) also be given a seat among the mighty. Weak states have some vocal power in numbers, but no clout or control.

This weakness represents a shift from the past, when the numerical majority of the Global South enabled it to exercise greater power within the UN than any of its members could have wielded individually. Nonalignment had further enhanced that influence because the Soviet Union had often sided with the developing states in the General Assembly, particularly on decolonization issues. Now, however, the locus of power is firmly lodged in the U.S.-dominated Security Council, and the United States can veto most important resolutions originating in the General Assembly, where the Global South commands an overwhelming majority. This has intensified the developing countries' fears about many of the great powers' current activities within their territorial borders, such as "humanitarian" military intervention to cope with human suffering or to punish Global South governments that violate the human rights of their own people. That the great powers are developing a new generation of weapons of mass destruction while insisting that the Global South not participate in this arms race has also bred resentment. Thus, the Global South worries that the twenty-first century will witness "the reemergence of a more open and explicit form of imperialism, in which national sovereignty is more readily overridden by a hegemonic power pursuing its own self-defined national interest" (Bienefeld 1994). These concerns are rooted in past experience, because many developing countries felt betrayed and invaded when they became the battleground on which the superpowers conducted covert activities, paramilitary operations, and proxy wars. The Global South became the world's killing fields; more than 90 percent of the inter- and intrastate conflicts and 90 percent of the casualties in the past half-century occurred within it (see also Chapter 12).

Zones of Turmoil. More than two hundred and fifty violent conflicts of various magnitude have occurred in the Global South since the Cold War ended, claiming probably more than five million victims (Wallensteen and Sollenberg 1997, 339). Virtually every region of the world has experienced the horrors of these wars, yet *all* of the conflicts since 1989 occurred within and between the fragile states—and would-be states—of the Global South.

In the late 1990s the great powers—unlike the United States and the Soviet Union during the Cold War—have exhibited a growing reluctance to intervene in most of the deadly ethnonational clashes raging within many Global South countries. The genocidal war in Bosnia-Herzegovina, for example, escalated for more than three years before the United States and its NATO allies forced the combatants to the bargaining table, and it threatens to resume once those peacekeeping forces withdraw. Here, as elsewhere, the end of the superpowers' Cold War efforts to maintain a balance of power has reduced their willingness to become involved militarily in areas that were formerly seen as strategically important. Now the great powers are unlikely to intervene in the Global South unless vital interests (e.g., access to oil) or particular domestic considerations (placating ethnic group interests) demand action. This leaves the Global South highly vulnerable to violence, because since 1940 "enemies in civil wars have almost always failed to reach successful negotiated solutions to their conflicts unless an outside power guaranteed their safety during the ensuing transition period" (Walter 1997).

Arms Acquisitions. Faced with seemingly endless conflict at home or abroad, it is not surprising that the Global South has joined the rest of the world's quest to acquire modern weapons of war—including in some cases (China, India, Iraq, North Korea, Pakistan) nuclear weapons. As a result, the *burden of military spending* (measured by the ratio of military expenditures to GNP) is highest among those least able to bear it. In the Global South military spending typically exceeds expenditures on health and education; impoverished states facing ethnic, religious, or tribal strife at home are quite prepared to sacrifice expenditures for economic development in order to acquire weapons.

Until recently, few Global South states produced their own modern weapons of war; instead, they imported them. The United States and the Soviet Union were the principal weapons suppliers during the Cold War, often providing arms to would-be friends and allies as outright grants. Beginning in the 1970s, in the aftermath of the Vietnam War, the United States began to *sell* arms to others, particularly Middle Eastern oil-exporting countries such as Iran and Saudi Arabia whose newfound wealth enabled them to buy huge quantities of the most sophisticated conventional weapons. In addition, the United States targeted its sale of weapons at the volatile Middle East region to make it a bul-

Innocent noncombatants, especially women and children, are most often the primary victims of violent conflict in the Global South. Their protection has usually required humanitarian military intervention by an outside power. Shown here is a starving Somalian mother and child in 1997 waiting for relief supplies delivered by U.S. military aircraft to a refugee camp in Wafir, Kenya.

wark against communist expansionism, and supplied Israel with sophisticated weapons to protect it from a possible attack by newly armed Arab states. Elsewhere, the United States sold weapons as part of a program designed to shore up states facing communist threats (sometimes actual, sometimes imagined) without also having to supply American troops (as in Vietnam). Predictably, the Soviets often responded by supplying weapons to the neighbors of the U.S. arms recipients. In the Middle East, the Soviet Union became the chief weapons provider to the Arab states committed to the destruction of Israel, notably Syria and Iraq.

Global expenditures on the weapons of war dropped markedly following the Cold War's demise. Major reductions in states' relative burden of military spending followed. Between 1983 and 1993 the ratio for the world as a whole dropped from 5.7 percent to 3.3 percent (the lowest since 1960), and from 6.1 percent to 3.1 percent for the developing world (U.S. Arms Control and Disarmament Agency 1995, 24). As worldwide military spending declined, so did arms purchases from foreign suppliers.

However, in the Global South military spending has remained high where the ability to pay has remained high, especially in the Middle East and parts of Asia. Both Saudi Arabia, which had seen its share of the arms import market grow from 40 percent in the late 1980s to more than 55 percent in the early 1990s, and Kuwait became highly active in the Global South's growing weapons trade. The recent trend is toward the escalating expansion of military budgets and arms purchases throughout much of the Global South, alongside reductions in other, more stable regions (see Grimmett 1997 and Chapter 13).

As before, persistent conflict and insecurity are the primary reasons for weapons acquisition in many Global South states, and, particularly in these states, the human costs of preparing for war are exceptionally high. The Global South countries had hoped to reap the benefits of the **peace dividend** (the global savings from arms expenditure reductions made possible by the end of

136

the Cold War), anticipating that the savings the great powers realized as they cut their military expenditures would release large sums for use in bettering the economic and human condition of the world's less fortunate. But their hopes were quickly dashed. Although expenditures on the weapons of war were cut, the "dividends" were not "reinvested" to assist the Global South's economic development.

In Search of Wealth

The persistent underdevelopment of most developing states underlies their drive for greater wealth, a better life for their people, and a higher position in the hierarchy of global power. Breaking out of their dependent status and pursuing their own industrial development remains a foreign policy priority of most developing countries.

To this end, some (particularly those in Latin America) pursued development through an **import-substitution industrialization** strategy designed to encourage domestic entrepreneurs to manufacture products traditionally imported from abroad. Governments (often dictatorships) became heavily involved in managing their economies and in some cases became the owners and operators of industry. Import-substitution industrialization eventually fell from favor, in part because manufacturers often found that they still had to rely on Global North technology and even component parts to produce goods for their domestic markets. The recent preference is for **export-led industrialization,** based on the realization that "what had enriched the rich was not their insulation from imports (rich countries do, in fact, import massively all sorts of goods) but their success in manufactured exports, where higher prices could be commanded than for [Global South] raw materials" (Sklair 1991).

As exemplified by the newly industrialized economies, the shift toward export-led growth strategies has transformed many Global South countries from being suppliers of raw materials into manufacturers of products already available in the Global North. Thus a new international division of labor is emerging as production, capital, labor, and technology are increasingly integrated worldwide and decision making has become transnational. "The old ideas of national autonomy, economic independence, self-reliance, and self-sufficiency have become obsolete as the national economies [have] become increasingly integrated" (Dorraj 1995).

Not all Global South economies are positioned to survive in this highly competitive globalized market. Many of the least developed countries remain heavily dependent on raw materials and other primary products for their export earnings, and even some of the NIEs have not moved beyond the dependent development stage, as their export goods are in the old, declining industries of the Global North whose technology is easily transferred to the semiperiphery. Nonetheless, the future is certain: few Global South countries will be immune to the costs extracted by globalization of the rapidly expanding world economy. "While some may benefit from such integration and prosper, others may become more vulnerable to crises and fluctuations prevalent in capitalist economic cycles. Impoverished and dependent, . . . much of the [Global South] is ill-equipped to reap the benefits of global interdependence" (Dorraj 1995).

How to cope with dominance and dependence thus remains a key concern for many developing Global South countries. As they search for status and economic security, the Global South's key strategies in their relations with the Global North warrant attention.

A New International Economic Order. The emerging nations of the Global South were born into a political-economic order with rules they had no voice in creating. Beginning in the 1950s they began to seek the means to control their own economic futures, centering their efforts on the United Nations where their growing numbers gave them greater influence than they could otherwise command. In the 1960s they formed a coalition of the world's poor, the **Group of 77** (known in diplomatic circles simply as the G-77) and used their voting power to convene a United Nations Conference on Trade and Development (UNCTAD), which later became a permanent UN organization through which the Global South could express their interests concerning development issues.

A decade later the G-77 (now numbering more than one hundred twenty countries) again used its UN numerical majority to push for a **New International Economic Order (NIEO)** to counter the Liberal International Economic Order (LIEO) championed by the United States and the other capitalist powers since World War II. Motivated by the oil-exporting countries' rising bargaining "commodity power," the Global South sought to compel the North to abandon practices that they perceived as perpetuating dominance and dependence. Later, the heated debate between North and South shifted as the NIEO began to question who would govern the distribution of world wealth and how they would make their choices. Not surprisingly, the Global North rebuffed the South's reform efforts, and the North-South exchange gradually degenerated into a useless dialogue.

The Global South's determination to revise the existing rules is now little more than a footnote to the history of a struggle between rich and poor states. Many of the NIEO issues raised remain on the global agenda, as do key philosophical controversies about the extent to which states should manage international economic transactions. Whereas the liberal philosophy underlying the LIEO recommends limited government intervention, "economic nationalists" advocate that their states act aggressively to promote national prosperity. "The nationalist considers relative gain to be more important than mutual gain [and seeks] to change the rules or regimes governing international economic relations in order to benefit themselves disproportionately with respect to other economic powers" (Gilpin 1998). Clearly that competitive viewpoint remains popular in many Global South countries (as well as some in the North), even as privatization and a return to market mechanisms rather than state-run enterprises have become widely accepted as the most effective method for generating growth. As we will discover in Chapter 8, the tension between liberalism and mercantilism applies broadly to core contemporary issues in the world political economy.

Regional Trade Regimes. With the failure of reform envisioned by the NIEO, the integration of Global South countries into the globalization process will occur according to the rules dictated by the North. Are there alternatives? Can regional arrangements enable Global South states to take advantage of growing economic interdependence to achieve their development goals?

To promote growth through regional economic agreements, the global economy began in the 1990s to subdivide into three "trade blocs"—one in Europe (with the European Union as its hub), a second in the Americas (with the United States at the center), and a third in East Asia (with Japan and China dominant). Consider some recent developments:

- *In the Americas:* The North American Free Trade Agreement (NAFTA), formalized in 1993, brought Canada, Mexico, and the United States into a single free-trade area whose market size rivals that of the European Union. Plans envision early twenty-first-century regime expansion to create a hemisphere-wide free-trade area (in which tariffs among member countries are eliminated).

- *Also in the Americas:* The Mercosur agreement, which links Argentina, Brazil, Paraguay, and Uruguay (Latin America's largest trade bloc), and which hopes to incorporate the Andean Group (Bolivia, Colombia, Ecuador, Peru, and Venezuela) in its free-trade union.

- *In Asia:* The association of Asia-Pacific Economic Cooperation (APEC), an informal forum created in 1989 that now encompasses eighteen states (including the United States), has committed itself to creating a free-trade zone during the next twenty-five years.

- *Also in Asia:* The seven members of the Association of South-East Asian Nations (ASEAN), first established in 1967 by Brunei, Indonesia, Malaysia, the Philippines, Singapore, and Thailand and now including Vietnam, have agreed to set up a free-trade area by 2003.

- *In Africa:* The Southern African Development Community (SADC), formed in 1980 and now encompassing more than twelve countries, has pledged to develop a free-trade area and common currency by the end of the century.

Will the lofty expectations of these regional politico-economic groups be realized? Political will and shared visions have proven in the past to be indispensable elements in successful regional trade regimes. Economic complementarity is another essential component, as the goal is to stimulate greater trade among the members of the free-trade area, not simply between it and others. If one or more members export products that each of the others wants, the chances of the regime's success are greater; if, on the other hand, they all tend to export the same products or to have virtually no trade with one another (typically the case in Africa), failure is more likely.

Prospects for the success of regional trade regimes seem greatest when Global South countries cobble their futures to Northern states—but on terms that the North dictates (World Bank 1995a; see also Shaw 1994). That conclusion hardly augurs well for regional economic agreements as an effective method for balancing the North-South relationship.

Trade, Aid, Investment—or Nothing?

The developing countries have long pleaded for "trade, not aid" to improve their international position. The NIEs' experience supports the view that access to markets in the developed world is critical to economic growth in the Global South. However, market access has become increasingly difficult because domestic pressure groups in Global North countries have lobbied their governments to reduce imports of developing countries' products that compete with their own industries. Trade may be preferred to aid, but political barriers often prevent it.

Aid no longer offers a promising means for developing countries to increase wealth either. The end of the Cold War has propelled many former donor countries to oppose what some foreign aid critics see as "international welfare." Smith Hempstone, U.S. ambassador to Kenya, put the opposition's argument caustically when he opined in 1995 that with "the Soviets out of the game, we can no longer be blackmailed into giving money to projects which we know are not beneficial to the countries concerned."

Foreign aid comes in a variety of forms and is used for a variety of purposes. Some aid consists of outright grants of money, some of loans at concessional rates, and some of shared technical expertise. Although most foreign aid is bilateral—meaning the money flows directly from one country to another—an increasing portion is now channeled through international institutions such as the World Bank, and hence is known as "multilateral aid."

The purposes of aid are as varied as its forms. Security objectives are typically pursued through military assistance of one kind or another, but economic aid is also used for these purposes. The United States, for example, "paid" for military base rights in many Third World countries during the Cold War with both economic and military aid. In addition, America continues to target Israel and Egypt as major recipients to symbolize friendship, maintain a balance of power, and influence the Middle East peace process.

While disaster relief and other humanitarian purposes are also addressed through grants and loans, the economic development of the Global South has been a primary aim of most foreign aid since World War II. The assumption that development will support other goals, such as Arab/Muslim solidarity, commercial advantage, free markets, and democratization, rationalizes most donors' assistance programs. Today, however, some of these traditional justifications are under widespread attack in many donor countries, particularly in the United States which, until recently (when overtaken by Japan) provided more bilateral aid and more resources to multilateral institutions than any other donor. "The poor economic performance of many traditional aid recipients (and some aid agencies) has tried the patience of supporters of aid programs and increased skepticism about the effectiveness of aid" (World Bank 1996).

Virtually all Global North states (plus several Arab countries) provide large sums to developing countries each year. Nonetheless, the volume of aid has largely declined since the end of the Cold War (see Figure 5.2). Meanwhile, the number of recipients has increased as Russia and the other countries in transition have switched from being donors to recipients. Commonly stated goals that might give foreign aid new life include poverty reduction, human development, environmental protection, reduced military spending, enhanced economic management, development of private enterprise, enhancement of the role of women, and the promotion of democratic governance and human rights. Existing practice in Russia and Ukraine suggests that disarmament—specifically dismantling and storage of chemical and nuclear weapons—may also be facilitated with foreign aid support.

In all, however, the shift to market-oriented models has led many donors to conclude that foreign aid is no longer as needed, or even desirable. The emergent climate of opinion, moreover, has spawned "conditionality," demands that recipient countries must meet to receive aid. The result is that after growing for a number of years to its peak in the early 1990s, concessional assistance from official sources has been declining. "The poorest countries are not being protected from these declines, and the prospects for aid flows in the next few years appear dim. The decline is particularly worrisome at a time when many low-income countries lack access to capital markets and need assistance to better integrate their economies in the world economy, and when increasing democratization makes the prospect of poverty-reducing growth patterns more likely than ever before" (World Bank 1996, 28).

Developing countries have long chafed under the conditions or "strings" attached to donors' aid, believing that aid is their right and an obligation of rich countries in repayment for years of unequal exchange perpetrated through

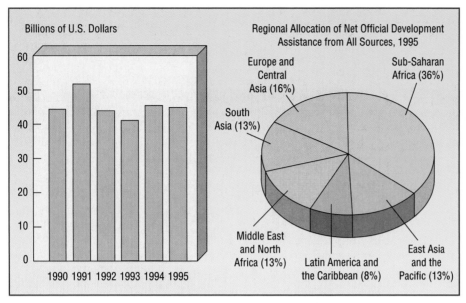

FIGURE 5.2

The Level and Regional
Distribution of Bilateral and
Multilateral Aid to Developing
Countries, 1990–1995

An increasing proportion of
foreign aid now goes to African
states, generally among the
poorest of the developing
countries. As the bar graph on
the left shows, the total volume
of global aid has declined,
despite an increase in the
number of needy aid
supplicants in the Global South.

Note: These figures include ODA and
official aid flows to economies in
transition.

SOURCE: World Bank (1996, vol. 1), 28.

colonialism and imperial rule. Consequently, they often view foreign aid as an instrument of neocolonialism and neoimperialism and have been especially critical of the conditionality imposed by the International Monetary Fund and other multilateral institutions in recent years.

Faced with the reality of diminishing foreign aid dollars, rich and poor states met in Copenhagen in 1995 at the UN Summit for Social Development, determined to find a way to stretch scarce resources. Although the neocolonial/neoimperial charge lurked in the background, the developing countries demonstrated pragmatism as they quickly supported a proposed "20:20 compact" for human development: Foreign aid donors would be asked to earmark 20 percent of the aid dollars for human development efforts, including meeting basic human needs; and in return, recipient nations would be expected to devote 20 percent of their own resources to similar efforts. Thus they recognized that without conditions, foreign aid might cease altogether.

The prevailing mood within the Global South has been a renewed search for other economic ways to escape deprivation and stagnant economic growth. Instead of relying on development assistance from the Global North, many Global South countries have sought to increase their export earnings and gain a share of global trade by seeking **foreign direct investment (FDI).** The goal of an FDI strategy for growth is encouraging private enterprise and multinational corporations to invest capital in domestic business ventures. The strategy has always been controversial, because with foreign investment has come external control, the erosion of governments' sovereignty, and, potentially, the removal of profits abroad (see Chapters 8 and 9). However, despite the risks, many developing countries have relaxed restrictions in order to increase foreign investors' activity. As World Bank records show, this has stimulated a surge in the flow of $938 billion of private capital to the Global South between 1990 and 1997 (see Figure 5.3). The impact has been substantial and has paved the way for the emerging markets of the Global South to expand their rates of economic development. Nonetheless, local industries in the Global South's domestic systems, which are threatened by the competition, maintain resistance as do

foreign direct investment (FDI)
ownership of assets
(physical facilities, such as
production plants and
equipment) in one country
by residents of another for
the purpose of controlling
the use of those assets.

141

FIGURE 5.3

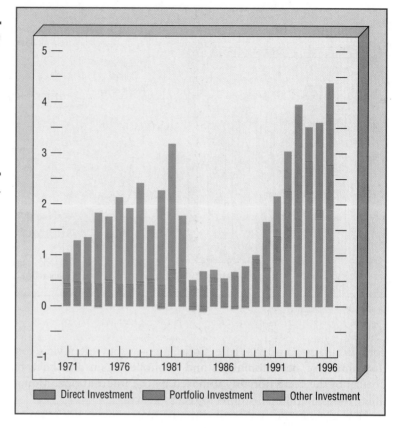

The Flow of Private and Corporate Investment to the Global South, 1971–1996

The Global South countries have turned to private capital to stimulate economic growth, and the penetration as a percent of their gross domestic product has been rapid. Overall, capital flows to developing countries have rebounded sharply in the 1990s from the depressed levels of the 1980s, with direct investment leading the way.

Note: Excludes major oil exporters. Because of limitations, these data may include some official flows.

SOURCE: International Monetary Fund (1997), 75.

those who point to the disruptions and income inequalities that these investments are causing within their homelands. These fears and consequences notwithstanding, an intensified push among the Global South developing countries to compete for investment capital in order to liberate themselves from dependence and destitution seems likely.

• • •

THE GLOBAL SOUTH IN THE NEW MILLENNIUM

The relationships between the world's developed and developing countries will no doubt continue to change in the globalized twenty-first century, but exactly how remains uncertain. A turn inward, toward isolationist foreign policies in the Global North, could lead to a posture of "benign neglect" of the South. Conversely, a new era of North-South cooperation could commence, dedicated to finding solutions to common problems, ranging from commercial to environmental and security concerns. Elements of both approaches are already evident, although the ultimate path that the Global North will choose in the new millennium is unclear.

Meanwhile, it is useful to remember the historical forces underlying the emergence of the Global South (the "Third World") as an analytical and political concept. Those who care to regard themselves as its members shared important characteristics and experiences. Most were colonized by people of another race, experienced varying degrees of poverty and hunger, and felt powerless in a world system dominated by the affluent countries that once, and perhaps still, controlled them. Considerable change occurred among the newly emergent states as the post-World War II decolonization proceeded, but much also remains the same. Thus, the concept "Third World" continues to describe "a state of mind" that will galvanize the Global South in the twenty-first century as it seeks to overcome the disorder and destitution that affect so many of its members.

KEY TERMS

Third World
First World
Second World
Global North
Global South
colonialism
decolonization
neocolonialism, neoimperialism
mercantilism
classical liberal economic theory
laissez-faire economics
Marxism-Leninism
world-system theory
self-determination
developing countries
gross national product (GNP)

developed countries
least developed of the developing
    countries (LLDCs)
barter
purchasing power parity (PPP)
newly industrialized economies
    (NIEs)
Asian Tigers
countries in transition
emerging markets
development
dependency theory
dualism
dependent development
basic human needs
absolute poverty

human development index (HDI)
gender inequalities
nonaligned states
Nonaligned Movement (NAM)
zero-sum
peace dividend
import-substitution
    industrialization
export-led industrialization
Group of 77
New International Economic
    Order (NIEO)
foreign aid
foreign direct investment (FDI)

SUGGESTED READING

Fallows, James. *Looking at the Sun: The Rise of the New East Asian Economic and Political System.* New York: Pantheon, 1994.

Handelman, Howard. *The Challenge of Third World Development.* Upper Saddle River, N.J.: Prentice Hall, 1996.

Landes, David S. *The Wealth and Poverty of Nations: Why Some Are So Rich and Some So Poor.* New York: W. W. Norton, 1998.

Packenham, Robert A. *The Dependency Movement: Scholarship and Politics in Dependency Studies.* Cambridge, Mass.: Harvard University Press, 1992.

Qadir, Shahid, ed. *Third World Quarterly: Journal of Emerging Areas,* five issues published annually. Oxford, Eng.: Carfax Publishing.

Schraeder, Peter J., Steven W. Hook, and Bruce Taylor. "Clarifying the Foreign Aid Puzzle," *World Politics* 50 (January 1998): 294–323.

Semmel, Bernard. *The Liberal Ideal and the Demons of Empire: Theories of Imperialism from Adam Smith to Lenin.* Baltimore: Johns Hopkins University Press, 1993.

Sklair, Leslie. *Sociology of the Global System,* 2nd ed. Baltimore: Johns Hopkins University, 1995.

Slater, Robert O., Barry M. Schultz, and Steven R. Dorr, eds. *Global Transformation and the Third World.* Boulder, Colo.: Lynne Rienner, 1992.

Todaro, Michael P. *Economic Development.* 6th revised ed. New York: Longman, 1997.

United Nations Development Programme. *Human Development Report 1998.* New York: Oxford University Press, 1998.

World Bank. *Global Economic Prospects and the Developing Countries 1997.* Washington, D.C.: The World Bank, 1997.

World Bank. *World Development Report 1998.* Washington, D.C.: The World Bank, 1998.

http://www.smplanet.com/imperialism/toc.html
The Age of Imperialism   Chapter 5 in *World Politics* begins with a discussion of European imperialism and its affects on the Global South. To extend your analysis of imperialism, review a Small Planet's Web site entitled "An Online History of the United States: The Age of Imperialism." Recommended by the History Channel, this site chronicles American expansion in the Pacific, the Spanish-American War, the Boxer Rebellion, and U.S. intervention in Latin America. See historic photos of the battleship *Maine,* maps of the regions, and portraits of the participants. Read letters, anti-imperialist essays from the past, and cartoons. You can even download movie clips.

When speaking of development issues, many U.S. citizens have trouble understanding the plight of the Global South. Use the following Web sites to familiarize yourself with these countries and the problems they face. For instance, choose a country from each of the following regions: Latin America, Asia, Africa, and the Middle East. Using the Web sites listed here, compare and contrast each of the countries in terms of political and economic structures. Keep the following questions in mind: What type of government does each country have? Which industrial revolution have they experienced? What primary goods does each country import and export? When you are finished, can you identify the biggest obstacles for each country in the development process?

http://www.georgetown.edu/LatAmerPolitical/home.html
Political Database of the Americas   Georgetown University, the Organization of American States, and the Canadian Foundation for the Americas have teamed up to bring you the "Political Database of the Americas." The database provides documentary and statistical political information on Latin America, including constitutions, electoral laws, political parties, legislative and executive branch information, and election data. There is also a section on international affairs where you can contact embassies and consulates. To practice reading Spanish, scan Costa Rica's national anthem in its native tongue.

http://www.sas.upenn.edu/African_Studies/AS.html
African Studies WWW   The University of Pennsylvania's African Studies Center has created a Web site that provides extensive links to country-specific information as well as a bulletin board that lists current events and important documents. They even have a multimedia archive where you can view African sculptures. Check out the "Alligator Head" from Nigeria. Why is the "Standing Male Figure" from Zaire impaled with so many blades?

http://coombs.anu.edu.au/WWWVL-Asian Studies.html
Asian Studies WWW Virtual Library   The resources in the Asian Studies WWW Virtual Library are divided according to global, regional, and country specific areas. With close to one million Web site visitors in four years they must be doing something right!

http://menic.utexas.edu/mes.html
The Center for Middle Eastern Studies   The Middle East Network Information Center at the University of Texas at Austin is an inclusive source for general as well as country specific information. Click on the "Arts and Culture" link and hear Arabic spoken on numerous radio stations. Or try your hand at "Interactive Arabic Texts" by accessing the "Modern Standard Arabic Page." You can practice your Arabic while continuing to develop your vocabulary.

The following Web sites provide general information on international development.

http://w3.acdi-cida.gc.ca/Virtual.nsf/pages/index
Virtual Library on International Development   A collection of links to international development resources.

http://www.unicc.org/unctad
United Nations Conference on Trade and Development (UNCTAD)   From the UNCTAD homepage, go to the "Least Developed Countries'" link and examine the backgrounds of the countries that the United Nations has deemed the poorest countries in the world. Then, view the "Activities" that UNCTAD has planned in order to help these countries. Do you think the "Trust Fund" will work?

CHAPTER 6

Universal and Regional Intergovernmental Organizations (IGOs)

CHAPTER TOPICS AND THEMES

- What are IGOs?

- The United Nations

- The European Union

- Other regional organizations

- Will the IGOs' web of interdependence propel globalization and transform world politics?

The 1648 Peace of Westphalia, which ended the Thirty Years' War, also ended the secular authority of the Pope by creating sovereign and independent territorial states. When European states started to integrate in the 1950s and later in February 1992 when the Maastricht treaty on European Union was signed, they moved a step away from the absolute sovereign control of states over their territory, and toward the reassertion of authority by supranational institutions.

The history of world politics for the past three hundred fifty years has largely been a chronicle of interactions among states, which remain the dominant political organizations in the world. States' interests, capabilities, and goals significantly shape world politics. However, the supremacy of the state has been severely challenged. Increasingly, world affairs are being influenced by organizations that transcend national boundaries—universal international organizations such as the United Nations and regional organizations such as the European Union. Diverse in scope and purpose, these actors perform independent roles and increasingly exert global influence.

In this chapter we examine the growth and influence of these transnational organizations. Chapter 7 examines a variety of other nonstate actors, such as ethnopolitical and religious movements and multinational corporations, which are also increasingly active on the world stage. The purpose of these chapters is not simply to describe these actors' existence, but to question the extent to which their activities undermine states' continuing autonomy. Thus the focus throughout will be on governments' capacity to manage global change, as well as the role of international organizations in the transformation of world politics.

There are two principal types of international organizations: **Intergovernmental organizations (IGOs)** are those whose members are states; **nongovernmental organizations (NGOs)** are those whose members are private individuals and groups. Neither type is unique to the twentieth century, although both are now more pervasive. The Union of International Organizations, which maintains comprehensive, up-to-date information on both types, records that their numbers increased sharply during the nineteenth century, as international commerce and communications grew alongside industrialization. In 1909, there were 37 IGOs and 176 NGOs. By 1960 there were 154 IGOs and 1,255 NGOs, and by 1997 these numbers had surged to 260 and 5,472, respectively (See Figure 6.1; *Yearbook of International Organizations 1996/97* Vol. 1, 1685).

In interpreting these trends, keep in mind that it is not easy to identify and measure international organizations. In principle, IGOs are defined by not only the fact that their members are states, but also by their permanence and institutional procedures; IGOs meet at relatively regular intervals, and have specified procedures for making decisions and a permanent secretariat or headquarters staff (Jacobson 1984), although they "do not have direct access to many of the material resources normally available to states" (Young 1995). If these criteria were relaxed, the number of IGOs would far surpass the two hundred and sixty "conventionally defined" organizations just cited, as would the number of NGOs. An additional 1,570 international bodies would qualify for inclusion as IGOs, as would more than 9,636 other nongovernmental associations that share some characteristics with NGOs (*Yearbook of International Organizations 1996/97* Vol. 1, 1684).

This growth in transnational organizations has created a complex network of overlapping memberships. In 1996, some two hundred countries and territo-

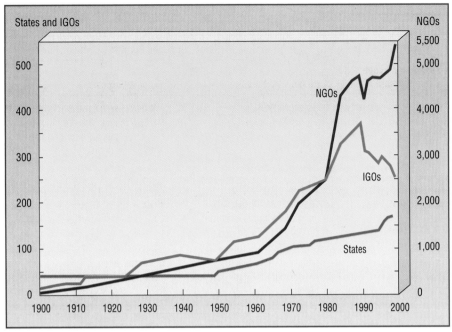

FIGURE 6.1

The Number of States, IGOs, and NGOs since 1900

The number of independent states has increased greatly in the twentieth century, especially since the decolonization movement began after World War II, but the number of intergovernmental organizations (IGOs) and especially nongovernmental organizations (NGOs) has grown even more rapidly.

SOURCES: States, United Nations and Freedom House; IGOs and NGOs, *Yearbook of International Organizations, 1996/97*, and moving averages from selected prior volumes.

ries had more than 135,000 different delegates representing them at the meetings of the 5,472 IGOs. The cooperative activities of these "networks of interdependence" (Jacobson 1984) span the entire range of global issues: trade, defense, disarmament, economic development, agriculture, health, culture, human rights, the arts, illegal drugs, tourism, labor, women's plight, education, debt, the environment, crime, humanitarian aid, civilian crisis relief, telecommunications, science, globalization, immigration, and refugees, to name just a few.

While more than 96 percent of all the transnational organizations now in operation are nongovernmental, the remaining 4 percent are more important because their members are states. The smaller subset of IGOs that governments create will remain preeminent as long as the preeminence of states themselves persists, because IGOs "derive their importance from their character as associations of states" (Jacobson 1984), which gives them whatever authority IGOs exercise.

IGOs are all composed of states, but vary widely in their purposes and breadth of membership. One study found that only eighteen qualify as general-purpose organizations, and of these only the United Nations approximated universal membership. The rest, making up more than 97 percent of the total, were limited in their membership and purposes (Jacobson 1984, 48). Table 6.1 illustrates these differences. The variation among the organizations in each subcategory is great, particularly with single-purpose, limited-membership IGOs. The North Atlantic Treaty Organization (NATO), for example, is primarily a military alliance, while others, such as the Organization of American States (OAS), promote both economic development and political reforms. Still, most IGOs engage in a comparatively narrow range of activities the purposes of which are usually economic and social, such as the management of trade, transportation, and other types of functional cooperation. In this sense IGOs

147

TABLE 6.1 A Simple Classification of Intergovernmental Organizations (IGOs)

Geographic Scope of Membership	Range of Stated Purpose	
	Multiple Purposes	Single Purpose
Global	United Nations World Trade Organization UNESCO Organization of the Islamic Conference	World Health Organization International Labor Organization International Monetary Fund Universal Postal Union
Interregional, regional, subregional	European Union Organization for Security and Cooperation in Europe Organization of American States Organization of African Unity League of Arab States Association of South East Asian Nations	European Space Agency Nordic Council North Atlantic Treaty Organization International Olive Oil Council International North Pacific Coffee Organization African Groundnut Council

are agents as well as reflections of global social and economic interdependence produced by the expansion of activities transcending state borders.

Nongovernmental organizations (NGOs) also differ widely. Due to their number and diversity, they are even more difficult than IGOs to characterize and classify. In 1997 the Union of International Associations categorized 10 percent of some 5,472 NGOs as universal membership organizations, with most of the remaining 90 percent classified as intercontinental or regionally oriented membership organizations. Functionally, NGOs span virtually every facet of modern political, social, and economic activity in an increasingly borderless globalized world, ranging from earth sciences to health care, language, history, culture, theology, law, ethics, security, and defense.

It is useful to think of NGOs as intersocietal organizations that help promote agreements among states on issues of international public policy. Many NGOs interact formally with IGOs. For instance, more than one thousand NGOs actively consult with various agencies of the extensive United Nations system and maintain offices in more than one hundred cities. The partnership between NGOs and IGOs enables both types to work (and lobby) together in pursuit of common policies and programs.

Although widespread geographically, NGOs are most active in the advanced Global North industrial democracies. "This is so because open political systems, ones in which there is societal pluralism, are more likely to allow their citizens to participate in non-governmental organizations, and such [democratic governments] are highly correlated with relatively high levels of economic development" (Jacobson 1984).

In this chapter, we will discuss some prominent and representative IGOs, including the United Nations, the European Union, and various other regional organizations. In Chapter 7 we shall investigate in greater depth the impact of NGOs.

Council, the Trusteeship Council, the Secretariat, and the International Court of Justice. In the General Assembly—the only organ that represents all the member states—decision making follows the principle of majority rule, with no state given a veto.

Unlike the Security Council, which is empowered by the UN Charter to initiate actions including the use of force, the General Assembly can only make recommendations. The founders of the United Nations did not foresee that this limited mandate would later be expanded to allow the General Assembly to participate with the Security Council in managing security. The General Assembly is also now the primary body for addressing social and economic problems, which have grown in number and importance.

In response to the challenge of managing these global problems, the United Nations has evolved into an extraordinarily complex set of political institutions. The United Nations also often relies heavily on the many nongovernmental organizations it helps to fund that are not under its formal authority. This involvement blurs the line between governmental and nongovernmental functions. Examples include the United Nations Children's Fund (UNICEF), the United Nations for Population Fund Activities, and the United Nations University, which fulfill their missions in part through nongovernmental organizations. Thus, today the United Nations is not one organization but a decentralized conglomerate of countless committees, bureaus, boards, commissions, centers, institutes, offices, and agencies. If any of these occupies a central role in the overall structure of the United Nations, it is the General Assembly.

The increase in UN bodies and activities paralleled the growth of international interdependence and cross-cutting linkages since World War II, and the ways in which the UN's growing membership used it to accomplish their own aims. Countries in the Global South, for instance—seizing advantage of their growing numbers under the one-state, one-vote rules of the General Assembly—began to guide UN involvement in directions of particular concern to them. This was reflected in the enormous growth of diverse affiliated agencies created to address the full array of the world's problems and needs.

The Global South countries' use of the UN forum to further their aims and interests regarding decolonization and economic development contrasted with the U.S. view of the United Nations as a platform for pursuing its own Cold War strategies. During the 1970s the United States suffered a series of defeats: In 1971 the General Assembly voted to seat Communist China. In 1974 the General Assembly extended permanent observer status to the Palestine Liberation Organization against U.S. opposition. In 1975 the General Assembly went on record branding Zionism "a form of racism and racial discrimination." And in 1983 the United States was the target of an overwhelmingly approved resolution deploring the U.S. invasion of Grenada.

This era of struggle between the Global South and the United States shifted when the Cold War ended. Although control of UN peacekeeping operations and financial support of UN operations no longer divided the Global North and the Global South in the same way they routinely did when the United States (and the Soviet Union) had a singular military agenda in mind and the developing countries had a quite different social, economic, and environmental one, differences remained. Today the less developed Global South countries continue to resist domination by the Global North even while protesting that the Global North increasingly ignores its needs.

North-South differences over perceived priorities are most clearly exhibited in the heated debate over the UN's budget. This controversy centers on how members should interpret the organization's Charter, which states that "expenses of the Organization shall be borne by the members as apportioned by the General Assembly."

The UN budget consists of three distinct elements: the regular budget, the peacekeeping budget, and the budget for voluntary programs. States contribute to the voluntary programs and some of the peacekeeping activities as they see fit. The regular program and some of the peacekeeping activities are subject to assessments.

The precise mechanism by which assessments have been determined is complicated, but historically assessments were generally allocated according to states' capacity to pay. Thus the United States, which had the greatest resources, contributed 25 percent of the regular UN budget, whereas several dozen extremely poor members paid the minimum (0.01 percent of the regular budget). The United States was also the prime contributor to UN peacekeeping and voluntary programs.

Resistance to this budgetary formula for funding UN activities has always existed. It has grown progressively worse, in large part because when the General Assembly apportions expenses, it does so according to majority rule. The problem is that those with the most votes (the less developed countries) do not have the money, and the most prosperous countries do not have the votes. Consider how wide these disparities had grown by comparing UN budget assessments and relative voting strengths in the General Assembly, based on the UN scale of assessments approved in December 1997 for the UN's 185 members between 1998 and 2000. The eight largest contributors to the United Nations will command only eight votes, although they are expected to pay 70 percent of its costs. At the other end of the spectrum, the poorest members, who collectively are asked to pay only 30 percent of UN costs, will command 177 votes. This long-standing situation, of course, led to many fierce financial disputes between the more numerous developing countries that wielded considerable influence over the kinds of issues on which the UN's attention and resources were focused, and the great powers' growing concern about the UN's priorities, administrative efficiency, and expenses. The wealthy members questioned if the payment formula was fair. They asked, did the existing budget procedures institutionalize a system of taxation without fair representation? The critics countered with the argument that the great-power members should bear financial responsibilities commensurate with their wealth and influence.

At issue, of course, was not simply money (which remained, with a 1998 total regular assessment at the comparatively paltry sum of less than $3 billion), but differences in images of what was important and which states should have political influence. Poor states argue that needs should determine expenditure levels rather than the other way around. Major contributors, sensitive to the amounts asked of them and the purposes to which the funds are put, did not want to pay for programs they opposed. The United States, in particular, was the most vocal about its dissatisfaction, and in the early 1990s refused to pay its assessments, and was still $1.3 billion in arrears in 1998. This obstructionism about how much the United States should pay was not inconsistent with past U.S. retributive policy. Earlier, the United States had gone even further to register its disapproval with what it saw as the anti-Western drift of many UN bodies by withdrawing from its membership in them. In the 1970s, for example, the Carter administration left the International Labor Organization in an attempt to influence the direction of its policies, and during the Reagan administration the United States also withdrew from the 159-member UNESCO (United Nations Educational, Scientific and Cultural Organization) in response to what it regarded as the politicization of the body and its hostility toward Western values (including, in particular, freedom of communication), thereby depriving UNESCO of one-fourth of its budget.

Even though the Global South countries usually managed to set the agenda in the General Assembly, like the United States they also regularly failed to pay for it or to spend time lobbying for political support from other important UN groups. In fact, in the 1990s about 90 percent of the Global South members were also in arrears.

Amidst these chronic cash-flow problems and rising complaints about the UN's "bloated bureaucracy" and inefficient administration, the largest contributor, the United States, refused to pay its financial obligations, and fell into arrears nearly $2 billion, on average, annually between 1993 and 1998. The U.S. Congress introduced legislation that sought to unilaterally lower the American contribution from 31 to 25 percent for peacekeeping, and in early 1997 passed a new law that would have cut the U.S. regular assessment by stages from 25 to 20 percent. At the same time, as a price for its continuing participation, the United States demanded massive streamlining reforms in the UN's budget, organization, and staff. Because the United Nations could not survive without the United States, it was in a good position at the time to get its requests for reorganization accepted. As one official put it, "It may happen that countries just throw up their hands and start to give in to the United States—the Europeans would be the first to go—if only just to keep the place rolling" (*Economist*, July 19, 1997).

In response to the crisis this pressure created, Secretary General Kofi Annan announced a "quiet revolution" of consolidation, delegating, and personnel cuts for the programs under his control, to reduce costs, correct corruption and waste, and allow for greater administrative efficiency. This included a $123 million reduction in the 1998–1999 biennium budget on the heels of a four-year freeze and the elimination of one thousand posts above the nearly two thousand positions previously cut (from twelve thousand in 1985) to reduce the staff an additional 25 percent, from ten thousand in 1996 to eight thousand. In addition, as a component of the highly detailed document entitled *Renewing the United Nations: A Programme for Reform*, Annan also begged the General Assembly to establish a commission to revise the mandates of the specialized agencies that are beyond his authority to reform (these kinds of changes require decisions by member states), and proposed that the members convene a Millennium Assembly in 2000 with a companion People's Assembly to define the twenty-first-century policy agenda and procedures for the UN. These massive reforms also cut the Secretariat's administrative costs by one-third, from 38 percent of the regular budget to 25 percent by 1999–2000, putting the savings into a development fund for poor countries. The overall budget was reduced to about $2.5 billion in 1998 and 1999, while holding the U.S. share to 25 percent; reducing Russia's (to 2.87 percent); increasing Japan's (to 20.6 percent), Germany's (to 9.6 percent), and Italy's (to 5.4 percent); and keeping China's below 1 percent. As Figure 6.3 shows, the reorganization plan merges the score of disparate programs into five categories and creates the UN's first Deputy Secretary General (Louise Frechette). The new budget

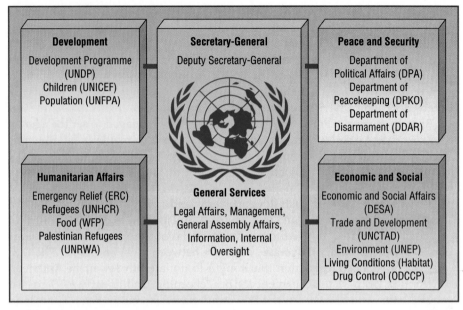

FIGURE 6.3

Secretary General Kofi Annan's Reform Proposal for Administration of the United Nations

To offset criticism and restore the United Nations to a sound financial footing that most members would likely fund, Secretary-General Kofi Annan pleaded in 1998, "Give us the tools and we will do the job." His pleas were heard, and he won acceptance for nearly all of his proposals to reorganize and streamline the many UN agencies under his authority. The cost-saving reforms "downsized" the organizational chart under a cabinet-style managerial chain of command, including the appointment of a French Canadian, Louise Frechette, as the first Deputy Secretary General in the UN's history. The reform package reorganized the UN's huge network of separate agencies, as this administrative restructuring chart prepared by the UN shows.

formula for the 185 members agreed to in December puts the UN financial house on a firmer if leaner foundation.

The future of the United Nations nonetheless remains uncertain. The U.S. Congress continues to resist paying America's arrears, and turned down a White House request for several billion dollars for the UN, intended to stop the criticism of the United States as a "deadbeat." The U.S. failure to meet its financial obligations undermines the faith of both America's friends and foes in the sincerity of the U.S. promise to support the UN and further threatens the UN's frail cohesion. To make matters worse, wide divergences among the General Assembly members continue to pose a well-entrenched obstacle to major changes in the way the UN works. However, given the promise of Kofi Annon's reform package and budget cutbacks, many supporters feel optimistic about the organization's long-term prospects, because past crises have been overcome and the UN's many important previous contributions to world peace and development have given most countries a large stake in its survival. The great gap between the mandates that the UN's members ordered, and the means they allowed for fulfilling them, may yet be closed, because failure would spell disaster.

The history of the United Nations' first fifty years reflects the fact that both rich countries and developing countries have successfully used the organization to promote their own foreign policy goals, and this proud fifty-year record has bred much loyalty and hopeful confidence in the UN's future capacity to manage an ever-changing and growing agenda (see Figure 6.4). The United Nations has been asked to address an expanding set of economic development and other nonmilitary issues, and its adaptive response has generated support from the members that demanded them. For example, the developing countries' interests were recognized in the host of world conferences and special General Assembly sessions held since the early 1970s (see Focus 6.2), even if these conferences frequently became forums for heated exchanges between North and South that limited their global problem-solving capability.

In the twenty-first century, the United Nations is likely to continue to play an active role in *both* the area of social and economic enhancement and in that of peace and security. As we will examine in Chapter 16, however, the prospects for future UN peacekeeping are uncertain, and the capacity for the globe's most powerful IGO to "identify, and focus on, what the United Nations can do best" (Boutros-Ghali 1995) in the social and economic realm is likely to be severely tested. The challenge will be great, because the United Nations is expected to serve the economic and social development needs of 185 states and 6 billion people with less money than the annual budget for New York State University (UNDP 1997, 93). In the last analysis, the United Nations can be no more than the mandates and power that the member states give to it. As one high-level UN civil servant, Brian Urquhart, described the world's political dilemma, "Either the UN is vital to a more stable and equitable world and should be given the means to do the job, or peoples and governments should be encouraged to look elsewhere. But is there really an alternative?"

• • •

THE EUROPEAN UNION: A MODEL REGIONAL IGO?

The tug-of-war between individual states and groups of states within the United Nations is suggestive of an underlying principle—IGOs are run by the states that join them. This severely inhibits the IGOs' ability to rise above interstate competition and independently pursue their own purposes. In the words of Inis Claude (1967), "The United Nations has no purposes—and can have none—of its own." This is even truer of other IGOs. Because they cannot act autonomously and lack the legitimacy and capability for independent global governance, IGOs are often viewed more as instruments of states' foreign policies and arenas for debate than as independent actors.

When states dominate international organizations, as in the UN, the prospects for international cooperation decline because, as realist theorists emphasize, states typically resist any organizational actions that compromise their vital interests. This limits IGOs' capability for multilateral decision making to engineer global change.

A rival hypothesis—that cooperation among powerful states is possible and that international organizations help produce it—emerges from neoliberal theory. This viewpoint is especially pertinent to the **European Union (EU),** known

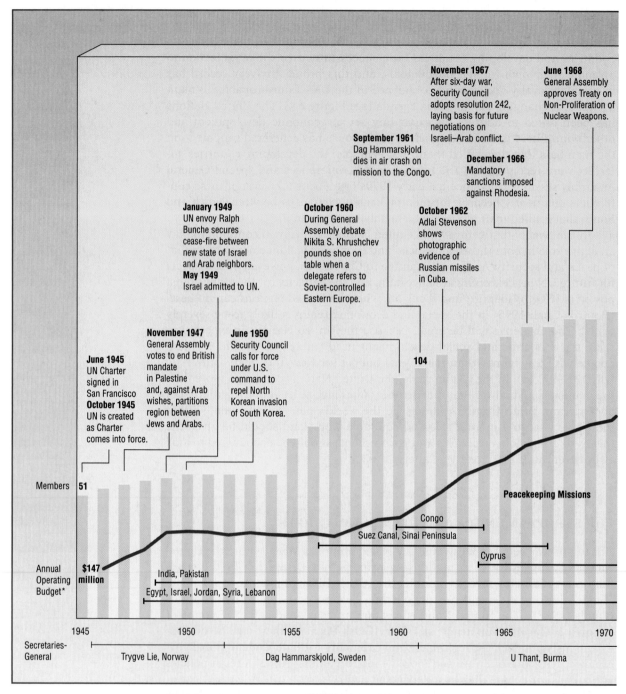

FIGURE 6.4

The UN at Fifty: A Look at Its First Half-Century

As the United Nations has grown from 51 countries in 1945 to nearly 190, its mission, its budget, and criticism of the way it operates have mushroomed, too. At fiftieth-anniversary ceremonies in New York in October 1995, world leaders offered prescriptions for making the UN a more effective force in the post-Cold War era. This figure highlights the major issues and developments in the UN's history since 1945.

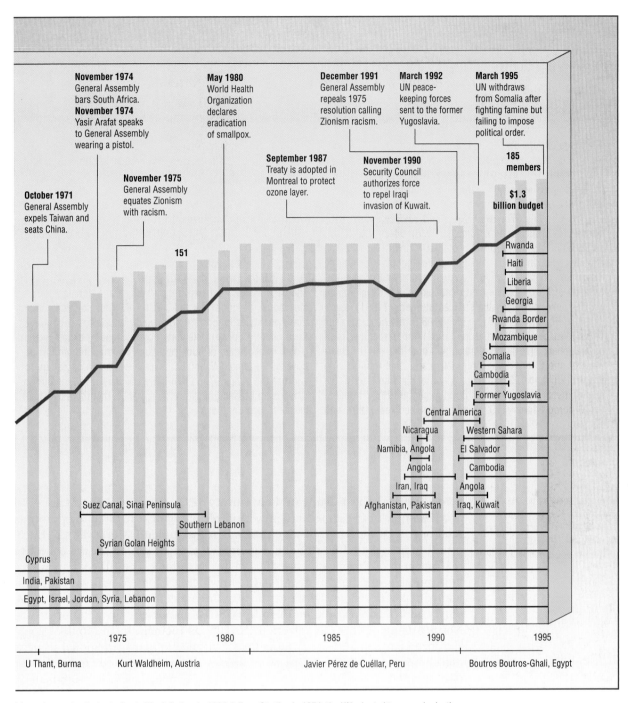

October 1971
General Assembly expels Taiwan and seats China.

November 1974
General Assembly bars South Africa.
November 1974
Yasir Arafat speaks to General Assembly wearing a pistol.

November 1975
General Assembly equates Zionism with racism.

May 1980
World Health Organization declares eradication of smallpox.

September 1987
Treaty is adopted in Montreal to protect ozone layer.

December 1991
General Assembly repeals 1975 resolution calling Zionism racism.

March 1992
UN peace-keeping forces sent to the former Yugoslavia.

November 1990
Security Council authorizes force to repel Iraqi invasion of Kuwait.

March 1995
UN withdraws from Somalia after fighting famine but failing to impose political order.

185 members

$1.3 billion budget

151

Rwanda
Haiti
Liberia
Georgia
Rwanda Border
Mozambique
Somalia
Cambodia
Former Yugoslavia
Central America
Nicaragua   Western Sahara
Namibia, Angola   El Salvador
Angola   Cambodia
Iran, Iraq   Angola
Afghanistan, Pakistan Iraq, Kuwait

Suez Canal, Sinai Peninsula
Southern Lebanon
Syrian Golan Heights
Cyprus
India, Pakistan
Egypt, Israel, Jordan, Syria, Lebanon

1975   1980   1985   1990   1995

U Thant, Burma   Kurt Waldheim, Austria   Javier Pérez de Cuéllar, Peru   Boutros Boutros-Ghali, Egypt

*Annual operating budget adjusted for inflation, in 1994 dollars. Starting in 1974, the UN adopted two-year budgeting.
Data after 1973 are the annual average for the corresponding two-year period.

SOURCE: *New York Times*, October 22, 1995, 8.

159

A Global Agenda
The Shifting and Multiple Issues the United Nations Faces

The range of subjects the United Nations addresses speaks to the agenda of issues especially important to the Global South. UN-sponsored world conferences that have raised global consciousness issues such as the human environment (1972), law of the sea (1973), population (1974, 1984, 1994), food (1974), women (1975, 1980, 1985, and 1995), human settlements (1976), basic human needs (1976), water (1977), desertification (1977), disarmament (1978 and 1982), racism and racial discrimination (1978), technical cooperation among developing countries (1978), agrarian reform and rural development (1979), science and technology for development (1979), new and renewable sources of energy (1981), least-developed countries (1981), aging (1982), the peaceful uses of outer space (1982), Palestine (1982), the peaceful uses of nuclear energy (1983), the prevention of crime and the treatment of offenders (1985), drug abuse and illicit trafficking in drugs (1987 and 1992), the protection of children (1990), the environment and economic development (1992), transnational corporations (1992), indigenous peoples (1992 and 1994), internationally organized crime (1994), social development (1995), housing (1996), and human rights (1993 and 1997).

The subjects of world conferences during the past two decades are in effect a list of "the most vital issues of present world conditions," whereas the conferences themselves "represent a beginning in a long and evolving process of keeping within manageable proportions the major problems of humanity" (Bennett 1988). In this the United Nations, spurred on by the Global South, can take some credit. Critics, however, charge that these expensive conferences and debates generate vague, do-good talk but not meaningful solutions; that many countries ignore the principled rhetoric the conference documents propose. Defenders counter that by exposing the global implications of such problems as crushing worldwide poverty, the United Nations arouses the concern necessary to address the dangers, and that if the UN were given the power it needs for meaningful global governance, members could alleviate these conditions.

European Community the collection of European states that solidified their collective governance, laying the foundation for the European Union.

before 1994 as the **European Community (EC).** The European Union is a good example of the sometimes powerful role of regional IGOs in international relations. It is important to note that it is rather unique. Moreover, the European Union is not a free-standing supernational organization for the collective management of European domestic and foreign affairs. The EU coexists with a large number of other European IGOs, in which it is nested and with which it jointly makes decisions. Of these, the fifty-three-member **Organization for Security and Cooperation in Europe (OSCE)** stands out, in addition to the North Atlantic Treaty Organization (NATO), as regional institutions of equal European partners, free of dividing lines, designed to manage regional security and promote the human rights of minorities through democratization. In this overlapping network of European IGOs, the EU nonetheless is prominent as the primary global example of a powerful regional institution.

The process of European integration began with the creation of the European Coal and Steel Community (ECSC) in 1951, the European Atomic Energy Community (Euratom) in 1957, and the European Economic Community (EEC) in 1957. Since the late 1960s, the three have shared common organizational structures, and, in successive steps, came to be called "the European Community." Its membership has grown and its geographical scope has broadened as the Union has expanded in a series of waves to encompass fifteen countries as of 1997: Belgium, France, Germany, Italy, Luxembourg, and the Nether-

Small island states such as Thuru Island in the Maldives may appear to be tiny paradises. However, they are exceptionally vulnerable to both natural catastrophes and human threats. If international organizations such as the United Nations will not help to protect them, who will?

lands (who were the original "Six"); Denmark, Ireland, and the United Kingdom (who joined in 1973); Greece (1981); Portugal and Spain (1986); and Austria, Finland, and Sweden (1995). In its April 1998 summit in Brussels, the EU reached a new milestone in its path toward enlargement when it formally opened negotiations aimed at bringing up to ten countries from eastern and central Europe plus Cyprus into its membership pending the applicants' ability to meet its economical social conditions for entry. This move will change the face of Europe, ending the continent's postwar division and increasing the EU's population by 50 percent. The EU also then agreed to a two-tier approach to expansion, with "slow-track" applicants engaged in "preparatory talks" to join the front rank if they quickly make the required reforms, and other countries such as Turkey, which had been seeking membership for thirty-four years, encouraged to continue negotiations.

Organizational Components and Decision-Making Procedures

The European Union organizationally consists of an Executive Commission, a Council of Ministers, a European Parliament, and a Court of Justice (see Figure 6.5). The Union's central component, the Council of Ministers, consists of cabinet ministers drawn from the EU's member states, who participate when the most important decisions are made. In this respect, the European Union is an association of states similar to the United Nations. But the EU is more than this, as evidenced by its other elements and decision-making procedures. In the process of "enlargement," the EU's authority over its members has grown so that the EU is truly much more than the sum of its parts.

Central among the other components of the European Union is the **European Commission,** which consists of twenty commissioners (two each from Britain, France, Germany, Italy, and Spain, and one each from the remaining member states). A professional staff of more than twenty-five thousand

European Commission the executive organ administratively responsible for the European Union.

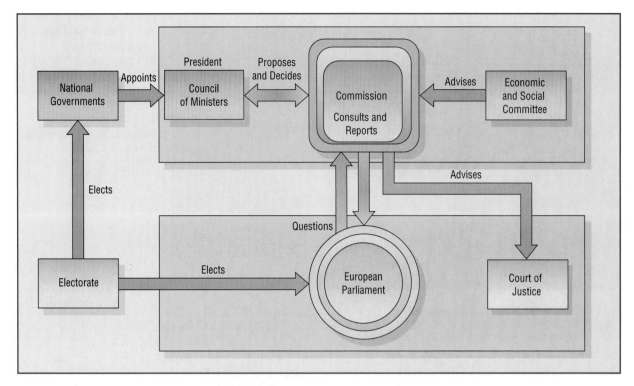

FIGURE 6.5

The Structure of the European Union

The European Union is a complex organization, with different responsibilities performed by various units. This figure charts the principal institutions and the relationships among them that collectively lead to EU decisions and policies.

SOURCE: Adapted from Taylor (1990), 112.

civil-service "Eurocrats," who in principle owe loyalty to the EU rather than to its national constituents, assists the Commission's administrative bureaucracy in proposing and directing decision making (by majority vote) for the EU and the Council of Ministers. The Commission proposes legislation, implements EU policies, and represents the European Union in international trade negotiations. It also manages the EU's budget, which, in contrast with most international organizations, derives part of its revenues from sources not under the control of member states.

The European Parliament is chosen by direct election of the citizenry of the EU's member states. Its more than six hundred delegates debate issues in the same way that national legislative bodies do under popular democracy, but its legislative powers are less pervasive than in a typical domestic parliamentary system. Still, the European Parliament is distinctive in that most international organizations' legislative bodies represent states (e.g., the UN General Assembly), not individual citizens or transnational political parties.

The Court of Justice is also distinctive in this respect. The court, consisting of fifteen judges, interprets EU law for national courts and rules on legal questions raised by the EU's institutions, or—in an important deviation from traditional practices—by individuals. Its decisions are binding, which also distinguishes the European Court of Justice from most other international tribunals.

Figure 6.6 illustrates the EU's decision-making processes. There are two procedures for the adoption of directives and regulations—consultation and cooperation. Which procedure is followed depends on the nature of the proposal, with the principal difference being that the European Parliament plays a greater role in the cooperative than in the consultative process. In both, however, the central role of the Commission is evident, as it has been the driving force behind European integration. That power was strengthened at the 1997 Amsterdam conference at which, after eighteen months of bargaining, the *Agenda 2000* accord reduced the decision process from twenty steps to three under a complex compromise formula designed to accommodate the diverse preferences of the EU's members.

Under the imaginative leadership of Jacques Delors, President of the Commission, the European Community in 1987 adopted the Single European Act, a major amendment to the 1957 Treaty of Rome that created the European Economic Community. The act eliminated members' veto power for most issues, in order to create, in principle, a true European "single" market on January 1, 1993. The goal at the time was a free flow of goods, services, people, and money—a market without internal borders similar to the United States. Although substantial progress toward the ideal was made at the 1997 Amsterdam summit, the new treaty failed to resolve many tough issues, including "stability pact" rules to stop governmental overborrowing under the planned single "euro" currency and the rules for Eastern enlargement. Obstacles to implementing the most ambitious part of the package, a monetary union for all EU countries, appeared at the time to delay progress. But in March 1998, momentum was regained when the EU crossed a historic hurdle by declaring eleven countries fit to join a single currency in January 1999, after years of determined efforts to slash deficits and debts. The European single currency, the euro, will make its debut on January 1, 1999, provided that remaining goals are met so that the eleven countries can hand over their national currencies to the new European Central Bank in Frankfurt.

Supranationalism or Pooled Sovereignty?

How, then, are the European Union's structures and decision-making procedures best described, as compared to the United Nations and other international organizations? The EU has the power to make some decisions binding on its members without being subject to their individual approval. In this sense it is a "supranational organization." That is, it is not an organization of or among states, but one that goes beyond them to supersede the individual countries that comprise it.

Although the EU incorporates some supranational elements, the term **pooled sovereignty** (Keohane and Hoffmann 1991) better captures its essence, as states remain paramount in its institutional structures and decision-making procedures. The transfers of full authority to a central body were until recently rather modest, and critical decisions are still made in the Council of Ministers where states dominate. Most EU decisions continue to depend on national governments for implementation. Sovereignty is nonetheless shared in the sense that decision-making responsibility is now spread among governments and between them and the EU's institutions.

pooled sovereignty legal authority granted by an IGO's members to make collective decisions regarding specified aspects of public policy heretofore held exclusively by each sovereign government.

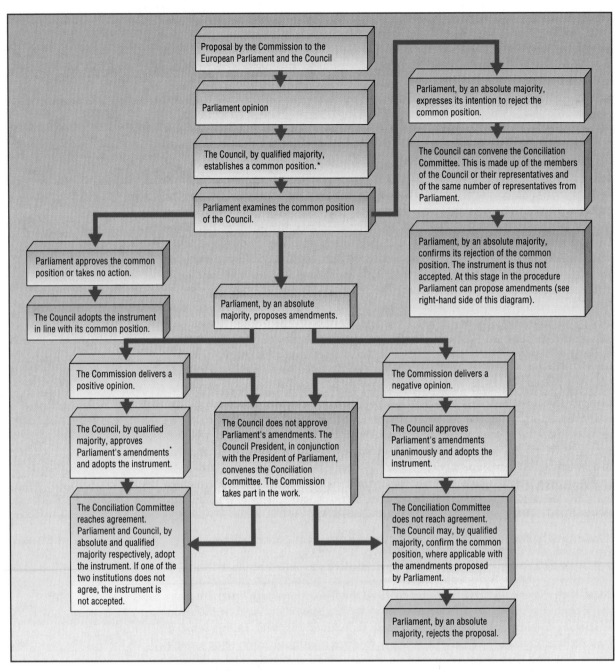

FIGURE 6.6

The Co-Decision Procedure for the European Union

The European Union uses two procedures—consultation and cooperation—to adopt regulations. The one chosen depends on the nature of the proposal being considered.

*The Council acts unanimously if its recommendation differs from that made by the Commission.

NB: (a) Each stage of the procedure is subject to time limits that run from the moment a common position is adopted.

(b) In addition to the co-decision procedure (Article 189b), there is also the cooperation procedure (Article 189c), which is similar but does not involve conciliation.

SOURCE: The European Commission Delegation to the United States.

Awareness that EU members decide by majority rule on some issues is critical to an understanding of pooled sovereignty. A major obstacle to effective decision making in the past was that most substantive proposals required unanimous approval. That rule enabled member states to protect their national interests as they alone defined them. For instance, France took advantage of this provision to thwart Community action in the late 1960s by simply refusing to send a minister to its meetings. The resulting impasse, called the "empty chair" crisis, spurred the development of new decision-making procedures.

Today, in a radical departure from past practices, and despite recurrent fears that a minority will block the will of the majority, reaching a consensus is easier because the European Union requires only a qualified voting majority on most internal market decisions (with votes weighted according to country size):

> Unlike [typical] international organizations, the European [Union] as a whole has gained some share of states' sovereignty: The member states no longer have supremacy over all other authorities within their traditional territory, nor are they independent of outside authorities. Its institutions have some of the authority normally associated with institutions of sovereign governments: On certain issues individual states can no longer veto proposals before the Council [of Ministers]; members of the Commission are independent figures rather than instructed agents. (Keohane and Hoffmann 1991, 13)

The EU's nature is also described by its functions. On the one hand, it is so distinctly different from traditional international organizations that it is virtually in a class by itself. On the other, it is self-evidently not (yet) a rival of the state as the dominant form of political organization, even in Europe. The legal meaning of sovereignty holds that the state alone has dominion over its affairs. The EU's authority is greatest in matters of economic and related external welfare issues, is limited in domestic political affairs, and has not expanded very far in military affairs. This was clearest in the EU's weak response to the 1991 Persian Gulf and Balkans wars and the 1996 dispute between Greece and Turkey over a set of Aegean islands—cases demonstrating that the collectivity was both unwilling and ill-equipped to act quickly and decisively to protect the region's threatened security interests. Its unresponsiveness during the Gulf crisis led Belgium's Foreign Minister Mark Eyskens to call Europe "an economic giant, a political dwarf, and a military worm."

Europe: An Economic Giant

Military security was uppermost in the minds of those who sought to forge a new Europe out of the ashes of World War II. Still, the EU has scored its most dramatic successes on the economic front. At the start of 1998 the European Union collectively represented a combined GNP of more than $6 trillion and a combined population of 375 million, making it the largest and richest single consumer market in the world. The EU's total gross domestic product and its population then exceeded those of the North American Free Trade Agreement, its closest economic rival, and the gap will widen if and when enlargement to an EU of twenty-six or more states is concluded.

As previously noted, the expanded European Union builds on previous precedents. In 1991 the seven members of the **European Free Trade Association (EFTA),** created in 1960 as a counterpoint to the European Economic Community, concluded a treaty with the EU to create the world's largest trading area. The agreement anticipated a single European "common market" that would have eliminated trade barriers among nineteen countries and nearly four hundred million people. Although the treaty did not allow the EFTA countries (then Austria, Finland, Iceland, Liechtenstein, Norway, Sweden, and Switzerland) power in setting EU trade policies, it set the stage for their participation in the benefits of the single market, eliminating barriers to the movement of money, products, and workers within the EU. In addition, the treaty eased the way for former EFTA members to join the EU as full partners, which Austria, Sweden, and Finland did in January 1995.

The EU's membership and geographical boundaries will expand further after the six new states accepted for fast-track membership at the December 1997 Luxembourg Summit (the Czech Republic, Cyprus, Estonia, Hungary, Poland, and Slovenia) are joined later by the five other states invited for inclusion on a slower track schedule for admission (Bulgaria, Latvia, Lithuania, Romania, and Slovakia). In addition, the EU continues negotiations with Norway, Switzerland, Turkey, and Malta, and sitting on the sidelines potentially seeking membership are Russia and the fourteen other CIS former Soviet republics, providing they can meet the democratic and economic requirements for inclusion. As Map 6.1 suggests, the probable expansion of the European Union would mend many of the geopolitical divisions of this once war-torn continent.

Beyond continuing discussions regarding formal enlargement, other countries have signed treaties that provide them with direct ties to the European Union. The EU is also linked to a large number of developing countries in Africa, the Caribbean, and the Pacific (ACP) through the **Lomé Convention,** first signed in 1975 and renewed, most recently in 1989, for a ten-year period. The Lomé IV Convention provides the ACP countries tariff-free access to the EU single market without the necessity of reciprocal concessions for EU exports to their economies. The EU's Center for Industrial Development also provides a commodity price stabilization scheme and foreign aid. In addition to the ACP countries, the EU has agreements with several other countries throughout the Global South and has signed a cooperative agreement with seven members of ASEAN (the Association of South East Asian Nations) covering trade, economic, and development issues.

Despite this legacy of successful integration and enlargement, the disintegrative forces of nationalism have constantly retarded progress. Resistance to the spirit and timetable of recent treaties reduced until recently supporters' optimism about achieving the goals required for establishment of a truly borderless common market, single currency, and monetary system. The rewards of integration and enlargement are huge, providing, in the words of German Foreign Minister Klaus Kinkel, the opportunity to spread "peace, democratic stability and prosperity across all of Europe." But those benefits are tied to equally huge costs and risks. The quest depends on finding compromise agreements acceptable to all the members, the prospects of which are diminished by the continuing differences between its more industrialized northern members and those in southern Europe. This was made evident in December 1997 when the EU members narrowly avoided a split over how they would coordinate their economic policies when they switch to the euro in 1999. The rupture was avoided when

Lomé Convention the series of agreements inspired by the NIEO movement that links forty-six developing countries to Europe to help the African, Caribbean, and Pacific (ACP) countries stabilize their export earnings and to provide them financial and technical assistance.

MAP 6.1

An Ever-Larger European Union?

In 1995 the European Union grew to fifteen members, and, as shown, the Brussels Summit in March 1998 redefined the European Commission's "Agenda 2000" package of plans to prepare for a much bigger membership of as many as twenty-six states. If the current applicants—and others—succeed in undertaking the significant economic and political reforms demanded by the EU for inclusion, the common "European home" could cover almost the entire continent in the early twenty-first century.

SOURCE: *International Herald Tribune*, 15 December 1997, p. 1.

the eleven members that will officially adopt the euro formed a special euro council to dovetail their economic policies while agreeing to debate decisions with the four members expected to keep their national currencies until at least July 1, 2002, the deadline by which national currencies are to be abolished.

The reforms first associated with the slogan "Europe 1992" promised to move the EU from a **customs union,** permitting the free movement of workers, to a genuine **common market,** in which the financial frontiers between member states are completely abolished. A genuine common market would require the removal of countless transborder inhibitions long apparent in Europe, including restraints on the free exchange of goods. It would also require the harmonization of product standards (e.g., uniform socket sizes for electrical appliances), variations in rules governing taxation and capital movements, regulations on transport standards (e.g., rules governing truckers' driving hours, rest periods, and driving teams), and the like. Such inhibitions safeguard national autonomy and perpetuate nationalistic rivalries; their elimination would further pool sovereignty within the EU. In this context, the substitution

customs union a market in which sovereign states agree to remove taxes on goods exported across the borders of the union's members.

of majority rule in the Council of Ministers for the previous practice of consensus decision making takes on added meaning. Majority rule, reaffirmed in the Single European Act, prevents individual states from vetoing key decisions.

Yet, as noted, because nationalistic resistance continue, more than a few skeptics predict that the EU's ambitious plans will ultimately fail or fall short of the goal of unity, as witnessed by the possibility that the proposed creation of an inner caucus of single-currency countries will open a new division between the EU's members. Although historical forces are driving the integration process forward and national governments have successfully implemented scores of directives issued by the Commission in social, environmental, economic, and monetary policy, many obstacles to the full union of a greater Europe remain.

Europe: A Political Dwarf and a Military Worm?

Since 1970 the EU's members have sought to construct a coordinated and common position on foreign policy issues. This collective spirit, known as **European Political Cooperation (EPC),** emerged at the Paris Summits of 1972 and 1974 to establish regular meetings between EU foreign ministers. Nonetheless, states often went their own way, and members failed to speak with a single voice on foreign policy issues.

Complex issues and barriers confront Europe's efforts to forge what is now known as EU's **Common Foreign and Security Policy (CFSP).** The doctrine's objectives are:

- To safeguard the common values, fundamental interests, and independence of the Union.
- To strengthen the security of the Union and its Member States in all ways.
- To preserve world peace and strengthen international security.
- To promote international cooperation.
- To develop and consolidate democracy and the rule of law, and respect for human rights and fundamental freedoms.

To fulfill these objectives, the EU must redefine and refine its foreign policy mission and identity, as well as reach consensus about its relationship with other European security organizations. Of these, the North Atlantic Treaty Organization (NATO) is the most important.

When the Soviet security threat and the Cold War ended, the EU's diverse members no longer had a common external challenge to unite them, and NATO's very survival became a subject of debate. Since then, however, the NATO allies have reaffirmed their commitment to a broadened agenda for the defense organization. At the October 1993 summit in Travemuende, Germany, the NATO defense ministers endorsed a U.S. plan known as the **Partnership for Peace (PFP),** which offered limited military NATO "partnerships" to virtually any European country interested, including Russia and the former Warsaw Pact states. The eager new partners began participating in NATO peacekeeping missions and crisis-management operations, even though they were not given the same commitment to defend their borders that NATO's full members were guaranteed. The new plan helped to alleviate fears that the alliance would disintegrate, given the hapless way in which the whole EU and NATO had slept when southern Europe was splintering in the former Yugoslavia prior to U.S. intervention. The PFP also prepared the way for the

1997 admission of Poland, Hungary, and the Czech Republic to full membership status, although this extensive enlargement heightened Russian fears of exclusion and encirclement (see Chapter 15). And the PFP laid the groundwork at the August 1997 Madrid Summit for creation of the **Euro-Atlantic Partnership Council (EAPC),** which replaced the PFP with "stronger, more cooperative partnerships . . . in decision taking through new mechanisms for consultations and political guidance 'on a qualitatively new level'" among fifty-one states.

The ten-country European military pact known as the **Western European Union (WEU)** is another symbol of the EU's proclaimed resolve to act in unity on defense problems. The WEU, which in 1994 made nine former Warsaw Pact countries associate partners, could eventually emerge as the military arm of the European Union and reduce European military dependence on the United States. The forty-member **Council of Europe,** founded in 1949 to promote greater unity and to safeguard Europe's cultural heritage, also plays an advisory role in European decision making. However, there is little urgency to develop closer military cooperation among EU members because NATO takes the lead in this area of policy making. The countries of Europe find themselves involved in a variety of overlapping security organizations, and critics point out that this very complexity interferes with the creation and coordination of a common European security policy (see Figure 6.7).

Closer cooperation on foreign and national security policy is a prerequisite to achieving the dream of a "United States of Europe." Differences continue to make a unified EU foreign and defense policy elusive, and even the form of a potential European government for a common European citizenship remains a divisive, unresolved issue. Still, the idea of a single Europe remains compelling for many Europeans who are haunted by the specter of European nationalities and states that have been fighting each other ever since the Pax Romana collapsed eighteen hundred years ago. Consolidation could be in Europe's future. But so could disintegration and the resurrection of intra-European discord and perhaps even a surge of civil wars.

• • •

OTHER REGIONAL ORGANIZATIONS

Since Europe's 1950s initiatives toward economic and political integration, a dozen or so regional economic schemes have been created in various other parts of the world, notably among states in the Global South. Most seek to stimulate regional economic growth. The major regional organizations in the Global South include:

- The Asia-Pacific Economic Cooperation (APEC) forum, created in 1989 as a gathering of twelve states without a defined goal. APEC's membership has grown to eighteen countries (including the United States) that collectively account for 40 percent of the globe's population and more than half of global gross domestic product. At its November 1994 meeting in Jakarta, APEC set for itself the explicit goal of free trade.

- The Association of South East Asian Nations (ASEAN), established in 1967 to promote regional economic, social, and cultural cooperation by seven founding members. ASEAN met in August 1995 to discuss the possibility of closer ties and an eventual merger between a planned free-trade zone among the ten countries in Southeast Asia and a similar zone that already

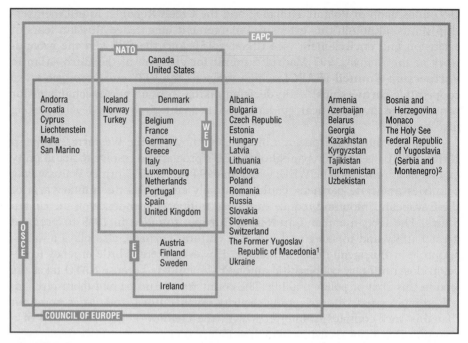

FIGURE 6.7

The Criss-Crossing Membership of Europe's Primary International Institutions, 1998

Since World War II, Europe has built, in a series of steps, an increasing number of political, military, and economic organizations, encompassing more and more countries throughout an enlarged geographic network of institutions. The overlapping architecture includes OSCE, NATO, EAPC, the Council of Europe, the EU, and the Western European Union defense organizations. As Anne-Else Holjberg in NATO's Political Affairs Division complained in 1997, "there is still a certain degree of rivalry between [these] different organizations," and the multilayered structure has made collective decision making difficult.

[1]Turkey recognizes the Republic of Macedonia by its constitutional name.
[2]Suspended.
SOURCE: *NATO Review*, Vol. 45 (July–August 1997), pp. 14–15.

exists between Australia and New Zealand. The purpose of this plan is to operate as a counterweight outside the orbit of Japan, China, the United States, and the other great powers.

- The Caribbean Community and Common Market (CARICOM), established in 1973 to promote economic development and integration among its fourteen members.

- The Council of Arab Economic Unity (CAEU), established in 1964 from a 1957 accord to promote economic integration among its twelve Arab members.

- The Economic Community of West African States (ECOWAS), established in 1975 to promote regional economic cooperation among its seventeen members.

- The Organization of the Islamic Conference (OIC), coordinates a large number of activities among fifty Islamic states (plus the Palestine Liberation Organization) for the purpose of promoting Islamic solidarity in economic, social, cultural and political affairs. While not technically a regional IGO, the OIC orchestrates preventive diplomacy, but does not condone the use of terrorism, and is not concerned with promoting fundamentalist Islamic religious principles.

- The Latin American Integration Association (LAIA), also known as *Asociación Latinoamericana de Integración* (ALADI), established in 1981 to promote freer regional trade among its eleven members.

- The Southern African Development Community (SADC), established in 1992 to promote regional economic development and integration among its twelve members.

- The South Asian Association for Regional Cooperation (SAARC), established in 1985 to promote economic, social, and cultural cooperation among its seven members.

It is hazardous to generalize about organizations as widely divergent in membership and sometimes in purpose as this list suggests (for comparisons with other regional IGOs, see the U.S. CIA 1998 *World Factbook*). None has achieved anything approaching the same level of economic integration and supranational institution building as the EU. The particular reasons underlying the modest success of the attempts vary, of course (see Chapter 16), but they share a common denominator: national leaders' reluctance to make politically costly choices that would undermine their personal popularity at home and governments' sovereignty. Nonetheless, these attempts at regional cooperation demonstrate many states' acceptance of the fact that they cannot individually resolve many of the problems that confront them collectively.

Because the state is clearly failing to manage many transnational policy problems, it finds itself ironically acting as the primary agent of the same cooperative management efforts that are eroding the state's power. Collective problem solving through the growth and expanding power of IGOs is likely to continue. Globalization and the force of a shrinking, borderless world are increasing the influence of international institutions, and, in turn, IGOs' expanding webs of interdependence are infringing on the power of states and changing the ways in which they network on the global stage. These IGOs and processes promise to transform world politics, which is why "almost any discussion of public policy nowadays seems to begin and end with the same idea: The state is in retreat [and] its power to rule is fading" (Crook 1997). Another set of agents in the transnational transformation and globalization of world politics—nonstate actors such as NGOs, ethnonational movements, and multinational corporations—are also highly active and increasingly influential. In Chapter 7 we turn our attention to their behavior and impact.

KEY TERMS

intergovernmental organizations (IGOs)
nongovernmental organizations (NGOs)
United Nations (UN)
collective security
consensus decision making
failed states
European Union (EU)
European Community (EC)

Organization for Security and Cooperation in Europe (OSCE)
European Commission
pooled sovereignty
European Free Trade Association (EFTA)
Lomé Convention
customs union
common market

European Political Cooperation (EPC)
Common Foreign and Security Policy (CFSP)
Partnership for Peace (PFP)
Euro-Atlantic Partnership Council (EAPC)
Western European Union (WEU)
Council of Europe

Coate, Roger A., and Craig Murphy, eds. *Global Governance* [Annual journal published quarterly]. Boulder, Colo.: Lynne Rienner.

Claude, Inis L., Jr., *Swords into Plowshares: The Problems and Progress of International Organizations.* New York: Random House, 1984.

Diehl, Paul F., ed. *The Politics of Global Governance: International Organization in an Interdependent World.* Boulder, Colo.: Lynne Rienner, 1997.

Keohane, Robert O. "International Institutions: Can Interdependence Work?," *Foreign Policy* 110 (Spring 1998): 82–96.

Kuehls, Thom. *Beyond Sovereign Territory.* Minneapolis: University of Minnesota Press, 1996.

Mingst, Karen A., and Margaret P. Karns. *The United Nations in the Post-Cold War Era.* Boulder, Colo.: Westview, 1995.

Murphy, Craig N. *International Organization and Industrial Change: Global Governance Since 1850.* New York: Oxford University Press, 1994.

Piening, Christopher. *Global Europe: The European Union in World Affairs.* Boulder, Colo.: Lynne Rienner, 1998.

Riggs, Robert E., and Jack C. Plano. *The United Nations: International Organization and World Politics*, 2nd ed. Belmont, Calif.: Wadsworth, 1994.

Ruggle, John Gerald. *Constructing the World Polity: Essays on International Institutionalization.* London: Routledge, 1998.

Taylor, Paul. *International Organization in the Modern World: The Regional and Global Process.* London: Pinter, 1993.

Weiss, Thomas G., David P. Forsythe, and Roger A. Coate. *The United Nations and Changing World Politics.* Boulder, Colo.: Westview, 1997.

WHERE ON THE WORLD WIDE WEB?

The following are examples of different international organizations' Web sites for intergovernmental organizations (IGOs) like those described in Table 6.1.

http://www.un.org/
The United Nations The United Nations (UN) is an IGO with global membership which performs multiple purposes. Visit the "Audio, Visual, Webcast" area from the UN's homepage for interesting pictures and sound videos.

http://www.imf.org/exteranl/about.htm
International Monetary Fund The International Monetary Fund (IMF) is an IGO with global membership that performs a single purpose. The IMF was created to promote international monetary cooperation and facilitate the expansion and balanced growth of international trade. It does this by promoting exchange stability by making monetary resources temporarily available to its members. Click on the "Lending" link on the IMF's homepage. Which countries have received the most IMF support? Why do you think this is so?

http://www.who.ch/
World Health Organization The main goal of the World Health Organization (WHO) is the attainment by all peoples of the highest possible level of health. They define health as the "state of complete physical, mental, and social well-being and not merely the absence of disease or infirmity." The WHO has been hailed as one of the best examples of how an international organization can benefit the world community. Review WHO's major achievements and the challenges it faces. Do you think it is possible for the WHO to achieve its goals? Do you agree with its expanded definition of health to include social well-being?

http://www.oas.org/
Organization of American States The Organization of American States (OAS) is an IGO with regional membership that serves multiple purposes. It is the "principal forum in the hemisphere for political, economic, and social dialogue." As you can see from the homepage, the OAS is concerned with issues such as democracy, human rights, trade, environment, and education. It sees its major challenges as drugs, corruption, poverty, and landmines. Explore one of these

challenges. How might the United States and other hemispheric countries differ in their views of the challenge and the best way to solve it?

http://www.nato.int

North Atlantic Treaty Organization The North Atlantic Treaty Organization (NATO) is an IGO with a regional scope and a single purpose. NATO is a military alliance which includes the European states, the United States, and Canada. It was originally formed to protect Europe from the Soviet threat after World War II. Since the end of the Cold War, it has been restructured and now has an auxiliary membership with the establishment of the Partnership for Peace (PFP). To see PFP's membership, click on "Welcome to NATO" link from the NATO homepage and then click on the "Partnership for Peace" area in the image map. What characteristics do the 27 PFP member countries share?

http://www.organic.com/Non.profits/Amnesty/index.html

Amnesty International Amnesty International (AI) is an international Nongovernmental International Organization (NGO) with a global reach and a specific purpose. Its activities are concentrated on prisoners around the world who are detained solely for their beliefs, color, sex, ethnic origin, language, or religion. Amnesty International advocates the release of all prisoners of conscience, the availability of a fair and prompt trial for political prisoners, and the abolishment of the death penalty, torture, and other cruel and inhuman treatment of prisoners. Go to "The Amnesty Gallery" and click on photos to read and hear real-life stories of individuals who were unjustly detained.

CHAPTER 7

Nongovernmental Actors on the World Stage

•••

The protection of the nation against destruction from without and disruption from within is the overriding concern. . . . Nothing can be tolerated that might threaten the coherence of the nation.

—HANS J. MORGENTHAU,
realist scholar, 1967

•••

Economic and technological forces all over the globe are compelling the world toward integration while ethnic and religious tensions tear nations apart.

—BILL CLINTON,
U.S. president, 1993

CHAPTER TOPICS AND THEMES

■ Nongovernmental organizations (NGOs): Their diversity and global role

■ Politically active minority-group challengers to the state:

- Ethnopolitical national groups
- The Fourth World in international relations: Indigenous and displaced peoples

■ Religious movements

■ International terrorists

■ Multinational corporations (MNCs)

■ NGOs and the strangulation of the state: Solution or problem for global stability?

A large number of people throughout the world regard themselves as participants in the international arena, because they are involved as members in one or more of the literally thousands of "nongovernmental organizations" (NGOs) (see Chapter 6). These are private international actors whose members are not states, but are instead volunteers drawn from the populations of two or more states who form organizations to promote their shared ideals and interests by influencing the policies of national governments and intergovernmental organizations (IGOs). These NGOs tackle many global problems such as disarmament, crime, environmental deterioration, and human rights abuses. Their contribution has often been impressively constructive to the promotion of high ideals. For example, NGOs such as Amnesty International, the International Chamber of Commerce, Greenpeace, the Red Cross, Save the Children, the World Wildlife Federation, and the Union of Concerned Scientists work with both states and IGOs, and their efforts have led to the successful creation of *regimes* or sets of rules that help to regulate many transnational problems. At the same time, a large number of NGOs are composed of minority racial or religious groups whose demands shake the sovereign control of fragile or failing states and lead to a devolution of power within many other strong states.

This chapter will bring into perspective **nonstate entities** as actors in world politics, a category that includes many types of actors.

> The term "nonstate entity" covers an enormously broad range of groups. On the most basic level, nonstate entities are associations of individuals and/or groups that are not established by agreements among states. This broad definition includes such disparate entities as transnational corporations and the business associations they establish to promote their interests, professional associations, ethnic groups, major religious organizations, terrorist groups, and social movements. (Riddell-Dixon 1995, 289)

While the stories of these diverse groups of NGOs are rich (and growing), this chapter will concentrate only on the major NGOs whose political pressure on states to accept their claims arouses the most debate worldwide. This selective focus is justified because today a small subset of increasingly active and self-assertive major **nonstate actors** provoke the most controversy. To simplify our task, we will thus examine four of the most visible politically active nonstate actors: ethnopolitical groups, religious movements, terrorists, and multinational corporations.

In examining these four major categories of NGO actors, consider whether world politics is undergoing a transformation as these political units compete for influence with the territorial state, which has been dominant for the past three centuries. The question is critically important because if, in the future, nonstate actors gain greater autonomy and power over states' resources and policy making, the state-centric structure of the international system will corrode, and the consequences of eroding state sovereignty are difficult to predict. The activities of these four NGOs have been responsible in many ways for increasingly calling into question the idea that the state has full and exclusive control over its destiny. NGOs are making borders porous and states vulnerable both to external pressures and to challenges from *within* their boundaries.

> Today the state-centric world no longer predominates. The skill revolution, the worldwide authority crises, and other sources of turbulence have led to

a bifurcation of the international system into two global structures, one the long-standing state-centric world of sovereign states and the other a complex multicentric world of diverse, relatively autonomous actors replete with structures, processes, and rules of their own in "globalized space." The actors of the multicentric world consist of NGOs, multinational corporations, ethnic minorities, subnational governments and bureaucracies, professional societies, incipient communities, and the like. Individually, and sometimes jointly, they compete, conflict, cooperate, or otherwise interact with the sovereignty-bound actors of the state-centric world. (Rosenau 1998, 159)

Let us look at the major NGOs to better evaluate whether they are contributing to the erosion of state sovereignty.

• • •

POLITICALLY ACTIVE MINORITY GROUPS: ETHNOPOLITICAL NATIONALISTS AND INDIGENOUS PEOPLES IN THE FOURTH WORLD

On the surface, the images of the all-powerful state and of governments as sovereign and autonomous rulers of unified nations are not very satisfactory. These images exaggerate the extent to which the state resembles a **unitary actor,** as realists often ask us to picture it. In truth, the unitary actor conception is misleading, because many states are divided internally and highly penetrated from abroad, and few are tightly unified and capable of acting as a single unit with a common purpose.

Many political scientists see a pressing "need to deal with the consequences of the declining ability of various governments to govern," and to confront the fact that one of the main forces contributing to "the erosion of effective government and of public confidence in government is the seeming insolvable nature of ethnic and religious differences that make political and social peace in more and more states a problematic exercise" (Shultz and Olson 1994). It has also been suggested that we must face the possibility that the "omnipotent state" of this century is a "historical anomaly" that "may be sickly and pale" because "nationalism is on the rise" (Mead 1995).

unitary actor the perception of states as culturally and racially homogeneous, solidified in their joint pursuit of common internal and foreign policy objectives.

Nationalism, Nationality, and Ethnicity

Although the state unquestionably remains the most visible actor in world affairs, **nationalism** and nationality are potent cultural factors defining the core loyalties and identities of many people that influence how states act. Many people pledge their primary allegiance not to the state and government that rules them, but rather to the politically active minority group with which they most associate themselves. One broad category of such national groups is **ethnopolitical groups** whose members share a common nationality, language, cultural tradition, and kinship ties. They view themselves as members of their nationality first and of their state only secondarily—a definition that follows the interpretation of E. K. Francis (1976) who maintains that "cultural affinities manifest in shared linguistic, religious, racial, or other markers . . . enable one community to distinguish itself from others." As Okwudiba Nnoli (1993) elaborates on the meaning of ethnonationalism, **ethnicity** is "a phenomenon associated with contact between cultural-linguistic communal groups . . . characterized by cultural prejudice and social discrimination. Underlying these characteristics are the feelings of pride in the in-group, and the exclusiveness of its members. It is a phenomenon linked . . . to forms of affiliation and identification built around ties of real or putative kinship."

Acknowledgment of the importance of **ethnic nationalism** (people's loyalty to and identification with a particular ethnic nationality groups) in world affairs reduces the relevance of the unitary state. Many states are divided, multiethnic societies made up of a variety of politically active groups that seek, if not outright independence, a greater level of regional autonomy and a greater voice in the social and foreign policies of the state. In the mid–1990s "of the world's 190 countries, 120 had politically significant minorities" (Gurr 1998, 199). Of 305 active minority groups that were at risk from persecution worldwide, 37 were ethnonational groups, 70 indigenous nations, and 44 national minorities. Relations between **ethnic groups** are also vitally important, as contact is customarily widespread between groups who define their identity by their common ancestry. These divisions and the lack of unity within states make thinking of international relations as exclusively interactions between unified states dubious.

The Fourth World. The globe is populated by an estimated six thousand separate indigenous nations, each of which has "a unique language and culture and strong, often spiritual, ties to an ancestral homeland. In most cases indigenous people were at one time politically sovereign and economically self-sufficient." Today there are an estimated 300 million indigenous people, more than 5 percent of the world's population (some have placed the number as high as 600 million) (Watson 1997, 389).

Indigenous peoples often feel persecuted because they are not permitted full political participation and representation in the states where they reside, and in some cases they feel that their livelihoods, lands, cultures, and lives are threatened. This segment of global society is conventionally referred to as the **Fourth World** to heighten awareness of "native" or "tribal" **indigenous peoples** within many countries, the poverty and deprivation that confronts them, the state's occupation of the land from which they originate, and the methods to combat discrimination these movements are pursuing (Wilmer 1993). Aroused nationalists are now fighting back across the globe in rebellion against the injustice, misery, and prejudice they perceive the state to have perpetrated against them. The pervasiveness of ethnic nations alongside states is so commonplace that many feel the voice of the people behind the indigenous national movements they lead must be given its due.

Fourth World liberation movements are active in many countries throughout the globe. "For most indigenous peoples, the central issue in this clash of civilizations is land" (Watson 1997). Most seek a state or, more often, a regional government, of their own. In part, this quest is inspired by and is a reaction to the evidence that between 1900 and 1987 about 130 million indigenous people were slaughtered by state-sponsored **genocide** in their own countries (Rummel 1994). As Table 7.1 shows, friction escalating to war between indigenous nations and the state occurs in many countries. In other areas, conflicts below the threshold of overt armed violence are heated and activism appears to be growing.

This is not to suggest that all indigenous groups are bent on tearing existing states apart, or on using violence to attain power. The members of many such

Fourth World a term used to recognize that native nationalities reside in many so-called united states who, although often minorities, occupied the state's territory first and refuse to accept their domination. In rebellion against discrimination, they see the state as "divisible" and either seek to create a new state for themselves by splitting existing states or to gain greater political freedom to govern themselves. This term is also sometimes used to describe the "poorest of the poor" less developed countries of the Global South.

Many subnational groups of nations and indigenous peoples reside on the territory of existing states which govern them. To protect their human rights and national identity, Fourth World groups have organized meetings such as the World Conference of Indigenous Peoples in Rio de Janeiro, Brazil, in May 1992. As a result of their lobbying, the UN named 1993 the International Year of the World's Indigenous Peoples.

movements are divided about objectives, and militants who are prepared to fight for greater autonomy are usually in a minority within these groups. In fact, most Fourth World indigenous movements are committed to gaining substate autonomy, not sovereignty, and seek only more representative clout in redirecting the policies and allocation of resources within existing states. Increasingly, these repressed Fourth World minorities are using the conventional tactics of social movements (such as mass mobilization and protest), and are eliciting the support of NGOs and IGOs to pressure states to recognize their claims and protect their civil liberties and human rights. Moreover, a substantial number of indigenous movements in the last decade have negotiated settlements resulting in devolution by the state, in which the protagonists gained concessions for greater local political power in exchange for accepting the sovereignty of the state. Examples include the Miskitos in Nicaragua, the Gagauz in Moldova, most regional separatists in Ethiopia, and others in India's Assam region.

It is difficult to foresee what the post-Cold War wave of internal discontent and rise of politically active minority protests will ultimately bring. Many have spawned governmental decentralization, weakened the sovereign authority of states, and compounded leaders' difficulties in constructing a coherent foreign policy that adequately represents diverse ethnic and minority interests. But on the whole, **devolution**—the granting of political power to ethnopolitical national groups and indigenous peoples—has served more often to keep countries together rather than break them up. The devolution and decentralization of state control in response to minority discontent has *strengthened* the state in the European region where separatist movements have been especially rampant in the 1990s since the Cold War glue of state loyalties dissolved. For instance, the separatist Northern League has made electoral inroads, but devolution from Rome has solidified the national unity of Italy. Likewise, the September 1997 decision by three-fourths of Scotland's voters to establish their own parliament was interpreted by Scottish nationalists as a bold step toward dissolving the union with the United Kingdom by creating an independent Scotland with the size and wealth of Denmark or Ireland. However, here and

TABLE 7.1 States and Indigenous Peoples at War, 1996–1997

Country	Groups in Conflict	Group Objectives[1]	Year Begun
Myanmar (Burma)	Karens, Kayah, Mons, Shans	Autonomy or independence	1948
Myanmar	Wa	Autonomy or independence	1996
Pakistan	Mohajirs	Greater share of state power	1986
Papua New Guinea	Bougainvilleans	Autonomy or independence	1988
Philippines	Moros	Autonomy or independence	1970
Sri Lanka	Tamils	Independence	1985
Thailand	Malay Muslims	Cultural/religious autonomy	1981
North Africa and the Middle East			
Israel-Occupied Territories	Palestinians	Independence	1964
Iran, Iraq, Turkey	Kurds	Autonomy or independence	1984
Iraq	Shi'a	Greater share of state power	1991
Sub-Saharan Africa			
Angola	Cabindans	Independence	1992
Burundi	Hutus	Greater share of political power	1993
Central African Republic	Yakoma	Greater share of political power	1996
Congo (Brazzaville)	Lari, M'Boshi	Control of the state	1993
Ethiopia	Afars, Oromo	Regional autonomy	1991
Rwanda	Hutus	Regain control of the state	1994
Senegal	Casamançais	Regional autonomy	1982
Sierra Leone	Temne	Greater share of political power	1991
Sudan	Dinka, Shilluk, Nuba and others	Autonomy or independence	1983
Zaire (Democratic Republic of Congo)	Banyamulenge, easterners	Control of the state (rebels won May 1997	1996
Western Democracies and Japan			
Spain	Basques	Independence	1959
United Kingdom	Catholics in N. Ireland	Unification with Republic of Ireland	1968
Eastern Europe and Former Soviet States			
Azerbaijan	Armenians	Unification with Armenia	1988
Russia	Chechens	Autonomy or independence	1991
Asia			
Afghanistan	Pashtuns, Tajiks, Uzbeks, Hazaras	Greater share of state power	1992
Bangladesh	Chakma	Autonomy or independence	1975
Bhutan	Lhotshampas	Greater share of state power	1989
China	Uighers	Autonomy or independence	1980
India	Assamese	Autonomy or independence	1979
India	Bodos	Regional autonomy	1989
India	Kashmiris	Autonomy or independence	1990
India	Nagas	Independence	1952
India	Tripuras	Autonomy or independence	1952
Indonesia	East Timorese	Autonomy or independence	1975
Indonesia	Papuans	Autonomy or independence	1963
Laos	Hmong	Greater share of state power	1963–64
Latin America and the Caribbean			
Guatemala	Mayans	Greater share of political power	1972
Mexico	Mayans, Zapotecs, other indigenous peoples	Autonomy and greater share of political power	1994

[1]National people often claim the right to independence but settle for greater regional autonomy. Many members of the groups listed here do not support the use of armed violence as a means to achieve group objectives.

Note: Table created by Anne M. Pitsch and Ted Robert Gurr using the Minorities at Risk database. The Minorities at Risk web site is located at <http://www.bsos.umd.edu/cidcm/mar>.

elsewhere in Europe (as in France, where the state government in Paris has loosened its grip through devolution to pacify nationalist separatist movements by creating twenty-two new mainland regions with their own budgets), experience

> suggests that devolution has proved widely popular without generally leading to secession; indeed, it can help to hold a country together. When strong regional or national identities, silent or suppressed for many years, are suddenly given a voice, the paradoxical result has often been greater harmony and a greater desire to stick together rather than anguish, chaos and disintegration. The end of the Cold War and the inexorable rise of the European Union have both weakened the grip of Europe's main states but without threatening to break them up, except when involuntary unions fragmented after communists lost control. (*Economist*, September 20, 1997, 53)

Europe—one of the world's most stable but ethnopolitcally divided regions—could well signal the path other regions could travel in the twenty-first century.

Ethnopolitical Challengers to the State. The many Fourth World challengers to the state defy characterization because they are too diverse and distinctions between indigenous peoples and national minorities are hard to draw. Thus it is extremely difficult to classify and count the abundant variety of politically active movements by **nonstate nations** (Bertelsen 1977) struggling for power and/or statehood. While counting their numbers is difficult, perhaps the best way of making a rough estimate is by observing linguistic similarity. A huge number of ethnolinguistic divisions separate cultures. "Measured by spoken languages, the single best indicator of a distinct culture, all the world's people belong to 6,000 cultures; 4,000 to 5,000 of these are indigenous ones. Of the [nearly 6] billion humans on the planet, some 190 to 625 million are indigenous people" (Durning 1993, 81).

Still, this indicator may be somewhat misleading, since the belief systems and backgrounds that incite ethnopolitical movements by indigenous peoples are varied and often overlapping. Beyond language, these movements are based on numerous combinations of cultural, racial, and religious orientations. This is why indigenous ethnopolitical movements pursue many different goals.

One characteristic of ethnopolitical movements stands out as a defining attribute amidst these differences: Most transcend the existing borders that separate the more than 190 sovereign states currently recognized as independent under the rules of international law. Because indigenous peoples are scattered not only within state boundaries but also across them, they form transnational **cultural domains** that share a common intellectual heritage and place higher values on ideals other than patriotic loyalty to particular states (see Map 7.1). One scenario is that the future will be darkened by violent clashes between these transnational cultures or "world civilizations" every bit as destabilizing and destructive as the Cold War's East-West ideological clash. According to this proposition, first popularized by Samuel Huntington (1996), the main fault line dividing the globe and the chief source of international conflict "will not be primarily ideological or economic," but rather cultural, between "nations and groups of different civilizations." In his view, the coming **clash of civilizations**

clash of civilizations political scientist Samuel Huntington's controversial thesis that in the twenty-first century the globe's major civilizations will conflict with one another, leading to anarchy and warfare similar to that resulting from conflicts between states over the past six thousand years.

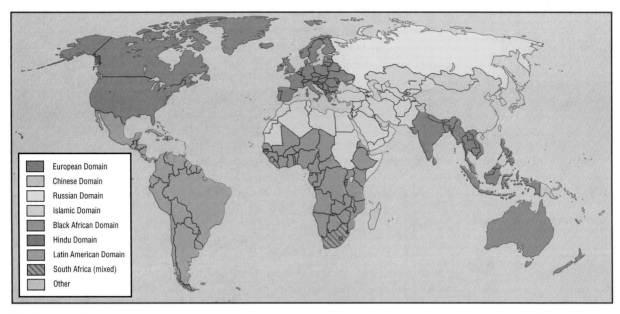

MAP 7.1

The World's Great Cultural Domains

The globe is culturally pluralistic, composed of at least eight distinct sets of value traditions. This map shows one estimate of the major cultural domains and areas where these are dominant.

SOURCE: Adapted from Chaliand and Rageau (1993), p. 37.

will be between and among seven or eight major civilizations (Western, Confucian, Japanese, Islamic, Hindu, Slavic-Orthodox, Latin American, and possibly African), as well as less influential ones such as a poorly integrated Afro-Caribbean tradition.

National Disintegration and Global Instability

In many cases, Fourth World political activism has resulted in the devolution of state sovereignty and fragmentation of the territorial integrity of existing states. In those countries where indigenous minority groups have gained a grant of internal self-government, the achievement of a measure of quasi-autonomy and a homeland relatively secure from persecution has fostered the protection of human rights and, ironically, has strengthened the state because formerly separatist peoples have been provided joint institutions of governance. However, in less stable countries balkanization, disunion, and even anarchy has resulted.

When people identify with the culture of their nationality more intensely than they do with their country, separatist revolts by peoples struggling for **self-determination,** the pursuit of self-rule, can be expected. Keep in mind that indigenous peoples are highly mobilized because "they were largely pushed to inaccessible and unproductive lands by earlier waves of colonization [and] now find that even these lands are coveted by outsiders" (Watson 1997). In response, they have pursued self-determination to protect themselves and control the re-

181

sources of their territories. This quest for greater self-governance can some-times be achieved through the peaceful separation of formerly unified states, as almost happened in November 1995 when a slim majority of Quebec's voters upheld Canadian unity, and *did* occur in Czechoslovakia on December 31, 1992, when that country split peacefully, through the so-called "velvet divorce," into the independent Czech Republic and Slovakia. However, aroused nationalist passions can also escalate to violence, as evidenced by the bloody warfare that racked the former Yugoslavia beginning in 1991. Both the Bosnian Serbs and Croats committed atrocities in the name of **ethnic cleansing**—a program of terror, destruction, and murder designed to force out the rival nationality. The tribal warfare in Burundi, Somalia, and Rwanda also epitomizes the horror that results when ancient hatreds erupt into warfare.

These divisions of states into segregated fragments along ethnic and cul-tural lines are different from the *political* partitions that resulted in the division of Korea, Vietnam, Germany, and China into separate states. Many states, in short, are inherently fragile, because they are weak coalitions of multiple na-tionalities that can splinter (Chatterjee 1993). Consider the degree to which mi-nority groups compose many states; for example, the share of indigenous popu-lations in Bolivia is 70 percent; Peru, 40 percent; Mexico, 12 percent; the Philippines, 9 percent; Canada, 4 percent. Cultural diversity is also captured by the number of distinct languages spoken in "megadiversity" countries, of which Indonesia's 670, Nigeria's 410, India's 380, Australia's 250, and Brazil's 210 are exceptional examples (Durning 1993, 83, 86). To speak of these states as cultur-ally, linguistically, or politically "united" would be an exaggeration. Forging a consensus behind a consistent foreign policy is a challenge for many nationally diverse countries, because a definition of state interests that represents the di-vergent needs of minority populations is inherently difficult.

The long-term conflict between the Palestine Liberation Organization (PLO) and the state of Israel illustrates the potential for very different kinds of consequences to result from the existence of Fourth World ethnic pluralism. For four decades the Palestinian nation sought by every means available, in-cluding terrorism and war, to create a state from the territories that Israel claimed and controlled. That search destroyed life but failed to create indepen-dence. Then, through dialogue and negotiation, they sought to produce a com-prehensive peace accord in September 1993. Israel and Jordan then agreed to permit the Palestinians to form a government and create a new state in the West Bank territory, which was returned to them by Israel. The accord symbol-ized the possibility for nationalities to become independent states through dis-cussion and compromise rather than force and provides a potential model for other independence movements. But the peace process fell apart in the wake of the assassination of Israeli Prime Minister Yitzhak Rabin by a Jewish extremist in November 1995.

Racism and intolerance could spawn a new era of tribal terrorism and war-fare. In this grim scenario, the lack of the Cold War stalemate to hold such eth-nic conflicts in check will render states powerless to suppress ancient rivalries and animosities. The ethnic wars between Armenians and Azerbaijanis in 1993, which brought Russia, Turkey, and Iran perilously close to combat, and the sep-aratist revolt in Georgia to create an independent state of Abkazia, foreshadow future transpolitical ethnic turmoil in many other places. Russia appears par-ticularly vulnerable to ethnopolitical revolts in the nine republics where Rus-sians make up less than fifty percent of the population. If and where disintegra-

Hate and hostility have traditionally led to terrorism and genocide. Racial and ethnic prejudice have commonly led to intercommunal warfare, such as the U.S. government's policy of expulsion and extermination of Native Americans, Fascist Germany's annihilation of 6 million Jews, and Japan's death marches and enslavement of those it conquered in the early victories of World War II. More recently, in 1994 ethnic conflict escalated to genocide in Rwanda as the Hutu militia attacked the Tutsi, and later as the Tutsi-dominated Rwandan Patriotic Front retaliated against the Hutus. This photo depicts the results of one such bloodbath, where as many as 1 million Tutsis died.

tion results in the future, the earth's territorial boundaries will have to be redrawn by cartographers.

Although **interethnic competition** is a phenomenon that dates back to Biblical times, it is a plague of the post-World War II era. Some of the most explosive flashpoints in the world are the products of disputes between groups in multiethnic and culturally heterogenous countries, such as Afghanistan, Belgium, Canada, Nigeria, Russia, Somalia, Spain, Sri Lanka, and the United Kingdom, to name a few. Ethnopolitical cleavages have produced a surge of serious conflicts since 1945. According to *The Minorities at Risk Project* (see Gurr 1993), over three hundred ethnopolitical minority groups facing discrimination have been involved in serious, often violent, struggles between 1945 and 1997, and the trend has steadily accelerated since the 1960s (see Figure 7.1). Consider 1994, a year in which "all but five of the 23 wars fought [were] based on communal rivalries and ethnic challenges to states. About three-quarters of the world's refugees, estimated at nearly 27 million people, [were] in flight from or [were] displaced by these ethnic conflicts. Eight of the United Nations' 13 peacekeeping operations [were] aimed at separating the protagonists in ethnopolitical conflicts" (Gurr 1993, 350).

The inherent **ethnocentrism** underlying ethnonationalism—the belief that one's nationality is special and superior and that others are secondary and inferior—breeds ethnic conflict. Nationalists find it easy to condone marginalizing and oppressing "outside" nationalities, and ethnocentric peoples are prone to

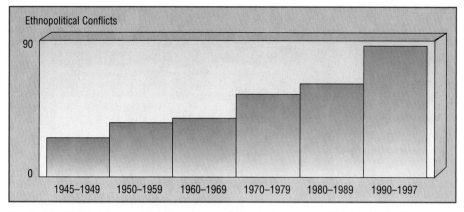

FIGURE 7.1

Ethnopolitical Minority Groups Involved in Serious Conflicts since 1945

Since World War II, over three hundred ethnopolitical groups have been involved in serious conflicts. The frequency of these cultural conflicts has steadily risen, reaching epidemic proportions since the Cold War ended. Ethnic conflicts are now a primary cause of mass violence in the world.

SOURCE: *Minorities at Risk Project*, with data provided courtesy of Ted Robert Gurr, updating his previous studies (1994, 1997, 1998).

reject conciliation and compromise with other nationalities. This barrier to co-operation and its conflict-generating consequences was highly evident between 1993 and 1995 in the crumbling peace talks and escalating warfare in the Balkans, as negotiations among the Serbs, Croats, and Bosnians produced no concessions until NATO used force to propel the combatants to the bargaining table. In December 1997 it appeared that this barrier to the resumption of fighting would collapse after the external peacekeeping forces from NATO began to withdraw, but the probability of a blood bath declined when the United States, France, and their interventionary troops pledged to continue to police the explosive situation.

If ethnonationalist values spread and intensify, it is possible that violence will spread also. If so, the forces of disunion and disintegration could overwhelm the power of the state, which has previously bound diverse nationalities into a common purpose. To the extent that conflict within and between ethnically disunited and divided states becomes a major axis on which twenty-first-century world politics revolves, the power and independence of the state can be expected to decline exponentially in a new era of global anarchy or lawlessness (Barber 1995). The perils should not be underestimated. As Russian Foreign Minister Andrei V. Kozyrev warned the United Nations in September 1993, the threat of ethnic violence today is "no less serious than the threat of nuclear war was yesterday." The existence of over three hundred politically active national minority movements in two-thirds of the globe's states (Gurr 1998) alongside three to five thousand ethnolinguistic groups in the world (Nietschmann 1991) punctuates the potential peril of future separatist rebellion, as does the evidence that between 1945 and 1997 about one-third of all armed conflicts were internal resistance or secession revolts (see Chapter 12).

RELIGIOUS MOVEMENTS

In theory, religion would seem a natural worldwide force for global unity and harmony. Yet millions have died in the name of religion. The Crusades between the eleventh and fourteenth centuries were originally justified by Pope Urban II in 1095 to combat Muslim aggression, but the fighting left millions of Christians and Muslims dead and, "in terms of atrocities, the two sides were about even [as both religions embraced] an ideology in which fighting was an act of self-sanctification" (*Economist*, January 5, 1996). Similarly, the "not-so-holy wars" in the religious conflicts during the Thirty Years' War (1618–1648) between Christian Catholics and Protestants killed nearly one-fourth of all Europeans.

A large proportion of the world's nearly 6 billion people is estimated to be members of **religious movements**—politically active organizations based on strong religious convictions. At the most abstract level, a religion is a system of thought shared by a group that provides its members an object of devotion and a code of behavior by which they can ethically judge their actions. This definition points to commonalities across the great diversity of organized religions in the world, but it fails to capture that diversity. The world's principal religions vary greatly in the theological doctrines or beliefs they embrace. They also differ widely in the size of their followings, in the geographical locations where they are most prevalent (see Map 7.2), and in the extent to which they engage in political efforts to direct international affairs.

These differences make it risky to generalize about the impact of religious movements on world affairs. Those who study religious movements comparatively note that a system of belief provides religious followers with their main source of identity, and that this identification with and devotion to their religion springs from the natural human need to find a set of values with which to evaluate the meaning of life and the consequences of choices. Unfortunately this need sometimes leads believers of a religious creed to perceive the values of their own religion as superior to those of others, which often leads to intolerance. The proponents of most religious movements believe that their religion should be universal—that is, accepted by everyone throughout the world. To confirm their faith in their religious movement's natural superiority, many organized religions actively proselytize to convert nonbelievers to their faith, engaging in evangelical crusades to win followers of other religions over to their beliefs. Conversion is usually achieved by persuasion, through missionary activities. But at times conversion has been achieved by the sword, tarnishing the reputations of some international religious movements (see Focus 7.1).

In evaluating the impact of religious movements on international affairs, it is important to distinguish carefully the high ideals of their doctrines from the activities of the people who head these religious bodies. The two realms are not the same, and each can be judged fairly only against the standards they set for themselves. To condemn what large-scale religious movements sometimes do administratively when they abuse the principles of the religions they manage does not mean that the principles themselves deserve condemnation. Moreover, although many students of international relations draw a causal linkage between the activities of religious movements and the outbreak of political conflict and violence (Juergensmeyer 1993; Schwartz 1997), this does not apply to all religions. Consider the Hindu ideology of tolerance of different religions, which teaches that there are many paths to truth, and accepts pluralism among

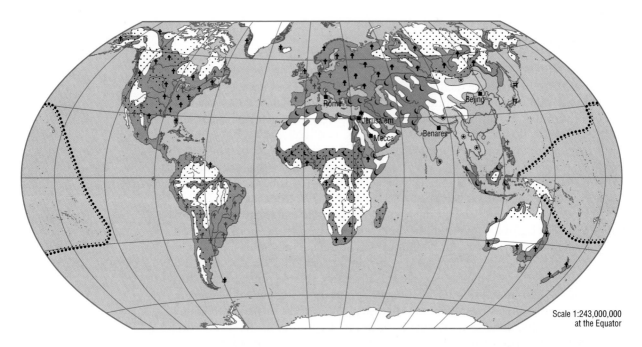

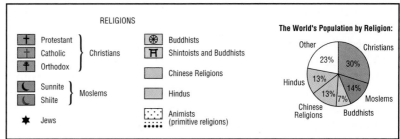

RELIGIONS

✝ Protestant	}	
✝ Catholic	Christians	
✝ Orthodox	}	
☾ Sunnite	} Moslems	
☾ Shiite	}	
★ Jews		

⊛ Buddhists

⊓ Shintoists and Buddhists

Chinese Religions

Hindus

Animists (primitive religions)

The World's Population by Religion:

Other 23%
Christians 30%
Moslems 14%
Buddhists 7%
Chinese Religions 13%
Hindus 13%

M A P   7 . 2

The Geographic Concentration of the World's Principal Religions

People everywhere seek a power higher than themselves to give meaning and purpose to their lives, and accept one or another theological doctrine for these purposes. There are powerful reasons for the quest, because life for many people is shallow without a deity to respect and a code of conduct to honor. This map shows where ten of the world's major religious affiliations have attracted a dominant following.

SOURCE: Adapted from *International Herald Tribune World Atlas*. Copyright, 1994 Lieber Kartor AB and Maps International AB, Stockholm.

diverse populations. Similarly, Buddhism preaches pacifism, as did early Christianity, which prohibited Christians from serving in the armies of the Roman Empire (later, by the fourth century, only Christians were permitted to serve, as church and state became allies). But the propensity for religious institutions to subordinate their beliefs to the state in order to survive and increase public popularity notwithstanding, many observers maintain that otherwise pacificist and humanitarian religions at times are inclined to oppose each other violently, despite their professed tolerant doctrines. When they do, religious movements

Religious Movements

Forces for Transnational Peace and Harmony, or Catalysts to Holy Wars?

High ideals inspire the believers of nearly all the world's major religious movements. Indeed, many of the principles they espouse are very similar: reverence for the sanctity of life, acceptance of all people as creations of the deity as equal (regardless of race or color), and the need for self-sacrifice and compassion. These are noble ideals. They speak to universals across time and place—to enduring values in changing times. Moreover, they recognize no boundaries for their eternal validity—no north, south, east, or west—but only true virtue wherever found, and the relevance of moral precepts (e.g., the prohibition of killing and the value of working for the betterment of humankind) throughout the entire world.

If all the world's great religious movements—approximately 1.8 billion Christians, 972 million Muslims, 733 million Hindus, 315 million Buddhists, and 18 million Jews—espouse universalistic ideals that accept all people's rights, why are some of those same religions often seen as sources of international conflict—of exclusivism, hatred, terror, and war? Sociologists of religion answer that it is because these same universalistic religions are managed by organizations that often adopt a particularistic outlook (see Juergensmeyer 1993; also Schwartz 1997). They conceive the world and history through an ideological lens that views one true deity protecting a single people against inferior others. This outlook inspires an ethic that justifies violence, plunder, and conquest, in part because outsiders tend to be seen as threatening rivals, whose loyalty and allegiance to other deities represents a challenge to their own religion's claim of universality. In a word, religious movements often practice intolerance—disrespect for diversity and the right of people to freely embrace another religion's beliefs. The next logical step is for fanatics to paint these imagined enemies as evil, unworthy of mercy, and to justify brutal violence against them.

This inclination of extremist religious movements to evoke prejudice and aggression leads some realist theorists of international politics to conclude that such movements are more a menace than a pacific influence (despite the fact that paganistic and atheistic societies recognizing no higher deity have equally long violent histories of waging wars under transcendental logic against external enemies and their own people). Observing that most wars have been fought in the name of religion, these realist critics ask the world to acknowledge the viciousness and mean-spiritedness of followers who betray their religion's humanistic and global values by championing a style of religious thought that denies that morality is about nourishing life, not destroying it.

become sources of international tension, especially when they become radical—heavily involved in political action on a global scale and fanatically dedicated to the promotion of their cause. The leaders of **extreme militant religious movements** are convinced that those who do not share their convictions must be punished, and that compromise is unacceptable. Richard Shultz and William Olson explain:

> While not all radical religious movements involved in politics are alike, they share certain similar characteristics:
>
> 1. Militant religious political movements tend to view existing government authority as corrupt and illegitimate because it is secular and not sufficiently rigorous in upholding religious authority or religiously sanctioned social and moral values.
>
> 2. They attack the inability of government to address the domestic ills of the society in which the movement exists. In many cases the religious movement substitutes itself for the government at the local level and is involved in education, health, and other social welfare programs. . . .

187

Religion, politics, and violence are seldom seen as contributing to one another. But in many countries, religious bodies are supported by the armies of the state and the state supports the transnational activities of religious movements. Consider South America, for instance, where the powerful Roman Catholic Church has often worked hand in hand with the governments the church supports. At the same time, proponents of "liberation theology" have joined forces with revolutionary groups in the so-called "Marxist-Catholic alliance" to bring about reforms in the repressive governments they oppose.

3. They subscribe to a particular set of behavior and opinions that they believe political authority must reflect, promote, and protect in all governmental and social activities. This generally means that government and all of its domestic and foreign activities must be in the hands of believers or subject to their close oversight.

4. They are universalists; unlike ethnic movements, they tend to see their views as part of the inheritance of everyone who is a believer. This tends to give them a transstate motivation, a factor that then translates their views on legitimacy of political authority into a larger context for action. In some cases, this means that international boundaries are not recognized as barriers to the propagation of the faith, even if this means the resort to violence.

5. They are exclusionists; they relegate all conflicting opinions on appropriate political and social order to the margins, if they do not exclude them altogether. This means second-class citizenship for any nonbeliever in any society where such a view predominates.

6. Finally, they are militant, willing to use coercion to achieve the only true end. (Shultz and Olson 1994, 9–10)

Although militant religious movements are not the only nonstate actors whose ideologies and activities may contribute to violence, many experts believe that they tend to stimulate five types of international activities. The first is **irredentism**—the attempt by a dominant religion or ethnic group to reclaim territory in an adjacent region once possessed but later lost from a foreign state that now controls it. Force is often rationalized for this purpose. The second is **secession** or **separative revolts**—the attempt by a religious (or ethnic) minority to break away from an internationally recognized state. Here, again, force is sometimes used, often with arms and aid supplied by third parties that support the secessionist goals. When these separative revolts succeed, states disintegrate into two or more new political units. The third type of international activity that militant religions tend to incite is **migration**—the departure of religious minorities from their countries of origin to escape persecution. Whether they move by force or by choice, the result—a fourth consequence of militant religion—is the same: The emigrants create **diasporas** or communities that live abroad in host countries but maintain economic, political, and emotional ties with their homelands. Finally, a fifth effect of militant religions is **international terrorism** in the form of support for radical coreligionists abroad.

If we critically inspect the compound consequences of the activities of militant religious movements, we come away with the impression that religious movements not only bring people together but also divide them. Religious movements often challenge state authority, and religious-driven separatism can tear countries apart. The possible result, some predict, is that over time "the world may fracture into 500 states from the current 200" (UNDP 1994). Others put the ultimate number lower but talk of a new kind of state—something akin to "a corporate holding company—with the central government little more than a shell and power residing in the regions" (Davis 1994).

Against this prophecy, we must contemplate another dimension of the sometimes close connection between religions and states: Many states actively support particular religions while repressing minority religions (see Map 7.3). It is important to recognize just how closely states and religions are allied in many countries, with each reinforcing the other's power. And this observation, in turn, leads us to consider how terrorist groups sometimes influence the relationships between states and militant religions.

● ● ●

INTERNATIONAL TERRORISTS

Terrorist groups are another kind of nonstate actor on the global stage, whose activities exacerbate international tensions and undermine the state's authority and power. Like ethnopolitical national movements and religious groups, terrorist groups are difficult to identify because their motives, tactics, and membership differ widely. However, there are similarities. **Terrorism** is commonly defined as seeking to further political objectives through the threat or use of violence, usually in opposition to state governments.

Terrorism was known in ancient times, as seen in the assassination of tyrants in ancient Greece and Rome, and by the Zealots of Palestine and the Hashashin of medieval Islam. In the nineteenth century, terrorism became associated with anarchist bombings and with murders and destruction of property by nationalist groups such as the Armenians and Turks. Today terrorism is a strategy practiced by a diverse group of movements (see Table 7.2). The religious, ethnic, or political movements and minorities now practicing terrorism seek to obtain the advantages of the majority, and to extract revenge against those states and majority populations that the terrorist groups perceive as oppressors. Terrorist groups seek the political freedom, privilege, and property they think persecution has denied them.

Whereas religious fanaticism is responsible for approximately 20 percent of international terrorist incidents (James 1995, 6), the primary goals of most

terrorism criminal acts and threats against a targeted actor for the purpose of arousing fear in order to get the target to accept the terrorists' demands.

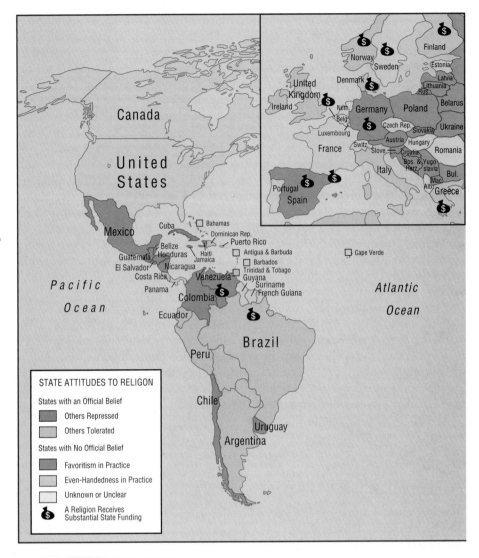

MAP 7.3

Caesar and God: State Support for Particular Religions in a Pluralistic World Community

Many states support particular organized religions and repress or merely tolerate others. This map displays the distribution of states' attitudes toward religion and shows the extent to which many countries try to encourage a given religious belief, while that religion also sustains the state.

SOURCE: Adapted from Kidron and Segal (1995), 110–11.

terrorist groups are independence and statehood. Terrorists are often the "international homeless," whose main objective is to obtain for themselves a territory and state they can control. But it would be a mistake to lump all terrorist movements together; although they share violent tactics, often crossing national borders, terrorist movements are more diverse than they are similar.

One increasingly active category of terrorist group is **international organized crime (IOC).** In the "borderless" globalized world, organized crime syndicates can easily use sophisticated computer and telecommunications technology to network with one another to expand their operations and profits. As Focus 7.2 illustrates, global gangsters are succeeding in the use of terror and death in pursuit of wealth. The drug cartels dealing in the illegal sale of cocaine are an example of the inability of law enforcement agencies to thwart these terrorist activities.

Another attribute of modern or "postmodern" terrorism (Laqueur 1998) has to do with the relationship of terrorists to the state. When viewing the activities of contemporary terrorist groups, it is safe to conclude that the actions

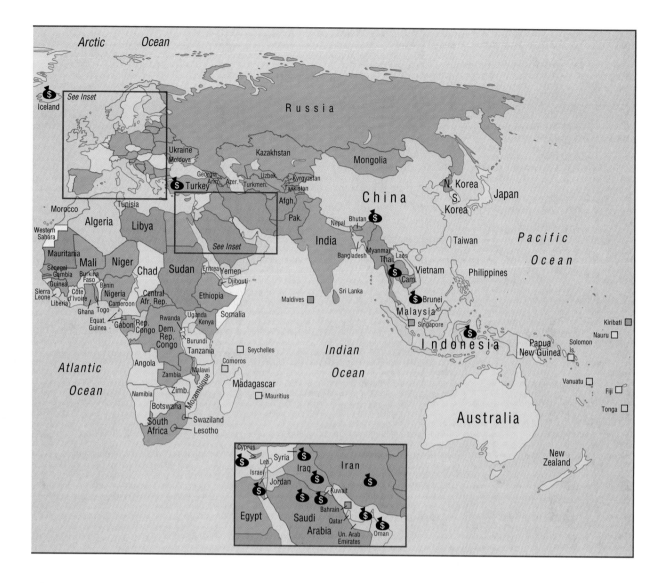

of most of these nonstate actors undermine the authority and sovereignty of existing states. However, **state terrorism** must also be included in any objective assessment, for some of the most ruthless acts of violent terrorism have been practiced by states' governments against people within their own borders. Historical examples of state terrorism include the "reign of terror" by the French revolutionary government in 1793 against the counterrevolutionary opposition, the violence practiced by Russian Bolsheviks after 1917 against their opponents (especially by the repressive regime of Joseph Stalin), and the actions of the genocidal Nazi regime of Adolf Hitler in Germany, which killed millions in the 1930s and 1940s. The state, in short, can and has fought back against opposition to its sovereign authority with terrorist tactics sometimes more militant and destructive than those used by insurgents and revolutionaries, and has used **state-sponsored terrorism** to support the governments' foreign policy goals against foreign adversaries. We should therefore not underestimate states' capacity and willingness to combat by force challengers to their sovereignty and perceived national interests.

state terrorism sovereign states' use of their armed forces and police to rule through fear and terror over targeted population groups and minorities within their borders.

state-sponsored terrorism formal assistance, training, and arming of *foreign* terrorists by a state in order to achieve foreign policy goals.

The following descriptions of modern terrorist movements are provided by the U.S. Department of State's Office of the Coordinator for Counterterrorism. Although not exhaustive, they convey the degree to which terrorist groups seek a combination of religious, ethnic, and political goals that generally aim to challenge the authority of existing states.

Group	Description
• Abu Nidal Organization (ANO)	Led by Sabri al-Banna, the ANO was headquartered in Iraq (1974–1983), Syria (1983–1987), and now Libya, and operates internationally to coordinate the activities of various other Muslim terrorist groups.
• Armed Islamic Group	An extremist group that seeks to overthrow the secular Algerian government and replace it with an Islamic state.
• Basque Fatherland and Liberty (ETA)	Founded in 1959, the group, which was once committed to Marxism, seeks to create an independent homeland in Spain's Basque region.
• HAMAS (Islamic Resistance Movement)	Emerging in 1987 from the Palestinian branch of the Muslim Brotherhood, HAMAS pursues—often by violent means—the goal of an Islamic Palestinian state in place of Israel.
• Hizballah (Party of God)	Radical Shia religious group seeking to establish an Iranian-style Islamic Republic in Lebanon.
• Kach and Kahane Chai	Stated goal is to restore the biblical state of Israel and to halt the peace process in Palestine. A right-wing Jewish extremist who was a member of Eyal (an offshoot of the radical Kach movement) assassinated Israeli Prime Minister Yitzhak Rabin in November 1995.
• The Party of Democratic Kampuchea (Khmer Rouge)	Communist insurgents hoping to destabilize the Cambodian government. Under Pol Pot's leadership, a campaign of genocide killed more than 1 million people in the late 1970s.
• Provisional Irish Republican Army (PIRA)	Radical group formed in 1969 as the secret armed wing of Sinn Fein, the legal political movement seeking to remove British forces from Northern Ireland and unify Ireland.
• Sendero Luminoso (Shining Path)	Guerrilla insurgency formed in the late 1960s by a former university professor whose stated goals are ridding Peru of foreign influences, destroying existing Peruvian institutions, and replacing them with a peasant revolutionary regime.

• • •

MULTINATIONAL CORPORATIONS

multinational corporations (MNCs) private businesses headquartered in one state that invest and operate extensively in other states.

Multinational corporations (MNCs)—business enterprises organized in one society with activities in another growing out of direct investment abroad—are a fourth type of nonstate actor. Since World War II, MNCs have grown dramatically in scope and potential influence with the expansion of the world political economy. As a result, they have provoked considerable discussion, at times animosity, and at other times enthusiastic acceptance. As advocates of liberal free trade and as active contributors to the globalization of world politics, MNCs generate both credit for the positive aspects of free trade and globalization and blame for their costs.

The numbers and immense size of MNCs add to the controversy surrounding their role and impact. By the mid–1990s more than 38,500 MNCs worldwide with more than 250,000 foreign affiliates generated $5.2 trillion in global sales, outpacing worldwide exports of goods and services and accounting for one-fifth of the globe's $25 trillion economy (*World Investment Report 1995* 1995, 3–4; Francis 1997, 8). MNCs also employed more than 73 million people, roughly 10 percent of all paid employees outside of agriculture and nearly

Where the Creed Is Greed
The Threat of the Global Network of Organized Crime

In November 1994 the United Nations sponsored a conference in Naples, Italy, to confront a growing menace: the emergence of international organized crime (IOC). Attended by more than eight hundred delegates from 136 countries and thirty international organizations, the conference alerted the international community to the growth of what then UN Secretary General Boutros Boutros-Ghali termed an "empire of criminals," whose criminal activities range from slavery to trafficking in weapons, human organs, toxic waste, illegal drugs, and nuclear materials.

International organized crime represents a new kind of nonstate actor—new in the sense, according to Claire Sterling (1994) in *Thieves' World,* that criminal organizations that were once local (such as the Italian-Sicilian Mafias, the Japanese Yakuza, the Chinese Triads, and the Colombian cocaine cartels) are now internationally linked in a global network that cooperates to exploit the institutional weaknesses of a decentralized state system. According to Sterling's evidence, a "planetwide criminal consortium" has been established that is without precedent, running by its own rules, outside the law, to victimize the international community. The motive is not to promote ideological beliefs or religious creeds, but pure profit: the search for easy money, by any means necessary. This code of conduct accepts violence as an honorable necessity. As Sterling sees it, "the Mafia and its confederates are the ultimate terrorists of our times."

The absence of an animating ideology beyond wealth does not mean that international organized crime groups and ethnic and terrorist groups are disconnected, however:

> Just as criminal organizations search out opportunities in the midst of ethnic conflict, ethnonational movements likewise find advantages in their associations with organized crime or in developing their own criminal capabilities.
>
> Ethnonational minority groups pursuing either separation from or political realignment within an existing state require resources. Through arrangements with organized crime, these

movements can gain access to arms, information, and the means to help finance their operations. There is ample evidence that this is happening in Peru, Turkey, Lebanon, the Balkans, and elsewhere. An illustrative example of these types of interconnections is found in the links in heroin trafficking from Southwest Asia. Here Afghan groups, usually Pathans, have links to Pakistani, Iranian, or Indian groups who help in production and transiting. These groups, in turn, have links to Kurdish or Palestinian groups that help move heroin through Iran, Lebanon, or Turkey to Europe. In return, the various resistance movements in Turkey, Iran, and Afghanistan receive capital with which to fund their operations. They are convenient relationships.

Criminal organizations likewise find advantages in these ties. The presence of violent ethnic conflict and government turmoil provides opportunities and incentives for criminal activities. In situations where government and law enforcement [are] ineffective, criminal organizations thrive. In Pakistan, for example, government authority is excluded from tribal areas, and it is precisely in these areas where organized drug production and smuggling are most evident. Burma shows a similar pattern. In Peru, Colombian drug traffickers work with the Sendero Luminoso [terrorists] to impair government enforcement efforts, not only against drug smuggling, but also against the very presence of government itself.

IOCs benefit from other by-products of ethnic conflict, state dissolution, and borderless globalization. One such by-product is the population migration these conflicts generate. European countries harboring large refugee populations have identified a spectrum of organized criminal activities taking place within these communities, and the immigrant groups themselves are frequently the victims of these criminal ventures. Ethnic diaspora communities abroad serve as operational bases and safe havens for criminal organizations. (Shultz and Olson 1994, 28–29)

---

twenty percent of the employees in the Global North (*World Investment Report 1994* 1994, xxiii). Each MNC job also typically generates additional jobs. The Nike footwear company, for example, employs about 9,000 people on its core staff but another 75,000 through subcontracting. Conservatively, then, MNCs can be expected to generate one additional job for each job in the corporation, bringing the number of jobs associated with MNCs to at least 150 million.

TABLE 7.3 The World's Top Twenty Banks, 1996
(ranked by revenues)

Rank	Transnational Bank	Revenues (millions of dollars)
1	Bank of Tokyo-Mitsubishi, Japan	$46,451
2	Deutsche Bank, Germany	39,413
3	Crédit Agricole, France	34,620
4	Citicorp, U.S.	32,605
5	Gan, France	32,260
6	Industrial Bank of Japan, Japan	30,208
7	HSBC Holdings, Britain	28,860
8	Sanwa Bank, Japan	27,973
9	ABN AMRO Holding, Netherlands	27,651
10	Crédit Suisse, Switzerland	27,647
11	Chase Manhattan Corp., U.S.	27,421
12	Société Générale, France	26,010
13	Crédit Lyonnais, France	25,180
14	Banque Nat. De Paris, France	24,125
15	Fuji Bank, Japan	24,071
16	Sumitomo Bank, Japan	22,811
17	Natl. Westminster Bank, Britain	22,784
18	Sakura Bank, Japan	22,693
19	Bankamerica Corp., U.S.	22,071
20	Dresdner Bank, Germany	21,489

SOURCE: *Fortune* (August 4, 1997), F16–17.

The MNCs' expansion has been facilitated by **transnational banks (TNBs)** whose revenues and assets are primarily generated by financial transactions in the international economy. These have become major forces in the world political economy and have contributed to the globalization process that has led to financial integration worldwide at the same time that it has made international banks critical to global economic stability (as the collapse of lending following occasional banking crises and the costs of re-capitalizing, reorganizing, or liquidating insolvent banks by foreign countries illustrates). In 1995 the combined assets of the world's twenty largest banks exceeded $8.4 trillion (Malkin 1995, 1). And international banking is highly profitable: the revenues of the world's top twenty commercial banks in 1996 exceeded $566 billion (see Table 7.3). These investments funnel transnational trade and the penetration of states into one another's economies, thereby re-ducing the significance of national borders by transferring capital through international loans and investments that can transform low-income coun-tries' economies. Reflecting other global economic trends in the mid-1990s before the "Asian flu" financial crises in 1998, 30 percent of the world's top twenty TNBs were headquartered in Japan and 25 percent were headquar-tered in France.

Through their loans to the private sector, TNBs have made capital highly mobile and expanded the capacity of MNCs to lead the way in converging the incomes, tastes, lifestyles, and consumer products in the global marketplace. As MNCs have grown in scope and power, concern has understandably been raised about whether their efforts to remove national barriers to foreign investments and trade is undermining the ability of seemingly sovereign states to control their own economies and therefore their own fates and cultures. Is it possible

Multinational Corporations in World Politics
A Balance Sheet of Claims and Criticisms

FOCUS 7.3

MNCs have been alternately praised and condemned, depending on how their performance is viewed. The record is mixed and can be evaluated differently in terms of different criteria. Below is a "balance sheet" summarizing the major arguments, pro and con.

Positive

- Increase the volume of world trade.
- Assist the aggregation of investment capital that can fund development.
- Finance loans and service international debt.
- Lobby for free trade and the removal of barriers to trade, such as tariffs.
- Underwrite research and development that allows technological innovation.
- Introduce and dispense advanced technology to less developed countries.
- Reduce the costs of goods by encouraging their production according to the principle of comparative advantage.
- Generate employment.
- Encourage the training of workers.
- Produce new goods and expand opportunities for their purchase through the internationalization of production.
- Disseminate marketing expertise and mass advertising methods worldwide.
- Promote national revenue and economic growth; facilitate modernization of less developed countries.
- Generate income and wealth.
- Advocate peaceful relations between and among states in order to preserve an orderly environment conducive to trade and profits.
- Break down national barriers and accelerate the globalization of the international economy and culture and the rules that govern international commerce.

Negative

- Give rise to oligopolistic conglomerations that reduce competition and free enterprise.
- Raise capital in host countries (thereby depriving local industries of investment capital) but export profits to home countries.
- Breed debtors and make the poor dependent on those providing loans.
- Limit the availability of commodities by monopolizing their production and controlling their distribution in the world marketplace.
- Create "sanctuary markets" that restrict and channel other investments to give MNCs an unfair advantage.
- Export technology ill suited to underdeveloped economies.
- Inhibit the growth of infant industries and local technological expertise in less developed countries while making Global South countries dependent on Global North technology.
- Conspire to create cartels that contribute to inflation.
- Curtail employment by driving labor competition from the market.
- Limit workers' wages.
- Limit the supply of raw materials available in international markets.
- Erode traditional cultures and national differences, leaving in their place a homogenized world culture dominated by consumer-oriented values.
- Widen the gap between rich and poor countries.
- Increase the wealth of local elites at the expense of the poor.
- Support and rationalize repressive regimes in the name of stability and order.
- Challenge national sovereignty and jeopardize the autonomy of the states.
- Create cartels with other MNCs that share markets in order to cut competition.

that MNCs are shaking the very foundations of the present international system? Or is this question perhaps based on exaggerated estimates of the MNCs' influence and therefore unwarranted?

The benefits and costs attributed to MNCs as they have risen to a position of prominence since World War II have been many and complex, and this has made them highly controversial nonstate actors (see Focus 7.3). Here we examine four major issues: MNCs' global reach and economic power, their effects on host and home countries, their involvement in politics, and their long-run influence on world politics.

MNCs' Global Reach and Economic Power

The modern MNC characteristically maintains an elaborate overseas network of affiliates to coordinate manufacturing and marketing globally. The creation of the European Economic Community (EEC) in 1957 stimulated this form of business organization and the internationalization of production that it fostered. Because the original six EEC members hoped to create a common external tariff wall around their common market, it made economic sense for U.S. firms to build production facilities in Europe. In this way they could remain competitive by selling their wares as domestic rather than foreign products, with their additional tariff costs. Ultimately, "the primary drive behind the overseas expansion of today's giant corporations is maximization of corporate growth and the suppression of foreign as well as domestic competition" (Gilpin 1975).

The reasons for direct investments overseas are more complex than this explanation suggests. According to *product-cycle theory*, overseas expansion is essentially a defensive maneuver designed to forestall foreign competitors and thus maintain the global competitiveness of domestically produced products. This theory views MNCs as having an edge in the initial stages of developing and producing a new product but then having to relocate production abroad to protect export markets from the foreign competitors that naturally arise as the relevant technology becomes more widespread or imitated. In the final phase of the product cycle, "production has become sufficiently routinized so that the comparative advantage shifts to relatively low-skilled, low-wage, and labor-intensive economies. This is now the case, for example, in textiles, electronic components, and footwear" (Gilpin 1975; see also Vernon 1971).

The world's giant producing, trading, and servicing corporations have become the agents of the globalization of production. Table 7.4 illustrates their economic and perhaps political importance in world politics, ranking firms by annual sales and states by GNP. The profile shows that 37 percent of the world's top one hundred economic entities are MNCs. Among the top fifty entries, multinationals account for only nine, but in the next fifty, they account for twenty-eight. Their financial clout thus rivals or exceeds that of many countries; indeed, "sales of the ten largest corporations exceed the combined GNP of the 100 smallest countries" (*World Watch* 9 [January/ February 1996], 37).

Although the growth of multinational firms is a global phenomenon, the Global North is home to about 90 percent of MNC parent corporations. Historically, the United States has been the home country for most of the largest multinationals, and in 1996 was the headquarters for 162 of the globe's 500 largest MNCs, followed by Japan (126), France (42), Germany (41), and Britain (34) (*Fortune*, August 4, 1997, F1). Together these five liberal democracies account for 80 percent of all parent corporations, and also account for a similar share of both the stock and flow of foreign direct investment.

Foreign direct investment (FDI)—formally defined as "ownership of assets in one country by residents of another for purposes of controlling the use of those assets" (Graham and Krugman 1995)—measures the investment activities of MNCs. The "stock" of FDI reflects the accumulation of past patterns of MNC investments, as revealed, for example, in the value of factories and equipment built up over a period of time. The "flow" of FDI reveals MNCs' current

Rank	Country/Corporation	GNP/Sales (billions of dollars)	Rank	Country/Corporation	GNP/Sales (billions of dollars)
1	United States	6387.7	51	AT&T (U.S.)	74.5
2	Japan	3926.6	52	NIPPON LIFE INS. (Japan)	72.6
3	Germany	2004.8	53	Israel	72.6
4	France	1289.2	54	MOBIL (U.S.)	72.3
5	Italy	1134.9	55	DAIMLER-BENZ (Ger.)	71.6
6	United Kingdom	1042.7	56	BRITISH PETROLEUM (Br.)	69.9
7	China*	630.2	57	MATSUSHITA ELEC. (Japan)	68.1
8	Canada	574.8	58	VOLKSWAGEN (Ger.)	66.5
9	Spain	533.9	59	DAEWOO (S. Korea)	65.2
10	Brazil	471.9	60	SIEMENS (Ger.)	63.7
11	Russia	343.4	61	CHRYSLER (U.S.)	61.4
12	Mexico	324.9	62	Malaysia	60.0
13	Korea	338.0	63	NISSAN MOTOR (Japan)	59.1
14	Netherlands	316.4	64	Venezuela	58.9
15	India	262.8	65	ALLIANZ (Ger.)	56.6
16	Switzerland	254.0	66	U.S. POSTAL SERVICE (U.S.)	56.4
17	Argentina	244.0	67	Pakistan*	55.6
18	Australia	229.6	68	Singapore	55.4
19	Taiwan	222.0	69	PHILIP MORRIS (U.S.)	54.6
20	Sweden	216.3	70	Philippines	54.6
21	Belgium	213.4	71	UNILEVER (Br./Neth.)	52.1
22	Austria	183.5	72	FIAT (It.)	50.5
23	GENERAL MOTORS (U.S.)	168.4	73	SONY (Japan)	50.3
24	FORD MOTOR (U.S.)	147.0	74	Colombia	50.1
25	MITSUI (Japan)	144.9	75	DAI-ICHI MUTUAL LIFE INSURANCE (Japan)	49.1
26	Mitsubishi (Japan)	140.2	76	IRI (It.)	49.1
27	Iran*	138.2	77	NESTLÉ (Switzerland)	48.9
28	Denmark	137.6	78	TOSHIBA (Japan)	48.5
29	Indonesia	136.9	79	HONDA MOTOR (Japan)	47.0
30	ITOCHU (Japan)	135.5	80	ELF AQUITAINE (Fr.)	46.8
31	SHELL GROUP (Br./Neth.)	128.2	81	TOMEN (Japan)	46.5
32	Turkey	126.3	82	BANK OF TOKYO-MITSUBISHI (Japan)	46.5
33	South Africa*	125.2	83	VEBA GROUP (Ger.)	45.3
34	Thailand	120.2	84	Ireland	44.9
35	EXXON (U.S.)	119.4	85	TOKYO ELEC. POWER (Japan)	44.7
36	SUMITOMO (Japan)	119.3	86	New Zealand	44.6
37	Norway	113.5	87	TEXACO (U.S.)	44.6
38	TOYOTA MOTOR (Japan)	108.7	88	SUMITOMO LIFE INSURANCE (Japan)	44.1
39	WAL-MART STORES (U.S.)	106.1	89	SUNKYONG (S. Korea)	44.0
40	Hong Kong	104.7	90	NEC (Japan)	43.9
41	Ukraine	99.6	91	ELECTRICITE DE FRANCE (Fr.)	43.7
42	Finland	96.2	92	STATE FARM INSURANCE COS. (U.S.)	42.8
43	Poland	87.3	93	Chile	42.4
44	GENERAL ELECTRIC (U.S.)	79.2	94	DEUTSCHE TELECOM (Ger.)	41.9
45	NISSHO IWAI (Japan)	78.9	95	PHILIPS ELECTRONICS (Neth.)	41.0
46	NIPPON TELEGRAPH AND TELEPHONE (Japan)	78.3	96	UNION DES ASSURANCES DE PARIS (Fr.)	40.7
47	Portugal	77.7	97	PRUDENTIAL INS. COS. OF AMERICA (U.S.)	40.2
48	Greece	76.7	98	FUJITSU (Japan)	40.0
49	IBM (U.S.)	75.9	99	E.I. DU PONT DE NEMOURS (U.S.)	39.7
50	HITACHI (Japan)	75.7	100	DEUTSCHE BANK (Ger.)	39.4

SOURCES: MNC data: *Fortune* (August 4, 1997). F-4, F-5; GNP data: Seven Seas Mailing Lists <http://www.mightymall.com/sevenseas/facts.html>. Missing data (indicated by asterisk) based on *World Bank Atlas 1996* 1995, 18–19.

investment transactions. The FDI stocks thus reveal the current structure of global production and the primary locus of economic activity, while FDI flows provide insight into their changing patterns.

In the mid-1990s, the MNCs' *new* FDI exceeded about $230 billion each year (Francis 1997, 8). Building on the past accumulation, most foreign investment stock today is heavily concentrated in the Global North, which is the source of most investment capital (outflows) and its favored target (inflows). In particular, the Japan-European Union-North America triad dominates global investments, as it does the interregional flow of global trade (see Chapter 8). This pattern replaces an earlier "bipolar" investment configuration, in which the United States and a handful of European countries (acting independently of one another) dominated the investment world. By the end of the 1980s, however, Europe began increasingly to act as a unified entity, and Japan actually surpassed the United States, with much of its investment directed at the United States itself.

The current tripolar investment pattern emerged from the corporate preferences of each partner to consolidate its own market hold and to gain a foothold in the other two regions. The United States and the European Union have shown a preference for investing in each other rather than Japan, and Japan has preferred the United States to Europe. The result is a serious imbalance between Japan and the other two partners, with the outward flow of stocks from Japan much greater than the inward flow. Because of these imbalances, competition among the three economic blocs, as well as political struggle, is likely to become increasingly fierce (Thurow 1992).

As the market strategies of major corporations in the United States, Europe, and Japan pursued control of their existing markets and expansion in new regional markets, they also adopted strategies that sought to construct regionally integrated core networks of affiliates clustered around their home countries. This has led to the creation of regionalized networks for production and marketing across many industries as the cartellike market-sharing arrangements of globe-spanning MNC networks converged practices but hindered openly competitive markets.

As a result of this clustering strategy, foreign direct investment is now increasingly regional, and local markets are protected in opaque ways. Each of the principal host countries in eastern Europe and the Global South receives the bulk of its funds from a single member of the investment triad, typically the one geographically closest to it. The effect is to reinforce—perhaps to cause—the growing regionalization of the world political economy across a range of dimensions, not only in investment but also in finance, labor, and trade (Doremus et al. 1998; see also Chapter 8).

Although the Global North is both home and host to most FDI stock, the Global South's share of FDI flows increased during the 1970s, plummeted during the debt crisis of the early 1980s, and expanded again in the 1990s as the emerging economies became increasingly favored targets. Today, "the lion's share of international financial flows has continued to go to capital-abundant states" in the Global North (Heredia, 1997) (see Chapters 5 and 9).

The Effects of MNCs on Home and Host Nations

In addition to their global reach and economic power, MNCs' domestic impact on both home and host countries is a matter of widespread concern. MNCs allegedly exercise their power at great cost to their home or parent countries. Charges against them include shifting productive facilities abroad to avoid labor unions' demands for higher wages. According to this view, because capital is more mobile than labor, the practice of exporting production from industrially advanced countries to industrially backward countries—where labor is cheap and unions weak or nonexistent—causes structural unemployment in the advanced countries. Others contend, however, that MNCs help reduce balance-of-payments deficits, create new employment opportunities, promote competition in both domestic and foreign markets, and reduce rather than widen income inequalities between rich and poor states and within both.

If home countries have incurred both costs and benefits, have host countries shared similar experiences? "As privileged organizations," David E. Apter and Louis W. Goodman (1976) note, MNCs "hold a unique position among growth-inducing institutions able to affect the direction of development." This implies that MNCs may promote development as much as they impede it. It is nonetheless true that countries in the Global South historically viewed MNCs with suspicion. This attitude has changed noticeably in recent years. MNCs are more important to the developing countries' overall GNP and to their most advanced economic sectors than they are to the developed states' economies, and realization of the opportunities their investments can create has altered the traditional fear in the Global South of MNCs as neocolonial agents that endanger national sovereignty and undermine local prosperity. Global South countries from Mexico to Malaysia are "rolling out the welcome mat for global companies in the quest for rapid growth" (Francis 1997), despite the many risks and costs that MNCs' penetration incur (Heredia 1997).

Politics and Multinational Corporations

A lingering concern regarding MNCs' role is their involvement in the domestic political affairs of local or host countries. In some instances this concern has extended to MNCs' involvement in the domestic politics of their home countries, where they actively lobby their governments for more liberal trade and investment policies that will enhance the profitability of their business activities abroad. In turn, both host and home governments have sometimes used MNCs as instruments in their foreign policy strategies.

Perhaps the most notorious instance of an MNC's intervention in the politics of a host state occurred in Chile in the early 1970s. There, International Telephone and Telegraph (ITT) tried to protect its interests in the profitable Chiltelco telephone company by seeking to prevent the election of Marxist-oriented Salvador Allende as president and later by seeking his overthrow. ITT's efforts to undermine Allende included giving monetary support to his political opponents and, once Allende was elected, pressuring the U.S. government to disrupt the Chilean economy. Eventually Allende was overthrown by a military dictatorship.

At times MNCs' practices have been embarrassing to home countries—as when the West German government found that a German firm had sold mustard gas manufacturing equipment to Libya. On other occasions they seemed to defy the home country—as when the French subsidiary of Dresser Industries of Dallas, Texas, exported energy technology to the Soviet Union in defiance of a U.S. government effort to thwart the sale.

In addition, MNCs often lobby their home governments for policies that back their disputes with host governments, although they are not always successful in these endeavors. The U.S. stipulation, made in the early 1970s, that foreign aid would be cut to any country that nationalized U.S. overseas investments without just compensation is representative of the tendency for home-state governments to support their own MNCs' overseas activities.

More broadly, MNCs have assisted in promoting free trade. In this sense, they have been active participants in the process by which governments have reached agreements on rules liberalizing economic transactions in the global marketplace, and active participants in the globalization process.

However, at another level, MNCs headquartered in one country have sometimes worked at cross-purposes with their parent governments by serving the wishes of the host government. During the 1973–1974 oil crisis, for example, the governments of the Organization of Petroleum Exporting Countries (OPEC) received assistance from the multinational oil companies to achieve OPEC's goal of using oil as a political weapon against the West. As the corporations reaped huge profits, their home countries suffered greatly.

The political role of the MNC in home and host countries is difficult to characterize, and varies around the globe. Perhaps the conclusion that best describes its impact is one that pictures the MNC not only as a threat to state power, but also as "a stimulant to the further extension of state power in the economic realm" (Gilpin 1985).

> Only the state can defend corporate interests in international negotiations over trade, investment, and market access. Agreements over such things as airline routes, the opening of banking establishments, and the right to sell insurance are not decided by corporate actors who gather around a table; they are determined by diplomats and bureaucrats. Corporations must turn to governments when they have interests to protect or advance. (Kapstein 1991–1992, 56)

Still, the blurring of the boundaries between internal and external affairs adds potency to the political role that MNCs unavoidably play as actors at the intersection of foreign and domestic policy, and the symbolic invasion of national borders by MNCs can be expected to arouse the anger of many local nationalists who fear the loss of income, jobs, and control to foreign corporate interests.

MNCs' Influence

Because multinationals often make decisions over which national political leaders have little control, a fourth significant issue regarding MNCs is whether their influence will lead to the erosion of the international system's major structural foundation—the principle that the state alone is sovereign.

The question of control is especially pertinent to countries in the Global South, although it is not limited to them. As one senior U.S. foreign policy official declared at the time of the Dresser Industries controversy, "Basically we're in an impossible situation. You don't want to get rid of the advantages of this international economic system, but if you try to exercise control for foreign policy reasons, you cut across sovereign frontiers."

Bemoaning the suspicion that multinationals "steal" U.S. technology and fail to "generate or retain wealth and quality jobs within [U.S.] borders," the U.S. Office of Technology Assessment in 1993 called for new rules to "balance

Many nationalists blame multinational corporations for the problems of their countries economies and social conditions. Foreign firms often face a backlash. In 1995, Hindu nationalists in India—the world's largest democracy—protested economic reforms that would open the country's borders to liberal trade and investment. These and other opponents pledged to drive some of the world's best-known brands out of the Indian market.

interests . . . between nations and firms" (Dentzer 1993). However, the MNCs' complex patterns of ownership and licensing arrangements make the problem unmanageable, because it is often difficult to equate the MNCs' interests with particular national jurisdictions (Reich 1990). General Electric, for example, one of the most "American" of all U.S. MNCs, has co-production agreements with Nuovo Pignone of Italy, Mitsubishi and Hitachi of Japan, and Mannessmann and AEG Telefunken of Germany, and in 1998 Daimler-Benz of Germany and the Chrysler Corporation in the United States agreed to a merger that stimulated a wave of new international merger negotiations among other automobile manufacturers. Controlling such a complex pattern of interrelationships, joint ventures, and shared ownership for any particular national purpose is nearly impossible. Part of the reason is that "about one-third of the 1996 world $6 trillion trade in goods and services occurs within multinationals—from one branch to another, [and] trade between different multinationals accounts for another third of world trade" (Francis 1997, 8). Joint production and **strategic corporate alliances** to create temporary phantom "virtual corporations" complicates the problem of identity. "The internationalization of the economy–which the U.S. spearheaded–has rendered obsolete old ideas of economic warfare," Richard J. Barnet, coauthor of *Global Reach* (Barnet and Müller 1974), observed in 1982. "You can't find targets any more, and if you aim at a target you often find it's yourself."

The multinationals' potential long-run influence is depicted in *Global Dreams: Imperial Corporations and the New World Order:*

The emerging global order is spearheaded by a few hundred corporate giants, many of them bigger than most sovereign nations. Ford's economy is larger than Saudi Arabia's and Norway's. Philip Morris's annual sales exceed New Zealand's gross domestic product. The multinational corporation of 20 years ago carried on separate operations in many different countries and tailored its operations to local conditions. In the 1990s large business enterprises, even some smaller ones, have the technological means and strategic vision to burst old limits—of time, space, national boundaries, language, custom, and ideology. By acquiring earth-spanning technologies, by developing products that can be produced anywhere and sold everywhere, by spreading credit around the world, and by connecting global channels of communication that can penetrate any village or neighborhood, these institutions we normally think of as economic rather than political, private rather than public, are becoming the world empires of the twenty-first century. The architects and managers of these space-age business enterprises understand that the balance of power in world politics has shifted in recent years from territorially bound governments to companies that can roam the world. As the hopes and pretensions of government shrink almost everywhere, these imperial corporations are occupying public space and exerting a more profound influence over the lives of ever larger numbers of people. (Barnet and Cavanagh 1994, 14)

Whether the corporate visionaries who manage the MNCs will help to create a more prosperous, peaceful, and just world—as free-trade liberal theorists hope and others, whose interests are threatened by a new globalized political economy, fear—is debatable. "For some, the global corporation holds the promise of lifting [humankind] out of poverty and bringing the good life to everyone. For others, these corporations have become a law unto themselves; they are miniempires which exploit all for the benefit of a few" (Gilpin 1975).

The existence of multinational corporations "has become a fact of life. They are now permanent—and influential—players in the international arena" (Spero and Hart 1997). Because of MNC's "globalized financial markets have greatly heightened the structural power of capital holders and reduced the policy options open to governments" (Heridia 1997), MNCs' challenge to the existing international system of states should not be taken lightly. The UN Commission on Transnational Corporations forcefully poses the issue:

A growing number of international norms has produced a body of international soft law on transnational corporations; it is, however, limited in scope and does not adequately match the globalization of business activity. In an era of globalization, it is increasingly difficult to distinguish between national and international issues of governance. The capacity of governments to manage their economies and achieve national objectives in areas ranging from fiscal policy to environmental control is being strained by the growing importance of transnational corporations in the international economy. Many issues related to corporate responsibility cannot be resolved satisfactorily in the context of a single national legal regime. . . . The effective and stable governance of international economic relations requires not only the unleashing of market forces and private enterprise, but also effective international instruments to deal with the broad range of issues related to the globalization of business activity–problems that are beyond the capacity of national regimes of governance. (Commission on Transnational Corporations 1991, 33)

• • •

NONSTATE ACTORS AND THE STRANGULATION OF THE STATE

Because ethnopolitical movements, religious groups, and international terrorists—along with international organizations and multinational corporations—sap the state's authority, they also challenge the very institutional pillars on which the contemporary state system is built. An adequate conceptualization of contemporary world politics must acknowledge the influence of nonstate actors, because, as political theorist Richard Falk argues, it is misleading "to view the world as consisting of territorial units each exerting supreme authority within its borders, but not elsewhere." Falk explains:

> Even if a few states can still defend their territory against an invading army, not even the most powerful can protect its people and cities against a devastating surprise attack by guided missiles, and none can control the flow of images and ideas that shape human tastes and values. The globalized "presence" of Madonna, McDonald's and Mickey Mouse make a mockery of sovereignty as exclusive territorial control. A few governments do their best to insulate their populations from such influences, but their efforts are growing less effective and run counter to democratizing demands that are growing more difficult to resist. . . . Interdependence and the interpenetration of domestic and international politics, the mobility and globalization of capital and information, and the rising influence of transnational social movements and organizations are among the factors that make it anachronistic to analyze politics as if territorial supremacy continues to be a generalized condition or a useful fiction. In particular, sovereignty, with its stress on the inside/outside distinction as between domestic and international society, seems more misleading than illuminating under current conditions. (Falk 1993, 853)

This by no means indicates that the era of state dominance is over, however. States retain a (near) monopoly on the use of coercive force in the international system, and they continue to shape the transnational interactions of nonstate actors. The state still molds the activities of nonstate actors more than its behavior is molded by them. It "may be anachronistic, but we have yet to develop an alternative form of societal organization that is able to provide its members with both wealth and power" (Kapstein 1991–1992). It is also true that "a gain in power by nonstate actors does not necessarily translate into a loss of power for the state" (Slaughter 1997). We must conclude that whereas it would be premature to abandon the focus on the state in international politics, it would be equally mistaken to exaggerate the state's power as a determinant of the globe's fate and dismiss the expanding role that nonstate actors are playing within the tightening web of interdependent globalization that is eroding the power of states. We cannot ignore the shifts occurring "away from the state—up, down, and sideways—to supra-state, sub-state, and, above all non-state actors—new players that have multiple allegiances and global reach" (Slaughter 1997; also Mathews 1997). The next chapter examines how trade and currency issues are changing in the new globalized market, making it difficult to distinguish corporations, countries, and other actors.

KEY TERMS

nonstate entities/actors
unitary actor(s)
nationalism
ethnopolitical groups
ethnicity
ethnic nationalism
ethnic groups
Fourth World
indigenous peoples
genocide
devolution
nonstate nations

cultural domains
clash of civilizations
self-determination
ethnic cleansing
interethic competition
ethnocentrism
religious movements
extreme militant religious
  movements
irredentism
secession or separative revolts
migration

diasporas
international terrorism
terrorism
international organized crime
  (IOC)
state terrorism
state-sponsored terrorism
multinational corporations
  (MNCs)
transnational banks (TNBs)
foreign direct investment (FDI)
strategic corporate alliances

SUGGESTED READING

Appiah, Kwame Anthony, and Henry Louis Gates, Jr., eds. *The Dictionary of Global Culture*. New York: Knopf, 1997.

Barnet, Richard J., and John Cavanagh. *Global Dreams: Imperial Corporations and the New World Order*. New York: Simon & Schuster, 1994.

Carment, David, and Patrick James, eds. *Peace in the Midst of Wars: Preventing and Managing Ethnic Conflicts*. Columbia: University of South Carolina Press, 1998.

Cederman, Lars-Erik. *Emergent Actors in World Politics: How States and Nations Develop and Dissolve*. Princeton, N.J.: Princeton University Press, 1997.

Connor, Walker. *Ethnonationalism: The Quest for Understanding*. Princeton, N.J.: Princeton University Press, 1994.

Doremus, Paul N., Simon Reich, William Keller, and Louis W. Pauly. *The Myth of the Global Corporation*. Princeton, N.J.: Princeton University Press, 1998.

Gurr, Ted Robert, and Barbara Harff. *Ethnic Conflict in World Politics*. Boulder, Colo.: Westview, 1994.

Huntington, Samuel P. *The Clash of Civilizations and the Remaking of World Order*. New York: Simon & Schuster, 1996.

Rudolph, Susanne Hoeber, and James Piscatori, eds. *Transnational Religion and Fading States*. Boulder, Colo.: Westview, 1997.

Smith, Anthony D., ed. *Nations and Nationalism: Journal of the Association for the Study of Ethnicity and Nationalism*. (Published three times annually.) New York: Cambridge University Press.

Williams, Phil, ed. *Transnational Organized Crime*. (Annual journal published quarterly.) London: Frank Cass.

Wilmer, Franke. *The Indigenous Voice in World Politics*. Newbury Park, Calif.: Sage, 1993.

http://www.partal.com/ciemen/ethnic.html
Ethnic World Survey Divided according to continent, this site has links to information on all ethnic groups. In Asia, read about the conflict between Tibet and China and Kashmir and India. In Europe, review the conflicts that the Basques have with the Spanish government, and that the Corsicans have with the Italian authorities. In the Americas, examine the combative Pipil in El Salvador and the Mayans in Mexico. By exploring this Web site, you will be amazed at the extent and number of ethnic groups. Why do you think that some ethnic groups turn to violence and others do not?

http://www.halcyon.com/FWD/fwdp.html
Fourth World Documentation Project The Center for World Indigenous Studies has created this Web site to document and make available important materials relating to the social, political, strategic, economic, and human rights situations that indigenous peoples face. The site is divided according to region and has links to international agreements and resolutions.

http://www.nativeweb.org
NativeWeb The NativeWeb has both a resource and community center. Research the native peoples of the world by clicking on the "Nations/Peoples" link in the resource center, or visit the community center and discuss current issues on the message board. You can also partake in an on-line chat.

http://weber.u.washington.edu/~madin/
Academic Info Religion Ever wonder what the difference is between Baha'i and Zoroastrianism? Find out by visiting the Academic Info Religion Web site. This site links you with Internet resources for the study of the world's religions. Click on the "World Scriptures" and then "Religious Texts" to read passages from the Koran and the Old and New Testaments. Compare and contrast Taoist, Zen, Mormon, Hindu, Gnostic, and Nag Hammadi texts. If your tastes lean more toward mythology and alchemy, you will find that here, too.

http://www.usis.usemb.se/terror/rpt1997/index.html
Patterns of Global Terrorism, 1996 The U.S. Department of State compiled a Web site that reviews 1996 region-specific information on terrorism. See "Appendix B" of the Web site for background information on specific terrorist groups.

http://www.terrorism.com/terrorism/research.html
Terrorism Research Center This site is a good source for research on terrorism and links to other Web sources on terrorism. Look at the "Terrorist Profiles" for profiles of groups and the "Definition of Terrorism" controversy. Keep in mind that one group's "freedom fighters" may be another group's "terrorists."

CHAPTER 8

Trade and Monetary Issues in a Globalized Political Economy

•••

We are in the midst of cataclysmic change that will result in a new map of power and influence, a map being drawn by the big emerging markets [which] pose unprecedented challenges to American global leadership.

—JEFFREY E. GARTEN,
former U.S. Under Secretary of Commerce for International Trade, 1997

•••

The idea of economic competition among nations is flawed. Companies compete. But economically, countries depend on each other.

—ROBERT J. SAMUELSON,
political economist, 1998

CHAPTER TOPICS AND THEMES

- The shifting global setting for international economic conditions
- Liberalism and mercantilism: A clash of values regarding free trade and monetary management
- Can a free-trade regime flourish without a liberal hegemon?
- New institutions to manage free international trade
- Liberalism, mercantilism, and hegemony in the international trade system
- Liberalism, mercantilism, and hegemony in the international monetary system
- Emerging state and regional trade policies
- The destiny of the global political economy: Triumph or trouble?

As the United Nations convened in the 1997 opening session, leaders faced an unfamiliar opportunity. Much of the world was savoring a surge in economic growth made possible largely by the removal of the Cold War's ideological chains and the economic distortions great-power rivalries had caused. Growing international trade was transforming the ways people were living and interacting. Newly affluent people and emerging middle classes were basking in the freedom of a promising future. Much of the world now set its sights on generating even more prosperity, while confronting the awesome task of reducing the huge gap between the rich and poor and of preserving the peace that allowed such vigorous economic growth. The world concentrated on finding new ways of making money, not war.

The quest for wealth is an ageless pursuit. Because it provides the means by which many other prized values can be realized, the successful management of economics lies at the center of how governments define their national interests. What practices (and the underlying philosophies that justify them) should they embrace to regulate commercial and monetary activities within their borders? And what policies should each state adopt to influence trading and financial exchanges with other states?

These are the principal concerns of **political economy.** To introduce this topic, this chapter will first look at the ways in which the international political economy has evolved. This will allow us to then investigate how trade and monetary activities in today's growing globalized marketplace are creating new issues, and the promise and peril that reside in how these issues will be addressed in the twenty-first century.

political economy the study of the relationship between politics and economics.

• • •

THE GLOBAL CONTEXT FOR INTERPRETING CONTEMPORARY WORLD ECONOMIC CHANGE

Rapid changes in the world force people to think about and interpret world politics in fresh ways. Of all the many changes, perhaps none has been more profound and far reaching than the post-World War II phenomenon known as **globalization**—"the increasingly close international integration of markets both for goods and services, and for capital" (IMF 1997). The growth of the interdependence of states' economies can be viewed as the recent culmination of a trend that began more than a century ago, but its current level is unprecedented. As states' economies have become more closely linked, basic ideas about states, markets, trade, and currency exchange mechanisms are being reexamined. **International political economy**—"the study of the inequality in power and wealth between peoples and nations and the patterns of collective power and learning that change this inequality" (Isaak 1995)—has gained prominence as an area of investigation because it is at this vortex of politics and economics that controversies in world politics often find their most heated expression. The contests between rich and poor, Global North and Global South, and supplier and producer have risen to prominence. While some might say that the **high politics** governing military confrontation, superpower struggle, and the quest for national security in an insecure strategic environment remain a necessary preoccupation, most would also agree that the turbulent world of **low politics,** where the economic game of world politics is played out, has assumed new relevance. The strong undercurrents in the latter are reshaping the former. The dramatic growth of international trade and the increasingly interlocked nature of the world's economy compel attention to economic transactions. Today, high interest rates in one country lead to high interest rates in others, and a stock market free fall starting in Asia will spread to New York and London. Depression abroad means recession at home. Inflation is shared everywhere, and it seems to be beyond the control of any single actor. The balance of fiscal power is now as pertinent to national security and quality of life as the global balance of military power. These are some of the consequences of the growing international interdependence known as "globalization."

Globalization has led to theoretical rediscovery of political economy as an approach to understanding contemporary world affairs, and to the reexamination of such classic mid-nineteenth-century studies as John Stuart Mill's *Principles of Political Economy* and Karl Marx's *A Contribution to the Critique of Political Economy*. This reconsideration stems from the growing awareness that the conventional categories of politics and economics can no longer be separated. They do not form a meaningful dichotomy. The two realms are insuperably joined in an era of globalization that challenges states, because now "much of politics is economics, and most of economics is politics" (Lindblom 1979).

In this transformed context politics (states) and economics (markets) are merging. The growth of world trade, which is projected to exceed $8 trillion annually by the year 2000 (Schott 1996) and is expanding at a rate that far exceeds that of world output, is the most visible symbol and cause of globalization and interdependence. World trade properly deserves our primary attention, as do the dynamics of the floating **international monetary system** through which foreign currencies and credits are calculated when capital moves across borders through trade, investments, and loans. For inquiry, we need to first step backward and understand how globalization is influencing ideas about states' trade and monetary policies, which are rooted in past thinking. As the World Bank (1997) observes, "Around the globe, the state is in the spotlight. Far-reaching developments in the global economy have us revisiting basic questions about government: what its role should be, what it can and cannot do, and how best to do it." Accordingly, in this chapter we will focus on the critical role of the United States in shaping the contest between liberalism and mercantilism as alternative political economy philosophies underlying the different trade and monetary strategies states pursue in their quest for power and wealth.

The Shadow of Past Commercial Policy Philosophy

In July 1944, forty-four states allied in war against the Axis powers met in the New Hampshire resort community of Bretton Woods. Their purpose was to devise rules and new institutions to govern international trade and monetary relations after the war. As the world's preeminent economic and military power, the United States played the leading role. Its proposals were shaped by its perception of the causes of the 1930s' economic catastrophe and its beliefs about the role the U.S. dollar and economy should play in the postwar world. The United States sought free trade, open markets, and monetary stability—all central tenets of what would become the "Bretton Woods system"—based on the theoretical premises of **commercial liberalism** that advocates free markets with few barriers to private trade and capital flows.

commercial liberalism an economic theory advocating free markets and the removal of barriers to the flow of trade and capital as a locomotive for prosperity.

Britain also played an important role at the conference. Led by John Maynard Keynes—whose theories about the state's role in managing inflation, unemployment, and growth influenced a generation of economic thinking throughout the capitalist world—the British delegation won support for the principle of strong state action by states facing economic problems. That ideology conforms less closely with liberalism than with the principles of **mercantilism**, which assign states a greater role than markets in managing economic interactions and accepts protectionist trade policies to expand exports and limit imports as a strategy for acquiring national wealth.

mercantilism a popular theory in the seventeenth century preaching that trading states should increase their wealth and power by expanding exports and protecting their domestic economy from imports.

Despite these differences, the rules established at Bretton Woods reflected a remarkable level of agreement and governed international economic relations for the next twenty-five years because they rested on three political bases (Spero and Hart 1997). First, power was concentrated in the rich Western European and North American countries, which reduced the number of states whose agreement was necessary for effective management by restricting the potential challenges by Japan, the Global South, and the then-communist states of Eastern Europe and the Soviet Union. Second, the system's operation was facilitated by the dominant states' shared preference for an open international economy with limited government intervention. The onset of the Cold War helped cement Western unity, because a common external enemy led the Western industrial countries to perceive economic cooperation as necessary for both prosperity and security. That perception promoted a willingness to share economic burdens. Third, Bretton Woods worked because the Cold War encouraged the United States to assume the burdens of leadership and others to willingly accept that leadership to ensure American military support.

The political bases of the Bretton Woods system crumbled in 1972 when the United States suspended the convertibility of the dollar into gold and abandoned the system of fixed currency exchange rates at its core. Since then, when floating exchange rates and growing capital mobility have made monetary mechanisms unstable, more chaotic processes of international economic relations have materialized. Still, commercial liberalism's preference for market mechanisms over government intervention remains widely accepted today. Democracy and the urge to privatize and otherwise reduce government regulation of markets has spread worldwide since the Cold War collapsed, and multinational corporations are fulfilling the former role of the political pillars in the continuing support and strength of the liberal rules of the global trade regime. Thus it is still useful to characterize the contemporary international economic system as a **Liberal International Economic Order (LIEO)**—one based on such free market principles as openness and nondiscriminatory trade.

This is not to suggest that all states consistently support the liberal tenet that governments should not interfere by managing trade flows because they are prone to making misguided decisions. That principle is under attack within many states, including some of liberalism's unenthusiastic proponents, which are pressured domestically to protect industries and employment at home. When the president of the United States calls the king of Saudi Arabia to secure a multibillion-dollar sale of U.S.-built passenger jets—as Bill Clinton did—free trade is victimized. When the European Union risks the failure of a seven-year multilateral effort to reduce trade barriers rather than abandon a system of expensive agricultural subsidies that protects inefficient domestic producers from foreign competition—as did occur—mercantilism reigns supreme. States and markets continue to coexist in tension with one another, as they always have in a world of competitive sovereign states. Globalization has not erased this urge to compete, because states fear that **interdependence**—a condition of mutual sensitivity and mutual vulnerability (Keohane and Nye 1989)—will compromise their sovereignty and security. "Sensitivity" means that changes in one society are readily transmitted to another through their mutual interactions (e.g., inflation), and governments cannot control their transnational reverberations. "Vulnerability" results when changes in the policies (e.g., trade embargoes) of one state politically affect another. Interdependence thus encourages states to maximize their gains through international exchanges while minimizing their sensitivity and vulnerability. States' trade policies are naturally influenced by the selfish desire to increase the domestic benefits of international economic transactions and to lessen their adverse consequences, even if this will undermine the expansion of a global capitalist economy propelled by free trade.

The Clash between Liberal and Mercantile Values

How should states rationally cope in the globalized political economy to best manage economic change? The choices inspire different philosophies and policies. They force governments to attempt to reconcile the overriding need for states to cooperate with others in trade liberalization if they are to most effectively increase their country's wealth with each state's natural competitive desire to put its own welfare first.

Commercial Liberalism. Liberalism and mercantilism are competing ideologies based on "fundamentally different . . . conceptions of the relationships among society, state, and market" to which most controversies in international political economy are ultimately reducible (Gilpin 1998). A comparison of the logic behind the two theoretical traditions can help us to appreciate why a reconciliation or balance is so hard to achieve, why particular protectionist domestic interests sacrifice collective prosperity in order to maximize their own parochial gains, and why others criticize mercantilism as self-defeating.

theory a set of conclusions derived from assumptions (axioms) and/or evidence about some phenomenon, including its character, causes, and probable consequences and their ethical implications.

Commercial liberalism as a *political* **theory** explains economics by building on the presumption of humankind's natural inclination to cooperate in order to increase prosperity and enlarge individual liberty under law. Consequently, it is closely related to liberal theory as described in Chapter 2, which is based on the assumption that individuals usually act in rational, unemotional ways, recognizing that through mutually beneficial exchanges and compromise among individuals all can benefit.

Adam Smith, the eighteenth-century political economist who helped define the precepts of classical liberalism as well as modern-day economics, used the metaphor of the unregulated market's "invisible hand" to show how the collective or public interest can be served by humans' natural tendency to "truck, barter, and exchange" in pursuit of private gain. Hence the importance of "free" markets, which produce collective as well as private gain. David Ricardo, a nineteenth-century British political economist, added an important corollary to this thinking as applied to the international economy. Ricardo demonstrated conclusively that when all states specialize in the production of those goods in

Comparative Advantage and the Gains from Trade

Start with two countries, such as Japan and the United States. Each produces cameras and computers. Assume that the hypothetical figures below show output per hour for workers in each country.

	Worker Productivity	
	Japan	United States
Units of output per hour, cameras	9	4
Units of output per hour, computers	3	2

Clearly Japan has an absolute advantage in both products, as Japanese workers are more productive in turning out cameras and computers than the American workers are. Does this mean the two countries cannot benefit by trading with one another? If trade does occur, should each country continue to allocate its resources as in the past? The answer to both questions is no.

Each country should specialize in that item in which it has the greatest comparative cost advantage or least comparative cost disadvantage, and trade for others. Because Japan is three times more productive in cameras than computers, it should direct more of its resources into that industry. One cost of doing so is lost computer output, but Japan can turn out three additional cameras for every computer given up. The United States, on the other hand, can obtain only two computers.

Like their Japanese counterparts, American workers are also more productive in making cameras than computers. Still, U.S. resources should be directed to computers because the United States is at a smaller disadvantage compared with Japan in this area. If the United States specializes in computers and Japan in cameras and they trade with one another, each will benefit. The following scenario shows why.

Begin with one hundred workers in each industry before specialization:

Japanese Output	United States' Output
Cameras: 900	Cameras: 400
Computers: 300	Computers: 200

Shift ten Japanese workers from computer to camera production; shift twenty American workers from camera production to computers:

Japanese Output	United States' Output
Cameras: 990	Cameras: 320
Computers: 270	Computers: 240

Trade eighty Japanese cameras to the United States; trade thirty American computers to Japan:

Japanese Benefits from Trade	United States' Benefits from Trade
Cameras: 910	Cameras: 400
Computers: 300	Computers: 210

By shifting Japanese resources into the production of cameras and U.S. resources into computers, the same total inputs will cause camera and computer output to rise ten units each. The reason is because resources are now being used more efficiently. Benefits to both countries can be realized when each trades some of its additional output for the other's. Japan ends up with more cameras than before specialization and trade and the same number of computers, while the United States finds itself with more computers and the same number of cameras. More output in both countries means higher living standards.

The message derived from the logic of comparative advantage is clear. If all countries were to concentrate on those products they can produce most efficiently, the world's output and income would increase, and everyone's standard of living would rise.

which they enjoy a **comparative advantage** and trade them for goods in which others enjoy an advantage, a net gain in welfare for both states, in the form of higher living standards, will result. The principle of comparative advantage would become a touchstone for advocacy of free trade and the popularity of liberal (open) international economic systems (see Focus 8.1). Benjamin Franklin summarized the liberal premise more than two centuries ago: "No nation was ever ruined by trade."

Liberals such as Smith, Ricardo, and Franklin believed that markets work best when free of government interference. They reasoned that economic processes governing the production, distribution, and consumption of goods and services operate according to certain natural laws. They saw **politics** or the exercise of power as necessary if crass, and argued that while governments often performed their key tasks poorly, they had the capacity to overcome their historic proclivity to abuse power and could instead become engines for prosperity—providing they would not exercise a heavy hand in regulating the marketplace. (Today people subscribing to these views are described as conservatives, not liberals. The tenets described here are those of "classical" liberalism.) The hallmark of commercial liberal theory, then, is its commitment "to free markets and minimal state intervention. . . . Liberals believe economics is progressive and politics is regressive. Thus they conceive of progress as divorced from politics and based on the evolution of the market" (Gilpin 1998).

Transferred to the international level, these principles argue that trade and other forms of economic relations "are a source of peaceful relations among nations because the mutual benefits of trade and expanding interdependence among national economies will tend to foster cooperative relations. . . . A liberal international economy will have a moderating influence on international politics as it creates bonds of mutual interests and a commitment to the status quo" (Gilpin 1998).

There is a fly in this liberal ointment, however. Although commercial liberal theory promises that the "invisible hand" will maximize efficiency so that everyone will gain, it does not promise that everyone will gain equally. Instead, "everyone will gain in accordance with his or her contribution to the whole, but . . . not everyone will gain equally because individual productivities differ. Under free exchange, society as a whole will be more wealthy, but individuals will be rewarded in terms of their marginal productivity and relative contribution to the overall social product" (Gilpin 1998). This applies at the international level as well: The gains from international trade may be distributed quite unequally, even if the principle of comparative advantage governs. Commercial liberal theory ignores these differences, as it is concerned with **absolute gains** rather than **relative gains.** Other theorists, however, are more concerned with the distribution of economic rewards.

Mercantilism. Mercantilism is an economic philosophy deeply entrenched in the long story of states' quest for power and wealth. Its theoretical underpinnings prompted Adam Smith to write his famous critique in *The Wealth of Nations*, and its practice prompted rebellious American colonists to dump British tea into the Boston harbor in 1773.

Mercantilism advocates government regulation of economic life to increase state power and security. It emerged in Europe as the leading political economy philosophy after the decline of feudalism and helped to stimulate the first wave of Europe's imperialist expansion, which began in the fifteenth century. Accumulating gold and silver was seen as the route to state power and wealth, and imperialistically acquiring overseas colonies was seen as a means to that end.

While states no longer try to stockpile precious metals, many continue to intervene in the marketplace. In the contemporary context, then, **neomercantilism** refers to "a trade policy whereby a state seeks to maintain a balance-of-trade surplus and to promote domestic production and employment by reducing imports, stimulating home production, and promoting exports" (Walters and Blake

absolute gains a condition in which all participants in exchanges become better off.

relative gains a condition in which some participants benefit more than others.

1992). Its advocates are sometimes called "economic nationalists." For them, states must compete for position and power, and economic resources are the source of state power. From this it follows that "economic activities are and should be subordinate to the goal of state building and the interests of the state. All nationalists ascribe to the primacy of the state, of national security, and of military power in the functioning of the international system" (Gilpin 1998).

As an ideology of political economy, mercantilism shares much in common with political realism: Realists and mercantilists both see the state as the principal world actor; both view the international system as anarchical; and both dwell on the aggressively competitive drive of people and states for advantage. "Economic nationalists . . . stress the role of power in the rise of a market and the conflictual nature of international economic relations; they argue that economic interdependence must have a political foundation and that it creates yet another arena of interstate conflict, increases national vulnerability, and constitutes a mechanism that one society can employ to dominate another" (Gilpin 1998).

While commercial liberals emphasize the mutual benefits of cooperative trade agreements, mercantilists are more concerned that the gains realized by one side of the bargain will come at the expense of the other. For them, relative gains are more important than both parties' absolute gains. An American economic nationalist, for instance, would complain about a trade agreement that promised the United States a 5 percent growth in income and the Chinese 6 percent. Although the bargain would assure an eventual increase in U.S. living standards, its position compared with China's would erode. Indeed, projected over the long run, such seemingly small differences would eventually lead to China's replacement of the United States as the world's largest economy—an outcome highly unacceptable to American economic nationalists. Calculations such as these explain why achieving mutual gains through international cooperation often encounters stiff resistance from domestic groups seeking to protect their profits from foreign competition. It also explains why specific, negatively affected domestic producers lobby for mercantilist measures, and why they sometimes succeed against the unorganized interests of consumers who benefit from free trade.

Protectionism is the generic term used to describe a number of mercantilist policies designed to "protect" domestic producers from the influx of foreign goods. The following are some common protectionist strategies:

- **Beggar-thy-neighbor policies** seek to enhance domestic welfare by promoting trade surpluses that can be realized only at other countries' expense. They reflect a government's efforts to reduce unemployment through currency devaluations, tariffs, quotas, export subsidies, and other strategies that adversely affect its trade partners. These protective strategies encourage unequal exchanges between exporters and importers (see Chapter 5).

- **Import quotas** unilaterally specify the quantity of a particular product that can be imported from abroad. In the late 1950s, for example, the United States established import quotas on oil, arguing that they were necessary to protect U.S. national security. Hence the government, rather than the marketplace, determined the amount and source of imports.

- **Export quotas** result from negotiated agreements between producers and consumers and restrict the flow of products (e.g., shoes or sugar) from the former to the latter. An **orderly market arrangement (OMA)** is a formal

protectionism barriers to foreign trade, such as tariffs and quotas, that protect local industries from competition.

agreement in which a country agrees to limit the export of products that might impair workers in the importing country, often under specific rules designed to monitor and manage trade flows. The Multi-Fiber Arrangement (MFA) is an example of an elaborate OMA that restricts exports of textiles and apparel. It originated in the early 1960s, when the United States formalized earlier, informal **voluntary export restrictions (VERs)** negotiated with Japan and Hong Kong to protect domestic producers from cheap cotton imports. The quota system was later extended to other importing and exporting countries and then, in the 1970s, to other fibers, when it became the MFA.

- Import and export quotas are representative of a broader category of trade restrictions known as **nontariff barriers (NTBs)** that discriminate against imports without direct tax levies. As complex societies strive to protect the welfare of their citizens through numerous and often complex government regulations regarding health and safety, foreign-produced goods frequently cannot compete. NTBs are now a more important form of trade protectionism than tariffs that impose taxes on commodity imports to shelter *particular* domestic industries from foreign competition.

- Among developing countries, whose domestic industrialization goals may be hindered by the absence of protection from the Global North's more efficient firms, the **infant industry** argument is often used to justify mercantilist trade policies. According to this argument, tariffs or other forms of protection are necessary to nurture young industries until they eventually mature and lower production costs to compete effectively in the global marketplace. Import-substitution industrialization policies, once popular in Latin America and elsewhere, often depended on protection of infant industries (see Chapter 5).

- In the Global North, *creating* comparative advantages now motivates the use of what is known as **strategic trade policy** as a neomercantilist means of ensuring that a country's industries will remain competitive. Strategic trade is a form of industrial policy that targets government subsidies toward particular industries so as to gain a competitive edge over foreign producers.

The theory of realism helps to account for states' impulse to practice mercantilist and neomercantilist protectionism. Recall that realism argues that states often shun cooperation because international anarchy without global governance creates fear. Threatened states mistrust one another's motives. Moreover, in the self-help international system, states alone are responsible for their survival and well-being. As a result, uncertainty about others' expansionist aims encourages each state to spend "a portion of its effort, not forwarding its own good, but in providing the means of protecting itself against others" (Waltz 1979).

The insecurity that breeds competition rather than cooperation is often exhibited in international economic relations. Those who see states' power and wealth as inextricably linked conclude that "even if nation-states do not fear for their physical survival, they worry that a decrease in their power capabilities relative to those of other states will compromise their political autonomy, expose them to the influence attempts of others, or lessen their ability to prevail in political disputes with allies and adversaries" (Mastanduno 1991). Thus many states are "defensively positional actors" that seek not only to promote their domestic well-being but also to defend their rank (position) in comparison with others (see Grieco 1995).

The relative gains issue speaks to the difficulties of achieving international cooperation under anarchical conditions, and explains why some domestic producers vigorously oppose liberal (open) international economies despite the evidence that free trade promotes economic growth (Quinn 1997). Different countries therefore practice dissimilar economic policies. Some endorse free trade, and others impose protectionist barriers; some see an unregulated market as the best method for protecting the greatest good for the greatest number; others seek to tilt the playing field to their own advantage.

Hegemony: A Precondition for Economic Order and Free Trade?

Hegemonic stability theory, a blend of liberalism and mercantilism, holds that when a **hegemon** ascends so that a preponderance of military and economic power is held in the hands of a single state, international economic stability based on liberal principles can materialize to alleviate the fears of nationalistic mercantilists. Unlike mercantilism, this realist worldview follows the logic of long-cycle theory (see Chapter 4) in viewing the balancing of power among competing actors in anarchy as the key to global economic order, but accepts the likelihood that order can best emerge at those phases in the long-term redistribution of global power when an all-powerful single hegemon uses its position to enforce free-trade rules. Hegemonic stability theory thus "assumes that a liberal economic system cannot be self-sustaining but must be maintained over the long term through the actions of the dominant economy" (Gilpin 1998).

Hegemony is the ability to "dictate, or at least dominate, the rules and arrangements by which international relations, political and economic, are conducted" (Goldstein 1988). In the world economy it occurs when a single great power garners a sufficient preponderance of material resources so that it can dominate the international flow of raw materials, capital, and trade (Keohane 1984).

From its preponderant position, a hegemon is able to promote rules for the whole global system that protect the hegemon's own interests. Hegemons such as the United States (and Britain before it), whose domestic economies are based on capitalist principles, have championed liberal (open) international economic systems, because their comparatively greater control of technology, capital, and raw materials has given them more opportunities to profit from a system free of mercantilist restraints. When they have exercised that power by enforcing such free-trade rules, the hegemon's economies typically have served as "engines of growth" for others in the "liberal train."

However, historically hegemons have also had special responsibilities. They have had to coordinate states' **macroeconomic policies,** manage the international monetary system to enable one state's money to be exchanged for others', make sure that countries facing balance-of-payments deficits (imbalances in their financial inflows and outflows) could find the credits necessary to finance their deficits, and serve as lenders of last resort during financial crises. When the most powerful liberal states could not perform these tasks, they have often backtracked toward more closed (protected or regulated) domestic economies, and in doing so have undermined the open international system that was previously advantageous to them (Block 1977). This kind of departure historically has made tariffs, monetary regulations, and other mercantilist policies more widespread, and thereby undermined the LIEO regime. In short, hegemonic

macroeconomic policies the study of aggregate economic indicators such as GDP, the money supply, and the balance of trade that governments monitor to measure changes in the national economy.

collective goods goods such as safe drinking water from which everyone benefits.

states have not only had the greatest capacity to make a free-trade regime succeed but in the past they have also had the greatest responsibility for its effective operation and preservation. To interpret whether hegemonic stability theory is likely to hold in the future, a closer look at the theory's logic is useful.

The Hegemonic Pillars of Free Markets and Free Trade. Nearly all economic theories accept particular principles about the preconditions for the creation of a regime fostering the free movement of goods across national borders. A core concept that informs discussion is known as public or **collective goods.** These are benefits everyone shares and from which no one can be excluded selectively. National security is one such collective good that governments try to provide for all of their citizens, regardless of the resources that individuals contribute through taxation. In the realm of economic analysis, an open international economy permitting the relatively free movement of goods, services, and capital is similarly seen as a desirable collective good, inasmuch as it permits economic benefits for all states that would not be available if the global economy were closed to the free trade.

According to hegemonic stability theory, the collective good of an open global economy needs a single, dominant power—a hegemon—to remain open and liberal. If a hegemon does not exist or is unwilling to use its power to provide this collective good, states will be tempted to free ride rather than contributing to the maintenance of the liberal international economy. And if enough states take this easy route when no hegemon is present to support the structure of free trade, the entire structure may collapse.

The analogy of a public park helps us to clarify this principle. If there were no central government to provide for the maintenance of the park, individuals themselves would have to cooperate to keep the park in order (the trees trimmed, the lawn mowed, and so on). But some may try to come and enjoy the benefits of the park without pitching in. If enough people realize that they can get away with this—that they can enjoy a beautiful park without helping with its upkeep—it will not be long before the once beautiful park looks shabby. Cooperation to provide a public good is thus difficult. This is also the case with the collective good of a liberal international economy, because many states that enjoy the collective good of an orderly, open, free market economy pay little or nothing for it. These are known as **free riders.** A hegemon typically tolerates free riders, partly because the benefits that the hegemon provides, such as a stable global currency, encourage other states to accept the leader's dictates. Thus, both gain, much as liberalism sees the benefits of cooperation as a "positive-sum" outcome because both sides to a bargain stand to gain from their exchanges. If the costs of leadership begin to multiply, however, a hegemon will tend to become less tolerant of others' free riding. In such a situation cooperation will increasingly be seen as one-sided or zero-sum because most of the benefits come at the expense of the hegemon. Then the open global economy will crumble amidst a competitive race for individual gain at others' expense.

Charles Kindleberger (1973), an international economist, first theorized about the need for a preponderant liberal hegemon to maintain order and stability. In his explanation of the 1930s Great Depression, Kindleberger concluded that "the international economic and monetary system needs leadership, a country which is prepared, consciously or unconsciously, . . . to set standards of conduct for other countries; and to seek to get others to follow them, to take on an undue share of the burdens of the system, and in particular

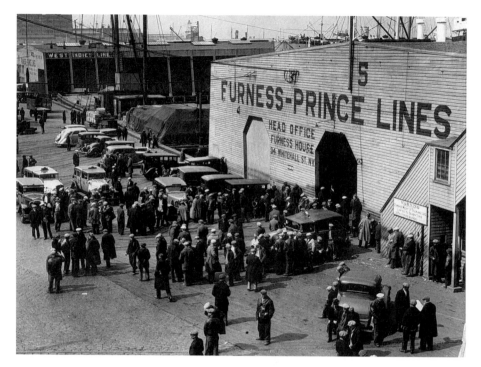

Britain's inability to provide for world order and stability and the United States' disinclination to assume this leadership role after World War I plunged the world into the Great Depression—a severe drop in business activity, production, and capital investment that led to high rates of corporate failure. As international trade dried up in its wake, harbor activity in port cities slowed to a crawl, and longshoremen such as those pictured here found themselves without work.

to take on its support in adversity." Britain played this role from 1815 until the outbreak of World War I in 1914; and the United States assumed the British mantle in the decades immediately following World War II. In the interwar years, however, Britain was unable to play its previous leadership role, and the United States, although capable of leadership, was unwilling to exercise it. The void, Kindleberger concluded, was a principal cause of the "width and depth" of the Great Depression throughout the world in the 1930s.

The Causes of Hegemonic Decline. Although hegemonic powers benefit from the liberal economic systems that their power promotes, the very success of liberalism eventually erodes the pillars which support it.

> Economic competition and the price mechanism drive the market economy toward ever higher levels of productive efficiency, economic growth, and the integration of national markets. In time, the market produces profound shifts in the location of economic activities and affects the international redistribution of economic and industrial power. The unleashing of market forces transforms the political framework itself, undermines the hegemonic power, and creates a new political environment to which the world must eventually adjust. With the inevitable shift in the international distribution of economic and military power from the core to rising nations in the periphery and elsewhere, the capacity of the hegemon to maintain the system decreases. Capitalism and the market system thus tend to destroy the political foundations on which they must ultimately rest. (Gilpin 1987, 77–78)

The leading economic power's ability to adapt is critical to maintenance of its dominant position. Britain was unable to adapt, and fell from its top-ranked position. Is the United States destined to suffer the same fate? Many contend that the signs of U.S. hegemonic decline should not be ignored.

- In 1947, the United States accounted for nearly 50 percent of the combined gross world product. By 1960, its share had slipped to 28 percent, by 1970 to 25 percent, and by 1980 to 23 percent. Since then the proportion has ranged between 22 and 26 percent, but is projected to decline at the end of the twenty-first century (IMF 1997).

- Since the late 1970s, average annual GNP growth rates in Europe, China, Japan, and the Newly Industrialized Economies have typically outstripped that of the United States; the U.S. is no longer the world's biggest economy— it is second behind the European Common Market (Thurow 1998).

- The U.S. share of world industrial output of both "sunset industries," such as steel and automobiles, and "sunrise industries," such as microelectronics and computers, has declined.

- Since the 1970s, labor productivity has grown more rapidly in Europe and Asia than in the United States.

- The U.S. share of world financial reserves declined abruptly as the United States moved from being the globe's greatest creditor country in 1980 to the world's largest debtor by 1990. It "remains the biggest debtor nation in history" (D. White 1998). The European Union's "creation of the euro will end America's monetary dominance" as the globe's lender of last resort with a stable currency to prime the pump monetarily for trade (Bergsten 1997), and for the first time since 1945 "investors and financiers will have a viable alternative to the U.S. dollar" (Thurow 1998).

- U.S. dependence on foreign energy sources, first evident in the early 1970s, has continued unabated in the 1990s.

- The U.S. investment in public infrastructure in 1997 was lower than that of all the other G-7 industrialized economies (*Harper's* 994, January 1997, 15), and the United States is "losing its ability to compete with other economies because of its low savings rates and insufficient investment in education" (Thurow 1998).

Thus in all the areas essential to hegemony—control over raw materials, capital, and markets, and competitive advantages in production—U.S. preponderance has waned.

Some "declinist" analysts accept Paul Kennedy's (1987) thesis that **imperial overstretch** will be the cause of America's fall from prominence, as "The United States now runs the risk that the sum total of [its] global interests and obligations is nowadays far larger than the country's power to defend them all simultaneously." This prediction derives from a principle suggested by past hegemonic experiences, namely "that a power that wants to remain number one for generation after generation requires not just military capability, not just national will, but also a flourishing and efficient economic base, strong finances and a healthy social fabric, for it is upon such foundations that the country's military strength rests in the long term" (Kennedy 1992).

Kennedy's popular declinist thesis was attacked by critics who saw the parallels between the American and earlier British experiences as unfair and as unappreciative of continuing U.S. dynamism (see, e.g., Nye 1998). Still, the rise of economic rivals to U.S. hegemonic leadership, partly as a result of America's low domestic savings rate and poor educational performance, does

imperial overstretch Paul Kennedy's thesis that hegemons decline because they make global commitments in excess of their ability to fulfill them.

not bode well for continuing U.S. economic dominance. "The decline . . . of the U.S. share of world exports, and of world GNP, or more narrowly of world production of manufactures" (Strange 1996) are the primary reasons why "competitiveness" became such a key theme in the Clinton administration's economic policy.

An undisputed hegemonic power typically can afford to be less concerned about its relative power position than others. It is therefore less likely to attempt to maximize its share of the global market than are aspiring hegemons or other economic powers threatened by an erosion in their relative power. As a hegemon's dominance erodes, however, its behavior on trade and other issues can be expected to change. The United States once tolerated—indeed, encouraged—other states to practice mercantile policies as it sought to cement Western solidarity during the Cold War. Today it is less willing to assume the burdens of maintaining the liberal international economic order it once championed.

The Uncertain Consequences of Hegemonic Decline. What happens when a hegemon's preponderant power declines? Domestically we would expect it to abandon carrying the torch of commercial liberalism as the forces of economic nationalism gain politically. Internationally, hegemonic stability theory predicts that disorder will result, because hegemonic leadership is "The cement that holds the system together" (Gilpin 1987). In extreme instances, armed conflict may follow; for example, the hegemonic decline of Britain and the absence of U.S. leadership may have precipitated the two world wars of the twentieth century (see Gilpin 1981).

An orderly and stable world political economy existed from the end of World War II until the early 1970s, when U.S. hegemony was unchallenged. Since then, however, American dominance has waned, and international economic relations have been wracked by periodic crises and instability. Still, the system has not collapsed, as it did in the years between World Wars I and II. Is this because the processes of hegemonic decline have yet to play themselves out? Or, as some would argue, is the decline of American power a myth? Or is it because the institutions and rules put into place to govern the liberal order during the period of American hegemony have now taken on a life of their own? The last view is the most convincing one to commercial liberals, who believe that the rise of a liberal international regime and embedded network of complementary institutions to support its open rules explains the persistence of economic order and growth, even though American hegemony may be fading (Strange 1996).

The power of that conviction resides in the fact that the commercial liberalism institutionalized in the original Bretton Woods system is continuing to gain strength, *despite* the relative decline of U.S. hegemony. True, "America's defection could throw the process into reverse" (Bergsten 1997). However, even in the absence of a U.S. hegemon pushing for trade liberalization, and even in the possible face of the declining U.S. hegemon succumbing to the temptations of (free-riding) mercantilism, trade liberalization is now too deeply entrenched for it to collapse easily. The free-trade regime has too many supporters, including powerful multinational (or, more accurately, "global") corporations, for it to need a single hegemonic protector to preserve free trade as it did in the past two hundred years. Institutionalized globalization has progressed to a level that makes the continuation of a liberal trading system likely, because too many states and multilateral institutions have an enormous stake in its preservation.

International regimes are created when states devise rules for cooperation even under international anarchy. Although most of the liberal international regimes (rules and institutions) that govern international trade today first developed during the era of U.S. dominance, they have continued to flourish. "By providing more information, establishing mechanisms for monitoring and generating shared expectations, institutions can create an environment in which interstate cooperation is possible even without a single dominant leader" (Krasner 1993). Thus the persisting liberal international trade regime may explain why the magnitude and extent of disruptions predicted by the relative decline of U.S. power have not materialized, and why, perhaps, the strength of the free-trade regime no longer depends on the existence of an all-powerful hegemon.

To better probe that hypothesis and understand the likely future of global economics, let us now inspect how those international trade and monetary rules have evolved from mere pledges to reduce trade barriers to become entrenched customary policy practices.

• • •

LIBERALISM, MERCANTILISM, AND HEGEMONY IN THE INTERNATIONAL TRADE REGIME

In the period immediately following World War II, when the United States became the world's new hegemon, it simultaneously became the preeminent voice in international trade affairs. The liberal trading system the United States chose to promote drew on the painful lessons of the 1930s. The zero-sum, beggar-thy-neighbor policies associated with intensely competitive economic nationalism were widely seen as the major cause that deepened and perpetuated the economic depression of the 1930s. Removing barriers to trade became a priority and led to the recurrent rounds of trade negotiations that cumulatively produced remarkable reductions in tariff rates. As the large U.S. market was opened to foreign producers, other countries' economies grew, and rising trade contributed to the climate that encouraged others to open their markets also.

That movement toward free trade progressed in a series of steps. At the time of the Bretton Woods negotiations, the United States envisioned a new International Trade Organization (ITO) that would seek lower restrictions on trade and set rules of commerce. The organization was stillborn, however. The proposed trading scheme, popularly known as the "Havana Charter," failed to win the approval of the U.S. Congress: "Protectionists opposed the arrangement for being too liberal, and liberals were against it for being too protectionist. . . . Without U.S. support the ITO was dead" (Isaak 1995).

Without the ITO, the United States needed to find another institutional base from which to create and enhance a liberalized trade regime. It turned to the **General Agreement on Tariffs and Trade (GATT)** that, after its birth in the late 1940s, became the principal international organization designed to promote and protect free trade in the postwar Liberal International Economic Order.

GATT was never intended to be a formal institution with enforcement powers. Instead, a premium was placed on negotiations and reaching a consensus to settle disputes among parties to the agreement, which was first and foremost a commercial treaty. As the trading system changed and disputes multiplied, though, GATT—under pressure from the United States—increasingly became involved in dispute settlement following increasingly legalistic procedures.

GATT an international organization affiliated with the United Nations that promotes international trade and tariff reductions.

Those rules put into law an evolving regime whose primary mission has been increasing free trade.

Hegemonic Power and the Changing Free-Trade Regime

The United States, the principal catalyst to the GATT negotiating rounds, opened its own market to others and tolerated their free riding. For example, the United States knowingly acquiesced in Japan's protectionist trade practices and Europe's discrimination against many U.S. exports, because restoring European and Japanese economic vitality was the first U.S. foreign policy goal. In the poisoned Cold War atmosphere, the long-term economic benefits of their revitalization outweighed the short-term costs. Thus the United States not only permitted but actually encouraged others' relative gains.

The high point in the momentum toward a liberal trade regime in industrial products occurred with the mid-1960s Kennedy Round of negotiations, but they did not deal with agriculture. Although trade in agriculture fell beyond the purview of GATT as originally conceived, it was becoming increasingly important. The European Economic Community's (EEC) "egregiously mercantilist" (Babai 1993) Common Agricultural Policy (CAP) posed the immediate challenge. By maintaining politically acceptable but artificially high prices for farm products produced within the EEC, CAP curtailed American agricultural exports to Europe, which had become a major U.S. trade partner. Disagreements on this issue began to raise doubts among U.S. policymakers about the ultimate wisdom of promoting expansionist economic policies from which others benefited.

As Europe (and later Japan) challenged U.S. economic prowess, a rising tide of protectionist forces bombarded Congress with trade restriction demands designed to insulate the United States from foreign economic competition. The liberal trade regime came under attack and was now threatened. To cope with growing protectionist sentiments in the United States, the Nixon administration sought authority from Congress to negotiate lower tariff barriers with other countries. This congressional concession to the president laid the basis for the Tokyo Round of multilateral trade negotiations, concluded in 1979 after nearly six years of bargaining.

The Tokyo Round began in a radically different environment from that of the previous GATT sessions. The value of world trade had grown exponentially. The level of economic interdependence among the world's leading industrial countries had reached unprecedented levels. Tariffs no longer posed the principal barriers to trade, and the United States no longer remained an unchallenged hegemon. In this new setting, addressing the new protectionism—the rise of nontariff barriers to trade (NTBs) that discriminate against imports without direct tax levies beyond the scope of international regulation—and reducing barriers to free trade in agricultural products took on greater urgency.

The Tokyo Round produced a series of standards of conduct ("codes") directed at the increasingly troublesome NTBs. It also granted an exception to the principle of reciprocity when it approved of a Generalized System of Preferences (GSP), which granted developing countries preferential access to markets in the Global North. Still, the developing countries, many of which were not members of GATT, generally shunned the accords because of their belief that the Tokyo negotiations preserved the North's protectionist practices that deprived them of market access. Furthermore, the Tokyo Round did not clearly reaffirm the principles underlying GATT and the liberal trade regime (Krasner 1979). Nor did it deal with the growing incidence of neomercantilist and strategic trade practices that were of special concern to the United States. In fact, GATT's rules and procedures were increasingly irrelevant to the changes taking place in the trade regime, which meant they were often ignored.

By the end of the Tokyo Round, it was clear that the promise and practice of free trade diverged widely. Spectacular increases in Japan's exports and overall economic performance during the 1960s and 1970s posed especially formidable challenges not only to the United States but also to the premises of liberalism. As the Asian Tigers and others imitated Japan's neomercantilist behavior, the Liberal International Economic Order and the shared interests and values that once bound North America and Western Europe began to unravel. Europe challenged the GATT principle of **nondiscrimination**—"the core notion that each national government would grant equal treatment to the products of all others adhering to the GATT system." By definition, the European Community was "an enormous exception," as "its members agreed to grant one another more favorable (i.e., duty-free) market access than they granted to outsiders" (Destler 1995).

U.S. determination to reverse its burgeoning trade deficit explains why the Reagan administration abandoned its previous free-trade leadership and embraced *fair trade* as an alternative. It charged that "the playing field was tilted" against American producers by other governments' mercantilist practices and claimed that "the process of reciprocal liberalization under the GATT was increasingly biased against the United States." Because "other countries relied more heavily on nontariff barriers and other industrial policies than did the United States . . . critics of U.S. trade policy began to emphasize reciprocity in *levels* of protection—or comparable market access—rather than just reciprocal *changes* in the level of protection" as a negotiating tool in GATT (Bayard and Elliot 1994). This U.S. threat to close its market followed hegemonic stability theory in predicting that as the costs of leadership begin to outweigh its benefits, a declining hegemon's acceptance of absolute gains from trade would be replaced by complaints about trade competitors' relative gains.

Over the next decade the United States launched a multipronged strategy to right what it saw as the wrongs of the liberal trade regime it had once championed. It fought for a new round of multilateral trade negotiations with a specific mandate to address issues of growing concern to the United States; it pursued unilateral strategies that smacked of the same mercantilist principles it deplored in others; it lobbied to liberalize trade in services and to promote the foreign direct investment and protection of intellectual property rights—goals that primarily benefited (multinational) firms in the United States; and it moved to create regional free-trade zones to balance the European Union and the potential rise of other competitors. The new response became highly visible in the **Uruguay Round** of negotiations, which began in 1986. Barriers to trade in services (insurance, for example), intellectual property rights (such as copyrights on computer software, music, and movies), and investments (stocks and bonds) were put on the agenda as new issues, and no state stood to gain as much from these provisions as the United States.

The long-standing issue of world trade in agriculture had previously evolved outside of the main GATT framework. Agricultural trade was especially controversial because it is deeply enmeshed in the domestic politics of producing states, such as the United States and some members of the European

Union, for which the global market is an outlet for surplus production. At the core of differences on agricultural trade are the enormous government subsidies that some leading producers pay farmers to keep them competitive internationally. During the Uruguay Round, the United States reversed its prior silence when it aggressively proposed to phase out all agricultural subsidies and farm trade protection programs within a decade. Its proposal gained some support, but stiff European opposition created an impasse in the Uruguay Round negotiations, causing the original 1990 target date for conclusion of the talks to be missed. (In the process, GATT earned a reputation as the "General Agreement to Talk and Talk.") Three years later, when the negotiations finally ended, the United States could claim a measure of success on agricultural issues, as the EU and others agreed to new (but limited) rules on export subsidies, domestic subsidies, and market access.

Global South states figured prominently in several Uruguay Round issues, particularly agriculture and textiles. Trade-related intellectual property rights (TRIPs), one of the new issues confronted at Uruguay, was another. The United States (and other Northern states) wanted protection of copyrights, patents, trademarks, microprocessor designs, and trade secrets, as well as prohibitions on unfair competition. When developing countries also vigorously resisted these efforts to enforce standardized intellectual property regulations throughout the world, no significant headway was made. During the negotiations, U.S. initiatives regarding trade-related investment measures (TRIMs) and services (such as banking and insurance) and its efforts to abolish European restrictions on non-European (read American) movies and television programs also met widespread resistance.

However, the United States ultimately won in its efforts to modernize GATT. Despite disagreements and disappointments—after prolonged bickering and in nothing less than a crisis atmosphere—the frustrated GATT negotiators finally struck a bargain. Their product in the prolonged and bitter Uruguay Round negotiations was the creation of a new organization with "teeth"—a **World Trade Organization (WTO)** whose purpose is to monitor the implementation of trade agreements and settle disputes among trading partners. The agreement was the most comprehensive trade deal in history, covering everything from paper clips to jet aircraft. The very bulk of the document symbolized its breadth: "The Final Act signed in Marrakesh, Morocco, on 15 April, 1994 weighed 385 pounds and included over 22,000 pages" (Jackson 1994, 131).

The new World Trade Organization represented a breathtaking step in free-trade management. The WTO extended GATT's coverage to products, sectors, and conditions of trade not previously covered adequately. The WTO also enhanced previous dispute-settlement procedures by making the findings of its arbitration panels binding on the domestic laws of participating nations (GATT's findings were not binding). And the WTO dealt with the problem of free riding by being available only to states that belong to GATT, subscribe to all of the Uruguay Round agreements, and make market access commitments (under the old GATT system, free riding was possible when some small states were permitted to benefit from trade liberalization without having to make contributions of their own). Finally, the WTO embodied certain "legislative powers" that removed the need for prolonged negotiations that result in large "packages" embracing multiple concessions, as in previous multilateral negotiating sessions. Now it is possible simply to amend existing rules one at a time.

Thus, the WTO extended the GATT structure in a manner consistent with what was once envisioned for the failed ITO, as there is now "an explicit treaty-charter agreement establishing an international organization for trade, which can take its place beside the other Bretton Woods organizations" (Jackson 1994).

Fear of failure and its consequence for the trade regime and individual countries' economic and political stability provided important incentives for the accord's acceptance, which proponents hailed as a big step toward keeping the liberal trade regime afloat in an increasingly competitive and globalized world economy. The anticipated payoff of lower free-trade barriers figured prominently. Analysts predicted that the Uruguay Round would stimulate expansion of global output by billions of dollars in the decade ending in 2003. The agreement was no less important for the United States. U.S. Trade Representative Mickey Kantor predicted that the pact would generate two million jobs for American workers over the next decade. President Clinton claimed that the agreement would "cement our position of leadership in the new global economy."

In the end, then, the Uruguay Round that created the World Trade Organization had struck a blow for liberalism. It may also have struck a blow for hegemony because the agreement that outlawed a great deal of free riding (neomercantilism) was to the U.S. hegemon's advantage, as the United States derived greater relative gains from the successful conclusion of the pathbreaking multilateral negotiations. The irony of this step toward trade liberalization was that the new rules and institutions incorporated in the 132-member World Trade Organization made it increasingly difficult and costly for the United States to extricate its economy from the growing force of the global economy on which U.S. prosperity increasingly depends. Trade liberalization is thus likely to continue, with or without U.S. support, because "globalization and multinationalization have reduced the powers of all governments to regulate behavior and set independent economic policies. Companies are no longer wedded to any one economy" (Thurow 1998). As former U.S. Trade Representative Mickey Kantor predicted in November 1997, "There will still be progress, because there are companies around the world that share an interest in getting rid of the political obstacles to doing business. The only question is whether those deals will be struck with us, or around us."

• • •

MONETARY MATTERS: CAN REGIMES PROMOTE TRADE AND GROWTH?

States cannot trade as they wish. The flow of exports (and imports) depends on many factors, such as the level of tariffs, quotas, and duties of others that restrict sales abroad and, of course, changes in global demand and prices for the goods and services that countries' producers sell in the global marketplace. The mechanisms operative for setting the currency exchange rates by which the value of traded goods are priced are another key structural factor that heavily influences international trade. Indeed, the **monetary system** is crucial for international trade, for without a stable and predictable method of calculating the value of sales and foreign investments, those transactions become too risky, causing trade and investment activity to fall.

When they met at Bretton Woods, leaders in the capitalist West were vividly aware of the need for a reliable mechanism for determining the value of countries' currencies in relation to one another. They recognized that this was a necessary precondition for trade, and, from it, economic recovery and prosperity. The negotiating parties agreed that the postwar monetary system should be based on **fixed exchange rates,** and assigned governments primary responsibility for enforcing its rules. In addition, they foresaw the need to create what later became the International Monetary Fund (IMF), to help states maintain equilibrium in their balance of payments and stability in their exchange rates with one another. The International Bank for Reconstruction and Develop-**World Bank,** was also created to aid recovery from the war.

Today the IMF and World Bank are important, if controversial, players in the global monetary and financial systems. Their primary missions are to promote Global South development and serve as "lenders of last resort" when its member states face financial crises, providing those seeking assistance meet the often painful "conditions" requiring domestic adjustments to strengthen their liberal economies' export markets. In the period immediately after World War II, these institutions commanded too little authority and too few resources to cope with the enormous devastation of the war. The United States stepped into the breach.

The U.S. dollar became the key to the hegemonic role that the United States eagerly assumed as manager of the international monetary system. Backed by a vigorous and healthy economy, a fixed relationship between gold and the dollar (pegged at $35 per ounce of gold), and the U.S. commitment to exchange gold for dollars at any time (known as "dollar convertibility"), the dollar became "as good as gold." In fact, others preferred dollars to gold for use in managing their balance-of-payments and savings accounts. Dollars earned interest, which gold did not; they did not incur storage and insurance costs; and they were needed to buy imports necessary for survival and postwar reconstruction. Thus the postwar economic system was a dollar-based system with the dollar a "parallel currency" universally accepted as the "currency against which every other country sold or redeemed its own national currency in the exchange markets" (Triffin 1978–1979). Dollars became the international reserve used by monetary authorities in most countries, as well as the primary "working balances" used by private banks, corporations, and individuals for international trade and capital transactions.

To maintain the value of their currencies, central banks in other countries either bought or sold their own currencies, using the dollar to raise or depress their value. Thus the Bretton Woods monetary regime was based on fixed exchange rates, and ultimately required a measure of government intervention for its preservation (see Focus 8.2).

To get U.S. dollars into the hands of those who needed them most, the Marshall Plan provided Western European states billions of dollars in aid to buy the U.S. goods necessary for rebuilding their war-torn economies. The United States also encouraged deficits in its own balance of payments as a way of providing **international liquidity** (reserve assets used to settle international accounts) in the form of dollars.

In addition to providing liquidity, the United States assumed a disproportionate share of the burden of rejuvenating Western Europe and Japan. It supported European and Japanese trade competitiveness, permitted certain forms of protectionism (such as Japanese restrictions on importing U.S. products), and condoned discrimination against the dollar (as in the European Payments Union, which promoted trade within Europe at the expense of trade with the

World Bank also known as the International Bank of Reconstruction and Development (IBRD), the World Bank is the globe's major IGO for financing economic growth in the Global South.

A Primer on Exchange-Rate Systems

Without a world government, there is no common international currency for carrying on financial transactions and settling international accounts. If states want to trade or engage in other financial transactions with one another, a mechanism must be devised to determine their monies' relative value. The international monetary system establishes that framework. Its goal is stability in the value of national currencies combined with the flexibility necessary to adjust relative values when circumstances require it.

Currency rates of exchange express the value of one currency, such as the German mark, in relation to another, such as the U.S. dollar. There are three types of systems: fixed, floating, and managed.

- A *fixed exchange-rate system* is one in which a government sets the value of its currency at a fixed rate in relation to others' money. The gold standard of the late nineteenth century is an example. National currency values were defined in terms of gold, whose coinage was used as money. The "invisible hand" of the gold market adjusted their relative values, righting imbalances in their balance of payments—at least in theory. In practice, Britain bore a disproportionate share of the burden of ensuring a stable monetary system.

  The Bretton Woods system was also designed as a fixed exchange-rate system. The United States set the value of its currency at $35 per ounce of gold, and other nations priced their currencies in relation to the dollar, maintaining value within narrowly defined boundaries. Theoretically, devaluations were permitted if necessary to maintain equilibriums in states' trade and payments and stability in the system as a whole. In practice, Bretton Woods depended critically on the hegemonic power of the United States.

- A system of *floating exchange rates* replaced Bretton Woods in the early 1970s. The link between the dollar and gold was cut. Market forces, rather than government actions, were expected to adjust the relative value of states' currencies to reflect the underlying strengths and weaknesses of their economies. Theoretically, they would more or less automatically adjust imbalances in their trade and payments with one another. Actually, state intervention again proved necessary to ensure monetary stability and flexibility. Without a hegemonic power to perform these tasks, policy coordination among the world's principal economic powers is required, but this, too, has proven elusive.

- The European Union has been committed to a *managed exchange-rate system* since it undertook creating the single European currency, the euro. The European Monetary System (EMS) links the currencies of EU members whose governments pledge to stabilize currency values through government intervention if necessary. In practice, the system has proven stable, when EU governments have exercised the necessary will to operate it effectively.

United States). The United States willingly incurred these leadership costs and others' free riding because subsidizing economic growth in Europe and Japan would widen the U.S. export markets and strengthen the West against communism's possible popular appeal.

Although this system, with the United States operating as the world's banker, worked well, the costs grew as the enormous number of dollars held by others made the U.S. economy increasingly vulnerable to financial shocks from abroad. As the British had discovered before them, U.S. leadership made devaluing the dollar without hurting U.S. allies difficult; nor could inflationary or deflationary pressures at home be managed without impairing allies abroad. This reduced the United States' ability to use the normal methods available to other states for dealing with the disruption caused by deficits in a country's balance of trade, such as adjusting interest and currency exchange rates (see Focus 8.3).

As early as 1960 it was clear that the dollar's top currency status could not be sustained by U.S. hegemony. A number of developments combined to de-

A Primer on Trade and Payments Balances

Trade is the most important international economic transaction for many states. A deficit in the **balance of trade** results from an imbalance between imports and exports, that is, when a state buys more abroad than it sells. The merchandise balance measures only the value of goods bought and sold abroad. Trade in services, which has grown rapidly in recent years, must be added to get a complete picture of the balance between imports and exports.

The **balance of payments** is a more inclusive summary statement of a state's financial transactions with the rest of the world. In addition to imports and exports, the balance of payments includes such items as foreign aid transfers and the income of citizens employed abroad who send their paychecks home. The current account measures trade in goods and services plus investment income and payments (e.g., money from and to multinational corporations) and government transactions. The capital account measures foreign na-

tionals' investment of resources abroad and in the home country. The balance of payments is the sum of the balance of trade and the current and capital accounts.

A balance-of-payments surplus occurs when more money flows into a country than out of it; a balance-of-payments deficit is the reverse. A deficit requires some kind of corrective action. Policies that modify either the level of imports or the value of one's currency relative to that of others are possible options, but neither is without costs.

Broadly speaking, there are three (painful) methods a country can use to correct a payments deficit (Isaak 1995). It can embark on deflationary policies at home by raising interest rates or adopting tight budgets. It can restrict the outflow of money by imposing higher tariffs, import quotas, or other mechanisms. Or it can increase its international liquidity by borrowing in capital markets or liquidating its foreign exchange reserves.

stroy the monetary system. First, the costs of extensive U.S. military activities, foreign economic and military aid, and massive private investments produced increasing balance-of-payments deficits. Second, the possibility of a U.S. devaluation of the dollar made others less confident in it and less willing to hold dollars as reserve currency. The Global North's increasing monetary and financial interdependence permitted the central bankers and finance ministers from the leading economic powers to devise various *ad hoc* solutions (such as currency swaps) to deal with their common problems and to create Special Drawing Rights (SDRs) in the IMF (reserve assets popularly known as "paper gold") to grow international liquidity by means other than increasing the outflow of dollars from the United States. Third, Europe and Japan had completely recovered, and because recovery made their currencies convertible again, U.S. monetary dominance and the dollar's privileged position were increasingly unacceptable politically; the return to convertibility meant that alternatives to the dollar (such as the German mark and Japanese yen) as media of savings and exchange were now available.

Although the United States sought to stave off challenges to its leadership role, its own deteriorating economic situation as a consequence of the costs of its global military involvements made it increasingly difficult. Mounting inflation—caused in part by the unwillingness of the Johnson administration to raise taxes to pay for either the Vietnam War or the "Great Society" domestic engineering initiative—drove up the price of U.S.-produced goods and reduced their relative competitiveness overseas. In 1971, for the first time in the twentieth century, the United States suffered a trade deficit of $2 billion, which worsened the next year. Predictably, demands by industrial, labor, and agricultural

floating exchange rates a
system where market forces
rather than government
intervention determine the
value of currencies.

stagflation a situation in
which economic stagnation
and high inflation occur at
the same time and the usual
tendency for an economic
downturn to drive down
prices does not occur.

interests for protectionist trade measures grew. Simultaneously, the U.S. position in the global marketplace was deteriorating, as its share of international trade declined and Europe's and Japan's increased. America could no longer unilaterally regulate international monetary affairs.

The United States aggressively sought to shore up its sagging position. In August 1971 President Richard M. Nixon abruptly announced that the United States would no longer exchange dollars for gold. He also imposed a surcharge on imports into the United States as part of a strategy designed to force a realignment of others' currency exchange rates. These startling and unexpected decisions shocked the other Western industrial countries, which had not been consulted, and promptly ended the Bretton Woods system.

With the price of gold no longer fixed and dollar convertibility no longer guaranteed, the Bretton Woods system gave way to a much larger set of liberal rules and oversight institutions based on **floating exchange rates.** Market forces, rather than government intervention, were now expected to determine currency values (see Focus 8.4). The theory underlying the major change is that a country experiencing adverse economic conditions will see the value of its currency decline in the marketplace in response to the choices of traders, bankers, and businesspeople. This will make its exports cheaper and its imports more expensive, which in turn will pull its currency's value back toward equilibrium—all without the need for central bankers to support their currencies. In this way it was hoped that the politically humiliating devaluations of the past could be avoided.

Policymakers did not foresee that the new rules would introduce an unparalleled degree of uncertainty and unpredictability into international monetary affairs. Two "oil shocks" induced by the Organization of Petroleum Exporting Nations (OPEC) and the subsequent debt crisis that many Global South countries and others faced raised apprehension about the viability of an international economy clumsily managed by various groups of industrial states and quasi-official negotiating forums. These fears were compounded by the absence of hegemonic U.S. leadership and the beginning of the erratic and nerve-wracking fluctuation of the dollar's value.

These fears proved to be well-founded. Global economic recession followed each oil shock. Ironically, however, inflation persisted. **Stagflation** was coined as a term to describe the strange and strangled situation. In response, the leading industrial powers relied on fiscal and monetary adjustments to stimulate economic recovery and to avoid politically unacceptable unemployment levels. But after the second oil shock triggered unprecedented inflation and the longest and most severe economic downturn since the 1930s Great Depression, efforts shifted to controlling inflation through strict monetarist policies (i.e., policies designed to limit the money supply in the economy). Large fiscal deficits, sharply higher interest rates, and higher unemployment rates followed.

All the Global North countries suffered these problems, which also spread to the Global South developing countries that borrowed extensively from abroad to pay for the increased cost of energy. Borrowing was possible because the billions of "petrodollars" flowed to the oil-producing states, and private banks and various multilateral institutions "recycled" them. In the process, however, many states assumed ominous debt burdens just when interest rates on loans climbed. The 1980s threat of massive defaults by countries unable to service their debts pushed the international monetary regime to the brink of crisis, and the debt problem persisted afterwards (see Figure 8.1).

Why Do Exchange Rates Fluctuate?

Money works in several ways and serves different purposes. First, it must be acceptable, so that people earning it can use it to buy goods and services from others. Second, it must serve as a store of value, so that people will be willing to keep some of their wealth in the form of money. Third, it must be a standard of deferred payment, so that people will be willing to lend money knowing that when the money is repaid in the future, it will still have purchasing power.

Inflation occurs when the government creates too much money in relation to the goods and services produced in the economy. As money becomes more plentiful and thus less acceptable, it cannot serve effectively as a store of value or as a medium of exchange to satisfy debts. Governments work to ensure that their currencies do the jobs they are intended to do. This means, among other things, that they try to maintain an inflation-free environment.

In the international monetary system, movements in a state's exchange rate occur in part when changes occur in assessments of its underlying economic strength or the ability of its government to maintain the value of its money. A deficit in a country's balance of payments, for example, would likely cause a decline in the value of its currency relative to that of others. This happens when the supply of the currency is greater than the demand for it. Similarly, when those engaged in international economic transactions change their expectations about a currency's future value, they might reschedule their lending and borrowing. Fluctuations in the exchange rate could follow.

Speculators—those who buy and sell money in an effort to make it—may also affect the international stability of a country's currency. Speculators make money by guessing the future. If, for instance, they believe that the Japanese yen will be worth more in three months than it is now, they can buy yen today and sell them for a profit three months later. Conversely, if they believe that the yen will be worth less in three months,

they can sell yen today for a certain number of dollars and then buy back the same yen in three months for fewer dollars, making a profit.

Speculators base their decisions on a number of factors. One is their reading of the health of the currency in which they are speculating. If they believe the U S. dollar is weak because the U.S. economy itself is weak, they may conclude that policymakers will permit the dollar to depreciate. A closely related consideration is whether a government is perceived as having the political will to devise policies that will ensure the value of its money, particularly against inflationary pressures. If speculators think it does not, they would again be wise to sell dollars today and buy them back tomorrow at the (anticipated) lower price. In the process, speculators may create self-fulfilling prophecies: They may "prove" that the dollar needs to depreciate in value simply because of the volume of seemingly unwanted dollars offered for sale. The globalization of finance now also encourages managers of investment portfolios to move funds from one currency to another in order to realize gains from differences in nations' interest rates—including their anticipation of how interest rates might change.

In the same way that governments try to protect the value of their currencies at home, they try to protect them internationally by intervening in currency markets. Their willingness to do so is important to importers and exporters, who depend on orderliness and predictability in the value of the currencies they deal in to carry on their transnational exchanges. Governments intervene when countries' central banks buy or sell currencies to change the value of their own currencies in relation to those of others. Unlike speculators, however, they are pledged not to manipulate exchange rates so as to gain unfair advantage. Whether they can affect their currencies' values in the face of large transnational movements of capital is, however, increasingly problematic.

High U.S. interest rates compared with other countries contributed not only to the Global South's debt burden but also to the rising demand for the U.S. dollar. Renewed U.S. economic growth, a sharp reduction in inflation, and the perception of the United States as a comparatively safe haven for financial investments also helped to restore faith in the dollar. Foreign investors therefore rushed to acquire the dollars necessary to take advantage of profitable investment opportunities in the United States, driving the mid-1980s value of the

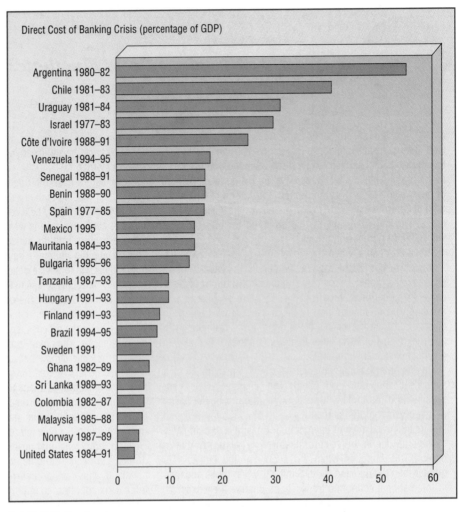

Direct Cost of Banking Crisis (percentage of GDP)

FIGURE 8 . 1

Currency Concerns: The Spread of Costly Banking Crises throughout a Globalized and Unstable International Monetary System

Many countries have experienced serious banking crises as a result of their inability to manage debt, inflation, interest, and income in a turbulent international monetary environment. Between the late 1970s and mid-1990s, no less than one hundred major episodes of bank insolvency occurred in ninety developing and transition countries, partly as a consequence of their increasing exposure to external financial pressures. The disastrous debt generated by trade and monetary disruptions forced governments to suffer direct losses often in excess of 3 percent of gross domestic product. The wave of new banking failures that swept Asia in 1997–1998 illustrate the continuing likelihood of future currency crises.

SOURCE: World Bank (1997), 68.

dollar to new heights (see Figure 8.2). This situation contrasted sharply with the 1970s when fears of the huge U.S. foreign indebtedness drove the exchange rate lower.

For the United States, the dollar's appreciation was a mixed blessing because it increased the cost of U.S. exports to foreign buyers, reducing the com-

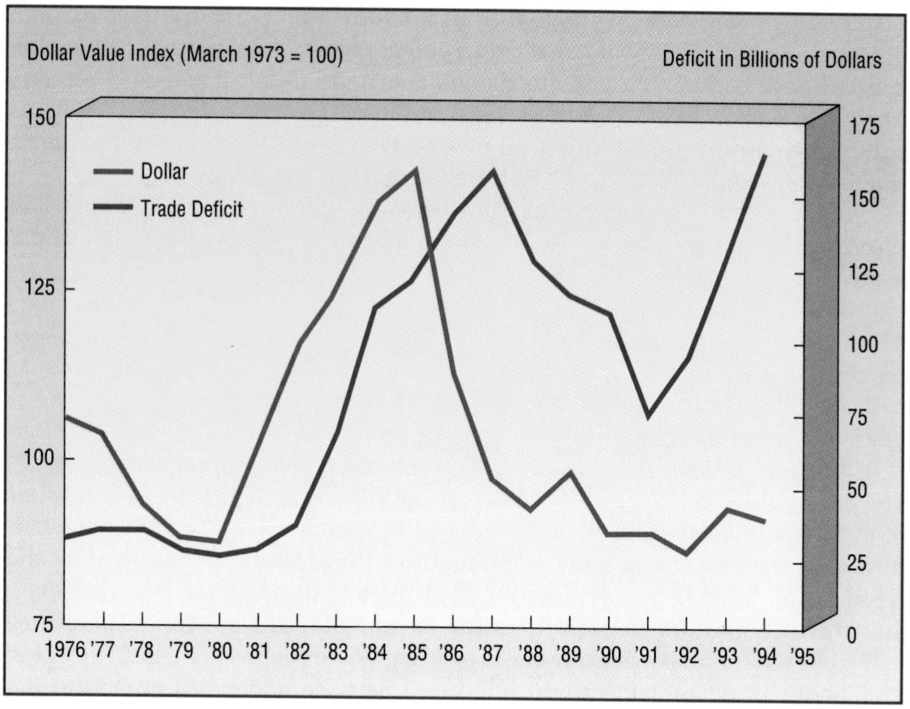

Dollar Value Index (March 1973 = 100)   Deficit in Billions of Dollars

FIGURE 8.2

The Dollar and the U.S. Trade Deficit, 1976–1994

In the post-Bretton Woods monetary system of floating exchange rates, the value of the dollar has fluctuated widely, causing uncertainty in the monetary system and disorder in the trading system. Since the mid-1980s the leading industrial democracies have sought to manage the monetary system by coordinating their domestic economic policies, but their efforts generally have failed. Note also the relationship of the dollar's value to U.S. trade balances. When the dollar has soared (in the mid-1980s), American firms that produce for export are pummeled as their goods are no longer competitive in overseas markets; when U.S. imports grow, huge deficits occur in U.S. merchandise trade with the rest of the world. The dollar fell sharply in the latter half of the 1980s, causing a reduction in the deficit but not its elimination. In the 1990s the trade deficit again rose sharply, even as the dollar remained low.

Note: The index is the weighted average value of the U.S. dollar against the currencies of ten other major industrialized countries, based on average monthly rates for the corresponding year.

SOURCE: Dollar exchange rates, Federal Reserve System; merchandise trade deficit from *Economic Report of the President* (1994), 386.

petitiveness of American products in overseas markets. Tens of thousands of jobs were lost, and record trade deficits ($122 billion in 1985, $145 billion in 1986, and $160 billion in 1987) occurred as imports from abroad became relatively cheaper and hence more attractive to American consumers.

The budget deficit of the U.S. government also climbed to record levels at this time, topping $200 billion each year. To deal with the deficit and help fund its staggering military expenditures, the Reagan administration began to borrow both at home and abroad at a record rate. In only five years, as the debt climbed and interest payments on it compounded, the United States went from being the world's biggest creditor to being its largest debtor. By the early 1990s interest payments on the national debt (the accumulation of past deficits) alone surpassed the government's *combined* expenditures on agriculture, education, the environment, foreign aid, law enforcement, and transportation (Fry, Taylor, and Wood 1994, 257). Faced with rising debts and interest payments on them, American leaders were constrained in dealing with other economic problems and by criticism from the American people, who feared the prospect of diminished living standards.

In a normally functioning market, the combination of a strong dollar and severe trade imbalance would set in motion self-corrective processes that would return the dollar to its equilibrium value. Growing U.S. imports, for example—although beneficial to America's trade partners in generating jobs and thus stimulating their return to economic growth—should create upward pressure on the value of others' currencies. Conversely, a drop in U.S. exports should ease the demand for dollars, thereby reducing the dollar's value in exchange markets. These mechanisms did not work as they should have because high U.S. interest rates persisted as a result of continuing high military spending.

In response to the growing awareness of the extent to which the health of others' economies depended on the value of the dollar internationally (which in turn depended on the underlying strength of the U.S. economy), in 1985 the **Group of Five** (or **G-5**—composed of the United States, Britain, France, Japan, and West Germany) met secretly in the Plaza Hotel in New York. There they agreed to mount a coordinated effort to bring down the overvalued U.S. dollar. The landmark agreement proved important because it signaled an end to the United States' benign neglect toward the vulnerabilities of global interdependence and committed the major economic powers to greater collective coordination of their economic policies through management of exchange rates internationally and interest rates domestically.

Japan now also became a full partner in international monetary management, a move that led to formalization of the **Group of Seven** (the **G-7,** consisting of the G-5 plus Canada and Italy). The G-7 holds annual summits to address both economic and political problems, and in 1997 invited Russia to participate in the common forum of leading industrial democracies. However, the G-7's meetings between 1985 and 1998 failed to inspire much confidence in the group's ability to coordinate global monetary policy. It appears that the G-7 (or what President Clinton renamed at the twenty-third meeting in 1997 the "Summit of Eight") continues to remain incapable of making "hard economic choices at home. Each government's emphasis on dealing with seemingly intractable domestic problems . . . constrains joint efforts to stimulate global economic growth or to manage monetary and trade relations, preventing G-7 governments from pursuing disciplined and synchronized fiscal and monetary policies" (Ikenberry 1993).

In the absence of true collective management of global monetary conditions, it appears likely that the volume of world trade and the activities of currency speculators (who use sophisticated global electronic technologies and rely on about two thousand "hedge funds" to make profits in currency trading) will increasingly determine national currency values. Over $1.3 trillion in currency trading occurs each day—a transfer of wealth greater than France's GNP or one-fourth of the world's 1997 $9 trillion *yearly* trade in goods and services. International sales of stocks and bonds have mushroomed as well. This globalization severely reduces states' individual or collective capacity to control the value of their currencies in exchange markets. It was this that prompted Alan Greenspan, Chair of the Federal Reserve system responsible for U.S. monetary

When a country's banks go bankrupt and its economy collapses, foreign capital flees in panic, and the financial crisis spreads rapidly throughout the globe as lenders attempt to limit losses. No worldwide central bank exists to cushion the crash and restore confidence by providing temporary loans or closing banks with bad loans. Money problems in one country lead to money problems in others, provoking currency depreciations and plunges in stocks prices at home and abroad. Pictured here are stock brokers reacting to the January, 1998 plummet of Hong Kong stocks that caused the key indexes elsewhere in Asia, London, Frankfurt, New York, and Paris to fall.

policy, to lament that the U.S.'s ability to prop up the dollar by buying it in foreign exchange markets "is extraordinarily limited and probably in a realistic sense nonexistent." The globalization of finance and the removal of barriers to transnational capital flows have also, in Greenspan's words, exposed "national economies to shocks from new and unexpected sources, with little if any lag."

Many proposals have been advanced for reforming the international monetary system. Reforms are needed to help cushion the aftershocks of the rapid movement of investment funds among countries that creates booms and busts, such as the 1980s Latin American debt crisis and the global crisis that followed on the heels of the 1997–1998 flow of capital from Asia. Some see reversion to the "gold standard" operative before World War I as preferable to the current system of floating exchange rates with highly fluctuating currencies. Others recommend something like the Bretton Woods system of fixed but adjustable rates. What these and other proposals seek is a mechanism for currency stability and flexibility on which prosperity through trade depends, and which the current system has failed to achieve. "There is little agreement on what to do about the exchange rate system. All appraisals conclude that the performance of the world economy could be improved if policy discipline were strengthened and if the frequency and size of exchange rate misalignments could be reduced. But there is little consensus on how to bring that about" (Goldstein 1995). With global democratization, few governments are insulated from domestic pressures to sacrifice such goals as unemployment reduction for exchange-rate stability, so it seems likely that floating exchange rates, with all their costs and uncertainties, are here to stay (see Eichengreen 1996).

The European Monetary System (EMS), launched in 1979 by the European Community, blends elements of the Bretton Woods system of fixed exchange rates and the post-Bretton Woods system of floating rates. Short-term fluctuations are guided by the marketplace, but the EMS requires that political consultations precede realignments of European currencies. Hence it is a "managed" system aimed at eliminating all eighteen EU national currencies by 2002, replacing them with the single "euro" currency, which would reduce Europeans' need for foreign exchange reserves and raise the value of the euro against the U.S. dollar. This currency integration could serve as a model for *global* monetary management, provided that the many disappointments until recently the European Union experienced in its journey to a single currency can be avoided.

The European Union's determination to create a Europe-wide central bank and currency based on a system of managed exchange rates began to bear fruit as the eruo went into effect in 1999 for most EU members. Nonetheless, it is an unlikely precursor of a new global monetary regime. On the contrary, the regionalization of the European monetary system reinforces other trends in the world political economy that portend potentially divisive conflict on economic policy. At the same time, global interdependence portends the further expansion of free-trade regions, the increasing influence of global (multinational) corporations in the promotion of liberal trade, and the continuing rejection (however painful domestically) of closed markets under the mounting collective pressure of multilateral institutions such as the World Trade Organization. In December 1997, mobilized by the Asian fiscal crisis, the WTO hammered out a last-minute pact to open the members' banking, insurance, and securities markets to more foreign competition. That kind of agreement could represent the future.

• • •

COMMERCIAL TUG OF WAR: LIBERAL FREE TRADE AND MERCANTILE PROTECTIONISM

The exponential growth of world trade in the second half of the twentieth century has contributed measurably to an unprecedented rise in global economic prosperity. Between 1970 and 1998 the value of world trade has grown at an average rate of 4.8 percent annually, and is expected to expand between 1999 and 2002 at an average yearly rate of 6.7 percent. In the same period, world real GNP has increased each year an average 3.7 percent, and is projected to grow an average of 4.5 percent each year between 1999 and 2002 (IMF 1997, 205). Reductions in barriers to free trade are expected to accelerate these trends, specifically if world trade continues to expand three times faster than real world output did in 1997 (*Economist*, March 28, 1998) (see Figure 8.3). The World Bank (1995a) predicts "trade integration"—the difference between growth rates in trade and gross national (or gross world) product—will bind national economies ever more tightly in interdependent economic relationships.

These projections assume that the process of liberalizing the global political economy will continue. Progress, however, remains problematic if the forces of neomercantilism also remain vibrant. Although hegemonic stability theory would predict that a U.S. leadership decline will inevitably be followed by the liberal trade regime's *closure*, a collapse of free trade is unlikely. The liberal trade regime endures with the support of global institutions such as the World Trade Organization and liberal regional regimes such as **Free Trade Area of the Americas (FTAA),** consisting of the thirty-four democracies of

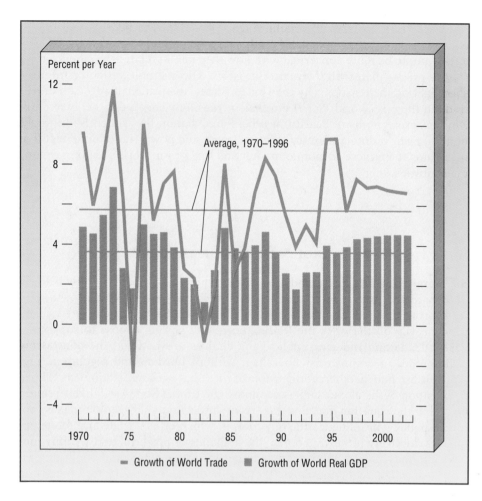

F I G U R E   8 . 3

Global Economic Prospects: The Growth of Trade and Wealth

World trade has expanded almost without interruption each year since 1970, rising more than 9 percent between 1995 and 1998. This has contributed to robust economic growth, which is expected to continue above the historically high 4 percent yearly average rate between 1995 and 1998. However, although trade integration is deepening, the benefits of a favorable global economy are unevenly distributed, as some countries are not participating in the expansion at the same level as the global trend in trade and output.

Note: Figures beyond 1997 are projections.

SOURCE: International Monetary Fund (1997, 2, 205).

North and South America. Many states see advantages in rejecting mercantilism and accepting instead the **most-favored-nation (MFN) principle** (which holds that the tariff preferences granted to one state must be granted to all others exporting the same product) as well as the **reciprocity** norm (countries will reduce their own tariffs in return for another's reductions) and *nondiscrimination* rule (goods produced at home and abroad are to be treated the same).

Free trade is attractive only if everyone can benefit. Recall that the principle of comparative advantage is a central tenet of free trade, because specialization and trade are viewed as permitting trading states to enjoy a higher standard of living than they would otherwise (review Focus 8.1). Still, as we have seen, many states remain tempted to enhance their domestic well-being by protectionist means even though, according to commercial liberalism, their relations with their trade partners will be undermined, reducing the benefits free trade would otherwise provide to both. If neomercantilism spreads, the preservation of the free-trade regime is unlikely throughout the twenty-first century.

The simultaneous pursuit of liberalism and mercantilism today shows states' determination to reap the benefits of interdependence while minimizing its costs. It also reveals the tension between states and markets, between the

most-favored-nation (MFN)
GATT principle guaranteeing unconditional nondiscriminatory treatment in trade between contracting parties; in 1997 U.S. Sen. Daniel Patrick Moynihan introduced legislation to replace the term with "normal trade relations" to better reflect its true meaning.

235

promise that everyone will benefit and the fear that the benefits will not be equally distributed. As noted earlier, the absence of world government encourages states to be more concerned with how they fare in relation to others—their *relative gains*—than with their *absolute gains*. These simple yet powerful ideas shed light on the reasons why the United States, the principal advocate of free trade in the post-World War II era, has increasingly engaged in neomercantilism and protectionism. Fearful of others' free riding, the United States looks more like an "ordinary country" than a hegemonic power, despite the fact that it remains the largest economic market and one of the world's leading exporting countries.

• • •

THE FATE OF FREE TRADE: TRIUMPH OR TROUBLE?

Six premises dictate the boundaries within which the global economy is likely to vary in the future. First, free trade contributes to economic growth, and trade protection reduces prosperity in the long run. Second, the future will depend heavily on the rules the leading economic powers choose to support to govern trade and monetary policy; the choices are between the contrasting philosophies of commercial liberalism without burdensome regulation, and mercantilist and neomercantilist approaches that seek protectionism. Third, the position of the globe's largest economy, the United States, will likely remain pivotal in the equation, for how this (rising or declining?) hegemon makes economic policy will influence the direction in which others' trade and monetary policies are likely to move. Fourth, the activities of powerful and wealthy mobile multinational corporations in foreign investment and trade will increasingly determine economic flows; these activities and pressure for continuing trade liberalization are increasingly beyond the control of state governments, whose sovereign power is eroding. Fifth, nonstate commercial and monetary actors (e.g. transnational banks) will provide much of the lubrication that can keep the global trade engine humming. Finally, globalization is likely to accelerate, and as competition expands wealth and reduces the costs of both products and labor, the economic fate of the globe's nearly 6 billion people will be tied together in increasingly interdependent ties, making the welfare of any one important to the welfare of all.

Emerging State and Regional Trade Policies

To anticipate the future, we can look at the unilateral strategies of individual countries and at the regional strategies of groups of countries or blocs.

Unilateral Strategies. In the past, the United States led the way to the decline of protectionist tariffs in the industrialized world (see Figure 8.4). However, the United States has not consistently advocated free trade; in reaction to its increasingly shaky global position in 1998, it began to practice "aggressive unilateralism" by retaliating against states perceived to be engaging in unfair trade practices. Earlier, the Omnibus Trade Act incorporated a bellicose "Super 301"

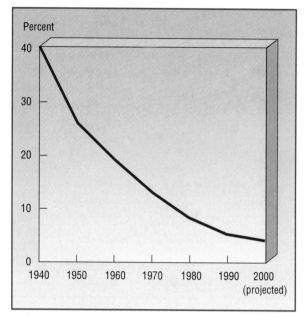

FIGURE 8.4

The Decline of Tariffs in the Industrialized Countries, 1940 Projected to 2000

Tariffs have declined dramatically since the peak period of economic nationalism in the 1930s. With average tariff levels among industrialized countries projected to decline to only 5 percent by 2000 (compared with 40 percent in 1940), tariffs have become a comparatively unimportant restraint on international trade.

source: Office of the U.S. Trade Representative and the Center for International Economics, as aggregated by *Time*, December 27, 1993, 16.

provision that *required* the president to identify countries believed to be engaging in unfair trade practices and to force them to either negotiate remedies or face U.S. retaliation. This is symptomatic of the fragility of commitments to free trade, because the Super 301 provision was "almost unanimously viewed abroad as a clear violation of the GATT" (Walters and Blake 1992). Since then, however, the United States has begun to act under the milder, less accusatory "ordinary" 301 legislation (which does not carry automatic retaliatory penalties), but has still initiated nearly one hundred complaints, with the European Union (23 percent) and Japan (13 percent) the most frequent targets. U.S. efforts to liberalize trade in relation to its partners were successful in about half the cases (Bayard and Elliott 1994, 58–65).

The continuing trade imbalance between Japan (long viewed as the preeminent neomercantilist power) and the United States—which runs into the tens of billions of dollars each year—reinforced the U.S. assertion that Japan's protectionist trade policies closed the Japanese market to U.S. exports. American firms particularly resent Japan's intimate government-business alliance and its cross-share holding practice known as *keiretsu*, which results in informal corporate bargains that make foreign penetration difficult. Nonetheless, nearly thirty new trade agreements were subsequently reached under a mix of 301 and Super 301 retaliatory threats that have permitted American exports to Japan to increase considerably in recent years. These bilateral sectional agreements included the Structural Impediments Initiative (SII), launched in 1989 shortly after Japan was named as one of three countries engaging in unfair trade practices under Super 301 (Brazil and India were the others). Hence, U.S. trade policy reflects twin instincts: to push for trade liberalization in foreign markets, and to cushion the impact of imports on the U.S. economy and employment rate. The stakes are high; in 1997 the Commerce Department estimated that one in five U.S. jobs were supported by trade. Awareness of this dependence

237

The Japanese regard foreign products as inferior to those produced domestically. This makes it difficult for those who export to Japan to compete with local firms, even if their products are of equal or superior quality. The Japanese perpetuate this restraint on trade by labeling retail goods with little flags that show the country of origin and by placing imported goods in separate sections of stores.

fast-track negotiating authority a concession by the U.S. Congress permitting the president to negotiate reciprocal tariff-reduction agreements with other countries which, when granted, enables the United States to reach bilateral trade treaties more easily.

was behind the Clinton administration's elusive 1997 search for **fast-track negotiating authority** from Congress. "At issue," Clinton argued, "is America's leadership and credibility in the eyes of our competitors." Clinton's failure to obtain from Congress greater power to negotiate trade agreements illustrated the power of domestic trade protectionists and the fragility of free-trade agreements, despite the strongly pro-free-trade support of U.S. corporations who complained that without fast-track authority, huge opportunities for new trade deals would be lost and the U.S. economy would be hurt. "I'm concerned," reported one U.S. manufacturer, "that we'll end up exporting jobs rather than products" (Stevenson 1997).

How the U.S. trade partners and rivals view the American commitment to free trade will shape their own trade policies, and whether they will choose free trade over protectionism. Tough negotiations and countercharges plague U.S.-China export flows, as well as the relationship between many other active partners to international trade. With many countries debating the merits of open markets and free trade, the question remains: Which will govern the rules of trade in the twenty-first century, mercantilism or free trade?

Regional Strategies. In addition to the temptation to reject the free-trade regime by turning to unilateral trade agreements, the United States has led the way toward building regional arrangements in response to its changing position in the global political economy. These include the 1984 Caribbean Basin

Initiative to reduce tariffs and provide tax incentives to promote industry and trade; free-trade agreements with Israel and Canada concluded in 1987 and 1989, respectively; and the **North American Free Trade Agreement (NAFTA),** signed by Canada, Mexico, and the United States in 1993.

NAFTA's purpose was to intertwine Mexico and Canada with the United States as a prelude to a wider Western Hemispheric economic partnership, in part to balance the challenge of the emerging European-wide common market. This challenge began to grow in the mid-1980s when European leaders committed to creating a single market and followed this with the Maastricht agreement to develop a single European currency. With enlargement of its membership eastward accepted in 1998, the European Union escalated its push toward the creation of a continent-wide economic union.

In the Pacific Rim, the Asia-Pacific Economic Cooperation (APEC) forum, whose eighteen members make up half the world economy, has agreed to achieve "free and open trade and investment" by the year 2020. Already the growing antagonism between the United States and China on security as well as economic issues stands as an obstacle to the goals of making APEC the world's largest free-trade area. Meanwhile, the United States and the thirty-three Western Hemispheric democracies agreed at the 1994 Miami Summit of the Americas to build a Free Trade Area of the Americas (FTAA) in that region by 2005. The highly successful Mercosur free-trade zone in the cone of South America and the ASEAN free-trade region in Southeast Asia are the other major multilateral regional trading blocs (see Map 8.1).

Although many feel that NAFTA and other regional free-trade zones are consistent with GATT's rules, others fret that they violate the nondiscrimination principle by moving away from free trade toward closure. In particular, the fear is pervasive that further development of regionalized markets or blocs centered on Asia, Europe, and North America could split globalized trade into competitive trade blocs. Already more than one-third of world trade takes place *within* four major regions (see Figure 8.5), with nearly half of all Asian exports going to other Asian countries, and exports within the European Union accounting for 60 percent of all the EU's trade (Curtis 1998, A12). The United Nations vocalized this fear in its world economic survey, observing in 1991 that "Today the question is not whether these blocs will be formed, but rather how encompassing they will be and how to ensure that they will not harm the [global] trading system."

The ultimate impact of the trend toward regionalization of the world political economy, both nationally and globally, remains uncertain. Some analysts, pointing to the dispute settlement provisions of NAFTA and its side agreements on the environment and other matters, see that agreement as the precursor of future efforts to negotiate settlements on issues that will likely undermine the free-trade regime and thereby plague world growth in the years ahead. Others are concerned with the possible impact of the economic regional centers on security relationships. One line of reasoning—which builds on the logic of strategic trade theory—suggests that "bitter economic rivalry" is a likely outcome of a triangular world political economy because of fear that "there can be *enduring* national winners and losers from trade competition" (Borrus et al. 1992). The result would be mercantile rivalry among the world's principal trading blocs, in which "fear of one another" may be the only force binding them together.

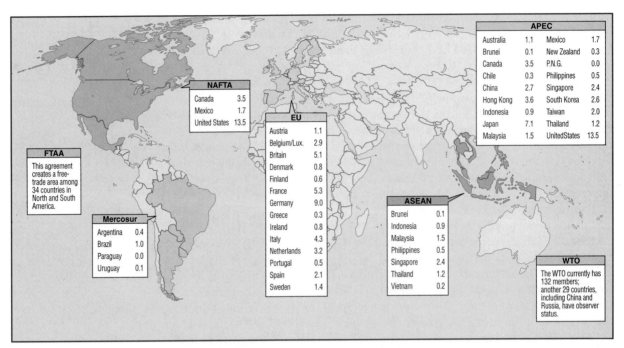

MAP 8.1

Regional Free-Trade Blocs: Building Blocks or Road Blocks for Economic Growth?

Dynamic rates of economic growth have recently occurred in a number of regions where agreements have been reached to reduce tariff barriers. This map identifies the six major regional free-trade blocs that have dedicated themselves to even greater trade liberalization, as promoted by the 132-member World Trade Organization (WTO), and records the percentage of total world trade of the member countries of the primary trading blocs in 1996.

Note: Numbers represent percentage of world trade. FTAA = Free Trade Area of the Americas; NAFTA = North American Free Trade Agreement; EU = European Union; ASEAN = Association of South East Asian Nations; APEC = Asia–Pacific Economic Cooperation; WTO = World Trade Organization.

SOURCE: *Economist*, Vol. 344, September 27, 1997, p. 23.

Those outside the globe's three major regional trading blocs have ample reason to be concerned about this regionalization. "For the developing countries, the prospect of a world divided into separate regional centers is disconcerting. It leaves too many countries out of the system altogether, and even those it encompasses are left relatively weaker as their bargaining power is divided. So, even though developing countries in the past have regarded the GATT as a `rich man's club,' today they see it as a guardian for the clear and fair rules they need if they are to enter the international arena successfully" (Philips and Tucker 1991). Beyond GATT, and now the 132-member WTO, however, developing countries have also spawned a growing number of regional economic cooperation schemes of their own, as discussed in Chapter 5. But their chances of superseding existing bilateral and multilateral agreements are poor.

Global Economic Destiny?

The United States, Europe, and Japan have advocated quite different philosophies toward states and markets over the years, and their policies have evolved as

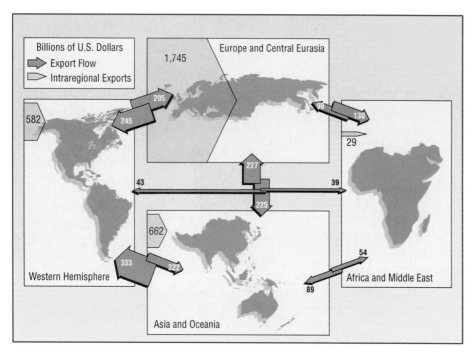

FIGURE 8.5

The Regionalization of International Trade: Share of Exports within and between Major Areas

Increasingly, trade is concentrated within particular regions more than between them. The flows are not even, as in 1996 the dollar value of exports varied in direction and balance across the major trade regions.

Note: Width of arrows scaled to dollar value of exports.

SOURCE: *Handbook of International Economic Statistics* (1997), 134.

their circumstances in the global economy have changed over time. At times, Japan has embraced mercantilism (even as it talked of liberalization), the United States has touted liberalism (even as it practiced mercantilism), and Europe historically has stood midway between the two (but looked more inward than outward). Increasingly, economic nationalism "could propel the preeminent economic powers—and the rest of the world with them—into an era of *'real-economik'*, in which parochial economic interests drive governments to pursue marginal advantage in an international system marked by growing interdependencies" (Peterson 1998). Whether a collision of these competing capitalisms can be averted is questionable, especially if the relative position of American economic power declines; this possibility and other recent changes "do not augur well for the level of cooperation necessary to avoid the neomercantilist confrontation that could flow from competing national policies" (Peterson 1998).

The architecture of a Liberal International Economic Order constructed at Bretton Woods a half-century ago appeared to depend not only on a consensus about the appropriate shape of the world political economy but also on U.S. leadership. The United States is still the dominant state in the world political economy and continues to perform many hegemonic functions: It tries to maintain a comparatively open market for others' goods, manage the international monetary system, provide capital to would-be borrowers facing financial stress, and coordinate economic policies among the world's leading economies. Today, however, U.S. willingness to absorb the costs of leadership has waned, and its ability to affect global economic outcomes in preferred directions is simply not what it once was. Both the United States and the world must adjust to the decline of American hegemony, and must resist the temptation to return to mercantilist free riding and protectionist trade practices.

However, a new wave of mercantilism and trade wars is not preordained. A number of other important developments are also likely to influence the future

China has a booming free-market economy under communist political control, and its vast market is now closely tied to the global economy. China is seeking membership in the 132-member World Trade Organization, at the same time that the WTO is insisting, as a price for membership, that China make large-scale concessions that would allow foreign companies to sell stock, deliver packages commercially, and sell telecommunications across the breadth of China. Much of the future may hinge on whether negotiations can integrate China into the free-trade regime.

direction of the world political economy, and these, in combination, are likely to sustain and strengthen the liberal free-trade regime that has contributed to global economic growth. World commerce has become globalized; global financial flows outstrip trade transactions within countries; and market forces almost everywhere are now being given a freer reign to determine economic outcomes. With trade growing rapidly in the absence of barriers, and with the expansion of free-trade areas, pressure to preserve the liberal trade regime has increased. Multinational corporations are playing a larger role in the continuing growth of commercial liberalism worldwide, and they are supported in this aspiration by the powerful World Trade Organization, the conversion of eastern Europe and China to acceptance of freer trade, and the opening up of free-riders' markets to exports. All these developments suggest that the prospects for the momentum of commercial liberalism to gain strength are promising.

Some theorists believe that the spread of liberal market philosophies will eliminate the need for new institutions to cope with the changed and changing world political economy. Others caution that the unregulated market should not be considered the ideal and universal arrangement for economic activity, because coordinating institutions are needed to manage sustained growth (Hollingsworth and Boyer 1997). The task of reaching agreement about economic principles is made more daunting by the absence of a true consensus about what the world political economy should look like, as the continuing contest between liberalism and mercantilism (as well as the conflict between rich and poor countries) illustrates. Furthermore, the globalization of commerce and finance increasingly seems to shape, rather than be shaped by, states' policies—thus challenging the sovereign prerogatives of states themselves.

The shape of the future thus remains uncertain. If liberals are correct, the process of rapid globalization already on the horizon will multiply concerns about interdependence and integration and, with that, the prospects for economic prosperity and political harmony. If mercantilists are right, however, an emerging era of geo-economics will increase states' vulnerability, and thus the likelihood of political conflict and states' efforts to dominate others. What the future holds is hard to foresee, because the various rules for trade and currency are likely to change in the twenty-first century, and these changes will undercut the usefulness of past economic philosophies. The world seems to be spinning out of control in a sea change of rapid globalization that hides the decisions that affect our daily lives. In the next chapter we will examine further how *globalization* is entangling the functions of governments and markets and making it difficult to tell the difference between countries and corporations.

K E Y   T E R M S

political economy
globalization
international political economy
high politics
low politics
international monetary system
commercial liberalism
mercantilism
Liberal International Economic
 Order (LIEO)
interdependence
theory
comparative advantage
politics
absolute gains/relative gains
neomercantilism
protectionism
 • beggar-thy-neighbor policies
 • import quotas
 • export quotas

• orderly market arrangement
 (OMA)
• voluntary export restrictions
 (VERs)
• nontariff barriers (NTBs)
• infant industry
• strategy trade policy
hegemonic stability theory
hegemon
hegemony
macroeconomic policies
collective goods
free riders
imperial overstretch
international regimes
General Agreement on Tariffs and
 Trade (GATT)
nondiscrimination
Uruguay Round
World Trade Organization (WTO)

monetary system
fixed exchange rates
World Bank
international liquidity
balance of trade
balance of payments
floating exchange rates
stagflation
Group of Five (G-5)
Group of Seven (G-7)
Free Trade Area of the Americas
 (FTAA)
most-favored-nation (MFN)
 principle
reciprocity
fast-track trade negotiating
 authority
North American Free Trade
 Agreement (NAFTA)

S U G G E S T E D   R E A D I N G

Andrews, David M., and Thomas D. Willett. "Financial Interdependence and the State: International Monetary Relations at Century's End," *International Organization* 51 (Summer 1997): 479–511.

Burch, Kurt, and Robert Denemark, eds. *Constituting International Political Economy*. Boulder, Colo.: Lynne Rienner, 1997.

Caporaso, James A., and David P. Levine. *Theories of Political Economy*. New York: Cambridge University Press, 1992.

Eichengreen, Barry. *Globalizing Capital: A History of the International Monetary System*. Princeton, N.J.: Princeton University Press, 1996.

Frankel, Jeffrey. *Regional Trading Blocs in the World Economic System*. Washington, D.C.: Institute for International Economics, 1997.

Gilpin, Robert. "Three Ideologies of Political Economy," pp. 277–95 in Charles W. Kegley, Jr. and Eugene A. Wittkopf (eds.), *The Global Agenda*, 5th ed. New York: McGraw-Hill, 1998.

Greider, William. *One World, Ready or Not: The Manic Logic of Capitalism*. New York: Simon & Schuster, 1997.

Irwin, Douglas A. *Against the Tide: An Intellectual History of Free Trade*. Princeton, N.J.: Princeton University Press, 1996.

Milner, Helen. "International Political Economy: Beyond Hegemonic Stability," *Foreign Policy* 110 (Spring 1998): 112–24.

Strange, Susan. *The Retreat of the State: The Diffusion of Power in the World Economy*. Cambridge, Eng.: Cambridge University Press, 1996.

Spero, Joan Edelman, and Jeffrey Hart. *The Politics of International Economic Relations*, 5th ed. New York: St. Martin's Press, 1997.

Thurow, Lester C. *Head to Head: Coming Economic Battles among Japan, Europe, and America*. New York: Morrow, 1992.

WHERE ON THE WORLD WIDE WEB?

http://g8.cuonline.edu/
Summit of the Eight and World Affairs Project This Web site offers you the ability to hear and see segments of the Summit of the Eight (formerly G-7) conference held in Denver, Colorado, June 1997, as well as interviews with leading scholars. See interviews with U.S. Secretary of State Madeleine Albright and Secretary of the Treasury Robert Rubin or audiovisual segments from the Chinese unification and the handing over of Hong Kong in July 1997.

http://www.oecd.org/
Organization for Economic Cooperation and Development The Organization for Economic Cooperation and Development (OECD) began with the purpose of rebuilding war-ravaged economies after World War II and administering the distribution of Marshall Plan's aid. Today, the OECD promotes policies that contribute to the expansion of world trade on a nondiscriminatory basis. The OECD provides a forum in which the governments of the twenty-nine member states can compare their experiences and further the principles of a market economy. From the OECD's homepage, you can access the largest source of comparative statistical data on the industrialized countries. Look at the "Frequently Requested Statistics" to compare economies.

http://www.wto.org/
World Trade Organization The World Trade Organization (WTO) is an IGO with global membership which performs multiple purposes. It was established January 1, 1995, and expands the General Agreement on Trade and Tarriffs (GATT). The WTO's main purpose is to administer trade agreements between countries, monitor trade policies, and provide technical assistance and training for developing countries. Unlike many international organizations, the WTO has a mechanism for settling international disputes with limited enforcement abilities. Click on the "Dispute Settlement" link on the homepage and then review "Overview of the State-of-Play of WTO Disputes." In how many disputes is the United States the defendant? In how many is the United States the complainant?

http://www.usitc.gov/tr/tr.htm
Trade Resources The United States International Trade Commission (USITC) has created an information referral service for those seeking information related to international trade and investment. Interested in investing in a chemical company in Canada? Want to export tractors to Russia? This Web site provides Internet resources to help those interested in international trade and investment to obtain information on their client country, research various products, access trade assistance, understand patent law, or view international law.

CHAPTER 9

Globalization and the Impact of Vanishing Borders

> ●●●
> *If we try to close up our economy, we will only hurt ourselves. Protectionism is simply not an option because globalization is irreversible.*
>
> —BILL CLINTON,
> *U.S. president, 1997*

> ●●●
> *There is a saying that all politics is local. But increasingly, all local politics has global consequences. And those global consequences, in turn, affect the quality of local life everywhere.*
>
> —KOFI ANNAN,
> *Secretary-General of the United Nations, 1998.*

CHAPTER TOPICS AND THEMES

- A global village?
  - The telecommunications and computer revolutions
  - The globalization of information and ideas
  - Transnationally contagious disease in a borderless globe

- The globalization of finance

- The globalization of trade

- The globalization of production

- The globalization of labor

- Globalization and the state: What future?

At the dawn of the new millennium, many global trends are moving in divergent directions. Stock prices throughout the world surge as investors move capital at lightning speed across borders to buy equities, but a later sell-off in Asia causes panic and selling in New York and London. In a failing East African state, another family member falls victim to tribal war. As the Federal Reserve System lowers U.S. interest rates, skittish currency traders sell billions of dollars and buy yen and "euros." A German manufacturer shifts production overseas, substituting foreign workers without trade unions for local ones. The liberalization of previously closed economies in eastern Europe adds millions of consumers to the world marketplace. University students in Istanbul chat with their friends on cellular phones as they sip raki in a local bar. Clad in Levi jeans and Calvin Klein shirts, their counterparts in Bangkok rock to the music of Hootie and the Blowfish.

Goods, money, people, technology, and ideas are moving across national borders at an accelerating pace. The world is rapidly becoming interconnected, linked tighter and tighter into a single, integrated community and market. This movement and interaction across frontiers is uniting the world, generating new levels of wealth in a cutthroat marketplace, and making national boundaries and governments less important. This process poses both possibilities and problems, creating many winners but also many losers. It is leading to the simultaneous integration and disintegration of states, to the growth of some states' power and the erosion of the authority of many other states.

Together, these divergent trends are increasing the connectedness of the world and changing it in the process; their compound effect appears to be creating a new "global" era. "The presumed erosion of national economies and societies raises a question mark over the potential political power of the state: Both 'inside' and 'outside' territorial borders, the power of governments and institutions to shape the economic and social environment in which they find themselves appears to have waned" (Amoore et al. 1997).

This transformation is the product of trends in the world economy that commenced more than a century ago. It is referred to throughout the world as **"globalization,"** shorthand for a cluster of related phenomena.

> The term "globalization" has served as an arresting metaphor to provide explanation, meaning and understanding of the nature of contemporary capitalism, though not all of the processes that currently come under the rubric of globalization are new. It is meant to suggest a number of analytically distinct phenomena and developments within the international system, while combining them into a single overarching process of change. Considerable attention centers on the application of new (often information-based) technologies to the production process and parallel changes in management, organization and communications at corporate, societal and state levels. (Amoore et al. 1997, 179)

The deepening economic, political, social, and cultural contacts across borders that are characteristic of globalization are making state borders and governments increasingly less meaningful as barriers. It is understandable, therefore, that globalization is so controversial. It portends two very different possible futures. In one optimistic scenario, **neoliberal theory** sees sovereignty is at bay as the globalization of markets and cultures transcends contemporary geopolitical boundaries and erodes the meaning of national identity, creating "global citizens" who assign loyalty to the common interests of all peoples. In

globalization according to the International Monetary Fund, "the increasingly close international integration of markets both for goods and services and for capital."

neoliberal theory a philosophy that maintains that peaceful change with prosperity can be encouraged through cooperation in institutions that knit the states and peoples of the world together into a true global community.

the other, more pessimistic, forecast, states will compete with one another although their goals are essentially the same: to attain or retain the trappings of independence from and control over the homogenizing forces now sweeping the world. This competition will divide the world as countries become more alike, making some wealthy and stable but others poorer and fragile. The cascading cross-border activities that make for global interdependence will be considered disruptive and will represent "a fundamental qualitative change in the international system, predicting perhaps the end of the nation-state" (Reinicke 1997).

The economic side of globalization dominates the headlines of financial pages and computer trade journals. It is found in "that loose combination of free-trade agreements, the Internet, and the integration of financial markets that is erasing borders and uniting the world into a single, lucrative, but brutally competitive, marketplace" (T. Friedman 1996). The causes and consequences of globalization extend beyond economics, though. Globalization stems from "the onrush of economic and ecological forces that demand integration and uniformity and that mesmerize the world with fast music, fast computers, and fast food—with MTV, Macintosh, and McDonald's, pressing nations into one commercially homogenous global network: one McWorld tied together by technology, ecology, communications, and commerce" (Barber 1995). Globalization implies nothing less than a redistribution of global economic power "which will increasingly translate into a redistribution of political power" (Schwab and Smadja 1996).

In this and the next two chapters we will examine the diverse forces propelling the rapid globalization now sweeping the world, and explore whether the globalized "new economy" will sweep away the old order based on sovereign states. In considering whether the state will have a future (see Focus 9.1), this chapter will look most at the economic influence of international trade, investment finance, production, and labor and their impact on markets, growth, and global governance. Chapters 10 and 11 broaden the coverage to encompass the demographic (population) and ecopolitical (environmental) dimensions of a globalizing world. All three chapters repeatedly ask how globalization is likely to affect the well-being of the states and people of the Global North and South, as well as the prospects for cooperation and conflict. Before looking at globalization's consequences, we must first inspect its causes.

• • •

A GLOBAL VILLAGE?

Rapid and unrestrained communication is a hallmark of the **global village**—a metaphor used by many futurologists to portray a world in which borders will vanish and the world will become a single community. The major source of this global transformation is the growing speed and flow of communications, because "by drastically reducing the importance of proximity, the new technologies change people's perceptions of community" (Mathews 1997). Do cellular phones and other means of transnational communication portend consensus, and, perhaps, an integrated global village? Will life in the emergent wired global village be an improvement over what we now know? Or is the vision of such a global village, in which shared information breeds understanding and peace, mere mythology?

global village a popular image used to describe the growth of awareness that all people share a common fate, stemming from a macro perspective that views the world as an integrated and interdependent whole.

Will Globalization Doom the Future of the State?
The Debate as Conducted at the 1997 Salzburg Seminar

Journalist Neal R. Peirce attended the fiftieth Salzburg (Austria) Seminar, which convened to contemplate the state's future in the face of transformative globalization. He issued this provocative summary of the debate, which defines well the nature of globalization and leading propositions about its causes and likely consequences

Is the nation-state at the end of its 500-year run? Is it about to succumb to rapid-fire economic globalization, resurgent regions or to ethnic and tribal rivalries?

Not entirely, say midcareer professionals from some 32 nations who came here in March [1997] to debate the nation-state's furture at the elegant 18th-century palace that has been the site of the Salzburg Seminar for 50 years.

Whether from advanced or undeveloped, Western or Eastern nations, most participants agreed we'll still need nation-states to give people identity, raise taxes, provide social safety nets, protect the environment and guarantee internal security.

But for a peek into the deep uncertainties of the 21st century and the astounding array of forces now undermining the nation-states, this conference was a remarkable tour de force.

Leading the parade of transformative change are globalization and its accomplices. The computer and telecommunications revolutions enable instant worldwide communications to create new relationships, new economics, whether central governments like them or not.

Multinational corporations now assemble goods from plants across the globe and have moved heavily into services, too—law, accounting, advertising, computer consultation—as if the world were borderless.

Financial markets are also globalized. Where nation-states once sought to set exchange rates, private traders now control currency flows—at a scarcely believable level of $1.3 trillion a day.

The nation-states fatefully shrank their own power by creating supernational institutions such as the United Nations, World Trade Organization and World Bank. Each creates its own cadres of civil servants unaccountable to any single state.

Now comes a rise of influential, globally active nongovernmental organizations—the NGOs—ranging from Greenpeace to Amnesty International to animal rights groups. They got official UN recognition at the Rio Earth Summit in 1992; now they're negotiating to get a voice in official UN deliberations. Yet the NGOs, like multinationals, are mostly based in Europe and North America, feeding off cutting-edge technology, setting new global standards without much accountability to anyone.

Globalization is creating immense wealth. Yet countries unwilling or unequipped to become technologically connected—many in Africa today, for example—face "marginalization," another word for isolation and poverty.

At the Salzburg sessions there was real unease about globalization—a fear that the world order now emerging would be too cruel, too amoral, too exclusive in its power-wielding.

Anil Saldanha, a corporate executive from India, gave voice to these concerns.

"Man is not well," Mr. Saldanha said. "He is going through a process of insularity—insecurity, fright, fear. He doesn't know what's thrust on him, he must cope. So we need to look inward, to express our individuality, spirituality. If we do not put a human face on globalization, bring humanity to the forefront, we may not have far to go."

A global market does not create a global community, another speaker commented.

Yet the conference made it clear that the erosion of the nation-state is not only coming from above, it's creeping up from below.

One force is the rise of subnational regions impatient with the bureaucracy and unresponsiveness of large national governments. Nimble city-states—the "Asian tigers" of Hong Kong, Taiwan and Singapore, for example—have been recent models of success. In 1970, four U.S. states had trade offices abroad. Now virtually all do and all have official standing in the World Trade Organization.

Ethnic, racial and religious groups grasping for power are perhaps an even greater pressure from below. The end of the Cold War untapped myriad ethnic nationalistic tensions.

Indeed, we may end up with more nation-states. The United Nations had 166 member "states" in 1991. It now has 185, and it could one day end up with 400 or more, just because of ethnic diversions. But how many will be viable nations? And what does the developed world do about the collapse of countries worlds removed from its sleek globalization?

New hybrid structures—African, Asian or Latin American emulations of the European Union, for example—may be needed.

Perhaps we'll see forms of community as unknown now as the nation-state was when it burst on the scene in the 16th century.

SOURCE: Neal R. Peirce, "Does the Nation-State Have a Future?" *International Herald Tribune*, April 4, 1997, p. 9.

The revolution in telecommunications has contributed to the death of distance, as virtually instantaneous communications are possible nearly everywhere. Here, in a remote and desolate region of northern Kenya, a Samburu warrior makes a call on his cellular telephone.

The Telecommunications Revolution

Cellular phones are becoming available worldwide, enabling many among the estimated 50 percent of the world population who have never before made a phone call to communicate instantly with others ("Wireless Phones Ring Off the Hook" 1995, 7). This is one element of a larger revolution in telecommunications that is shrinking our world. "The death of distance as a determinant of the cost of communications will probably be the single most important economic force shaping society in the first half of the next century," according to the *Economist* (September 30, 1995, 5–6). "It will alter, in ways that are only dimly imaginable, decisions about where people live and work; concepts of national borders; patterns of international trade. Its effects will be as pervasive as those of the discovery of electricity."

The PC and the Internet

Computers are a second symbol of globalization. They are also its most potent agents. No area of the world and no arena of politics, economics, society, or culture is immune from the pervasive influence of computer technology. Even victims of ethnopolitical conflict and natural disasters in the most remote corners of the world are connected to others by the laptop computers that relief workers from the International Federation of Red Cross and Red Crescent Societies bring with them.

More than 150 million computers are in use today; more than 90 percent are personal computers (PCs), which have replaced the mainframes of yesteryear. Their number is growing by as many as 18 to 20 million annually (Lopez, Smith, and Pagnucco 1995, 35). Miniaturization has propelled their rapid spread. Microprocessors in today's PCs are incredibly small and growing more powerful at an exponential rate. "Computers owe their growth and impact to a phenomenon dubbed Moore's Law (after Gordon Moore, the founder of Intel), which says that computing power and capacity double every eighteen months. This exponential growth has led to the digital revolution, and it has only just begun" (*Economist*, July 1, 1995, 4).

The freedom people enjoy with personal computers and their ability to tap into emerging technologies without government intervention is most apparent on the Internet. Individuals routinely "surf the Net" without constraints, creating a global, electronic web of people, ideas, and interactions—a **cyberspace**—unencumbered by state borders (see Focus 9.2). Governments are not bystanders in the emerging technology of the future, however. Under pressure from the German government, one on-line service company, CompuServe—concerned about the use of the Internet to transmit offensive sexual and neo-Nazi materials—temporarily cut access to more than two hundred sex-related Internet news groups (arguing it was unable to stop transmissions on a selective basis). The United States has also taken new steps toward regulating the rapidly expanding telecommunications industry. A law passed in early 1996 to promote competition contained a provision requiring television manufacturers to incorporate technology into their sets that will enable parents (or others) to block reception of particular stations or programs.

Because the United States spawned the Internet, is home to more PCs than any other country, and is at the forefront of the telecommunications revolution, its influence on the emerging technology of the future is substantial. America's information capabilities probably provide the most potent basis for continued U.S. global influence in culture, politics, and military affairs in the next century (Nye and Owens 1996).

Although computer technology and the Internet are agents of rapid globaliziation, wide differences exist in countries' ability to shape (and be shaped by) a computer-driven, technocratic world. As shown in Map 9.1, the spread of the Internet is confined almost exclusively to the Global North and some of the emerging markets, notably those in Asia. Thus the revolution in computer technology adds to the promise that globalization will be uneven—benefiting some while putting others at a disadvantage. In addition, the growing global electronic network has spawned a new condition known as **virtuality**—"the ability to create a fictitious world using one's computer and to conceal one's identity in dealing with others," and it is "a more diffuse danger" with uncertain costs (Moisy 1997).

The Media: Markets or Monopoly?

Ours is often described as the "information age," but a remarkably large portion of the information we receive is controlled by a remarkably small number of media sources. According to Freedom House, within states, of 187 governments, 92 own the television broadcasting structure outright, and 67 have part ownership (*U.S. News & World Report*, November 11, 1996, 48). Ownership of the *world's* media sources, in comparison, is increasingly concentrated in a few giant national and multinational corporations. In the early 1980s they numbered about fifty; by the mid-1990s they had been reduced to twenty. Although thousands of other sources of information about politics, society, and culture are available, their influence is comparatively negligible. In the United States, for example, despite more than twenty-five thousand media outlets, only "23 corporations control most of the business in daily newspapers, magazines, tele-

The Internet
Cyberspace Pros and Cons

The Internet was developed in the late 1960s at the initiative of the U.S. Department of Defense. Its intent was to enable scientists and engineers working on military contracts to share computers, resources, and ideas—the latter through "e-mail," a way of sending messages electronically. Designed to survive a nuclear war, information was transmitted in small "packages" through different routes, making it difficult to eavesdrop on the data and messages sent.

The popularity of the Internet spread slowly throughout the academic world, which by the mid-1980s was its principal user. Two innovations then revolutionized the ease with which the Internet could be used, propelling its popularity beyond academe. One was Swiss software engineer Tim Berners-Lee's invention of the World Wide Web and "hypertext" to link documents with one another. The other was a software program known as Mosaic (written primarily by Marc Andreesen, an undergraduate student at the University of Illinois), which provides user-friendly access to the "Web" and the "Net."

In 1994 commercial companies surpassed universities as the leading users of the Internet. Today it is the functional equivalent of the "information superhighway" telecommunications specialists have long anticipated and promised.

Use of the Internet has grown—fueled by the growth of personal computers in homes and businesses—from less than 100,000 Internet hosts in 1988 to 15 million in 1997 (*Time*, May 19, 1997, 68). Concerns about its uses and abuses surfaced, and questions about whether and how governments might exert control over the "Net" inevitably followed. Here are contrasting viewpoints about the culture of cyberspace and the concerns it raises.

THE ETHOS OF INDEPENDENCE AND INDIVIDUALITY

The [Internet] classic user takes a libertarian stance, is suspicious of government, disdainful of politicians, and actively hostile towards those who would screw up his paradise with indiscriminate advertising, stupid questions, and "newbie" (naive newcomer) behavior. . . .

Fundamental to the Internet credo are the protection of free speech and the right of every group to be heard. . . .

Enthusiasts see the Internet as a sort of digital Utopia, not because everything on it is admirable, but because it is there at all. The Internet defies centralized authority; its mantra is "do your own thing."

—*The Economist* 336 (July 1, 1995): 14

THE INTERNET ELITE

Theoretically, anyone can post information, but the reality is that the main content of the Internet . . . is controlled by governments, corporations, and academic institutions. . . . The ease with which it is possible to alter information—or merely to shade the truth by selectively culling out unfavorable information—is a real concern. . . . Who will be the custodians of the world's information?

. . . Although the Internet supposedly is available to anyone with a modem and the will to use it, the profile of users is skewed by race, gender, income, and age. . . . Access may be unlimited in theory, but it is restricted by the cost of technology and the steep learning curve for computer neophytes. . . . If electronic communication is the future, what will become of the vast majority of people who can only stand by and watch the worldwide exchange of electrons?

. . . There are disturbing social implications of a future in which human communication increasingly takes place through electronic media. . . . Work will be done at home and transmitted by modem; shopping will be done over the World Wide Web and paid for by debits to our electronic bank accounts. Even entertainment will take place through the computer screen.

. . . No one is examining the question of whether a world split between an elite minority of information-empowered people interacting electronically and a majority mired in information poverty is in anyone's best interests. Do we really want to choose between a "successful" but soulless electronic existence and disenfranchisement?

—H. W., "The Internet Elite," *Bulletin of the Atomic Scientists* 51 (July/August 1995): 44–45

vision, books, and motion pictures" (Bagdikian 1992, 4). As corporate America merges its media sources into ever larger but fewer units (as witnessed, for example, by the Disney Corporation's buyout of ABC television), fewer and fewer corporate executives control what Americans hear and see about the world around them. Critics worry that the American people have become a "captive

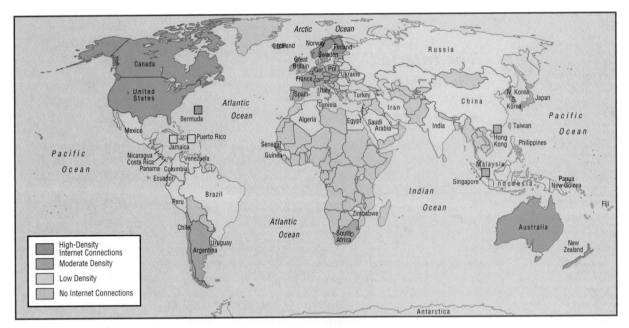

MAP 9.1

Uneven Spread: Global Connections to the Internet

The information age has made it possible for people, corporations, and institutions to communicate with one another and transact business throughout the globe almost instantaneously, but access to this technology is uneven. Information technology has spread rapidly throughout the Global North, while much of the Global South lags far behind.

SOURCE: *Time* (1995), 81.

audience," subject to limited information from limited sources. Nonetheless, the promise of profits and the ability to exercise influence over "news, information, public ideas, popular culture, and political attitudes" spur the corporate giants and their investors onward (Bagdikian 1992).

The media's impact on the global diffusion of Western culture is widely recognized. However, its impact on public affairs is more difficult to trace. Scholars generally agree that the media have the capacity to *set the agenda* of public discourse about political affairs. In the process of **agenda setting,** they also often shape public policy. Particular power is attributed to CNN (Cable News Network), the twenty-four-hour television news channel beamed around the world. For example, its global broadcasts of squalor and violence were often viewed as a catalyst to the humanitarian intervention in Somalia and to NATO's proactive military effort to bring the disputants in Bosnia to the bargaining table. These reassuring examples of the positive contribution of information technology to international peacekeeping aside, some caution that this "virtual diplomacy" has limitations. One critic has described the impact of CNN and the media this way:

> In foreign policy circles these days one often hears that the advent of instantaneous and global technology has given the news media far greater influence in international relations than ever before, robbing diplomacy of its rightful place at the helm in the process. Observers of international affairs

agenda setting the thesis that by their ability to identify issues, the communications media determine the problems that receive attention by governments and international organizations.

call it the CNN curve. . . . It suggests that when CNN floods the airwaves with news of a foreign crisis, it evokes an emotional outcry from the public to "do something." Under the spell of the CNN curve, goes this refrain, policymakers have no choice but to redirect their attention to the crisis at hand or risk unpopularity, whether or not such revision is merited by policy considerations. (Neuman 1995–1996, 109)

Control of television and other media sources by the United States and a small number of European countries became the focus of hot dispute with the Global South during the 1980s. Dissatisfied with the media coverage it received from Global North news agencies and resentful of Northern domination of other forms of communication, Global South leaders demanded a **New World Information and Communication Order (NWICO)** to create a new regime with fair rules to right the imbalance of the information flows from North to South that painted what they perceived to be an unfavorable image of the South. This image, they believed, fostered Northern values, such as consumerism and conspicuous consumption, that perpetuated the South's dependence on the North. As the North–South conflict brewed, the United States withdrew from the United Nations Educational, Scientific, and Cultural Organization (UNESCO), in part due to its role in promoting the new communications order.

The NWICO has since receded on the global agenda, but the issues remain very much alive in nongovernmental organizations concerned about the concentration of so much media power in so few hands. In 1995 Hollywood was able to beam the Academy Awards around the world to over a billion people, and American evangelist Billy Graham preached via electronic links to a similar number in over 185 countries. The new global information infrastructure is "especially disturbing because dominance in 'global' products implies not just the ability to ship products around the world, but dominance in cultural exports. This dominance provides the potential to displace indigenous culture with a tide of largely Western, largely consumerist, global conformity. Perhaps globalization is just a nice word that multinational corporations use to hide their efforts to infect the entire world with the cultural virus of commercialism" (Mowlana 1995).

Whatever its true character, the $600 billion global telecommunications industry is without question the major vehicle for the rapid spread of ideas, information, and images worldwide. It also plays a role in the transfer of institutions and generation of income, as exhibited by the World Trade Organization's World Telecom Pact, scheduled to go into force in 1998. Issued by nearly seventy countries, the accord to open the industry to the free market creates a new regime that ends government and private telecommunication monopolies in many states and is expected to pump new funds into the global economy by slashing phone costs to consumers and creating countless jobs. Estimating that liberalization could add $1 trillion, or 4 percent, to the value of world economic output over the next decade, WTO Director-General Renato Ruggiero proclaimed that the accord "is good news for the international economy, it is good news for businesses and it is good news for the ordinary people around the world" (*International Herald Tribune*, February 17, 1997, 1). Many, of course, agree with this assessment, and see global telecommunications liberating minds, expanding choices, penetrating societies closed to diplomatic communication, and creating a single, more united, homogenized global culture. Others disagree, however. They note that the airwaves can communicate divisive messages as well as unifying ones; what is said is more important than how much is said, and division rather than global solidarity can be created when particular values are disseminated.

One counterpoint to the "McWorld" of transnational media consumerism is "Jihad"—a world driven by "parochial hatreds," not "universalizing markets" (Barber 1995). In this context, it is sobering to note that the Ayatollah Khomeini, author of the revival of Islamic fundamentalism that swept the shah of Iran from power in 1979, "combined his access to networks of mosques and bazaars with that of electronic communication and cassette tapes" to carry on a successful long-distance bid to create an Iranian theocracy (Mowlana 1995).

Hence, because globalized communications and information may be used as tools for conflict and revolution as well as for community and peace, the creation of "a world without boundaries where everybody will know everything about everybody else" may not necessarily be a better world (Moisy 1997). We must ask, would the world be better or worse if people throughout the globe were to become "rootless, atomistic individuals floating free of any ties to society, . . . a world without ties of history, language, culture and kinship, in which it is costless for people and objects to move around?" (*Economist*, September 20, 1997, 29).

Global Health or Global Infection?

Humankind and the threat of disease have always coexisted uneasily. For example, in Kikwit, Zaire, the deadly Ebola virus—after lying dormant for twenty years—broke out and ravaged its victims with massive hemorrhaging and certain death. Globalization not only heightens awareness of health risks, but actually multiplies them. Truck drivers in India are primary agents for the AIDS (acquired immune deficiency syndrome) epidemic in that country and elsewhere in Asia. Rapid urbanization in much of the world also contributes to the rapid spread of diseases. Growing numbers of refugees forced into unsanitary camps are ravaged by cholera and other diseases that can prove as deadly as the violent ethnic conflicts they flee. Excessive population growth forces people to move into habitats where unknown microorganisms and killer viruses await them. Millions of airline travelers share cabin-sealed environments filled with the carriers of potentially fatal diseases. A shrinking globe, in short, has made the spread of disease across borders rapid, frequent, and difficult to control:

> It is somewhat ironic that, in the face of an ongoing biomedical revolution, traditional diseases are making a comeback and new microbes are evolving to challenge human immune systems. The World Health Organization estimates that one-quarter of the world's population is subject to chronic intestinal parasitic infections. Of the nearly twenty million annual deaths due to communicable diseases, resurgent tuberculosis kills three million people annually, malaria two million, and hepatitis one million. In addition, the AIDS virus, estimated to have infected more than 750,000 people in North America, has infected between 13 and 15 million people worldwide. More than 8,000,000 are infected in Sub-Saharan Africa, and in South Africa one-fifth of the adult population will be HIV positive by the year 2000. (Pirages 1998, 393)

Many also view narcotic use as a disease. The illicit use of drugs is widespread, hugely profitable, and difficult to control in a borderless world. Fueled by major production and distribution complexes in the Andes and southwest and southeast Asia, the narcotics industry generates profits estimated at $400 billion annually (Mathews 1997, 57). As profits have grown, traffickers' power has expanded, leading to other worrisome developments. Among them are "the [widening] impact of the illicit drug trade on illegal economic structures and processes in major producing or transit countries; the increasing political corruption in such countries; the growing intrusion of narcocriminal enterprises into the realm of the state and the law . . . ; the successes of narcotics businesses in innovation, avoiding detection, and increasing operating efficiency; and . . . the growing transnational cooperation among criminal empires that deal in drugs and other black-market items" (Lee 1995). It is not an exaggeration to posit that globalization has contributed to the rise of international organized crime (IOC) syndicates (see Chapter 6).

Global Migration

The movement of populations across frontiers has reached unprecedented proportions, producing a **global migration crisis.** It raises a host of moral issues, such as the ethnic balance inside host countries, the meaning of citizenship and sovereignty, the distribution of income, labor supply, xenophobia, the impact of multiculturalism, protection of basic human rights and prevention of exploitation, and the potential for large flows of migrants and refugees to undermine democratic governance and state stability. Particularly troubling is the moral inconsistency between liberal democracies that simultaneously defend the fundamental right of refugees to emigrate and the sacred right of sovereign states to control their borders (see Weiner 1995).

As "national sovereignty is eroded from above by the mobility of capital, goods and information across national boundaries" (Sandel 1996), whether existing institutions of global governance are able to cope with globalization's multiple challenges is a hotly contested issue. Meanwhile, the capacity of the state to cope with the forces of rapid change is also being tested. As we turn our attention to the globalization of finance, trade, production, and labor, we will find further evidence that "globalization is uneven. It unites but it also divides, creating winners here and losers there." And in an anarchical international political system, "there is no global civil society that can be called on to support global governance" (Sørensen 1995). Like politics and markets, then, politics and the process of globalization are intimately intertwined, as "even the most powerful states cannot escape the imperatives of the global economy" (Sandel 1996). Meanwhile, realization of truly civic-spirited community in the global village remains elusive.

• • •

THE GLOBALIZATION OF FINANCE

Global finance encompasses "all types of cross-border portfolio-type transactions—borrowing and lending, trading of currencies or other financial claims, and the provision of commercial banking or other financial services. It also includes capital flows associated with foreign direct investment—transactions involving significant control of producing enterprises" (Cohen 1996). The **globalization of finance** refers to the increasing transnationalization or centralization of financial markets through the worldwide integration of capital flows. The central characteristic of the emerging consolidated system of financial arrangements is that it is not centered on a single state. Thus globalization implies the growth of a single, unified world market. While telecommunications specialists talk about the "death of distance," financial specialists talk about the "end of geography," which "refers to a state of economic development where geographic location no longer matters in finance" (O'Brien 1992).

Evidence of financial globalization abounds. Although trade has grown dramatically since World War II, the volume of cross-border capital flows has increased even more. Financial flows now exceed trade in merchandise by twenty to forty times, and the gap continues to widen. Cross-border transactions in bonds and equities have increased at an astonishing rate over the past twenty years:

> [In 1986], about $190 billion passed through the hands of currency traders, in New York, London and Tokyo every day. By 1995 daily turnover had reached almost $1.2 trillion. In 1990, $50 billion of private capital flowed into emerging markets; [in 1997] that figure was $336 billion. These bald figures confirm what every financier from Wall Street to Warsaw will tell you: that the world's capital markets have been transformed. Even larger sums of money are moving across borders, and ever more countries have access to international finance. (*Economist*, October 25, 1997, 87).

Further evidence of financial globalization is the astonishing recent increases in the daily turnover on the foreign exchange market. On many days, *private* currency traders often exchange more than $2 trillion to make profits through **arbitrage** on the basis of minute shifts in the value of states' currencies, and their activity continues to climb steadily. Consequently, interconnected markets require more than ever a reliable system of money to conduct business across borders while coping with an array of fluctuating national currencies. "It has become a well-known fact that the daily turnover on the currency markets now often exceeds the global stock of official foreign exchange reserves—so what chance have central banks in influencing exchange rates by buying and selling currency in the markets?" (*Economist*, September 10, 1997).

As the transnational economy becomes integrated, "most national central banks are now irrelevant [because] the world's money is essentially controlled by three key institutions: the U.S. Federal Reserve Board, the Bank of Japan, and the German Bundesbank, and global capital markets centered in London, Tokyo and New York are facilitating increased internationalization in every area of finance" (Thurow 1998). "National" securities markets have also lost their meaning as a consequence of the globalization of finance. National securities markets have been integrated. Foreign investors' activities in U.S. stock markets during the 1980s increased by more than $300 billion. They also set new records in Japan, growing from 4.6 billion yen in 1980 to more than 54 billion in 1987. Between 1980 and 1990 the market value of shares (known as "capitalization") on world stock markets increased from $2.5 to $8.2 trillion. "New York's capitalization doubled, London's more than tripled, and Tokyo's increased tenfold" (Sobel 1994, 50–51). Amidst this growth in transactions, a rise

arbitrage the selling of one currency (or product) and purchase of another to make a profit on the changing exchange rates; traders ("arbitragers") help to keep states' currencies in balance through their speculative efforts to buy large quantities of devalued currencies and sell them in countries where they are valued more highly.

or fall in any national security market now routinely causes a similar change in the others' indexes. In addition, new financial instruments have emerged, leading to new markets in which they are bought and sold. "Derivatives" are one example. These are complex financial instruments that combine speculation in "options" and "futures" designed to hedge against volatility in financial markets, but they require no actual purchase of the underlying securities (stocks and bonds). Derivatives now account for trillions of dollars in cross-border transactions and "are rapidly becoming one of the most globalized financial markets" (Cerny 1994, 331, 334).

As these illustrations suggest, markets are being profoundly transformed by the rapid acceleration of financial globalization. We may not yet have experienced the end of geography, but clearly financial globalization "has put governments distinctly on the defensive, eroding much of the authority of the contemporary sovereign state" (Cohen 1996). What explains these changes? Analysts generally agree that three critical developments account for the globalization of finance. First, the oil crisis of 1973–1974 and the OPEC decade that followed unleashed a rapid increase in global financial flows and stimulated new patterns of global investments and new financial management procedures. Second, beginning in the 1970s and accelerating in the 1980s, the basic philosophy governing financial and capital movements began to accept the value of "deregulating" markets in adherence with commercial liberalism's tenet that markets operate best when free of government interference. Third, "the computerization of finance" (O'Brien 1992) became "the electronic equivalent of nuts and bolts that [altered] the culture of production, competition, and innovation . . . in all of the other sectors of economy and society" (Cerny 1994) because financial transactions and contracts across borders could be processed instantly on a computer screen.

Many economists see the increased mobility of capital as proof that markets become more efficient as they are widened. From their perspective, the exploding volume of international financial transactions encourages deregulation and liberalization of global markets and the convergence of monetary and fiscal policies, particularly in the Global North. This is known as the **capital mobility hypothesis**—that the free or unregulated flow of money across borders is influential in the globalization of finance. A corollary hypothesis is that the technological revolution has created **electronic cash** in the form of global electronic debit and credit systems, "smart" credit cards, and true digital money, and that in the new **digital world economy** "the risks of fraud, money-laundering, and other financial crises are markedly increased" (Kobrin 1997).

A contributing factor to the transnational movement of capital has been the growing preference of states to relax legal constraints on international capital. As Figure 9.1 reveals, the rules governing foreign capital transactions have been progressively liberalized, speeding the globalization of finance:

> In addition to liberalizing trade, more countries are also gradually removing restrictions on cross-border movements of capital, either unilaterally or as part of regional initiatives. The number of countries with liberal or mostly liberal capital regimes has grown from nine to thirty in the past two decades, while the number of countries with relatively restrictive rules has dropped sharply, from 73 to 53. (World Bank 1997, 134)

FIGURE 9.1

The Global Diffusion of Liberal Rules Governing Foreign Capital Transactions

Many countries are loosening restraints on international capital, and this has encouraged the globalization of finance.

Note: Data are for 102 industrial and developing countries. *Liberal* means no restrictions; *mostly liberal* means a few restrictions by industry; *partly liberal* means many restrictions on the size and timing of transactions; *restrictive* means that domestic investment by foreigners or foreign investment by domestic residents requires official approval; *very restrictive* means that all cross-border transactions require official approval.

SOURCE: World Bank (1997), 135.

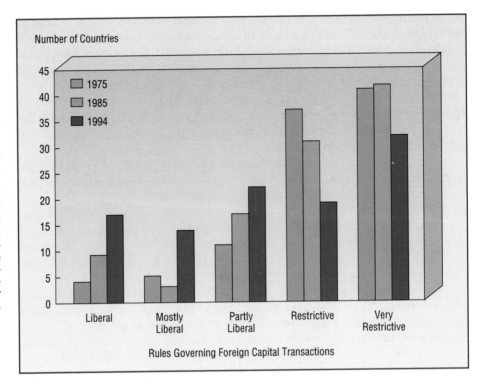

Note, however, that wide differences exist between states and regions in the receipt of international capital.

> Just as countries differ markedly with respect to growth in trade, so there is considerable disparity in countries' ability to attract foreign capital. Although worldwide private and official capital flows have expanded by about a factor of ten in the past two decades, developing regions have fared unequally in attracting these flows. Much of the expansion has been in private flows, and among developing regions most of these go to East Asia and Latin America. One estimate suggests that more than half the population of the developing world has been little touched by this aspect of globalization. (World Bank 1997, 134)

Because the accelerating mobility of capital means that financial markets are no longer centered within states, the globalized financial system is not subject to regulation by any one state in particular. Most states are losing their grip on their capacity to control the flow and level of finance in their national economies. The globalization of finance has expanded the power of private markets and corporations no longer tied to any one country, "thereby increasingly undermining state power itself and institutionalizing that of the global marketplace. . . . Having set up the conditions in which more open international financial markets were established in the 1970s and 1980s, [states] are now having difficulty controlling their own creations" (Cerny 1994).

Thus, as financial globalization has taken on a life of its own, states' economic policy choices are constrained—much as **realist theory** argues that the distribution of military power constrains their choices in the quest for self-preservation against competitors' weapons. In other words, the international mobility of capital has modified states' circumstances by rewarding some actors and punishing others much as military power once did; it also undermines the **neorealist theory** that states are autonomous, unitary actors free to regulate their internal economic affairs: Globalization limits "the ability of governments to restrict—or even control—economic activity" (Thurow 1998).

States' diminishing ability to regulate financial markets, control the international conduct of national business enterprises, and manage the global character of their national economies was vividly illustrated by the Global South's debt crisis in the 1980s. In the wake of excessive borrowing to repay their loans from foreign sources, many Global South countries discovered how much they could be victimized by "capital flight" during the worldwide 1980s recession, when the money they needed to service the interest payments owed on their growing debt simply failed to materialize. Their sovereignty was put at risk by their dependence on foreign finance. The crisis—as well as the plunging currencies and stock markets that put east Asian "tiger" economies in a deep freeze in 1998—call into question the soundness of the international financial and banking system and dramatically underscore the extent to which all countries had become *mutually sensitive* and *mutually vulnerable* in a globalized, interdependent financial world. This example suggests the growing need for more routinized multilateral mechanisms for policy coordination and cooperation to cope with potential future crises as global finance becomes increasingly interlocked through massive cross-border transactions beyond the immediate reach of state regulation.

• • •

THE GLOBALIZATION OF TRADE

Technological changes have led to the integration of states' economic markets. However, the extraordinary pace at which the countries of the world have linked their markets can be attributed to more than the increased speed of transport and communication. The organization of markets at a global level, and the convergence of commodity prices across countries, has been driven by the worldwide reduction of tariff rates that has made the expansion of international trade possible. Recall that:

> After World War II, the General Agreement on Tariffs and Trade (GATT) was created by the international community, along with the IMF, the World Bank, and other international organizations. Based on the principles of multilateral cooperation, the GATT had a mandate to roll back tariffs from their prewar peaks and to continue reducing them in the future. The GATT was extremely successful in 1947 in the first Geneva Round in reducing tariffs by 35 percent. Successive rounds in the 1950s, 1960s (the Kennedy Round), and the 1970s (Tokyo Round) and the recent Uruguay Round have virtually eliminated tariffs on manufactured goods. The World Trade Organization (WTO), which succeeded GATT in 1994, is currently engaged in

realist theory the view that states are unitary global actors in relentless competition with each other for position and prosperity in the international hierarchy, dedicated to the promotion of their own interests at the expense of other states.

neorealist theory the new realist theory that the behavior of competitive states is shaped by changes in the distribution of global power more than by changes in their domestic systems.

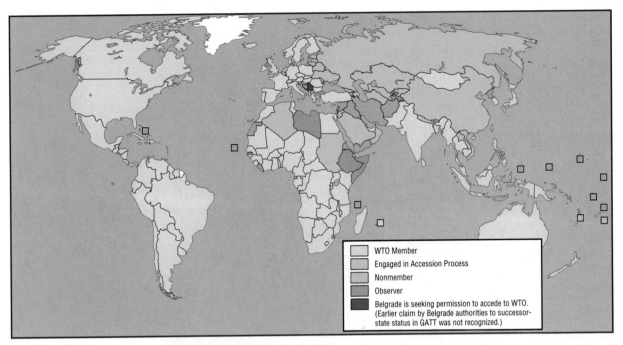

MAP 9.2

A Globalized Trading System: Countries Affiliated with the World Trade Organization

Most states are already members of the World Trade Organization, whose purpose is to promote free trade throughout the world. Most of the remaining states are applicants, and when (and if) they join, the volume of trade will climb, contributing further to the integration of the world market.

Notes: Independent states that are effectively part of the customs territory of other countries and dependent areas are not shown. Serbia and Montenegro have asserted the formation of a joint independent state, but this entity has not been formally recognized as a state by the United States. Boundary representation is not necessarily authoritative.

SOURCE: *Handbook of International Economic Statistics* (1997).

reducing nontariff barriers and protection, including in areas not covered by the GATT. (IMF 1997, 113)

The WTO has enlarged its membership, and the 132 countries that have agreed to adhere to its free-trade rules are spread across the globe, with important applicants such as China eagerly seeking entry (see Map 9.2). If and when this expansion process is complete, the globalization of trade will escalate even further and faster.

In historical perspective, the globalization of trade serves as testimony to the wisdom of **commercial liberalism,** which held that trade liberalization to remove barriers to exports would permit the free trade crucial to growing prosperity. The reduction of tariff rates since World War II (see Chapter 8) permitted international trade and world output to grow hand in hand. Growing international trade has propelled widespread advances in global welfare during the past half-century, and its expansion has been particularly rapid recently. Even during the early 1990s, when the world experienced a recession in economic growth, world trade growth barely slowed (see Figure 9.2). Despite the 1997 Asian financial crisis, world trade volume grew by 9.5 percent in real terms that year, above the 5 percent increase in 1996 and the second highest rate in more

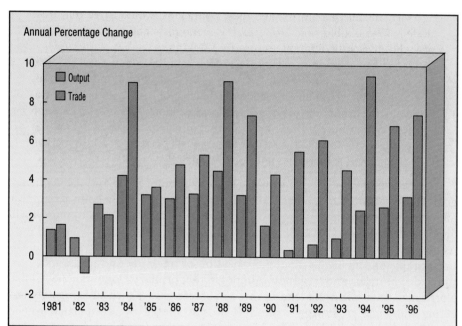

Annual Percentage Change

FIGURE 9.2

Growth of World Output and Trade, 1981–1996

Since the early 1980s, the growth of world trade has consistently outpaced the growth of world economic output. As a result, states' domestic welfare has become more tightly intertwined as states have become more closely integrated into the global political economy.

SOURCE: *World Economic and Social Survey* 1995 (1995), 35.

than 20 years (*Economist* March 28, 1998, 5). The growth and globalization of trade has pushed economic growth to new highs, which many experts believe will continue into the next century (see also Fig. 8.3).

Trade globalization through the liberalization of trade rules has truly transformed the way the world works, thinks, and consumes. It has altered peoples' standards of living, as the volume of goods and services crossing borders has climbed with reductions in the obstacles to free trade. As two reports summarize,

> If shop windows everywhere seem to be filled with imports, there is a reason. International trade has been growing at a startling pace. While the global economy has been expanding at a bit over 3 percent a year, the volume of trade has been rising at a compound annual rate of about twice that. In 1996 some $5.2 trillion of goods was sent from one country to another, up from $2 trillion a decade earlier. Foreign products, from meat to machinery, play a more important role in almost every economy in the world, and foreign markets now tempt businesses that never much worried about sales beyond their nation's borders. . . .
>
> Time was when trade flows were of interest mainly to economic experts and executives of big corporations. But over the past few years, the movement of goods and services across national boundaries has become the subject of intense public attention all over the world. To the public at large, trade is the most obvious manifestation of a globalizing world economy. . . .
>
> Measured by the volume of imports and exports, the world economy has become increasingly integrated in the years since the Second World War. A fall in barriers to trade has helped stimulate this growth. The volume of world merchandise trade in 1997 was about 16 times what it was in 1950, while the world's total output is only five-and-a-half times as big. The ratio of world exports to GDP has climbed from 7 to 15 percent.

Virtually all economists, and most politicians, would agree that freer trade has been a blessing. However, the economists and politicians would probably give quite different reasons for thinking so. . . .

What lies behind this explosion in international commerce? The general worldwide decline in trade barriers, such as tariffs and import quotas, is surely one explanation. The economic opening of countries that have traditionally been minor players in the world economy, such as China and Mexico, is another. A third force behind the import-export boom has passed all but unnoticed: the rapidly falling cost of getting goods to market.

(*Economist*, November 8 and 15, 1997, p.85)

There is a serious downside to the globalization of trade and the economic growth it has stimulated, however. As shown in Chapter 8, the gains from trade are uneven because "capitalism is motivated by inequality: the economically fit are expected to drive the economically unfit out of existence" (Thurow 1998). As a result, domestic protectionist measures designed to cushion or curtail the unfavorable effects of the rapid globalization of trade abound in the most victimized countries and regimes. Although the primary winners, the Global North has often taken the lead in these neomercantilist measures, usually targeting the rapidly growing economies in the Global South—particularly in Asia. For the Newly Industrialized Economies (NIEs) in Asia and other emerging markets, however, the globalization of trade has become the preferred route to economic advancement, and they have energetically sought to attract multinational corporations' foreign direct investment to help them better compete for exports in the global market, despite the costly consequences for the poor (see also Chapter 5).

Trade Integration: Winners and Losers

Trade integration is the difference between growth rates in trade and gross domestic (or gross world) product. As trade integration grows, so does interdependence. As the data in Figure 9.3 show, the 1990s have witnessed not only growth in trade integration but also a spectacular increase in the *speed* of integration, as growth in trade has consistently outpaced growth in production. The pace of integration has been sharply higher in the Global South than in the North, reflecting the Global South's increasing contribution to trade growth—a trend expected to continue (see Figure 9.3). This also means that the Global South is becoming increasingly important to growing economic prosperity in the Global North. Still, wide—and predictable—differences exist within the Global South and the countries in transition. Eastern Europe, Central Asia, and East Asia have experienced the most rapid integration into the world political economy. North Africa, Sub-Saharan Africa, and the Middle East lag far behind (World Bank 1997).

The differences among these groups reflect their historical experiences and the different strategies of development each has chosen (see Chapter 5). They also reflect changes in technology and consumer demands in a global economy. High-technology electronic goods (i.e., data-processing equipment, telecommunications equipment, and semiconductors and microprocessors) make up an increasing proportion of trade in manufactured goods. Here, the twenty-eight advanced Global North economies have cornered the market as the major supplier, accounting for nearly 80 percent of world exports in goods and services in 1996 (IMF 1997, 120). The United States and Japan lead the pack, followed by

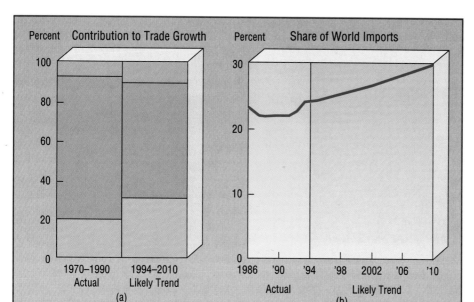

FIGURE 9.3

The Global South in World Trade

In recent years, international trade has grown more rapidly than the production of goods and services. The Global South's contribution to world trade growth and its rising share of world imports reveal its growing importance to the world political economy.

SOURCE: World Bank (1995a), 58.

western Europe. But these patterns are changing rapidly, creating new winners not only in products but also among producers.

As noted, the Global South's share of world trade, both now and projected into the future, is growing (from 23 percent in 1985 to 29 percent in 1995). Its share of manufactured-product exports is growing as well, having increased by 10 percent (to 22 percent) between 1980 and 1993. But its share of total exports of new products as a result of the recent industrialization they have undergone has grown even more—from less than 12 percent in 1980 to more than 28 percent in 1995 (IMF 1997, 72-73, 120). This is the area in which Asia surpasses all others. Three Asian "tigers" and now the new "cubs" (Malaysia and Thailand) account for nearly two-thirds of all developing country exports of new products (new products account for nearly one-third of the total output of manufactured goods—twice the level for the United States). In short, Asian NIEs and emerging markets, well integrated with rapid technological upgrading of exports into the globalization of trade, have been winners.

Trade in services also promises to make new winners. Because the United States enjoys comparative advantages in this area, it has been a strong advocate of bringing services under the liberalizing rules of the World Trade Organization, as noted in Chapter 8. Trade in services has already expanded more than threefold since 1980, with the Global North reaping most of the benefits, even though the Global South has increased its share of this growing trade even more rapidly. The spread of information technology and the comparatively lower wage costs in developing economies are among the reasons why the World Bank predicts that developing countries will capture 25 percent of world trade (and one-third of global GDP) by 2020 (*Economist*, September 13, 1997,

Globalization is sped by the rapid expansion of computer technology. Intel is the world's largest manufacturer of computer chips, tiny microprocessors fifty thousand times faster than the first computers. On the left, a worker inspects computer chips as they come off the assembly line. Globalization is also sped by the availability of cheap, low-wage labor in some countries, which take advantage of their peoples' low wages to make products highly competitive in the globalized marketplace. On the right, a child labors at near slave wages in Bangladesh, producing goods that cost less than those made where labor unions protect workers. Such practices have mercantilist nationalists and free-trade critics up in arms, even though open global markets encourage them.

7). In the case of services, then, it appears that—at least for the time being—North and South will both reap the growing profits from the globalization of trade.

It would be terribly inaccurate to picture trade globalization as a panacea for poverty, however. It is not proving to be a path to wealth for many developing countries, and wide disparities exist among them in their trade linkages to the world. Simply put, most Global South countries see themselves as victims of an integrated trade world. "Globalization is proceeding largely for the benefit of the dynamic and powerful countries" (UNDP 1997), and the Global South's poorer countries are not participating in the advantages that globalization is providing the winners. The losers, "poor countries and poor people," often find their interests neglected. Focus 9.3 vividly defines the painful costs of trade globalization for the Global South's poor countries, as described by the United Nations Development Program (UNDP). While the shares of world exports of the Asian NIEs and the rapidly industrialized economies have increased between 1968 and 1996, the shares of most of the other 127 developing countries have been "roughly flat or have declined," and their "integration with the world economy has been rather slow" (IMF 1997, 73–74). If globalization is to continue, and it appears highly likely, then perhaps in the long run "globalization's success" will depend on large "transfers of capital, tangible and intangible alike," from the Global North to the Global South (Reinicke 1997).

• • •

THE GLOBALIZATION OF PRODUCTION

In the early 1990s Ford Motor Company launched a program called Ford 2000. Its purpose is to transform the world's second-largest industrial firm into its first

Globalization
Producing Poor Countries and Poor People?

Globalization has come at a severe cost to many poor countries, as the United Nations Development Program observes:

A dominant economic theme of the 1990s, globalization encapsulates both a description and a prescription. The description is the widening and deepening of international flows of trade, finance and information in a single, integrated global market. The prescription is to liberalize national and global markets in the belief that free flows of trade, finance and information will produce the best outcome for growth and human welfare. All is presented with an air of inevitability and overwhelming conviction. Not since the heyday of free trade in the 19th century has economic theory elicited such widespread certainty.

The principles of free global markets are nevertheless applied selectively. If this were not so, the global market for unskilled labor would be as free as the market for industrial country exports or capital. Global negotiations are moving rapidly toward a free world market in foreign investments and services. But intervention in agriculture and textiles, an obstacle to developing countries, remains high. Lacking power, poor countries and poor people too often find their interests neglected and undermined.

Globalization has its winners and its losers. With the expansion of trade and foreign investment, developing countries have seen the gaps among themselves widen. Meanwhile, in many industrial countries unemployment has soared to levels not seen since the 1930s, and income inequality to levels not recorded since the last century.

A rising tide of wealth is supposed to lift all boats. But some are more seaworthy than others. The yachts and ocean liners are indeed rising in response to new opportunities, but the rafts and rowboats are taking on water—and some are sinking fast.

Inequality is not inherent in globalization. Because liberalization exposes domestic producers to volatile global markets and to capital flows that are large relative to the economy, it increases risks—but it also increases potential rewards. For poverty eradication the challenge is to identify policies that enable poor people to participate in markets on more equitable terms, nationally and globally.

Globalization has many aspects. . . . Its economic impact on poor nations and poor people is staggering.

For the world the benefits of liberalization should exceed the costs. During 1995–2001 the results of the Uruguay Round of the GATT (General Agreement on Tariffs and Trade) are expected to increase global income by an estimated $212–$510 billion—gains from greater efficiency and higher rates of return on capital, as well as from the expansion of trade.

The overall gains obscure a more complex balance sheet of winners and losers. Projected losses are heavily outweighed by the gains, but those losses will be concentrated in a group of countries that can least afford them—and for some the costs will be significant. The least developed countries stand to lose up to $600 million a year, and Sub-Saharan Africa $1.2 billion.

This scenario has disturbing implications for poverty and human welfare. Foreign exchange losses will translate into pressure on incomes, a diminishing ability to sustain imports and increased dependence on aid at a time when aid itself is under severe pressure. Revenue from trade will be lost, undermining the capacity of governments to develop the economic and social infrastructure on which sustained reduction in human poverty depends.

SOURCE: UNDP (1997), 82–83.

truly international corporation. Management control will no longer be centered in Dearborn, Michigan, but rather dispersed throughout the world. Already Ford's chairman Alex Trotman—himself from Scotland—proudly proclaims that "there's not an American in charge of any of our national companies in Europe." Ford anticipates changes in its product line as well. Unlike most multinational corporations today, which manufacture and sell products tailored for particular regional markets (such as the Toyota corporation), Ford intends to develop manufacturing capabilities that reduce duplication in different national settings. This will also permit greater standardization and move it along the path toward a "world car." Reduced costs and greater efficiency are the goals.

Ford's plan to develop a truly international corporation is arguably the "highest stage" of corporate development. According to Harvard University's Christopher Bartlett, MNCs evolved through four stages. The initial period was one of corporate colonialism, when European MNCs directed their investments toward colonies. This was followed, after World War II, by the nationalistic period, in which U.S. companies dominated the manufacture of goods and sold them in foreign markets. Today, as noted, most multinationals are stressing manufacturing and selling products tailored for particular regional markets. From a management point of view, MNCs' overseas operations are "appendages" of a centralized hub. Ford's plans to move into the fourth stage of MNC development would disperse the hub, much as production facilities themselves are now dispersed worldwide. MNCs are replacing national corporations, because the sales of large corporations are geared to the global market and a large proportion of their revenues are generated from sales outside the countries where they are headquartered.

What needs to be added to this picture is the modern mobility of the MNCs mode of production. Beginning in the 1980s, the MNCs began to move their manufacturing plants overseas to meet the cost of competition in foreign markets. This led to a trend toward **strategic corporate alliances** with foreign companies in the same industry. As political economist Neil Richardson observes,

> Some of these are long-term partnerships, anchored in equity ownership—thus, Ford now owns 25 percent of rival Mazda while Honda owns 20 percent of rival Rover. Other alliances are more transient and project-specific, giving rise to the term "virtual corporations." Generally speaking, there are two purposes these various alliances can serve. First, an alliance with a rival may serve to achieve economies of scale. The Chrysler-Mitsubishi assembly plant in Illinois produces virtually identical cars under different nameplates for the two companies. (Originally the Diamond-Star assembly plant in Normal, Illinois, was equally owned by each firm. In 1991, Chrysler sold its half of the plant to Mitsubishi on the condition that certain Chrysler components continue to be used there and that Chrysler-badged vehicles continue to be produced there.) Second, an alliance can allow each firm to complement the other's most distinctive talents and simultaneously learn from its partner's expertise. In addition, these alliances are often complex: Mitsubishi works with Chrysler in North America and meanwhile cooperates in far-flung electronic and automotive ventures with Germany's Daimler-Benz and in automobile coproduction with the Volvo-Renault alliance in the Netherlands.
>
> These cases show that states are being drawn into disputes that are given new form by the growth of those global alliances. Policymakers can easily misunderstand the consequences of their [efforts to arrest foreign imports when] they are seemingly oblivious to the mobility of relevant firms even as they futilely expend diplomatic good will in sometimes rancorous negotiations with other governments. . . .
>
> What is a member of the U.S. Congress to think when lobbied by the "Big Three" U.S. automakers for much higher tariff protection against Japanese minivans? Would the official know that Ford and Nissan jointly produce a minivan in the United States already? That the Dodge Colt minivan is imported from Japan? Would she or he appreciate that, because Japanese minivans have only a very small market share in the United States, Detroit would gain little from such a diplomatically costly decision?

Few government leaders in the major trading states are likely to have such trade expertise. (N. Richardson 1995, 286–287, 289)

As the multinational corporation has evolved, it has been the primary agent of the globalization of production, propelling as well the extraordinary growth in trade and capital mobility witnessed during the past half-century. "While in the 1960s and 1970s foreign direct investment closely correlated with world output and trade, it expanded at an average of 16 percent annually between 1985 and 1995, compared with 2 percent and 7 percent, respectively, for output and trade" (Reinicke 1997, 128). As shown in Chapter 7, today there are more than 38,500 multinational parent companies, many now linked with each other in **virtual corporations** and alliances of co-ownership and coproduction. These corporate networks of MNCs pursue truly global strategies for financial gain, often through long-term supplier agreements and licensing and franchising contracts through the MNCs' international alliances and joint foreign direct investment strategies; today "about 70 percent of world trade is intra-industry or inter-firm" (Reinicke 1997, 128). As they funnel large financial flows across national borders, these global corporate conglomerates are integrating national economies into a single global market. The outward flow of **foreign direct investment (FDI)** stock attributable to their more than 250,000 foreign affiliates has increased rapidly between 1970 and 1995, from less than $12 billion to an estimated $2.4 trillion (*Economist*, September 20, 1997, 29; *World Investment Report 1995* 1995, 9). Most of this investment in search of profits remains in the Global North, which is also the primary source and target of the outward flow of FDI.

foreign direct investment according to the United Nations, like plant and equipment, FDI also implies "a lasting involvement in the management of enterprises in the recipient economy." In contrast, *equity investment* flows such as stock ownership are typically more speculative in nature and respond quickly to changing perceptions of risk and reward.

The reason for the concentration of FDI in the North is self-interest: Profits are MNCs' primary motivation, and their investment returns are likely to be greatest in the Global North, where a combination of affluence and political stability reduces investment risks. Still, the Global South is the recipient of considerable, and rapidly growing, FDI. Although the amounts fluctuate on a yearly basis, the 1990s have generally seen a return to the expansive pattern of 1971 to 1981, when a growing number of developing countries came to be viewed as targets of investment opportunity, and inflows between 1990 and 1997 totaled $938 billion (*Newsweek*, November 10, 1997, 35).

Net private capital flows to developing countries (excluding the Asian NIEs) averaged about $150 billion a year over 1993–96 and almost hit $200 billion in 1996—nearly a sixfold increase from the average annual inflow over 1983–1989. In fact, capital flows to one country, China, were larger in 1996 than they were to all developing countries as recently as 1989. These capital inflows roughly doubled in relation to developing country GDP between 1985 and 1996. Unlike in the 1970s and early 1980s when most capital flows represented bank lending, the largest flows in recent years have been in equity and portfolio investments. Such private capital flows rose from a low of 1/2 of 1 percent of developing country GDP in 1983–1989 to 2–4 percent of GDP in each of the years 1994–1996. Foreign direct investment has posted the largest rise. This has flowed overwhelmingly toward the emerging market countries that have been experiencing relatively fast economic growth. Asian developing countries received almost twice the net private capital inflows as a percentage of their GDP that African countries received over 1990–1996. Liberalization of financial markets in both recipient and source countries has helped to spur this growing capital market integration. Successful developing countries increasingly have lifted controls

The developing countries once shunned foreign investments, fearing their adverse economic and political consequences, but no longer. Even Vietnam, once a bitter communist enemy of the capitalistic United States, now welcomes American investment dollars.

on cross-border flows, especially on capital inflows, and removed restrictions on payments for current account transactions. (IMF 1997, 73)

The impact of foreign direct investment on creating an interconnected global capital market extends beyond money. With it comes technology, managerial expertise, and employment opportunities. Champions of MNCs view these as contributions to the development of less developed economies. Not surprisingly, many Global South countries often actively seek MNC investment capital and the other perquisites that flow from it. MNCs are especially important to those who seek to emulate the economic success of the Newly Industrializing Economies, which depend on an ability to sustain growth in exports. Foreign capital is critical to this goal.

Foreign investment is not without costs, however. With it comes MNC political influence, for example, which sometimes skews the political process in questionable directions (see Korten 1995). Critics of MNCs also worry that the presumed economic benefits of FDI gloss over the adverse economic consequences. "They see these giant corporations not as needed agents of economic change but more as vehicles of antidevelopment. Multinationals, they argue, reinforce dualistic economic structures and exacerbate domestic inequalities with wrong products and inappropriate technology" (Todaro 1994). (See Focus 9.4.)

Critics contend that MNCs exact a cost not only on the Global South but also on the Global North (recall Focus 7.4). They note that while corporate executives often have a "broad vision and understanding of global issues," they have little appreciation of, or concern for, "the long-term social or political consequences of what their companies make or what they do" (Barnet and Cavanagh 1994; see also Barnet and Müller 1974). These allegedly include a host of maladies, including environmental degradation, a maldistribution of global resources, and social disintegration. Further, critics complain that MNCs are beyond the control of national political leaders.

The formidable power and mobility of global corporations are undermining the effectiveness of national governments to carry out essential policies

Inappropriate Products in a Homogenizing World

In the 1970s, babies in Third World nations were dying when they might have been thriving. The apparent culprit: ersatz mother's milk made from powder. The Nestlé Company, a Swiss-based multinational, had identified Third World mothers as a high-growth marketing opportunity. Nestlé baby formula was aggressively pushed as the "modern" way to feed infants.

In the developed world, baby formula works fine. It may not be as good as mother's milk, but it's reasonably close. As long as the bottles and rubber nipples for the formula are properly sterilized, the mixing water reasonably pure, and the mixing proportions right, babies do well on it. But in Third World villages in the 1970s, pure water was the exception, not the rule, and the need for sterilization was hard to explain and seldom practiced. Beyond that, the formula was cheap by First World standards, but expensive by Third World reckonings. That makes it fatally tempting to stretch the powder by diluting it too much, thus degrading the nutritional value.

Health care professionals and missionaries working in the Third World were outraged, and they communicated their sadness and anger to Nestlé, which did nothing, and to governments, which didn't seem to care. Nestlé had threatened no nation's security, broken no laws.

But nutritionists and activists in the industrialized world did care, and condemnation of Nestlé's marketing practices became widespread. As word got out, the cause was taken up by nearly one hundred private organizations in sixty-five states. A transnational economic boycott of Nestlé products was launched, coordinated by a U.S.-based transnational citizen coalition, the Infant Formula Action Committee (INFACT).

Whether the boycott had much economic effect on Nestlé's bottom line is hard to pin down. But it became a public relations nightmare for a company that liked to be known for its warm and cuddly hot chocolate and its candy-counter Crunch bars. The INFACT-led transnational campaign ultimately forced Nestlé to abandon its Third World marketing practices, and in 1981 it led to the passage of a World Health Organization code of conduct governing the marketing and sale of infant formula.

SOURCE: Lopez, Smith, and Pagnucco (1995), 33.

on behalf of their people. Leaders of nation-states are losing much of the control over their own territory they once had. More and more, they must conform to the demands of the outside world because the outsiders are already inside the gates. Business enterprises that routinely operate across borders are linking far-flung pieces of territory into a new world economy that bypasses all sorts of established political arrangements and conventions. (Barnet and Cavanagh 1994, 19)

Nonetheless, some corporate visionaries extol multinational corporations' transnational virtues and the positive contribution they claim MNCs make by encouraging replacement of narrow nationalistic values with those of a truly global culture. To the extent that this influence is operative, MNCs' globalization of production and investment will lead to the transfer of people's loyalties from individual countries to the world as a whole. By challenging "the operational sovereignty of a government, that is, its ability to exercise sovereignty in the daily affairs of politics" (Reinicke 1997), the globalization of production builds bridges across the politics that divide states—providing a common ground for people to cooperate. This would fulfill the humanist vision of international harmony resulting from acceptance of everyone's shared humanity and destiny. "There are no longer any national flag carriers," in the words of

Kenichi Ohmae, a Japanese management consultant. "Corporations must serve their customers, not governments."

• • •

THE GLOBALIZATION OF LABOR

In his manifesto on the evils of capitalism, Karl Marx urged the workers of the world to unite, throwing off the chains imposed by the oppressive owners of capital. The assumption was that workers everywhere shared a common purpose and vision. But that is no longer true. As the liberalization and rapid integration of markets throughout the world proceed, labor markets will be profoundly affected. Competition—not solidarity—has intensified. Because the spread of globalization is uneven, some employees will be winners, many others losers.

As recently as the 1970s one-third of the world's workers were insulated from the rest of the world through centralized economic planning, as in the former Eastern bloc, and through restrictive trade barriers and the regulation of capital markets elsewhere. "Today, three giant population blocs—China, the republics of the former Soviet Union, and India—with nearly half the world's labor force among them, are entering the global market, and many other countries from Mexico to Indonesia have already established deep linkages. By the year 2000 fewer than 10 percent of the world's workers are likely to be cut off from the economic mainstream" (*World Development Report 1995* 1995, 50).

Accommodating the influx of new workers will be difficult. Already "the world is experiencing the worst employment crisis since the 1930s," according to a former U.S. Secretary of Labor. "Almost one-third of the Earth's 2.8 billion workers are either jobless or underemployed, and many of those who are employed work for very low wages with little prospect for advancement" (Marshall 1995). Europe suffers chronic unemployment, with as much as 12 percent of the labor force idle. Unemployment and **underemployment** rates are lower in the United States, but the real wages of most U.S. workers have fallen over the past two decades. Mass unemployment characterizes conditions in many of the countries in transition, while in much of the Global South employment growth has slowed and wage rates have fallen.

The costs of deteriorating employment are high. "Globalization has exposed a deep fault line between groups who have the skills and mobility to flourish in global markets and those who either do not have these advantages or perceive the expansion of unregulated markets as inimical to social stability" (Rodrik 1997). High levels of joblessness produced by global economic integration result in human suffering and hopelessness, rising inequality within and between countries, and deteriorating social cohesion, domestic disintegration, and corroding democratic institutions. Growing global interdependence in one country affects the economic circumstances of workers in others as well:

> During that first era of openness, labor was far more mobile than today (it was a time of mass migration). Now highly skilled and professional workers are mobile, either physically or via computer, but most countries no longer welcome unskilled immigrants.
>
> Meanwhile, companies that once were anchored in their communities can easily pick up and relocate. In fact companies which do not go where

underemployment a condition critics trace to trade globalization in which a large portion of the labor force works short hours at low pay in occupations below their skill level.

they can manufacture and operate most efficiently will soon be overtaken by those which do.

So capital can move, but labor can't; business executives are in a strong bargaining position, but workers aren't; and the result is pretty much what you would expect. (Hiatt 1997, 8)

Multinational corporations have been a primary vehicle of growing global interdependence that benefits some workers at the relative expense of others' wages. This forecast about the success of the rich and powerful that makes workers the losers, and that makes "the hollowing of the middle class a feature of income distribution in many countries" (Rodrik 1997), has been fulfilled in the global economy; "wage inequality between skilled and unskilled labor is a global trend." Part of the reason is because MNCs easily move manufacturing sites and technical know-how to developing countries, where labor is cheap. Of the 8 million jobs created by MNCs between 1985 and 1992, 5 million were in the Global South. In countries as diverse as Argentina, Barbados, Botswana, Indonesia, Malaysia, Mauritius, Mexico, the Philippines, Singapore, and Sri Lanka, multinationals account for one-fifth of the manufacturing sector employment (*World Development Report 1995* 1995, 62). These workers have benefited from the new job opportunities created. In a world of highly mobile capital, however, this also makes unskilled laborers with low wages, and the countries where they are employed, vulnerable. "Many developing countries fear that increased competition for funds by other developing countries will lead to a rise in footloose investments, prone to leave at the slightest shock. . . . This problem is especially acute in low-skill industries such as garments and footwear, where firm-specific knowledge is slight and exit costs are low."

Such fears, born of experience, are all too real in the Global North. Workers there also fear losing their jobs due to cheap imports made possible by lower-cost production in the Global South or because the companies they work for will relocate abroad. The irony is that economic growth has been rekindled since the recession of the early 1990s. For many, however, this has been a time of "jobless growth." And even if they keep their jobs, employees often blame cheap foreign labor for their own lack of pay hikes and resultant stagnating living standards.

Wage rates differ widely throughout the world. It is difficult to assess the impact of wage rates in different countries on one another, because labor trends are affected not only by trade but also by technological developments, trends in labor productivity, and migration. However, economic theory does predict that, as a result of international trade, the wage rates in poor countries will eventually be pulled up somewhat. Meanwhile, wage rates *for unskilled workers* in rich countries will come down. "The logic behind this is that trade affects the relative rewards of factors of production by changing the relative price of goods. Opening up to trade increases the price of labor-intensive goods in poor, labor-rich countries, which, as a consequence, shift their resources to the production of labor-intensive goods. This, in turn, raises demand for labor in poor countries, and hence raises relative wages. As relative prices of goods converge in rich and poor countries, so do wages" (Diwan and Revenga 1995). In short, as a consequence of trade, wage rates should tend toward convergence. For some, this means a gain in welfare; for others, it means lost income.

Empirical studies of wage rates in different countries support these expectations (for a summary, see Diwan and Revenga 1995). They also show that increased competition from producers in developing countries are responsible in

Free trade and globalization are seen as threats to the job security of some workers, who seek protection to preserve their employment in vulnerable, relatively uncompetitive sectors of the global market. In 1993 American domestic workers demonstrated against the North American Free Trade Agreement (NAFTA). If such protests succeed around the globe, free-trade agreements are likely to unravel.

part for declining wages for labor and growing income inequality in Australia, Canada, and the United States, as well as for the persistence of high levels of unemployment in Europe. Where analysts disagree is in their determination of what part trade competition plays in these problems. "Most analyses conclude that trade with developing countries can explain only 10 to 30 percent of the industrial countries' labor market difficulties, but some studies come up with more extreme results—on both sides of the argument" (Diwan and Revenga 1995).

With protectionist sentiments widespread in the Global North, countries in the Global South worry that their own hopes for economic advancement cannot be realized unless and until the Global North relaxes its multitude of restrictive trade barriers. Interestingly, however, concern for the impact of low wage rates is no longer confined to the Global North. Faced with the prospect of huge numbers of low-wage Chinese workers entering the work force, some Global South countries have also embraced protectionist trade practices. Thus the challenge of globalization promises to shape the global political agenda in the twenty-first century.

• • •

GLOBALIZATION AND THE STATE: WHAT FUTURE?

Rapid globalization, fueled in large measure by technological revolutions, is likely to continue. Analysts differ on whether globalization is desirable or despicable, however, depending in part on the scenarios about the future world order that globalization will help create and the political perspectives that inform their worldviews. Some analysts focus on the benefits of globalization for economic well-being; others focus on its unevenness and the prospects for marginalizing large numbers of peoples and states. Some focus on the challenge globalization poses to an international system founded on the sovereign terri-

For Richer or for Poorer?
Debating Globalization's Uneven Payoff

As globalization has narrowed distance between the world's people, some have gained and others have lost ground. The "global village" is not proving to be an equally hospitable home for everyone. The losers resisting "corporate citizenship" or "stakeholder capitalism" are mounting a backlash, even though "no one can predict globalization's outcome" (Pfaff 1996). "Globalization rides mankind, but drives people to take refuge from its powerful forces" (Schlesinger 1997). Winners play down the costs of global integration, while protectionist nationalists deny its benefits, and the debate about its uncertain impact has intensified without resolution as the debaters have hardened their positions without listening to the counterarguments:

> The debate about globalization is largely a dialogue of the deaf. On one side, ivory-tower economists tout the benefits of increased trade and cross-border investment, while ignoring (or at least downplaying) the costs. On the other hand, the critics of free trade and open capital markets acknowledge the gains from closer integration, often displaying at best an elementary grasp of economics. (*Economist* 343, June 21, 1997, 82)

The key question is really about fairness, ethics, and justice, not about the benefits of free trade, which both rich and poor countries recognize as they competitively seek to gain a larger share of the market. The evidence about the costs and payoffs is mixed because globalization refers to different phenomena, and the outcomes are open to rival interpretation. Dani Rodrik, a specialist on the controversy, has sought to separate "sense and nonsense in the globalization debate." He points out some relatively unrecognized features of the process, noting that:

- In reality, national economics retain a considerable degree of isolation from each other, and national policymakers enjoy more autonomy than is assumed by most writings on the erosion of sovereignty.
- A substantial volume of literature on the relationship between trade and inequality exists, much of which contradicts the simplistic view that Americans or Europeans owe their deteriorating fortunes to low-wage competition from abroad.
- Due to the increased importance of trade, the options available to national policymakers have narrowed appreciably over the past three decades.
- There is an . . . unmistakably positive correlation between a nation's openness to trade and the amount of its spending on social programs. . . . International economic integration thus poses a serious dilemma: Globalization increases the demand for social insurance while simultaneously constraining the ability of governments to respond effectively to that demand. Consequently, as globalization deepens, the social consensus required to keep domestic markets open to international trade erodes. (Rodrik 1997)

Many things are unclear, but it is certain that globalization is not an altogether "win-win" situation. Therefore, the debate will continue.

---

torial state; others are more hopeful about the state's resilience and the prospects for global governance to cope with the challenge of steering globalization in rewarding directions. We can expect the controversies about globalization's alleged virtues and vices, benefits and costs, to heighten as finance, population, trade, labor, and culture continue to converge globally (see Focus 9.5)

Globalization, as the term itself suggests, has been a worldwide phenomenon, albeit uneven. The intensification of interdependence has been most pronounced among the countries of the Global North and the emerging economies of East Asia, which have reaped most of its economic benefits. But because it is uneven, globalization also threatens to widen the gulf between the world's rich and poor countries. This is true even within the Global South, which already stands at some distance from the high-consumption societies of the North.

If the borderless world rewards entrepreneurs, designers, brokers, patent owners, lawyers, and dealers in high-value services, then East Asia's commitment to education, science, and technology can only increase its lead over other developing economies. By contrast, their relative lack of capital, high technology, scientists, and skilled workers, and export-oriented industry makes it difficult for poorer countries to partake in the communications and financial revolution. . . . Some grimmer forecasts suggest the developing world may become more marginalized, partly because of the dematerialization of labor, raw materials, and foodstuffs, partly because the advanced economies may concentrate upon greater knowledge-based commerce among themselves. . . .

As we move into the next century the developed economies appear to have all the trump cards in their hands—capital, technology, control of communications, surplus foodstuffs, powerful multinational companies—and, if anything, their advantages are *growing* because technology is eroding the value of labor and materials, the chief assets of developing countries. (Kennedy 1993, 223–25)

But is technology also eroding the ability of even the rich states to control their economic and political fortunes? Certainly a world of vanishing borders challenges the territorial state, but states still rule and govern the institutions and laws that shape changes in the world economy. States remain the globe's major political unit, and some observers see the power of the state as strong as ever, even in the era of global interdependency that has forced states to reorganize themselves to more effectively manage international transactions (see Gelber 1998). Globalization may even strengthen the size and economic power of states. The age of "big government" is not "dead."

At the beginning of this century government spending in today's industrial countries accounted for less than one-tenth of national income. [In 1997] in the same countries, the government's share of output was roughly half. Decade by decade, the change in the government's share of the economy moved in one direction only: up. During war it went up; during peace it went up. Between 1920 and the mid-1930s, years of greatly diminished trade and international economic contact, it went up. Between 1960 and 1980, as global trade and finance expanded, it went up. Between 1980 and 1990, as this breeze of globalization became a strong wind, it went up again. Between 1990 and 1996, as the wind became a gale, it went up some more (*Economist*, September 20, 1997, 7).

The expansion of governmental control over states' spending notwithstanding, globalization has arguably reduced the sovereign control of states over activities within their borders and their relations with other states and nonstate actors.

Globalization reduces the capacity of states to exercise political power over the territory in which private-sector actors operate. This loss of control probably means that, "Probing further into the future, including the future of the nation-state itself, one must recognize that globalization has ended the nation-state's monopoly over internal sovereignty, which was formerly guaranteed by territory. This change deprives external sovereignty of its functional value. The nation-state as an externally sovereign actor in the international system will become a thing of the past" (Reinicke 1997).

International regimes such as those that evolved after World War II to promote global governance in monetary and trade affairs may also prove effective as management strategies for coping with the globalization challenge. A key issue is whether states can find a focal point, a norm, around which cooperation could coalesce. Liberal theorists, who focus on the mutual gains stemming from international cooperation, are optimistic about the possibilities. Realists and neomercantilists, who are concerned more with relative gains than absolute gains, are more pessimistic.

There is another troublesome side to globalization: its impact on the global environment. This chapter began by asking whether globalization is the route to a global village—one free of conflict and intent only on improving villagers' welfare—or whether this is mere mythology. *Global pillage* is an alternative description of the probable consequences that will flow from cascading globalization. The costs of rapidly accelerating consumption promoted by free trade and the ethos of consumerism are not sustainable. Will that force—the possibility of destroying the planet's very life-support systems—ultimately doom humanity's future? The next two chapters investigate possible answers to this question.

KEY TERMS

globalization
neoliberal theory
global village
cyberspace
virtuality
agenda setting
New World Information and
    Communication Order (NWICO)

global migration crisis
globalization of finance
arbitrage
capital mobility hypothesis
electronic cash
digital world economy
realist theory
neorealist theory

commercial liberalism
trade integration
strategic corporate alliances
virtual corporations
foreign direct investment (FDI)
underemployment

SUGGESTED READING

Baylis, John, and Steve Smith, eds. *The Globalization of World Politics.* Oxford, Eng.: Oxford University Press, 1997.

Berger, Peter L. "Four Faces of Global Culture," *The National Interest* 49 (Fall 1997): 23–29.

Drucker, Peter F. "The Global Economy and the Nation-State," *Foreign Affairs* 76 (October 1997): 159–171.

Gelber, Harry. *Sovereignty Through Interdependence.* Cambridge, Mass.: Kluwer Law International, 1998.

Keohane, Robert, and Elinor Ostrom, eds. *Local Commons and Global Interdependence: Heterogeneity and Cooperation in Two Domains.* London: Sage Publications, 1995.

Mittelman, James H., ed. *Globalization: Critical Reflections.* Boulder, Colo.: Lynne Rienner, 1997.

Moisy, Claude. "Myths of the Global Information Village," *Foreign Policy* 107 (Summer 1997): 78–87.

Reinicke, Wolfgang H. "Global Public Policy," *Foreign Affairs* 76 (November-December 1997): 127–38.

Rodrik, Dani. *Has Globalization Gone Too Far?* Washington, D.C.: Institute for International Economics, 1997.

Sachs, Jeffrey. "International Economics: Unlocking the Mysteries of Globalization" *Foreign Policy* 110 (Spring 1998): 97–111.

Schaeffer, Robert K. *Understanding Globalization.* Oxford, Eng.: Rowman & Littlefield, 1997.

Wienner, Jarrod, ed. *Global Society: Journal of Interdisciplinary International Relations.* Three issues published each year. Oxfordshire, Eng.: Carfax Publishing.

http://itl.irv.uit.no/trade_law/

International Trade Law Monitor An example of the globalization of markets is the extent that international trade laws are expanding. The International Trade Law Monitor allows you to access documents by subject or treaty (convention). As you will note, many links refer to the Internet which has greatly increased the globalization of the marketplace. Read the U.S. framework and European Union initiative in electronic commerce. What are the similarities? What are the differences? Can you imagine a world of "electronic signatures" and "e-cash"?

http://www.labornet.apc.org/labornet

LaborNet Workers of the world unite! LaborNet provides Internet services, labor news from around the world, and Internet training to those interested in workers' causes. What to be a sympathetic striker? Click on the "Strike Page" and find out the who, what, where, and why of current strikes anywhere in the world. This Web site also has extensive links to international labor unions. Want to form a student union organization? This is the place to look for support and more information. It also gives the reader a sense of how the Internet has contributed to the globalization of labor.

http://china.si.umich.edu/telecom/telecom-info.html

Telecom Information Resources on the Internet The University of Michigan has produced a Web site that references information sources related to technical, economic, public policy, and social aspects of telecommunications (voice, data, video, wired, wireless, cable television, and satellite). Do you want to be the first person on the block who is able to videoconference from your home computer? Click on "Internet Telephony" and find out how to get started. Want the link to every television and radio broadcaster in the world? Click on "Broadcasters." While you are at it, count how many broadcasters are in each country. You will be amazed at the number in the United States. If you are worried about security on the Internet, worry no more. There is also a link to "Network Security." This site has it all.

http://infomanage.com/International/Trade/

InfoManage—International Trade InfoManage hosts a Web site that allows you to access information on trade resources for any country or region of the world. It also has links to the world's stock exchanges, currency converters, and other sites of interest. Try some of the currency converters to see how the dollar is doing compared to other currencies.

CHAPTER 10

World Demographic Patterns, Problems, and Possibilities

•••

If fertility remained at current levels, [world] population would reach the absurd figure of 296 billion in just 150 years. . . . There are six billion of us already, a number the world strains to support.

—BILL McKIBBEN,
futurist, 1998

•••

For many countries population growth is "a question of survival because it eats into economic progress to an extent that, unless it is rapidly checked, we get pushed two steps backward every time we advance one step forward."

—RAFIG ZAKARIA,
UN Commission on Population and Development, 1996

CHAPTER TOPICS AND THEMES

- The earth's carrying capacity
- The tragedy of the global commons
- The demographic dimensions of globalization: Characteristics and trends
- The causes of global population patterns and problems
  - Epidemic viruses: The global spread of AIDS and other diseases
  - Demographic momentum, overpopulation, and demographic transitions
- Migration and the global refugee issue
- The demography of development and of national security
  - Resource depletion and scarcity: Global food security and sustainable development
  - Population policies: The international response
- The plight of women: Gender inequalities as a global problem
- A crowded planet and a shrinking world: Optimists, pessimists, and the future

The globalization of the world is bringing people together, making them increasingly interconnected and interdependent. Distance is diminishing in a crowded "global village." Population growth is altering how people interact and threatens to transform humanity's long-term prospects for survival. These changes raise new questions and create new issues. How many people can the earth support? The planet's **carrying capacity**—its ability to support human and other life forms—is not infinite. However, human ingenuity and rapidly advancing technology have continuously stretched the boundaries. As a result, the earth will doubtless accommodate the growth projected for today's 6 billion inhabitants into the next century. But at what cost—to human freedom, human welfare, and the environment?

The **tragedy of the commons** is a metaphor that highlights the potential impact of human behavior on the planet's resources and its delicately balanced ecological systems. First articulated in 1833 by English political economist William Foster Lloyd and later extended to contemporary problems by human ecologist Garrett Hardin, the metaphor refers to nineteenth-century English villages, where the green was common property on which all villagers could graze their cattle. Freedom of access to the commons was a cherished village value, and sharing the common grazing area worked well as long as the number of cattle did not exceed the land's carrying capacity. Should that happen, the pasture would be ruined and the number of cattle the common property could sustain would be drastically reduced.

Which path would the village herders take—preserving the village green or ruining it? In the absence of restraints on human freedom—and assuming the villagers were driven by the profit motive—herders had a maximum incentive to increase their herds as much as possible. Although the village green eventually would be destroyed if they all behaved this way, in the short run the addition of one more animal would produce a personal gain whose costs would be borne by everyone. Self-interest thus encouraged all herders to increase their herds indiscriminately and discouraged self-sacrifice for the general welfare. In the end, however, the collective impact of their individual efforts to maximize private gain led to more cattle on the village green than it could sustain, with the inevitable result: destruction of the common property. "Ruin is the destination toward which all men rush," Hardin (1968) concluded, "each pursuing his own best interest in a society that believes in the freedom of the commons."

The tragedy of the commons provides insight into numerous environmental issues (see Soroos 1998), ranging from excessive fishing of the oceans by a few at the expense of others to transboundary pollution caused when industries spew toxic wastes into the atmosphere. More broadly, the metaphor is a kind of shorthand for situations in which "people so impinge on each other in pursuing their own interests that collectively they might be better off if they could be restrained, but no one gains individually by self-restraint." Thus the commons are a part of a broader set of situations "in which some of the costs or damages of what people do occur beyond their purview, and they either don't know or don't care about them" (Schelling 1978).

The freedom to procreate is a major "unregulated" freedom of choice. "The most important aspect of necessity that we must now recognize," Hardin (1968) wrote, "is the necessity of abandoning the commons in breeding. Freedom to breed will bring ruin to all. . . . The only way we can preserve and nurture other and more precious freedoms is by relinquishing the freedom to breed, and that very soon. . . . Only so, can we put an end to this aspect of the tragedy of the commons."

Not everyone will agree with the **ethics** Hardin's arguments imply (see also Hardin 1993). Indeed, few decisions are more intensely personal or more intimately tied to the social and cultural fabric of a society than those about marriage and the family. Furthermore, just as the ultimate carrying capacity of the global ecosystem has proved elastic, the impact of unregulated population growth on social well-being and environmental quality remains unclear. Nonetheless, the balance of both theory and evidence from **demography** points to a world in which unrestrained population growth will result in lost economic opportunities, environmental degradation, domestic strife, and incentives—perhaps imperatives—for governmental restraints on individual choice. A globe interdependent ecopolitically as well as economically is certain to share the consequences.

This chapter and the next explore how changes in demography, the environment, and resources influence world politics. Here the focus is on demographic variables—how global trends in births, deaths, migration, and their correlates are likely to shape the world's future. This sets the stage for Chapter 11, which examines the relationship between environmental and resource trends and the widely shared goals of security and development.

ethics the criteria by which right and wrong behavior and motives are distinguished.

demography the study of population changes, their sources, and their impact.

• • •

GLOBAL DEMOGRAPHIC PATTERNS AND TRENDS

The dramatic growth in world population in the twentieth century is historically unprecedented. It took 2 million years before world population reached 1 billion in 1804; 2 billion was reached in 1927. Since then, additional billions have been added even more rapidly: 3 billion was reached by 1960, 4 billion in 1974, and 5 billion in 1987 (see Figure 10.1). The sixth billion was added on the eve of the next century. How is this possible? Because world population grows by nearly ten thousand *each hour of every day* and is increasing at a record pace, "we add a New York city every month, almost a Mexico every year, almost an India every decade" (McKibben 1998, 56). In fact, more people will be added to the world's population in the last fifth of the twentieth century than at any other time in history. If present trends continue uninterrupted, world population will grow to 7.5 billion in 2015, stand at 9.8 billion in 2050, and reach 10 billion only a few years later—about the time most of today's college students in the Global North will be drawing on their retirement benefits. Indeed, most students reading this book will have witnessed the largest population surge ever to have occurred in a single generation—theirs.

As difficult as it may be to imagine a world with half again as many people as today, 10 billion is less than what was once projected for the middle of the next century. The latest projection—what the United Nations calls its "medium variant" (the middle line among the three population projections in Figure 10.1)—depends on the assumption that the world fertility rate will continue to decline, as it has for more than a decade, and will eventually settle at a point where couples only replace themselves. Without that, population growth could be much more rapid in the first half of the twenty-first century, reaching 11.9 billion in the year 2050 (the top line in Figure 10.1), nearly five times the 1950 population. In either case, world population will continue to grow throughout the twenty-first century and into the twenty-second. On the other hand, should

World Population Growth, 1750 to 1995 and Projected to 2050

World population in the twentieth century has grown from fewer than 2 billion people to nearly 6 billion, with each billion added in less time than the previous billion. Between 2 and 4 billion more will be added between now and the fifth decade of the twenty-first century. Changes in world fertility rates will determine the exact number.

SOURCE: Adapted from United Nations (1995), 101, 226–27, 234–35, 242–43.

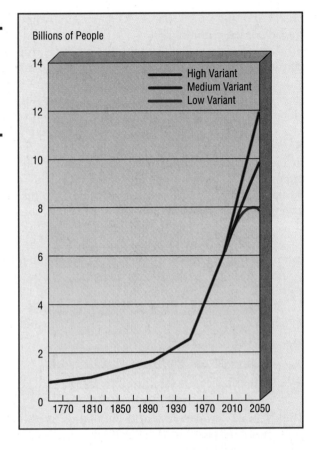

world fertility slow more rapidly, world population would also grow more slowly and eventually settle at a level much lower than now seems most likely (the bottom line in Figure 10.1).

The rapid growth of world population after reaching 2 billion in 1927 is described by a simple mathematical principle articulated in 1798 by the Reverend Thomas Malthus: Unchecked, population increases in a geometric or exponential ratio (e.g., 1 to 2, 2 to 4, 4 to 8, etc.), whereas subsistence increases in only an arithmetic ratio (1 to 2, 2 to 3, 3 to 4). When population increases at such an accelerating rate, the compound effect can be staggering (see Focus 10.1). Consider, for example, how money deposited in a savings account grows as it earns interest not only on the original investment but also on the interest payments. If each of our ancestors had put a mere ten dollars in the bank for us two hundred years ago, and it accrued a steady 6 percent annual interest, today we would all be millionaires! Population grows in the same way: It is a function of increases in the original number of people plus those accruing from past population growth. Thus a population growing at a 1 percent rate will double in sixty-nine years, while a population growing at a 2 percent rate will double in only thirty-five years. (The impact of different growth rates on doubling times can be calculated by dividing sixty-nine by the percentage of growth.)

Worldwide, the rate of population growth peaked at just over 2 percent in the late 1960s and then declined to just under 1.6 percent by the mid-1990s. Hence the projection that world population in 2050 will be far less than once thought. Not all countries will share equally in the phenomenon, though. In

Understanding Growth Rates
The Secret of the Persian Chessboard

The way I first heard the story, it happened in ancient Persia. But it may have been India, or even China. Anyway, it happened a long time ago. The Grand Vizier, the principal adviser to the King, had invented a new game. It was played with moving pieces on a board of 64 squares. The most important piece was the King. The next most important piece was the Grand Vizier—just what we might expect of a game invented by a Grand Vizier. The object of the game was to capture the enemy King, and so the game was called, in Persian, *shahmat—shah* for king, *mat* for dead. Death to the King. In Russia it is still called *shakhmaty,* which perhaps conveys a lingering revolutionary ardor. Even in English there is an echo of the name—the final move is called "checkmate." The game, of course, is chess.

As time passed, the pieces, their moves and the rules evolved. There is, for example, no longer a piece called the Gand Vizier—it has become transmogrified into a Queen, with much more formidable powers.

Why a king should delight in the creation of a game called "Death to the King" is a mystery. But, the story goes, he was so pleased that he asked the Grand Vizier to name his own reward for such a splendid invention. The Grand Vizier had his answer ready: He was a humble man, he told the King. He wished only for a humble reward. Gesturing to the eight columns and eight rows of squares on the board he devised, he asked that he be given a single grain of wheat on the first square, twice that on the second square, twice *that* on the third, and so on, until each square had its complement of wheat.

No, the King remonstrated. This is too modest a prize for so important an invention. He offered jewels, dancing girls, palaces. But the Grand Vizier, his eyes becomingly lowered, refused them all. It was little piles of wheat he wanted. So, secretly marveling at the unselfishness of his counselor, the King graciously consented.

When the Master of the Royal Granary began to count out the grains, however, the King was in for a rude surprise. The number of grains starts small enough: 1, 2, 4, 8, 32, 64, 128, 256, 512, 1024. . . . But by the time the 64th square is approached, the number becomes colossal, staggering. In fact the number is nearly 18.5 quintillion grains of wheat. Maybe the Grand Vizier was on a high-fiber diet.

How much does 18.5 quintillion grains of wheat weigh? If each grain were 2 millimeters in size, then all the grains together would weigh around 75 billion metric tons, which far exceeds what could have been stored in the King's granaries. In fact, this is the equivalent of about 150 years of the world's present wheat production. . . .

SOURCE: Carl Sagan (1989), 14.

fact, rapid population growth in the Global South is the most striking demographic development in the post-World War II era, and its consequences will continue to be felt well into the future.

During the next fifty years the developed and the developing worlds alike will experience declining population growth rates, but the incremental contributions of the Global South to expanding world population will actually increase. "Whereas 79 percent of the annual increase in world population between 1950 and 1955 originated in the less developed regions, 95 percent of the increment between 1990 and 1995 originated in those regions [see Figure 10.2]. It is expected that by 2045–2050 all of the net population growth in the world will arise in the less developed regions, as the population of the more developed regions is expected to be declining in absolute numbers" (*World Economic and Social Survey 1995* 1995, 147). The world has become, and will remain, demographically divided. To better understand the inevitability of this prediction, and how demographic developments will affect world politics, we must go beyond the simple arithmetic of population growth to explore its dynamics.

FIGURE 10.2

The Demographic Divide, 1950–2050

Nearly all of the world's population growth in the next half-century will occur in the Global South, with Africa growing most rapidly. By the middle of the twenty-first century, the absolute number of people in the Global North is expected to be declining.

Note: Projections are based on United Nations medium variant estimates shown in Figure 10.1.

SOURCE: Adapted from United Nations (1995), 213–14, 588, 674.

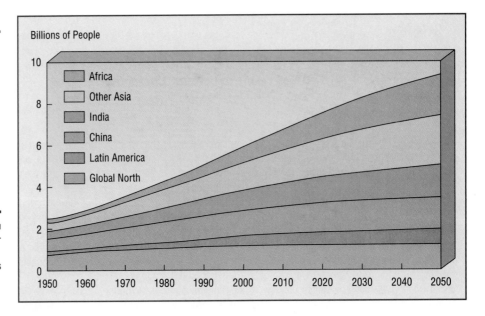

• • •

POPULATION DYNAMICS: THE CAUSES OF GLOBAL POPULATION TRENDS

In Austria, the population growth rate in 1995 was 0.1 percent. This is an annual rate similar to that of other Global North countries, where births and deaths have nearly stabilized and population growth is thus near zero. In Kenya, on the other hand, the growth rate in 1995 stood at 3.3 percent, which is typical of other Global South countries (*1995 World Population Data Sheet*). The differences between Austria and Kenya illustrate why today's population surge is confined to the developing countries, where sharply lower death rates since World War II have resulted from advances in medical science, agricultural productivity, and public sanitation. The paradox—illustrated in Figure 10.2—is that population growth is occurring in precisely those countries least able to support a burgeoning number of people. High fertility rates in much of the Global South combined with the sheer number of children that will be born explain why ever-wider differences between North and South are expected in the new millennium.

Fertility Rates

The world **fertility rate** (the average number of children born to a woman in her lifetime) is estimated to have been 3.1 in 1995. In the developed world the rate stood at 1.6, which is below **replacement-level fertility** (2.1 children per woman, or roughly one couple replacing themselves with two children). In the developing world, however, it stood at 3.5 (and even higher—at 4.0—if China, which has restrictive population policies, is excluded) *(1995 World Population Data Sheet)*. These numbers are sharply lower than in the 1960s and 1970s, thus helping to slow the rate of world population growth to its present level.

Still, world population cannot stabilize until the world fertility rate falls to replacement level. Yet throughout much of the Global South, the preferred family size remains far in excess not only of the replacement level but also of the present world fertility rate of 3.1 percent. Among the world's largest states, for example, China is the only Global South country that has achieved the replacement plateau, while four-fifths of the remaining ones continue to experience fertility rates higher than the present world rate. The numbers are especially startling in Africa south of the Sahara (e.g., Nigeria), where the region's fertility rate stood at 6.2 in 1995.

The developing countries' high fertility rates derive from a variety of sources. Besides the pleasures that children provide, cultural traditions and religious norms often encourage the bearing of children, ascribing prestige and social status to women based on the number of children they bear and typically placing special value on male offspring. Politics also exerts a force, as many governments deliberately encourage women to have large families, "arguing that this adds to the country's military strength. 'Bear a child,' posters in Iraq proclaimed, 'and you pierce an arrow in the enemy's eye.' Countries such as Iraq and Libya offer many incentives for larger families, as do the Gulf states and Saudi Arabia, anxious to fill their oil-rich lands with native-born rather than foreign workers" (Kennedy 1993).

Economics is perhaps the most potent force, with many children adding to a family's labor force today and providing future security for parents who live in societies that have no public programs for the elderly. When the infant mortality rate is high, the incentives to have many offspring are even greater: The larger the number of children born, the greater the chance that some will survive. Infant and child (under-five) mortality rates have declined dramatically in the past three decades (*The State of the World's Children 1995* 1995, 55), but improvements have been slowest where poverty and population growth are most pervasive. In Sub-Saharan Africa, for instance, one out of every ten children born will die before reaching the age of one, and in South Asia one out of eight will die before age five (*The State of the World's Children 1995* 1995, 84).

Epidemic Virus: The Global Spread of HIV/AIDS

Although infant and child mortality rates remain discouragingly high in much of the developing world, at least the direction is downward. Not so with the spread of the **human immunodeficiency virus (HIV)**, the virus that causes **AIDS (acquired immune deficiency syndrome).** Are world death rates thus destined to rise in the future, reversing the upward trend in world population?

Since the onset of the AIDS pandemic in the late 1970s, the UN estimates the occurrence of new infections to be 16,000 each day and 5.8 million each year. The current number of those already HIV-infected is believed to be 40 million. Because 30 million of those infected are alive today (Garrett 1998, 141), the number of infected people continues to increase each year. As many as 150 million will be infected with the fatal virus by the year 2000 (Pear 1997, 1; *Vital Signs 1997*, 84-85). Two-thirds of those infected live in Africa, but the virus is now spreading rapidly in South and Southeast Asia where 6 million people were believed to be HIV-infected in 1997. More than 90 percent of new infections occur in the developing countries of the Global South, but the contagion respects no borders and is a truly global epidemic, killing throughout the world (see Map 10.1).

Like other infectious diseases (such as Lassa fever, Ebola, and mad cow disease), AIDS and its control must be viewed as a global issue, since "bacteria parasites, and viruses exploit appropriate ecospheres wherever they find them, regardless of national boundaries" (Garnett 1988).

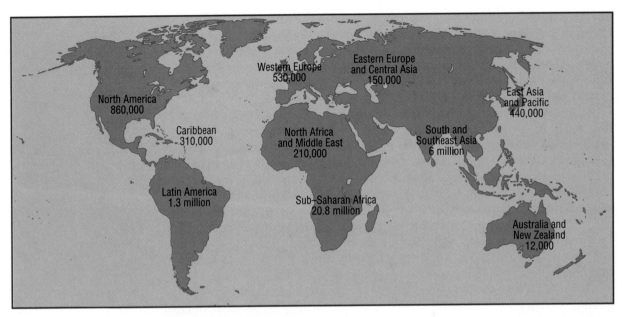

MAP 10.1

A Grim Portrait of a Silent Killer: The Global Spread of HIV—the Virus That Causes AIDS

In 1997, the United Nations doubled its previous estimates of new cases of HIV infection. The estimated number of people who will die from AIDS worldwide was put at 2.3 million in 1997—up more than 50 percent from the 1.5 million who died from the disease in 1996. Africa is at the epicenter of the pandemic, but as shown, no region of the world is unaffected by the rapid spread of this killing disease.

SOURCE: *International Herald Journal*, November 27, 1997, p.1.

The spread of AIDS is difficult to predict because many cases go undiagnosed or unreported, particularly in the Global South. Furthermore, the virus that causes AIDS is hard to detect because of its long incubation period. The length of time between HIV infection and the onset of AIDS averages about ten years. Consequently, even if HIV infections could be immediately halted, the AIDS pandemic would continue to spread. "It is hard to imagine the expansion of this deadly disease halting, because 75 percent of new infections are the result of heterosexual contact, and about 3,500 women are infected each day and 25–35 percent of all infants born to HIV-infected women become infected before or during birth, or through breastfeeding" (*Vital Signs 1997*, 84). HIV/AIDS has a certain, dark future, because "about 10 percent of all new infections are in children under 15, and more than half, the remainder, are in people 15 to 24" (Pear 1997, 6).

As the cumulative impact of HIV infections grows, the societal costs of AIDS climb, and the ruinous economic effects in particular regions pose a threat to the entire global market economy. Already AIDS adds heavy burdens to overtaxed health-care systems in many poorer countries. In some African cities, for example, over half of those hospitalized are HIV-infected (*The State of the World Population 1995* 1995, 51). In addition, AIDS' impact on social structures and economic performance is more devastating than its victims' number suggests, as its spread mostly affects young and middle-aged people. Thus income generation, family caregiving, and food production in countries where agriculture remains heavily labor intensive will all be affected. Increased mortality among younger age groups also follows; in many African countries life expectancy will be cut by more than twenty-five years by 2010 (Brown, Lenssen, and Kane 1995, 98).

As AIDS spreads, its ravages may cause negative population growth rates. Still, it will seldom reduce national population growth, even in countries where HIV infections are highest, as these countries also have the highest population growth rates and the momentum propelled by high growth rates in the past. AIDS will take a heavy toll, but it will not stop the world's relentless march toward a population of 10 billion people.

Population Momentum

The surge in the Global South's population in this century is easily explained: It resulted from a combination of high birth rates and rapidly falling death rates. But to understand the population surge projected for the next century—when birth rates throughout the world will decline—we have to understand the force of **population momentum,** the continued growth of population for decades into the future because of the large numbers of women now entering their childbearing years. Like the inertia of a descending airliner when it first touches down on the runway, population growth simply cannot be halted even with an immediate, full application of the brakes. Instead, many years of high fertility mean that more women will be entering their reproductive years than in the past. Not until the size of the generation giving birth to children is no larger than the generation among which deaths are occurring will the population "airplane" come to a halt.

The impact of the existing base population on future growth was made evident in 1996. That year, world population increased even though the rate of growth (1.4 percent) fell from the record high of 2.2 percent in 1963: "The 2.2 percent growth rate in 1963 yielded 69 million more people, but the 1.4 percent growth rate in 1996 produced an additional 80 million," swelling the global total to 5.77 billion (*Vital Signs 1997*, 80). Hence, the momentum created by the past population base limits the significance of a declining growth rate.

Western Europe and Sub-Saharan Africa illustrate the force of population momentum. Africa's age and sex profile is one of rapid population growth, as each new age group (cohort) contains more people than the one before it. Thus, even if individual African couples choose to have fewer children than their parents, Africa's population will continue to grow because there are now more men and women of childbearing age than ever before. In contrast, Europe's population profile is one of slow growth, as recent cohorts have been smaller than preceding ones. In fact, Europe has moved beyond replacement-level fertility to become a "declining" population, described by low birth rates and a growing number of people who survive middle age. A product of an extended period of low birth rates, low death rates, and increased longevity, Europe's age structure is best described as that of a "mature" or "old" society.

As the Global North generally ages, much of the Global South continues to mirror the Sub-Saharan African profile. Because each cohort is typically larger than the one before it, the number of young men and women entering their reproductive years will also grow. Figure 10.3 projects the consequences of the Global South's now proportionately larger fertile age groups and shows why the

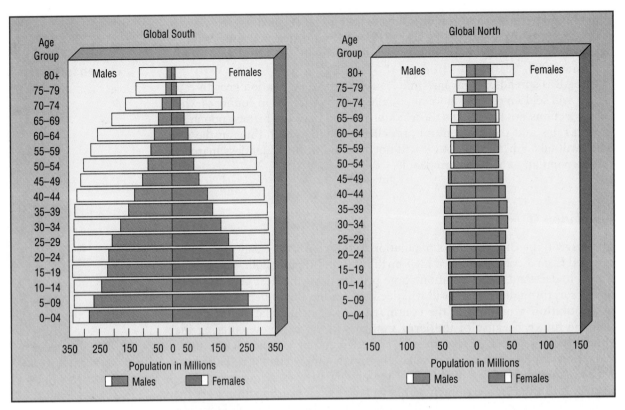

FIGURE 10.3

Population Pyramids for the Global North and South, 1995 and 2050

As the population of the Global South ages, those comprising today's large cohorts will contribute to future population growth, as will the even larger number of childbearing children they leave behind. Increased longevity will also add to the Global North's population momentum, but the magnitudes will be comparatively inconsequential because the number in each age group has not expanded in recent years.

SOURCE: Adapted from United Nations (1994a), 25, 73.

demographic momentum already in place will produce quite different population profiles in the developed and the developing worlds.

The momentum of prior population growth explains why world population will continue to grow for many decades into the future. If replacement-level fertility were reached worldwide around the year 2050, it would still not lead to a steady-state population for at least a century. By this time, world population will have grown to more than 11 billion people. If replacement-level fertility is not reached by this time, or if fertility rates stabilize somewhat above the replacement level, the world's ultimate population will be even larger. The reverse is also true, meaning that a world population well below 11 billion is possible if fertility rates somehow stabilize below 2.1 (refer back to Figure 10.1). The obvious question, then, is how to reduce current fertility levels to the replacement level—or less. The demographic transition, which describes population changes over time nearly everywhere in the world, suggests some answers.

The **demographic transition** describes the change that Europe and, later, North America experienced between 1750 and 1930, when a condition of high birth rates combined with high death rates was replaced by low birth rates and low death rates. The transition started when death rates began to fall—presumably due to economic growth, rising living standards, and improved disease control. Although the potential for substantial population growth was high, birth rates soon began to decline as well. During this phase of the demographic transition, population growth slowed. In fact, growth rates rarely exceeded 1.5 percent per year.

The demographic transition is now underway virtually everywhere in the world (Lutz 1994). The experience of the Global South, however, differs from that of Europe and North America. Death rates declined precipitously following World War II rather than mirroring the slow, long-term declines of the Global North, largely as a result of more effective "death-control" measures introduced by the outside world. A population explosion inevitably followed. The experience of the Indian Ocean island of Mauritius illustrates the interplay of changing birth and death rates as underlying long-term factors in demographic transitions. Following the eradication of malaria and the introduction of modern medical technology after World War II, the death rate dropped abruptly; however, birth rates remained high, and the population of Mauritius grew rapidly. It was not until the fertility rate fell much later, when the average number of children born to each woman declined from six to less than three, that the growth rate of Mauritius's population slowed (Lutz 1994). India provides another example of the barriers to slowing the rate at which population increases until the full effects of a demographic transition occur. Even though India's total fertility rate dropped from 4.3 in 1985 to 3.2 in 1996, because of India's already massive population size "close to 25 million babies were born there" that year, and despite the drop in fertility, "India's population is expected to reach 1 billion by 2000" (*Vital Signs 1997*, 80).

There are two ways to explain the changes in birth and death rates that occur with the demographic transition. One argument says that the decline in death rates itself stimulates a decline in birth rates. This implies that societies eventually reach an "equilibrium" in their mortality and fertility rates.

> When death rates fall because of advances in medicine and better living conditions, the equilibrium is disturbed. The population grows unless birth rates adjust to the new mortality conditions and also decline. The fact that it may take many years after mortality falls for fertility to fall is explained as a perception lag—that is, the time it takes couples to realize that more of their children will live to adulthood, and therefore, to feel secure that they can have fewer births and still achieve their desired number of surviving children. (Lutz 1994, 8)

A second explanation of the demographic transition holds that "modernization" produces declines in both mortality and fertility. According to this argument, birth rates decline because economic growth alters people's preferred family size. In traditional societies children are economic bonuses; as modernization proceeds, they become economic burdens, inhibiting social mobility and capital accumulation. The move from large to small families, with the associated decline in fertility, is therefore usually exhibited when modernization takes place.

Eventually birth and death rates both reach very low levels. With fertility rates near the replacement level, low population growth (or none at all) follows.

The "equilibrium" and "modernization" explanations of demographic transitions are not mutually exclusive. They may in fact be at work simultaneously in much of the Global South, where declines in death and birth rates have often occurred in tandem. Mauritius is again instructive: The halving of its fertility rate in a single decade occurred "on a strictly voluntary basis—the result of high levels of literacy and education for women—together with successful family-planning programs" (Lutz 1994). Both arguments, then, contain the seeds of population policies that may help move the world fertility rate toward the replacement level.

The demographic transition paradigm, in both its equilibrium and modernization variants, assumes that replacement is the endpoint at which fertility levels will ultimately rest. The high and low global population projections in Figure 10.1 suggest the consequences of stabilization either above or below replacement level—and some current evidence supports both possibilities.

The demographic transition involves four phases: (1) high birth rate, high death rate; (2) high birth rate, falling death rate; (3) declining birth rate, relatively low death rate; (4) low birth rate, low death rate. Yet in such different places as Costa Rica in Central America, Tunisia in North Africa, and Sri Lanka in South Asia, some countries are seemingly stuck somewhere between the second and third stages of the transition: Death rates have fallen to very low levels, but fertility rates seem to have stabilized well above replacement level. Does the reason lie in social attitudes toward family size remaining unchanged by modernization, unlike in Europe and North America? Or, unlike in Mauritius, is it caused by inadequate education and family-planning programs? In both cases, women's role in society may be critical, a point to which we will return.

A second puzzle that conventional theories of demographic transitions do not account for is the possibility of a fifth phase: declining birth rates even in the face of low death rates. Western Europe's fertility rate has not stabilized at the replacement level, as the demographic transition paradigm predicts, but instead has fallen steadily over the past two decades and now stands at 1.5 *(1995 World Population Data Sheet)*. As a result, a secular decline of the continent's population is now in motion, which will eventually lead to a Europe with markedly fewer people than today. A "birthless Germany," for example, faces the prospect of having 15 million fewer people by 2030—and a simultaneous dramatic increase in the number of people over sixty (Walker, 1995b, 13). Declining fertility rates in western Europe are not easily explained, but they do lead to intense policy disputes, as many believe the region is committing "demographic suicide."

Eastern Europe and Russia have also experienced sharp fertility-rate declines since the end of the Cold War, but here they have been accompanied by rising mortality and falling average life expectancy. Russia faces nothing short of a population "implosion." The fertility rate, which averaged just over the replacement level a few years ago, has fallen to only 1.4, and life expectancy plummeted between 1990 and 1995 "from 64 to 57 for men and from 74 to 70 for women, due largely to cardiovascular disease, accidents, murder, suicide, and excessive consumption of alcohol" (*Vital Signs 1997*, 80). The grim birth and death statistics reflect the bleak reality of life. Now free to leave, many in eastern Europe and the former Soviet Union have opted to migrate elsewhere—

often to western Europe, adding another critical variable to the demography of world politics.

Migration

Fertility, mortality, and *migration* are the three basic demographic variables that determine all population changes. Migration figures less prominently in long-range population projections, but is nonetheless politically important and pervasive in many countries. Britain and France, for example, continue to receive large numbers of immigrants from their former colonies, while Israel has absorbed a flood of immigrants, particularly from Russia. The Middle Eastern oil producers also have received large numbers of migrants in recent years. And the United States, historically a refuge from religious and political persecution and a mecca of economic opportunity, continues to provide a home for millions from throughout the world. The 1980s witnessed the largest immigration into the United States since early in the twentieth century. But there was an important difference: In the early part of the century nearly all of the immigrants came from Europe; in the 1980s, 80 percent came from Asia and Latin America, stimulated in part by the end of the Vietnam War and political turmoil and civil strife in Cuba, El Salvador, Guatemala, Haiti, and Nicaragua.

● ● ●

THE GLOBALIZATION OF POPULATION DYNAMICS AND TRENDS

Immigration is now the principal cause of U.S. population growth. There, as in other host countries, the influx of immigrants largely originating in the Global South promises to transform society. Thus the consequences of a burgeoning world population cannot be confined to the Global South, although most effects are now felt there and will continue to be felt there most strongly. The economic, environmental, political, and social consequences of a world population that promises to grow by more than half in the next half-century will be widely shared.

The Causes and Consequences of Migration

Migrants are of two types: refugees and those in search of economic opportunity. **Refugees** are individuals whose race, religion, nationality, membership in a particular social group, or political opinions makes them targets of persecution, and who escape by living outside the country of their origin or nationality and are unable to return to it. According to the United Nations High Commissioner for Refugees, the world's refugee population has grown steadily since 1960, swelling especially rapidly since 1992 to an all-time high of 27.4 million in 1995 (see Figure 10.4). Combined, the totals between 1960 and 1996 exceed 294 million refugees, not counting another 3.3 million **returnees** (former refugees who have returned home) and another 20 to 30 million **internally displaced people** "living in refugee-like situations in their own countries" (*Vital Signs 1997*, 82). One estimate of the magnitude of this problem suggests that of the "at least 47 million people [who] have abandoned their homes in fear for their lives and livelihoods, more than half are refugees in their own countries" (Kidron and Segal 1995, 103).

refugees people who flee for safety to another country because of a well-founded fear of persecution.

internally displaced people people involuntarily uprooted from their homes but still living in their own countries.

FIGURE 10.4

The Globe's Growing Refugee Population

The number of refugees receiving assistance from the United Nations has risen exponentially between 1961 and 1996, as nearly 300 million have fled their home countries to avoid persecution. This mass exodus is a symptom of human rights abuses worldwide and a symbol of the globalization process that is making for a borderless world.

SOURCE: United Nations High Commissioner for Refugees.

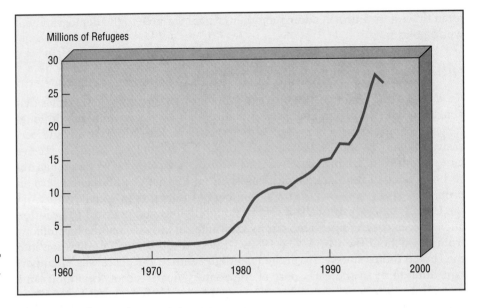

The number of *legal immigrants* is more difficult to determine but is believed to be in excess of 100 million, while the number of *illegal immigrants* is probably around 10 million. Thus "about 125 million people live outside the countries where they were born—it is as if the entire population of Japan had packed up and left" (Kane, 1995a).

In Search of Freedom. Refugees and displaced persons alike are often the victims of war. The Persian Gulf War, for example, created a refugee population of 5 million. The war in Afghanistan caused a peak flight of 6.3 million people, and civil conflict and genocide in Rwanda left more than 1.7 million still classified as refugees in 1997 (*Vital Signs 1997*, 82). The persecution, ethnic cleansing, and armed conflict that accompanied the breakup of the former Yugoslavia uprooted nearly 3 million victims, moving Europe to the list of continents with large numbers of refugees for the first time since World War II.

War—particularly communal rivalries and ethnic conflicts, which account for a large proportion of the world's refugees and displaced people—may be the force that propels some to make the difficult decision to flee their own homelands. If we understood the causes of war (a topic explored in detail in Chapter 12) we could better understand the underlying roots of what many now see as a global migration crisis (Weiner 1995).

Human rights abuses must figure prominently in any assessment of why millions of people make the difficult decision to leave. "Refugees know that they cannot expect, at home, the protection of the police, access to a fair trial, redress of grievances through the courts, prosecution of those who violate their rights, or public assistance in the face of disaster. . . . Forcing people to flee is a violation of the human right to remain peacefully in one's home. The direct denial of other basic rights, including the rights of civilians not to be targeted in military actions, often provides the immediate impetus for flight" (Newland 1994).

Demographic variables and their correlates apply to migrants in search of economic opportunity as well as refugees.

In search of safety and freedom, more than 200,000 refugees flooded into Tanzania after civil war erupted in Rwanda in April 1994. Sparked by the death of the country's president in a suspicious plane crash, ethnic conflicts between the Hutu majority and Tutsi minority led to genocide as well as mass migration before the year was out.

In virtually every instance of conflict or poverty today, factors like unmanageable population growth, unsustainable development, even disease and illiteracy have fermented over time in a volatile cocktail of insecurity. It is this combination of factors that ultimately brings people to the sometimes hopeful, but often desperate, hour of departure. . . .

It is significant that countries with stable populations and high levels of education and public health demonstrate a resilience against war and overt persecution and rarely experience refugee and migrant outflows. Many countries ravaged by high infant mortality, low literacy, eroding farmland, and hunger, on the other hand, are highly susceptible to the despots, the politically motivated bigotry, and the extremist politics that eventually force people out, and in fact they have recently seen people leave at record rates. (Kane, 1995a, 6, 10; see also Homer-Dixon 1998)

In Search of Opportunity. Legal migrants—particularly young people in the Global South without productive employment—are among those leaving at record rates. Germany and the United States are favored host (receiving) states, but nearly all of the states in western Europe and Japan have experienced a rising tide of migrants in recent years. Migration also occurs within the Global South. In fact, the bulk of today's migrants move from one developing country to another in search of opportunity (Weiner 1995). But everywhere the pattern is the same: People leave poorer states in search of higher-paying jobs in richer states.

Migrants traveling to faraway lands often take jobs shunned by local inhabitants. Typically this means they earn less than the native people but more than they would earn in their homelands, even when performing the same tasks. Host countries sometimes welcome migrants (as Europe did during the 1970s' "guest worker" era) not only because they accept low wages for undesirable jobs, but also because in many places the host pays little if anything for migrants' health, education, and welfare needs. On the other hand, the home (sending) countries sometimes encourage people to emigrate as a way of reducing unemployment or dealing with other problems (as in the case of Cuban emigration to the United States). Often, however, many of those who leave their home states are the best educated and most talented, causing a serious "brain drain" that is rarely, if ever, reversed.

Migrants typically send considerable portions of their income to their families at home. "By the end of the eighties, remittances [money sent home] amounted to more than $65 billion a year according to a World Bank study, second only to crude oil in their value to the world's economy, and larger than all official development assistance. Almost half of this money went to developing countries" (Kane 1995a, 34). The Persian Gulf War forced some 2.5 million immigrant workers (and their dependents) to flee Iran, Iraq, and Kuwait, causing a hardship for other governments (principally Egypt, Jordan, and Yemen) when remittances from their nationals working abroad dried up and the workers required repatriation (United Nations 1994b, 107).

Backlash: Migrants under Nationalist Fire. Although receiving countries can benefit economically from migration (see Passel and Fix 1994), the influx of foreigners has become a matter of growing controversy everywhere.

> In many countries, citizens have become fearful that they are now being invaded not by armies and tanks but by migrants who speak other languages, worship other gods, belong to other cultures, and, they fear, will take their jobs, occupy their land, live off the welfare system, and threaten their way of life, their environment, and even their polity. . . . Virtually every country in western Europe now has a right-wing antiforeign political party or movement. . . .
>
> The sense of crisis is not confined to advanced industrial societies. . . . In portions of Pakistan, India, Bangladesh, Thailand, Mauritania, Senegal, Congo, Nigeria, and Libya, local citizens or their governments have turned against foreigners. (Weiner 1995, 2–3)

xenophobia the suspicious dislike, disrespect, and disregard for members of a foreign nationality, ethnic, or linguistic group.

With **xenophobia** (fear of foreigners) on the rise, many among the growing number of refugees seeking asylum are finding the doors to safe havens closing. Security concerns stimulated by terrorist fears are sometimes at work—as in the United States, where many believe the New York World Trade Center bombing would not have occurred had immigration controls been tighter. More often, asylum seekers "are seen as migrants looking for better economic conditions rather than as refugees with a well-founded fear of being persecuted" (United Nations 1994b). Those seeking political refuge in the United States also have suffered "guilt by association," as a wave of illegal immigrants has contributed to the rising tide of anti-immigrant sentiments in a nation born of immigrants (see Clad 1994; Passel and Fix 1994). Thus thousands of refugees from Haiti and Cuba, who earlier would have found safe haven in the United States, have been repatriated to their homelands or otherwise denied a chance to apply for political **asylum** in the United States.

asylum the provision of sanctuary to safeguard refugees escaping from the threat of persecution in the country where they hold citizenship.

The end of the Cold War contributed to these increasingly restrictive practices. Once the United States willingly accepted those seeking to escape communist rule as a way of scoring points in the Cold War contest, but no longer (see Kirschten 1994). Pakistan has also shut its door to the surge of refugees from the long, bloody civil war between pro- and anti-Marxist forces in Afghanistan, and many Southeast Asian states have become less hospitable to

Vietnamese asylum seekers, forcing many to return to a homeland they once rejected. Meanwhile, Germany has altered its constitution to make granting asylum more restrictive; and the United States has begun to reduce the annual number of new arrivals and to assail the family-based criteria long used to open America's doors to others.

A combination of *push* and *pull* factors has propelled migration to the forefront of the globalization of population dynamics. **Human rights** violations, environmental degradation, international war, and ethnonational clashes and **atrocities** within states—all in some sense related to the Global South's rapidly expanding population—*push* millions beyond their homelands. They also are *pulled* abroad by the promise of political freedom and economic opportunity elsewhere, particularly in the Global North. Indeed, "the growing demand for immigration to the North from the South is related to the 'shrinking' of the world (through revolutions in communication and transport), reduction in economic obstacles to labor movements (despite the increase in political barriers), and the growing reach and absorptive power of international capitalism (even as economic politics in the North has turned more inward-looking and nationalistic)" (Sen 1994). Population growth may encourage outward migration, but "to try to explain the increase in immigration pressure by the growth rate of total population in the [Global South] is to close one's eyes to the deep changes that have occurred—and are occurring—in the world in which we live, and the rapid internationalization of its cultures and economies that accompanies those changes." Nonetheless, to many Northern societies, immigration has become *the population problem,* and shutting the door is increasingly viewed as a solution.

Migration is the primary dimension through which the globalization of population dynamics occurs, but it will also be felt in other ways, including national security considerations, social and economic stresses on development, food production and distribution, and environmental degradation.

The Demography of National Security

In 1996, 98 percent of the growth in world population occurred in the developing countries, and this disproportionate rate of increase is projected to continue (*Vital Signs 1997*, 80). As rapid population growth in the Global South makes the countries of the developed world a declining fraction of world population, concerns about the consequences for Global South security have risen. Realists argue that a country's population size is an important source of political power. The shrinking of the world's more economically prosperous states, as low fertility rates and aging populations in the Global North make it difficult to maintain large armies, may reduce their military power relative to the Global South, whose abundant youth can provide ample supplies of soldiers to fight the wars of the twenty-first century.

Ironically, Global South economic progress over the next several decades may also accelerate a shift of the balances of power toward those experiencing rapid population growth. For some, in fact, power is already perceived to have shifted toward those most prone to reject the North's values and challenge its interests. This is particularly so when demographic changes are coupled with rapid economic growth in the newly industrialized economies and elsewhere in the Global South. "Simple arithmetic demonstrates Western folly," a deputy secretary in Singapore's Foreign Ministry has written. "The West has 800 million people;

human rights the political rights and civil liberties recognized by the international community as inalienable and valid for individuals in all countries by virtue of their humanness.

atrocities brutal and savage acts against targeted citizen groups or prisoners of war, defined as illegal under international law.

the rest make up almost 4.7 billion. . . . No Western society would accept a situation where 15 percent of its population legislated for the remaining 85 percent" (cited in Connelly and Kennedy 1994).

Varying fertility rates among various ethnic populations will also have internal and international consequences. In Israel, for example, the Jewish population may one day become the minority, as fertility rates among Arabs and Palestinians within Israel's borders outstrip those of Israeli Jews. Similar trends are evident in South Africa, where the white population is already outnumbered and is expected to account for only about 10 percent of the total population by the year 2020, compared with the 20 percent it accounted for in the early 1950s (Eberstadt 1991).

The influence of demographic changes within societies in stimulating domestic strife and external conflict is difficult to measure but imprudent to ignore. Lebanon—wracked by violent civil conflict and foreign military intervention for nearly fifteen years beginning in the mid-1970s—is a case in point. There, competing Muslim religious sects enjoyed more rapid population growth than the Christian population, upsetting a delicately balanced, if rigid, political structure that could not contain the resulting sectarian tensions. This led to death, destruction, and the exodus of one-third of the Lebanese population (Kane 1995a). In South Africa, on the other hand, the black-majority government has an opportunity to prove that flexible policies within a democracy can balance competing interests deeply rooted in ethnic and demographic differences. Time will tell.

AIDS poses a wholly different security issue. Beyond its social and economic costs, foreign and defense policy analysts worry about the political and military implications of the spreading disease. In parts of Thailand one-fifth of twenty-one-year-old military recruits are now infected—and this in a country where AIDS was virtually unknown in 1987 (*World Health Report 1995* 1995, 29). National defense readiness will weaken as HIV/AIDS spreads among military personnel. Ensuring safe blood supplies for the military, especially in countries with inadequate medical equipment, is a related concern. More broadly, countries where the incidence of AIDS is high are prone to instability; leaders could fall, victims of the disease's impact, resulting in power struggles among ministerial-level bureaucrats who themselves could become HIV-infected (Hamilton 1994).

The Demography of Development, Food Security, and Environmental Preservation

The impact of population growth on economic development, food security, and environmental quality has long been in dispute—and remains so. Two broadly defined groups of analysts approach these issues quite differently. Taking their name and orientation from Thomas Malthus and his classic *Essay on the Principle of Population* (1798), **neo-Malthusians** believe that world population is pushing against the earth's resources, straining its ability to meet the needs of this generation and the next. Neo-Malthusians—many of whom are human ecologists sometimes called "growth pessimists"—routinely point to a host of disconcerting facts about the present global condition: "Since Malthus wrote, the human population has grown by a factor of six, and total human energy use by a factor of one hundred or so. . . . The forest cover of the earth has been cut by a third and the area of undisturbed wetlands by half. The composition of the atmosphere has been altered by human-generated pollution. Hundreds of mil-

lions of people have starved to death; thousands of species have gone extinct"
(Meadows 1993).

In contrast with the pessimism of neo-Malthusians, **cornucopians**—many
of whom are economists and otherwise known as "growth optimists"—emphasize quite different global trends:

- Global life expectancy more than doubled this century from thirty to sixty-
  four years, while global infant mortality fell from 170 infant deaths per
  1,000 births in 1950 to just 60 in 1990. Rapid population growth has occurred not because human beings suddenly started breeding like rabbits
  but because they finally stopped dropping like flies.

- Despite a tripling of the world's population in this century, global health
  and productivity have exploded. Today human beings eat better, produce
  more, and consume more than ever. . . .

- "Overpopulation" is a problem that has been misidentified and misdefined.
  The term has no scientific definition or clear meaning. The problems typically associated with overpopulation (hungry families, squalid and over-
  crowded living conditions) are more properly understood as issues of
  poverty. . . .

- Although some blame dwindling natural resources for the reversals and
  catastrophes that have recently befallen heavily populated low-income
  countries, such episodes are directly traceable to the policies or practices of
  presiding governments. (Eberstadt 1995, 8)

Compelling as the neo-Malthusian and cornucopian perspectives may be,
the range of opinion and conviction separating them is less clear than the labels
themselves suggest. Furthermore, determining which perspective is "right" is
difficult, as history does not provide a clear answer. As noted in Chapter 5, for
example, the absolute gap in income between North and South continues, but
the gap in human development between rich and poor countries has narrowed.
Moreover, the relative economic position of many countries within the Global
South has improved with time, as their gross economic products have grown
more rapidly than their populations, but the total number of people living in
absolute poverty continues to grow. Even in Sub-Saharan Africa—which in the
last decade has experienced sharp declines in economic growth coupled with
the world's most rapid population growth—it is too easy to attribute financial
woes to rising population.

What applies in Africa applies elsewhere: Population alone is not the cause
of current problems; instead, it is one factor that aggravates other problems,
including ill-advised government policies, political instability, unsustainable resource consumption, and inadequate technology. We can better appreciate
these interactions by examining how the globalization of demographic trends
and population dynamics affects economic development, food security, and environmental preservation.

The Demography of Development. Dependent children (those younger than fifteen) in the Global South typically make up about 35 percent of the total population (compared with 20 percent in the developed world) (World Bank 1997,
16–17). This means there are fewer than two working-age adults for each child
under fifteen in developing countries compared with more than three in the
Global North. Such a large proportion of dependent children burdens public

services, particularly the educational system. It also encourages the immediate consumption of economic resources rather than their reinvestment in the social infrastructure to promote future economic growth.

As the children mature, the demands for new jobs, housing, and other human needs multiply. However, the resources to meet them are typically scarce and inadequate. On a global scale, as many as 1.3 billion people will be added to the workforce in the Global South between 1995 and 2020 (*The State of the World Population 1994* 1994, 2). In places such as Mexico this means that 1 million new jobs must be created every year to absorb the wave of young people entering the labor market. Failure to do so worries political leaders not only in Mexico but also elsewhere, notably the United States, because the youths who do not find jobs will likely turn to the United States, the streets, or revolution (Moffett 1994).

The search for employment propels internal as well as international migration, contributing to the rapid urbanization occurring throughout the world, but especially in the Global South. "The UN expects that between 1990 and 2025 the number of people living in urban areas will double to more than 5 billion, and that 90 percent of that growth will be in developing countries" (*Economist*, March 31, 1998, 4). By the turn of the century, half of the world's 6 billion people will live in cities, three-fourths of them in the developing countries. "Another billion—or the equivalent of about sixty more cities the size of New York—will be added by the year 2025. New York itself, the [world's largest] city in 1950, may not even make the list by 2025, as it is overtaken by swelling [Global South] capitals like Jakarta and Manila" (Moffett 1994, 30).

New York, London, and Shanghai were the only cities with populations of 10 million or more in 1950. According to the United Nations, by the mid-1990s the number had grown to fifteen—eleven of them in the Global South—with even larger "megacities" and "supercities" on the horizon. Lagos, Nigeria, an "urban agglomeration" (in UN parlance) of 9.7 million in 1994, will increase to more than 24 million by 2015; São Paulo, Brazil, with 16 million will grow to 21 million; and Bombay, India, will increase its rank from the world's sixth largest urban agglomeration to the second (behind Tokyo) as it nearly doubles in size to 27.4 million between 1994 and 2015. Increasingly, the fate of these and other exploding cities in the Global South will determine the fate of countries and whole regions (Linden 1996).

The growth of urban areas is not necessarily bad in itself, but the speed of today's urbanization often is, as it overwhelms the capacity of local governments to keep pace with the demands that accompany urban growth. "It took London 130 years to climb from 1 to 8 million residents. Mexico City covered the same distance in just thirty years, between 1940 and 1970. Sixteen years later the city's population had doubled to 16 million" (Moffett 1994, 31). Thus in Mexico City and elsewhere, rapid urbanization severely taxes the capacity for effective governance. Millions of urban dwellers live in crowded, cramped hovels in sprawling shantytowns and squatter settlements amid mounting garbage dumps, without adequate water or sanitation, without access to adequate health care or education and other social services, and in the constant shadow of pervasive crime and violence. And the environmental and health hazards multiply. Cars, for example, are proliferating more rapidly than people in many Global South cities and add to the pollution of urban areas worldwide. So crushing are the burdens of urban life in many developing countries that one analyst described it as "a close approximation of hell on earth" (Cairncross 1994).

The untoward consequences of urbanization are not confined to city dwellers. Urbanization increases pressures on local agricultural systems as well, because there are fewer hands in the countryside to feed the growing number of mouths in the city. Furthermore, food prices in urban areas are often purposely depressed by governing elites. This has the dual effect of diminishing farmers' incentives to produce while also encouraging them to abandon their lands in search of a better future in the city. Pressures to import food follow. By 2030 ten Global South countries (India, Bangladesh, Indonesia, Iran, Pakistan, Egypt, Ethiopia and Eritrea, Nigeria, Brazil, and Mexico) are expected to require some 190 million tons of imported grains—an amount equal to nearly all of world grain exports in 1994 (Brown 1995, 115). All ten have rapidly growing urban agglomerations, which in many cases will be three or four times as large in 2030 as they are now.

As fertility rates in the Global South decline, the number of children under fifteen will also steadily decline. If the experience of Europe, North America, and especially Japan is a guide, this should lead to economic gains (Woods 1989). Ironically, however, the demographic life cycle also portends that the countries now most burdened by a rapid population growth among young people will also be those with an increasing number of older dependents. During the next half-century, the population pyramid for developing regions shown in Figure 10.4 will begin to turn upside down due to declining birth rates and increased longevity. This will tip the "dependency ratio"—those no longer economically productive and thus dependent on others in the work force—away from younger people toward the elderly. Urbanization will further increase the social burdens of the world's growing number of elderly people by breaking down the extended families that in traditional societies provide social security for older people. The experience of the Global North demonstrates that there is a distinct disadvantage to this long-term demographic change, as demands for social services, particularly expensive health care, will multiply, burdening the Global South in yet another way (see Focus 10.2).

The aging population in the Global North is especially striking in Japan, where the demographic transition began later than elsewhere but was completed more rapidly. While Sweden today is the "oldest" nation, with nearly one-fifth of its citizens sixty-five or older (Kinsella 1994, 6), Japan is the most rapidly aging, with the highest life expectancy in the world. Elderly persons are expected to make up one-fourth of Japan's population by 2025. Already most Japanese workers are over forty.

As Japan continues to age, it will confront troublesome questions about its ability to continue the vigorous economic productivity and high domestic savings rates that have stimulated the projection of its economic power abroad. The Japanese term "child shock" dramatizes the growing crisis forecast by the decline in workers and growth in pensioners. The Japanese government and private-sector groups have joined forces to promote pronatalist attitudes among the Japanese people to raise fertility rates. However, unlike similar efforts undertaken during the 1930s (when war between Japan and the United States loomed on the horizon), the response to these contemporary efforts to stimulate birth rates has been unenthusiastic.

The "Graying" of Nations

Every month, the present world total of 360 million persons aged 65 and over increases by 800,000. Three decades from now, the world's elderly are projected to number 850 million. This unprecedented growth of the older population has already changed the social and political landscape in industrialized nations, and will increasingly bear upon policies and programmes throughout the developing world. Although issues of health care policy and reform vary enormously among and within continents, most national decisions in the health arena are already—or soon will be—affected by the momentum of population aging.

. . . A majority of today's growth in the numbers of elderly is occurring in the developing countries. The speed of aging is likewise more rapid there than in the industrialized world; while it took 115 years for the proportion of elderly to rise from 7% to 14% in France, the same change in China will occur in fewer than 30 years. The high fertility rates that prevailed in most developing countries from 1950 until at least the early 1970s ensure that the ranks of the elderly will continue to swell during the next four decades.

Related to the demographic transition is the epidemiological transition. This concept refers to a long-term change in major causes of death, from infectious and acute diseases on the one hand to chronic and degenerative diseases on the other. We know that the average individual's risk of becoming disabled rises with age. As entire populations age, the societal prevalence of disability is also likely to increase. And as we live to higher and higher ages, the debate is brewing: does longer life translate into healthier life, or are individuals spending a greater portion of their later years with disabilities, mental disorders, and disease?

. . . Because the oldest consume disproportionate amounts of health care and long-term services, provision of those services will become more costly. Many health systems today are being economically squeezed by the competing desires to keep pace with a growing elderly population and to expand basic coverage to all segments of society. Countries throughout the world are looking beyond their borders for clues about restructuring their health systems, avoiding primary reliance on institutional care, and promoting family care and home care for their aging populations.

SOURCE: Kinsella (1994), 6.

Providing for the increasing number of dependent elderly people relative to the number of productive workers is also a political concern elsewhere in the Global North. In western Europe the wisdom of pursuing pronatalist policies to reverse the projected decline in its overall population has been intensely debated. Much of the dialogue has turned on questions of individual versus collective welfare. Advocates of pronatalist measures are concerned with the "continued vitality of national populations that do not replace themselves: No children, no future, is the key phrase." National pride, concern for the country's place among the world powers, and the prominence of European culture in a world where non-European countries grow much faster also motivate pronatalists.

Opponents of pronatalist measures, on the other hand, "dismiss as exaggerated the specter of Europe as a decrepit society of ruminating octogenarians" (van de Kaa, 1987). They "attach no special value to their own cultures" and oppose stimulating population growth in a world where overpopulation is already a serious problem. They believe that "economic resources rather than military resources or population size determine a country's international standing" and that "economic integration is a much more effective way to maintain Europe's international position than stimulating the birth rate" (van de Kaa, 1987). Finally, they question whether it makes sense to stimulate births when Europe al-

The frontiers of food science have not yet been reached, optimists believe, because many breakthroughs can be expected that will expand yields and productivity. Shown here is "cow power"—a farmer in Tienman, China, cultivating a field. Researchers in Africa have developed a new breed of cow that is strong enough for field work without reducing its capacity to produce milk and reproduce.

ready suffers from chronic high unemployment. "With modern technology eliminating jobs, workers are encouraged to work shorter hours, part-time, or retire early, and immigration is halted," the argument continues, "so why should we have more people?" (van de Kaa 1987).

The Demography of Global Food Security. The gloomiest of Thomas Malthus's predictions, made two centuries ago, is that the world's population will eventually outstrip its capacity to produce enough food to sustain its growing numbers. Malthus based his prognosis on what he regarded as the simple mathematical fact that population grows exponentially while agricultural output grows only arithmetically. He did not foresee that agricultural output would also grow at an increasing rate due to technological innovations.

Increases in the world's food output have been especially remarkable since World War II, far outstripping the largest-ever expansion of world population. The greatest gains occurred as a result of the increased productivity of farmers in the Global North. However, the South also obtained impressive results by expanding the acreage devoted to agriculture and, later, by introducing new high-yield strains of wheat and rice—what we now call the "green revolution." By the 1980s Indonesia, once a massive importer of food, had largely been removed from the import market; and India, once regarded as a permanent candidate for the international dole, had actually become a modest grain exporter.

Continued growth in world food production is uncertain, yet it is necessary if output is to keep pace with an expanding world population and improved living standards. A former secretary of the U.S. Department of Agriculture describes the challenge in drastic terms: "In the next two to four generations, world agriculture will be called on to produce as much food as has been produced in the entire 12,000-year history of agriculture" (Freeman 1990, 16).

Cornucopians—who point with pride to the continued growth of food production since 1980 (see Figure 10.5)—argue that continued advances can be expected as current resources are used more efficiently and high-yield farming practices continue to spread. They cite as evidence the **green revolution** resulting from scientific advances since the 1950s, such as pest-resistant hybrids, that have raised crop yields per acre substantially for key grains such as rice, maize, wheat and rye. And they foresee few reasons why cross-breeding, biotechnology, and genetic engineering should fail to boost yields considerably in the future, while at the same time introducing new, efficient methods for protecting the environment from destruction. Among the impressive record of past accomplishments are:

- Rice plants that resist the tungaro virus and thus will produce another 7 million tons of rice per year.

- Wheat plants with the strongest resistance yet to the pervasive rust diseases, one of the worst pests that attack wheat crops all over the world. . . .

- A genetically engineered copy of the natural pork growth hormone that produces hogs with half as much body fat, which means more healthful pork, and raised with one-fourth less feed grain. Think of pork growth hormone as the equivalent of producing millions of extra tons of feed corn from laboratory bacteria instead of ploughed-down wildlife habitat.

- Cloned and tissue-cultured Georgia yellow pine, planted in Brazil, which can produce sixteen times as much pulpwood per hectare per year as a Swedish natural forest. Each acre of the high-yielding trees can protect fifteen wild acres from being logged. . . . (Avery 1995, 67–68)

Neo-Malthusians counter these claims, arguing that agricultural and other biological systems such as ocean fisheries will be unable to meet rising demand, jeopardizing realization of the goal of global **food security** (continued access by all people to enough food for an active, healthy life). They point to several disturbing trends to illustrate their concern:

food security the availability of sufficient food for an adequate diet, in contrast to food insecurity (the lack of access to enough food, or, at worst, famine).

- Although food production has increased steadily, per-capita production has generally stagnated (see Figure 10.5).

- The world's fish catch peaked at 100 million tons in 1989—a level believed to be near the maximum sustainable yield of ocean fisheries—and has since grown little, with most increased output attributed to aquaculture (fish farming) (Brown, Lenssen, and Kane 1995, 32–33). The world's rangelands are under similar pressure, as they are grazed beyond their capacity to regenerate (Brown and Kane 1994).

- The world's carryover stocks of grain ("the amount in the bin when the new harvest begins"), which in effect provide the world with a food-security buffer during lean years, has dropped to levels not seen since the 1970s, when grain prices doubled in the face of a global food crisis (Brown et al. 1996, 8).

Neo-Malthusians point to other developments that suggest a less-than-rosy future, including the impact of rising affluence on global food supplies and the resources required to provide them. As wealth increases, people move up the **food ladder,** shifting their preferences from beans and rice to steak and chicken, asparagus and apricots. The culinary preferences of more affluent people also translate into proportionately higher demands on agricultural lands and water resources. Still, ascending the food ladder is the shape of things to come.

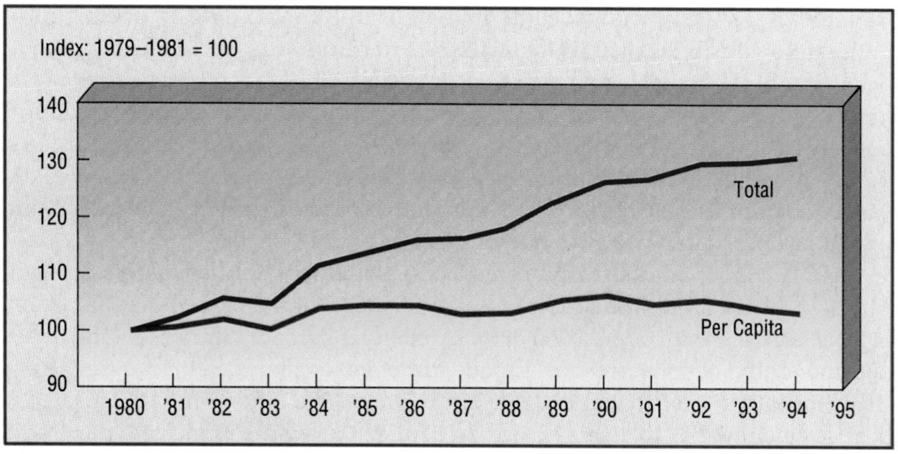

Index: 1979–1981 = 100

FIGURE 10.5

Total and Per-Capita Food Production, since 1980

World food production has grown by nearly 30 percent since the early 1980s, but per-capita production has remained stagnant. The difference between the trends is largely accounted for what is eaten up by population growth.

SOURCES: Adapted from *FAO Yearbook: Production 1990* (1991, 39–40, 49–50); *FAO Yearbook: Production 1994* (1995), 39, 49.

China's meat consumption is currently rising by 3 million tons (and 10 percent) per year. Chinese meat consumption has traditionally been very low, but rising per-capita incomes are putting more meat within the reach of many more consumers. Indians do not eat much meat because of their predominant Hindu religion, but the demand for dairy products is rising by 2 million tons per year. Indonesia is Islamic, so its residents do not eat pork, and it has no extensive grazing lands for beef, but poultry consumption is rising at double-digit rates. All told, Asia's diet upgrading is the biggest surge in farm resource demand the world has ever seen. . . . And each ton of added protein demand will require three to five added tons of grain and oilseed production to provide feed to produce the additional animal protein. (Avery 1995, 51–52)

Thus, even as world population growth begins to level off, pressures on world food systems will continue their forward momentum.

Can the world's food-producing systems sustain the growing demand stimulated by population growth and rising affluence? Lester Brown, a prominent neo-Malthusian, and his associates at the Worldwatch Institute warn that the earth's carrying capacity is limited and that its limits are rapidly approaching (see, e.g., Brown et al. 1996; Postel 1994). They argue that diminishing returns from fertilizer applications combined with soil erosion, growing water scarcity, and other environmental stresses already undermine the ability of national agricultural systems to provide for a growing world population.

China—which accounts for more than one-fifth of humanity—is especially worrisome. Drawing on the experience of Japan, South Korea, and Taiwan, Brown (1995) argues that the transformation of China from an agricultural to an industrial society will cause its food consumption to quickly outstrip production. Increasingly, then, China will have to turn to the world marketplace to feed its billion-plus residents. Evidence is seen in China's food imports from the United States, which tripled in 1995, contributing to record U.S. agricultural exports in excess of $50 million. American farmers doubtless profited, but in a tightly integrated world market based on free-trade logic, prices everywhere can be expected to rise sharply as demand exceeds supply. Who feeds China may thus determine who goes hungry.

Africa's experience already seems to vindicate neo-Malthusians' pessimism. The continent's food production increased by less than 2 percent annually during the 1970s, but its population grew by nearly 3 percent. Starvation and death became daily occurrences in broad stretches of the Sahel, ranging from Ethiopia in the east to Mauritania in the west. The situation was repeated a decade later when, in Ethiopia in particular, the world witnessed the tragic specter of tens of thousands suffering and dying from malnutrition and famine at a time of unprecedented food surpluses worldwide.

As population growth has moved in concert with environmental degradation, Sub-Saharan Africa has experienced the tragedy of the commons in all of its most remorseless manifestations. Civil strife, ethnic bloodletting, and war have characterized post-colonial Africa, as conflicts affecting tens of millions of people have ravaged one-third or more of the countries in the region since the 1970s. In some cases, as in Ethiopia, Somalia, and the Sudan, food was actively used as a political weapon. The UN/U.S. humanitarian intervention in Somalia in 1992–1994 sought to curb these practices, but with limited success. Thus the words of Shun Chetty of the UN High Commission for Refugees retain their tragic pertinence: "He who controls roads controls food. He who controls food controls the people."

Growth optimists reject the Malthusian analogy as applied to Africa, particularly the prophecy that excessive population growth causes food deficits. War is not the *consequence* but the *cause* of famine, malnutrition, and starvation, cornucopians argue. "Famines come about when political systems fail to encourage agriculture and distribution successfully. And those political failures have a pattern: They occur in centralized, authoritarian systems. Free-market economics do not produce famines" (Avery 1995). Asia's recent experience also seems to vindicate cornucopian logic. The continent's per-capita food production has outstripped that of all other world regions since the early 1980s, with China and Vietnam leading the pack as each moved toward market-based agricultural systems—and this despite large population increases.

Still, millions go hungry each day. The World Resources Institute (1994, 108) estimates that at the beginning of the 1990s nearly 800 million people in Africa, Asia, Latin America, and the Middle East—representing 20 percent of humanity—suffered chronic undernutrition. Neo-Malthusians urge that, on moral grounds alone, population growth must be stemmed so that those who now suffer most can be relieved. In practice, however, the issue is not a lack of food but its maldistribution. According to the microeconomic principle known as **Engel's law,** poorer families typically spend a much higher percentage of their budget on food than do higher-income groups. Yet the ability to acquire more food depends on having the income necessary to buy it. "Most people who stop eating do so not because there is insufficient food grown in the world but because they no longer grow it themselves and do not have the money to buy it" (Barnet 1980). From this perspective, poverty—not overpopulation—is the cause of the food deficits so many countries and people experience. But

Engel's law the Marxist economist Friedrich Engel's principle of consumption, which predicts that poor people spend their limited income on necessary goods, whereas the rich spend wealth on unnecessary luxuries.

what causes poverty? And what are its cures? Neo-Malthusians and cornucopians both speak to this issue, and both offer prescriptions for dealing with it. But who is right?

The Demography of Environmental Preservation. Neo-Malthusians stress environmental degradation in assessing the adverse consequences of population growth. Excessive consumption in the Global North also falls under their indictment. Unless both are curbed, they argue, **ecological overshoot**—exceeding the earth's carrying capacity—will surely follow.

Once again, growth optimists do not accept the pessimists' arguments or conclusions. Still, a kind of global consensus has converged around the wisdom of **sustainable development,** which says that the present generation's needs must be met without compromising the ability of future generations to meet theirs. This concept will figure prominently in the analysis in Chapter 11, which examines in greater detail how global environmental and resource trends affect world politics. Here that discussion is anticipated by emphasizing that the links between population growth and environmental stress—like connections between population growth and economic development generally—are not easily unraveled. Population growth doubtless has adverse environmental consequences, but the relationship is not straightforward.

> Many other factors—government policies, the legal system, access to capital and technology, the efficiency of industrial production, inequity in the distribution of land and resources, poverty in the South, and conspicuous consumption in the North—may work separately or together to buffer or increase humankind's impact on the environment. The potential for reducing the effect of population growth depends largely on altering factors such as these that compound the environmental impact of human activity. (World Resources Institute 1994, 27–28)

Thus the environmental toll of population growth and rising affluence seemingly binds humanity in a common fate. Still, as the tragedy of the commons suggests, not everyone will share the costs equally. Herein lies what many describe as the "planetary predicament," as the costs of environmental stress affect the Global North and South quite differently.

Soil erosion, desertification, and deforestation are worldwide phenomena, but they are often most acute where population growth and poverty are most evident (see McKibben 1998). The search for fuelwood is a major source of deforestation and a primary occupation in developing countries. Deforestation and soil erosion also occur when growing populations without access to farmland push cultivation into hillsides and tropical forests ill-suited to farming. In the Sahel area of Africa, growing populations of livestock as well as humans hastened the destruction of productive land, producing a desert that led to famine—a graphic illustration of the tragedy of the commons. And the danger extends beyond Africa: Recent estimates put the amount of land affected by **desertification** at 1.2 billion hectacres—an area equivalent to the size of India and China combined. "That's about 17 percent of the planet's total land area, and the process appears to be accelerating" ("Environmental Intelligence" 1994, 7).

Logic suggests that excessive population growth produces excessive environmental stress. In fact, the consumption patterns associated with affluence are even more debilitating. "A typical resident of the industrialized . . . world uses fifteen times as much paper, ten times as much steel, and twelve times as much fuel as a [Global South] world resident" (Durning 1991, 161).

sustainable development economic growth engineered by policies and practices that do not destroy the environment to subsidize quick development and short-term profits for producers.

desertification the creation of deserts due to soil erosion, overfarming, and deforestation, which convert cropland to nonproductive, arid sand.

A consuming society is also a throwaway society. "The Japanese use 30 million 'disposable' single-roll cameras each year, and the British dump 2.5 billion diapers. Americans toss away 180 million razors annually, enough paper and plastic plates and cups to feed the world a picnic six times a year, and enough aluminum cans to make six thousand DC-10 airplanes" (Durning 1991, 161). Each American threw away an average of 1,460 pounds of garbage in 1988, and the amount is expected to grow to nearly 1,800 pounds per person by 2010 (Young 1991, 44). As the mountains of garbage grow, disposing of it has become increasingly difficult.

If people and wealth both cause environmental stress, what will the twenty-first century bring, as both population growth and rising affluence are already on the horizon?

• • •

POPULATION POLICIES: OPTIMISTS, PESSIMISTS, AND THE INTERNATIONAL RESPONSE

More than two decades have passed since the world community convened its first World Population Conference to address the world's growing population, then already concentrated in the Global South. Meeting in Bucharest in 1974, many delegates from the Global South concluded from Europe's and North America's demographic transitions that declining fertility rates flowed more or less automatically from economic growth. Thus they understandably prescribed policies that focused on economic development and not on population control. They called on the Global North for assistance in their economic development, reasoning that the population problem would then take care of itself. The slogan "development is the best contraceptive" reflected the prevailing view. Many in the Global North, on the other hand, advocated a more direct attack on what they saw as "the population problem"—namely, excessive population growth that erodes economic opportunities and imperils other values.

A decade later, a second World Population Conference was held in Mexico City. By then a new consensus had converged around the critical importance of family planning. Curiously, the United States, previously a major advocate of this viewpoint, departed from this emerging global consensus. Reflecting the conservative political sentiments prevalent in Washington at the time, the U.S. delegation asserted that free-market principles should take precedence over government intervention in economic and population matters. The Reagan adminstration also vigorously opposed abortion as an approach to family planning. China became the object of special ire, prompted by a television exposé of its family-planning practices, which included "human rights abuses . . . [ranging] from mandatory sterilization and abortion to forced insertions of IUDs, all committed in the name of slowing the country's runaway population growth" (Moffett 1994). The United States now withheld support for multilateral as well as bilateral efforts to assist family-planning programs in developing countries, slowing their spread throughout the Global South.

Although the views of the United States in 1984 clearly represented a minority perspective, they reflected growing dissatisfaction with earlier neo-Malthusian analyses of the global ecopolitical implications of population growth. Instead, the U.S. position in Mexico City reflected that of cornucopians, who argue that human ingenuity has developed resource-saving (or -substituting) innovations in response to shortages created by population growth, so that population growth is a stimulus, not a deterrent, to economic advancement.

The United States reversed its course following Bill Clinton's election in 1992. Restrictions that denied U.S. funds to some family-planning organizations because of abortion-related activities were lifted almost immediately. Bilateral and multilateral aid designed to support population activities soon began to flow more liberally. The Clinton administration also embraced the premise—effectively denied during the 1980s—that population pressures aggravate social, economic, and environmental problems and may cause political instability. Robert D. Kaplan's (1994) shockingly pessimistic account of "the coming anarchy" in West Africa, stimulated by overpopulation and environmental degradation, not only captured the attention of Washington policymakers but also encapsulated their convictions.

The debate between optimists and pessimists continues. By 1994, however, when the United Nations convened its third decennial world population conference in Cairo, it had moved in new directions. As suggested by the conference title, "International Conference on Population and Development (ICPD)," population and development were now placed on the same track. Thus the ICPD moved beyond population numbers and demographic targets, embracing instead the view that population stabilization can be achieved only in the larger context of human development and sustainable economic growth. The conference paid particular attention to the critical role of women in both population control and the development process.

The Subordinate Status of Women and Its Consequences

The road to Cairo was marked by signposts that increasingly depicted the right of women to control their own bodies and reproductive fate as a basic human right, recognizable under international law (see Focus 10.3). It was also marked by incontrovertible evidence that women's status in society, and especially their education, have an important influence on preferences toward family size.

> Having an education usually means that women delay marriage, seek wage-paying jobs, learn about and have more favorable attitudes toward family planning, and have better communication with their husbands when they marry. Educated women have fewer infant deaths; high infant mortality is associated with high fertility. Similarly, when women have wage-paying jobs, they tend to have fewer children (and conversely, women with fewer children find it easier to work). (Population Reference Bureau 1981, 5)

Nevertheless, as measured by the UN's **gender empowerment index,** women throughout the world continue to be disadvantaged relative to men across a broad spectrum of educational statistics, such as literacy rates, school and college enrollments, and targeted educational resources. Women also enjoy less access to advanced study and training in professional fields, such as science, engineering, law, and business. In addition, within occupational groups, they are almost always in less prestigious jobs, they face formidable barriers to political involvement, and everywhere they receive less pay than men. Although these and other gender differences have narrowed in recent years, in most countries **gender inequalities** remain firmly rooted.

gender empowerment index, the UN Development Program's attempt to measure the extent of gender equality across the globe's countries, based on estimates of women's relative economic status, high-paying employment, and access to professional and parliamentary positions.

Addressing women's rights is difficult because the issues touch deeply entrenched as well as widely divergent religious and cultural beliefs. In many Islamic countries, for example, women must hide their faces with veils in public, and women and men are often completely separated in social and religious ac-

Human Rights and Women's Rights
A Quarter-Century of Progress

Over the past twenty-five years, women's civil rights and re-productive rights have made notable incursions into the international legal and human rights agendas. . . .

1968, United Nations International Conference on Human Rights (Teheran)

The United Nations explicitly addresses the issue of "human reproduction." The Teheran Declaration states: "Parents have a basic human right to decide freely and responsibly on the number and spacing of their children and a right to adequate education and information in this respect. "

1974, World Population Conference (Bucharest)

From "parents," the focus shifts to "couples and individuals," who have a right to the "means" as well as the information and education needed to decide on the number and spacing of their children. The notion of responsibility is also introduced: "The responsibility of couples and individuals in the exercise of this right takes into account the needs of their living and future children, and their responsibilities towards the community."

1975, International Women's Year Conference (Mexico City)

Launching the UN Decade for Women, the conference emphasizes reproductive choice, bodily integrity, and reproductive autonomy: "The human body, whether that of woman or man, is inviolable, and respect for it is a fundamental element of human dignity and freedom."

1979, Convention on the Elimination of All Forms of Discrimination against Women (the Women's Convention)

An unambiguous goal of the convention is equality between women and men in their right and ability to control reproduction. The convention's thirty articles address educational, economic, social, cultural, civic, and political discrimination. Article 12 refers to women's reproductive rights and calls on countries that have ratified the convention to "take all appropriate measures to eliminate discrimination against women in the field of health care in order to ensure, on a basis of equality of men and women, access to health care services, including those related to family planning." Article 16 urges the elimination of "discrimination against women in all matters relating to marriage and family relations."

1984, World Population Conference (Mexico City)

Conference recommendations emphasize the responsibilities of governments and individuals alike: "The experience of the past ten years suggests that governments can do more to assist people in making their reproductive decisions in a responsible way." Making family planning more available is viewed "as a matter of urgency."

1992, United Nations Conference on Environment and Development (Rio)

Agenda 21, the draft of the meeting's official document, includes discussion of family planning and highlights quality, calling for "women-centered, women-managed, safe and accessible, responsible planning of family size and services."

1993, United Nations World Conference on Human Rights (Vienna)

The Vienna Declaration includes nine paragraphs on "The Equal Status and Human Rights of Women," and, for the first time, violence against women is recognized as a human-rights abuse.

1994, International Conference on Population and Development (Cairo)

ICPD Programme of Action "reaffirms the basic human right of all couples and individuals to decide freely and responsibly the number and spacing of their children and to have the information, education, and means to do so."

SOURCES: *The State of the World Population 1994* (1994), 19; *The State of the World Population 1995* (1994), 2.

tivities. These traditions are difficult to understand in many Western countries. On the other hand, Western conceptions of feminism and women's rights, typically focused on social, political, and economic equality of the sexes, are foreign to women elsewhere, where the issues are personal and the goals prag-

In August 1995, women representing the different cultures of the world held the "peace torch" during the opening ceremony for the Nongovernmental Organization Forum on Women at the Olympic Stadium in Beijing. The forum was held in conjunction with the United Nations Fourth World Conference on Women, which met in Beijing from September 4–15.

matic: "access to capital, the right of inheritance, basic education for girls, a voice in the political establishment and medical systems that let them make choices, especially in reproductive health" (Crossette 1995).

Despite the pitfalls and minefields, the ICPD Programme of Action—endorsed by 180 countries—addressed issues of gender equality and "empowerment" as well as women's reproductive rights. This was a historic step toward global recognition of the critical role that women play in both development and population stabilization. Noting that "in all parts of the world, women are facing threats to their lives, health, and well-being as a result of being overburdened with work and of their lack of power and influence," the conference also called for "the elimination of all kinds of violence against women."

In 1995, in Beijing, the United Nations convened its fourth World Conference on Women, the largest-ever gathering of women. Many of the issues regarding women's rights, along with the arguments provoked by differing religious and cultural traditions (including some thought to have been resolved in Cairo), resurfaced during the conference. Nonetheless, its very occurrence continued to focus attention on gender issues and the concept of **gender empowerment**—the conviction that "only when the potential of all human beings is fully realized can we talk of true human development" (UNDP 1995).

A World Population Plan of Action

Surprisingly, the Cairo debates paid little attention to many issues which by then had become common fare in global population forums—perhaps because the contentious issue of abortion rights commanded center stage during the conference. Among the standards were issues of environmental quality, resource conservation, demographic sources of political instability and ethnic conflict, urbanization, and structural inequalities between the Global North and South. Many did figure into the goals articulated in the ICPD Programme of Action. Nonetheless, others now also emerged prominently among the key objectives around which a global consensus was achieved:

- Establishing a long-term goal of stabilizing population growth levels consistent with sustainable development;
- Establishing an international partnership for sustainable development that recognizes the responsibility of the North to address wasteful resource use in conjunction with the South's addressing high rates of population growth;
- Developing a comprehensive approach for national efforts and international assistance programs that includes:
  —addressing the unmet need and demand for family planning and reproductive health services;
  —strategies for preventing HIV/AIDS infection;
  —child survival and women's health needs;
  — the need to advance the rights and economic, political, and social roles of women;
  —improving the education of girls and women; and
  —increasing male responsibility in family planning and childrearing.
- Mobilizing institutional capability and financial resources necessary to implement the above goals. (U.S. Department of State *Dispatch* 5, Supplement no. 8 [September 1994], 9)

The Programme of Action also set out specific goals to be achieved by 2015 that deal with access to primary school education, family-planning services, reproductive health, infant and under-five mortality, maternal mortality, and life expectancy.

The proposals contained in the Programme of Action are only recommendations and thus not binding on governments. Indeed, few could be expected to act on all of them, particularly given the enormous resources their realization demands. By the end of this century, the expenditures on family planning alone are expected to balloon to $10 billion, nearly double the amount spent in the early 1990s. Even greater sums would be required to meet the goals of increased access to primary education and to health care (including that required by the growing number of HIV/AIDS patients). Global South countries cannot be expected to meet these demands by themselves, and others—meaning governments in the Global North—will be asked to supplement their resources. However, domestic political support for foreign aid among donor countries has virtually disappeared.

Mounting a sustained effort to stem the growth of world population thus remains a formidable challenge. But the goal itself is no longer in dispute—a rather remarkable achievement given the comparatively short time in which the "population problem" has been on the global agenda and the disparate interests and values that motivate states' behavior on the issues it encompasses. As neo-Malthusian Lester Brown (1994) observes, "The delegates [to the Cairo conference] rejected the idea that human numbers could be allowed to continue growing until they reached 10 to 14 billion as projected, and opted instead for an ambitious Plan of Action to stabilize population at a much lower level. Perhaps the boldest initiative ever undertaken by the United Nations, the Plan reflects a justifiable sense of urgency, and an awareness that growing human demands are already exceeding some of the earth's natural limits."

A PRESCRIPTION FOR OPTIMISM OR PESSIMISM?

Neo-Malthusians and cornucopians paint quite different visions of our future. Might both be right? Rapidly expanding populations stress environmental systems, exacerbate poverty, and encourage reproduction to hedge against the future. Economic development, on the other hand, discourages large families, stimulating reduced birthrates and hence declining population growth rates. So, too, do government family-planning policies. Where each of us choose to focus attention—dictated by our perceptual lens—will in turn frame our policy prescriptions.

The world community has made great strides in recent decades in recognizing the complex causes and consequences of rapid population growth. Whether it has the will and shared vision to cope with the problems and expand the possibilities remains to be seen. Meanwhile, an interdependent and rapidly globalizing world promises that none will be immune to world population trends and dynamics. As a prominent American policy analyst (Steinbruner 1995) recently concluded, "Both the scale and composition of [the] population surge [facing the world during the next half-century] will have consequences powerful enough not just to affect, but perhaps even to dominate, conceptions of international security."

KEY TERMS

carrying capacity
tragedy of the commons
ethics
demography
fertility rate
replacement-level fertility
human immunodeficiency virus
    (HIV)
acquired immune deficiency
    syndrome (AIDS)
population momentum

demographic transition
refugees
returnees
internally displaced people
xenophobia
asylum
human rights
atrocities
neo-Malthusians
cornucopians
green revolution

food security
food ladder
Engel's law
ecological overshoot
sustainable development
desertification
gender empowerment index
gender inequalities
gender empowerment

SUGGESTED READING

Buvinić, Mayra. "Women in Poverty: A New Global Underclass," *Foreign Policy* 108 (Fall 1997): 38–52.

Carrying Capacity Network. *The Carrying Capacity Briefing Book*. Washington, D.C.: Carrying Capacity Network, 1997.

Cassen, Robert. *Population Policy: A New Consensus*. Washington, D.C.: Overseas Development Council, 1994.

Castles, Stephen, and Mark J. Miller. *The Age of Migration: International Population Movements in the Modern World*. New York: Guilford, 1993.

Cohen, Joel E. *How Many People Can the Earth Support?* New York: Norton, 1997.

Ehrlich, Paul, Anne H. Ehrlich, and Gretchen C. Daily. *The Stork and the Plow*. New York: Putnam, 1995.

Kritz, Mary M., Lin Lean Lim, and Hania Zlotnik, eds. *International Migration Systems: A Global Approach*. New York: Oxford University Press, 1992.

McKibben, Bill. "The Future of Population: A Special Moment in History," *Atlantic Monthly* 28 (May 1998): 55–78.

Ryan, Frank. *Virus X: Tracking the New Killer Plagues Out of the Present and Into the Future*. Boston: Little, Brown, 1997.

Switzer, Jacqueline Vaughn, with Gary Bryner. *Environmental Politics: Domestic and Global Dimensions*, 2nd ed. New York: St. Martin's Press, 1998.

Watts, Sheldon. *Epidemics and History: Disease, Power, and Imperialism*. New Haven, Conn.: Yale University Press, 1998.

World Bank. *Confronting AIDS: Public Priorities in a Global Epidemic*. New York: Oxford University Press, 1997.

WHERE ON THE WORLD WIDE WEB?

http://www.census.gov/cgi-bin/ipc/popclockw
World POPClock Projection The U.S. Census Bureau's "World Population Clock" projects the world population every second of every day. Once you arrive at this Web page, scan the number of people in the world. Then, hit the "Reload" button on the top of your Web browser. How many more people were born into the world in the time that it took you to *read* the number of people in the world? Click "Reload" again. How many more people were born?

http://www.census.gov/ipc/www/idbnew.html
International Data Base The U.S. Census Bureau offers you the chance to use their computerized data bank to examine the demographic data for all countries of the world. From their homepage you can look at the "Summary Demographic Data" to see totals in population and rates of growth for each country. What is more interesting, however, is to compare countries according to their population pyramids. Click on "IDB Population Pyramids." First, choose the United States. What age groups had the largest concentration of people in 1997? Does this change in the year 2025? What about in the year 2060 (when you will probably be retired)? Is there a big difference between male and female populations? Now, choose a country in Africa. How is the pyramid for your selected country different from the one for the United States? How does it change across time? What conclusions can you draw about the problems each of the countries may face given the number of citizens within different age categories at the different time periods?

http://www2.macroint.com/dhs/
Demographic and Health Surveys Through funds provided by USAID, the Demographic and Health Surveys Program conducts national surveys on fertility, family planning, maternal and child health, and household living conditions. This Web site provides excellent data for each country. When you click on the "Fact Sheets" you will find country-specific information: average level of education of the women interviewed, age when they were married, age when they first gave birth, their desire for children, their knowledge of family planning, and various other areas of interest. Compare and contrast the statistics from countries in Africa, Asia, or the Middle East. Do these figures surprise you?

http://www.womensnet.org/beijing/
Beijing 95: Women, Power, and Change WomensNet brings you a Web site devoted to the implementation and follow-up of the 1995 United Nations' Fourth World Conference on Women. Through this site, interested individuals can read the "Final Report on the Fourth World Conference on Women" or examine the influence that nongovernmental organizations had on the issues presented at the conference and some of the problems they experienced. For an exercise, read the "Platform for Action Summary." Then, examine one of the following issues at length: poverty, education, health, violence, economy, power, armed conflict, human rights, media, environment, or "The Girl Child." Explore the Web links provided to gather more information.

http://www.unicef.org/voy/meeting/fir/girhome.html
Voices of Youth UNICEF has created an interactive Web site so that you can explore the issues and plight of "The Girl Child" as she grows up in the world—if she is allowed to grow up! Then take a quiz, discuss the issues, or learn how to take action.

Ecological Security and the Preservation of the Global Commons

•••
As the world enters the next millennium, human civilization is undergoing profound changes that are often difficult to perceive. Energy use is very much at the foundation of these crucial changes; energy supply and security—and the viability of the electric power industry—will play a large part in determining our planet's future.

—MAURICE F. STRONG, *Chairman, Earth Council, 1997*

•••
It is time to accept firm limits for reducing carbon dioxide to combat global warming. We are all in this together. No country can opt out of global warming or fence in its own private climate.

—TONY BLAIR, *British Prime Minister, 1997*

CHAPTER TOPICS AND THEMES

- Environmental security and sustainable development
- The ecopolitics of energy
- The ecopolitics of the atmosphere
  - Global warming: Its causes and costly consequences
  - The Kyoto Protocol to slow the effects of carbon dioxide and other gases
- The ecopolitics of forests and biodiversity
- Trade, the environment, and sustainable development
- How can environmental security be sustained?

When American astronauts first viewed the earth from the Apollo space-craft, they remarked to millions of listeners about the "blue planet" they saw through their small windows and how the clouds and continents flowed into one another without regard to the political boundaries humans had imposed on a pristine planet. Those images are still often replayed. However, the improvement in space technology has also enabled us to see from afar uncomfortable images—of atmospheric poisons that encircle the globe; of violent winter and summer storms pounding islands and continents with relentless fury; of massive holes in the ozone shield that protects humans from dangerous ultraviolet rays; of vanishing forests and widening deserts. The same satellite technology enables military commanders to target their opponents in warfare, in order to defend national borders.

Warfare can clearly be laid at the doorstep of humankind. Are environmental problems also our doing? Is the growth in world population during this century and projected for the next responsible for recurrent and irrefutable images of a global environment under stress? Or are the consumption patterns of the world's wealthy the primary culprits? There is no consensus on these issues, as explained in Chapter 10. Not surprisingly, then, there is no more consensus on how states ought to respond to rapid environmental change than on how they should deal with profound demographic, economic, and political transformations.

This chapter explores global environmental challenges and responses to them, broadly described in the concept of **ecopolitics**—the intersection of ecology and politics. Ecology deals with the impact of human activity on the environment. Politics, as we have seen, is concerned with the exercise of power. Ecopolitics, then, centers on how political actors influence perceptions of, and policy responses to, their environments.

Peoples and states today face a broad range of environmental and resource challenges. This discussion will cover a limited yet representative sample including issues related to nonrenewable resources, common properties, and renewable resources—in seeking to understand how ecology and politics interact to shape our future. Not surprisingly politics emerges as a powerful force that permeates all dimensions of environmental and resource issues, ranging from the evaluation of scientific evidence to prescriptions for dealing with that evidence. The text goes on to examine the alternative strategies states have adopted for coping with environmental stress in an anarchical international system and how environmental issues are linked to other values that states prize, notably security and economic and social well-being.

• • •

ENVIRONMENTAL SECURITY AND SUSTAINABLE DEVELOPMENT: AN OVERVIEW

"Security" means freedom from fear. It also means freedom from risk and danger. During the Cold War, fear of nuclear holocaust haunted much of the world. Security was equated with "national security," which typically connoted freedom from the fear, risk, and danger posed by the threat of war. This required the development of national strategies for coping with the struggle for power

National Security and Environmental Security
Competing or Complementary?

The traditional concept of national security that evolved during the Cold War viewed security as a function of the successful pursuit of interstate power competition. . . . Environmental security represents a significant departure from this approach to national security. It addresses two distinct issues: the environmental factors behind potentially violent conflicts, and the impact of global environmental degradation on the well-being of societies and economies. The idea that environmental degradation is a security issue when it is a cause of violent conflict appears to be consistent with the traditional definition of national security. However, . . . [the] focus on threats that do not involve an enemy state or political entity disturbs many theorists and practitioners of national security, for whom the only issues that should be viewed as "security" issues are those that revolve around conflict itself. . . .

The case for environmental security rests primarily on evidence that there has been serious degradation of natural resources (fresh water, soils, forests, fishery resources, and biological diversity) and vital life-support systems (the ozone layer, climate system, oceans, and atmosphere) as a result of the recent acceleration of global economic activities. These global physical changes could have far-reaching effects in the long run.

Each of these environmental threats to global well-being is subject to significant empirical and scientific uncertainty. . . . The uncertainties . . . are comparable, however, to those associated with most military threats that national security establishments prepare for. Military planning is based on "worst-case" contingencies that are considered relatively unlikely to occur, yet military preparations for such contingencies are justified as a necessary insurance policy or "hedge" against uncertainty. . . .

The relationship between scarce natural resources and international conflict is not a new issue. But unlike traditional national security thinking about such conflict, which focuses on nonrenewable resources like minerals and petroleum, the environmental security approach addresses renewable resources—those that need not be depleted if managed sustainably.

SOURCE: Porter (1995), 218–20.

central to realist thinking. Today many analysts urge a broader conception of what constitutes security at both the state and global levels.

One view suggests that threats to national security should encompass actions or events that "degrade the quality of life for the inhabitants of a state . . . or narrow the range of policy choices available to the government of a state or . . . private, nongovernmental entities (persons, groups, corporations) within the state" (Ullman 1983). This is the politics of scarcity, which predicts that future international conflict will likely be caused by resource scarcities—restricted access to food, oil, and water, for example, rather than by overt military challenges.

Compelling as this unconventional viewpoint may be, scarcity continues to be studied primarily from a state-centric ecopolitical perspective. To broaden the definition of national security, pushing our vision beyond borders and their protection, **environmental security** is a useful concept. Focusing on the transboundary character of challenges to preserving the global environment, it recognizes that "threats to global life systems such as global warming, ozone depletion, and the loss of tropical forests and marine habitats are just as important to the future of humankind as the threat of nuclear catastrophe" (Porter and Brown 1996) (see Focus 11.1). Because environmental degradation undercuts states' economic well-being and the quality of life all governments seek for their citizens, it invites a **neoliberal** interpretation of how states can cooperate with IGOs and NGOs to cope with environmental challenges (Zacher and Matthew 1995). Because the effort by the neoliberal **epistemic community** to redefine security moves beyond realism's popular state-centric fundamental conceptions of world politics, the enterprise is understandably controversial.

Global environmental issues pose another controversy, one that engages the competing perspectives of cornucopians and neo-Malthusians. Cornucopians believe that if free markets and free trade are practiced, ecological imbalances that threaten humankind will be corrected. For them, prices are the key adjustment mechanism that in time produces the greatest good for the greatest number. Neo-Malthusians, on the other hand, share more in common with liberal internationalists and mercantilists. For them, markets' failure to account for the cost of excessive exploitation of both renewable and nonrenewable resources requires intervention by nonmarket agents. More fundamentally, it requires revision of the "dominant social paradigm," which says "first, that the free market will always maximize social welfare, and second, that there is not only an infinite supply of natural resources but also of 'sinks' for disposing the wastes from exploiting those resources. . . . Humans will not deplete any resource, according to this world view, as long as technology is given free rein and prices are allowed to fluctuate enough to stimulate the search for substitutes, so absolute scarcity can be postponed to the indefinite future" (Porter and Brown 1996).

The dominant social paradigm—a view shared by cornucopians—is under serious attack by environmental activists. It is also under attack internationally. **Sustainable development** is now perceived as an alternative to unlimited growth, a concept that enjoys widespread support among governments and a broad range of NGOs that are particularly active in shaping the global environmental agenda. Its heritage is traceable to *Our Common Future,* the 1987 report of the World Commission on Environment and Development, popularly known as the Brundtland Commission after the Norwegian prime minister who chaired it. The commission concluded that the world cannot sustain the growth required to meet the needs and aspirations of the world's growing population unless it adopts radically different approaches to basic issues of economic expansion, equity, resource management, energy efficiency, and the like. Rejecting the "limits of growth" maxim popular among neo-Malthusians during the 1970s, it emphasized instead "the growth of limits." The commission defined a "sustainable society" as one that "meets the needs of the present without compromising the ability of future generations to meet their own needs."

The Brundtland Commission report is an important landmark in the rapid emergence of environmental issues as global concerns. The process began in earnest in 1972, when the UN General Assembly convened the first United Nations Conference on the Human Environment in Stockholm. Conferences have since been held on a wide range of environmental topics, with scores of environmental treaties negotiated and new international agencies put into place to promote cooperation and monitor environmental developments (Haas, Keohane, and Levy 1993).

A second milestone in the challenge to the dominant social paradigm is the **Earth Summit,** which took place in Rio de Janeiro, Brazil, in 1992—the twentieth anniversary of the Stockholm conference on the environment. Formally known as the United Nations Conference on Environment and Development (UNCED), the meeting brought together more than 150 states, fourteen hundred

The Making of an Ecological Disaster
The Aral Sea

The Aral Sea [in Central Asia] is dying. Because of the huge diversions of water that have taken place during the past thirty years, particularly for irrigation, the volume of the sea has been reduced by two-thirds. The sea's surface has been sharply diminished, the water in the sea and in surrounding aquifers has become increasingly saline, and the water supplies and health of almost fifty million people in the Aral Sea basin are threatened. Vast areas of salty flatlands have been exposed as the sea has receded, and salt from these areas is being blown across the plains onto neighboring cropland and pastures, causing ecological damage. The frost-free period in the delta of the Amu Dacrya River, which feeds the Aral Sea, has fallen to less than 180 days—below the minimum required for growing cotton, the region's main cash crop. The changes in the sea have effectively killed a substantial fishing industry, and the variety of fauna in the region has declined drastically. If current trends continue unchecked, the sea would eventually shrink to a saline lake one-sixth its 1960 size.

This ecological disaster is the consequence of excessive abstraction of water for irrigation purposes from the Amu Dacrya and Syr Dacrya rivers, which feed the Aral Sea. Total river runoff into the sea fell from an average fifty-five cubic kilometers a year in the 1950s to zero in the early 1980s. The irrigation schemes have been a mixed blessing for the populations of the Central Asian republics—Kazakhstan, Kyrghyz- stan, Tajikistan, Turkmenistan, and Uzbekistan—which they serve. The diversion of water has provided livelihoods for the region's farmers, but at considerable environmental cost. Soils have been poisoned with salt, overwatering has turned pastureland into bogs, water supplies have become polluted by pesticide and fertilizer residues, and the deteriorating quality of drinking water and sanitation is taking a heavy toll on human health. While it is easy to see how the problem of the Aral Sea might have been avoided, solutions are difficult. . . .

. . . The Central Asian republics (except for Kazakhstan) are poor: their incomes are 65 percent of the average in the former Soviet Union. . . . The regional population of thirty-five million is growing rapidly, at 2.7 percent a year, and infant mortality is high. The states have become dependent on a specialized but unsustainable pattern of agriculture. Irrigated production of cotton, grapes, fruit, and vegetables accounts for the bulk of export earnings. Any rapid reduction in the use of irrigation water will reduce living standards still further unless these economies receive assistance to help them diversify away from irrigated agriculture. Meanwhile, salinization and dust storms erode the existing land under irrigation. This is one of the starkest examples of the need to combine development with sound environmental policy.

SOURCE: *World Development Report 1992* (1992), 38.

nongovernmental organizations, and some eight thousand journalists. A program of action agreed on at Rio, *Agenda 21*, embodies a political commitment to a broad range of environmental and development goals. Prior to the Earth Summit, the environment and development had been treated separately—and often regarded as being in conflict with each other, as development frequently imperils and degrades the environment (see Focus 11.2). Now the concept of *sustainability* galvanized a simultaneous treatment of environmental and development issues. Recognition of the interrelatedness of global welfare issues continued at the 1994 Cairo International Conference on Population and Development (ICPD), where population and development were again placed on the same track. Acceptance of the proposition that all politics—even global politics—are local, and that protection of the earth's environment is a primary international security issue, was reaffirmed at the 1997 **"Rio Plus Five" UN Earth Summit**. A warming, polluted globe requires a global remedy, and for that reason environmental security is an issue destined to stay atop the twenty-first century global agenda.

Deforestation and inappropriate farming techniques often lead to degradation of soils, causing excessive erosion and desertification, as shown in the left-hand picture. Appropriate farming techniques, such as Indonesia's traditional methods of terracing farmlands illustrated on the right, can limit the damage, even in a densely populated and growing society.

Because sustainability means living off the earth's interest without encroaching on its capital, it draws attention to meeting current needs without depriving future generations of the resources necessary for their survival. Literally hundreds of books and articles have asked how this ambitious goal can be achieved. A common thread throughout this literature is that sustainability cannot be realized without dramatic changes in the social, economic, and political fabric of the world as we now know it. Is that possible? Are individuals willing to sacrifice personal welfare for the common good? Will they sacrifice now to enrich their heirs? The **tragedy of the commons** metaphor, described in Chapter 10, provides little basis for optimism, whether applied to individuals or states, because greed by some in the absence of regulation leads to everyone's destruction. Add to this the anarchical structure of the international system—which, as noted in Chapter 8, discourages states from cooperating with one another out of fear that some will gain more than others—and it becomes clear that while environmental issues and challenges often transcend national boundaries, they remain hostage to institutions too week to effectively manage the threat to global security and welfare.

To better understand the multiple tensions that global environmental problems pose in an anarchical world and how competing perceptions of security and markets shape responses to them, we turn our attention to three interrelated clusters of problems on the global ecopolitical agenda: oil and energy, climate change and ozone depletion, and biodiversity and deforestation. The first involves conflict over a scarce, nonrenewable resource in the tradition of commonplace definitions of national security. The other two broaden the net to encompass what many analysts regard as threats to environmental security within the **global commons.** The latter two clusters illustrate the problems and pitfalls that state and nonstate actors face as they seek sustainable development of common properties and renewable resources. Following this we will examine the controversy surrounding the impact of international trade on sustainable development.

THE ECOPOLITICS OF ENERGY

In April 1990, the average price for a barrel of internationally traded crude oil was less than fifteen dollars. Five months later—stimulated by Iraq's invasion of the tiny oil sheikdom of Kuwait—it was more than forty dollars. For the third time in less than two decades, the world suffered an "oil shock" as the price paid for the most widely used commercial energy source skyrocketed.

Oil and National Security

The Persian Gulf War underscored the importance of oil to the economic security of states dependent on foreign energy supplies and hence to their national security. For example, U.S. President George Bush—under whose multilateral leadership Iraq's aggression was foiled—never openly admitted that oil was the main reason for his decision to oppose Iraq's Saddam Hussein, but he did acknowledge that short-sighted energy policies had made the United States unduly dependent on Middle Eastern oil to fuel its industrial economy.

Oil also figured prominently in Iraq's own security calculations and hence in Saddam Hussein's decision to invade Kuwait. Iraq's eight-year war with Iran, which ended in 1988, had caused severe domestic economic dislocations and a mounting foreign debt burden. Lower oil prices, caused in part by increased production by other OPEC members, made it more difficult for Iraq to meet its obligations. The Iraqi dictator turned to aggression as a quick fix for his country's economic ills by attempting to seize the vast wealth of Kuwait, including its $100 billion in foreign assets. Political goals also motivated Saddam Hussein, including his aspiration to dominate the Arab world. Thus, control over Kuwaiti oil was a means to an end as well as an end in itself. The effort once more plunged the Middle East into open warfare, causing worldwide alarm that mobilized nearly forty countries to support the UN-authorized military response to Iraq's aggression.

The Persian Gulf War culminated two decades of Middle Eastern turmoil in which access to its valued energy resources often figured prominently. That concern remains. Indeed, it is not an exaggeration to suggest that prospects for global prosperity and peace depend on the preservation of order in the volatile Middle East, whose oil is especially critical to the economic fortunes of the Global North. Ensuring access to the region's oil is thus a national security priority for the developed countries. At issue is the ability to protect the region's vast oil fields from terrorist or other attacks, to avert a repetition of the internal political disruptions that have often plagued the region, and to secure the sea lanes along which oil is shipped.

Global Patterns of Energy Consumption

The criticality of oil to the Global North generally and the United States in particular is evident from the disproportionate share of world energy resources they consume. Europe uses more than twice as much energy per capita as the Global South, while Canada and the United States use more than six times as much (*BP Statistical Review of World Energy* 1995, 36). The differences parallel the gap between the world's rich and poor countries, apparent on so many other dimensions of contemporary world politics.

Because energy consumption is critical to the production of goods and services, it is closely correlated with changes in economic activity. From the 1930s to the 1980s, the world's demand for energy increased at almost the same rate as did the aggregate world gross domestic product, reflecting the industrial countries' substitution of energy for labor to facilitate production and transportation. Energy efficiencies typically differed widely among the industrial countries. The United States in particular, whose energy policies depressed the price of energy below its true cost, became not only the most profligate energy consumer but also the most inefficient. Japan and Europe continue to use energy more efficiently today than does the United States. The pattern is evident elsewhere, where other states with similar economic profiles also exhibit widely different energy use patterns. On the whole, however, the world (including the United States) has made great strides since the oil crises of the 1970s and early 1980s in the efficiency with which it uses nonrenewable energy resources.

Despite increased efficiency, demand for oil continues its upward spiral. Use of oil hit an all-time high of 3.3 billion tons (64 million barrels per day) in 1996, as rising global demand pushed prices above $20 a barrel for the first time since the Gulf War. The increase of global demand for fossil fuels, which provide about 85 percent of the world's commercial energy (*Vital Signs 1997*, 46), was spurred in large measure by the Global South, which sees energy as the key to its economic development and higher standards of living (see Figure 11.1). The inescapable if uncomfortable fact is that rising affluence and growing populations in the Global South will propel rising demand for energy from fossil fuels even if per-capita levels of consumption remain unchanged. Urbanization will also play a role, with a greater use of motor vehicles accounting for much

FIGURE 11.1

World Oil Demand, 1994 and 2010

World demand for oil is expected to surge by one-third between 1994 and 2010, growing from 68 million barrels per day to 91 million barrels. Most of the growth in demand will come from the Global South, which will soon consume more than two-fifths of world oil supplies.

SOURCE: *World Economic and Social Survey 1995* (1995), 168.

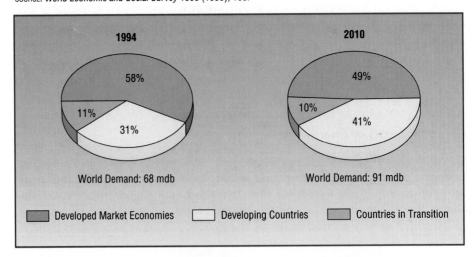

of the increase in the demand for oil. The demand for energy exerted by economic growth in Asia will be especially strong. Oil consumption in the region surpassed that of western Europe in 1994 and will surpass North American consumption within a decade (*World Economic and Social Survey 1995* 1995).

As demand for oil and other commercial energy grows in the Global South, the environmental consequences may prove dire. This concern underlies the indisputable fact that the world's dependence on fossil fuels is a critical cause of many environmental stresses that the world now faces. How did we get into this situation?

Oil Becomes King

Little more than a century ago, fuelwood was the principal energy source. As the mechanical revolution altered the nature of transportation, work, and leisure, coal began to replace fuelwood. Early in the twentieth century, coal became the dominant source of energy throughout the world. New technological developments, particularly the internal combustion engine, then spurred the shift away from coal to oil and, somewhat less so, natural gas. The United States, well endowed with petroleum resources, led the development of oil-based technologies, above all in the automotive and petrochemical industries. Oil now rapidly outpaced coal as the main energy source, and dependence on oil began its rapid rise.

In 1950, when world population stood at roughly 2.5 billion people, world energy consumption was 2.5 billion tons of coal-equivalent energy. Although population increased rapidly during the next quarter-century, energy use increased almost twice as fast, stimulating rapid economic growth (Brown 1979). Rapidly rising production made oil the world's principal source of commercial energy. Everywhere the reasons for the shift to oil were the same: It was cleaner and less expensive than coal. From the end of the Korean War until the early 1970s, world oil prices actually declined compared with the prices of other commodities.

Despite growing dependence on oil, the long-term stability of world oil prices is striking. As Figure 11.2 shows, World War I was followed by a notable spike in the price of oil. Otherwise its price remained stable during this century. As the price of other commodities and manufactured goods rose, oil became relatively cheaper. It therefore made good economic sense to use it in large quantities.

A small group of multinational corporations (known as the "majors") were the chief actors in propelling the worldwide shift from coal to oil. Their operations encompassed every aspect of the business, from exploration to the retail sales of products at their gas stations. Their search for, production of, and marketing of low-cost oil were largely unhindered. Concessions from countries in the oil-rich Middle East and elsewhere were easy to get. The communist states were virtually the only oil-producing countries that barred them. The oil companies were thus able to maintain the price of oil at a level profitable for themselves, even though it declined relative to other commodities. An abundant supply of oil at low prices facilitated the recovery of western Europe and Japan from World War II and encouraged consumers to use energy-intensive technologies, such as the private automobile. An enormous growth in the world-wide demand for and consumption of energy followed.

The continuing search for and exploitation of new oil deposits were needed to meet the high growth in demand. The incentives for developing petroleum

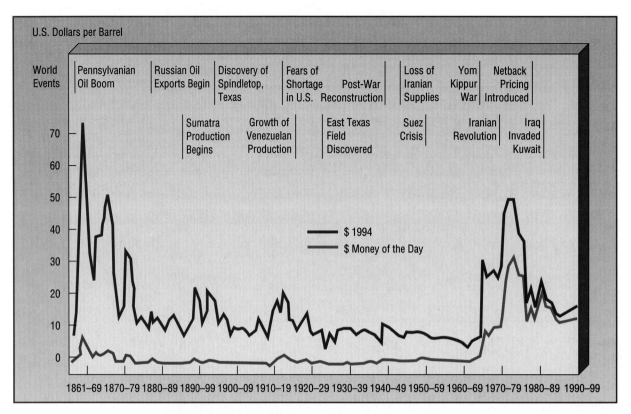

FIGURE 11.2

Crude Oil Prices since 1861

World oil prices have remained comparatively steady during this century, thus reducing the cost of oil relative to other commodities. The two oil shocks of the 1970s and 1980s caused a sharp upturn in oil prices, which then receded until 1996.

SOURCE: *BP Statistical Review of World Energy* (1995), 12; *Vital Signs 1997*, 46; *Economist* (March 28, 1998), 17–18.

reserves outside the Middle East waned, however, as the real cost of oil failed to keep pace with increases in the cost of other commodities, goods, and services. And incentives for developing technologies for alternative energy sources, such as coal, were virtually nonexistent. Eventually this contributed to the rise of OPEC as an important actor in the energy market, as alternatives to the resources it controlled could not easily be replaced. For nearly a decade—until the global price of oil plunged sharply in the mid-1980s—the oil cartel was a pivotal actor not only in energy markets but also in the world political economy generally.

Running on Empty: Is Energy Security an Elusive Goal?

Oil will play the principal role in the global energy picture well into the next century and perhaps beyond. This raises questions about OPEC's potential future role as a price setter and production leader. The historical record leads us to be cautious in predicting the cartel's future role, but signs point toward its continuing importance. The threat is not that another oil crisis is inevitable soon, because although oil is an exhaustible energy resource, it is unlikely that scarcities will develop in the near future. Comfort can be taken in the fact that "historically, additions to global oil reserves have outpaced production" (Emerson 1997).

> The problem is not that we are about to "run out" of oil. The problem is that the world's conventional oil resources are concentrated in relatively few countries who are able to manipulate the economic scarcity of oil to their advantage and to the disadvantage of other countries and who have done so in the past. Our best estimates of the totality of the world's conventional oil resources indicate that OPEC countries own more than half of them. Published, credible estimates of OPEC's share range from a low of 55 percent to a high of 64 percent. The difference is due to greater optimism on the part of analysts at the US Geological Survey about the extent of petroleum resources in the former Soviet Union and, to a lesser extent, in the United States, Canada, Mexico, and China.
>
> Because OPEC members are drawing down their reserves at half the rate of the rest of the world's oil producers, it seems almost inevitable that OPEC's share of the world oil market will grow. For example, the US Energy Information Administration predicts that OPEC's share of the world oil market will rise from its current level of 42 percent to reach 48 percent by 2005, and will climb to 52 percent by 2010. (Greene 1997, 18)

These trends mean that OPEC is critical to global oil supply, the Middle East is critical to OPEC, and countries such as the United States that depend on oil imports from this volatile, instable source to fuel their growth are highly vulnerable to disruptions.

Despite sensitivity to OPEC's past and potential future role, it is noteworthy that world oil prices remained comparatively low following the Persian Gulf War, despite the embargo of Iraqi oil and the reduction in exports from the former Soviet Union caused by the collapse of much of its productive capability. Those price trends may persist. Based on technological developments that have reduced the cost of finding new oil deposits, "oil production could rise another 20–30 percent before peaking sometime between 2005 and 2015. Major, sustained price increases appear unlikely . . . barring a political cataclysm in the Middle East" (*Vital Signs 1997*, 46). However, whereas this forecast is good news for individual consumers and the world political economy in the short run, it does little to pave the way toward a postpetroleum energy system. Nor does it alleviate states' security concerns because of the unequal distribution of proven and prospective oil reserves. The security challenge arises not simply from the possibility of another episode of supply and price disruptions like those caused by the first oil shock in 1973–1974, but also from the chronic balance-of-payments and debt problems caused by dependence on foreign energy sources. It is noteworthy that many of the most indebted countries in the Global South are also those most heavily dependent on imported energy.

Oil derived from unconventional sources (such as tar sands and shale) and renewable forms of energy (such as solar, tidal, and wind power; geothermal energy; and bioconversion) are among the alternatives to oil that may someday become viable technologically and economically. Their development would reduce dependence on oil from the volatile Middle East and reduce anxieties over possible scarcity. However, the comparatively low price of oil—and its projected stability—discourages their development. Meanwhile, coal, natural gas,

FIGURE 11.3

Ratio of Fossil-Fuel Reserves to Production

At 1994 levels of production, world coal reserves will last much longer than those for oil or natural gas—until about 2040, because the continuing discovery of new reserves can be expected to outpace the world's steady increases in production and consumption.

SOURCE: *BP Statistical Review of World Energy* (1995), 36.

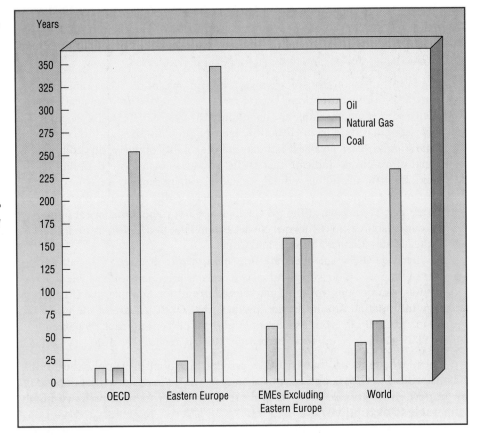

hydropower, and nuclear power are the principal alternatives to oil. Each, however, faces economic and political uncertainties and poses its own environmental risks.

Coal. Coal is the chief fossil-fuel alternative to oil. Based on the current ratio of reserves to production, oil will last only until about 2040, but coal will last for more than two centuries (see Figure 11.3). Coal now accounts for 27 percent of the world's primary energy use, compared with 40 percent for oil and 23 percent for natural gas.

Although trade in coal increased sharply during the 1980s, most is consumed where it is produced, making it less susceptible to supply disruptions than oil. China, the United States, and the former Soviet Union account for nearly 60 percent of world coal reserves and are its largest consumers. China tops the list; to fuel its rapid economic expansion, China's coal use has risen 50 percent since 1985, and coal now accounts for three-fourths of the country's total commercial energy supply.

Although the use of coal increased sharply in the aftermath of the first oil shock, the social costs—known as **externalities**—associated with its widespread use are substantial. Coal is a major pollutant of the atmosphere, for example, as it contributes heavily to the acidification of precipitation and to the release of carbon that contributes to global warming. As a result of environ-

externalities the side effects produced by economic activities, especially costs such as pollution.

mental concerns and tighter regulations, coal is an unattractive alternative to oil worldwide. Nonetheless, in some countries, such as China, it is still a major energy source, sparking the ire of those who must bear the consequences.

Natural Gas. Natural gas is cleaner and more convenient to use than either oil or coal (see Flavin 1992). Based on the current ratio of reserves to production, natural gas supplies will last for more than sixty years. Unlike coal, however, natural gas is distributed very unevenly on a regional basis, which means that its continued development will depend on export trade.

The two largest natural gas markets are the United States and Russia. In 1994 the two countries consumed, respectively, 29 percent and 18 percent of production. Russia is also a major producer of gas and possesses the largest reserves, with 34 percent of the world's proven reserves in 1994. The United States, on the other hand, has less than 4 percent of world reserves (*BP Statistical Review of World Energy* 1995, 18). Historically the United States has met virtually all of its need for gas from domestic sources. It seems likely, though, that it will have to look increasingly to imports to sustain its high demand. As with oil, the Middle East is a likely source, as it holds nearly one-third of the world's proven reserves but consumes only 6 percent of world production.

Getting gas from the wellhead to consumers is a primary problem. Pipelines are the preferred method of transport, but they are massive and expensive engineering projects that also pose environmental dangers and thus encounter resistance. Liquefied natural gas is an alternative—perhaps the only one for transshipment from the Middle East to North America or to the growing European and Japanese markets—but experts disagree about its safety. That concern, combined with cost considerations and sensitivity to dependence on OPEC sources, has limited the development of liquefied natural gas. Still, because natural gas produces considerably less carbon emissions than either coal or oil, its attractiveness will grow, providing incentives to increase its use throughout the world.

Wind, Water, Earth, and Sun. Wind power, the fastest growing energy source in the 1990s, is expanding by 25 percent a year, but still generates less than 1 percent of the globe's electricity. This technology appears likely to improve as new wind turbines become available. In contrast, hydropower, which harnesses water to generate electricity and now supplies one-fifth of the world's electricity (Brown et al. 1998, 179–80), has the great advantage of not contributing to pollution. However, limits on water availability, prohibitive financial costs, and controversies about land management and soil loss due to dam construction restrict hydropower development as an alternative to fossil fuels. This is the primary reason that water-generated electricity accounts for less than 3 percent of global energy use. Geothermal energy—heat from the center of the earth—is costly but growing as another energy source; 250 power plants supply more than seven thousand megawatts of electricity in twenty-two countries, which, nonetheless, is less than 1 percent of the world's total power. Finally, the use of **photovoltaic (PV) cells**—semiconductors that convert sunlight into electricity—has expanded rapidly in the 1990s as new technology has reduced the cost of this clean energy source. Solar-cell energy provides more than ninety megawatts of electricity worldwide, and this nonpolluting source is particularly efficient in supplying energy in developing countries where approximately 2 billion people live without access to electricity (*Vital Signs 1997*, 48–55).

Wind, water, earth, and sun thus seem destined to grow as sources for meeting the globe's increasing need for energy, despite the great financial expenses for their continued development.

Nuclear Energy. In 1996 436 nuclear reactors throughout the world provided about 7 percent of the globe's energy, and an additional thirty-seven new reactors were under construction (while eighty-six were dismantled). Those in operation combined to generate 343,586 megawatts of energy, with the highest consumption in the United States, followed by France, Japan, and Russia (*Vital Signs 1997*, 48; U.S. CIA 1997, 107).

Among known technologies, nuclear energy was once seen as the leading alternative to fossil-fuel dependence, but that is no longer the case. Technical and financial problems have forced some countries to reduce or abandon their programs, and in others the political climate has turned markedly against nuclear power, with safety a principal point of contention. Three well-publicized nuclear accidents—in the United States at the Three Mile Island nuclear power plant in Pennsylvania in 1979, at Chernobyl in Ukraine in 1986, and at the Monju fast breeder reactor in Japan in 1995—dramatized the risks and seemed to vindicate the skeptics who had warned of the dangers posed by nuclear energy.

Catastrophe was averted at Three Mile Island, but even without the threatened meltdown of the reactor core, the accident released the largest-ever level of radioactive contamination by the U.S. commercial nuclear industry. At Chernobyl, however, catastrophe did strike. Thousands are believed to have been killed; hundreds of thousands were forced to evacuate their homes; and the radioactive fallout—"the equivalent of ten Hiroshima bombs"—"left a swath of agricultural land the size of Holland permanently poisoned" (Dobbs 1991, 10). Radioactive fallout spread beyond the Ukraine as well, multiplying the geographical scope and number of those ravaged by the catastrophe and its long-term consequences. Nine years after the disaster, it was estimated that "Chernobyl will be the longest, most high-tech and expensive environmental cleanup the world has attempted—costing billions of dollars and taking perhaps one hundred years to complete" (Rupert 1995). And in Japan, political support for nuclear power has steadily fallen since the Monju accident.

Concerns about the risks of nuclear power extend beyond the safety of nuclear energy as a means of generating electricity. How and where to dispose of highly radioactive nuclear wastes, for example, is a contentious and unresolved issue virtually everywhere. No safe procedure for handling radioactive nuclear waste—some of which remains dangerous for hundreds of thousands of years—has yet been devised. In the meantime, large quantities have accumulated, posing a substantial threat to environmental safety. The end of the Cold War has compounded the issue, as the dismantling of both nuclear weapons and the facilities that produced them requires means of disposal. The cry of local communities is often "not in my back yard" (NIMBY is the popular acronym). The issue is no less contentious internationally, as disposal of nuclear and other toxic wastes figures prominently on the global ecopolitical agenda as a divisive issue between the Global North (which prefers to dump wastes outside its own territory) and the Global South (which would prefer not to be the dump—but often is).

A related fear is that countries that do not now possess nuclear know-how might acquire it, thus gaining the means to develop nuclear weapons.

While proliferation is essentially a national security issue, it is linked technologically to nuclear power production for peaceful purposes. Nuclear-generating facilities produce weapons-grade material, specifically highly enriched uranium and plutonium. Neither of these materials, which can be used to create a nuclear weapon, is used commercially as fuel in the current generation of nuclear power reactors. Still, the fear persists that eventually weapons-grade material will place within reach the construction of tens of thousands of nuclear bombs. It was this concern that prompted the United States (with the help of South Korea and Japan) to give North Korea—a longtime political-military adversary—nuclear reactors less susceptible to nuclear weapons production than the path North Korea was following in its indigenous nuclear program.

The brief exploration of the "energy problematique" demonstrates the centrality of the politics of scarcity in contemporary world politics. In an environmentally interdependent world without strong global governing institutions, where actions anywhere have external costs almost everywhere, the challenge of managing the global commons has reached unprecedented levels. Common property resources and their preservation *will* be a core concern and security issue in the twenty-first century.

• • •

THE ECOPOLITICS OF THE ATMOSPHERE

The scores of government negotiators and nongovernmental representatives who converged on Rio de Janeiro in 1992 came in the wake of the hottest decade on record. For years scientists had warned that **global warming**—the gradual rise in world temperature—would cause destructive changes in world climatological patterns and that rising sea levels, melting glaciers, and freak storms would provoke widespread changes in the globe's political and economic systems and relationships. Perhaps because they had been burned by the heat of the 1980s, negotiators agreed at Rio to a Framework Convention on Climate Change whose purpose was to address the human causes of climate change by reducing emissions of carbon dioxide and other "greenhouse" gases.

Three years later, new data and technology narrowed the disagreement about the important questions concerning the extent of climate change, and two thousand of the world's top climate scientists concluded that the balance of evidence showed a discernible human influence. In response, in December 1997 more than 160 governments sent representatives to Kyoto, Japan to negotiate a new agreement to curb the pollutants blamed for global warming.

Climate Change

Although major gaps in knowledge remain, few climate scientists think the world can afford to wait for answers. The changes are substantial, and threatening. Most scientists believe that the gradual rise in the earth's temperature, especially evident since the onset of the industrial revolution, is caused by an increase in human-made gases released into the atmosphere, altering its insulating effects. The atmosphere permits radiation from the sun to penetrate to the earth, but gas molecules form the equivalent of a greenhouse roof by trapping heat remitted from earth that would otherwise escape into outer space.

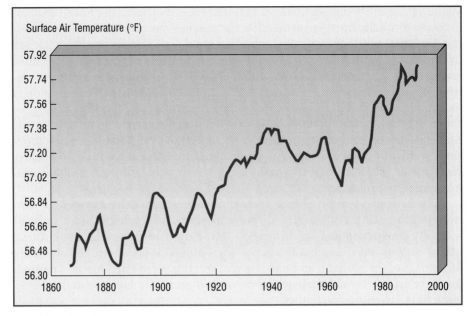

FIGURE 11.4

Courting Disaster as a Global Heat Wave Warms the Earth: How Temperatures Have Risen since 1860

The World Meteorological Organization (WMO) monitors average global surface temperatures at thousands of sites around the world, and its records strongly indicate that so-called global warming is not a myth. For nearly 150 years, the globe's temperature has seesawed up and down, usually by tiny fractions of degrees. But since the mid-1970s, the mercury has largely been on the rise, and the WMO predicts that the average global surface temperature could jump 3.6 degrees by the end of the twenty-first century—more than triple the rise of the past one hundred years.

Note: Five-year averages of global temperatures.

SOURCE: Repetto and Lash, World Resources Institute, *Foreign Policy* (Fall 1997), 93.

Carbon dioxide (CO_2) accounts for the bulk of **greenhouse gases,** with chlorofluorocarbons (CFCs) composing much of the rest. As the amount of these gases released into the atmosphere has grown, the global temperature has risen. As shown in Figure 11.4, the temperature of the atmosphere at the earth's surface has increased nearly a half degree since 1950, and nine of the hottest years since record keeping began in 1866 have occurred since 1987, with 1997 the warmest of the century (Warrick 1997).

The globe's temperature is now between 0.3 and 0.6 degrees Celsius higher than it was in 1880, and is projected to further increase by 3.5 degrees Celsius by 2100 if preventive action is not taken (Soroos 1998, 475). Although carbon dioxide is the principal greenhouse gas, concentrations of methane in the atmosphere are growing more rapidly. Methane gas emissions arise from livestock populations, rice cultivation, and the production and transportation of natural gas. Interestingly, the largest concentrations of methane are not in the atmosphere but locked in ice, permafrost, and coastal marine sediments. This raises the possibility that warming will cause more methane to be released into the atmosphere, which would then reinforce the process because of methane's strong warming potential.

Since some greenhouse gases stay aloft for long periods and because the oceans store a huge amount of heat, warming will continue and persist irreversibly for centuries even after accumulation stops. Consequently, the observable change in the climate, at any time before equilibrium is restored, will be much less than what emissions up to that point have made inevitable. Put simply, the climate problem will always be worse than it appears to be. (Repetto and Lash 1997, 85)

Critics of the thesis that human activity causes global warming believe that the rise in global temperature is part of the cyclical pattern changes the world has experienced for tens of thousands of years. That view has been steadily discredited, however. Since 1988, hundreds of atmospheric scientists from around the world organized several United Nations agencies to study global climate change. The team, known as the **Intergovernmental Panel on Climate Change (IPCC),** first conclusively stated in 1995 its belief that global climate trends are "likely to be entirely due to natural causes," that humans are to blame for at least part of the problem, and that the consequences are likely to be very harmful and costly. The implications were self-evident: Without significant efforts to reduce the emission of greenhouse gases, global temperatures could rise by as much as 6 degrees Fahrenheit by the year 2100, a huge increase equivalent to that which ended the last ice age. Even at the lower end of its estimates (1.4 degrees Fahrenheit), the rise would be faster than any experienced in recorded human history.

According to the IPCC, the world has already entered a period of climatic instability likely to cause "widespread economic, social, and environmental dislocation over the 21st century." The effects of continued temperature rises could be both dramatic and devastating:

- Sea levels could rise up to three feet, mostly because of melting glaciers and the expansion of water as it warms up. That will flood vast areas of low-lying coastal land, including major river deltas; most of the beaches on the U.S. Atlantic Coast; part of China; and the Maldives island, the Seychelles, and the Cook and Marshall islands. More than 1 million people could be displaced, and 30 million would be put at risk of at least one flood per year.

- Winters would get warmer . . .warm-weather hot spells such as the 1995 summer heat wave that killed five hundred people in Chicago would become more frequent and more severe.

- Rainfall would increase globally, but only the areas already prone to flooding would flood more often and more severely, with freak storms such as the 1997 El Niño surge of storms in the Pacific and the 1997 flooding in the Dakotas becoming more common. Since water evaporates more easily in a warmer world, drought-prone regions would become even dryer. As oceans heat, hurricanes, which draw their energy from warm oceans, would become even stronger.

- Entire ecosystems would vanish from the planet, and a hotter earth would drive some plants to higher latitudes and altitudes and require farmers to irrigate and change their crops and agriculture practices.

- The combination of flooding and droughts will cause tropical diseases such as malaria and dengue fever to flourish in previously temperate regions that were formerly too cold for their insect carriers.

Climate-Change Culprits. It is clear that the politics of agreements to reduce the threat of global warming are charged because the economics and financial stakes are enormous and every proposal generates stiff opposition. However, the basic physical dynamics behind the problem are rather simple. Carbon dioxide emissions are the principal culprits in global warming. That is, when released through combustion to generate energy, carbon reacts with oxygen to form the carbon dioxide (CO_2) greenhouse gas that traps heat in the atmosphere, which in turn makes surface temperatures rise.

CO_2 emissions from the burning of fossil fuels have climbed steadily, rising fourfold since 1950. The industrial Global North states generally are the principal sources of global carbon emissions, accounting for 73 percent of global CO_2 emissions (*Fortune* December 8, 1997, 113); the United States emits more CO_2 into the atmosphere than any other state. In large measure because of its big buildings, 100 million cars, and relatively inefficient industries, the U.S. carbon dioxide emissions per person are nearly four times those in western Europe, and five times the world average. Elsewhere, China is a major and growing source of concern because coal emits more atmospheric pollutants than other fossil fuels, and three-fourths of China's energy for its fast-growing economy comes from coal. China now accounts for about 15 percent of all greenhouse gas emissions, making it the fastest-growing major contributor to global warming, even though its emissions per person remain one-seventh of those in the United States.

To combat the danger of accelerating global warming, more than 160 states signed the 1992 **UN Framework Convention on Climate Change,** which seeks to contain greenhouse gases at levels that will avoid threatening climate change, and aims to return emissions to 1990 levels by 2000. But that agreement did not go far enough and most industrial countries were expected to miss their targets for reductions; in fact, yearly emissions were predicted to reach "9 billion tons by 2010—49 percent above 1990 levels" (*Vital Signs 1997,* 58). To strengthen the 1992 Climate Change Treaty, the 1997 **Kyoto Protocol** was reached, requiring twenty-eight industrial countries to reduce their greenhouse gas emissions from 1990 levels between 2008 and 2012. If adhered to, the United States would cut emissions by 7 percent, the European Union by 8 percent, and Japan by 6 percent, and the Protocol asked China, India, and other developing economies to voluntarily set sizable reduction targets.

Coal is a major source of atmospheric sulfur and nitrogen oxides as well. These pollutants return to earth, typically after traveling long distances, in the form of **acid rain,** which adds to the acidification of lakes, the corrosion of materials and structures, and the impairment of ecosystems. Acid rain is a serious problem in much of China. Because the oxides that cause it are also transboundary pollutants, China's domestic energy policies have become a major irritant in its relations with its neighbors, particularly South Korea and Japan (see Map 2.1 in Chapter 2). Nonetheless, China plans to increase the amount of coal it burns by nearly 900 million tons a year by 2010. Other Asian states are following in its path, including populous India which, like China, has sizable coal deposits. Already China and India account for 14 percent of global greenhouse gas emissions. In addition, their combined share of carbon dioxide emissions is expected to grow to 25 percent in the next fifteen years (Tefft 1995, 8).

Global emissions of carbon dioxide and other greenhouse gases are rising and contributing to global warming. The long-term consequences are grim; if the earth continues to heat, oceans will rise and land will be submerged. Pictured here is the Bering Glacier at the edge of Vitus Lake in Alaska, which according to Greenpeace has shrunk about forty feet in length during the past century due to global warming.

The Science and Politics of Climate Change. Global climate change contains the elements of a classic tragedy of the commons: It was intended by none yet is seemingly beyond the control of all who must bear its costs. Four strategies are available for avoiding the ruin common properties face when excessively exploited for private gain:

1. *Voluntary restraints*, which come about "through education about the ecological consequences of irresponsible actions and by bringing social pressures to bear on members of the community who have not moderated their actions" (Soroos 1998).

2. *Regulations* that restrict the use of common properties, including penalties for violators.

3. *Partitioning* of the common property so that those who profit from the common property also pay the costs of excessive exploitation.

4. *Common ownership* of the property, which limits access to those with a share in ownership and who in turn share in the profits. "Under such an arrangement, the community as a whole would not only receive all the profits but also absorb all the costs of [excessive exploitation]" (Soroos 1998).

Each of these strategies for averting a commons tragedy has counterparts in states' efforts to cope with the environmental challenges they collectively face. In the case of climate change, however—arguably the most threatening of all—global efforts remain confined to largely voluntary restraints. Because education and social pressures are particularly important here, the role of the IPCC in determining that the world has already entered a period of climatic instability due to rising temperatures takes on added significance. As one prominent environmentalist observed, "The IPCC's influence stems from its unique design.

329

It combines in a single institution independent scientists acting on their professional knowledge with policymakers acting on behalf of governments. Science is separated and protected from political tinkering and at the same time thrust under policymakers' noses. Without realizing what they were doing, governments created in the IPCC an institution that forces them to confront a phenomenon many—if not most—would prefer to ignore" (Mathews 1996).

The Kyoto Protocol of 1997 amending the 1992 Earth Summit set an ambitious goal: stabilizing the overall concentration in the atmosphere of greenhouse gases as well as reducing their emissions worldwide. Despite the expectations generated, many experts criticized the treaty's modest goals (Warrack 1998), and little progress has been made in realizing the voluntary restraints agreed to. European states, previously at the forefront of efforts to reduce carbon emissions, began to waffle and the United States interpreted the treaty's provisions to mean that carbon emissions could actually *increase* if they were offset by reductions in other emissions. Thus, the subtle shift from "binding limits" to rather vague "targets" and "goals" threatens to reduce the impact of the accord. Furthermore, most Global South countries have not adopted any targets, despite rapid increases in their own greenhouse gas emissions. And the agreement will not take effect until fifty-five states representing 55 percent of 1990 emissions levels ratify it, which has not yet happened.

The dispute between the Global North and South centers on how to deal with a problem colored by widely discrepant perceptions and political interests. The South sees the North—correctly—as the primary culprit in previous greenhouse emissions, while the North sees the South—also correctly—as the primary source of rising emissions, thus negating any benefits that might be realized by altering its own behavior today. Since 1988 greenhouse emissions from the Global South have increased 71 percent (*Time*, April 13, 1998, 199). Rising levels of coal burning by China and India alone could undermine any efforts to deal with long-term problems.

The developing world said, basically, "hell-no!" to the Kyoto Protocol, in large measure in reaction to the Global North's perceived unwillingness to bear the costs of reshaping their $1 trillion dollar fossil fuel economies (Warrack 1998, 31). Friction generated by the search for financial profit at the expense of environmental protection and by disagreements between North and South thus continue to undermine the prospects for the global community to set binding limits on greenhouse emissions in the future at such follow-on conferences as that in Buenos Aires in November 1998.

Ozone Protection

States' efforts to cope with depletion of the atmosphere's protective **ozone layer** share similarities with the story of climate change. In this case, however, an international regime has emerged and has been progressively strengthened as scientific evidence pointing toward the environmental damage caused by human activity continues to mount.

Ozone is a pollutant in the lower atmosphere, but in the upper atmosphere it provides the earth with a critical layer of protection against the sun's harmful ultraviolet radiation. Scientists have discovered a marked depletion of the ozone layer—most notably an "ozone hole" over Antarctica which grows at times to be larger than the continental United States—and they have conclusively linked the thinning of the layer to chlorofluorocarbons, a related family of compounds known as halons, hydrochlorofluorocarbons (HCFCs), methyl bromide, and other chemicals. Depletion of the ozone layer exposes humans to increased health hazards of various sorts, particularly skin cancer, and threatens other forms of marine and terrestrial life. The release of many ozone-depleting gases also adds measurably to the accumulation of greenhouse gases that threaten dramatic climate change through global warming.

Scientists began to link halons and CFCs to ozone depletion in the early 1970s. Even before their hypotheses were conclusively confirmed, the **United Nations Environment Programme** (a UN agency created in the aftermath of the 1972 Stockholm conference) sought some form of regulatory action. The scientific uncertainty surrounding the issue eased the sense of urgency some felt, and differences between the interests of the chemical industry in the United States (where bans were placed on some CFCs, such as aerosol propellants) and Europe (where they were not) slowed efforts to devise controls. Nevertheless, in 1985 the Vienna Convention on Protection of the Ozone Layer, whose purpose was to control ozone-modifying substances, was concluded. This landmark decision "represented the first international effort to deal formally with an environmental danger before it erupted" (Benedick 1991).

Two years later an even more significant agreement was reached, the Montreal Protocol on Substances That Deplete the Ozone Layer, signed by twenty-three states and the Commission of the European Community. The signatories agreed to reduce their CFC emissions to one-half of their 1986 levels by the turn of the century. The agreement was widely heralded, as its parties accounted for more than 80 percent of global CFC emissions. Even further cuts were proposed later, with an agreement for a 1996 phaseout of CFC production in the Global North and in the Global South by around 2010. Subsequent agreements called for the phaseout of HCFCs. Originally developed because they were believed to be ozone-friendly alternatives to CFCs and a bridge to further scientific breakthroughs, HCFCs will be phased out completely by 2030 under current agreements (although many European states would prefer to speed up the timetable). Agreement was also reached in late 1995 to completely eliminate by 2010 production of methyl bromide, an ozone-depleting chemical widely used as an all-purpose pesticide.

The rapid move since 1985 to restrict the use of ozone-depleting chemicals contradicts the behavior the tragedy of the commons metaphor would lead us to expect. Rather than exploiting a common property (the atmosphere), states have successfully put their long-term collective interests in environmental protection ahead of short-term individual interests in protecting investments and jobs in the chemical industry.

As remarkable as this achievement is, implementation of the ozone regime still faces challenges. Notably, in spite of reductions in CFCs over the past decade, the ozone hole over Antarctica has continued to expand. Nature will eventually mend the atmospheric damage done by prior ozone-depleting chemical emissions, but it will take decades. Meanwhile, under the current international regime, depletion of the protective ozone shield is expected to accelerate before it begins to regenerate itself. An increase in sulfur particles due to volcanic eruptions (such as Mount Pinatubo in the Philippines in 1991 and Mountserrat in 1997) and the burning of fossil fuels are contributing factors. The use of HCFCs as transition chemicals may also be debilitating. Although these compounds do not last as long as CFCs (whose ozone-depleting chemical reactions can last a century or more), they do most of their damage in ten to twenty years—precisely the time frame in which the ozone shield is already at greatest risk (Gurney 1996)—and they contribute markedly to global warming. Some states, however, notably the United States, are unwilling to shorten the time frame for elimination of HCFCs so as to permit the industries that have heavily invested in alternatives to CFCs to recover their investments (Porter and Brown 1996).

A second issue turns on the differing interests of developed and developing countries. Global production of CFCs has declined sharply in this decade as the largest producers (and consumers) prepared for their complete phaseout. This, for the most part, has now been achieved. Production in the Global South, on the other hand, is surging. Demand is growing for refrigerators, air conditioners, and other products using CFCs. Current CFC production in the Global South is still comparatively low. However, as it increases between now and 2010, it will offset the gains realized by stopping production in the North. Developed countries agreed to provide aid to the developing countries to help them adopt CFC alternatives, but thus far they have failed to provide all of the resources promised. Without this support, many in the Global South may not be able to keep their end of the global bargain. Meanwhile, a significant illegal trade in both virgin and recycled CFCs has emerged, threatening to further undermine the positive effects of the ozone regime (Porter and Brown 1996).

Despite these challenges to the ozone regime, it stands as a significant achievement in international environmental cooperation. Can it serve as a model for breakthroughs on other issues, notably climate change? The success of the ozone initiative is widely attributed to the growing body of scientific evidence supporting the theory, combined with what some see as the absence of a significant requirement for changes in behavior or substantial costs. However, containing other environmental threats more characteristically meets resistance because the costs to vested interests are excessive. Again, consider the example of global warming. "There's a better scientific consensus on this than any other issue I know—except maybe Newton's second law of dynamics," observed D. James Baker of the U.S. National Oceanic Administration. "Man has reached the point where his impact on the climate can be as significant as nature's" (Warrick 1997). Yet, despite this consensus about the benefits of reducing the effects of global warming, many countries have failed to ratify the 1997 Kyoto Protocol to bolster the 1992 Climate Change Convention, and developing countries such as China and India are not even required to make a binding commitment to its provisions. Hence global efforts to avert the tragedy of the commons on atmospheric issues are inadequate. Continued conflicts are predicted in efforts to negotiate new treaties to protect forests and the earth's biological heritage.

• • •

THE ECOPOLITICS OF FORESTS AND BIODIVERSITY

The world's forests play a critical role in the earth's complex ecological systems as well as in humankind's relationship with the environment and its well-being. Forests are intimately tied to preserving the earth's biodiversity and to protecting the atmosphere and land resources. For these reasons they have been the object of global attention. Some rules have emerged to guide global behavior in the preservation of biodiversity, but issues concerning forests have proven much more difficult to address.

Forests

Are the world's forests at risk of destruction through commercial exploitation or at the hands of local populations? Information is inconclusive, but estimates based on trends during the 1980s point toward considerable **deforestation** in the United States and throughout much of the Global South. Each minute, on average, 52 acres of the world's forests are lost (*Time*, April 13, 1998, 199). Destruction of tropical rain forests in such places as Brazil, Indonesia, and Malaysia is a matter of special concern, as much of the world's genetic heritage is found there (see Map 11.1). This is a matter of *international* concern, a contentious issue. Commercial logging to sell lumber and other wood products in the global marketplace is a major cause of deforestation, but "why the virgin forest is being cut down is not so much the simple pursuit of profit but a set of perverse economic incentives. . . . The sort of policies that might help countries reduce their rate of deforestation are the sort of policies that are likely to promote economic growth. The desire to promote economic growth stands in the way of efforts to stop deforestation, despite the evidence that in the long run the countries that limit the rates at which they cut their forests are the one that expand their rates of economic growth the fastest (*Economist*, March 21, 1998, 10–11).

> **deforestation** to the World Resources Institute, "the permanent depletion of the ground cover of trees to less than 10 percent."

The representatives sent to the Earth Summit hoped to secure an easy victory on a statement of principle for global forest conservation, but opposition quickly developed to the principle that all countries were responsible for protecting—in the global interest—national forests. The Global South objected vigorously.

Led by Malaysia—a principal exporter of tropical wood products—the South resisted an effort to establish the legal principle that the world's forests are a common property resource, the "common heritage of mankind." Malaysia and others in the Global South feared that accepting that principle as applied to forests would give the Global North "some right to interfere in the management of the tropical forest countries' resources." In the end, the Earth Summit dropped "both the idea of international guidelines for forest management and any reference to trade in 'sustainably managed' forest products" (Porter and Brown 1996). The situation today is largely unchanged. The **International Tropical Timber Organization (ITTO)** remains the principal international forum for addressing transnational issues (notably trade) in timber products, but it is dominated largely by the timber interests themselves.

Meanwhile, population growth and demands for increased well-being contribute to higher rates of deforestation. This sometimes results in desertification, which renders the land useless both for production and as habitat for wildlife. Based on previous trends, it has been estimated that an area about the size of one-fourth to one-half of an American football field is deforested each time another person is added to the world population. This means that the addition of another billion people will require between 1.2 million to 2.5 million square kilometers of additional land for food production and other uses (J. Cohen 1995, 338). In the Global North, reforestation has alleviated some of the danger. This is not the case in many cash-starved Global South countries, which sell timber for income and to make room for their growing populations

MAP 11.1

Forests and Rain Forests

Deforestation is a global phenomenon, but the rate of deforestation is much higher in the Global South than in the North. Tropical forests in Central and South America, Africa, and Southeast Asia have disappeared at an alarming rate.

SOURCE: Seager (1995), 72–73.

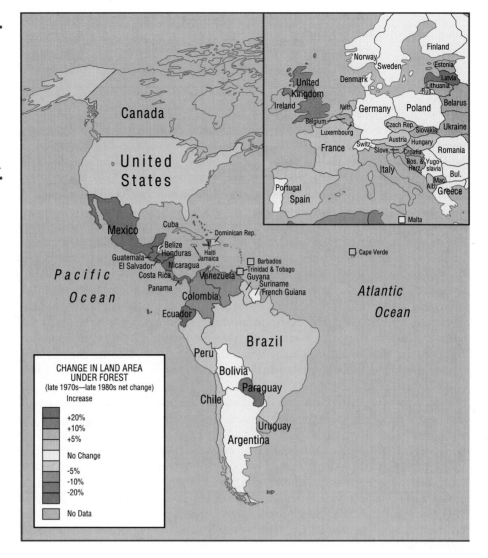

seemingly without concern for the long-term consequences of the destruction of their forests. The World Wide Fund for Nature, a London-based environmental NGO, called 1997 "the year the world caught fire," complaining that more tropical forests were deliberately burned that year than in any other year in recorded history, 80 percent by multinational corporations clearing land for planting or development. Up to 12.4 million acres of forest were burned in Indonesia and Brazil alone in what the WWF termed a "planetary disaster that is destroying our insurance for the future."

The clearing and burning of tropical rain forests to make room for farms and ranches is especially troublesome from the viewpoint of climate change. Green plants routinely remove carbon dioxide from the atmosphere during photosynthesis. The natural processes that remove greenhouse gases are destroyed when forests are cut down, and, as the forests decay or are burned, the amount of CO_2 discharged into the atmosphere increases. This makes deforestation doubly destructive. Furthermore, the cattle raised on the newly deforested land add to the staggering volume of methane released into the atmos-

334

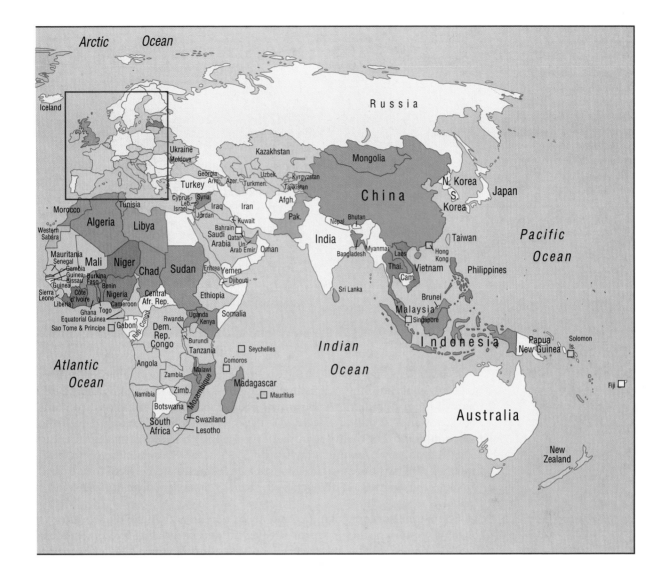

phere, which also contributes to global warming. Nonetheless, the World Resources Institute reports that the rate of tropical deforestation during the 1980s was so rapid that "an area three times the size of France was converted to other uses" (Knickerbocker 1994, 7).

Biodiversity

Biodiversity, or biological diversity, is an umbrella term that refers to the earth's variety of life. Technically it encompasses three basic levels of organization in living systems: genetic diversity, species diversity, and ecosystem diversity. As a practical matter, until recently public attention has been focused almost exclusively on preserving species diversity. Efforts to protect endangered species from extinction and conservation programs designed to protect old-growth forests, tall-grass prairies, wetlands, coastal habitats, coral reefs, and similar areas are illustrative.

Destruction of the world's forests contributes to climate change through global warming and threatens the earth's biodiversity and genetic heritage. Lumbering for commercial purposes exacts a toll on forests, but deforestation due to the expansion of agriculture to meet the needs of a growing population may be a more critical threat.

Forests, especially tropical forests, are especially important to preserving biodiversity because they are home to countless species of animals and plants, many of them still unknown. Scientists believe that the global habitat contains between 8 and 10 million species. Of these, only about 1.5 million have been named, and most of them are in the temperate regions of North America, Europe, Russia, and Australia (Edwards 1995, 215). Destruction of tropical forests, where two-thirds to three-fourths of all species are believed to live, thus threatens the destruction of much of the world's biological diversity and genetic heritage.

Some experts worry that, due mainly to human activities, "the world is on the verge of an episode of major species extinction, rivaling five other documented periods over the past half-billion years during which a significant portion of global fauna and flora were wiped out," each time requiring "ten million years or more for the number of species to return to the level of diversity existing prior to the event." Others doubt the imminence of a massive die-out, pointing out that only a small fraction of the earth's species have actually disappeared over the past several centuries (World Resources Institute 1994, 147). Indeed, cornucopians argue that species extinction may not be bad news, as new species may evolve that will prove even more beneficial to humanity (McKibben 1998).

Threats to biodiversity have implications for all species. Therefore the issue resembles threats to other common property resources. However, biodiversity's distributional characteristics make it different from other issues. In particular, because the earth's biological heritage is concentrated in the tropics, the Global South has a special interest in this issue. It also has a growing concern about protecting its interest in the face of recent developments. "Traditionally, the genetic character of the many species of plants and animals have been considered a part of the common heritage of humankind, but increasingly they have become the objects of an enclosure movement that is seeking to enclose, privatize, and reduce the building blocks of life to marketable products" (Miller 1995).

Toward Enclosure: The Stakes. Multinational corporations in the Global North are major players in the **enclosure movement** (the claiming of common properties by states or private interests). In India, for example, products from the neem tree "for centuries . . . have been used locally for medicine, contraception, toiletries, timber, fuel, and insecticide. Its chemical properties have never been patented in India, but since 1985 U.S. and Japanese firms have taken out more than a dozen U.S. patents for a variety of neem compounds" (Miller 1995). Ironically, local Indian populations must now compete with MNCs for products long readily available to them, often at sharply higher prices.

Pharmaceutical companies have also laid claim to resources in the Global South. They actively explore plants, microbes, and other living organisms in tropical forests for possible use in prescription drugs. "This is a lucrative field; about 25 percent of the prescription drugs used in the United States have active ingredients extracted or derived from plants" (Miller 1995, 110). An example of a particularly successful project was Eli Lilly's development of drugs from the rosy periwinkle found in Madagascar's rain forest to treat childhood leukemia. Sales of the drugs amounted to about $100 million annually—although Madagascar received nothing for the use of its biological resource. Averting repetition of Madagascar's experience is a central concern among developing countries.

The rapid growth of biotechnology has added incentives for preserving the earth's biological diversity so as to maintain a wide gene pool from which to develop new medical and agricultural products. At the same time, however, **genetic engineering** in the industrialized world to develop hybrid seeds for new plants threatens the loss of biodiversity. The uneven distribution of biological resources is related to these developments (see Map 11.2 for identification of those locations where most of the species on earth are concentrated). Farmers and scientists increasingly must look to the Global South for primitive germ plasm (the genetic material containing hereditary information).

> They assume that, as with the high seas, this primitive germ plasm is the common property of humankind. These genetic resources are used to produce genetically altered seeds for the international market. Since these are now patented and are private property, they can then be sold back to [Global South] consumers. The genetically altered seeds often need expensive additives such as chemical fertilizers and pesticides, which are often environmentally as well as financially costly. The picture for [Global South] agriculture deteriorates further when developing-country farmers focus on hybrid varieties to the detriment of, and at the risk of causing the disappearance of, the old varieties. (Miller 1995, 112)

Toward Preservation: The International Response. Biodiversity has been a focus of global attention since the 1972 Stockholm conference. Between then and the 1992 Earth Summit, several conferences were held and agreements were reached on a number of issues, including many of special concern to developing countries. In addition, bilateral agreements have set important precedents for possible alternative arrangements for dealing with the competing interests at stake. Among the most innovative was an agreement between Costa

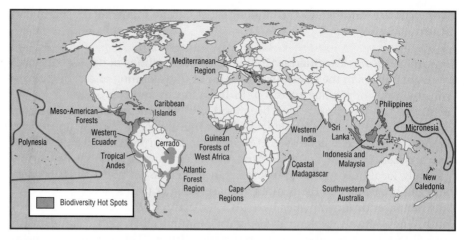

MAP 11.2

Biodiversity Hot Spots: Bang for the Conservation Buck?

According to the United Nations, about fifty thousand plant and animal species become extinct each year. Saving endangered species for future generations has been difficult, but Conservation International urges increasing the effort and suggests that a big payoff could result from targeting a relatively small number of areas in which species are concentrated. This map pinpoints seventeen biodiversity "hot spots" covering only 2 percent of the land where more than half of the earth's species are found.

SOURCE: *U.S. News & World Report*, February 24, 1997, p. 43.

Rica and Merck Corporation, the world's largest pharmaceutical firm. The company agreed to pay for access to Costa Rica's rich tropical forests for drug-related research and to compensate Costa Rica with royalty payments for any products resulting from this research.

What set the Earth Summit apart from previous biodiversity efforts at the international level was the special treatment now given the issue. For instance, a separate Convention of Biodiversity set forth a comprehensive framework for preservation of biodiversity. The road to the convention was rocky, however, as the Global North and South repeatedly clashed. Especially contentious was a proposal to use a recently created **Global Environment Facility (GEF)** within the World Bank (a joint enterprise with the UN Environment [UNEP] and Development [UNDP] Programmes) as the instrument for resource transfers from North to South to meet the objectives spelled out in the biodiversity convention as well as in other Earth Summit documents. This controversy was largely due to the developing countries' belief that the World Bank heavily favors the interests of the Global North, which is its principal source of funds.

Ratified by 161 countries, the **Convention on Biodiversity** spells out guidelines for sharing the profits of biotechnology between the Global North and South. It also commits governments to devise national strategies for conserving species and habitats, protecting endangered species, expanding protected areas and repairing damaged ones, and promoting public awareness of the need to protect the earth's heritage.

Still, much remains to be done. Although food production is rising and most people are living longer and healthier lives,

These gains are threatened by a growing scarcity of fresh water and a loss of topsoil and productive farmland. According to the UN, one-third of the world's population does not have an adequate supply of clean water, and two-thirds will be deprived of it by 2010 unless action is taken. Some 3.7 billion acres of farmland—nearly 30 percent of the world's vegetated surface—are now degraded to some degree.

Air and water quality is generally improving in rich countries. But despite substantial reforestation in those countries and a recent slowing of deforestation globally, forest loss continues worldwide.

Each year, according to the United Nations, an area the size of Nepal is cut or burned. Ocean pollution threatens the health and livelihood of the two-thirds of humanity living near coastlines, and about 60 percent of commercial fisheries are overfished or fully fished and in danger of depletion. Toxic chemicals still pose significant threats. (Stevens 1997, 4)

The obstacles to overcoming the human habits that have reduced environmental security are many. Part of the problem is due to the fact that scientific uncertainty about how (or even whether) species can be saved abounds. Balancing the interests of those who seek access to genetic materials with those of others with a stake in sharing in the profits of biotechnology must still be resolved. And agreements on mechanisms to finance the obligations contained in the treaty and creating an institutional mechanism to oversee its implementation must still be reached. As one environmental specialist astutely observes, "governments of most nations . . . recognize the need for rules to preserve those aspects of the global environment that are beyond the jurisdiction of any state." However, they "often balk at agreeing to specific regulations and complying with them" to avert environmental tragedies (Soroos 1998). At the conclusion of the 1997 "Rio Plus Five" Earth Summit, observers sadly noted that "with some important exceptions, environmental trends [had] changed little since the 1992 Rio gathering" (Stevens 1997), and the magnitude of the corrections needed to preserve the global commons is huge (see Focus 11.3).

• • •

TRADE, THE ENVIRONMENT, AND SUSTAINABLE DEVELOPMENT

This chapter began by posing the question of whether national security and environmental security are compatible objectives. A similar contrast may be drawn between free trade and sustainable development. Do these values complement one another, or are they in conflict? The question is especially pertinent in a rapidly globalizing world in which trade increasingly links politics, economics, societies, and cultures in complex interdependencies.

Liberal economic theory argues that free trade produces benefits. If all states specialize in the production of goods in which they enjoy comparative advantages and trade them with others who enjoy similar advantages in other products, all will prosper. Following this logic, commercial liberals conclude that free trade increases prosperity, and wealth contributes to the capacity to manage the environment well. "Growth enables governments to tax and to raise resources for a variety of objectives, including the abatement of pollution and the general protection of the environment. Without such revenues, little can be achieved, no matter how pure one's motives may be" (Bhagwati 1993).

Post-Rio Report Card on a Sustainable Global Commons

There has been some progress toward a healthy environment, but without significant change, the goal of "sustainable development" espoused at the 1992 Earth Summit may be difficult to reach.

Poverty

Gaps between rich and poor continue to grow. More than 1.1 billion people—20 percent of the world's population—live on the equivalent of less than $1 a day.

Consumption

Twenty percent of the world's people consume 80 percent of its resources. Some large developing countries are moving rapidly toward high-consumption lifestyles.

Population

Fertility rates are declining more rapidly than expected in most regions, but population-growth rates still strain natural resources in some countries.

Forests

Forest loss has declined, but 13.7 million hectares of forest—about the size of Arkansas—are cut or burned yearly.

Fresh Water

One-fifth of the world's population lacks access to safe water. By 2025, two-thirds of the population could live in countries facing moderate or severe water stress.

Oceans

About 60 percent of fish stocks are overfished or fully fished. Marine pollution continues to pose a serious problem.

Climate

Global emissions of carbon dioxide, and other greenhouse gases, are rising.

Energy

Rapid growth in fossil-fuel use in many developing countries is leading to severe pollution. Energy consumption is projected to more than double by 2050.

Land

World food production is rising, but more than 800 million people still suffer from hunger and malnutrition. Pesticides, poor farming methods, and desertification—the degradation of drylands—have taken a heavy toll.

Toxics

About 3 million tons of toxic and hazardous waste crosses national borders each year.

Biodiversity

About 50,000 plant and animal species are lost each year.

SOURCE: United Nations, as summarized in the *Christian Science Monitor,* June 24, 1997, p. 11

Environmentalists question commercial liberal economists' logic, especially because they see economic growth and environmental protection as goals at cross-purposes. "Free traders seek to maximize profits and production without regard for considerations that represent hidden social and environmental costs [and fail to appreciate] that growth is increasing environmental costs faster than benefits from production—thereby making us poorer, not richer" (Daly 1993).

Beyond the issue of the gains from and costs of trade, environmentalists and liberal economists differ in their assessments of the wisdom of using trade to promote environmental standards (see Focus 11.4). Liberal economists see such efforts as market distortions, while environmentalists view them as useful instruments for correcting market failures, such as markets' inability to

Free Trade and Sustainable Development
An Oxymoron?

The links between trade and the environment raise three main questions.

1. What are the environmental effects of trade liberalization?

The fear that these effects are generally negative has led to calls for amending trade policies to take explicit account of environmental goals. Recent controversies have concerned the negative effects of the . . . North American Free Trade Agreement [NAFTA] on air and water quality in Mexico and the southwestern United States, of liberalized cassava exports to the [EEU] on soil erosion in Thailand, and of exchange rate depreciation on deforestation in Ghana. But using trade restrictions to address environmental problems is inefficient and usually ineffective. Liberalized trade fosters greater efficiency and higher productivity and may actually reduce pollution by encouraging the growth of less-polluting industries and the adoption and diffusion of cleaner technologies.

In these and other examples, the primary cause of environmental problems is not liberalized trade but failure of markets to price the environment appropriately. . . . Indeed, modifying trade policies to deal with environmental problems may worsen degradation. Thus, restricting the export of logs, as in Indonesia, raises returns to the domestic wood-processing industry and may contribute to inefficient and high-cost production that could worsen deforestation. Usually, more direct instruments than trade policies are available for combating deforestation, soil erosion, or industrial pollution. . . .

2. Should trade policies be used to influence environmental standards in other countries?

The arguments noted above apply here as well and are strengthened by another consideration: Some variation in environmental standards across regions and countries is justified by differences in priorities and in capacities to assimilate pollutants or cope with resource degradation. When countries (typically, the bigger and richer ones) use trade policy to impose their environmental standards, the effect is to protect domestic producers from foreign competition. Applying the same standards to domestic production and imports may be justified when, as with cars or pesticides, consumption leads to environmental damage. But even there, environmental concerns do not warrant uniformity across countries.

Evidence shows that developing countries do not compete for foreign investment in "dirty" industries by lowering their environmental standards. . . . Rather, anecdotal data . . . suggest the opposite: Because it is cheaper for multinational corporations to use the same technologies as they do in industrial countries, these firms can be potent sources of environmental improvement.

3. Should trade policies be used to enforce or implement international environmental agreements?

Trade measures to implement environmental agreements include the Montreal Protocol, which phases out ozone-depleting chemicals; the Basel Convention for controlling the transboundary movement and the disposal of hazardous wastes; and the Convention on International Trade in Endangered Species (CITES), which supports the embargo on ivory trade. The use of trade instruments could be justified in some of these cases. For instance, restricting trade in hazardous and toxic wastes . . . is appropriate if the capacities of many countries to monitor and dispose of these wastes are in doubt. But in most countries, the scale of such trade is small in comparison with the volume of hazardous wastes being generated domestically. Therefore, the concern should be to minimize the production of these wastes and to devise ways of ensuring their safe disposal. A total ban on all trade in hazardous and toxic wastes would be counterproductive because it would prevent the development of collective arrangements for treatment and disposal, even where individual countries, as in western Europe, can specialize in safe and low-cost disposal.

The ban on trade in ivory to protect the African elephant also involves difficult tradeoffs. Available evidence shows that ivory prices have fallen and poaching has declined since the ban became effective. But countries such as Botswana, South Africa, and Zimbabwe have argued that the ivory ban, by raising prices in the long run, will simply make poaching more lucrative. . . . These countries also claim that the ban discriminates against their efforts to manage their elephant herds sustainably by using revenue from hunting and tourism to enrich local people and finance law enforcement.

SOURCE: *World Development Report 1992* (1992), 67.

incorporate the externalities of environmental exploitation (e.g., atmospheric pollution by chemical companies). Some countries, however, particularly in the Global South, view the use of trade mechanisms to protect the environment as yet another way in which the rich states block entry into lucrative Northern markets, thus keeping the South permanently disadvantaged (Durbin 1995).

Trade-offs must sometimes be made between goals that, in principle, seem designed for the same end—namely increasing human well-being. However, another interpretation maintains that trade encourages states to live beyond their means. It "magnifies the ecological effects of production by expanding the market for commodities beyond national boundaries. . . . It allows nations that have depleted their resource bases or passed strict laws protecting them to reach past their borders for desired products, effectively shifting the environmental impacts of consumption to someone else's backyard" (French 1994).

What happens when everyone does the same thing? The tragedy of the commons metaphor suggests a bleak future. Is ruin the destination toward which humankind rushes?

● ● ●

TOWARD SUSTAINABILITY

Sustainable development promises a much brighter future. Although the goal remains distant and elusive, the acceptance of the concept by governments and nonstate actors throughout the world invites environmentally sensitive responses to the challenges posed. Differences between the rich countries of the Global North and the rapidly growing states in the Global South will continue to spark controversy. Contention will be especially pronounced on issues involving the transfer of resources and technology—as called for to deal with climate change, ozone depletion, biodiversity, and a host of other specific problem areas. This controversy will arise in part from differing perceptions as to who is responsible for what.

There is little doubt that the Global South, faced with rapidly growing populations and rising affluence, poses increasingly serious environmental challenges. Nonetheless, the trend is already "toward better environmental policies, increased investment in environmental infrastructure and technology, and the pursuit generally of economic development alternatives that minimize environmental impacts" (Helman 1995).

The Global North poses serious environmental challenges as well, as its consumption levels far exceed those of other states. Interestingly, though, as the industrialized countries move into the information age and their economies shift away from "dirty" manufacturing to much cleaner service-oriented activities, the adverse environmental consequences of their economic activities will diminish, or at least they will decline locally. Trade with other states, however, will ensure continuing pressures on global resources and the environmental burdens they pose.

The key to solving the dilemma posed by the stress that economic growth places on the environment may rest on replacing our current ideas about markets with the concept of a steady-state economy. "A steady-state economy is one whose throughput [the speed at which resources are consumed] remains constant at a level that neither depletes the environment beyond its regenerative capacity nor pollutes it beyond its absorptive capacity" (Daly 1993). This is sustainable development (qualitative improvements) without growth (quantitative increases in the use or consumption of materials), in its essence. "An economy that is steady in scale may still continue to develop a greater capacity to satisfy human wants by increasing the efficiency of its resource use, by improving social institutions, and by clarifying its ethical priorities—but not by increasing resource throughput." Is the world ready for such a revolution in thinking? Even if it is, can the revolution be achieved? As one futurist put the question,

> The bottom-line argument goes like this: the next fifty years are a special time. They will decide how strong and healthy the planet will be for centuries to come. . . . so it's the task of those of us alive right now to deal with this special phase, to squeeze us through the next fifty years. . . . We need in these fifty years to be working simultaneously on all parts of the equation—our ways of life, on our technologies and on our population. (McKibben 1998, 78)

K E Y   T E R M S

ecopolitics
environmental security
neoliberal
epistemic community
sustainable development
Earth Summit
"Rio Plus Five" 1997 UN Earth
  Summit
tragedy of the commons
global commons
externalities
photovoltaic (PV) cells

global warming
greenhouse gases
Intergovernmental Panel on
  Climate Change (IPCC)
UN Framework Convention on
  Climate Change
Kyoto Protocol
acid rain
ozone layer
United Nations Environment
  Programme

deforestation
International Tropical Timber
  Organization (ITTO)
biodiversity
enclosure movement
genetic engineering
Global Environment Facility
  (GEF)
Convention on Biodiversity

S U G G E S T E D   R E A D I N G

Audley, John J. *Green Politics and Global Trade.* Baltimore: Georgetown University Press, 1997.

Benedick, Richard Elliot. *Ozone Diplomacy: New Directions in Safeguarding the Planet.* Cambridge, Mass.: Harvard University Press, 1998.

Choucri, Nazli, ed. *Global Change: Environmental Challenges and International Responses.* Cambridge, Mass.: MIT Press, 1993.

D'Amato, Anthony, and Kirsten Engle. *International Environmental Law Anthology.* Cincinnati: Anderson Publishing, 1996.

Goldsmith, Edward, and Peter Bunyard, eds. *The Ecologist.* Journal published six times each year. Cambridge, Mass.: MIT Press.

Gore, Al. *Earth in the Balance: Ecology and the Human Spirit.* Boston: Houghton Mifflin, 1992.

Ostrom, Elinor. *Governing the Commons: The Evolution of Institutions for Collective Action.* Oxford, Eng.: Oxford University Press, 1992.

Repetto, Robert, and Jonathan Lash. "Planetary Roulette: Gambling with the Climate," *Foreign Policy* 108 (Fall 1997): 84–98.

United Nations Environment Programme. *Global Environment Outlook.* New York: Oxford University Press, 1997.

World Resources Institute. *World Resources 1997–98.* New York: Oxford University Press, 1998.

Young, Oran R., ed. *Global Governance: Drawing Insights from the Environmental Experience.* Cambridge, Mass.: MIT Press, 1997.

http://www.earthtimes.org/

Earth Times It's not easy being green. To help, read the Earth Times. This daily electronic newspaper is devoted to the environment, sustainable development, population, and current affairs.

http://www.ran.org/ran

Rainforest Action Network The mission of the Rainforest Action Network is to protect the Earth's rainforests and support the rights of rainforest inhabitants through education, grassroots organizing, and nonviolent direct action. Visit the network's Web site and learn about the threats the rainforests face and read about the campaigns that this group is waging. Take a quiz to see how proficient you are on rainforest issues. Lastly, learn what you can do to help protect the rainforests. You can also buy the "Kids Resource Guide" for your favorite child—or for *your* "inner child."

http://ioc.unesco.org/iyo/

1998 International Year of the Ocean The United Nations has declared 1998 as the International Year of the Ocean. They would like you to become aware of ocean issues and consider the actions needed to protect our ocean heritage. Through this Web site, examine different national contributions, see what international nongovernmental organizations are doing, discuss the issues with other concerned individuals—and request some really nice stamps or free stickers.

http://iisd1.iisd.ca/

IISDnet The International Institute for Sustainable Development (IISD) has produced a Web site to help readers learn about the concept of sustainable development, give information on some hot topics, explore issues in environmental management, and show how businesses can turn sustainability into a competitive advantage. There is also a link to multimedia resources. A very interesting part of the site is a "Sustainable Development Timeline." Click on the link and follow how society has tried to integrate protection of the environment by establishing healthy societies and economies. Is there a specific event that you believe has crystallized global thinking on sustainable development? Which decade do you believe has seen the greatest advances toward sustainable development? Follow some of the timeline links and read about the organizations that have been on the forefront of environmental protection.

http://www.wwf.org/action/lite/
frame_climate.htm

The Road to Kyoto Conference The World Wildlife Foundation (WWF) has monitored and evaluated the International Climate Change Convention held in Kyoto, Japan in December 1997. Read the daily journals or the press releases from the WWF. See how the foundation scored the five key nations and the European Union (EU) on five different criteria. (Australia, Canada, and the United States get the worst marks.) Do you believe that the WWF's assessment is fair? After reviewing the scorecard, visit the "Climate Solutions" link. How would you evaluate the WWF?

http://www.worldwatch.org/

The Worldwatch Institute One of the leading publications on the environment is now online. The Worldwatch Institute is dedicated to fostering the evolution of an environmentally sustainable society. Scan the most recent articles from the *WorldWatch* magazine or access alerts and press briefings.

Armed Conflict between and within States

CHAPTER TOPICS AND THEMES

■ Continuities and change in the use of force

■ Why states wage war: Rival theories of the causes at
the individual, state, and global levels of analysis

● Is human nature responsible?

● The domestic determinants of national aggression

● The global system and cycles of war and peace

■ Armed conflict within states: Civil wars, uncivil
methods

■ Terrorism

■ The tragic human costs of violent conflict

Daily, the media report human activity in which force is used to settle disputes. Since 1945 not a single day has gone by without war, and the end of the Cold War has not reduced its frequency. For example, in 1996 thirty-six armed conflicts were active in twenty-nine locations throughout the world, in such places as Afghanistan, Algeria, Cambodia, Chechnya, Liberia, Peru, Sri Lanka, Sudan, and Turkey (Wallensteen and Sollenberg 1997, 339–40). Given its widespread occurrence, it is little wonder so many people equate world politics with violence.

In *On War*, Prussian strategist Karl von Clausewitz advanced his famous dictum that war is merely an extension of diplomacy by other means—"a form of communication between countries," albeit an extreme form. This insight underscores the realist belief that **war** is an instrument for states to use to resolve their disputes. War, however, is the deadliest instrument of conflict resolution, and its onset usually means that persuasion and negotiations have failed.

In international relations, **conflict** regularly occurs when actors interact and disputes over incompatible interests arise. In and of itself, conflict (like **politics**—the exercise of influence) is not necessarily threatening because *war* and *conflict* are different. Conflict may be seen as inevitable and occurs when two parties perceive differences between them and seek to resolve those differences to their own satisfaction. Some conflict results whenever people interact and may be generated by religious, ideological, ethnic, economic, political, or territorial issues; therefore we should not regard it as abnormal. Nor should we regard conflict as necessarily destructive, since it can promote social solidarity, creative thinking, learning, and communication—all factors critical to the resolution of disputes (Coser 1956). However, the costs of conflict *do* become threatening when the partners turn to arms to settle their perceived irreconcilable differences. When that happens, violence occurs, and we enter the separate sphere of warfare.

This chapter explores the challenge that armed conflicts pose in world affairs, examining the character, causes, and magnitude of international violence, as well as changes in it over time. It investigates three primary ways that **armed force** (combat between the military forces of two or more states or groups) is most often used: *wars* between states, *civil wars* within states, and *terrorism*. The next chapters consider the ways in which states and other global actors respond to this challenge and the major approaches they have taken for managing armed conflict.

● ● ●

ARMED CONFLICT IN THE WORLD: CONTINUITIES AND CHANGE

Our understanding of the amount of armed conflict occurring globally depends in part on the definitions scholars use to establish types and thresholds. One broad measure of war provides a disturbing estimate that includes both national and foreign incidents of armed conflict resulting in death to both soldiers and civilians (see Figure 12.1). It shows that

> As the 20th century races to a close, it already stands out as the most productive *and* destructive century on record. No other comes close to it in terms of social progress—in the education, health, and wealth it has pro-

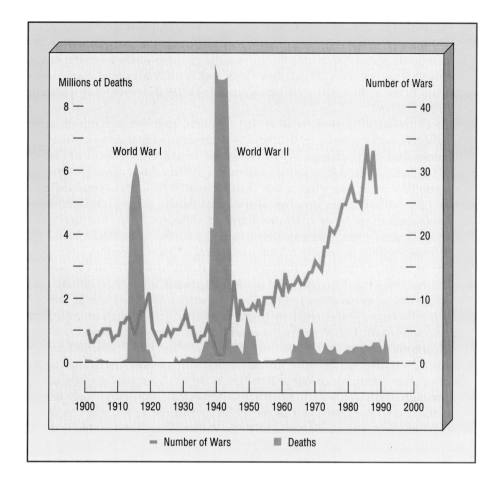

FIGURE 12.1

The Changing Wages of War in the Twentieth Century

The one hundred years between 1900 and 2000 have been deadly, with death and destruction frequent and widespread. More than 250 wars have occurred, and their frequency has risen. Twentieth-century wars have taken the lives of nearly 110 million people—a death toll that has climbed as weapons have increasingly made civilian noncombatants the primary victims. "By one analysis, the number of war deaths during the post-1945 period has been more than twice that in the nineteenth century and seven times that in the eighteenth century" (Kane 1995a, 19).

SOURCE: Sivard (1996), 7.

vided for the population. Yet it is also evident that no other century on record equals the 20th in uncivilized civil violence, in the number of conflicts waged, the hordes of refugees created, the millions of people killed in wars, and the vast expenditures for "defense."

With four years still to go, this modern century has already been responsible for 250 wars and 109,746,000 war-related deaths, a number somewhat larger than the total current population of France, Belgium, Netherlands, and the four Scandinavian countries, Denmark, Finland, Norway, and Sweden. Since mid-century, wars have become more frequent and much more deadly. There have been six times as many deaths per war in the 20th century as in the 19th. (Sivard 1996, 7)

These grim statistics can be put into perspective by observing the trends evident since 1945. The definitional criteria used by such behavioral or scientific studies as the Correlates of War (COW) project at the University of Michigan (Small and Singer 1982) and the Peace and Conflict Research project at Uppsala University in Sweden (Sollenberg and Wallensteen 1998), focus on *major* armed conflicts (more than one thousand battle deaths). Defined by this measure, from the end of World War II through 1997 we observe no less than the *initiation* of 142 separate wars. In the same 1945–1997 period the number of wars *under way* between countries (not counting foreign interventions into civil wars or wars for independence from colonial rule) was, on average, 2.5 annually (Kane 1995b, 110–12). The number of these major armed conflicts peaked in 1994 at thirty-four, with over three times as many erupting that year as occurred during the 1950s (when they averaged eleven each year) and twice as many as took place during the 1960s (when they averaged fifteen each year).

These frequencies show that armed conflicts have been common since World War II, and suggest why in 1995 UN Secretary General Boutros Boutros-Ghali described the contemporary international system as a "culture of death." The size, location, and frequency of armed conflicts have shifted when the international system has shifted, but their destructiveness has remained constantly high; consider the number of the most deadly armed conflicts *under way*—those claiming more than one hundred thousand lives. For the 1945–1997 period, each year on average there were 9 such wars, and their frequency was relatively stable, averaging 8.5 each year in the 1960s, 7.3 in the 1970s, and 10.1 in the 1980s; in the 1990s, the number has declined from 11 in 1991 to 7 in 1994 (Kane 1995a) and 1 at the start of 1998 (*Defense Monitor* 27 1998, 3).

Of particular concern to international security are global trends in wars *between* established states (such as Iraq's 1990 attack on Kuwait and the Gulf War that followed). Armed interstate conflicts that cross borders and result in one thousand or more battle fatalities have been far less frequent between 1945 and 1997 than all types of armed conflicts in general. According to the Worldwatch Institute, since World War II, 103 such interstate wars were under way annually during this period, with, on average, 2.5 occurring each year in the 1950s, 2.6 in the 1960s, 2.9 in the 1970s, 3.1 in the 1980s, and 1.3 in the 1990s (Worldwatch database diskette 1995; Wallensteen and Sollenberg 1997, 339). This tells us that although the post-World War II period has not been peaceful, most armed conflicts have been civil wars *within* states instead of wars *between* two recognized countries. While we will look separately at internal wars, let us first look more closely at the characteristics and causes of armed conflicts between states.

The Changing Character of Armed Conflict between States

Over the course of history, armed conflicts have changed in response to innovations in military technology and their dispersion throughout the globe. In the twentieth century, increasingly destructive modern weaponry has transformed contemporary warfare in major ways:

- First, although the duration of interstate wars steadily increased between 1816 and World War II, wars have been shorter since 1945. Presumably, the capacity to inflict massive destruction has brought many armed conflicts between countries to an end sooner.

- Second, the average number of countries involved in major wars has fallen sharply since World War II (*Defense Monitor* 27 1998, 1–2). This is observable both in the types of and number of countries that participate in armed conflicts.

- Third, armed conflicts have become increasingly concentrated geographically and now usually involve the less developed countries. Since 1945, more than 90 percent of wars have been in the Global South (Kane 1995b, 110).

Iraqi dictator Saddam Hussein in 1991 financed a plan to rapidly develop a nuclear weapons arsenal, for use against the United States and its allies. Nuclear proliferation appeared to be an omen for the future when in 1998 India and Pakistan became nuclear powers. This prompted fears that other countries would follow and that the so-called nuclear peace that has prevailed for more than fifty years might end.

- Fourth, *large-scale* armed conflicts involving many participants have become less frequent, reversing the historic pattern that characterized the nineteenth century (when war between the great powers was more common, included more participants, and often took a large toll in human lives).

- Fifth, the goals of many states have changed since previous centuries about waging war, perhaps as a consequence of the destructiveness of wars, their financial costs, and security danger. "A large number of the most powerful states," writes British diplomat Robert Cooper (*International Herald Tribune*, September 18, 1997, 8), "no longer want to fight or conquer. Acquiring territory is no longer of interest. Acquiring subject populations would be for most states a nightmare."

This last change raises questions as to why wars between the great powers have ceased.

Nuclear Weapons and the Obsolescence of Great-Power War?

Paradoxically, during the past half-century the world's most powerful countries have been the most constrained in their use of military strength against one another. Some people believe that the creation of nuclear weapons has produced this outcome. For example, British Prime Minister Winston Churchill articulated this thesis in 1953 when he confessed that on occasion he had "the odd thought that the annihilating character of [nuclear weapons] may bring an utterly unforeseeable security to mankind. . . . It may be that when the advance of destructive weapons enables everyone to kill anybody else no one will want to kill anyone at all." Whatever its causes, peace among the great powers has prevailed since 1945, with a "zone of peace" emerging among them alongside a "zone of turmoil" in the rest of the world (Singer and Wildavsky 1993).

deterrence a military strategy
whose primary purpose is to
prevent a foreign adversary's
attack.

In early 1992, U.S. President George Bush observed at the United Nations that "today the threat of global nuclear war is more distant than ever before." As Melvin Laird, U.S. Secretary of Defense in the Nixon administration, observed, "Nuclear weapons . . . are useless for military purposes." This does not assure us, however, that the threat of wars of mass destruction has disappeared. Increasing numbers of countries in the globe's large "zone of turmoil" are now stockpiling weapons of mass destruction, overtly or covertly, for defense and, possibly, aggression (see Chapter 13). Admittedly, many countries are very risk averse when it comes to actually using these lethal weapons, because doing so could easily result in their own destruction. However, even though most nuclear states seek not to win but rather to avoid loss, there is no guarantee that **deterrence** (dissuasion by means of military threat) will succeed forever, or that a radical regime that acquires nuclear weapons will not use them. By the laws of probability, moreover, the longer nuclear arsenals exist, the more probable it is that a nuclear exchange will occur: the question is not *if*, but *when*. The odds of a nuclear holocaust occurring through a fatal error (whether of judgment, miscalculation, or accident) are high. The limits to rationality under conditions of crisis heighten the potential dangers, as do the unreliable decision-making procedures of large-scale organizations and the probability of "close call" accidents (Sagan 1993). If these pessimistic considerations are included in assessments of the future, then we must question if the world has escaped nuclear devastation largely by sheer luck—"less a consequence of intelligent policy than a fortunate concatenation of conditions" (Singer 1991).

These apocalyptic thoughts suggest that the widespread belief that nuclear weapons have preserved peace—a *pax atomica*—may be a fanciful myth (see Vasquez 1991). Also questionable is the corollary proposition that as "the fear of escalating nuclear power reaches further down, [it will inhibit] also the use of lesser force for lesser ends and goals" (Majeed 1991). If the trends in armed conflicts since 1945 tell us anything, it is that recourse to force is likely to continue, even if the proportion of armed conflicts between states declines relative to internal armed conflicts within states. Destruction and death remain rampant. People, it seems, remain willing to kill through organized violence, especially in the Global South.

What ends motivate human beings to continue to resort to force, given the unspeakable casualties? The question provokes a more fundamental set of related questions about the causes of aggression generally. Accordingly, it is useful to review contending theories about the sources from which armed conflicts arise.

• • •

THE CAUSES OF ARMED CONFLICT: RIVAL THEORIES

levels of analysis the
interpretation of the sources
of international phenomena
that looks at influences
from individuals, the
characteristics of states, or
the global system.

Throughout history efforts have been made to explain why states resort to force. Inventories of war's origins invariably conclude that they are incomplete (see Blainey 1988; Howard 1983; Vasquez 1993; Waltz 1954), in part because most agree that war is rooted in multiple sources at various **levels of analysis.** For our purposes, the most plausible causes are divided here into three major levels or categories: individuals, states, and the global system.

In a sense, all wars between states originate from the decisions of national leaders, whose choices ultimately determine whether armed conflict will occur. We must therefore consider the relationship of war to individuals and their choices, and for this, questions about human nature are central.

The repeated outbreak of war has led some, such as psychologist Sigmund Freud (1968), to conclude that aggression is an instinctive part of human nature that stems from humans' genetic programming and psychological makeup. Identifying *Homo sapiens* as the deadliest species, **ethologists** (those who study animal behavior in order to understand human behavior) such as Konrad Lorenz (1963) similarly argue that humankind is one of the few species practicing **intraspecific aggression** (routine killing of its own kind), in comparison with most other species, which practice **interspecific aggression** (killing only other species, except in the most unusual circumstances—cannibalism in certain tropical fishes being one exception). Ethologists are joined in their interpretation by those **realists** who assume that the drive for power is innate and cannot be eliminated. They therefore accept the conclusion suggested by Charles Darwin's theories of evolution and natural selection: Life entails a struggle for survival of the fittest, and natural selection eliminates the traits that interfere with successful competition, such as **pacifism,** which rejects the right of people to kill in order to obtain power.

Many question these theories on both empirical and logical grounds. If aggression is an inevitable impulse deriving from human nature, then should not all humans exhibit this genetically determined behavior? This, of course, is rarely the case; many individuals are consistently nonaggressive, and most, adhering to the ethical position that killing is evil, neither murder nor accept others' killing on behalf of the state. In addition, genetics does not explain why individuals may be belligerent only at certain times. Social Darwinism's interpretation of the biological influences on human behavior can be countered by examining why people cooperate and act morally. As James Q. Wilson (1993) argues, Darwinian **survival of the fittest** realist theory overlooks the fact that "the moral sense must have adaptive value; if it did not, natural selection would have worked against people who had such useless traits as sympathy, self-control, or a desire for fairness in favor of those with the opposite tendencies."

Although the **nature-nurture controversy** regarding the biological bases of aggression has not been resolved (see Caspary 1993; Nelson 1974; Ridley 1998; and Somit 1990), most social scientists now strongly disagree with this realist premise and conclude that war is a learned trait, part of humankind's cultural heritage rather than its biological nature. The 1986 *Seville Statement,* endorsed by more than a dozen professional scholarly associations, maintains that "it is scientifically incorrect" to say that "we have inherited a tendency to make war from our animal ancestors," "that war or any other violent behavior is genetically programmed into our human nature," "that humans have a 'violent brain,' " or "that war is caused by 'instinct' or any single motivation" (see Somit 1990). Political scientist Ted Robert Gurr (1970) expresses the thesis, supported by behavioral research that "[t]he capacity, but not the need, for violence appears to be biologically entrenched in humans." Aggression is a propensity acquired early in life as a result of **socialization** and, therefore, is a learned rather than biologically determined behavior.

realists those who uphold the theory underlying the belief that states are driven to compete for power through war and imperialsim because of human nature, which is flawed by the urge to engage in aggression.

pacifism the liberal idealist school of ethical thought that takes seriously the Judeo-Chrisitan command "Thou shall not kill" and recognizes no conditions that justify the taking of another human's life, even when authorized by a head of state.

nature-nurture controversy the issue of whether human behavior is determined more by the biological basis of "human nature" than it is nurtured by the environmental conditions that humans experience.

Individuals' willingness to sacrifice their lives in war out of a sense of duty to their leaders and country is one of history's puzzles. "The fog of war" is what the Russian author Leo Tolstoy and others have called the fact that people will give their lives in struggles, large and small, whose importance and purpose are sometimes not understood. Clearly, this self-sacrifice stems from learned beliefs that some convictions—such as loyalty to the state—are worth dying for. "It has been widely observed that soldiers fight—and noncombatants assent to war— not out of aggressiveness but obedience" (Caspary 1993). This, however, does not make human nature a cause of war, even if such learned habits of obedience are grounds for participation in the aggression authorized by others, and even if at times the mass public's jingoistic enthusiasm for aggression against foreign adversaries encourages leaders to start wars.

Many scholars using behavioral methods to study international relations question the belief that entire nationalities are predisposed to war—that **national character** predetermines national aggression. National character— the shared attributes and values of members of a nationality—can express itself in different ways and can also change. Sweden and Switzerland have managed conflict without recourse to war since 1809 and 1815, respectively, whereas formerly they were aggressive. And until its invasion by China in 1949, Tibet had negotiated its foreign disputes peacefully for eight hundred consecutive years. This suggests that violence is not an inborn characteristic of particular peoples that predestines periodic outbreaks of aggression. Many states have escaped the tragedy of war; in fact, since 1500 more than one in five have never experienced war (Sivard 1991, 20). This variation across states over five centuries suggests that war is not endemic and unavoidable: "A vision of a ubiquitous struggle for power or of a determining systemic structure explains recurrence without accounting for non-recurrence or the great deviations from an average pattern of recurrence"(Holsti 1991).

Nobel Prize-winner Ralph Bunche, a U.S. policymaker, argued before the United Nations that "there are no warlike people—just warlike leaders." Similarly, St. Thomas More declared in the sixteenth century that "the common folk do not go to war of their own accord, but are driven to it by the madness of kings." But explaining the role of leaders in making war is not quite that simple, as leaders usually make foreign policies within groups. The social-psychological and bureaucratic setting for decision making and the global environment may exert "an influence independent of the actions and beliefs of individual policymakers. . . . War seems less like something decision makers choose than something that somehow happens to them," even as it happens "through them," through the choices they make (Beer 1981).

The decision for war is better explained, then, not by individual leaders' aggressiveness or by aggressive national character, but by the many political pressures that influence the government leaders who "ultimately decide the great questions of war and peace" (Holsti 1991). Therefore, it is relevant to ask, what domestic factors encourage policymakers to "choose war"—to see foreign aggression as the most **rational choice** for realizing foreign policy goals.

The Second Level of Analysis: States' Internal Characteristics and War Involvement

Conventional wisdom holds that variations in states' governments, sizes, ideologies, geographical locations, population dynamics, ethnic homogeneity, wealth, economic performance, military capabilities, and level of educational attainment influence whether they will engage in war. Drawing on the possibility suggested by Russian political theorist Peter Kropotkin in 1884 that "the word *state* is identical with the word *war*" and the evidence that war has contributed to the rise of the state (Porter 1994), we need to examine some theories addressing the internal characteristics of states that influence leaders' choices regarding the use of force. Implicit in this approach to explaining armed conflict at the **state level of analysis** is the assumption (embraced by "the comparative study of foreign policy" perspective relied on to discuss foreign policy decision making in Chapter 3) that differences in the types or classes of states will determine whether they will engage in war. To argue that the prospects for war are influenced most heavily by national attributes and the types of leaders making decisions for states is to challenge the neorealist premise that international circumstances are the most powerful determinants of warfare, and that domestic factors have no influence.

Duration of Independence. New states are more likely to initiate wars than are mature states (Wright 1942). Newly independent countries typically go through a period of internal political upheaval, which often serves as a catalyst to external aggression. Drives to settle long-standing internal grievances and territorial disputes by force often follow the acquisition of independence: Between 1945 and 1992, all but one of sixty civil wars were fought in emergent nations, and nearly one-fourth of them became internationalized as the bloodletting expanded across borders (Singer 1991, 59, 79). Because the national upheavals and revolutions that produce new states are most common in the newly formed countries of the Global South, it is not surprising that these states "are much more likely to be involved in international conflict" (Gurr 1994).

Cultural Determinants and the Decay of Moral Constraints. The cultural and ethical traditions of their peoples strongly influence the international behavior of modern countries. In the state system governed by the rules championed by realism, moral constraints on the use of force do not command wide acceptance. Instead, most governments have encouraged their populations to accept whatever decisions their leaders deem necessary for national security, including warfare against adversaries (see Focus 12.1).

To those theorists who embrace a cultural interpretation, the penchant for warfare does not evolve in a vacuum but is produced by the ways in which societies shape their populations' beliefs and norms. Many governments, through the educational programs they fund in schools and other institutions, indoctrinate values in their political culture that condone the practice of war. Ironically, in a world of diverse national cultures, the messages of obedience and of duty to make sacrifices to the state through such **cultural conditioning** are common. States disseminate the belief that their right to make war should not be questioned and that the ethical principles of religious and secular philosophies prohibiting violence should be disregarded. Consequently, critics stress the existence of powerful institutions that prepare individuals to subconsciously accept warfare as necessary and legitimate.

Poverty. A country's level of economic development also affects the probability of its involvement in war. Historically, the most warlike states have been poor, and this pattern persists, as the locale of warfare has shifted since 1945 to the

The Feminist Critique of Realism
Cultural Numbing and Violence

Advocates of the cultural origins of war argue that most people in most societies live an everyday experience of disengagement, or "numbness," which disinclines them to oppose their leaders' decisions to wage war. The modern state thus organizes its society to accept war and "builds a culture that affirms death" and accepts senseless carnage (Caspary 1993). In contrast, critics operating from the perspective of **feminist theories** of international relations argue that the foundation of war worldwide, alongside cultural numbing, is rooted in the masculinist ethos of realism, which prepares people to accept war and to respect the warrior as a hero (see especially Enloe 1993 and Tickner 1997). Gender roles, they assert, supported by realist values contribute to the prevalence of militarism and warfare:

> According to feminist critics, international relations theory as it has evolved incorporates "masculinist" prejudices at each of its three levels of analysis: man, the state, and war. Realists are "androcentric" in arguing that the propensity for conflict is universal in human nature ("man"); that the logic and the morality of sovereign states are not identical to those of individuals ("the state"); and that the world is an anarchy in which sovereign states must be prepared to rely on self-help, including organized violence ("war"). Feminist theorists would stress the nurturing and cooperative aspects—the conventionally feminine aspects—of human nature; they would expose the artificiality of notions of sovereignty, and their connection with patriarchy and militarism; and they would replace the narrow realist emphasis on security, especially military security, with a redefinition of security as universal social justice. (Lind 1993, 37)

We need to take seriously the potentially powerful cultural origins of armed conflict. Does history support the theory that the prevailing dominant cultural systems in the world, rooted in realism, glorify the state and aggression and, as a consequence, make violence more probable?

developing countries at the Global South's periphery. As U.S. Secretary of Defense Robert S. McNamara explained in 1966, "there is no question but that there is evidence of a relationship between violence and economic backwardness."

Before we conclude that poverty always breeds war, however, we must note that the *most* impoverished countries have been the least prone to start wars with their neighbors. The poorest countries cannot vent their frustrations aggressively because they lack the military or economic resources to do so. Thus the poorest states, like the wealthiest, cannot afford to wage war, but for quite different reasons. The former lack the means; the latter hold weapons too destructive to use.

This pattern does not mean that the poorest countries will always remain peaceful. If the past is a guide to the future, then the impoverished countries that develop economically will be those most likely to acquire arms and engage in future external wars. In particular, many studies suggest that states are likely to initiate foreign wars *after* sustained periods of economic growth—that is, during periods of rising prosperity, when they can most afford them (Cashman 1993). This signals danger if countries in the Global South develop rapidly and the new resources are directed toward armament rather than investments in sustained development, as India and Pakistan chose to do in 1998.

Many people believe that "violence begets violence"—that once aggression is accepted, fighters are prone to practice armed conflict in the future against foreign or domestic enemies. Pictured here are guerrilla units in Afghanistan preparing for a military attack against the ruling Afghan government. Funding for the fighters who ousted Soviet troops from Afghanistan provided a springboard for today's eager terrorists, conditioned by past experience and training to use force to achieve their objectives against foes, unconcerned that their aggression might be immoral.

Militarization. The age-old question of whether the acquisition of military power leads to war or peace is as timely as ever on the eve of the twenty-first century. As Chapter 13 explains, the race for the most advanced military technology in the highly industrialized countries is no longer confined there. It is now highly active in the Global South where the developing countries are racing to acquire weapons. In the 1990s the poorer states in the Global South have been the biggest customers in the global trade in arms, purchasing 60 to 70 percent of all arms (Sivard 1996, 14). As a result of this military expansion, a key question is whether this dispersion of weapons will also increase the probability of new wars.

As developing countries in the Global South accumulate the economic resources to equip their military establishments, many experts believe that war will become more frequent before it becomes less so. This prediction stems from the evidence that fundamental changes in military capability are an important determinant of the onset of war (Vasquez 1993), especially as reflected in the historical pattern in Europe.

During its transition to the peak of development, Europe was the location of the world's most frequent and deadly wars. The major European states armed themselves heavily and were engaged in warfare about 65 percent of the time in the sixteenth and seventeenth centuries (Wright 1942). Between 1816 and 1945, three-fifths of all interstate wars took place in Europe, with one erupting on average every other year (Singer 1991, 58). Not coincidentally, this happened when the developing states of Europe were most energetically arming in competition with one another. Perhaps as a consequence, the great powers—those with the largest armed forces—were the most involved in, and most often initiated, war (Cashman 1993). Since 1945, however, with the exception of war among the now-independent units of the former Yugoslavia, interstate

355

war has not occurred in Europe. As the European countries have moved up the ladder of development, they have moved away from war with one another (internal conflict is another matter).

In contrast, the developing countries now resemble Europe prior to 1945. If the Global South follows the European pattern, the immediate future may well witness a peaceful, developed world surrounded by a violent less developed world.

Economic System. Does the character of states' economic systems influence the frequency of warfare? The question has provoked controversy for centuries. Particularly since Marxism took root in Russia following the Bolshevik revolution in 1917, communist theoreticians claimed that capitalism *was* the primary cause of war—that capitalists practice imperialism and colonialism. According to the **communist theory of imperialism,** capitalism produces surplus capital. The need to export it stimulates wars to capture and protect foreign markets. Thus **laissez-faire capitalism**—economies based on the philosophical principle of free markets with little governmental regulation of the marketplace— rationalized militarism and imperialism for economic gain. Citing the demonstrable frequency with which wealthy capitalist societies engaged in aggression, Marxists believed that the only way to end international war was to end capitalism.

Contrary to Marxist theory is commercial liberalism's conviction that free market systems promote peace, not war. Defenders of capitalism have long believed that free market countries that practice free trade abroad are more pacific. The reasons are multiple, but they center on the premise that commercial enterprises are natural lobbyists for world peace because their profits depend on it. War interferes with trade, blocks profit, destroys property, causes inflation, consumes scarce resources, and encourages big government and counterproductive regulation of business activity. By extension, this reasoning continues, as government regulation of internal markets declines, prosperity will increase and fewer wars will occur (see also Chapter 8).

The evidence for these rival theories is, not surprisingly, mixed. Conclusions depend in part on perceptions regarding economic influences on international behavior, in part because alternative perspectives focus on different dimensions of the linkage. This controversy was at the heart of the ideological debate between East and West during the Cold War, when the relative virtues and vices of two radically different economic systems (socialism and capitalism) were uppermost in people's minds. At the time, communists cited the previous record of wars initiated by capitalistic countries (e.g., Germany, Japan, and the United States in Vietnam) to lend credence to the Marxist interpretation, while ignoring the pacificity of other capitalist states such as Switzerland.

Marxist theory also did not explain communist states' embarrassingly frequent use of force. The Soviet Union invaded Finland in 1939 and Afghanistan in 1979; North Korea attacked South Korea in 1950; Communist China attacked Tibet in 1959; Vietnam invaded Cambodia in 1975; and Cuba intervened militarily in Africa in the 1980s. Moreover, communist states repeatedly clashed with one another during the Cold War (e.g., China and the Soviet Union in 1969, China and Vietnam in 1979 and 1987, the Soviet Union and Hungary in 1956, and the Soviet Union and Czechoslovakia in 1968). Communist or socialist systems participated in roughly 25 percent of all interstate wars between 1945 and 1967, even though only about 15 percent of all countries had

communist theory of imperialism the Marxist-Leninist economic interpretation of imperialist wars of conquest as driven by capitalism's need for foreign markets to generate finance.

socialist economies (Cashman 1993, 133). Thus the thesis that socialist or communist states are inherently nonaggressive failed empirically.

Communism's failure to produce economic prosperity also hastened its rejection in eastern Europe and in the very heartland of the communist experiment, the Soviet Union. With capitalism's triumph over communism, a phase of history appeared to have ended (Fukuyama 1992b). By 1998 only Cuba and North Korea still fully endorsed communist *economic* principles; although communism could yet prove resurgent, all other former advocates appear committed to free market economies.

The end of the Cold War did not end the historic debate about the link between economics and war. The issue of economic influences on international behavior remains, and this basic theoretical question is likely to command increasing interest, especially given the "shift in the relevance and usefulness of different power resources, with military power declining and economic power increasing in importance" (Huntington 1991a; see also Chapters 8 and 9).

Type of Government. Realist and especially **neorealist theories** discount the importance of government type as an influence on war and peace. Not so with liberalism, especially **neoliberal theories,** which disagree stridently. Indeed, the liberal tradition assigns great weight to the kind of political institutions that govern states as a factor that powerfully shapes the kinds of foreign policies states formulate. Recall that neoliberalism predicts that "free" democratically ruled governments and free trade will promote peaceful interstate relations. This perspective uses this prophecy to prescribe that states *should* reform their governments and economies by liberalizing them (giving citizens power through the ballot to choose their leaders and commercial enterprises freedom to conduct business with minimal government interference in the marketplace). Liberty in governance and the economy are seen as beneficial—not only because human dignity and civil liberties are virtues in their own right, but because when embraced in policy choices, these values produce consequences that make for a better life. According to liberal theorists, liberal political and economic institutions promote cooperation, peace, and prosperity.

This belief and policy recommendation is rooted deeply in liberal intellectual history. It follows the argument carefully advanced by the eighteenth-century German philosopher Immanuel Kant, whose influential essay, *Perpetual Peace,* published in 1795, summarized the basis for liberal theory's view of how lasting peace between sovereign, competitive states could be created, even under conditions of global anarchy that would otherwise encourage conflict and war. Kant reasoned that a democratic form of government, which permits all people to vote in freely contested elections so that leaders are chosen by popular vote among a citizenship enjoying civil rights and civil liberties, produces foreign policy decisions that are far less inclined to initiate wars than do centrally ruled dictatorships and monarchies. Indeed, when a government is accountable to the people, Kant predicted, heads of state will be reluctant to wage war because public opinion will restrain rulers. Why? Wars are fought by common people, who as soldiers are asked to die for their country, and the mass public bearing the human and financial costs of wars made by leaders crave peace and prosperity more than death and poverty. In democracies, where the voice of the people is heard, opposition to unnecessary warfare abroad deters an adventuresome ruler from choosing to use armed force. Hence, Kant's solution to the problem of war was to recommend that states

neoliberal theories the "new" liberal theories stressing the critical impact of free governments and free trade in promoting peace and prosperity through democratically managed institutions, following the liberal world politics philosophies of Immanuel Kant, Thomas Jefferson, James Madison, and Woodrow Wilson.

give power to the people to democratically control their fates and fortunes. If liberal democracy (and free trade) spread worldwide, world politics would become peaceful, and a truly new world order would emerge.

Kant was joined by other liberal reformers, such as Thomas Jefferson, James Madison, and Woodrow Wilson in the United States—all of whom believed that an "empire of liberty" (as Madison pictured a growing community of liberal democracies) would be one freed of the curse of war, and that if democratic institutions spread throughout the world, the entire past pattern of belligerent international relations would be replaced by a new pacific pattern.

These liberal and neoliberal predictions have been fulfilled by the passage of time since they were first advanced. "We now have solid evidence that democracies do not make war on each other" (Russett 1998). Much research has been conducted that convincingly shows that "Although preventive war has been the preferred response of declining authoritarian leaders, no democracy has ever initiated such a war" against another democratic state (Schweller 1992). True, democracies experience disagreements with each other often, and one or more of the disputing parties have become boiling mad over the issue; but they have always resolved their differences at the bargaining table rather than on the battlefield (Dixon 1994; Doyle 1997; Lake 1992). The demonstrated capacity of democracies to settle their disputes peacefully provides the cornerstone for what is known as the **democratic peace** proposition (Ray 1995). This proposition holds that democratic governance *is* a strong pillar of international peace, and that if and when the globe is ruled by a larger and larger proportion of democratic governments, lasting peace within this enlarged liberal community will result. As Bruce Russett summarizes,

democratic peace the liberal theory that lasting peace depends on the deepening of liberal democratic institutions within states and their diffusion throughout the globe, given the "iron law" that democracies do not wage wars against each other.

> Democracies are unlikely to engage in any kind of militarized disputes *with each other* or to let any such disputes escalate into war. In fact, they rarely even skirmish. Since 1946 pairs of democratic states have been only one-eighth as likely as other kinds of states to threaten to use force against each other, and only one-tenth as likely actually to do so. Established democracies fought *no wars* against one another during the entire 20th century. . . . The more democratic each state is, the more peaceful their relations are likely to be. Democracies are more likely to employ "democratic" means of peaceful conflict resolution. They are readier to reciprocate each other's behavior, to accept third-party mediation or good offices in settling disputes, and to accept binding third-party arbitration and adjudication. Careful statistical analyses of countries' behavior have shown that democracies' relatively peaceful relations toward each other are not spuriously caused by some other influence such as sharing high levels of wealth, or rapid growth, or ties of alliance. The phenomenon of peace between democracies is not limited just to the rich industrialized states of the global North. It was not maintained simply by pressure from a common adversary in the Cold War, and it has outlasted that threat. (Russett 1998, 244–45)

The "democratic peace" proposition is based on a theoretical explanation of the influence of democracy in foreign policy making, as well as a prediction about democratization's potential impact on world politics in the future. Again, Russett summarizes the thinking behind this neoliberal argument.

> The phenomenon of democratic peace can be explained by the pervasiveness of normative restraints on conflict between democracies. That explanation extends to the international arena the cultural norms of live-and-let-

live and peaceful conflict resolution that operate within democracies. The phenomenon of democratic peace can also be explained by the role of institutional restraints on democracies' decisions to go to war. Those restraints insure that any state in a conflict of interest with another democracy can expect ample time for conflict-resolution processes to be effective, and that the risk of incurring surprise attack is virtually nil. These two influences reinforce each other. The spread of democratic norms and practices in the world, if consolidated, should reduce the frequency of violent conflict and war. Where normative restraints are weak, democratic institutions may provide the necessary additional restraints on the use of violence against other democratic states.

To the degree that countries once ruled by autocratic systems become democratic, the absence of war among democracies comes to bear on any discussion of the future of international relations. The statement that in the modern international system democracies have almost never fought each other represents a complex phenomenon: (1) Democracies rarely fight each other (an empirical statement) because (2) they have other means of resolving conflicts between them and therefore don't need to fight each other (a prudential cost-benefit statement), and (3) they perceive that democracies should not fight each other (a normative statement about principles of right behavior), which reinforces the empirical statement. By this reasoning, the more democracies there are in the world, the fewer potential adversaries democracies will have and the wider the zone of peace. (Russett 1998, 244–45)

In viewing the promising prospects for a democratic peace, it is important to note that its proponents do not see democratization as a panacea. Neoliberals qualify the assessment. They acknowledge that democracies do sometimes start wars and are not always pacific in dealing with other states—"It appears that democracies fight as often as do other types of states" (Morgan and Schwebach 1992; Small and Singer 1976; Wright 1942), because they have often been engaged in "defensive" or preventive wars against aggressive dictatorships. Moreover, democracies have actively practiced imperialism by taking colonies by force and have frequently used covert and overt military intervention in the internal affairs of other states—both democratic and nondemocratic (Kegley and Hermann 1997). "Democracies are nearly as violence-prone in their relations with authoritarian states as authoritarian states are toward each other. But the relations between stable democracies are qualitatively different" (Russett 1998). The democratic peace specifies only that democracies seldom, if ever, fight *each other*. Ballots serve as a barrier against the use of bullets and bombs by one democracy against another.

Faith in democratization as an antidote to armed conflict has grown in the past several decades, not only as a result of growing recognition of research findings, but also in association with the global diffusion of democratic governance. As described in Chapter 3, recently there has been a resurgence of democracy (see Figure 12.2). Between 1974 and 1991, roughly one-third of the countries on the planet converted their political systems to democratic rule. Since then, the surge of democratic reforms has continued. According to annual measures of each state's degree of freedom, provided by the influential research organization Freedom House, at the beginning of 1998 the number of "free" democratically elected governments respecting political rights and civil

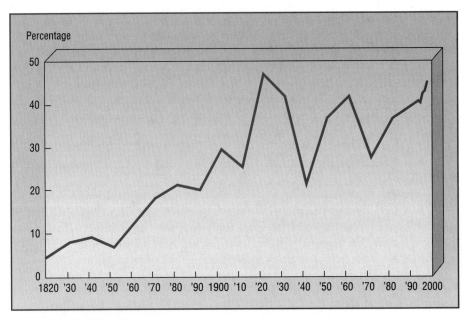

FIGURE 12.2

The Percentage of the World's Governments since 1800 That Are Fully "Free" Democracies

Throughout most of modern history, states have been ruled by monarchies, despots, dictators, and autocrats. But beginning in the twentieth century, democratization has spread sporadically in a series of waves—with an increasing percentage of the world now ruled by democratic institutions that support civil liberties and empower voters to restrict leaders' freedom to initiate wars.

SOURCE: Polity III data (Jaggers and Gurr 1995), as extended by Freedom House since 1993 as calculated by Harvey Starr.

liberties had risen to 81 states, or 45 percent of the globe's countries (and an additional 54 of the globe's 117 elected governments were "partially free").

This wave of democratization since the 1970s has provoked speculation that Western liberal democracy eventually will become universal, "the final form of government" (Fukuyama 1992b). As the growth of democracy spreads to the Global South, hope has risen that the transition to democratic rule will usher in a new era of truly peaceful world politics. Indeed, this liberal doctrine has been embedded in the foreign policy of the United States and the other liberal democracies in the Group of Seven (G-7) (i.e., Britain, Canada, France, Germany, Italy, and Japan, alongside the "eighth" member, the fledgling Russian democracy), which have defined the promotion of democracy elsewhere as one of their central purposes and strategies for preventing future wars. In President Clinton's 1994 State of the Union Address, for example, he cited the absence of war between democracies as a justification for promoting democratization around the globe, and this neoliberal principle has been endorsed by the World Bank, the International Monetary Fund, NATO, the European Union, and now the United Nations, all of which advocate defining democracy as a "human right" or entitlement that all states are obligated to protect (see Chapter 16).

Although the experience of Western Europe since World War II has helped make "the enlargement" of the liberal democratic community a policy goal, predicated on the discovery that democratic states will not engage in war with one another, we must still be cautious of quick assumptions that democracy will necessarily serve as an altogether reliable barrier to war in the twenty-first century. Fragile new democracies sometimes fall prey to internal instability, as ethnic and national passions spill over into turmoil, and at times have put into office leaders who stepped on the human rights of the people who elected them. And the fact that leaders in elective democracies are accountable to public approval and electoral rejection does not guarantee that they will not use force to settle disputes with other democracies:

> It was, after all, the democratization of conflict in the nineteenth century that restored a ferocity to warfare unknown since the seventeenth century; the bloodiest war in American history remains the one fought between two (by today's standards flawed) democracies—the Civil War. Concentration camps appeared during another conflict between two limited democracies, the Boer War. World War I was launched by two regimes—Wilhelmine Germany and Austria-Hungary—that had greater representation and more equitable legal systems than those of many important states today. And even when modern liberal democracies go to war they do not necessarily moderate the scope of the violence they apply; indeed, sensitivity to their own casualties sometimes leads to profligate uses of firepower or violent efforts to end wars quickly. Shaky democracies fight each other all the time. . . . We must remind ourselves just how peculiar the wealthy and secure democracies of the West are, how painful their evolution to stability and the horror of war with each other has been. Perhaps other countries will find short-cuts to those conditions, but it would be foolish to assume they will. (E. Cohen 1995, 39)

Thus it would be premature and overly optimistic to assume that the growth of democracy will automatically produce a more peaceful world.

Yet another concern is the frequency with which democratic states have intervened militarily, not only in authoritarian states but in other democratic states as well, in order to force democratic reform. Waging wars to spread democracy, as Woodrow Wilson did when he sent U.S. Marines into Mexico "to teach them to elect good governments," will not make for a more peaceful world. And the democratic peace could collapse because "countries do not become mature democracies overnight. More typically, they go through a rocky transitional period, where democratic control over foreign policy is partial, where mass politics mixes in a volatile way with authoritarian elite politics, and where democratization suffers reversals. In this transitional phase of democratization, countries become more aggressive and war-prone, not less, and they do fight wars with democratic states" (Mansfield and Snyder 1995).

Nationalism. Nationalism—love of and loyalty to a nation—is widely believed to be the cauldron from which wars often spring (Van Evera 1994; see also Chapters 4 and 7). "The tendency of the vast majority of people to center their supreme loyalties on the nation-state," political scientist Jack S. Levy explains, is a powerful catalyst to war. When people "acquire an intense commitment to the power and prosperity of the state [and] this commitment is strengthened by national myths emphasizing the moral, physical, and political strength of the state and by individuals' feelings of powerlessness and their consequent tendency to seek their identity and fulfillment through the state, . . . nationalism contributes to war" (Levy 1989a).

The connection between nationalism and war suffers from a long history (see Focus 12.2), but it has been especially pronounced in the twentieth century. The English essayist Aldous Huxley once termed nationalism "the religion

nationalism sentimental devotion to the welfare of one's own nation, without concern for the common interest of all nations and states in the global community.

Nationalism and War

Karl Deutsch, a German-born political scientist who taught for many years at Harvard University, described nationalism and its connection to armed conflict with these moving words:

Nationalism is an attitude of mind, a pattern of attention and desires. It arises in response to a condition of society and to a particular stage in its development. It is a predisposition to pay far more attention to messages about one's own people, or to messages from its members, than to messages from or about any other people. At the same time, it is a desire to have one's own people get any and all values that are available. The extreme nationalist wants his people to have all the power, all the wealth, and all the well-being for which there is any competition. He wants his people to command all the respect and deference from others; he tends to claim all rectitude and virtue for it, as well as all enlightenment and skill; and he gives it a monopoly of his affection. In short, he totally identifies himself with his nation. Though he may be willing to sacrifice himself for it, his nationalism is a form of egotism written large. . . .

Even if most people are not extreme nationalists, nationalism has altered the world in many ways. Nationalism has not only increased the number of countries on the face of the earth, it has helped to diminish the number of its inhabitants. All major wars in the twentieth century have been fought in its name. . . .

Nationalism is in potential conflict with all philosophies or religions—such as Christianity—which teach universal standards of truth and of right and wrong, regardless of nation, race, or tribe. Early in the nineteenth century a gallant American naval officer, Stephen Decatur, proposed the toast, "Our country! In her intercourse with foreign nations, may she be always in the right, but our country, right or wrong." Nearly 150 years later the United States Third Army, marching into Germany following the collapse of the Nazi regime, liberated the huge concentration camp at Buchenwald. Over the main entrance to that place of torture and death, the Nazi elite guard had thoughtfully written, "My Country, Right or Wrong." (Deutsch 1974, 124–25)

In confronting the impact of nationalism on armed conflict, we need to recognize its dual character: It is a force that (1) binds nations and nationalities together in common bonds, and (2) divides nation against nation, nationality against nationality, and is used to justify armed conflicts against other nations.

---

of the twentieth century." Today, nationalism is particularly virulent and intense, and arguably, with racism, "the most powerful movements in our world today, cutting across many social systems" (Gardels 1991).

Most armed conflicts today are fed by nationalist sentiments that promote "war fever . . . accompanied by overt hostility and contempt toward a caricatured image of the enemy," out of which sadistic violence and genocide have historically emanated (Caspary 1993). This entrenched linkage leads some to argue that "Nationalism has often generated aggression abroad [and] has given us some three dozen costly wars in the Middle East since 1945" (Yoder 1991). And the danger could escalate. Nationalism's threat to world order led former Soviet President Mikhail Gorbachev to warn in May 1992 that "the demons of nationalism are coming alive again, and they are putting the stability of the international system to the test. Even the United States itself is not immune from the dangerous nationalism."

This discussion of the characteristics of states that influence their proclivity for war does not exhaust the subject. Many other potential causes internal to the state exist. But however important domestic influences might be as a source of war, many believe that the nature of the international system is even more critical.

The Third Level of Analysis: Cycles of War and Peace in the Global System

Classical realism emphasizes that the roots of armed conflict rest with human nature. In contrast, neorealism sees war springing from changes at the **global level of analysis,** that is, as a product of the decentralized character of the international system that requires sovereign states to rely on self-help for their security.

International anarchy may promote war's outbreak, but it fails to provide a complete explanation of its occurrence. To capture war's many structural determinants, we must consider how and why systems change. This requires us to explore the impact of the distribution of military capabilities, balances (and imbalances) of power, the number of alliances and international organizations, and the rules of international law. At issue is how these factors—the system's characteristics and institutions—combine to influence changes in war's frequency. We will examine many of these factors in Chapters 15 and 16. Here we focus on cycles of war and peace at the international level and the structural determinants of armed conflict.

Does Violence Breed Violence? The adage "violence breeds violence" reflects the notion that the seeds of future wars are found in past wars. From this perspective World War II was an outgrowth of World War I, and the successive wars in the Middle East were seemingly little more than one war, with each battle stimulated by its predecessor. Because the frequency of past wars *is* correlated with the incidence of wars in later periods, war appears to be contagious and its future outbreak inevitable. If so, then something within the dynamics of world politics—its anarchical nature, its weak legal system, its uneven distribution of power, inevitable destabilizing changes in the principal actors' relative power, or some combination of structural attributes—makes the state system a war system.

Those believing in war's inevitability often cite the historical fact that war has been so repetitive. We cannot, however, safely infer that past wars have *caused* later wars. The fact that a war precedes a later one does not mean that it caused the one that followed.

Nor does war's recurrence throughout history necessarily mean we will always have it. War is not a universal institution (see Etzioni 1968; Kluckhohn 1944; Mead 1968; Sumner 1968); as we have seen, some societies have never known war, and others have been immune to it for prolonged periods. Moreover, since 1945 the outbreak of armed conflicts *between* states has declined, despite the large increase in the number of independent countries. This indicates that armed conflict is not necessarily inevitable and that historical forces do not control people's freedom of choice or experiences.

Power Transitions. This notwithstanding, when changes have occurred in the major states' military capabilities, war has often resulted. Although not inevitable, war has been likely whenever competitive states' power ratios (the differentials between their capabilities) have narrowed. Dubbed the **power transition theory,** this structural explanation holds that

> an even distribution of political, economic, and military capabilities between contending groups of states is likely to increase the probability of war; peace is preserved best when there is an imbalance of national capabilities between disadvantaged and advantaged nations; the aggressor will

global level of analysis an approach that emphasizes those properties of the entire global system—such as its geographic features (oceans, mountains), the distribution of resources (income, military capabilities, energy supplies), institutions (IGOs and NGOs), and norms (laws of war)—that influence states' foreign policy choices and patterns of interaction.

363

come from a small group of dissatisfied strong countries; and it is the weaker, rather than the stronger, power that is most likely to be the aggressor. (Organski and Kugler 1980, 19)

During the transition from developing to developed status, emergent challengers can achieve through force the recognition that their newly formed muscles allow them. Conversely, established powers ruled by risk-acceptant leaders are often willing to employ force to put the brakes on their relative decline. Thus, when advancing and retreating states seek to cope with the changes in their relative power, war between the rising challenger(s) and the declining power(s) has become especially likely. For example, the rapid changes in the power and status that produced the division of Europe among seven powers largely equal in military strength are often (along with the alliances they nurtured) interpreted as the tinderbox from which World War I ignited.

As explained in Chapter 15, rapid shifts in the global distribution of military power have often preceded outbursts of aggression, especially when the new distribution nears approximate parity (i.e., equality) and thereby tempts the rivals to wage war against their challengers. According to the power transition theory, periods in which rivals' military capabilities are nearly balanced create "the necessary conditions for global war, while gross inequality assures peace or, in the worst case, an asymmetric, limited war" (Kugler 1993). Moreover, transitions in states' relative capabilities can potentially lead the weaker party to start a war in order either to overtake its rival or to protect itself from domination. Presumably, the uncertainty created by a rough equilibrium prompts the challenger's (usually unsuccessful) effort to wage war against a stronger opponent. Equally persistent is the power transition theory's observation that advantages have shifted from the attacker to the defender: "In earlier centuries the aggressor seemed to have a 50–50 chance of winning the war, but this no longer holds. The chances of the starter being victorious are shrinking. In the 1980s only 18 percent of the starters were winners" (Sivard 1991, 20). As in the past (e.g., Japan's attack and subjugation of China in 1931 and 1937), there are notable exceptions: "Since 1945, six out of twenty wars have secured decisive advantage for the initiator (the Vietnam, Six Day, Bangladesh, Yom Kippur/Ramadan, Falklands, and Persian Gulf wars)" (Ziegler 1995).

Cyclical Theories. If war is recurrent but not necessarily inevitable, are there other international factors besides power transitions that might also explain changes over time in its outbreak? The absence of a clear trend in its frequency since the late fifteenth century, and its periodic outbreak after intermittent stretches of peace, suggest that world history seesaws between *long cycles* of war and peace. This provides a third structural explanation of war's onset.

The more recent formal analysis of such cycles is known as **long-cycle theory.** As noted in Chapter 4, its advocates argue that cycles of world leadership and global war have existed over the past five centuries, with a "general war" erupting approximately once every century, although at irregular intervals (Modelski 1987b; Modelski and Thompson 1996; Thompson 1988). Long cycle theory seeks to explain how an all-powerful invisible hand built into the system's dynamics causes such peaks and valleys. Although this theory embraces many contending explanations (see Goldstein 1988), they converge on the proposition that some combination of systemic properties (economic, military,

long-cycle theory an interpretation of world history that focuses on repeating patterns of interstate behavior, such as the outbreak of systemwide general wars at regular intervals, after long periods during which other patterns (global peace) were dominant.

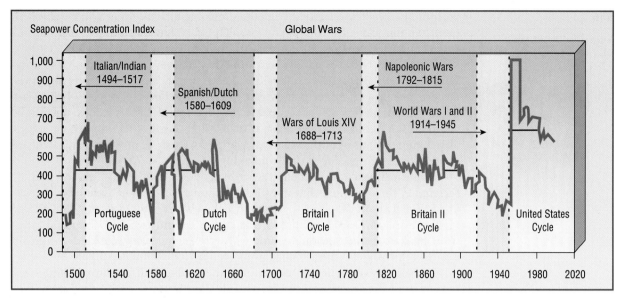

FIGURE 12.3

The Long Cycle of Global Leadership and Global War, 1494–2000

Over the past five hundred years, five great powers have risen to control the international system by dominating it. However, none of these powerful states (except Britain) has managed to reign for long. The past pattern shows that within a generation, the leader's grip on top-dog status has slipped, and in time new rivals have risen to challenge their leadership. About every one hundred years, a global war has erupted to settle the contest. The troubling question is whether this long cycle of war can be broken in the future and whether humankind will again experience a global war to determine which great power will lead.

SOURCE: Adapted from Modelski (1987a), 6.

and political) produce the frequency with which major wars have erupted periodically throughout modern history.

The long-cycle perspective is based on the fact that a great power has risen to a hegemonic position about every one hundred years. Using as a measure of dominance the possession of disproportionate sea power, we observe regularly appearing intervals of hegemony (see Figure 12.3). Portugal and the Netherlands rose at the beginning of the sixteenth and seventeenth centuries, respectively; Britain climbed to dominance at the beginning of both the eighteenth and nineteenth centuries; and the United States became a world leader at the end of World War II. During their reigns, these hegemonic powers monopolized military power and trade and determined the system's rules. Yet no hegemonic power has retained its top-dog position for more than three or four decades. In each cycle, overcommitments, the costs of empire, and ultimately the appearance of rivals led to the delegitimation of the hegemon's authority and to the deconcentration of power globally. As challengers to the hegemon's rule grew in strength, a "global war" has erupted after a long period of peace in each century since 1400. At the conclusion of each previous general war, a new world leader emerged dominant (Modelski 1978, 1987b), and the cyclical process began anew.

Such deterministic theories have intuitive appeal. It seems plausible, for instance, that just as long-term downswings and recoveries in business cycles profoundly affect subsequent behaviors and conditions, wars will produce aftereffects that may last for generations. The idea that a country at war will become exhausted and lose its enthusiasm for another war, but only for a time, is known as the **war weariness hypothesis** (Blainey 1988). Italian historian Luigi da Porto expresses one version: "Peace brings riches; riches bring pride; pride brings anger; anger brings war; war brings poverty; poverty brings humanity; humanity brings peace; peace, as I have said, brings riches, and so the world's affairs go round." Because it takes time to move through these stages, alternating periods of enthusiasm for war and weariness of war appear to be influenced by learning, forgetting, and aging.

Empirical tests of cyclical theories produce conflicting results. Quincy Wright (1942) suggested that if cycles exist, intervals between major outbreaks of war last about fifty years. In contrast, Lewis F. Richardson (1960a) and Pitirim Sorokin (1937) estimated that cycles extend over two hundred years from peak to peak (although both were somewhat skeptical and cautioned against attaching too much causal importance to their time estimates).

The validity of cyclical interpretations depends in part on the methods used to measure war's frequency and magnitude. For example, the Correlates of War research project traced cycles in the frequency and character of war between states, breaking the state system since 1815 into six historical periods, with 1848, 1881, 1914, 1945, and 1989 marking the significant turning points scholars conventionally identify in contemporary history. Table 12.1 summarizes the data for the outbreak of interstate wars exceeding one thousand battle deaths, facilitating comparisons across these six successive periods. Measured in this restricted way, the data show that 187 interstate wars erupted between 1816 and 1997, but that the frequency was fairly stable over time until the last period (1989–1997), when these kinds of wars between states greatly declined. Furthermore, if we take the expanding number of countries in the system into account, the frequency of the outbreak of wars since 1816 "actually declines from four per state per decade prior to World War II to two per state per decade since [and even less since the Berlin Wall was dismantled in 1989]. And if we control not for the number of states but the number of *pairs*, the decline appears even more dramatic" (Singer 1991, 57).

TABLE 12.1 Frequency with Which 187 Wars between States Have Begun over Six Historical Periods, 1816–1997

Period	Key System Characteristic	Number of Wars Initiated	System Size (average number of states)
1816–1848	Concert of Europe	33	28
1849–1881	Wars of European unification	43	39
1882–1914	Resurgent imperialism	38	40
1915–1944	The Great Depression	24	59
1945–1988	The Cold War	43	117
1989–1994	Post-Cold War multipolarity	6	182

SOURCES: Data for 1816–1988 provided courtesy of the Correlates of War project under the direction of J. David Singer and Melvin Small. Data for 1989–1997 are for wars that "concerned 'classical' interstate conflict, where two internationally recognized countries were waging an armed battle," based on Sollenberg and Wallensteen (1998), and Freedom House for the number of independent states.

This evidence fails to establish the existence of a cycle in war's onset since 1815 (Singer 1981). Moreover, because "no cyclical patterns are apparent when we examine the military experiences of the individual nations which participated in several wars" (Small and Singer 1972), it is doubtful that the international system automatically produces recurrent cycles in wars between sovereign states.

Thus, when we adjust for the increasing number of independent states, the post-World War II and post-Cold War eras appear comparatively more peaceful than do the periods that preceded them. Or do they? A somewhat different picture emerges when attention focuses on the number of wars *under way*, rather than on the number of wars that start. (This measure takes into account the fact that many wars continue, or last, over two or more years.) Interstate war has been in progress almost continuously since the Congress of Vienna in 1815. Although there were eighty-four years between 1816 and 1997 in which no interstate wars began, there were only twenty in which none was in progress (Small and Singer 1982, 149; Singer 1991, 60–75; Wallensteen and Sollenberg 1998). The so-called outbreak of peace in the post-Cold War era is not mythical, however, as only four large-scale wars were under way between states in the 1989–1997 period. Thus, the available evidence "suggests not so much that discrete wars come and go with some regularity, but that, with *some* level of such violence almost always present, there may be certain periodic fluctuations in the amount of that violence" (Small and Singer 1982).

From several theoretical standpoints, therefore, we must question claims that warfare in the twenty-first century—whether long and destructive or short and less costly—is structurally predetermined. The historical record provides a basis for assuming that the war system may be disappearing, and that peace between countries is possible. Both long periods of peace and long periods of warfare have existed in the past, and either could follow in the approaching new millennium. But the most recent trends show promise that classical war between states is ceasing to dominate world affairs.

If the disappearance of war is possible over the long run, armed conflict and violence may persist *inside* established states. We now turn from our exploration of the multiple causes of armed conflicts between states to examine armed conflicts within states.

● ● ●

ARMED CONFLICT WITHIN STATES

Civil wars—wars within states—have erupted far more frequently than have wars between states. It is these armed struggles that most often capture news headlines worldwide. The *New York Times Magazine* (May 7, 1995, 28), for example, featured a story concluding that "for just about the first time since 1815, no great powers are at one another's throats [but] civil wars and snarling savageries continue on both sides of the Equator." There is a basis in fact for this assertion. Between 1989 and 1997, internal armed conflicts over government (civil wars) or over territory (state formation conflicts) have been the most common, by far. In this period, 103 civil wars erupted, in comparison with only six between states. At the start of 1998, 21 civil wars were raging, and *no* armed "cross-border armed conflicts were under way" (*Defense Monitor* 27 1998, 1–3).

TABLE 12.2 The Frequency and Severity of Civil Wars, 1816–1997

Period	Number of Civil Wars Begun	System Size (average number of states)	Battle Deaths	Number (percent) of Civil Wars Internationalized through Large-Scale Military Intervention
1816–1848	12	28	93,200	3 (25%)
1849–1881	20	39	2,891,600	1 (5%)
1882–1914	18	40	388,000	3 (17%)
1915–1945	14	59	1,631,460	4 (29%)
1946–1988	60	117	6,222,020	14 (23%)
1989–1997	103	182	1,740,000	8 (8%)
Totals	227		12,966,280+	31 (14%)

SOURCE: Data for 1816–1988 provided courtesy of the Correlates of War project under the direction of J. David Singer and Melvin Small; 1989–1997 frequencies are based on Wallenstein and Sollenberg (1997) and deaths on Sivard (1996).

Civil wars resulting in at least one thousand civilian and military deaths per year occurred 227 times between 1816 and 1997 (Small and Singer 1982; Singer 1991, 66–75; Wallensteen and Sollenberg 1997). Their outbreak has been somewhat irregular. Although at least one civil war was begun in "only" eighty-four (less than half) of these years, over time civil war has become increasingly frequent (see Table 12.2). Of the civil wars since 1816, 72 percent began after 1945, with the frequency steadily climbing each decade in this period. Other inventories support this impression, estimating that "more than two-thirds of all armed conflict in the world since 1945 has taken the form of civil wars" (K. Holsti 1995, 320–21; see also SIPRI 1998). However, this trend (Sivard 1996) is, in part, a product of the increase in the number of independent states in the international system, which makes the incidence of civil war statistically more probable. Nonetheless, civil wars stem from similar emerging conditions, and are "generally waged around three issues":

- First, many minority ethnic groups are seeking greater autonomy or the creation of an independent state (e.g., Kurds in Turkey and Chechens in Russia).

- Second, wars are fought over control of the state. During the Cold War, the East and West fueled many such conflicts. Although superpower sponsorship has ended, fighting continues in Afghanistan and Angola. Wars over state control are also driven by ethnic, clan or religious differences (as in Rwanda and Algeria).

- Finally, several armed conflicts are occurring where national government has either badly eroded or completely broken down. In these "failed states" (such as Liberia and Somalia) the line between political struggle and economic banditry is blurred. (Sivard 1996, 17)

The number of civil wars *under way* provides a different picture of its worldwide spread. Referring to the same inventories cited in Table 12.2, we see that between 1816 and 1997 civil wars were in progress somewhere in the world about 90 percent of the time. Domestic, not international, war *is* the most familiar form of armed conflict today. During the five-year period from 1989 to 1993, a total of ninety conflicts were active in at least one year in sixty-one locations around the world, and none of these were "truly international" (Gleditsch 1995, 586). In June 1994, *all* of the thirty-six wars then being fought were civil wars, twenty-one of which had begun more than a decade earlier (*Harper's* 289 July 1994, 11).

A notable characteristic of civil wars is their severity. The number of lives lost in civil violence has remained high since the Napoleonic Wars ended in 1815, and casualty rates show an alarming growth, especially since World War II. One symptom of the climbing lethality of civil rebellions is that ten of the fifteen most destructive civil wars between 1816 and 1980 occurred in the twentieth century; of those ten, seven have occurred since World War II (Small and Singer 1982, 241). "The most savage conflicts occur in the home" is a cliché that captures this ugly reality, as genocide and other indiscriminate attacks aimed at depopulating entire regions in mass slaughter have become commonplace in recent civil wars. That grim aspect was illustrated in Rwanda, where "the Hutu government incited citizens to a genocidal slaughter, resulting in the murder of an estimated 500,000 people in a month's time" (Sivard 1996).

A second core characteristic of civil wars is their duration.

> Most of today's wars are civil wars. The dominant pattern is of rumbling conflicts that, from time to time across a decade, erupt viciously into action. . . . For the most part, modern [internal] war resembles a slow torture, [offering] few triumphs. . . . They simply continue. More than half the wars of the 1990s lasted more than five years, two-fifths lasted more than ten years and a quarter for more than twenty. The action is often fitful. (D. Smith 1997, 14).

A third characteristic of civil wars is their resistance to negotiated settlement. Making peace among rival factions that are struggling for power, driven by hatred, and poisoned by the inertia of prolonged killing that has become a way of life is very difficult. Civil wars rarely result in the decisive victory of one faction over another. The pattern of civil wars is that domestic enemies are rarely able to end the fighting through negotiated compromise at the bargaining table; most end on the battlefield:

> Unlike interstate wars, civil wars rarely end in negotiated settlements. Between 1940 and 1990 55 percent of interstate wars were resolved at the bargaining table, whereas only 20 percent of civil wars reached similar solutions. Instead, most internal wars ended with the extermination, expulsion, or capitulation of the losing side. In fact, groups fighting civil wars almost always chose to fight to the finish unless an outside power stepped in to guarantee a peace agreement. If a third party agreed to enforce the terms of a peace treaty, negotiations always succeeded regardless of the initial goals, ideology, or ethnicity of the participants. If a third party did not intervene, these talks usually failed. (Walter 1997, 335)

The growing frequency, severity, length, and indeterminate conclusion of the civil wars in the last decade of the twentieth century are accounted for by the multiple causes of these prolonged domestic disputes raging throughout the globe.

The Causes of Civil War

Civil wars stem from a wide range of ideological, demographic, religious, ethnic, economic, social-structural, and political conditions. Civil war and revolution have simultaneously been defended as instruments of justice and condemned as the immoral acceptance of violent change. They contain ingredients of both. Those who engineered the American, Russian, and Chinese revolutions claimed that violence was necessary to realize social change, political freedom, and independence; the powers from whom they sought liberation berated the immorality of their methods.

Internal Rebellion and Secessionist Revolts. Among the sources of civil war, internal violence is a reaction to frustration and **relative deprivation**—people's perception that they are unfairly deprived of the wealth and status that they deserve in comparison with advantaged others (Gurr 1970). When people's expectations of what they deserve rise more rapidly than their material rewards, the probability of conflict grows. That, of course, applies to most of the countries in the Global South today, where the distribution of wealth and opportunities is highly unequal. Note in this context that the seeds of civil strife are often sown by national independence movements. "More than two thirds of all the armed combat in the world between 1945 and 1995 were manifestations of the state-creation enterprise" (K. Holsti 1995, 22). In the aftermath of the Cold War, unrest and discontent—long held in check at the point of a bayonet— have been released, and secession revolts have escalated as a result (Gurr 1998).

Nationalism and "Neonationalism." Nationalism today is widely regarded as an especially potent cause of war within states as noted earlier (see also Chapter 7). However, the conditions prevailing today lead many to believe that nationalism will incite "wars of states against nations, wars of succession, and major armed uprisings to oust governments" (K. Holsti 1995) at unprecedented levels. The potential magnitude of nationalism-inspired revolutionary war is great:

> More than 95 percent of the world's . . . states are multinational, that is, composed of many nations, some unconsenting. These . . . states assert sovereignty over the world's three thousand to five thousand nations and peoples. . . . State governments [are pitted] against guerrilla insurgencies and indigenous nations. Most of these wars are over territory, resources, and identity, not ideology. They are hidden from most people's views because the fighting is against peoples and countries that are not even on the map. (Nietschmann 1991, 172–73)

If nationalism is a powerful influence on internal wars, what is termed **neonationalism** adds a new element to this traditional cause. Neonationalism and the localized conflicts it spawns differ from the nationalism previously seen in the Global South.

> Earlier stages of Third World nationalism tended to revolve around the national liberation experience, the zeal engendered by the throwing off of colonial ties. . . . Neonationalism is the product of more recent decades, going beyond classical nationalism and [including] separatist subnationalism; that is, the expression of communal/ethnic aspirations of groups within the nation-state that are unhappy with their lot: Shiites in Iraq, Sikhs in India, Unighur Turks in Chinese Turkestan. It involves strong new drives toward separatism: the Moros in the Philippines, Georgians in the [former] Soviet Union, Catholics in Northern Ireland, Hungarians in Romania, Biafra in Nigeria, even Quebec in Canada. (Fuller 1991–1992, 14–15)

relative deprivation the inequality between the wealth and status of individuals and groups, and the outrage of those at the bottom about their perceived exploitation by those at the top.

370

This kind of destabilizing "hypernationalism" is malign because the neonationalist doctrines are used "to justify or motivate large-scale violence [or] the conquest or subjugation of other nationalities" (Snyder 1993). The civil strife that erupted in Albania, Liberia, Serbia, Sudan, and Rwanda in the mid-1990s is symptomatic of the new wave of fractional conflicts that neonationalism has ignited. The future is foretold by the recent (1990–1995) past, during which half the countries that experienced a civil war were those in which ethnic minorities comprised 10 to 50 percent of the population (D. Smith 1997, 30).

Ethnonational Conflict. Since World War II, civil wars provoked by ancient ethnic and racial hatreds have been commonplace in multiethnic states. Between 1945 and 1981, 258 cases of **ethnic warfare** were observed, 40 percent of which involved high levels of violence (Carment 1993, 141). More recently, this armed conflict has reached epidemic proportions. Ted Robert Gurr (1994, 351–52) estimated that 26,759,000 refugees were fleeing the fifty major ethnonational conflicts that were occurring in 1993–1994, each of which was responsible for an average of eighty thousand deaths. Most of the victims were innocent children. Between 1983 and 1993, some 10 million children died in civil strife (Kane 1995a, 20), and the rate of killing of innocent civilian noncombatants continues to climb. Brutal assaults on civilians, including children, are escalating, and it is estimated that "today more than 90 percent of all casualties are non-combatants" (Sivard 1996, 17). Of the 40 million refugees worldwide, just over half are **displaced people**—refugees within their own countries—and "women and children are more likely to be made refugees than men" (D. Smith 1997, 26).

As U.S. President Bill Clinton observed in his June 7, 1994, speech before the French National Assembly, militant ethnic nationalism was "on the rise, transforming the healthy pride of nations, tribes, religious and ethnic groups into cancerous prejudice, eating away at states and leaving their people addicted to the political painkillers of violence and demagoguery." Chan Heng Chee, Singapore's former ambassador to the United Nations, in 1993 described the opinion shared by most experts when she observed that "with the end of the

Children have often been the major victims of civil strife. This photo, which received the World Press Award in 1985, depicts children caught in the ethnonational and religious civil war in Beirut, the capital of Lebanon—a country whose population is about two-thirds Muslim and one-fourth Christian, with each faction divided into further sects.

Cold War . . . the new problems haunting us will be instability arising from ethnic and religious turmoil. . . . The fault line will . . . to a large extent coincide with racial and ethnic divisions." The danger, warns Irish author Conor Cruise O'Brien (1993), resides in the fact that ethnonationalism "is something for which people are prepared to kill and die in large numbers, as Serbs, Croats, and Bosnian Muslims [did in the former Yugoslavia], and as, at an even more primordial level, warlike Somalian clansmen are doing." Thus, much of the internal revolt and ethnic warfare currently sweeping the world is less inspired by political motives and economic aims than it is by deeply rooted ethnic animosities. Ethnopolitical clashes differ greatly from the anticolonial secessionist and separatist movements of the past, and instead are often waged by irregular and private gangs committing atrocities against their neighbors.

Failed States. Many fledgling governments are fragile and fall apart as they fail to effectively manage the regulatory power sovereignty under international law gives them to govern affairs within their territorial borders. Mismanagement by failed government administration is causing an epidemic of **failing states** throughout the globe, as disarray, discontent, and disorder have mobilized desperate populations living in conditions of anarchy to rebel. The civil wars percolated by state failure have caused as many as 113 states to dissolve or fragment into separate units between 1955 and 1994 according to the U.S. Central Intelligence Agency's "State Failure Task Force" report. As Map 12.1 shows, in 1996 no less than another sixteen states were "high-risk" countries vulnerable to destruction through civil rebellion against a feeble government.

failing states those governments that are in danger of losing the loyalty of their citizens, who are rebelling against corruption and administrative failure, and in the process tearing the country into separate political parts.

The causes of state failure and civil disintegration are multiple, but failed states share some key characteristics. Among them, the CIA "State Failure Task Force" report finds that

- Democracy generally lowers the risk of state failure; autocracy increases it.
- Poor democracies, however, are more unstable than either rich democracies or poor nondemocracies, and poor democracies that don't improve living standards are exceptionally vulnerable.
- The best predictor of failure is high infant mortality.
- High levels of trade openness seem to inoculate any kind of regime against failure. States that have fair rules allowing a high degree of international trade gain stability.
- The existence of a "youth bulge"—a large proportion of young adults in the population—increases the risk of ethnic war because large pools of underemployed youth are easily mobilized into action.
- Mass killings are often associated with low levels of trade openness, in part, because countries with little foreign trade are usually of little concern to the international community. (Zimmerman 1996, 46)

Inasmuch as many of the 190 sovereign states in the world have one or more of these attributes, it is likely that failing states will grow as a problem in the globalized twenty-first century, as the pressures of globalization (see Chapter 9) contribute to the conditions that are causing civil wars and state failure.

The Economic Sources of Internal Rebellions. The destabilization caused by rapid growth also helps to account for the ubiquity of internal war (see Olson

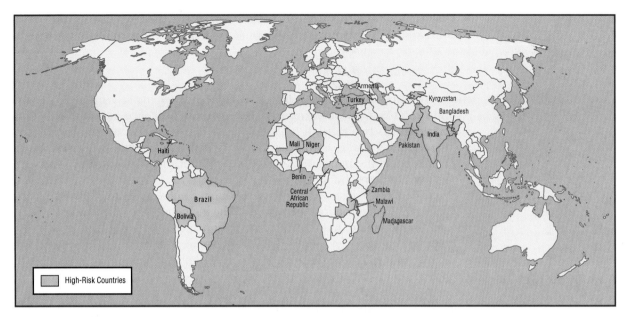

MAP 12.1

"Failing States" Threatening to Fall Apart, 1996

The U.S. CIA "State Failure Task Force" identifies sixteen "high-risk" countries vulnerable to dissolution as a result of mismanagement and civil revolt. *State failure*, defined as revolutionary or ethnic wars, mass killings and disruptive regime changes, threatens to increase the number of countries in the twenty-first century, as failing states splinter into newly emergent states. The United Nations estimates that by 2025 there may be as many as five hundred sovereign states in the world.

SOURCE: U.S. Central Intelligence Agency, from Zimmerman, 1996, 4.

1971). In contrast with what intuition might suggest, civil violence often erupts in countries in which conditions are improving, not deteriorating. "Economic modernization," former U.S. Secretary of State Henry Kissinger suggested, "leads to political instability rather than political stability." When modernization generates rising expectations that governments are unable to satisfy, civil war often follows. This is the essence of *relative deprivation* as a cause of internal violence, as people who feel themselves to have been denied resources they deserve are often inclined to use force in acts of rebellion (Gurr 1970).

Having observed rapid growth as a source of civil war, we must not ignore the persistence of poverty as an ancient and continuing cause. Desperation has fomented domestic insurrection throughout all periods of history, and today, even in the period of democratization and economic growth through free trade and free markets, misery among those not sharing in the benefits is breeding revolt. "The chief causes of conflict remain—overwhelming poverty in cities and the dominance of a narrow elite in rural areas." This is made evident by the fact that 57 percent of the armed conflicts between 1990 and 1995 erupted in the poor countries ranking "low" on the UN Human Development Index (HDI; see Chapter 5), and another 34 percent in the "medium-human-development" countries, in contrast to only 14 percent in the "high" countries providing relative prosperity, health and education for their citizens" (D. Smith 1997, 48, 50). As Sadaka Ogata, the UN High Commissioner for Refugees, concluded in December 1997, "to establish a more peaceful, prosperous and secure world, poverty must be eliminated and income differentials reduced."

The International Dimensions of Civil War

It is tempting to think of civil war as stemming exclusively from conditions within countries. However, external factors often influence internal rebellions. "Every war has two faces. It is a conflict both between and within political systems; a conflict that is both external and internal. [It is undeniable that] internal wars affect the international system [and that] the international system affects internal wars" (Modelski 1964).

We can distinguish several phases that have influenced the linkage between changes in the international system and the incidence of civil war. First, the effects of imperialism, industrialization, nationalism, and ideology provoked the comparatively high levels of civil war between 1848 and 1870. Second, the breakup of the European colonial empires contributed to the frequent incidence of civil war between the end of World War II and the 1960s. And today, the discipline imposed by Cold War bipolarity has disappeared, removing states' fear that turmoil within their borders will precipitate military intervention by the great powers.

Because the great powers have global interests, historically they have been prone to intervene militarily in civil wars to support friendly governments and to overthrow unfriendly ones. When they did, wars within states became internationalized. But today it is often difficult to determine where an internal war ends and an international one begins. In an interdependent, increasingly borderless world, the difference between involvement and intervention is difficult to distinguish. The two types of armed conflict are closely linked. As Table 12.2 reveals, between the Congress of Vienna (1816) and the tearing down of the Berlin Wall (1989), nearly one in five civil wars has become an interstate war through intervention by an external power. More than three-fifths of these large-scale military interventions have occurred since 1945. During the Cold War, many entanglements of the United States (e.g., Lebanon, the Dominican Republic, Korea, Vietnam, Grenada, and Panama) and the Soviet Union (e.g., Hungary, Ethiopia and Afghanistan) were responses to internal instability. Even today, the Global South remains the site of most violent conflicts and military and humanitarian interventions in the world. In response to the tragic fate of the innocent victims, the United Nations and NATO have intervened in multilateral operations to stop the carnage (see Chapter 16).

Many analysts believe that domestic conflicts become internationalized because leaders who experience internal opposition are inclined to provoke an international crisis in the hope that their citizens will become less rebellious if their attention is diverted to the threat of external aggression. This proposition has become known as the **diversionary theory of war** (see Focus 12.3).

The diversionary theory of war is based on the expectation that external war will result in increased domestic support for political leaders. "To put it cynically, one could say that nothing helps a leader like a good war. It gives him his only chance of being a tyrant and being loved for it at the same time. He can introduce the most ruthless forms of control and send thousands of his followers to their deaths and still be hailed as a great protector. Nothing ties tighter the in-group bonds than an out-group threat" (Morris 1969).

The argument is logical. However, the relationship between civil and international conflict is, in practice, more complex. In general, the available evi-

The Diversionary Theory of War
Is There a Connection between Civil Strife and External Aggression?

If leaders assume that national unity will rise when an external threat exists, they may seek to manage domestic unrest by initiating foreign adventures. Indeed, many political advisers counsel this as a solution. For instance, the realist theorist Niccoló Machiavelli in 1513 advised leaders to undertake foreign wars whenever turmoil within their state became too great, and he was echoed by the legal theorist Jean Bodin in 1593, who argued that "the best way of preserving a state, and guaranteeing it against sedition, rebellion and civil war is . . . to find an enemy against whom they can make common cause." Hermann Goering, Adolf Hitler's adviser, advocated the same idea in Nazi Germany, contending: "Voice or no voice, the people can always be brought to do the bidding of the leaders. That is easy. All you have to do is tell them they are being attacked and denounce the pacifists for lack of patriotism." Similarly, John Foster Dulles (1939), who later became U.S. Secretary of State, recommended "The easiest and quickest cure of internal dissension is to portray danger from abroad."

Whether leaders actually start wars to offset domestic conflict is an empirical question. Many studies have examined the proposition, but few confirm it (see Morgan and Bickers 1992). It seems reasonable to assume that "war with the outside is sometimes the last chance for a state ridden with inner antagonisms to overcome these antagonisms" (Simmel 1956), and that "statesmen may be driven to a policy of foreign conflict—if not open war—in order to defend themselves against the onslaught of domestic enemies" (Haas and Whiting 1956). Yet we cannot demonstrate that leaders undertake these diversionary actions for this purpose. "The linkage depends," political scientist Jack Levy (1989b) concludes, "on the kinds of internal conditions that commonly lead to hostile external actions for diversionary purposes." For example, "democratic states are particularly likely to use force externally during an election year, especially when the election occurs at a time of economic stagnation" (Ostrom and Job 1986). This linkage does not always hold, however. In most cases "where civil unrest preceded external conflict, war was not usually initiated by the strife-torn state. Instead, most wars were initiated by outside powers, with the internally troubled state in the role of the victim" (Cashman 1993).

dence urges that we question the diversionary theory of war. Perhaps the most compelling reason for some doubt is that "when domestic conflict becomes extremely intense it would seem more reasonable to argue that there is a greater likelihood that a state will retreat from its foreign engagements in order to handle the situation at home" (Zinnes and Wilkenfeld 1971).

• • •

TERRORISM

Terrorism poses another alarming kind of violence in the contemporary world. The instruments of terror are varied and the motivations of terrorists diverse, but "experts agree that terrorism is the use or threat of violence, a method of combat or a strategy to achieve certain goals, that its aim is to induce a state of fear in the victim, that it is ruthless and does not conform to humanitarian norms, and that publicity is an essential factor in terrorist strategy" (Laqueur 1986).

Some terrorist activities, such as the 1995 bombing of the U.S. federal government building in Oklahoma City, begin and end in a single century. Many, however, cross national borders. In the early 1990s terrorists targeted citizens and property in a large percentage of countries, with the incidents spread randomly throughout the globe (see Map 12.2).

terrorism premeditated, politically motivated violence perpetrated against noncombatant targets by subnational groups or clandestine agents, usually intended to influence an audience.

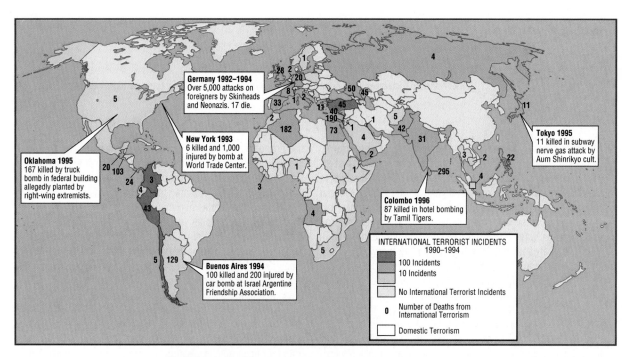

Germany 1992–1994
Over 5,000 attacks on foreigners by Skinheads and Neonazis. 17 die.

New York 1993
6 killed and 1,000 injured by bomb at World Trade Center.

Oklahoma 1995
167 killed by truck bomb in federal building allegedly planted by right-wing extremists.

Tokyo 1995
11 killed in subway nerve gas attack by Aum Shinrikyo cult.

Colombo 1996
87 killed in hotel bombing by Tamil Tigers.

Buenos Aires 1994
100 killed and 200 injured by car bomb at Israel Argentine Friendship Association.

INTERNATIONAL TERRORIST INCIDENTS
1990–1994

100 Incidents

10 Incidents

No International Terrorist Incidents

0   Number of Deaths from International Terrorism

Domestic Terrorism

M A P 1 2 . 2

The Global Spread of International Terrorist Incidents, 1990–1994

Dan Smith of the Oslo International Peace Research Institute (PRIO) argues that "terrorism is warfare by another name—the low level, low intensity use of violence for political ends." Terrorists use a variety of methods, and as this map shows, in the 1990s terrorism is a global problem.

SOURCE: Dan Smith, Director, International Peace Research Institute (PRIO) in Oslo, Norway, as cited in Smith, *The State of War and Peace Atlas*, 3rd rev. edition (Copyright, Dan Smith and Myriad Editions, Limited, 1997). New York: Penguin USA, 375 Hudson Street, 10014, 1997, pp. 22–23.

Although terrorism has always been practiced, it emerged as a significant international problem in the 1960s (Kidder 1990) and grew to epidemic proportions in the 1970s and 1980s. Figure 12.4 shows the changing frequency of terrorism in today's world, the general trend suggesting an increasing level of transnational terrorist activity since 1968, followed by a decline since 1987. International terrorist attacks fell during 1997 to 304 separate terrorist acts. This was the lowest annual total in twenty-four years (the 1997 casualty rates also showed a falling level similar to those in recent years; 221 people were killed and 693 were wounded, the U.S. Department of State reported).

Terrorism is a tactic of the powerless against the powerful. Thus it is not surprising that political or social minorities and ethnic movements sometimes turn to acts of terrorism on behalf of their political causes (see Chapter 7). Those seeking independence and sovereign statehood, such as the Basques in Spain, typify the aspirations that animate terrorist activity. Religion also sometimes rationalizes the terrorist activities of extremist movements, such as the efforts of the Sikh groups who wish to carve out an independent Sikh state called Khalistan ("Land of the Pure") from Indian territory, and of the Islamic extremist group HAMAS to destabilize Israel and sabotage a negotiated peace between Israel and its Arab neighbors. In 1994 attacks by secular terrorist groups declined, while terrorist activities by radical Islamic groups increased

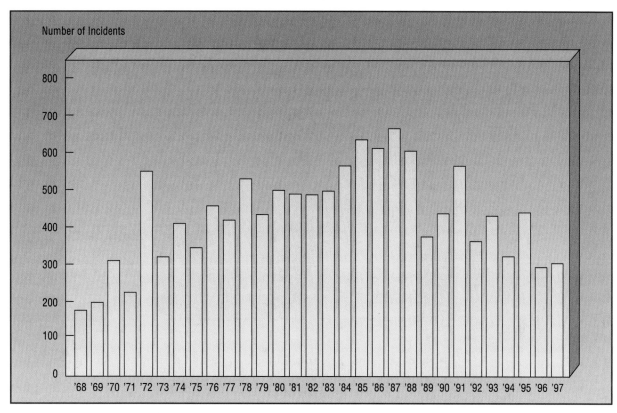

FIGURE 12.4

International Terrorist Incidents, 1968–1997

The frequency of international terrorist activity has changed over time since 1968, and the number of incidents each year has ranged between 174 (in 1968) and 665 (in 1987). These activities appear entrenched, but vary over time.

SOURCE: Office of the Coordinator for Counterterrorism, U.S. Department of State.

(U.S. Department of State 1995), and in November 1995 right-wing Jewish fanatics in the Kach religious terrorist group assassinated Israeli Prime Minister Yitzhak Rabin to derail the peace process in Palestine.

In the industrialized world, terrorism often occurs where discrepancies in income are severe and where minority groups feel deprived of the political freedoms and privileges enjoyed by the majority. In the urbanized areas of the industrialized world, guerrilla warfare—normally associated with rural uprisings—is not a viable route to self-assertion, but terrorist tactics are.

Consideration of terrorists' motives often obscures the perception of terrorism as a disease: One person's terrorist may be another person's liberator. Ironically, both governments and countergovernment movements claim to seek liberty, and both are labeled terrorists by their opponents.

Those who are described as terrorists, and who reject that title for themselves, make the uncomfortable point that national armed forces, fully supported by democratic opinion, have in fact employed violence and terror on a far vaster scale than what liberation movements have as yet been able to attain. The "freedom fighters" see themselves as fighting a just war. Why

377

The world has paid a fearful price for the random violence that modern terrorism inflicts. The point of terrorist campaigns is to make people feel unsafe and unsure, and to succeed, terrorists fight outside the accepted rules of war by threatening to strike anywhere, at any time, at anyone, without warning. Shown here is an innocent bystander being evacuated from the scene of a September 1997 terrorist attack in Israel.

should they not be entitled to kill, burn, and destroy as national armies, navies, and air forces do; and why should the label "terrorist" be applied to them and not to the national militaries? (O'Brien 1977, 56–57)

The difference between nationalistic "freedom fighters," whose major complaint is that they lack a country, and governments claiming to protect freedom, often lies in the eye of the beholder. This problem makes the definition of a terrorist group less obvious and more controversial, as what most distinguishes terrorists groups from liberation movements is the outcome—which faction succeeds or fails in a political struggle for power. We must keep in mind that those who are willing to use violence and terror outside the rules of warfare that have evolved over time tend to be condemned or praised, depending on whether those who condemn or praise accept or reject their cause.

The popularity of the slogan that "one person's terrorist is another's freedom fighter" notwithstanding, there is a difference. Terrorists are defined by the *means* (terror) they use, and freedom fighters by the *end* (civil liberty) they pursue. Because freedom can be fought for by moral and legal methods that respect the immunity of noncombatant targets, freedom fighters are different from terrorists, who are prepared to use violence against unarmed civilians and to promote good causes by evil methods.

Although many terrorist groups today are undeniably seeking sovereignty, a broader definition of terrorism would acknowledge that many governments undertake terrorist acts, sometimes against their own people and sometimes by supporting terrorism against other established sovereign states (see Crenshaw 1990). In fact, some states underwrite the activities of terrorist movements that advocate philosophies they embrace (or challenge the security of rival states). States have often financed, trained, equipped, and provided sanctuary for terrorists whose activities serve their foreign policy goals (see Chapter 7). The practice of such *state terrorism* is among the charges that the United States leveled in the 1980s against Cuba, the Soviet Union, Syria, Iraq, and Libya, among others.

Similarly, others accused the United States of sponsoring terrorist activities in Vietnam, Chile, El Salvador, Nicaragua, and elsewhere (Schlagheck 1990).

Although many terrorist sanctuaries have disappeared with the end of the Cold War,

> it is unlikely that international terrorism is a passing and transitory phenomenon. The trend toward the weakening of central authority in governments, the rise in ethnic and subnational sentiments, and the increasing fractionalization of the global political process point toward its growth as a form of political protest and persuasion. Classic balance-of-power diplomacy is of little utility in dealing with it, for violent acts of small groups of people, or individuals, are difficult for governments to control. International terrorism is likely to continue and to expand because in the minds of many of its perpetrators it has proven to be "successful." (Pierre 1984, 85)

Indeed, the dangers of terrorism have not waned. Libyan leader Col. Muammar Qaddafi warned in July 1993, "Whatever takes place in America—and you will see a lot more terrorism there—is a function of perceived injustices in other parts of the world. . . . Acts of terrorism in America will be the answer, and they will be more and more violent and spectacular for television purposes around the world." The terrorist threat thus thrives, as shown by the wave of suicide bombing in the Middle East that provoked world leaders to attend a "summit of the peacemakers" conference in March 1996. "The use of terror is more widespread and more effective than is generally recognized" (*Economist*, March 2, 1996, 338), and the threat is likely to escalate if terrorists use nuclear, biological, or chemical weapons for political blackmail. And it will persist for other reasons. One reason is that **postmodern terrorism** is likely to expand because the globalized international environment without meaningful barriers allows terrorists to practice their ancient trade by new rules and methods, while at the same time encouraging state-sponsored terrorism as a substitute for warfare and making the most advanced countries the most vulnerable (Laqueur 1998). Another is the rapid spread of new weapons and technology, and their easy transport across borders, which provide unprecedented opportunities for terrorists to commit atrocities and to change their tactics in response to successes in countering them. A third is the growing difficulty in a globalized system of detecting and deterring the attacks of disciplined globalized terrorist networks that are generously funded by international organized crime (IOC) syndicates to facilitate their profit in the narcotics trade (see Chapter 7). And still another is the moral ambiguity that surrounds the activities of extremist militia groups, who are glorified by some in the media for their independence and defiance of governing authority, especially in democracies protecting the rights of citizens to carry arms and express their grievances. Governments often seem reluctant to exercise the political will necessary to destroy terrorism:

postmodern terrorism to Walter Laqueur, the "improved prospects" of the "many terrorisms" now made possible for an expanding set of diverse actors with new weapons "to sow panic in a society, to weaken or even overthrow the incumbents, and to bring about political change."

> Terrorism continues, and will continue, because terrorists and their supporters make distinctions of class and race and other divisions of mankind, subordinating the humanity of their victims to the purposes of their cause, giving credit to the political smoke that thinly masks acts of pure bloodlust. And it continues because those who should know better refuse to recognize the distinction between aggression and rightful defense, forswearing power as if it itself were evil, when clearly it is neither good nor evil but falls easily into the service of either.

Refusal to make such distinctions and to hold to them is why . . . terrorists are given the Nobel Peace Prize, and why the press refers to their retainers who attack kindergartens as "fighters." . . . It is why terrorists know that the world is safe for them, that they have a good chance of success and even honor. (Helprin 1995, A14)

● ● ●

THE HUMAN TRAGEDY OF VIOLENT CONFLICT

War exacts a terrible toll on human life, commemorated publicly by black flags of mourning fluttering from the homes of the war dead and memorials at grave sites. Monuments honor the courage of the soldiers who gave their lives in their countries' wars. At the beginning of this century approximately 90 percent of war casualties were military; today about 90 percent of the world's war victims are innocent civilians (UNDP 1994, 47). UNICEF reported, in *The State of the World's Children 1992*, that more than 1.5 million children were killed in wars during the 1980s, and more than 4 million were "physically disabled—limbs amputated, brains damaged, eyesight and hearing lost—through bombing, land-mines, firearms, torture. Five million children are in refugee camps because of war: A further 12 million have lost their homes."

The tragic human consequences of violence are also revealed daily by the efforts of individuals and families seeking to escape its scourge. These are the victims of armed conflict who can be observed fleeing from one country in hopes of finding refuge, and perhaps a better life, in another country. The refugee asylum problem has now assumed global dimensions, as noted in Chapter 10. Of the twenty largest source countries of refugees in 1995, nineteen were embroiled in internal armed conflict. Religious preference, ethnic origin, and the expression of political dissent are some of the factors that motivate refugees, but armed conflict—along with poverty, persecution, and the pain of hunger and starvation—remains a paramount cause.

The ravages of war are not confined to its human victims, however. Some of its costs are economic, leaving the survivors to pay for the debts and damages. Other costs are ecological, as illustrated by the 1991 Persian Gulf War; although blackened skies have now cleared, the environmental damage may take decades to undo.

Could it be that a world so ingenious in perpetrating violence also will learn that war and violence are too costly, too destructive to continue? If so, can it discover viable paths to peace? The chapters that follow examine some of the solutions that policymakers and concerned citizens have proposed.

KEY TERMS

war
conflict
politics
armed force
deterrence
pax atomica
levels of analysis

ethologists
intraspecific aggression
interspecific aggression
realists
pacifism
survival of the fittest
nature-nurture controversy

socialization
national character
rational choice
state level of analysis
cultural conditioning
feminist theories
communist theory of imperialism

laissez-faire capitalism	power transition theory	ethnic warfare
neorealist theories	long-cycle theory	displaced people
neoliberal theories	war weariness hypothesis	failing states
democratic peace	civil wars	diversionary theory of war
nationalism	relative deprivation	terrorism
global level of analysis	neonationalism	postmodern terrorism

SUGGESTED READING

David, Steven R. "Internal War: Causes and Cures," *World Politics* 49 (July 1997): 552–76.

Delmas, Philippe. *The Rosy Future of War*. New York: Free Press, 1997.

Doyle, Michael W. *Ways of War and Peace: Realism, Liberalism, and Socialism*. New York: Norton, 1997.

Gilpin, Robert. *War and Change in World Politics*. Cambridge, Eng.: Cambridge University Press, 1981.

Hassner, Pierre. *Violence and Peace: From the Atomic Bomb to Ethnic Cleansing*. Budapest: Central European University Press, 1997.

Holsti, Kalevi J. *War, the State, and the State of War*. New York: Cambridge University Press, 1996.

Ignatieff, Michael. *The Warrior's Honor: War and the Modern Conscience*. New York: Henry Holt, 1998.

Porter, Bruce D. *War and the Rise of the State*. New York: Free Press, 1994.

Roy, A. Bikash. *Blood and Soil: War, Peace and Territorial Conflict*. Columbia: University of South Carolina Press, 1999.

Schechtenman, Bernard, and Martin Slann, eds. *Violence and Terrorism: Annual Editions*. Hightstown, N.J.: Dushkin/McGraw-Hill, 1998.

Suganami, Hidemi. *On the Causes of War*. New York: Oxford University Press, 1996.

Vasquez, John A. *The War Puzzle*. Cambridge, Eng.: Cambridge University Press, 1993.

WHERE ON THE WORLD WIDE WEB?

http://www.cfcsc.dnd.ca/links/wars/index.html
War, Peace, Security Guide The Canadian Forces College has created an information resource center on war and peace. Graphical links to armed forces, peace and disarmament sites, and military information are available. Visit the clickable "Map of World Conflicts" and choose two contemporary conflicts to explore. Who are the main combatants? What are the main issues? Can you identify any similarities between the two conflicts? Do you have any suggestions for resolving the conflicts? Are other international actors a help or a hindrance to the conflicts?

http://www.pbs.org/wgbh/pages/frontline/shows/tibet/
Dreams of Tibet PBS Online brings you a very educational Web site devoted to issues surrounding Tibet and its quest for independence. View the chronology of Tibet's history starting in the year 600 C.E., then read about Tibetan Buddhism and the Dalai Lama. Review interviews with actor Richard Gere, who is a "free Tibet" activist or Martin Scorses who directed the movie *Kundun* which is based on the biography of the Dalai Lama. You can also share your thoughts in a discussion forum.

http://cain.ulst.ac.uk/index.html
CAIN Web Service The Conflict Archive on the Internet provides information on "the Troubles" in Northern Ireland. There are links to the key events and issues, and you can also learn more about society in Northern Ireland.

http://www.incore.ulst.ac.uk/cds/countries/index.html
INCORE The Initiative on Conflict Resolution and Ethnicity has an Internet guide that allows you to examine the most recent international conflicts and nationalist movements in detail. Read about the Iraqi Kurds' quest for their own state. Find out what is happening in Kosovo, Serbia. There are links to prime sources, e-mail lists and newsgroups, news sources, maps, and nongovernmental organizations. You can also gather information according to theme. Want to learn about how war affects children? Visit the "Children and Conflict" link.

CHAPTER 13

The Changing Character of Military Power and National Security

CHAPTER TOPICS AND THEMES

- Power in international politics
  - What is "national security"?
  - How states' military capabilities compare
- The changing global distribution of power
  - International arms trade in the 1990s
  - The dispersion of modern weapons
  - The revolution in military technology
  - Unconventional biological and chemical weapons
  - Nuclear weapons proliferation: Problems and prospects
- The social and economic consequences of war preparations
- The great powers' national security strategies
  - The new U.S. security strategy
  - Russian strategy in the coming century
  - China's global clout and strategic posture
  - Japan's search for a strategy
  - Germany and the European Union search for a new strategic vision
- Can an insecure world escape the security dilemma?

The frequency and destructiveness of armed conflicts explain why states are preoccupied with threats to their security and why preparing for defense is so nearly a universal preoccupation. Because the anarchical international system requires that states rely on themselves for protection, **national security**—a country's psychological freedom from fear of foreign attack—is a paramount priority. As a result, policymakers typically assign national security the most prominent place on their foreign policy agendas.

This chapter examines why states often respond to perceived threats by arming. We begin by first considering the place of power in world politics. We then evaluate states' practices designed to diminish threats to their security, exploring in particular the great powers' security strategies in the context of general trends in military spending (and their domestic socioeconomic consequences), the arms trade, and weapons technology. Later chapters will use this discussion as a basis for exploring the dilemmas that armament acquisitions create, how states use weapons for coercive diplomacy, and which paths to peace realists and liberals advocate for escaping the danger of war.

• • •

POWER IN INTERNATIONAL POLITICS

What is this abstraction called **power,** the quest for which realists depict as states' primary motive? Although definitions abound, power remains an ambiguous concept (see Baldwin 1989; Claude 1962; Rothgeb 1993). Nonetheless, because most leaders are schooled in *realpolitik*, they conventionally operate from the traditional assumption that *power* gives states the ability to promote and protect national interests, to win in bargaining situations, and to shape the rules governing the international system. They are inclined to view power as a *political* phenomenon revolving around the capacity of one actor to persuade another to do what it otherwise would not. Thus, we will first evaluate this definition, which sees power as **politics**—the exercise of influence to control and dominate others.

When we view power as the means to control, it is reasonable to ask who is stronger and who is weaker, as well as which party will get its way and who will be forced to make concessions. These considerations invite the more fundamental question: What enables states to achieve their goals?

> **power** the factors that enable one state to coerce another; to realists, arms and military capabilities are the most important factor in determining which state will win a dispute.

The Elements of State Power

To determine the comparative power of states, analysts usually rank them according to the capabilities or resources presumed necessary to achieve influence over others. For such purposes, multiple factors (most significantly, military and economic capability) measure countries' relative **power potential.** If we could compare each state's total capabilities, according to this logic, we could then rank them by their ability to draw on these resources to exercise influence. Such a ranking would reveal the international system's hierarchy of power, differentiating the strong from the weak, the great from the marginal.

Of all the components of state power, military capability is usually thought to be the most important. Realists regard it as the central element in states' power potential. "Throughout history, the decisive factor in the fates of nations

383

has usually been the number, efficiency and dispositions of fighting forces," they argue. "National influence bears a direct relationship to gross national strength; without that, the most exquisite statesmanship is likely to be of limited use" (German 1960). Because realists assume that the ability to coerce is more important than the ability to reward or to purchase, they believe that military capability is a more important source of power than economic capability. By contrast, other strategic thinkers argue that in the next century, economic competition will be more critical to national strength than military competition. Accordingly, they insist the economic foundations of national security should receive primary emphasis.

Figure 13.1 presents two parallel rankings of the world's twenty most powerful states measured by their military spending and the size of their armed forces. Both rankings conform to what most people would likely regard as the world's most "powerful" states.

Power potential also derives from factors other than military expenditures and the number of soldiers. These include the size of a state's economy, its population and territorial size, geographic position, raw materials, degree of dependence on foreign sources of materials, technological capacity, national character, ideology, efficiency of governmental decision making, industrial productivity, volume of trade, savings and investment, educational level, and national morale and internal solidarity.

There is, however, no consensus on how best to weigh these factors. There is also no consensus as to what their relative importance should be in making comparisons, or what conditions affect the contribution that each makes in the equation that converts capabilities into influence. Although most analysts agree that states are not equal in their ability to influence others, few agree on how to rank their power potential. Consider what divergent pictures of the global hierarchy emerge when the relative capabilities of the great powers are ranked in other categories that realists also define as important (see Table 13.1). Clearly, strength is relative. The leading countries in some dimensions of power potential are not leaders in others, as power comes in many forms, and the global spread of technology has made it increasingly difficult to distinguish between powerful and weak states.

Inferring Power from Capabilities

Part of the difficulty of defining the elements of power is that their potential impact depends on the circumstances in a bargaining situation between actors in conflict, and especially on how leaders perceive those circumstances. Such judgments are subjective, as power ratios are not strictly products of measured capabilities. Perceptions also matter.

In addition, power is not a tangible commodity that states can acquire. It has meaning only in relative terms. As Chapter 14 explains, power is relational: A state can have power over some other actor only when it can prevail over that actor. Both actual and perceived strength determine who wins in a political contest. To make a difference, an adversary must know its enemy's capabilities and willingness to mobilize them for coercive purposes. For example, it must regard the opponent's threat to use military capabilities as credible. Intentions—especially perceptions of them—are critically important in this respect. The mere possession of weapons does not increase a state's power if its adversaries do not believe it will use them.

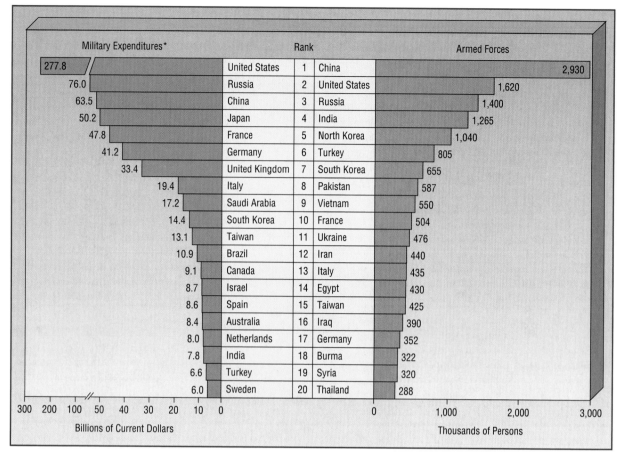

FIGURE 13.1

The World's Twenty Leading Military Spenders and Armed Forces, 1995

All states seek a measure of safety from war, and many "purchase" large armament arsenals and armies for this purpose. States vary widely in their ability and desire, however, and in the 1990s many countries, fearing excessive costs, *cut* their military expenditures and the size of their armed forces. In 1995 the United States was the globe's biggest spender, accounting for 32 percent of the world's total of $864 billion. At the same time, five countries (China, the United States, Russia, India, and North Korea) were the only countries with armies of more than 1 million soldiers; these five together accounted for nearly 30 percent of the world's total of 22.8 million soldiers.

*Note change and break in scale.

SOURCE: U.S. ACDA (1997), 5.

Historically, those with the largest arsenals have not necessarily triumphed in political conflicts. Weaker states often successfully resist pressure from their military superiors. Although Vietnam was weak in the conventional military sense, it succeeded against a vastly stronger France and, later, the United States. Similarly, the United States' superior military power did not prevent either North Korea's seizure of the USS *Pueblo* in 1968 or Iran's taking of American diplomats as hostages a decade later. The Soviet Union's inability, prior to its disintegration, to control political events in Afghanistan, eastern Europe, or

TABLE 13.1 The Power Potential of the Great Powers: The Top Ten Ranked by Five Measures

Territorial Size (thousand square miles)		Projected Population Size, 2025 (millions)	
1. Russia	6,590	1. China	1,523
2. Canada	3,850	2. India	1,385
3. China	3,700	3. United States	338
4. United States	3,620	4. Indonesia	277
5. Brazil	3,290	5. Pakistan	252
6. Australia	2,970	6. Nigeria	246
7. India	1,270	7. Brazil	225
8. Argentina	1,070	8. Bangladesh	194
9. Kazakhstan	1,050	9. Russia	153
10. Sudan	967	10. Mexico	137

Gross National Product, 1996 (billions of dollars)		Market Share of World Exports, Projected 1998 (percent)		Scientists and Engineers in Research (thousands)	
1. United States	6,388	1. United States	13.2	1. China	1,841
2. Japan	3,927	2. Germany	8.7	2. Russia	1,079
3. China	2,978	3. Japan	6.7	3. United States	949
4. Germany	2,005	4. China	6.5	4. Japan	813
5. France	1,289	5. France	5.4	5. Germany	492
6. Italy	1,135	6. United Kingdom	5.1	6. France	298
7. United Kingdom	1,043	7. Italy	4.7	7. India	244
8. Canada	575	8. Canada	3.1	8. United Kingdom	165
9. Spain	534	9. South Korea	2.6	9. Italy	120
10. Brazil	472	10. Singapore	2.5	10. South Korea	102

SOURCE: Territory and population, Population Reference Bureau; GNP, Seven Seas Web Site and *Handbook of International Economic Statistics* (1996); export shares, IMF (1997), 41; scientists, B. Hughes (1997), 80.

even its own constituent republics—despite an awesome weapons arsenal—shows that the impotence of military power is not peculiar to the United States.

Nonetheless, the quest for security through arms and the realist belief in military force remain widespread. Most policymakers assume that "while it could be a mistake to assume that political influence is proportional to military strength, it would be an even bigger mistake to deny any connection between the two" (Majeed 1991). Many believe that this is because military capability is a prerequisite to the successful exercise of **coercive diplomacy** (to be examined in Chapter 14), the employment of "threats or limited force to persuade an opponent to call off or undo an encroachment" (Craig and George 1990). The link between military power and foreign policy is intact even after the Cold War; in fact, it may be "more pervasive and more comprehensive than in earlier periods of history when war was less dangerous" (Majeed 1991). Perhaps it was this conviction that inspired U.S. President Bill Clinton to assert to the West Point graduating class in May 1993 that "[w]e have to ensure that the United States is ready, ready to win and superior to all other military forces in the world."

The Changing Nature of World Power

Military power is central in leaders' conceptualizations of national security. As noted in previous chapters, however, many analysts now argue that "the sources of power are, in general, moving away from the emphasis on military force and conquest that marked earlier eras. In assessing international power today, factors such as technology, education, and economic growth are becoming more important, whereas geography, population, and raw materials are becoming less important" (Nye 1990). In part this is because military force has often proven ineffectual, notably against belligerent revisionist states as well as politically mobilized nationalist and aggressive ethnic movements. Moreover, awareness of the importance of trade competitiveness to national standing has directed increasing attention to the nonmilitary dimensions of national security.

If we compare military-political and trade strategies as alternative methods for realizing national security, the latter may increasingly become more effective as a strategy for acquiring political power and material advancement. Since 1945 only a handful of states have borne the crushing costs of military expenditure, while the others have gained a relative competitive edge by investing in research on the development of goods to export abroad and conserving resources by relying on allies and global institutions to provide defense against potential threats. While the United States spent two-thirds of its research and development budget on military programs the past ten years, European countries spent two-thirds on development of new technologies for consumers and civilians at home and abroad (Sivard 1996, 40), and Japan's civilian product research exceeded 99 percent (Sivard 1996, 41).

Military expenditures extract other **opportunity costs** as well that retard economic growth and create fiscal deficits. According to the International Monetary Fund, "military spending crowds out both private and public investment." The **peace dividend** (the money saved if U.S. military outlays as a share of GDP had stayed at 1990 levels) comes to a hefty $345 billion, and if put to efficient use could pay big dividends for national strength. "Countries that made sharp cuts in military spending have also tended to reduce nonmilitary spending and their overall fiscal deficits while boosting social spending," the IMF reports (Koretz 1996). In addition to sacrificing other economic opportunities, this argument continues, military spending has direct costs, because expensive equipment quickly becomes outdated in the face of rapid technological innovations. This creates the need for even more sophisticated new weapons, the costs of which are staggering. Beyond the B-2 Air Force bomber, in production despite controversies about the need for its development ("costing four-and-a-half times its weight in gold"), the 1997 U.S. military budget included requests for development of the new Joint Strike Fighter that could cost $1 trillion and another $400 billion for six lesser-known new aircraft (*Defense Monitor*, April/May 1996, 1–2). Because "states can afford more 'butter' if they need fewer 'guns,'" Richard Rosecrance (1997) notes, "the two objectives sometimes represent trade-offs: The achievement of one may diminish the realization of the other," and the substantial costs of defense can erode national welfare—what policymakers hope to defend with military might. Conversely, commercial clout and trade competitiveness for national exports may contribute more than military might to national power in a globalized marketplace without barriers to trade; in that setting, trade bloc competition replaces the military and diplomatic struggles of the past. This thesis is a troublesome idea, to which we will return.

In addition to economic capability, other less tangible sources of national power now figure more prominently in calculations regarding national defense, including the media empires' "power over opinion" and control of global communications and information (Bell 1995). "Political leaders and philosophers have long understood that power comes from setting the agenda and determining the framework of a debate. The ability to establish preferences tends to be associated with intangible power resources such as culture, ideology, and institutions." These intangible resources constitute **soft power,** in contrast with the **hard power** "usually associated with tangible resources like military and economic strength" (Nye 1990). If soft power grows in relative importance, military force ratios will no longer translate into power potential in the way they once did.

• • •

THE QUEST FOR MILITARY CAPABILITIES

How people spend their money reveals their values. Similarly, how governments allocate their revenues reveals their priorities. Examination of national budgets discloses an unmistakable pattern: Although the sources of world political power may be changing, most states seek security by spending substantial portions of their national treasures on arms.

Trends in Military Spending

The weapons governments believe they require for national security are costly. Their willingness to purchase military protection has kept world military spending high. In 1995 the total stood at $864 billion, an amount exceeding more than $1.4 million each minute. However, world military spending could have been even higher had past levels continued. But in fact it has been trending downward, by 34 percent, since the peak-year high of $1.36 trillion in 1987.

Another impression results if the global outlay is measured in constant dollars to adjust for inflation. The 1995 level actually shows an *increase* over past levels, 2.6 times that spent in 1960, 1.8 times that of the 1970 total, and 1.2 times the 1980 level. These increases appear especially noticeable in the 1980s, but on closer inspection they extend the growth rates of world military expenditures exhibited throughout the twentieth century. Military spending has increased fifteenfold since the mid-1930s. The growth rate exceeds that of world population, the rate of expansion of global economic output, expenditures for public health to protect people from disease, and prices (U.S. ACDA 1997; Sivard 1991, 1993, 1996).

These aggregate figures require interpretation, because the global total spent for arms and armies conceals widely varying trends for particular groups of countries. Historically, the rich countries have spent the most money on arms acquisitions, a pattern that has continued. In 1995 the Global North spent $668 billion for defense, in contrast with the developing Global South's $197 billion. Thus, the developed countries' share of the world total is 82 percent. However, when measured against other factors, the differences are not so great. Both groups spent exactly 2.8 percent of their GNPs, on average, on weapons, but the Global North's military spending as a portion of government revenues stood at 9.2 percent and the Global South's at 13 percent. While these two groups' military spending levels are quite different, over time they are converging. The developed countries' expenditures declined 5.6 percent between 1985 and 1995, and the reduction of the developing countries fell only 1.7 percent. As Figure 13.2 reveals, the Global South's military expenditures in 1961 was about 7 percent of the world total, but by 1995 it had climbed threefold to almost 23

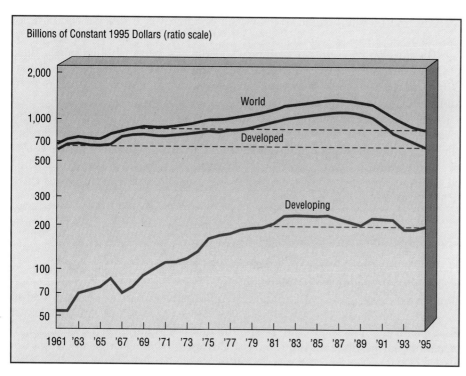

FIGURE 13.2

The Ebb and Flow of World Military Expenditures, 1961–1995

After peaking in 1987, total military spending fell about one-third by 1995. Most of this reduction was due to cuts by the Global North's developed economies (with the exception of the United States, whose defense budget exceeds the combined military expenditures of the next thirteen biggest spenders). In contrast, the expenditures of the Global South's developing countries have fluctuated since peaking in a 1982–1986 plateau, declining moderately after the 1991 Persian Gulf War and actually rising since 1993 to reach almost $200 billion or nearly a quarter of the total world in 1995 (U.S. ACDA 1997, 1–3; Sivard 1996, 5).

SOURCE: U.S. ACDA (1997), 1.

percent. This trend indicates that poor states are copying the past costly military budgetary habits of the wealthiest states (U.S. ACDA 1997, 2, 49).

There are equally mixed regional and national variations in these levels and growth rates. Between 1991 and 1995, with the fall of countries in transition, the decline of military spending (from 24 percent to 11.5 of the world share) in eastern Europe was the steepest, followed by the Middle East (–18 percent) and Central America (–12 percent), with declines in Africa (–6.4 percent), western Europe (–3.3 percent), and North America (–3 percent) being less steep. In the same period, military spending *rose* in Central Asia (+6.3 percent), South America (+5.2 percent), and Asia (+3.5 percent). The level of threats in each region from potential or actual wars within (and, less frequently, between) states, and the spread of conventional and advanced mass-destruction weapons, had much to do with the divergent trends. Similar variations in the growth rates of military expenditures across different regional organizations and military alliances are also exhibited. For instance, between 1985 and 1995 military expenditures for the OECD countries *fell* 1.7 percent, for OPEC 6.1 percent, for NATO 2.2

percent, and for the former Warsaw Pact countries 15.6 percent (U.S. ACDA 1997, 3).

The developing countries' military spending is extremely high given their poverty (see Chapter 5), resulting in large armies in the countries of the Global South that reflect their disproportionately large populations. Between 1960 and 1993, the armed forces of the developed Global North countries remained relatively constant at a little more than 10 million, and fell to 7.7 million in 1995. However, the total number of soldiers in uniform in the developing Global South nearly doubled, growing from 8.4 to 15 million—or to two-thirds of the total 22.8 million people in the armed forces in the entire world. Thirteen of the globe's twenty largest armies were in Global South countries (U.S. ACDA 1997, 7, 49).

Changes in Military Capabilities

The growing militarization of the Global South manifests itself in other ways as well. Military capabilities are now more widespread than ever. Part of the reason is because weapons-production capabilities are no longer concentrated in the industrial North. The Global South countries now are in the business of manufacturing modern aircraft, tanks, and missiles. A parallel change in the international arms trade and in the destructiveness of modern weapons has accelerated the spread of military capabilities throughout the globe.

The New Arms Bazaar: The Weapons Trade in the Late Twentieth Century. The international trade in arms, spurred by developing countries' energetic search for armaments commensurate with those of the industrial countries and their production of them for use at home and export abroad, has fueled the dispersion of military capability throughout the globe. In 1995, ninety-eight countries were the recipients of at least $5 million worth of imported weapons and the Global South's share of world arms exports was 6 percent, with $1.9 billion in sales (U.S. ACDA 1997, 23, 37).

Growth in the value of arms sales attests to the present character of arms trafficking. In 1961 world arms trade was valued at $4 billion. The traffic in arms imports thereafter climbed rapidly, peaking in 1987 at $82.4 billion, and then declined equally rapidly to $30 billion in 1996 (Grimmett 1997, 3-4; Sivard 1996, 50; U.S. ACDA 1997, 10, 100).

The Global South countries have been the leading market for the traffic in arms (see Figure 13.3). Erratic jumps exist in yearly distribution over the entire 1961–1996 period, and recent trends have followed this somewhat irregular cyclical pattern. The developed countries' share increased from 29 percent in 1985 to near equality in 1993 (45 percent), but since then their share has returned to the more traditional proportion of about one-third (U.S. ACDA 1997, 11).

Since the Cold War ended, the developing countries' total purchases (between 1989 and 1996, $206.5 billion) accounted for nearly three-fourths of the $284.8 billion of arms delivered worldwide (Grimmett 1997, 35, 36). Today, in the face of fierce competition among an expanding number of suppliers, the world's most advanced weapons are being transferred to the Global South. Weapons delivered by major suppliers to developing countries between 1989 and 1996 included 7,981 tanks and self-propelled cannon, 16,263 artillery pieces, 1,610 supersonic combat aircraft, 9,382 surface-to-air missiles, and a

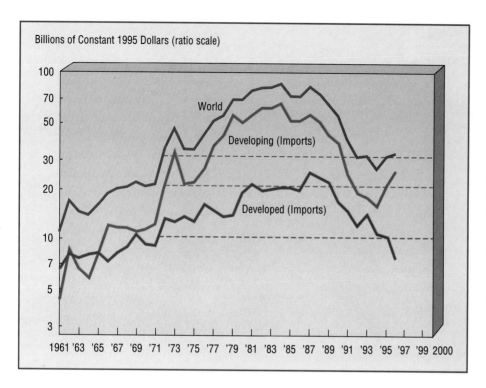

Billions of Constant 1995 Dollars (ratio scale)

FIGURE 13.3

The Rise and Decline of the Global Arms Trade since 1961

The purchase of delivered weapons (imports) has led to the globalization of military capabilities throughout the Global North and South. Between 1989 and 1996, arms sales to developing countries accounted for 72.3 percent of all arms deliveries worldwide, and sales included some of the most technologically advanced weapons of war available (Grimmett 1997, 32).

SOURCE: U.S. ACDA (1997), 10; for 1996, Grimmett (1997), 3–4, 57.

large number of warships, submarines, antishipping missiles, and other technologically advanced weapons systems (Grimmett 1997, 32–33, 76).

As noted, in 1996 nearly three-fourths of transnational arms shipments were imported by the less developed countries. However, the recipients are not spread evenly throughout the Global South. Arms deliveries to the *top ten* developing country recipients, as a group, between 1989 and 1996 alone totaled $121 billion, or two-thirds of the value of all arms deliveries ($186 billion) within the developing world. In rank order of the value of their purchases, those countries were Saudi Arabia, Egypt, Afghanistan, Iran, India, Taiwan, Iraq, South Korea, United Arab Emirates, and Syria, with Saudi Arabia and Egypt accounting for over one-third of the total (Grimmett 1997, 43, 65).

The Middle East has been the locus of intense strife and chronic national security problems. It still includes many pairs of competitive states. In the wake of the Persian Gulf War and the 1993 Israeli-Palestine peace accord, enduring rivalries remain between Egypt and Libya, Iran and Iraq, Iran and Saudi Arabia, Iraq and Kuwait, Iraq and Syria, Iraq and Turkey, and Israel and Syria, and these states' high level of activity in the global arms market has continued. Middle Eastern countries accounted for 11 percent of world arms imports in 1967. Between 1993 and 1996 the Middle East's proportion had mushroomed to 64 percent. Recently, Asia has joined the feverish rush to purchase arms, spending $22 billion (27 percent) of the global total of imports between 1993 and 1996, and this rise has escalated fears that an **arms race** similar to that of the Middle East will unfold there as well (Grimmett 1997, 60–61). Without "clearly defined boundaries between taking prudent defensive steps to prepare for future challengers, and taking action that could be seen as threatening to other countries," the Pacific Rim could explode in a regionwide conflagration (M. Richardson 1995).

arms race the buildup of weapons and armed forces by two or more states that threaten each other, with the competition driven by the conviction that gaining a lead is necessary for security.

The global arms trade is big business, and it remains brisk in many regions where perceptions of threats are intense. The Middle East, which accounts for more than two-thirds of global arms sales, is a prime example. Shown here are buyers examining a model of a warship at a defense exposition in Saudi Arabia in 1997. These "arms bazaars" are a regular feature of the global weapons market.

It is difficult to predict future trends in arms purchases. Shifts in procurement have regularly been rapid in response to war and perceived threats. States' proportionate share of total weapons purchases is likely to change, depending on the location of the globe's hot spots and each state's involvement in them. Aggregate levels of world arms imports are similarly likely to be influenced by the climate of political tension and the performance of the global economy, with activity fluctuating sharply from year to year, and with weapons imported at high levels in instable regions, in countries where the risk of civil war is high, and in situations where pairs of enemy states are engaged in arms races.

Alongside changing demands of arms importers, it is also important to observe changes in the activities of *arms suppliers*. During the Cold War the superpowers dominated the arms export market. Between 1975 and 1989 the U.S.-Soviet share of global arms exports varied between one-half and three-fourths, and the United States alone had cornered 40 percent of the world arms export market when the Cold War ended (U.S. ACDA 1997, 19). In that period the two superpowers together "supplied an estimated $325 billion worth of arms and ammunition to the Third World" (Klare 1994, 139). But with the demise of the Soviet Union, the United States reemerged as the unrivaled "arms merchant of the world" (a phrase used by U.S. President Jimmy Carter to deplore what he sometimes regarded as an unsavory business). Between 1990 and 1996, the United States accounted for a higher proportion of worldwide contracts to sell arms than any other supplier. The United States became the uncontested leader in the sale of military supplies to the world, agreeing to weapons export contracts between 1989 and 1996 of $123 billion, or 43 percent of the $286 total agreed to by suppliers worldwide (Grimmett 1997, 78–79). This contrasted sharply with the distribution exhibited among arms' suppliers in the closing years of the Cold War (1987–1990), when the United States captured less than a

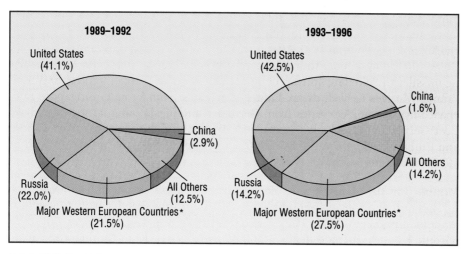

1989–1992

United States
(41.1%)

China
(2.9%)

Russia
(22.0%)

All Others
(12.5%)

Major Western European Countries*
(21.5%)

1993–1996

United States
(42.5%)

China
(1.6%)

All Others
(14.2%)

Russia
(14.2%)

Major Western European Countries*
(27.5%)

F I G U R E   1 3 . 4

The Shifting Competition among Arms Suppliers: The Exporters' Percentage of Arms Transfer Agreements, 1989–1992 and 1993–1996

Weapons are moved across borders when exporters sign agreements with countries to sell them. In the period between 1993 and 1996, the total value of all such arms transfer agreements ($136 billion) declined 27 percent from the preceding 1989–1992 period, when they had reached $188 billion. In both periods, the United States dominated the international arms trade, ranking first as the globe's leading exporter in weapons of war.

*France, United Kingdom, Germany, and Italy.

SOURCE: Grimmett (1997), 16.

quarter of the weapons suppliers' contracts (Grimmett 1995, 15). Figure 13.4 reports the magnitude of the changes in the export of arms in two periods since the end of the Cold War.

The arms sale agreements already under contract assure that the arms trade will remain vigorous in the future, and that the United States will continue to be the largest exporter, followed by the other great powers. In 1997, 85 percent of the globe's annual weapons exports were sold by the big five UN Security Council members (*Harper's* 294, June 1997, 13).

Although the top ten major suppliers dominate the global arms market, the number of new suppliers has grown steadily, as many developing countries also now produce arms for export. By 1990 more than sixty states had entered the business of "peddling arms" (Sivard 1991, 11). Still, most of these were small producers struggling for a share of the lucrative conventional armaments trade. In fact, for the countries in the Global South, the struggle has not been successful, as in 1995 they accounted for less than 6 percent of world arms exports (U.S. ACDA 1997, 18).

A consequence of the increased competition for arms markets is the relaxation of export controls. The United Nations Register of Conventional Arms, begun in 1991 to monitor the weapons exports and imports of countries, has not curbed their sale. Moreover, the illegal export of Western nuclear, ballistic missile, and chemical weapons technology has not abated. Diversification of suppliers, as well as the coproduction and codevelopment of weaponry through joint ventures among arms manufacturers in different countries, have ended many supplier–consumer ties that earlier had cemented patron-client diplomatic relationships. Every supplier, it seems, is now eager to sell to any purchaser. For example, in 1992 Russia sold $1.2 billion of its military hardware to China, including twenty-four advanced SU-27 fighters; China sold M-11 ballistic missiles to Pakistan; Taiwan bought 150 American F-16 jet fighters and sixty French Mirages as well as six Lafayette frigates from France; Singapore purchased five Type-62 corvettes from Germany; Indonesia bought most of the old East German navy; Thailand acquired six Jianhhu-class frigates from China; and China illegally acquired U.S. Patriot missiles reexported by Israel (Gordon 1993b; Klare 1993).

Motives for the Arms Trade. Economic gain is an important rationale for foreign military sales. Israel sells arms abroad to subsidize its arms production at home (Frankel 1987). The United States uses arms exports to offset its chronic balance-of-trade deficits, and to assure its lead in the lucrative arms business. In 1998 it assigned 6,493 full-time federal employees to handle U.S. arms deals and spent $477,300,000 on promotional activities for U.S. arms dealers (*Harper's* 295, February 1998, 13). Following the disintegration of the Soviet Union, Russia sought to raise desperately needed hard currency by selling at bargain-basement prices its one product mix still in demand— weapons, weapons technology, and weapons expertise. And this aggressive sales campaign continues as "a cash-starved defense industry is selling Russian weapons to the world—latest models included" (Khripunov 1997). Cash is also the primary motive among other arms suppliers, for whom ideological considerations are virtually nonexistent.

Because the sale of weapons is big business, arms manufacturers constitute a powerful domestic lobby for the continuation of arms sales. In the United States a "gunbelt" **military-industrial complex** profits at home and abroad from continued arms sales (Markusen, Hall, Campbell, and Deitrick 1991). At the same time, efforts to dismantle "the Cold War military economy" by ending "welfare" for the defense industry have encountered broad-based, coordinated resistance (Cahn 1995). As Lawrence J. Korb (1995a), who served as U.S. Assistant Secretary of Defense for five years in the Reagan administration, explained, "The military has succeeded in inflating the threat of our foes and downplaying the contribution of our allies." Andrew Cockburn (1995) described what he saw as the unjustifiably high U.S. military budget by noting "The problem is that the apparent goal of military spending is to direct as much money as possible into corporate coffers." In fact, many countries' civilian sectors are organized around preparations for militarization and arms manufacture and sales for the same reasons (Regan 1994).

The end of the Cold War ironically increased states' incentives to sell arms merely for profit. Nonetheless, many states continue to sell arms (or make outright grants) for time-honored purposes: to support friendly governments, to honor allies' requests, and to earn political loyalty. This was illustrated by U.S. arms export policy prior to and in the aftermath of the 1990 Persian Gulf War when America approved domestic arms manufacturers' export agreements to supply 58 percent of the $52 billion in arms transfers scheduled for delivery to the Middle East between 1989 and 1992, and 52 percent of $47 billion between 1993–1996, allegedly for the purpose of anchoring allies and preserving the military balance of power in the explosive region (Grimmett 1997, 48–49). However, the profit motive, fueled in part by the desire of defense contractors to

military-industrial complex the term coined by U.S. President Eisenhower to describe the coalition among arms manufacturers, military bureaucracies and top government officials, that promotes unnecessary defense expenditures for their own profit and power.

Many modern weapons are extremely expensive. The F-22 fighter jet is an example, with projected costs of more than $100 million each from Lockheed Martin, the manufacturer, to the United States. Critics of the military-industrial complex complain that the aircraft is an unnecessary subsidy because of the absence of enemy targets for the jet to attack. Others complain that to push for sales, the manufacturer's brochure contained a map of all the "potential threat" countries that possess the most advanced attack aircraft, but did not acknowledge that these so-called threats were actually U.S. fighter jets such as the F-16 and F-15 that America either sold or gave away, thereby generating an "arms trade boomerang" that reduced security. In 1997 Lockheed Martin requested an export license for the F-22 "stealth" jet.

maintain income in a less hostile strategic environment in which many states are reducing their defense budgets, also continues to drive the for-profit sale of weapons across borders. "The flourishing underground, or black market, trade [that supplied] the wars in the former Yugoslavia and in Somalia" (Sivard 1993) reveals the greed behind suppliers' activities.

The Strategic Consequences of Arms Sales. Whether the arming of other countries has accomplished all of its intended goals is open to dispute. During the Cold War, for example, the United States and the Soviet Union thought they could maintain peace by spreading arms to politically pivotal recipients. Between 1983 and 1987 the United States provided arms to fifty-nine less developed countries while the Soviet Union supplied forty-two (Klare 1990b, 12). Yet many of the recipients engaged in war with their neighbors or experienced internal rebellion. Of the top twenty arms importers in 1988, more than half "had governments noted for the frequent use of violence" (Sivard 1991, 17). The toll in lives from the wars in the Global South since 1945 exceeds tens of millions of people. Undoubtedly, the import of such huge arsenals of weapons from abroad aided this level of destruction. As the arms exporters "peddle death to the poor," they seldom acknowledge how this scouting for customers contradicts other proclaimed foreign policy goals. The U.S. arms export program, for example, undermines the current U.S. policy priority of promoting democracy because no less than one-third (eighteen) of the recipients of U.S. arms exports were nondemocratic governments, which purchased $13.25 billion (41 percent) of the total U.S. arms sold ($32.43 billion) in 1993 (Blanton and Kegley 1997, 94–95). Another report illustrates the contradiction between principles in the arms trade by observing that

> No sooner had the United Nations lifted its arms embargo against South Africa than Armscor, South Africa's state arms manufacturer, boasted that its weapons exports could double in a year. There was "nothing wrong," explained President Nelson Mandela, in selling arms abroad so that countries could "defend their sovereignty." And South Africa would make sure they did not get into the "wrong hands." Yet Mr. Mandela also wants to promote peace on a continent that his predecessors did so much to tear apart. As [the 1994] *Human Development Report* . . . points out, the two aims seldom make comfortable bed-mates.
>
> Too often, says the UNDP [UN Development Programme] report, the rich countries—and, by African standards, South Africa is one—offer aid and promote peace in poor countries with one hand while shoveling in death with the other. The United States, France and Britain between them sent $22 billion of aid to the poor world in 1992. The same three, plus China and Russia, the two other permanent members of the UN Security Council, also supplied 86 percent of all weaponry sold to poor countries in 1988–92. Rich-country governments often subsidize the exports of private arms makers; Mahbub ul Haq, the principal author of the report and a former finance minister of Pakistan, says the rich countries bluntly refused to tell him by how much. And many count the official "military assistance" they do admit to—meaning things like the sale of second-hand equipment or military training—as part of their "aid" for development.
>
> Nor—however scrupulous arms salesmen may be, and that is not their most famous quality—is it easy to tell who "the wrong hands" are. America spent the 1980s pouring guns into Somalia; it was by far the biggest supplier, followed by Italy. It then spent the 1990s trying to clear them out. In contravention of the UN arms embargo against it, South Africa happily sold guns, mortars and hand grenades to Rwanda for five years; France too sold the Rwandan government—whose militiamen have carried out the worst killings—mortars and light artillery, and gave technical help and French soldiers. (*Economist*, June 4, 1994, p. 43)

The inability of arms suppliers to control the uses to which their military hardware will be put is thus troubling. The United States armed both sides in several conflicts in the Global South since World War II, as did the Soviets. Moreover, loyalty is often a fragile commodity, and supplying weapons can backfire, as the United States discovered when the weapons it sold to Iraq were used against it by Saddam Hussein in the Persian Gulf War (Timmerman 1991). Likewise, in 1982 Great Britain found itself shipping military equipment to Argentina just eight days before Argentina's attack on the British-controlled Falkland Islands (Sivard 1982), and in 1998 U.S. military technology sold to China was exported to Pakistan, making possible its nuclear weapons test.

Trends in Weapons Technology

The widespread quest for armaments has created a potentially explosive global environment. The description is especially apt when we consider not only trends in defense expenditures and the arms trade but also in the destructiveness of modern weapons.

Nuclear Weapons. Technological research and development has radically expanded the destructiveness of national arsenals. The largest "blockbuster" bombs of World War II delivered a power of ten tons of TNT. The atomic bomb that leveled Hiroshima had the power of over fifteen thousand tons of TNT. Less than twenty years later, the former Soviet Union built a nuclear bomb with the explosive force of fifty-seven megatons (million tons) of TNT. As 1997 started, the world's seventeen thousand nuclear warheads collectively had the explosive force of nine hundred thousand Hiroshima bombs.

The use of such weapons could destroy not only entire cities and countries but, conceivably, the world's entire population. Albert Einstein, the Nobel Prize-winning physicist whose ideas were the basis for the development of nuclear weapons, was well aware of the threat they posed. He professed uncertainty about the weapons that would be used in a third world war, but was confident that in a fourth they would be "sticks and stones." He warned that inasmuch as "the unleashed power of the atom has changed everything save our modes of thinking . . . we thus drift toward unparalleled catastrophe."

The five principal nuclear-weapon states (the United States, the Soviet Union/Russia, Britain, France, and China) continuously refined the deadliness of their weapons through testing. Between 1945 and 1997 they detonated a combined total of more than two thousand nuclear explosions around the world, poisoning the planet with high levels of deadly radiation that will shorten the life spans of billions of people (D. Smith 1997, 72). The United States, which alone had conducted 1,030 nuclear tests (51 percent) in that period, suspended its testing program in August 1995, and France announced an end of its nuclear tests in January 1996. However, after the UN approved the Comprehensive Test Ban Treaty in September 1996, the United States began a round of controversial underground tests in July 1997, and in May 1998 India and Pakistan startled the world by conducting tests to announce that they were nuclear powers.

The nuclear arsenals of the United States and the former Soviet Union are particularly extensive and sophisticated. When World War II ended, the United States possessed the one atomic bomb still in existence. In 1967, at the height of the U.S. **strategic stockpile,** the United States had 32,500 warheads in its arsenal. In 1986, when the Soviet Union was at its peak, it had 45,000 (*Bulletin of Atomic Scientists* 49 [December 1993]: 57). In addition, during the Cold War the United States and the Soviet Union each deployed thousands of tactical nuclear weapons designed for the direct support of combat operations. Their combined arsenals ranged from 21,000 in 1961 to 46,000 in 1986 (WorldWatch web site).

strategic stockpile the inventory of nuclear warheads deployed for waging wars of mass destruction.

The 1987 Intermediate-Range Nuclear Forces (INF) treaty began the elimination of short- and medium-range delivery vehicles from Europe. At the end of 1995, the deployed nuclear stockpiles of the five major powers were estimated to total about 17,400 strategic warheads. The U.S. arsenal had 7,700 nuclear warheads, and Russia had 8,700. In addition, France stockpiled an estimated 482 warheads; China had 284; and Britain retained 234. To this should be added the 2,670 strategic warheads of three former Soviet Republics (Ukraine, Kazakhstan, and Belarus), as well as the 100 to 200 nuclear warheads held by India and Pakistan as well as Israel, an "undeclared" nuclear country.

Despite a worldwide surge in disarmament proposals since the end of the Cold War, some states continue to develop and refine their nuclear arsenal. On January 27, 1996, France tested its nuclear weapons in the Murura atoll of its South Pacific protectorate, Tahiti (an aerial photo of the shock waves during the test is shown here). Its decision to resume testing, justified by the proclaimed right to protect itself with weapons of mass destruction, provoked protests throughout the world. On January 29, 1996, France called a halt to its nuclear testing program and in February 1998 ratified the Comprehensive Nuclear Test Ban treaty. But India and Pakistan rejected this treaty, and in May 1998 began testing their nuclear weapons in a surprise move that threatened to encourage Israel, Iran, Iraq, and others to acquire nuclear weapons in a new chain-reaction nuclear arms race.

Technological Improvements and Weapon Delivery Capabilities. Advances in weapons technology have been rapid and extraordinary. Since the advent of the atomic age, with the "gravity bombs of 1945 . . . a whole warehouse of varied weapons, each with its own special purpose" has been created. These include:

> clean bombs; dirty bombs; bombs that burrowed into the earth, seeking underground command posts; bombs that went off undersea, seeking submarines; bombs that went off high over earth, to fry the brains of electrical devices with a huge shower of electromagnetic pulses; bombs that killed tank crews with radiation but didn't flatten towns or cities; bombs delivered by guidance so precise that they could destroy anything with a known location on or near the surface of the earth. . . . The results of this tireless invention were weapons powerful enough to threaten human life on the planet. (Powers 1994, 123)

Particularly deadly have been the technological refinements that enable states to deliver weapons as far away as nine thousand miles within one hundred feet of their targets in less than thirty minutes. In 1987, seven Western countries (Britain, Canada, France, Germany, Italy, Japan, and the United States) established the Missile Technology Control Regime (MTCR) to curtail the spread of missile technologies, especially those for the delivery of weapons of mass destruction. In 1993 the MTCR expanded its coverage to delivery systems for chemical and biological weapons. By December 1997 its formal membership included thirty-two states.

However, the MTCR is not a legally binding treaty, includes only a fraction of the missile-technology suppliers, and lacks an institution to monitor and enforce compliance with the voluntary agreement. Symptomatic of its weakness was the possession in 1993 of short- or medium-range surface-to-air missiles by twenty countries in the Global South, and the fact that seven of them have used missiles in warfare (Zimmerman 1994). Thus the highly threatening ballistic missile continues to be used outside meaningful international restraints.

Other technological improvements have broadened the spectrum of available weapons. The United States and Russia, for example, equipped their ballistic missiles with **multiple independently targetable reentry vehicles (MIRVs),** which enable a single missile to launch multiple warheads toward different targets simultaneously and accurately. One MIRVed U.S. MX (Peacekeeper) missile could carry ten nuclear warheads—enough to wipe out a city and everything else within a fifty-mile radius. The Minuteman III missile could carry three warheads with the equivalent of 300 kilotons explosive force; twenty-four missiles on each Trident submarine could carry eight warheads with an explosive force of one hundred kilotons. As a result of MIRVing, the number of deliverable nuclear warheads in the nuclear powers' arsenals increased far more rapidly than the number of delivery vehicles. Taking this capacity into account, before the superpowers agreed to the START II treaty to ban MIRVed intercontinental ballistic missiles, the world's combined nuclear inventory was nearly three times larger than the number of nuclear warheads in existence (in 1995, about 45,000).

Despite this effort to control missile capabilities, other kinds of technological improvements have led to steady increases in the speed, accuracy, range, and effectiveness of weapons. As Ruth Leger Sivard predicted,

> Now, with the improved yield-to-weight ratio, nuclear warheads can be incorporated in artillery shells with a weight of 95 pounds and a range of 18 miles. These have a yield of 2,000 tons of TNT equivalent. More powerful is the nuclear-headed cruise missile which weighs 2,650 pounds. Launched from a submarine at sea, it can travel 1,500 miles under its own power, and release up to 200,000 tons of explosives on the target. (Sivard 1991, 13)

New technologies also alter the character of weapons. Laser weapons, nuclear-armed tactical air-to-surface missiles (TASMs), Stealth air-launched cruise missiles (ACMs), and antisatellite weapons (ASAT) that can project force in and wage war from outer space, have become a part of the military landscape. In addition, a large number of innovative new weapons technologies are in use and under development—"wonder weapons" such as the so-called **nonlethal weapons** made possible by the **revolution in military technology (RMT)** so novel that they look like they belong in science fiction (see Focus 13.1). They include an ever-expanding inventory of "new frontier" weapons designed to fight the likely wars of the twenty-first century. They include plans to develop information-warfare squadrons to protect military computer networks from electronic sneak attacks, energy pulses to knock out or take down enemies without necessarily killing them, biofeedback beamed electromagnetic and sonic wavelengths that can modify the human behavior of targets (for example, putting people to sleep through electromagnetic heat and magnetic radiation), and underground **smart bombs** that at 1,000 feet per-second speed can penetrate a buried bunker and, at the proper millisecond after calculating the levels through which it crashes like a needle through flesh, detonate 500 pounds of explosive to destroy an adversary's inventory of buried chemical and biological weapons. Many of these advances in the technology of warfare are already highly developed (Cohen 1998).

nonlethal weapons the wide array of "soft-kill," low-intensity methods of incapacitating an enemy's people, vehicles, communications systems, or entire cities without killing either combatants or noncombatants.

revolution in military technology (RMT) the sophisticated new weapons technologies that make war fighting without mass armies possible.

The Next Generation of Weapons, Lethal and Nonlethal
A Revolution in Warfare

Technological breakthroughs have transformed the character of the battlefield of the twenty-first century. U.S. military planners speak loudly and hopefully of the **revolution in military affairs (RMA)**, the **military-technical revolution (MTR)**, and of "information age warfare." These concepts refer to the goal of seeking to increase military capabilities and effectiveness by seizing the opportunities created by microprocessors, instantaneous global communications, and precision-guided munitions technologies to confront and contain the armed conflicts of the future without relying on weapons of mass destruction. To advocates who seek a "kinder, gentler" type of warfare, the Revolution in Military Affairs promises to transform the ways wars will be fought and the way people think about them (E. Cohen 1998).

To alter the nature of warfare and the conduct of military operations, enthusiasts envision RMA and MTR developing in two stages:

> The first is based on stand-off platforms, stealth, precision, information dominance, improved communications, computers, global positioning systems, digitization, "smart" weapons systems, jointness, and use of ad hoc coalitions. The second may be based on robotics, nonlethality, psycho-technology, cyberdefense, nanotechnology, "brilliant" weapons systems, hyperflexible organizations, and "fire ant warfare." If this idea is correct, change that has occurred so far will soon be dwarfed by even more fundamental transformation. (Metz and Kievit 1995, vi)

Behind the technological revolution is the belief that nonlethal weapons are practical because they can obtain intelligence from computers and advanced technologies to enable precision strikes that can "blind, immobilize, and maintain the enemy at a distance while critical targets are identified, struck, and destroyed" (Tilford 1995; for an overview, see Kokoski 1994; also Schneider and Grinter 1995). The value of these weapons was illustrated dramatically during the Persian Gulf War by the United States' use of "smart" bombs that could drop down chimneys, stealthy aircraft that could elude radar detection, and an airborne tracking system that could scout Iraqi military installations and movements. Their advantages also were illustrated during the 1994–1995 U.S. military intervention in Haiti, where American soldiers carried miniature video cameras on their rifles, enabling them to broadcast live images back to their headquarters and—by satellite—to the Pentagon.

Talk of stealth, precision, information dominance, and missile defense anticipates a day when robots will replace soldiers in combat and unmanned aircraft will replace pilots roaming the globe with laser weapons to destroy ground and air targets, and "cyberdefense" through the use of "smart" and "brilliant" weapons systems will be able to make sophisticated decisions about when and how to act (Metz and Kievit 1995). In this revolution, nonlethal weapons figure prominently. Among the devices already available are "guns that shoot rubber pellets, wooden batons and tiny beanbags to disperse a crowd; stinger grenades that fire rubber pellets; sticky foam that immobilizes people; and another foam system that creates a sudslike barrier two hundred feet long, twenty feet wide, and four feet high, laced with tear gas" (Graham 1995). Today's arsenal includes lasers that can blind people from a distance and a variety of biological and chemical weapons. Some advocate using the latter, arguing that a day of fever, coughing, vomiting, and internal bleeding is preferable to incineration. Still in design is a next-generation missile capable of being retargeted in flight based on intelligence from the battlefield (Graham 1995).

The revolution in technology may make for a new kind of warfare. Will operations on the new battlefield be more humane? Advocates believe that by reducing the exposure of pilots to enemy anti-aircraft devices, precision-guided weapons can contain killing and deter adversaries while minimizing collateral casualties to civilians. However, critics question the effectiveness and ethics of remote and robotic killing with nonlethal arsenals.

Technological advances are likely to make orthodox ways of classifying weapons systems as well as prior equations for measuring power ratios obsolete. As an influential U.S. strategic report correctly predicted more than a decade ago:

> Dramatic developments in military technology appear feasible over the next twenty years. They will be driven primarily by the further exploitation of microelectronics, in particular for sensors and information processing,

and the development of directed energy. The much greater precision, range, and destructiveness of weapons could extend war across a much wider geographic area, make war much more rapid and intense, and require entirely new modes of operation. Application of new technologies to both offensive and defensive systems will pose complicated problems for designing forces and assessing enemy capabilities. (U.S. Commission on Integrated Long-Term Strategy 1988, 8)

For decades, a **firebreak** has separated conventional from nuclear wars. The term comes from the barriers of cleared land with which firefighters keep forest fires from racing out of control. In the context of modern weaponry, it is a psychological barrier whose purpose is to "prevent even the most intensive forms of conventional combat from escalating into nuclear war." As both nuclear and conventional weapons technologies advance, there is danger that the firebreak is being crossed from both directions—by a new generation of "near-nuclear" conventional weapons capable of "levels of violence approximating those of a limited nuclear conflict" and by a new generation of "near-conventional" **strategic weapons** able "to inflict damage not much greater than that of the most powerful conventional weapons" (Klare 1985).

The precision and power of today's conventional weapons have expanded exponentially, at precisely the moment when the revolution in military technology is leading to "the end of infantry" because, in the computer age "the sky has eyes, bullets have brains, and victory will belong to the country whose military has the better data network" (Ross 1997). Note also that even as the nuclear powers retain the capacity to turn cities into glass, they increasingly rely on a variety of new cyberstrategies to deter and demobilize enemies, and are turning to **virtual nuclear arsenals** for **deterrence** to prevent an adversary's attack. Examples include such futuristic weapons as the **electromagnetic-pulse (EMP) bomb,** which can be hand-delivered in a suitcase and can fry the enemy's computer and communications systems within an entire city; computer viruses of electronics-eating microbates that can eliminate a country's telephone system; and logic bombs that can confuse and redirect traffic on the target country's air and rail system. Also planned are **information warfare (IW)** or **infowar tactics** that deploy information-age technics "to disrupt the enemy's economy and military preparedness, perhaps without firing a shot." One example of these is the U.S. Air Force's Commando Solo psychological operations plane, which can "jam signals from the government television station and insert in its place a `morphed' TV program, in which the enemy leader appears on the screen and makes unpopular announcements, alienating him from his people" (Waller 1995).

Unconventional Weapons: Biological and Chemical. Biological and chemical weapons pose a special and growing threat. Each is sometimes regarded as a "poor man's atomic bomb," because they can be built at comparatively small cost and cause widespread injury and death. Despite the 1972 Biological Weapons Convention prohibiting the development, production, and stockpiling of biological weapons, "the United States, the United Kingdom, and Japan are known to have developed several types of biological weapons in the past (such stocks have since been destroyed), and Iraq and Syria are strongly suspected of stockpiling such weapons" (Fetter 1991) as is North Korea (Zimmerman 1994). Similarly, chemical weapons proliferation is a worldwide concern. In addition to Iran, Iraq, Russia, and the United States (the only states confirmed to

strategic weapons weapons of mass destruction that are carried on intercontinental ballistic missiles (ICBMs), submarine-launched ballistic missiles (SLBM)s, or long-range bombers and are capable of annihilating an enemy state.

virtual nuclear arsenals the next generation of "near-nuclear" military capabilities produced by the revolution in military technology that would put strategic nuclear weapons of mass destruction at the margins of national security strategies by removing dependence on them for deterrence.

deterrence to Kenneth Waltz, "to deter means to dissuade someone from doing something for fear of the consequences."

information warfare (IW) or **infowar tactics** attacks on an adversary's telecommunications and computer networks to penetrate and degrade an enemy whose defense capabilities depend heavily on these technological systems.

possess chemical weapons), twenty-one other countries—mostly in the Global South—are suspected to have produced chemical weapons (Stock and De Geer 1995, 340).

International law prohibits the use of chemical weapons: The 1925 Geneva Protocol banned the use of chemical weapons in warfare, and the Chemical Weapons Convention (CWC) signed by 164 countries by January 1998 required the destruction of existing stocks. Nevertheless, legal restraints do not assure that states will forgo them. Iran's and Iraq's use of gas in warfare demonstrated this, as did Egypt's use of chemical gas weapons in Yemen in the mid-1960s. Iraq even used chemical weapons in 1989 against its own Kurdish people. Thus the firebreak has already been breached.

A number of factors limit the use of chemical weapons, including weather conditions and the ability to defend against them. They are nonetheless capable of causing widespread death and suffering. The use of chemical weapons (gas) during World War I, for example, produced "about one hundred thousand battle fatalities and over one million total casualties" (Fetter 1991, 15). The proliferation of ballistic missiles among regional rivals in the Middle East, Asia, and elsewhere particularly raises the danger of their use because they enable chemical weapons to be readily delivered at great distances. The possibility that these weapons might be acquired and used by terrorists poses still another kind of threat.

The Proliferation Problem

Do arms acquisitions promote war? "Many amply supplied armed forces may incline governments to use force rather than to negotiate to resolve conflicts." Even so, "the possession of weapons does not guarantee their use" (Ball 1991). In fact, as Chapter 14 discusses, the primary purpose of arming is to *prevent* the use of force *(deterrence)*, not to encourage it. Hence, as Michael Klare (1987) reasons, "it would be foolish to argue that increased arms transfers automatically increase the risk of war—the decision to wage war is determined by numerous factors."

Still, Klare continues, "There is no doubt that the widespread availability of modern arms has made it *easier* for potential belligerents to choose the military rather than the diplomatic option when seeking to resolve local disputes." Huge arms purchases by Iraq, for example, may have set the stage for its invasion of Kuwait and the subsequent Persian Gulf War. Iraq bought $75 billion in military equipment during the 1970s and 1980s, or nearly 10 percent of all arms transfers. "The weapons . . . may have encouraged Saddam Hussein to believe that his invasion of Kuwait would not be challenged" (Ball 1991, 20). Thus, even if the arms trade and arms races do not necessarily make the world more violent, they do make it less secure (Johansen 1995). Hence the **proliferation** of arms is a serious global concern.

proliferation the spread of weapon capabilities from a few to many states in a chain reaction, so that an increasing number of states gain the ability to launch an attack on other states with devastating (e.g., nuclear) weapons.

Nuclear Weapons. The addition of new nuclear states is commonly referred to as the **Nth country problem.** The increase in the number of nuclear states is called **horizontal nuclear proliferation.** Increases in the capabilities of existing nuclear powers are referred to as **vertical nuclear proliferation.**

As Map 13.1 summarizes, in 1998 there were seven "official" members of the nuclear club—the United States, Russia, Great Britain, France, China, India, and Pakistan. In addition, Israel is a *de facto* or undeclared nuclear weapon state. Two others (North Korea, which agreed to freeze its nuclear pro-

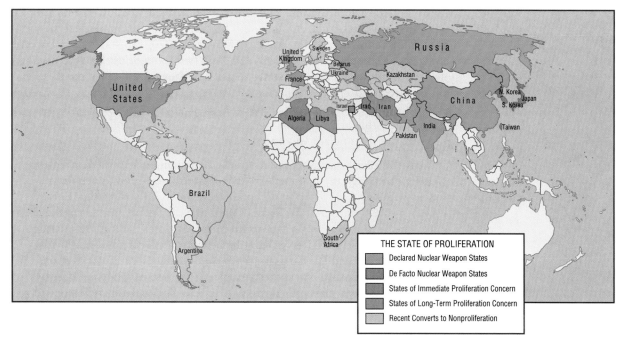

MAP 13.1

Nuclear States and the States Likely to Join the Nuclear Club

A number of countries are capable of producing nuclear weapons on short notice and are regarded as probable candidates for joining the "nuclear club" of declared nuclear weapon states. Others, such as Sweden, have long possessed the capability, but few experts consider them likely to seize the option. This map pictures the state of nuclear proliferation in 1998—a portrayal that may quickly become obsolete if Iran, Iraq, and other states build nuclear arsenals.

SOURCE: Projections based on predictions provided by the Arms Control Association.

gram in October 1994; and Iraq, which is subject to UN monitoring) are classifiable as "states of immediate concern." In addition, Iran and Libya warrant long-term concern because they are widely suspected of having secret nuclear weapons development programs in operation.

Most countries dread the **chain reaction arms race cycle** that might lead to widespread horizontal proliferation, which increases the likelihood that one or more states will choose to use nuclear weapons or that an accident or miscalculation will lead to catastrophe. Although estimates vary, experts agree that perhaps as many as thirty other states now have the economic and technological potential to become nuclear powers. By 2000, the number could grow to forty.

On the optimistic side of the ledger, seven states (Algeria, Argentina, Belarus, Brazil, Kazakhstan, South Africa, and Ukraine), once regarded as nuclear aspirants have now reversed their former position and joined the nonproliferation regime. On the pessimistic side, "If we totally ignore the mounting threats from nongovernmental groups and focus on nation-states alone, we can conclude that approximately twenty countries are either in or are knocking at the door of the nuclear club. . . . We may be looking at a world in which a third to a half of all countries have some hideous weapons of mass murder locked away in their arsenals" (Toffler and Toffler 1993).

chain reaction arms race cycle arms races propelled when states increase their military capabilities to offset the expected growth of their adversaries' capabilities, which prompts other states to increase their capabilities in self-defense—an interaction that produces an upward spiral in weaponry but reduces every state's security.

The Nonproliferation Regime. The **Nuclear Nonproliferation Treaty (NPT),** first signed in 1968, seeks to prevent further proliferation. Since the nonproliferation regime went into force on March 5, 1970, 186 states have become members. NPT membership is divided into two categories: nuclear weapon states and nonnuclear weapon states. Nuclear states were defined as those that manufactured and exploded a nuclear weapon prior to January 1, 1967. This definition included only China, France, Russia, the United Kingdom, and the United States—all of which are members of the NPT. All other parties to the agreement are nonnuclear weapon states.

> The NPT strikes a bargain between nuclear and non-nuclear weapon states. Under the treaty, the non-nuclear weapon states agree not to acquire nuclear weapons and to accept comprehensive International Atomic Energy Agency (IAEA) safeguards over all of their nuclear materials to ensure that they are used exclusively for peaceful purposes. In exchange, the nuclear weapon states agree to freely share the benefits of peaceful nuclear energy and technology and not t6o assist other states to acquire nuclear weapons. In addition, the nuclear weapon states pledged to pursue "good faith" negotiations toward an end to the arms race and toward general and complete disarmament. (Arms Control Association *Fact Sheet*, October 1, 1995, 1)

Despite the apparent success of the NPT, the obstacles to increased proliferation are fragile, as shown by the nuclear development programs of India and Pakistan in 1998. The incentives to join the nuclear club are strong for several reasons.

First, the materials needed to make a nuclear weapon are widely available. This is partly due to the widespread use of nuclear technology for generating electricity. Today hundreds of nuclear power and research reactors are in operation in dozens of countries throughout the world. In addition to spreading nuclear know-how, states could choose to reprocess the uranium and plutonium that power plants produce as waste for clandestine nuclear weapons production. By the year 2000, commercial reprocessing reactors could be producing enough plutonium to make thirty-seven thousand nuclear weapons (Sivard 1993, 13).

Second, the scientific expertise necessary for weapons development has spread with the globalization of advanced scientific training. "In the near future it will be possible to duplicate almost all past technology in all but the most forlorn of Third World backwaters, and much of the present state-of-the-art will be both intellectually and practically accessible" (Clancy and Seitz 1991–1992).

Third, export controls designed to stop technology transfer for military purposes are weak. "A large and growing number of states can now export material, equipment, technology, and services needed to develop nuclear weapons" (Potter 1992). In addition, the leaks in nuclear export controls make "a mockery of the long-revered nuclear nonproliferation regime" (Leventhal 1992). Conversion of peacetime nuclear energy programs to military purposes can occur either overtly or, as in the case of India and Pakistan covertly. The safeguards built into the nonproliferation regime are simply inadequate to detect and prevent secret nuclear weapons development programs.

The ease with which Pakistan made a successful end run around the technology-export controls of the United States and western European governments illustrates the problem of control. In 1979 Pakistan quietly bought all the basic parts—allegedly with funds supplied by the Libyan government—necessary for a uranium-enrichment plant. Similarly, UN inspectors discovered after the Persian Gulf War that Iraq was much closer to building an atomic weapon than previously suspected, despite UN restrictions against this and Iraq's continued pledge to adhere to the rules of the nonproliferation regime. Iraq managed to resist the efforts of UN inspections to freely investigate possible production and storage sites for weapons of mass destruction within Iraq, as called for by the peace agreement, throughout 1997 and early 1998. The Iraqi experience illustrates the obstacles to preventing the illegal proliferation of weapons, as does the record elsewhere. No less than eight countries have constructed secret nuclear production plants, underscoring the difficulties of managing effective inspections and monitoring nuclear developments (Albright 1993).

Fourth, other states have strong incentives to develop nuclear weapons similar to those once cited by the members of the nuclear club. French President Charles de Gaulle argued that, without an independent nuclear capability, France could not "command its own destiny." Similarly, in 1960 Britain's Labour Party leader Aneurin Bevan asserted that without the bomb Britain would go "naked into the council chambers of the world." And in 1993 North Korean President Kim Il Sung defiantly withdrew from the nonproliferation pact, refusing to allow even routine monitoring of his country's five declared nuclear sites at Yongbyon. The desire to act independently and to assert North Korea's power and independence were the primary motives. In response to President Clinton's June 1994 pledge that the United States "would not allow North Korea to develop a nuclear bomb," North Korea dug in its heels. Reluctantly, however, it agreed to freeze its nuclear development program in October 1994.

Many nonnuclear states want the same command of their own fate and the same diplomatic influence that the nuclear powers seem to enjoy. Why, non-nuclear states ask, should they heed a nonproliferation agreement that dooms them to others' domination and security guarantees? Consider Iran's sentiments: In January 1992 its spiritual leader, the Ayatollah Ali Khamenei, declared that the United States had no business questioning the nuclear weapons program designed to make Iran the most powerful military force in the Persian Gulf. "Iran's revolutionary Muslim people recognize no false hegemony for America or any other power," he exclaimed. Similarly, in November 1993, Pakistan's Prime Minister, Benazir Bhutto, asserted that "It is degrading and humiliating to expect Pakistan to roll back its nuclear program." Pakistan developed a nuclear capability, she explained, to deter India, its archenemy. India shouldered its way into the ranks of the nuclear powers in 1998 a month after Pakistan tested the Ghaura missle to counter the perceived threat of Pakistan and achieve the respect that India has long craved.

Nuclear Disarmament? Some see the end of the Cold War as an opportunity to begin eliminating nuclear weapons. In 1992 Russia advocated complete nuclear disarmament. Moreover, the United States and Russia undertook a number of important steps toward meaningful disarmament (see Chapter 15). This set the stage for expanding the nonproliferation regime. In accordance with the provisions of the Nonproliferation Treaty, 175 of its signatories met in the 1995 arms control conference in New York to decide, by majority vote, whether the NPT should remain in force indefinitely or be extended only for an additional fixed period or periods.

TABLE 13.2 **The Relative Burden, or Economic Costs to the Average Citizen, of States' Military Expenditures, 1995**

ME/GNP* (percent)	GNP per Capita (1995 dollars)					
	Under $200	$200 to $499	$500 to $999	$1,000 to $2,999	$3,000 to $9,999	$10,000 and Over
10 percent and over			Bosnia and Herzegov.† North Korea Iraq†	Serbia and Montenegro†	Oman Saudi Arabia Russia Croatia	Kuwait
5 to 9.99 percent	Sierra Leone Mozambique	Pakistan Sudan† Rwanda	Egypt	Jordan Botswana	Syria Libya Greece Bahrain	Israel Brunei Cyprus
2 to 4.99 percent	Burundi Chad Ethiopia	Gambia Laos Mauritania Cambodia Burkina Faso Haiti Guinea-Bissau Zambia Vietnam Central African Rep. India Mongolia Uganda Kenya Togo Nicaragua	Sri Lanka Zimbabwe Tajikistan Afghanistan† Macedonia Angola Liberia Congo Bolivia	Djibouti Morocco Turkey Burma Uzbekistan Ecuador Algeria Ukraine Azerbaijan Iran Swaziland Colombia Thailand Georgia China Moldova Namibia	Chile Lebanon South Korea Malaysia Slovakia Suriname Bulgaria Gabon Romania Uruguay Czech Republic Poland South Africa	Taiwan United Arab Emir. Singapore Qatar United States France United Kingdom Sweden Norway Portugal Australia Netherlands

The New York NPT Review and Extension Conference resulted in a consensus decision "to negotiate in good faith an effective nuclear disarmament, and to convene an extensive conference in twenty-five years to determine the duration of the treaty" (Epstein 1995). Nonetheless, it is unlikely that the nuclear threat will cease. "There's not a snowball's chance in hell we'll eliminate all nuclear weapons from the face of the earth," explains Matthew Bunn, editor of *Arms Control Today*. "That genie is long since out of the bottle and there's no chance of ever getting him back in." Moreover, a world nearing nuclear disarmament would not end the threat. "The problem is, if you eliminate them all, then any country that built just a few nuclear weapons would have enormous blackmail potential" (Davidson 1991).

• • •

THE SOCIAL AND ECONOMIC CONSEQUENCES OF MILITARY PREPARATIONS FOR WAR

Global patterns of military spending and arms acquisitions testify to the prevalence of the realist belief that power can be purchased. However, liberal and neoliberal challengers to this worldview ask: What are the effects of this belief

TABLE 13.2 *Continued*

ME/GNP* (percent)	GNP per Capita (1995 dollars)					
	Under $200	**$200 to $499**	**$500 to $999**	**$1,000 to $2,999**	**$3,000 to $9,999**	**$10,000 and Over**
1 to 1.99 percent	Tanzania Malawi	Mali Bangladesh Equatorial Guinea Guinea Ghana Benin Niger	Cameroon[†] Lesotho Indonesia Senegal Honduras Guyana Ivory Coast Cape Verde	Tunisia Fiji Peru Tukmenistan Belize Cuba Philippines Papua New Guinea Paraguay Panama Dominican Republic Guatemala Albania El Salvador	Argentina Trinidad and Tobago Brazil Hungary Venezuela Malta Estonia	Finland Germany Denmark Italy Canada Belgium Switzerland Spain Slovenia New Zealand Ireland
Under 1 percent	Bhutan[†] Zaire Somalia	Nepal Madagascar Sao Tome and Princ.[†]	Nigeria[†] Yemen[†]	Kyrgystan[†] Mexico Kazakstan Armenia Jamaica Costa Rica	Latvia Barbados Belarus Lithuania Mauritius	Japan Austria Luxemborg Iceland

Note: The relationship between states' economic output and military spending reveals that many of the countries whose citizens are heavily burdened by taxes to pay for defense are impoverished and unstable—compounding the reduction in security they experience. Fortunately for the most heavily burdened, there has been a "general tencency of burden ratios to decline in recent years" except for Global South developing countries (U.S. ACDA 1997, 32).

*Countries are listed within blocks in descending order of their military expenditures as a percentage of their gross national product.

[†]Ranking is based on a rough approximation of one or more variables, for which 1993 data or a reliable estimate is not available.

SOURCE: U.S. ACDA (1997), 31.

about security on national well-being? Do military expenditures and armaments promote national prosperity and security? Or are the consequences destructive?

The Burden of Defense

The **relative burden of military spending,** the ratio of defense spending to gross national product (GNP), is one way to measure the sacrifices that military spending requires. In 1995 the relative defense burden for the world as a whole fell to 2.8 percent, continuing a trend of consecutive reductions since 1986. The average among developed Global North and developing Global South countries both dropped to 2.8 percent—a historic low since 1960 (U.S. ACDA 1995, 24).

It is customary to show the wide range in states' willingness to pay a heavy burden for defense by grouping them according to the share of GNP they devote to the military and then juxtaposing this relative burden with their GNP for the average citizen. Such studies reveal wide variations. As shown in Table 13.2, some comparatively wealthy states (e.g., Kuwait, Israel, and Brunei) bear a heavy burden. In contrast, other states that provide a high average income for their citizens (e.g., Japan, Austria, and Luxembourg) have a low defense burden. Likewise, the citizens of some very poor countries (Sierra Leone, Mozambique, and

407

Chad) are heavily burdened, whereas those of others (Bhutan and Zaire) are not. Thus, it is difficult to generalize about the precise relationship between a country's defense burden and its citizens' standard of living, human development, or stage of development. Still, the available data do suggest two general patterns.

First, those most burdened by the costs of defense include a disproportionate share of poor countries experiencing civil or international war or security threats. Second, many of the countries least able to afford it bear a major share of the world's military burden. Because many of those countries least able to afford weapons make the greatest sacrifices to get them, it appears that the costs of arming for security pose "a formidable barrier" to the alleviation of poverty and suffering. The developing countries in the late 1980s "lost to the arms race in a single year the equivalent of 187 million human-years of income" (Sivard 1991, 11). This raises questions about the social costs of expenditures to prepare for war (see Focus 13.2 on pages 410–411).

"The problem in defense spending," as President Eisenhower observed in 1956, "is to figure how far you should go without destroying from within what you are trying to defend from without." Now the concern is how "downsizing" military establishments geared toward Cold War competition will affect employment levels and research, development, and production opportunities in defense-related industries. The goal of **defense conversion**—redirecting budgets from armaments to internal development—is "bedeviled by two conflicting objectives: how to shift firms out of defense and into civilian pursuits, and how to preserve a mobilization base to meet conceivable future defense needs" (Adelman and Augustine 1992). Even the absorption of large numbers of military personnel into the domestic economy has been a matter of concern on both sides of the one-time East–West divide.

Just as excessive military spending has its costs, conversion to a much smaller, "peace-maintaining" military posture may also exact a domestic economic toll. Perhaps this explains why the Clinton administration's fiscal 1994 defense budget did not abolish a single new weapons system. "There is a tendency," observes Robert Reno (1993), "to build an inventory of possible wars to match present levels of defense spending and present levels of manpower, [which is why] defense conversion in Russia will [also] be a very difficult undertaking."

Military Spending and Economic Development

How are military expenditures and economic growth linked? Many politicians and experts argue that a trade-off exists between "guns and butter"—between military spending and economic prosperity. Much evidence on the relationship points to "retarding effects through inflation, diversion of investment, use of scarce materials, misuse of human capital" (Sivard 1979). This is due to the tendency of defense expenditures to divert resources away from growth-promoting investments and to inhibit research and development in export-generating industries. One study, for example, found that every additional dollar spent on arms in the Global South reduced domestic investment by 25 cents and agricultural output by 20 cents (Klare 1987, 1279–180). Other studies agree, showing that in most developing countries, when military spending rises, the rate of economic growth declines (Deger and Smith 1983; also Lipow 1990; Payne and Sahu 1993; Väyrynen 1992) and debt increases (Snider 1991).

Despite this evidence, the **guns versus growth** issue remains controversial. "Previous research on the impact of military spending on the economy has produced disparate, inconsistent, and unstable results" (Chan 1987; cf. Sandler and Hartley 1995). A strong correlation does not hold for all countries. "The effects of military expenditure on the economy," conclude Ron P. Smith and George Georgiou (1983), "depend on the nature of the expenditure, the prevailing circumstances, and the concurrent government policies." In many advanced industrial economies, for instance, military spending stimulates economic growth, at least in the short run. This especially holds true during periods of unemployment, when the infusion of capital can provide jobs, training, and social infrastructure in the form of investments in highways, airports, communications, and the like.

The strain of military spending on economic growth, however, seems to be especially severe in many societies, particularly when it persists for many years (Väyrynen 1992; Ward, Davis, and Lofdahl 1995). Compare Japan with the United States and the former Soviet Union. Japan, relatively freed of the burden of funding militarization since the 1950s, expanded its economy greatly; the United States and the former Soviet Union, paying high costs for military power, fell behind economically. It appears that excessive military spending was a primary cause of the Soviet Union's demise. "No other industrialized state in the world [had] for so long spent so much of its national wealth on armaments and military forces. Soviet militarism, in harness with communism, destroyed the Soviet economy and thus hastened the self-destruction of the Soviet Empire" (Iklé 1991–1992, 28).

The end of the Cold War poses special problems for the United States, which now stands alone at the pinnacle of world power. What defense commitments and responsibilities should engage the United States now that the challenges of communist ideology and Soviet expansionism have disappeared? As noted in Chapters 4 and 8, there are no easy answers to these questions.

Maintaining a balance between military preparedness and economic revitalization presents a serious challenge not only to the United States, but also to the other major powers. A comparison of the great powers' new defense policies informs us about the ways states are thinking about national security as they prepare for the threats of the twenty-first century.

• • •

THE GREAT POWERS' NATIONAL SECURITY STRATEGIES

The threat of the Cold War turning hot has disappeared. In response, the superpowers have retired their strategic nuclear arsenals more rapidly than they have replaced them, and the size of those arsenals is scheduled to decline to their lowest levels in fifty years (see Chapter 15). As a consequence, the geostrategic landscape now bears little resemblance to the terrain of the early 1990s.

The transformed security environment has deprived the strongest states of a clear vision of how to protect their country's national interests and prosperity. In Washington, Moscow, Beijing, Tokyo, and Berlin, defense planners are struggling to construct strategies and defense doctrines.

As noted in Chapter 4, the choices range between the extremes of isolationist withdrawal from participation in world affairs to active international engagement. The options also require choices to be made between **unilateral** self-help

unilateral a go-it-alone, self-reliant strategy for dealing with threats from another actor or global problem, as opposed to multilateral approaches, which involve working with allies or collective problem-solving institutions.

Does Military Spending Reduce Citizens' Standards of Living?

The comparatively greater resources that military preparedness commands in relation to other problems has been a persistent concern to those seeking the best means to a secure and long life. Consider the following representative evidence that provides the basis for their concern about the trade-off between competing values, as seen by Ruth Leger Sivard (1996, 39):

> Governments are continually forced to make choices when allocating public funds. Some national priorities have begun slowly to shift in the direction of social development and away from excessive military budgets. Nevertheless, over half of the nations of the world still provide higher budgets for the military than for their countries' health needs; 25 countries spend more on defense than on education, and 15 countries devote more funds to military programs than to education and health budgets combined.

> The considerable sums still spent on the military could improve the quality of life of hundreds of millions of people in low-income countries. By choosing to direct public funds to unmet social needs, governments would alleviate the misery of poverty, and dispel the miasma of hunger, disease and illiteracy which stifles so many lives. The illustrations below suggest a number of alternatives to outlays for weapons (based on unit acquisition costs, as reported by the US Department of Defense).

Costs of Protection

Weapons	Dollars	Other Options
Seawolf nuclear-powered submarine to complement the current fleet of attack submarines.	$2,500,000,000	Immunization program with added vaccines and micronutrients for the world's children.
Intercontinental Stealth Bomber, designed for "time-critical" targets, nuclear and conventional.	$2,200,000,000	Supplying family planning services for one year to 120 million women in the developing world.
Aegis guided missile destroyer, intended for defense of aircraft carriers.	$969,000,000	One extra year of primary schooling for 11,400,000 girls in least developed countries.
Joint Stars, a 707-class aircraft modified to operate a target-attack radar system.	$387,000,000	A year's treatment for 400,000,000 children suffering from debilitating intestinal worms.
Hornet twin-engine strike fighter for fleet air defense.	$50,000,000	5,000,000 insecticide-treated nets for beds, to reduce malaria mortality.

actions on one end of the continuum, **multilateral** action with others on the other, and specialized **bilateral** alliances and ad hoc partnerships in between.

Based on the strongest powers' recent actions and statements, they appear to agree on certain fundamental priorities in the emerging twenty-first century:

- Forestalling a new major war is critical, because all other national security interests, such as prosperity, will be jeopardized if peace does not endure.

- Economic development will be of vital and growing importance to military security and to the position of each of the economic and military giants in the globe's future hierarchy of power.

These statistics show that countries often place a higher priority on defending their citizens from military attack than on protecting them from social, educational, and health insecurities. They also suggest that military spending reduces social welfare. The connection is not direct, but military spending and global deprivation are linked. Consider, for example, the military position of the United States among 160 countries across various indicators. America ranked *first* in military spending, military technology, number of overseas military bases, training of allies' armed forces, size of naval fleet and combat aircraft, and nuclear warheads and bombs. Yet on a number of popular measures of economic and social development, the United States ranked well below the achievements of many other countries. Examine the U.S. position in the global community of countries on various indices (Sivard 1996, 40):

U.S. Rank with 160 Other States

Social Development

Percent population with safe water	1
Percent births attended by trained personnel	2
Female and male literacy rate	4
GNP per capita	5

Economic–Social Standing

Public health expenditures per capita	8
Public education expenditures per capita	9
Public education expenditures per student	10
Maternal mortality rate	12
Infant mortality rate	13
Life expectancy	14
Percent school-age children in school	18
Under five mortality rate	18
Contraceptive prevalence	19
Percent infants with low birthweight	29
Population per physician	39
Students per teacher	39

These rankings suggest that high U.S. military spending has reduced the quality of American citizens' lives. Security in the broadest sense means security in the expectation that one will live a full life. Yet, do arms contribute to increased life expectancy or freedom from want? When expenditures for arms go up, so do disease, illiteracy, and suffering (Nincic 1982; Russett 1982; UNDP 1994). As U.S. President Dwight D. Eisenhower observed, "The world in arms is not spending money alone. It is spending the sweat of its laborers, the genius of its scientists, the hopes of its children."

- The world pyramid of power is moving toward a **multipolar** distribution, in which no hegemon will be dominant and three, four, or more great powers will share approximately equal military power.

multipolar a distribution of power with three or more power centers.

Given the prevailing consensus about these probabilities, what sort of national security response is most likely? We will look briefly at the emerging security policies of the five major great powers.

The United States' New Security Policies

A key to understanding U.S. national security policy is America's long-term economic decline relative to an ascending China, Japan, and Germany and an integrating European Union pursuing a common security policy. To many observers, if the eight straight years of the U.S. economy's expansion in the 1990s ends, America is destined to become more imperiled than imperial. To them, "the dawn of dominance" is at hand as "the American century" ends, because the United States has seen its share of world output fall steadily "to less than it was at the time of the Spanish-American War, when the United States first emerged as a world power"; remaining "the biggest debtor nation in history," America faces stagnating living conditions and diminishing expectations (D. White 1998). Simply put, the United States must confront the reality that it faces stiff trade competition, and its rivals' economies are growing at a pace that is threatening to cut into the U.S. share of the global financial pie. In the

411

Critics of excessive military spending cite the waste and fraud that often occur in defense contracts, claiming that unneeded weapons systems are produced as a result of lobbying by what President Dwight D. Eisenhower termed "the military-industrial complex." In 1995, Congress proposed spending almost $36 billion for the new B-2 bombers, over the objections of Senator John McCain (R-Arizona). McCain complained that "The prospect of utilizing the B-2 in a conventional role is akin to mosquito hunting with an elephant gun. It is neither practical nor cost effective."

long run, these trends could reduce U.S. influence and its ability to lead in world affairs, forcing the country to redefine its national security policy by making economic renewal at home a priority.

Yet this does not mean that military competition and threats will necessarily recede in importance, so that U.S. global strategy will shift in new directions. As former U.S. Secretary of State Lawrence Eagleburger explained in 1993, "The dangers of the period into which we are going can be as unpleasant, if not as bloody, as most of the first 50 years of this century." We are returning to the raucous multipolarity more reminiscent of the nineteenth century than of the past fifty years of the Cold War, he warned. Given this threat, military security will probably command as important a place in a new U.S. strategy as will trade, prosperity, and the promotion of free governments and markets throughout the world.

The trade-offs between these economic and military objectives have divided Americans about the appropriate U.S. response. Three schools of thought about America's role in world affairs have emerged:

> Neo-isolationists want the U.S. to deal only with threats to America's physical security, political independence, and domestic liberty. They find no such threats at present, and therefore argue that the U.S. should let other powers, and regional balances of power, take care of all the world's woes. Realists such as Henry Kissinger want the U.S. to continue to be the holder of the world balance of power, the arbiter of the main regional power groups, and the watchdog against all potential imperialistic trouble-makers. Internationalists want a greater role for multilateral institutions and more emphasis on human needs and rights, the environment and democracy. (Hoffmann 1992, 59)

The Clinton administration attempted to reconcile these divergent outlooks. Trying to strike a balance, Clinton argued in 1993 that "putting our economic house in order cannot mean that we shut our windows to the world." As he elaborated in December 1995, "problems that start beyond our borders can quickly become problems within them." This reality commends, as Clinton declared in his inaugural address, that "America must continue to lead the world. . . . When our vital interests are challenged, or the will and conscience of the international community is defied, we will act—with peaceful diplomacy whenever possible, with force when necessary."

But how to prepare militarily to act? To help define a post-Cold War strategy against unknown threats, the Clinton administration initiated a **Bottom Up Review (BUR).** Released in September 1993, it stressed the need for military preparedness, in order to:

- Deter the use of nuclear, biological, or chemical weapons against the United States, its forces, and its allies.

- Halt or at least slow the proliferation of such weapons.

- Deter and, if necessary, defeat major aggression in regions important to the United States.

- Be capable of fighting and winning two major regional conflicts nearly simultaneously, . . . while minimizing American casualties.

- Prepare U.S. forces to participate effectively in multilateral peace enforcement and unilateral intervention operations that could include peacekeeping, humanitarian assistance, counterdrug, and counterterrorism activities.

- Foster democratic values in other countries.

- Maintain technological superiority. (Collins 1994, 5–6)

Viewed in light of this *realpolitik* definition of its evolving defense doctrines, the United States has committed itself to relying heavily on military might while attempting to build liberal ideals into the definition of its goals. Labeling his policy "democratic realism," President Clinton explained in 1993 that the U.S. **engagement and enlargement strategy** would use U.S. power to help prevent or contain armed conflicts throughout the world and to "enlarge" the community of liberal democracies. Colin Powell, Chairman of the Joint Chiefs of Staff, elaborated: "The central idea in the strategy is the change from a focus on global war fighting to a focus on regional contingencies" through what Pentagon officials call **mid-intensity conflict (MIC).** Thus, U.S. national security policy reaffirms the commitment to being prepared to wage two major wars simultaneously and to being able to intervene militarily around the world, while at the same time avoiding war and selectively using U.S. troops in modest numbers to police tyranny and internal turmoil abroad. This **Clinton Doctrine** does not call for the United States to take on every burden throughout the world, but "to engage in some places and pass on others" (Dionne 1998). The purpose of U.S. power under the Clinton Doctrine is to uphold universal liberal ideals by actively promoting the spread of democratic governance, based on the **democratic peace** principle. This strategy also rests on the liberal tenet that American interests and security require liberal (free) trade in order to generate global prosperity because the prospects for peace among competitive states will improve when their continued economic growth depends heavily on an integrated and orderly global export market.

This broadened conception of national security preserves the traditional U.S. emphasis on a strong defense and on strategic deterrence, with a modestly reduced annual defense budget, from $268 billion in 1998 to $250 billion in

realpolitik the theoretical outlook prescribing that countries should prepare for war in order to preserve peace.

democratic peace the policy of preserving international peace by promoting the growth of democratic government worldwide, based on the observable law that democracies do not fight wars against each other.

2002. It aims at expanding military capabilities by developing a broad range of new conventional and nonlethal weapons to conduct precision raids on enemy targets made possible by the revolution in military technology (RMT). Moreover, it continues to emphasize coercive diplomacy, alliances, and arms sales as bargaining instruments to exercise influence abroad, while striking a balance between safeguarding peace through "assertive multilateralism" and "selective engagement." But the revised U.S. strategy places a renewed emphasis as well on containing the potential expansion of other great-power rivals and civil wars in the Global South by strengthening global institutions (NATO, the United Nations) and international law. In December 1997 President Clinton also revised the guidelines for the targeting of U.S. nuclear weapons that had been in place since 1981; seeking to adjust to the changing strategic climate, the new presidential directive formally recognized that no country could emerge as the victor in a major nuclear exchange by discarding the Cold War belief that the U.S. military must be prepared to fight and win a protracted nuclear war that could devastate the globe. To balance this reversal, as nuclear forces were being reduced, U.S. defense planners quietly began to expand "conventional" weapons seeking to develop a host of new weapons to deal with adversaries' research to augment strategic nuclear forces, "superhardened," "surface-buried" or "deeply buried" new targets with a host of new weapons (see Arkin 1997).

On the cusp of the chaotic twenty-first century, U.S. strategic thinking can be expected to seek flexibility in other ways as American leaders seek to adapt to the unknown dangers that lurk beneath the surface of turbulent global geostrategic waters. Limits on America's capacity to foresee the future—and limits on resources to take a unilateral approach to managing the new millennium's multiple security threats—suggest that construction of a coherent strategy resting on a clear vision is likely to prove an elusive goal for the United States in the future.

Russian Strategy in the Coming Century

Russia faces a precarious geostrategic future, fraught with threats to its security on many fronts. In a few days at the end of 1991, the Union of Soviet Socialist Republics (USSR) ceased to exist, and the Russian empire collapsed as Russia lost most of its satellite states. Overnight its superpower status vanished. Russia was no longer one of the world's foremost military powers with imperial ambitions and hopes of becoming the globe's next hegemon. The Soviet Union in 1991 had a population of 287 million people, a landmass of 8.65 million square miles, and an army of 5.5 million soldiers; today Russia's population is about 148 million people (and declining); it controls a landmass of 6.6 million square miles and an army of less than 1.2 million soldiers. Russia's army has lost its roar amidst a budget crisis in its slowly recovering new capitalistic market economy that has left Russia's soldiers poorly equipped and drained of morale. To add to this weakness, Russia has dismantled much of the awesome strategic nuclear stockpile that had been the backbone of its defense and deterrence strategy and the symbol of its military might, and it no longer benefits from the existence of the Warsaw Pact alliance to guard Russia's borders from external attack, facing instead an enlarged NATO alliance in its geopolitical backyard. On top of this reduction of Russia's defense position, Moscow must try to rule a federation of eighty-nine regions, with the pregnant threat of separatist independence movements led by ethnic minorities active in

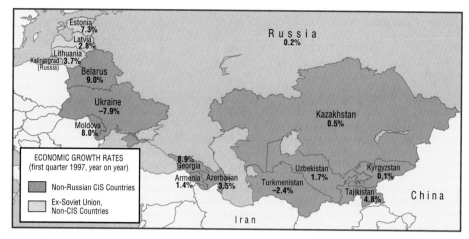

MAP 13.2

The Shriveling Geostrategic Situation of Russia

Russia has suffered a blow to its former imperial pride, as the collapse of the Soviet Union in 1991 has reduced the size of its territory by one-fourth and its population nearly in half. To add insult to injury, the postcommunist economic reforms have been slow to generate robust economic growth, and many ethnic minorities are rebelling—a revolt that could cause still further disunion. This map shows the geostrategic and geoeconomic divisions that the Kremlin faced in 1997.

SOURCE: *Economist*, May 24, 1997, p. 47.

many of the remaining regions in Russia's shrunken borders. As the danger of civil war percolates, fueled by the misery of stagnant growth rates, the picture of the strategic future is not pretty to those leaders peering at the Ex-Soviet disunion from the Kremlin (see Map 13.2).

Russian defense planners have no alternative but to attempt to adjust their national security strategies to these grim new realities. This has not been easy, and in the past, few great powers have experienced so painful an erosion of their power position—a **power transition** of unprecedented magnitude and rapidity—without experiencing a general war. Russia's sense of national security has plummeted, as Russia's December 1997 first post-Soviet security "concept" document candidly acknowledges. To manage the threats, internal strains, weaknesses, and crises, Russia has made a number of accommodative revisions of its strategy and goals in light of the fact that Russia is too poor and powerless to attempt to reestablish military or economic clout beyond its borders. In marked contrast to the Soviet Union's global ambitions, the largely inward-looking statement sets the following priorities for a new Russian security policy:

power transition a circumstance that occurs when the military capabilities of one great power fall relative to those of its nearest rival, often resulting in a war breaking out due to the escalating fears this transition tends to provoke.

- The most fundamental military reforms in the country's modern history will be undertaken. By 2000 the size of the Russian armed forces will be further cut below its reduced size of less than 1.2 million soldiers, and entire branches of the armed services will be eliminated. Moreover, the meager 1997 Russian defense budget ($20 billion annually, about 10 percent that of the United States and one-third that of Britain's) will be drastically cut, with the savings put to defense conversion to stimulate domestic economic recovery and put the country back on its feet.

- Smaller, more mobile and technologically adept fighting forces will be created to manage civil rebellions within Russia ("centrifugal aspirations that could tear the country apart") as well as along Russia's borders, in places such as war-torn Afghanistan and Chechnya where armed conflicts that undermine Russian security threaten to erupt. For this, Russian doctrine reserves the right to use military intervention in the so-called "near abroad" to preserve order.

- Russia will continue to dismantle its nuclear arsenal (with U.S. aid), in order to alleviate other powers' fears of resurgent Russian ambition and to honor its pledges to adhere to the START II disarmament agreement. Strategic nuclear weapons are impotent in solving the major security problems that Russia is likely to face, and therefore Russia's strategy places special emphasis on preventing the proliferation of weapons of mass destruction.

- Russian doctrine rules out using nuclear weapons against nonnuclear states, but repeals the **no first use** pledge made by Mikhail Gorbachev that Russia would not be the first to use nuclear weapons in the event of a conventional attack by those states that have nuclear weapons. Hence, for purposes of deterrence, Russia is prepared to use nuclear weapons in defense: Russia "reserves to itself the right to use all the means and powers it has in its possession, including nuclear weapons, if as a result of unleashing an armed aggression, there will appear a threat to the very existence" of the state.

- Russia will seek to cement its relationships with its European neighbors by creating institutions for democracy and a free market economy, and will attempt to end its isolation from the Asian-Pacific because "all of this is unacceptable as an influential European-Asian state."

These policies are designed to reduce the threat of foreign encirclement and/or international isolation. This requires attempting to speed the internal reforms to institutionalize democracy and a free market within Russia, so Russia can become a welcome, full-fledged member of the liberal democratic community and its leading institutions (the EU, NATO, the G-7, the OSCE, and the IMF). Moreover, the new policy seeks to cement cordial relationships with the other great powers, but especially the United States and China, on whom Russia's ultimate security depends heavily. Russia's **normalization of diplomatic relations** with China with a 1997 agreement to deepen the Sino-Russian strategic partnership (in part to respond to NATO enlargement), was representative of this bilateral approach. So, too, was the continuing diplomatic dialogue designed to build a Russo-American strategic alliance against possible emergent common threats, and Russia's December 1997 pledge to NATO to accelerate its military cooperation program with the goal of building a new twenty-first-century security partnership.

These departures from Cold War strategic doctrines exhibit an acute awareness that Russia's geostrategic position has declined. This sense of vulnerability explains Russia's professed desire to work cooperatively with others to preserve international security while it contends with security threats arising from ethnonational uprisings in Russia and along its borders. Russia seeks to forge a multilateral approach to its many security problems. This is evidenced by its 1996 military involvement of at least fifteen hundred troops in NATO peacekeeping operations in Bosnia—symbolically under the command of an

American general—while at the same time seeking to prevent NATO from expanding eastward to build a new wall around an isolated Russia.

China's Global Clout and Security Posture

China figures prominently in U.S. and Russian conceptions of security.

> The rise of China, if it continues, may be the most important trend in the world for the next century. When historians one hundred years hence write about our time, they may well conclude that the most significant development was the emergence of a vigorous market economy—and army—in the most populous country of the world. This is particularly likely if many of the globe's leading historians and pundits a century from now do not have names like Smith but rather ones like Wu.
>
> China is the fastest growing economy in the world, with what may be the fastest growing military budget. It has nuclear weapons, border disputes with most of its neighbors, and a rapidly improving army that may—within a decade or so—be able to resolve old quarrels in its own favor. The United States has possessed the world's largest economy for more than a century, but at present trajectories China may displace it in the first half of the next century and become the number one economy in the world. (Kristof 1993, 59)

China is an economic giant and potential military colossus bent on modernizing its maritime and air capabilities. Therefore, its rise and growing assertiveness have understandably heightened the concerns of the other great powers—especially Russia, which shares with China a four-thousand mile indefensible border; Japan in the China Sea; and the United States colossus. China seeks to reduce their fears about its rising capabilities as the globe's most populous and fastest growing free-market economy, destined to soon become one of the world's top three. China asserts that while it wants its rivals to treat the communist government with the respect due a great power, it seeks peaceful relations with all. In 1994 China signed an agreement with Russia to prevent accidental military clashes, and in 1997 it formalized the effort to assure Russian acceptance by signing a new strategic treaty of alliance for mutual defense. Following that initiative, later in 1997 China courted a new strategic partnership with the United States; at the October Washington Summit, President Jiang Zemin pledged to seek "common ground despite differences" in order to "share responsibility for preserving world peace and stability in the twenty-first century," and to underscore China's sincerity pledged to reign in nuclear and chemical exports and end sales of antiship cruise missiles to Iran.

China has taken still other steps to alleviate the concerns of Japan and the United States about how Chinese leaders might use the resources of an economy that has doubled every eight years for military purposes. That Beijing has greatly expanded its military spending in recent years has heightened these worries about a new Red Peril. Many skeptics believe the danger is more of a "red herring" and these fears are overblown, because China's defense spending and military capabilities remain comparatively low. To their mind, China is more interested in economic power and diplomatic stature than territorial expansion by force.

The direction of China's policies seems geared to ensuring its rise to prominence in the Pacific Rim, as shown by its military threats in 1996 against Taiwan. To this end, China has continued to arm, preserve its nuclear weapons,

China is an ascendent superpower with the capacity to intimidate its Asian neighbors and strike fear into distant great-power rivals who suspect that China's rise to the top position in the rankings of national economies will be followed by foreign aggressiveness as a method of restoring the Middle Kingdom to the global position China believes it deserves as the most powerful polity on the planet. Pictured here is a Chinese soldier expressing the defiant and assertive defense posture of the government in Beijing that conscripted him into military service to help regain the status and *suzerainty* (right to exercise influence over its neighbors) that most Chinese think China is due. Despite this aspiration, China's armed forces had to accept deep budget cuts in the 1990s so Beijing could spend more on economic growth.

and to equip the globe's largest standing army (3 million soldiers). At the same time, China seems committed to developing the strategic and military might that the Chinese believe its status as an economic giant justifies. This attitude is evidenced by China's resistance to its ASEAN neighbors' effort in 1995 to establish a nuclear-free zone in Southeast Asia.

However, despite its assertiveness and coercive diplomacy toward its neighbors China can be expected to concentrate on its internal development and trade relations, while seeking to contain domestic instability which threatens to tear apart national unity (especially if ethnic tensions and regional economic differences within China increase). Preserving domestic tranquility and growth is a priority.

As its power and wealth have grown, China has steadfastly refused to take instructions from its great-power rivals, insisting on its right to chart a foreign policy guided by its own perceptions of national interests. As yet, this does not mean that China is necessarily preparing for or planning foreign military engagement, as China argues that defense is the purpose of its military buildup and that its saber-rattling toward Taiwan and Macao are permissible actions toward rebellious provinces that are a part of sovereign Chinese territory. To find the safe place in the sun where China feels it belongs, China's national security strategy has sought as priority goals to:

- Lobby to see that the traditional international legal rule prohibiting external interference in sovereign states' domestic affairs is respected, to safeguard against foreign intervention to punish China for disregard of its citizens' human rights and civil liberties.

- Expand China's sphere of influence in the Pacific Rim to gain the respect of its Asian neighbors, which China regards as appropriate recognition of its status as the region's preeminent power.

- Pursue being allowed to join the other big powers' table on reasonable terms and with respect, by seeking membership in the World Trade Organization and other multilateral global institutions, in order to give China a greater voice in shaping those international organizations' future policies and decisions, and to prevent its isolation, demonization, and exclusion.

- Establish normalized cooperative diplomatic relations with the United States and deter that superpower from treating an ascendant China as an enemy to be contained in a new Cold War.

To the other great powers, these proclamations inspire divergent reactions. "Engagers" recommend efforts to further integrate China into the global economy, in the hope that this will allow China to become more prosperous and gradually become more liberal at home and reduce its hegemonial regional ambitions. "Containers" disagree, arguing that **appeasement** will fail by encouraging Chinese bellicosity, and that therefore a new **containment** policy is needed to curtail the Chinese threat before it becomes necessary to repel it by force. This reaction to China's growing clout calls, in short, for deterrence of China's potential imperial ambitions, while awaiting the day when liberal democracy comes alive within its borders to temper such pursuits.

The strategic situation for China is at a crossroads. At this historical juncture, it is certain that if China's vigorous rearmament and force-modernization program, inspired by reawakened nationalist pride, continue, China's arsenal will position it to play a dominant military role in Asia and the entire world. Napoleon Bonaparte counseled in the early nineteenth century that the world should "let China sleep" because, he predicted, when China awakens, "the world will tremble." China has now awakened.

Japan's Search for a Strategy

Japan is now an economic superpower—the second richest country on earth, just behind the United States (refer back to Table 13.1). On a per-person basis, in 1996 its citizens enjoyed an average income far exceeding that of the average American. Yet, Japan's "dramatic postwar ascent . . . has not been accompanied by a comparable rise in its international political and strategic weight" (Brown 1993). Since its defeat in World War II, Japan has adhered to the guidelines of the **Yoshida Doctrine,** in which Prime Minister Shigeru Yoshida argued that Japanese security policy should be to avoid international disputes, keep a low profile on divisive global issues, and concentrate on economic pursuits.

That preference continues to underlie the style behind Japan's strategic statements. But the new international setting has called into question the wisdom of this traditional posture—especially in light of the transformed distribution of power, with Russia's power having fallen, China's on the rise, and America's remaining predominant in the wake of the mid-1990s economic recovery. Particularly since America seems reluctant to lead in global governance, a larger role and presence are imminent, and are now being expressed.

Prime Minister Kiichi Miyazawa's policy departures in 1992 signaled the new direction that Japan's security policies are likely to take. He won passage of the Peacekeeping Operations Bill, which enabled Japan to deploy a self-defense force to participate in UN peacekeeping operations in Cambodia—the first use of Japanese armed forces abroad since World War II. Japan's acceptance of a large increase in its previous UN dues (17.98 percent in 1998, and 20.57 percent in 2000), its push for inclusion as a permanent member of the UN Security Council, and its rise to the top of the world's foreign aid donors also suggest growing Japanese international activism.

Japan seeks to discard its isolation and become an involved player in world affairs. Its rising defense expenditures and efforts to cement cordial relations

appeasement a strategy to deter a potential belligerent by making concessions.

containment a term coined by U.S. policymaker George F. Kennan for deterring Soviet Russia's expansionist aims by counterpressures, which has since become a general term used by strategists to describe the methods used to prevent an expanding great power from flexing its military muscles.

with its Asian neighbors also speak to this redirection. Japan in 1998 still adhered to its policy of spending no more than 1 percent of its gross national product on defense, and remained committed to its postwar constitution, which forbids remilitarization. But its Self-Defense Force is impressive, with 237,000 soldiers in uniform and the Pacific's largest navy. Although Japan does not have advanced offensive weapons such as long-range bombers and aircraft carriers, Japan has seventeen of the most sophisticated submarines. "Most analysts say that although Japan's air force and navy are numerically inferior to China's, they are more potent and will remain so for at least the next ten or twenty years" (M. Richardson 1995). This power worries Japan's neighbors, who remember well its violent imperialistic past. Postwar Japanese pacifism could, with this military clout, give way to resurgent militarism aimed at its simmering territorial disputes with both Russia and China. Regardless of the future use of this military power, Japan faces a wide range of security concerns, which would intensify if the troubled situation in northeast Asia (especially North Korea) worsens or the United States reduces its presence in Asia. These fears are likely to prompt continuing Japanese participation in the growing Asian arms race. However, predictions about Japan's emergence as a global military power with global ambitions began to disappear in late 1997 and 1998, when Japan's formerly robust economic growth rate slowed and the financial crisis spread to its beleaguered Asian neighbors. Fears elsewhere that the "American century" was giving way to a century of Japanese hegemony began to wane. A sluggish and stagnant Japanese economy coincided with growing recognition of the structural adjustments required for Japan to displace these fears. To recover, and to help prevent the deepening banking and economic crisis from spreading far beyond the Pacific and triggering a worldwide depression, Prime Minister Ryutaro Hashimoto inaugurated a deregulation plan that pledged to open the door to foreign trade and competition, and commited Japan to a revolutionary restructuring at home to reform the governmental protectionism and regulation that Japan had heralded in the high-roller 1980s as a superior brand of capitalism. That self-confidence was shattered in the mid-1990s when growth slowed, and massive debts accumulated. In response, Japan began to turn inward, and at the November 1997 Vancouver Asia-Pacific Economic Cooperation forum, Prime Minister Ryutaro Hashimoto humbly announced that Japan could not lend much help to its financially crushed neighbors, declaring, "We are certainly not arrogant enough to think we can take the role of locomotive for Asia."

As Japan's financial preeminence began to fade, Japan's security strategy sought to further tie Japan into the web of global institutions (the UN, the WTO, the G-7) on which it increasingly depended for preservation of the global order that had made its rise to prosperity possible. In the meantime, Japan stepped up its efforts to lead in foreign assistance to developing Global South countries; Japan perceives the poor's advancement as profitable investment in its own. Japan similarly sought to tie its security closer to America's by agreeing in 1997 to a new mutual defense treaty requiring Japanese troops to march with American troops in operations to keep the peace. A combination of bilateralism and multilateralism have thus replaced Japan's traditional preference for unilateralism in foreign affairs.

More problematically, with its neighbors arming to the teeth, Japan has begun to have second thoughts about nuclear weapons. It balked at the Clinton administration's attempt to press for a Japanese commitment to support the indefinite and unconditional extension of the nuclear nonproliferation treaty. This symbolic reversal of Japanese doctrine signaled the possibility of a radical departure in Japan's posture toward its future military role in the world. Indeed, as neorealists argue, it is extremely unlikely that Japan will refuse to develop military capabilities commensurate with its economic power and political ambitions.

Germany and the European Union Search for a Strategic Vision

Now united, Germany is likely to show signs of a new assertiveness once the immense costs of reunification and rebuilding the former German Democratic Republic are fully digested. Given its size, economic strength, and geographic location, the challenge for Europeans will be to find a way to absorb Germany within a broad European power-sharing arrangement. According to some analysts, however, Germany is too powerful to disappear into a wider European framework. It already accounts for almost one-third of the European Union's gross national product. In addition, its share of the EU budget is three times the contribution of Great Britain and twice the amount of Great Britain and France combined. Moreover, most European states' economies are heavily linked to Germany's economy and trade thereby giving Germany enormous leverage over the continent's economic growth. This extraordinary economic clout assures Germany's continued dominance within any emergent amalgamated European political entity, whether it is built around the federalist idea of a supranational government or some other, more modest pan-European institutional structure. In either case, there is no set of states in the European Union capable of balancing the power of a united Germany. "Too big for Europe, too small for the world" describes Germany's place in continental affairs.

If Germany's economic strength and diplomatic independence continue to grow, one consequence will be greater competition with the United States and other trade rivals. Yet this is not likely to result in a renewed push to flex German military muscle—even though Germany has one of the largest armies in Europe. Despite the parliamentary amendment to Germany's constitution, which permitted German troops to take part in international peacekeeping operations (e.g., the participation of four thousand Germans in the NATO-led Bosnian peacekeeping operations), an independent German military presence on the world stage is unlikely. Renewed militarism is even less so. Germany's armed forces are still deeply entrenched in and constrained by the joint command in NATO, the Western European Union, and its mutual Franco-German force structure. Because Germany remains a fervent advocate of the nuclear nonproliferation regime, economic rivalry is unlikely to culminate in military activity in the foreseeable future.

Germany likely will continue its effort to push for collective security with the military divisions it has created to assist multinational peacemaking units, both within Europe and globally. The drive to become a permanent member of the UN Security Council speaks to Germany's emphasis on multilateral approaches to international security; its armed force of 398,000 soldiers addresses its abiding desire to be prepared for defense. Similarly, Germany's continuing preference to rely on the United States and NATO for a nuclear guarantee reveals a preference for cooperative partnership in international security, even as fears that the United States may not always respond has made Germany prepare to shoulder Europe's post-2000 military burden. German leaders "have preferred to treat the cynical pleasures of *realpolitik* with suspicion and to believe that foreign policy could and should be grounded in defense of virtuous principles such as democracy, self-determination, free trade, and human rights" (*Economist,* September 20, 1993). A strong German aversion to militarism persists and is likely to shape Germany's security policies well into the next century. In this regard, German defense strategy differs from the posture the other great powers have assumed.

What is more, Germany remains the most enthusiastic supporter of integration and institutional approaches to the preservation of peace. Its security strategy subscribes unflinchingly to the tenets of **liberal institutionalism:** Germany has cast its fate on the spread of international organizations, European unification, international law, disarmament, and the promotion of democracy, free markets, and free trade as the most effective strategy for assuring that a twenty-first century peace will prevail. In that sense, Germany is the leading proponent of the European Union's quest to forge a common security policy. There are both dangers and opportunities embedded in that commitment, because by embracing the European Union's uniform defense position Germany has cast its fate with the EU's acceptance of NATO's pro-nuclear posture. This includes joining the core group of EU, NATO, and OSCE countries that see nuclear weapons as legitimate and NATO's first use of nuclear weapons doctrine to deter an attack as necessary (even though the July 1996 advisory opinion of the World Court challenged the legality of threatening to use nuclear weapons, and of their possession) (Marin-Bosch 1998). The wisdom or folly of Germany's strategy will be tested by the consequences that flow from the "nuclearization" of the EU's approach to national security.

● ● ●

THE SEARCH FOR SECURITY IN AN INSECURE WORLD

Preparation for war continues to command support from defense planners as an approach to peace. Rationalized by realism, the quest is understandable in a world where states alone remain responsible for their own self-defense. As President Eisenhower once noted, "until war is eliminated from international relations, unpreparedness for it is well nigh as criminal as war itself."

The fears produced by visions of national vulnerability also explain why many defense planners base their plans on worst-case analyses of others' capabilities and intentions. The urge to arm is further stimulated by defense planners' influence in the policy-making process of most countries and the tendency of political leaders to adopt the vocabulary and concepts of their military advisers.

Asking whether military preparedness endangers, rather than ensures, national security raises an uncomfortable question that challenges the prevailing approach to national security throughout much of the world's history. Yet many experts believe such questioning is justified (e.g., Porter 1995; UNDP 1994). To their way of thinking, now that fears of great-power war have receded, the economic and ecological dimensions of national security have assumed relatively greater prominence, and in the twenty-first century "security" should be defined more broadly so as to include both military and nonmilitary threats to human survival (see Focus 13.3).

Because a wide spectrum of problems has risen on political agendas, the concerns of today's foreign policymakers *are* arguably different and more di-

Redefining "Security" in the New World Order

Two authorities, Michael Klare and Daniel Thomas, call for new, broadened ways of thinking about national and international security and how they might be achieved.

> The concept of "security" must include protection against all major threats to human survival and well-being, not just military threats. Until now, "security"—usually addressed as "national security"—has meant the maintenance of strong military defenses against enemy invasion and attack. This approach may have served us well in the past, when such attack was seen as the only real threat to national survival; today, however, when airborne poisons released by nuclear and chemical accidents can produce widespread death and sickness (as occurred with the Bhopal and Chernobyl disasters), and when global epidemiological and environmental hazards such as AIDS and the "greenhouse effect" can jeopardize the well-being of the entire planet, this perspective appears increasingly obsolete. As individual economies become ever more enmeshed in the world economy, moreover, every society becomes more vulnerable to a global economic crisis. And, as modern telecommunications bring us all closer together, we are made acutely aware of the pain and suffering of those living under oppression, tyranny, and injustice.
>
> Given the fact that our individual security and well-being will depend to an ever-increasing extent on the world's success in mastering complex political, economic, environmental, and epidemiological problems, we must redefine "security" to embrace all of those efforts taken to enhance the long-term health and welfare of the human family. Defense against military aggression will obviously remain a vital component of security, but it must be joined by defenses against severe environmental degradation, worldwide economic crisis, and massive human suffering. Only by approaching the security dilemma from this multifaceted perspective can we develop the strategies and instruments that will be needed to promote global health and stability.
>
> Given the multiplicity of pressing world hazards, the concept of "national security" must be integrated with that of "world security." Until now, most people have tended to rely on the nation-state to provide protection against external threats, and have viewed their own nation's security as being adversely affected by the acquisition of power and wealth of other nations. Thus, in the interests of "national security," nation-states have often engaged in a competitive struggle to enhance their own economic and military strength at the expense of other nations' capabilities. This us-versus-them, zero-sum competition for security is naturally biased toward unilateral solutions to critical problems, frequently entailing military and/or economic coercion. In today's interdependent world, however, the quest for security is rapidly becoming a *positive-sum* process, whereby national well-being is achieved jointly by all countries—or not at all. (Klare and Thomas 1991, 3)

Approaches to the study of national security now frequently advocate putting these nonmilitary dimensions of the subject into the picture (for example, Shultz, Godson, and Quester 1997). At issue is whether this new way of organizing perceptions of national security is an idea whose time has come.

verse than they were just a short time ago. Though the danger of nuclear weapons and inter- and intrastate warfare continues, it would be foolish to neglect the dangers posed by such emergent threats as trade-bloc competition, neomercantilism, trade protectionism, the continuing impoverishment of the least developed countries, acid rain, deforestation, global warming, soaring population growth, the AIDS epidemic, international narcotic trafficking, the depletion of the earth's finite resources, and destruction of its protective ozone layer. These nonmilitary threats must command attention, as human survival may depend on addressing them.

However, the critical questions in an age of vulnerability to annihilation persist: How can states escape the prospect of destruction? How can they meet these emergent nonmilitary threats when the threat of warfare in a nationalistic age remains as pervasive as ever?

common security a concept advocating replacing the notion of states competing with one another for their own national security with collective security to promote the security of all states.

The security situation of the twenty-first century is unlikely to provide much room for maneuver. The world has yet to accept **common security** and *nonoffensive defense*, strategies that would eliminate offensive capabilities (Møller 1992). As demonstrated in the next chapter, many states still build weapons of attack for deterrence, even though conventional deterrence has failed frequently in the past. Moreover, contemporary deterrence theory remains based on the almost illogical premise that successful defense requires the continuing vulnerability of all states. Nonetheless, most believe that the threat system must be preserved to counter the threat.

Thus, security may depend as much on the control of force as on its pursuit. The next chapter examines the ways in which national leaders put armaments and arsenals to use for purposes of coercive diplomacy. It then evaluates the effectiveness of the bargaining strategies of coercive diplomacy on which states rely to defend themselves and to exercise influence over others.

KEY TERMS

national security
power
politics
power potential
coercive diplomacy
opportunity costs
peace dividend
soft power
hard power
arms race
military-industrial complex
strategic stockpile
multiple independently targetable reentry vehicles (MIRVs)
nonlethal weapons
revolution in military technology (RMT)
smart bombs
Revolution in Military Affairs (RMA)
military-technical revolution (MTR)

firebreak
strategic weapons
virtual nuclear arsenals
deterrence
electromagnetic-pulse (EMP) bomb
information warfare (IW)/infowar tactics
proliferation
Nth country problem
horizontal nuclear proliferation
vertical nuclear proliferation
chain reaction arms race cycle
Nuclear Nonproliferation Treaty (NPT)
relative burden of military spending
defense conversion
guns versus growth
unilateral
multilateral
bilateral

multipolar
Bottom Up Review (BUR)
realpolitik
engagement and enlargement strategy
mid-intensity conflict (MIC)
Clinton Doctrine
democratic peace
power transition
no first use
normalization of diplomatic relations
appeasement
containment
Yoshida Doctrine
liberal institutionalism
common security

SUGGESTED READING

Baldwin, David A. *Paradoxes of Power*. New York: Basil Blackwell, 1989.

Betts, Richard K. "The New Threat of Mass Destruction," *Foreign Affairs* 77 (January/February 1998): 26-41.

Brzezinski, Zbigniew. *The Grand Chessboard: American Primary and Geostrategic Imperatives*. New York: Basic Books, 1997.

Keller, William W., and Janne E. Nolan. "The Arms Trade: Business as Usual?" *Foreign Policy* 109 (Winter 1997–1998): 113–25.

Klare, Michael T., and Yogesh Chandrani, eds. *World Security: Challenges for a New Century*, 3rd ed. New York: St. Martin's Press, 1998.

Orme, John. "The Utility of Force in a World of Scarcity," *International Security* 22 (Winter 1997–1998): 138–67.

Pierre, Andrew J., ed. *Cascade of Arms*. Cambridge, Mass.: World Peace Foundation, 1997.

Rothgeb, John M., Jr. *Defining Power: Influence and Force in the Contemporary International System*. New York: St. Martin's Press, 1997.

Shultz, Richard, Roy Godson, and George Quester, eds. *Security Studies for the 21st Century*. Washington, D.C.: Brassey's, 1997.

Sinischalchi, Joseph. *Non-Lethal Technologies: Implications for Military Strategy*. Maxwell Air Force Base, Alabama: Air University, 1998.

Sopko, John F. "The Changing Proliferation Threat," pp. 78–88 in Charles W. Kegley, Jr. and Eugene R. Wittkopf, eds. *The Global Agenda*, 5th ed. New York: McGraw-Hill, 1998.

Waltz, Kenneth. "Thoughts about Virtual Nuclear Arsenals," *The Washington Quarterly* 20 (Summer 1997): 153–61.

WHERE ON THE WORLD WIDE WEB?

http://www.fas.org/asmp/
Arms Sales Monitoring Project Concerned with the global production and trade of weapons, the Federation of American Scientists monitors arms transfers and makes data available to the public through this Web site. Click on the "U.S. Arms Sales Table" to see which country is the biggest recipient of U.S. arms sales. See what was given to whom and for how much. Why do you think that certain countries got "freebies"?

http://www.webcom.com/ncecd/
National Commission for Economic Conversion and Disarmament Have you ever heard the slogan "We shall beat our swords into plowshares"? The National Commission for Economic Conversion and Disarmament, a nonprofit public education organization, takes the slogan seriously. This organization is dedicated to the transfer of military resources to civilian use. This Web site gives information on the costs associated with arms manufacturing and how resources can be better spent in other ways. Read the article that compares the exporting of arms to green technologies in the "Fact Sheets" or compare corporations and their conversion records. What is Washington's stance on this issue?

http://www.cdi.org/sc/javaclock.html
Military Spending Clock The Center for Defense Information, a nonprofit organization, has created a military spending clock. See what the U.S. government has spent on the military to date this year. See how much is spent every second, daily, and weekly.

http://sipri.se/projects/Milex/Introduction.html
SIPRI Military Expenditure Country Graphs The Stockholm International Peace Research Institute (SIPRI) monitors trends in military expenditures throughout the world. The SIPRI Web site allows the reader to compare military expenditures and the economic burden of the expenditures. Choose a country from the Middle East, Far East, and Africa. What do the trends indicate? How do they compare to the expenditures in European countries? What conclusions can you draw?

http://www.stimson.org/index.html
The Henry L. Stimson Center The Henry L. Stimson Center is a nonprofit, nonpartisan research center that concentrates on the intersection of national and international security policy and technology. The center provides information on chemical and biological weapons as well as nuclear proliferation. It houses important international agreements and searches for ways to eliminate weapons of mass destruction. It is a great site with tons of information.

CHAPTER 14

The Use of Coercive Diplomacy for Defense, Deterrence, and Bargaining

···

All diplomacy is a continuation of war by other means.

— CHOU EN-LAI,
Premier, The People's
Republic of China, 1954

···

We have grasped the mystery of the atom and rejected the Sermon on the Mount.

— OMAR N. BRADLEY,
U.S. General, Armistice
Day, 1945

CHAPTER TOPICS AND THEMES

- Coercive diplomacy as a necessary and widespread practice
- The security dilemma
- Nuclear deterrence and defense
  - Nuclear bargaining strategies and doctrines
  - The strategic situation
- Conventional forces and the future of deterrence
  - Military intervention
  - International crises and their management
- Sanctions as instruments of coercion
  - Boycotts as substitutes for weapons?
  - Why sanction?
- Diplomatic negotiation in lieu of military coercion?

It is impossible to pick up a newspaper without being reminded of a recurrent reality: people kill people. Likewise, it is impossible to read a newspaper without reading a story about political corruption–about one politician prostituting accepted law for personal gain. Nor is it possible to avoid headlines proclaiming that some country has done something horribly illegal and immoral to another in order to get its way. The media is loaded with unpleasant reminders that political life is not often lived by religious creeds and moral codes; the everyday global reality is not consistent with high ideals.

This chapter confronts this reality. It inspects the ways states and other transnational actors seek to survive, to prosper, and to get their way in a ruthless world where those with whom they must interact do not always play by the rules and are not always interested in behaving ethically. Instead, their primary motive is to get what they want—seeking, often, to (1) protect themselves from attack by others, (2) to persuade others to act contrary to their self-serving interests, and (3) to convince others to agree with contracts that are not to their advantage. This domain of everyday international behavior is called **coercive diplomacy.** In addition to diplomatic negotiation designed to settle disputes at the bargaining table, it involves the most newsworthy category of activities for defense, deterrence, and bargaining that capture the ways most people think that **politics** unfolds globally as states make attempts to get other actors to change their behavior against their will. The occasions are unavoidably common because often negotiators' efforts to peacefully resolve conflicts fail, and the actors involved then turn to coercive methods to get their way. How coercive diplomacy *should* be managed, however, poses a series of difficult choices, because the ethics and practical payoffs of potential decisions are unclear. This chapter will concentrate on three arenas in world politics in which coercive diplomacy is especially prominent: strategic bargaining for nuclear deterrence, the place of conventional weapons in coercion and defense, and the use of economic sanctions as a policy instrument in bargaining. The prominence of these bargaining tactics is a product of the influential impact of weapons and economic resources in the equation that separates winners and losers in interstate competition, and their mismanagement is a primary reason for the frequency of war (as argued in the concluding coverage of negotiation as a method of dispute management).

We look first at armaments and their changing role in interstate bargaining. This factor is pivotal to the survival capacity of coercively competing states, because, as documented in Chapter 12, one of the most disquieting long-term global trends is the exponential increase in the destructiveness of warfare and its human toll.

Preventing such human devastation is a primary security problem for all states—powerful and weak. As noted in Chapter 13, the traditional **realist** approach of most state defense planners to the danger of foreign aggression has been to build weapons systems and expand their country's military capabilities. However, in and of themselves arms will not assure peace, no matter how awesome the arsenal. To understand the predicaments that arming for war can create, the chapter first introduces the security dilemma that states face, and then examines the strategies states construct to prevent others from using arsenals against them, as well as how they use their military and economic resources in **bargaining** to exercise influence over other global actors.

realist an approach to world politics based on the assumption that all actors are naturally eager to compete, and that they see the acquisition of weapons as a means of winning against their rivals.

bargaining negotiation by states to try to settle their disputes without actually resorting to armed force.

• • •

THE SECURITY DILEMMA

What breeds the competition that propels states to seek security by preparing for war? The eighteenth-century French political philosopher Jean-Jacques Rousseau argued that "the state . . . always feels itself weak if there is another that is stronger. Its security and preservation demand that it make itself more powerful than its neighbors. It can increase, nourish, and exercise its power only at their expense. . . . Because the grandeur of the state is purely relative, it is forced to compare itself to that of the others. . . . It becomes small or great, weak or strong, according to whether its neighbor expands or contracts, becomes stronger or declines."

Concern for relative power derives from states' desire for self-preservation, national identity, freedom from the control of others, status, and wealth. They seek these under anarchical conditions that provide little protection from the hostile designs of others. Believing that their own strength will make them secure, many states attempt to build as much military might as their resources allow, often competing with one another in military capabilities.

Although states ostensibly arm for defensive purposes, their military might is often perceived as threatening. Alarmed, their neighbors are provoked to arm in response. Thus, as Rousseau observed, security is a relative phenomenon. Such fear and its reciprocated behaviors create a predicament known as the **security dilemma** (Herz 1951), defined as the consequences that result as "each party's power increments are matched by the others, and all wind up with no more security than when the vicious cycle began, along with the costs incurred in having acquired and having to maintain their power" (Snyder 1984).

security dilemma the chronic distrust that actors living under anarchy feel because, without sanctions or regulatory rules, rivals will do anything, including using aggression, to get ahead, with the result that all lose their security in a climate of mistrust.

Some scholars also describe the dynamics of this arms competition as the **spiral model** (Jervis 1976). The imagery is apt, as it captures the tendency of defense-enhancing efforts to result in escalating arms races that diminish the security of all. Sir Edward Grey, British foreign secretary before the First World War, described this process well:

> The increase in armaments, that is intended in each nation to produce consciousness of strength and a sense of security, does not produce these effects. On the contrary, it produces a consciousness of the strength of other nations and a sense of fear. Fear begets suspicion and distrust and evil imaginings of all sorts, till each government feels it would be criminal and a betrayal of its own country not to take every precaution, while every government regards every precaution of every other government as evidence of hostile intent. (Grey 1925, 92)

Despite the security dilemma that affects all states, leaders still refuse to accept vulnerability. Searching for strength, they often proceed from the assumptions that: (1) security is a function of power; (2) power is a function of military capability; and (3) military might is a measure of national greatness. Each of these suppositions is, of course, consistent with *realpolitik*.

Reformers in the liberal tradition question the logic by which states engage in competitive behavior that creates and sustains the security dilemma. To them, "the central theme of international relations is not evil but tragedy. States often share a common interest, but the structure of the situation prevents them from bringing about the mutually desired situation" (Jervis 1976).

To escape this predicament, **neoliberal** reformers call for changes in customary approaches to the problem of national security. Seeing weapons as "indefensible" (Lifton and Falk 1982), they argue that unarmed or defenseless countries enjoy a flexibility in their foreign policies that their armed neighbors do not. They are freed from the responsibilities that military power imposes and do not have to incur the costs of acquiring it. Although these countries might have to live in the constant shadow of others' missiles, they can take comfort in knowing that they are not the targets of the missiles. Appropriate in this context is John F. Kennedy's sober warning in 1963 that, in the event of another total war, regardless of how it might begin, those most heavily armed would automatically become its primary targets and victims.

Not surprisingly, realists are less than convinced by the liberals' views. Even if leaders and defense planners recognize the threats that arming for security provokes in others, they argue that international anarchy makes these threats inevitable. Since, by definition, there is no escaping a dilemma, the security dilemma explains why states sharing a common interest in security nonetheless engage in individual actions that prevent them from realizing it.

To understand how most states confront their lack of national security, we next describe the kinds of strategies they have created. We will first examine the ways the two leading military powers, the United States and the former Soviet Union, sought during the Cold War to prevent nuclear attack through their evolving strategic doctrines regarding **nuclear deterrence.** We will then look at the strategies that other less militarily powerful states have used for purposes of **conventional deterrence**—prevention of an attack with conventional, nonnuclear weapons. In pursuing these topics, although nuclear and conventional deterrence are often seen as the same, most theories of the former are guided by historical investigation of cases in the latter category (Harknett 1994). It is important to keep in mind the difference

> between strategic *nuclear deterrence* (the level at which the majority of the theorizing has occurred, at which the use of intercontinental thermonuclear weapons has been threatened, and at which deterrence is usually thought to have held) and *conventional* deterrence (the level that has received considerably less attention, at which, by definition, threats to use unconventional weapons of mass destruction are excluded, and at which deterrence, arguably, has been prone to fail). . . . The range of likely cost-benefit calculations shifts dramatically when the deterrent calculus of strategic nuclear warfare is compared with regional conventional conflict. (Haffa 1992, 9)

● ● ●

NUCLEAR DETERRENCE AND DEFENSE

The dropping of the atomic bomb on Japan on August 6, 1945, is the most important event distinguishing pre- from post-World War II international politics. In the blinding flash of a single weapon and the shadow of its mushroom cloud, the international arena was transformed from a balance-of-power to a balance-of-terror system.

In the following decades, policymakers in the nuclear states had to grapple with two central policy questions: (1) Whether they should use nuclear

neoliberal proponents of institutional reforms in governance, law, and economics as substitutes for warfare as an instrument of coercive diplomacy.

In the first true test of the awful destructive capabilities of atomic weapons on cities, American forces dropped an atomic bomb on Hiroshima on August 6, 1945, in an attempt to bring World War II to a speedy close. In an instant, what later became known as "the nuclear age" was ushered in and the Japanese city lay in ruins.

weapons, and (2) how to prevent others from using them. The search for answers has been critical, as the failure to deter a nuclear attack would result in unimaginable destruction.

The impact of a "limited" war with today's nuclear arms would not be limited. Studies of the immediate and delayed effects of nuclear war project a postnuclear environment too terrifying to contemplate (see Focus 14.1). Life as we know it could cease. The danger, moreover, persists: "If all planned cuts in nuclear weapons are implemented, in the year 2003 the world will still have as many as 20,000 nuclear weapons containing the explosive power of more than 200,000 Hiroshima bombs" (*Defense Monitor 22*, No. 1, 1993; 1) or, "after recent reductions, still over 700 times the explosive power used in the twentieth century's three major wars, which killed 44,000,000 people" (Sivard 1996, 5).

The threat of nuclear war was, and remains, particularly pertinent to the United States and Russia, today's two most heavily armed nuclear powers. Their decisions during the Cold War—the formative period that still casts its shadow on defense planning—shaped strategic thinking and doctrines both at home and elsewhere. In order to grasp the influence of past strategies on present ones, we need to first understand how the United States and the former Soviet Union used their most powerful weapons to deter each other. This will also allow us to understand the larger subject of which it is a part: how states conceive of deterrence as a method of coercive diplomacy for **signaling**—making threats in order to intimidate a potential enemy from using its weapons aggressively.

signaling in conflict situations, either explicit or implicit communication by states to reveal both their intentions and their capabilities.

Superpower Deterrence and Defense Policies

Although weapons of mass destruction have existed since World War II, the superpowers' postures toward them have evolved as technologies, defense needs,

The Aftermath of a Nuclear Attack
The View of Atmospheric Scientists

What would happen if even a fraction of today's nuclear weapons were used? Summarizing scientific studies, world-renowned researchers Carl Sagan and Richard P. Turco conclude that the planet would become uninhabitable:

> As bad as the prompt and local effects of nuclear war would be—the delayed and global consequences might be much worse. . . . Forest fires ignited in such a war could generate enough smoke to obscure the sun and perturb the atmosphere over large areas. . . . That smoke from the burning of modern cities would provide a still more serious threat. . . . Provided cities were targeted, even a "small" nuclear war could have disastrous climatic consequences; a global war, . . . might lower average planetary temperatures by 15 to 20°C, darken the skies sufficiently to compromise green plant photosynthesis, produce a witches' brew of chemical and radioac-

tive poisons, and significantly deplete the protective ozone layer. These effects, which had been almost wholly overlooked by the world's military establishments, [are] described as "nuclear winter." (Sagan and Turco 1993, 369)

It has been estimated that "the missiles on board a single [U.S.] SLBM submarine may be enough to initiate nuclear winter" (Quester 1992)—enough to end human existence. To defense planners, this prospect makes utilizing nuclear weapons for military purposes unthinkable. To the extent that nuclear states appreciate this fact, it reduces the purpose of nuclear weapons to one objective—deterring external aggression. However, if enemies do not believe that a sane nuclear arms state would actually use its weapons in retaliation against aggression, do those weapons become useless as a deterrent?

capabilities, and global conditions have changed. For analytical convenience, we can treat those postures in terms of three periods. The first began at the end of World War II and lasted until the **Cuban missile crisis.** U.S. nuclear superiority was the dominant characteristic of this period. The second began in 1962 and lasted until the breakup of the Soviet Union in 1991. Growing Soviet military capability was the dominant characteristic of this period (which meant that the United States no longer stood alone in its ability to annihilate another country without fear of its own destruction). The third phase began in 1992, as the former Cold War antagonists and other rising great powers began to restructure their forces and revise their strategic doctrines. To better understand this new thinking, we will first examine the superpowers' strategic policies during the precedent-setting Cold War period.

Cuban missile crisis the U.S. naval blockade of Cuba in October 1962 to force Soviet withdrawal of offensive missiles after the discovery of the Soviet's plan to deploy them.

Compellence, 1945–1962. Countries that enjoy military superiority often think of weapons as instruments for coercive bargaining—that is, as tools to be used for the political purpose of changing others' behavior. The United States, the world's first and, for many years, unchallenged nuclear power, was no exception. **Compellence** (Schelling 1966) described U.S. strategic doctrine when it enjoyed a clear-cut superiority in the nuclear balance of power. Compellence makes nuclear weapons instruments of political influence, used not for fighting but to get others to do what they might not otherwise do. Thus it refers to the use of nuclear weapons as instruments for "forceful persuasion" (George 1992), even if some question the ethics of a policy instrument that uses terror to pursue worthy ends such as peace (see Focus 14.2).

The United States sought to gain bargaining leverage after World War II by conveying the impression that it would actually use nuclear weapons. Its

Does War Necessitate Tragic, Even Evil, Action?

The Controversial Ethics of Peace Enforcement

FOCUS 14.2

During the American Civil War, Union General William Tecumseh Sherman declared that "war is hell." To end the war, he sought to literally make it hell by pursuing a ruthless "march to the sea" in the American South, ravaging civilians and their communities to force surrender. To put an end to killing, Sherman believed that killing must be devastating. Only by making war terrifying, he felt, could surrender be hastened.

Many since have adopted Sherman's scorched-earth strategy to demoralize a hostile civilian population in order to subdue its army leaders. They believe that terrorism—the wanton destruction of property and people—is the most effective method of bringing an adversary to its knees.

But where does this practice to stop war end and barbarism begin? To some there are no moral limits: The ends justify the terrible means. The savagery, of course, can never be justified to its victims. Critics argue that such strategies, which overlook the traditional right of innocent noncombatants to protection from genocide, violate international law and are crimes against humanity. Classic Christian theologians also condemn the philosophy that condones evil methods, maintaining that a right intention does not automatically justify any means to achieve it.

The debate over the ethics of cruel destruction as a strategy arose again in the closing days of World War II. At the insistence of the head of the Allied Bomber Command, Sir Arthur "Bomber" Harris authorized the devastation of the demilitarized German city of Dresden, "roasting at least twenty-five thousand of its inhabitants in the notorious firestorm," under the conviction that "bombing German cities simply for the sake of increasing terror" and "gunning down people fleeing the burning city the morning after the British raid" would speed a German surrender. However, after the deliberate attack on "city-center churches and palaces packed with refugees," German resistance to the Allies intensified. The strategy of terrorism by flattening cities backfired: "A year of saturation bombing had not brought an uprising" against Hitler and the Nazi regime (Jenkins 1995).

Yet many defense planners feel strongly that mass destruction can produce surrender. For example, the necessity of shocking the Japanese into submission was foremost among President Harry S Truman's reasons for dropping the atomic bomb on Japan. (When informed about the plan to use the bomb to force Japan's leaders into an immediate unconditional surrender, General Dwight D. Eisenhower expressed "grave misgivings" about using this "horrible and destructive" weapon, which he saw as "completely unnecessary" [Ambrose 1995].)

Experts in both defense and moral ethics remain divided as to the just means of limiting the evil of war. International law, too, reflects this division of opinion regarding the criteria that should govern the determination of the boundaries of legal conduct to coerce an aggressor's surrender. The issue of the ethical means of ending a war has not been resolved.

---

commitment a negotiator's promises during bargaining, designed to change the target's expectations about the negotiator's future behavior.

threatening posture regarding **commitments** in strategic negotiations was especially evident during the Eisenhower administration in the 1950s. To win political victories, Secretary of State John Foster Dulles practiced **brinkmanship,** deliberately threatening U.S. adversaries with nuclear destruction so that, at the brink of war, they would concede to U.S. demands.

Others went even further, seeing the new weapons of mass destruction as instruments for bargaining that could safely be used. For instance, to prevent the Soviets from also developing a hydrogen bomb, U.S. General Curtis Lemay, who would soon head the U.S. Strategic Air Command, in 1949 recommended "a nuclear Sunday punch," a preemptive strike against the Soviets. Lemay wanted to send "an armada of planes, carrying the entire Los Alamos stockpile (numbering more than one hundred atom bombs) to destroy seventy Soviet cities" (Stengal 1995). With hydrogen weapons, the damage would have been even more annihilating.

433

THE USE OF
COERCIVE DIPLOMACY
FOR DEFENSE,
DETERRENCE, AND
BARGAINING

When informed of the possibility of designing a hydrogen bomb, U.S. President Truman asked, "What the hell are we waiting for?" Politicians hailed the nuclear weapon as a defensive force. However, scientists such as Robert Oppenheimer—who headed the Manhattan Project, which produced the atomic bomb—maintained that the hydrogen bomb was inherently immoral because it was a weapon of genocide that, unlike the atomic bomb, was so destructive that its use could not be restricted to military purposes. More than two thousand nuclear-weapons tests have been undertaken since 1945, and testing has continued. Pictured here is a 1995 French atomic test in the South Pacific of a nuclear bomb smaller than the hydrogen bomb that, in 1952, created a three-mile fireball one thousand times more powerful than the bombs used by the United States on Hiroshima and Nagasaki. In 1997 the forty-five states possessing nuclear reactors agreed to a treaty that sought to ban future nuclear-weapons tests, but India's and Pakistan's tests in 1998 reduced the prospects for that ban holding.

Brinkmanship was part of the overall U.S. strategic doctrine adopted by the Eisenhower administration. Known as **massive retaliation,** it advocated the use of nuclear weapons to contain communism and Soviet expansionism. Massive retaliation was a **countervalue targeting strategy** because it aimed U.S. weapons at objects that the Soviets presumably valued most—their industrial and population centers. The alternative is a **counterforce targeting strategy,** which targets an enemy's military forces and weapons, thus sparing civilians from immediate destruction.

Massive retaliation and brinkmanship heightened Soviet fears. By 1949 the Soviet Union had broken the U.S. atomic monopoly. Thereafter, faced with U.S. belligerence, it pursued a twofold response. Following Nikita Khrushchev's rise to power in the mid-1950s, the Soviets ceased speaking of the usefulness of military power and instead pursued **peaceful coexistence** as an alternative nonmilitary strategy for continuing, by nonviolent economic and political means, the communist struggle with capitalism. Nonetheless, fearing that a nuclear exchange would destroy the Soviet Union but permit U.S. survival, Soviet leaders also expanded their nuclear arsenals. In 1957 the Soviet Union successfully launched the world's first space satellite *(Sputnik),* demonstrating its potential

counterforce targeting strategy the targeting of strategic nuclear weapons on particular military capabilities of an enemy's armed forces and arsenals.

peaceful coexistence the condition resulting from Soviet leader Nikita Khruschev's doctrine in 1956 proclaiming that capitalist and communist states could compete economically for growth without war.

ability to deliver nuclear weapons far beyond the Eurasian landmass. The super-powers' strategic competition thus took a new turn, as the United States for the first time began to face a credible military threat to its own geophysical security.

Mutual Deterrence, 1962–1983. As U.S. strategic superiority eroded, American policymakers began to question the usefulness of weapons of mass destruction for political bargaining, or for **peace enforcement** to coerce an adversary to stop fighting. They were horrified by the destruction that could result if compellence should provoke a nuclear exchange. In contrast to so-called **limited war,** waged without recourse to all weapons in a state's arsenal, the nearly suicidal Cuban missile crisis of 1962 dealt coercive diplomacy a serious blow, and undermined faith in **total war,** waged against an enemy's civilian population and economy to destroy its fighting spirit and capacity to continue. "With missiles, satellites and nuclear weapons, [it] was becoming recognized that there could be no return to the nineteenth-century belief that the military's first task is to keep war away from the country's civilians. In modern war, there are no civilians" (Drucker 1997, 170). After the near-miss Cuban encounter, the objective of nuclear weapons shifted to preventing an attack. That is, strategic policy shifted from compellence to deterrence.

Both superpowers also pursued **extended deterrence**, protecting not only their homelands but also targets outside their adversary's defense perimeter and alliance network, to prevent an attack on their allies. Extended deterrence was especially critical to the United States, as its allies were far from its own shores and geographically close to the Soviet Union. The United States repeatedly declared that it would defend its allies. However, the credibility of its guarantee to the NATO countries in particular was often questioned. Former U.S. Secretary of State Henry Kissinger punctuated this doubt when he noted in 1979 that the U.S. promise to defend Europe with nuclear weapons involved "strategic assurances that we cannot possibly mean or if we do mean, we should not execute because if we should execute, we risk the destruction of civilization." The dubious credibility of the U.S. deterrent led some critics to advocate "decoupling" Europe from the U.S. strategic security umbrella and encouraging individual NATO countries to develop their own nuclear capabilities.

Ironically, the shift from compellence to deterrence stimulated rather than inhibited the U.S.–Soviet arms race. A deterrent strategy depends on the unquestionable ability to inflict unacceptable damage on an opponent. It requires a **second-strike capability** that enables a country to withstand an adversary's first strike and still retain the ability to retaliate with a devastating counterattack. To ensure a second-strike capability and an adversary's awareness of it, deterrence rationalized an unrestrained search for sophisticated retaliatory capabilities. Any system that could be built was built, because, as President Kennedy explained in 1961, "only when arms are sufficient beyond doubt can we be certain without doubt that they will never be employed."

To characterize the strategic balance that emerged during the 1960s and early 1970s, policymakers coined the phrase **mutual assured destruction (MAD).** It described the superpowers' essential military stalemate. Mutual deterrence, based on the principle of assured destruction, assumed the military potential for and psychological expectation of widespread death and destruction by both combatants in a nuclear exchange. Peace—or at least stability—was viewed as the product of mutual vulnerability, which was seen in turn as a precondition for successful deterrence. Each superpower sought to preserve

435

THE USE OF
COERCIVE DIPLOMACY
FOR DEFENSE,
DETERRENCE, AND
BARGAINING

the other's second-strike capability, trusting that neither would then dare to attack the other at the price of its own subsequent destruction.

As the United States and the Soviet Union competed with each other, the differences in their strategic capabilities narrowed. By the early 1970s a *parity*, or equality, developed in the two superpowers' capabilities reinforcing the strategic assumptions of MAD. Thereafter, both armed not to gain superiority but to preserve a rough equivalence in their strategic arsenals.

The balance in the superpowers' arsenals laid the basis for negotiations on limiting strategic arms during the 1970s détente phase of the U.S.–Soviet rivalry. Two Strategic Arms Limitation Talks (SALT) agreements, both attempting to guarantee each superpower's second-strike capacity, were concluded during the 1970s. Although the pursuit of this shared goal posed difficulties, a precarious peace resulted. However, despite the superpowers' sometimes tacit, sometimes formal acceptance of the principles on which assured destruction rested, differences in their interpretation and practical application inevitably led to disagreements. As the strategic arms race continued into the 1980s, the concepts governing the competition began to revert from the principle of deterrence to the previous principle of compellence, which contemplated the actual use of nuclear weapons. Indeed, with superpower confrontation replacing cooperation, in the early 1980s a new debate raged regarding the role and purpose of nuclear weapons. Should nuclear weapons still be used exclusively for purposes of defense and deterrence? Or, assuming that a first-strike capability could be achieved, should they be used for offensive purposes?

Neither adversary had reason to trust the other. Each assumed that, unless deterred, its opponent would be tempted to use its arsenal for attack. As a result, bad faith and worst-case analyses governed the reformulation of strategic doctrines.

U.S. statements about the practicability of preemptive strikes and the "winnability" of a nuclear exchange alarmed the world. The atmosphere chilled as U.S. leaders spoke boldly of *damage limitation*. This concept was predicated on the belief that one way to avoid the destructive effects of nuclear weapons was to be the first to use them, destroying a portion of the adversary's weapons before they could be used in a retaliatory strike.

As U.S.–Soviet relations worsened, debate in the United States concerning the best way to protect national security with strategic weapons broke into polar positions. Although MAD continued to dominate the thinking of some, others advocated **nuclear utilization theory (NUTs),** an approach whereby nuclear weapons would not simply play a deterrent role, but could also be used in war. Such a posture was necessary, some U.S. policy advisers argued, because the Soviet Union was preparing to fight—and win—a nuclear war (Pipes 1977; c.f. Holloway 1983: Kennan 1984b). Furthermore, advocates of NUTs argued that use of nuclear weapons would not necessarily escalate to an unmanageable, all-out nuclear exchange. Instead, they reasoned that it was possible to fight a protracted "limited" nuclear war. By making nuclear weapons more usable, they argued, the United States could make nuclear threats more credible.

Proponents of MAD, on the other hand, held that deterrence remained the only sane purpose for nuclear weapons, and contended that any use of nuclear weapons—however limited initially—would surely escalate to an unrestrained exchange. "It is inconceivable to me," former U.S. Secretary of Defense Robert McNamara reflected, "that limited nuclear wars would remain limited—any

436

THE USE OF
COERCIVE DIPLOMACY
FOR DEFENSE,
DETERRENCE, AND
BARGAINING

decision to use nuclear weapons would imply a high probability of the same cataclysmic consequences as a total nuclear exchange." According to this view, the technical requirements necessary to wage a protracted limited nuclear war would surely exceed the human capacity to control it.

In addition, advocates of MAD felt that because the threatened use of even tactical nuclear weapons would lower the nuclear threshold, a nuclear strategy based on their utility in war made war more likely, thereby diminishing the weapons' deterrent capability. From this viewpoint, both superpowers were destined to live in a MAD world—even if, ironically, this meant remaining in the "mutual hostage relationship" in which their earlier weapons decisions had imprisoned them (Keeny and Panofsky 1981).

As the 1980s nuclear debate raged, U.S. and Soviet leaders both professed their commitment to avoiding nuclear war, viewing it as "unthinkable." This meant expanding the capabilities of both defensive and offensive systems. Thus each superpower continued developing and deploying the kinds of weapons that NUTs required—so-called discriminating low-yield nuclear weapons made possible by new technologies in guidance and precision. This weaponry prepared the contestants for warfare short of a massive, all-out nuclear attack and sought to provide them with effective deterrents against a conventional war.

This search for new weapons and new ideas to govern their use did little to calm fears, however. Instead, a vigorous peace movement swept Europe and North America, as mass publics on both sides of the Atlantic voiced their desire for an alternative to the threat posed by nuclear weapons. Accordingly, the purposes that NUTs strategists assigned nuclear arsenals fell into disfavor.

From Offense to Defense, 1983–1993. A new challenge to strategic thinking was launched in 1983, when U.S. President Reagan proposed building a space-based defensive shield against ballistic missiles. The **Strategic Defense Initiative (SDI),** as it was known officially, called for the development of a "Star Wars" **ballistic missile defense (BMD)** system using advanced space-based technologies to destroy offensive weapons launched in fear, anger, or by accident. The goal, as President Reagan defined it, was to make nuclear weapons "impotent and obsolete." Thus SDI sought to shift U.S. nuclear strategy away from reliance on offensive missiles to deterring attack—that is, away from dependence on mutual assured destruction, which President Reagan deemed "morally unacceptable."

From the start, scientists questioned the feasibility of SDI's technological fix to the security dilemma posed by strategic weapons. There was simply no assurance that a reliable system was possible (Slater and Goldfischer 1988). Critics warned that the projected costs in excess of $140 billion for SDI were prohibitive and that SDI was dangerous, capable of inducing an unwarranted sense of safety, when in fact it "almost surely would not work in the event of an all-out attack." Critics also warned that SDI would stimulate development of a new generation of offensive weapons designed to overwhelm the defensive ones, and that, in addition, it violated the Anti-Ballistic Missile (ABM) treaty of 1972 (Moore 1995).

Despite this uncertainty and questionable legality, the United States continued to support SDI even after the end of the Cold War and the demise of the Soviet Union. In the Bush administration's view, SDI still had a mission in providing "protection from limited ballistic missile assaults, whatever their source," rather than relying on "some abstract theory of deterrence." The Pentagon disagreed, pointing out the inability of a space-based system to protect against the

Strategic Defense Initiative (SDI) the so-called Star Wars plan conceived by the Reagan administration to deploy an antiballistic missile system using space-based lasers that would destroy enemy nuclear missiles before they could enter the earth's atmosphere.

437

THE USE OF
COERCIVE DIPLOMACY
FOR DEFENSE,
DETERRENCE, AND
BARGAINING

many other ways that an enemy can deliver tactical weapons, including "short-range missiles or intermediate-range ballistic missiles that fly slightly depressed trajectories" (Fetter 1991), or even in a hand-carried suitcase.

This argument notwithstanding, in late 1995 the Star Wars era continued. As Lawrence J. Korb, formerly a defense secretary in the Reagan administration, complained:

> Republicans seem determined to spend additional funds [on] revival of the Strategic Defense Initiative, now known as National Missile Defense. Support for strategic defense has become a litmus test of loyalty to the Reagan legacy. . . . Thus, almost in lockstep, Republicans in Congress are voting to double the amount currently spent [on missile defense, seeking] to throw some $40 billion or $50 billion at a multisite continental defense system, although there are serious doubts about necessity and cost-effectiveness and although such a system would violate the 1972 Antiballistic Missile Treaty, negotiated by a Republican president. (Korb 1995b, 29–30)

The Shifting Strategic Situation

Thus, in some respects strategic thinking continues to rely on MAD principles, as the Clinton administration in 1998 planned to clear the way for developing advanced *high-altitude* **theater missile defense (TMD)** systems that would undercut the Anti-Ballistic Missile (ABM) treaty outlawing such strategic defenses (Lewis and Postol 1997). The Cold War, the third global conflict of the twentieth century, concluded without bloodshed. Some attributed this remarkable achievement to the effectiveness of the superpowers' deterrence strategies—the intimidating power of their weapons, which made aggression suicidal—and to the rationality of leaders, inspired by their awareness that survival was preferable to victory. Others believe that the superpowers averted apocalypse *despite* their awesome arsenals and deterrence doctrines rather than because of them. In fact, many of the critics of strategic nuclear deterrence (e.g., Johansen 1991; Vasquez 1991) complain that the doctrine's validity is suspect because deterrence is the nonoccurrence of an event and by definition depends on **counterfactual arguments** that cannot be proven because they are not testable. According to this line of reasoning, "Although it can be argued that nuclear deterrence worked during the Cold War, we do not know that for sure. (The USSR may never have wished to invade Europe nor to attack the United States with nuclear weapons.) It is very difficult to prove deterrent successes because that would require showing why an event did not occur" (Haffa 1992).

Regardless of its causes, the halt to the Cold War rivalry has ended the former adversaries' need to prepare for war against each other. In a radical change, they now perceive their interests as being served by *reducing* their armaments, not increasing them, thus signaling the start of a new age. Not long after Mikhail Gorbachev assumed power in the Soviet Union in 1985, and shortly after Reagan's Star Wars speech, the superpowers negotiated a series of dramatic new arms control agreements (see Chapter 15). Reduced fears of an attack in Europe stripped away the rationale for tactical nuclear weapons. As a result, the precedent-setting Intermediate-Range Nuclear Forces (INF) treaty, followed by the Conventional Armed Forces in Europe (CFE) agreement, and then the *Strategic Arms Reduction Treaty (START)* hastened the emergence of a strategic setting less menaced by the spectre of global warfare. In this new

counterfactual arguments
thought experiments to consider the consequences that probably would have resulted had something happened that actually did not, such as speculating "what if Adolf Hitler had invaded Britain" or what if "John F. Kennedy had not been assassinated."

438

THE USE OF
COERCIVE DIPLOMACY
FOR DEFENSE,
DETERRENCE, AND
BARGAINING

setting, the superpowers began to shift their strategies from nuclear deterrence to mutual safety.

The consequences of the reductions since 1990 in the U.S. and Russian strategic nuclear arsenals by 1997 are depicted in Figure 14.1. As shown, their post-START disarmament initiatives will cut their diminished arsenals even further by the year 2003. If this "deep cut" occurs, the strategic situation in the twenty-first century will look radically different, requiring the rethinking of traditional assumptions underlying strategic doctrines.

Few expect a war between the great powers in the foreseeable future, although most expect wars to continue in the Global South. The great powers have sought to restructure their armed forces in order to cope with the kinds of threats and weapons with which adversaries will fight such wars. This invites additional reductions of nuclear (strategic) arsenals, U.S. help to the former Soviet republics to destroy their nuclear weapons, and collective great-power efforts to keep nuclear weapons out of the hands of aggressors. It also calls for increasing the capacity to wage conventional wars in emergent trouble spots. Military preparations have not ceased, but instead have been redirected toward short-term wars fought with increasingly sophisticated conventional weapons. The emerging strategies of the great powers now reflect their search for a new security architecture to contain regional conflicts and guard against the rising power of their rivals.

• • •

CONVENTIONAL FORCES AND THE FUTURE OF DETERRENCE

As noted in previous chapters, a number of states presently outside the circle of dominant military powers are striving to enter it as India and Pakistan did in 1998. With ambitiously expanding armament programs, their quest for nuclear weapons and the potential collapse of the nonproliferation regime would radically transform the globe's security climate. Joseph Kruzel, a former U.S. defense expert who tragically lost his life in August 1995 while seeking to negotiate a peaceful solution to the warfare in the Balkans, wrote:

> Nuclear proliferation in other parts of the world must be reckoned as a high probability. The [U.S.] Central Intelligence Agency estimated that in the early 1990s over fifty countries were working on nuclear, chemical, or ballistic missile capabilities. By the end of the century, some number of these states will certainly develop operational weapons of mass destruction and the means to deliver them. Because nuclear forces could serve as an effective deterrent against retaliation by an outside state, more and more states may be inclined to see nuclear weapons as a serious military option. A nuclear-capable Azerbaijan, for example, could invade Armenia and present the world with a *fait accompli* backed by the threat of using its own nuclear weapons against any third party that would presume to meddle.
>
> Given these political and technological trends, it appears likely that before the end of the twentieth century, a nuclear weapon will be detonated in anger somewhere on the planet. That event, the first use of nuclear weapons since August 1945, could lead to a rapid expansion of the nuclear club as countries with the technical know-how hasten to cross the threshold. Several states are also likely to develop or acquire intermediate-range

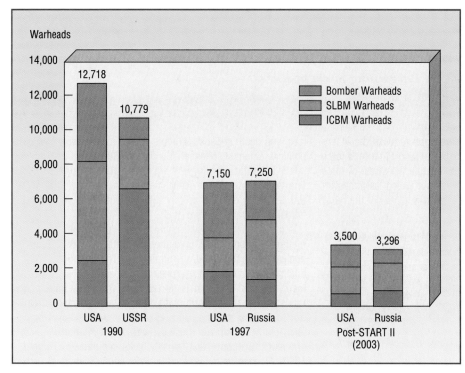

FIGURE 14.1

The Changing Strategic Balance,
1990, 1997, and 2003

The United States and Russia
have agreed to substantially
reduce the size of their nuclear
arsenals. They no longer
perceive huge inventories of
these weapons of mass
destruction as necessary for
survival. It remains to be seen
whether nuclear deterrence will
continue, and whether
technological advances will
allow other kinds of weapons
systems to keep the peace.

SOURCE: Adapted from the Stockholm
International Peace Research Institute (1997), 372.

delivery capabilities. Even if there is no actual use of nuclear weapons, the proliferation of fingers on nuclear triggers will almost inevitably change . . . attitudes toward defense against such weapons. (Kruzel 1993, 4)

By most assessments, controlling regional and ethnic violence is likely to provide the most compelling rationale for undertaking military action in the twenty-first century. The Global South is populated by many hypernationalist countries of growing military strength with an interest in controlling events in the areas where their primary security interests lie. This danger has increased the importance of conventional deterrence:

> The most important challenge for deterrence strategists may not be in deal-
> ing with the increased frequency of military conflict, but rather in dealing
> with an increased *variety* of sources of conflict. . . . The most important
> consequence of the end of the Cold War may be the recognition that the
> sources of conflict now emanate from less-clear and more-complex axes.
> Nationalist aspirations, religious cleavages, and resurgent authoritarian
> coups may all cut against established international political alignments.
> Now, and in the foreseeable future, the sources of war will have to be
> viewed across a variety of dimensions. (Harknett 1994, 102–3)

Many states today are highly agitated, and perceive military force below the threshold of nuclear weapons as an available means to achieve their political aims. Indeed, to the many states harboring historical grievances, armed coercion is a highly attractive option, as threats to initiate less destructive and less costly military actions with conventional weapons are far more likely to be

Low-Intensity Conflicts
Coercive Bargaining Short of War?

The destructiveness of modern weapons reduces the incentives for great and small powers alike to resort to armed force and increases the propensity to substitute the threat of force for its actual use. Still, violence has not ended, as states increasingly rely on low-intensity conflict (LIC) to get their way with others.

[Low-intensity conflict] is warfare that falls below the threshold of full-scale military combat between modern armies (of the sort that occurred in the Korean War and at the onset of the Iran-Iraq War). Under U.S. doctrine, low-intensity conflict encompasses four particular types of operations: (1) *counterinsurgency* [or] combat against revolutionary guerrillas . . . ; (2) *pro-insurgency* [or] support for insurgents . . . ; (3) *peacetime contingency operations* [or] police-type actions . . . ; and (4) *military "shows of force"* [which threaten] military maneuvers. (Klare 1988, 12)

Low-intensity conflict is today a symbol of warfare between the haves and have-nots, referring primarily to methods for combating terrorism, insurgency, and guerrilla activities in the Global South to protect the interests of the powerful. This type of warfare below the level of overt military operations by a state's regular army includes proxy wars, wars fought with mercenaries, psychological operations to terrorize the populace, and death squads. "What is crucial to recognize," notes political scientist Michael T. Klare (1988), "is that low-intensity conflict is a form of warfare in which *your* side suffers very little death or destruction, while the other side suffers as much damage as possible without producing undue hardship for your own society."

Low-intensity conflict characterizes the great powers' methods of combating "revolutionary strife, random violence, nuclear terrorism, and drug-running. . . . The strategy for conducting low-intensity war strikes at the heart of the development process, and that is its purpose. Physical attacks on roads, dams, and so forth, with the inevitable collateral damage to houses, schools, and hospitals, is accompanied by a psychological attack on those aspects of a revolutionary government's program that establish its legitimacy" (Barnet 1990). Despite its name, low-intensity conflict does not necessarily mean low levels of death or destruction. "The low-intensity conflict in Guatemala, for instance, . . . claimed well over one hundred thousand lives" (Klare 1988, 12).

In an interdependent world that is fraught with ethnic and religious rivalries, armed conflicts short of full-scale war are likely to erupt often, and great powers are likely to influence the outcomes of the conflicts with low-intensity bargaining tactics.

---

conventional war armed conflicts waged with nonnuclear naval, air, and ground weapons.

believed than are threats to initiate a nuclear war. **Conventional war** is a more credible bargaining chip because the risks are lower. Moreover, the odds of retaliation by the target are lower because "from a challenging country's perspective, conventional deterrent costs are likely to be viewed as highly suspect. Regardless of formidability, conventional deterrence will be perceived as threatening costs that can be contested" (Harknett 1994).

Deterrence is a risky game, and the strategies on which most states today depend do not give them reliable protection. Conventional force can be used for coercive purposes, and frequently is. The activity is not just practiced by weak states in the Global South; the use of conventional armed conflict short of war is a component of the great powers' bargaining strategies, as the **low-intensity conflict (LIC)** programs of the United States and others illustrate (see Focus 14.3).

The methods through which coercive diplomacy is pursued are varied, for both the goals of deterrence and compellence. To bring about changes in other actors' behavior, states may rely on words and deeds, usually attempting to combine both. They talk tough by making threats and often act tough by using their military capabilities.

It is difficult to generalize about the effectiveness of these strategies, which have worked in some situations but not others. Bargaining strategies depend on the issue, the reputation of the actor pursuing a strategy of coercive diplomacy, and the actor's commitment to its goals. The use of alternative strategies also varies with the purpose of the action. **Preventive diplomacy**—managing emergent threats by swiftly demonstrating intentions and capabilities—is one thing. The actual use of force in retaliation for acts deemed immoral, illegal, or threatening to national interests is another. Although those who initiate war often see it as a necessary instrument to pursuing national interests, it takes the game to a higher level. When push comes to shove, the escalation can either work or backfire. Consequently, the relationship between promises of rewards and military threats of destruction is complex. It works at times when the goal is war prevention as opposed to *peacekeeping* (stabilizing a threatening dispute) and *peace enforcement* (operations to deter terminated military hostilities from reigniting), and it fails at other times.

Military Intervention

Making military threats to coerce others can be done in many forms at many levels. However, the most frequent practice is **military intervention**—sending troops onto others' territory in order to influence developments and policies there. Coercive diplomacy sometimes moves from talking to bombing, and more frequently involves sending arms, armies, and aircraft to foreign territory. Interstate military interventions tap the frequency of states' use of limited armed force for bargaining with other states. Evidence suggests that this mode of coercive diplomacy has been common, if erratic, since World War II: altogether, 690 individual acts were initiated between 1945 and 1991 (see Figure 14.2). Collectively, they resulted in 2,400,000 fatalities, and on average, almost fifteen military interventions were undertaken each year (Tillema 1998). By another estimate, the United States initiated seventy-one such actions, and the Soviet Union twenty-five during the Cold War period ending in 1989 (Pearson, Baumann, and Pickering 1991, Table 1). Excluded from this count are an unknown number of the great powers' **covert operations**. If these were tallied in the total, the use of intervention would be even larger.

Conceptualizing foreign overt military intervention as a form of international behavior "most closely associated with international war," Herbert Tillema (1989) includes as instances "battles involving regular foreign military forces, at least on one side" that seldom result in more than one thousand fatalities. Interventions thus include "military operations undertaken openly by a state's regular military forces within a specific foreign land in such a manner as to risk immediate combat." They exclude "less-blatant forms of international interference such as covert operations; military alerts in place; shows of force; deployments of units not immediately prepared for combat; [and] incursions across international borders that do not involve occupation of territory . . ." (Tillema 1994). Conceived in this manner, intervention is a distinct category of

covert operations secret activities performed through clandestine means to realize specific political or military goals.

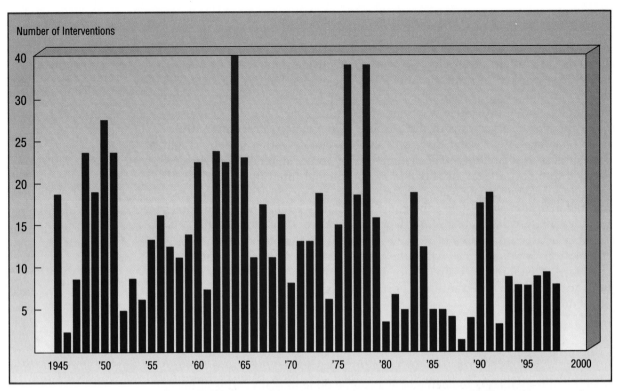

Number of Interventions

FIGURE 14.2

The Changing Incidence of Military Intervention in Coercive Diplomacy, 1945–2000

States have frequently sent their troops into the sovereign territory of other states in order to influence the target, despite the fact that military intervention has traditionally been prohibited by international law. This figure shows fluctuations in the frequency of intervention since 1945.

SOURCE: Based on Tillema (1998), with estimates since 1992 based on *Facts on File.*

militarized international behavior, which: (1) involves the use of force, (2) is intrinsically hostile in motive, (3) often results in the loss of soldiers' lives, and (4) is usually described by the target as an act of war.

As a result of frequent overt and covert activity, military interventions have often heightened international tension and led to war (thirty-five cases of third-party intervention occurred between 1816 and 1988, resulting in the internationalization of twenty-five civil wars; see Small and Singer 1982; Singer 1991, 60–75). The critical question about the use of military interventions for coercive diplomacy is their probable consequences. When states intervene, does this usually help peacekeeping, peacemaking, and preventive diplomacy by containing serious threats from escalating to full-scale war, or providing a calming influence in a war-torn or famine-stricken failing state (as Italy's 1997 humanitarian intervention into the impoverished, insurgent neighbor across the Adriatic Sea, Albania, aimed to restore order and alleviate suffering)? Or does intervention more often result not in pacification but in war? To consider this question, we need to look briefly at a sure consequence: Every past war has begun by an act of military intervention; the by-product of every military intervention is that it produces a crisis.

International Crises

Crisis is a commonly used word that describes a situation that has reached a critical stage. More precisely, a **crisis decision** in international affairs is a situation that (1) "threatens the high-priority goals of the decision-making unit, (2) restricts the amount of time available for response before the decision is transformed, and (3) surprises the members of the decision-making unit by its occurrence" (Hermann 1972). Most of the conspicuous military crises of our age, such as the Cuban missile crisis, the Berlin blockade, the Sino-Soviet border clash, and the Formosa Straits crisis, exhibited these attributes. Each contained the elements of surprise, threat, and time pressure, as well as the risk of war. None of these crises crossed the line into overt large-scale military hostilities, however; all were managed successfully. In contrast, many crises in the Global South were unsuccessfully managed and did escalate to war. Even with respect to crises between the great powers, the unbroken record of successful crisis management since 1945 should not necessarily instill confidence about the future. For crises to be managed successfully without escalating to war, governments, as rational actors, must be able to keep their quarrels within controllable bounds, and not let name-calling incite them to violence. There is no assurance that rationality will calm passions: "There is scant evidence that along with more lethal weapons we have evolved leaders more capable of coping with stress" (Holsti 1989). Crises can easily escalate to war because of the time pressures, inadequate information, fear and anxiety, and impulsive risk-taking that normally accompany decision-making procedures during threatening situations.

Crises result when one actor attempts to force an adversary to alter its behavior. "The strategy of coercive diplomacy . . . employs threats or limited force to persuade an opponent to call off or undo an encroachment—for example, to halt an invasion or give up territory that has been occupied" (Craig and George 1990). "Military power does not have to be used for it to be useful"; the threat of force may suffice by "coercing a country by demonstrating the quantity of force and highlighting the capability of, and intention to, use force" (Majeed 1991). "Coercive diplomacy offers the possibility of achieving one's objective economically, with little bloodshed, fewer political and psychological costs, and often with much less risk of escalation than does traditional military strategy" (Craig and George 1990).

The crises generated by coercive bargaining thus perform the function that war often traditionally played, namely, "to resolve without violence, or with only minimal violence, those conflicts that are too severe to be settled by ordinary diplomacy and that in earlier times would have been settled by war" (Snyder and Diesing 1977).

Figure 14.3 displays the distribution of 412 interstate crises between 1918 and 1994, revealing a continuous stream of changes "in the intensity of disruptive interactions between two or more states, with a heightened probability of military hostilities that destabilizes their relationships and challenges the structure of an international system" (Brecher 1993). Given this characteristic, it is understandable why the frequency of international crises is sometimes

crisis decision a choice made in highly threatening and potentially grave situations, involving elements of surprise, and restricted response time, by the highest level of authoritative decision makers.

443

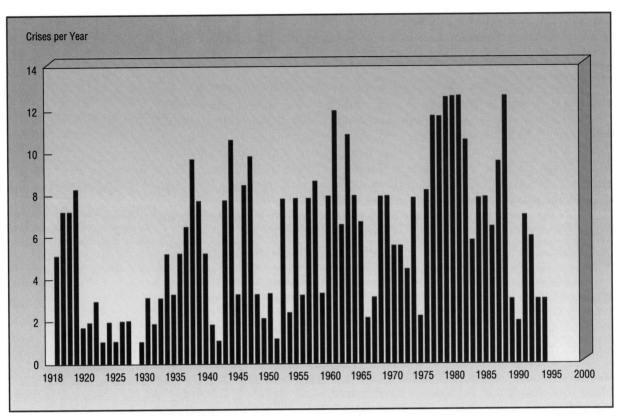

FIGURE 14.3

International Tension since World War I: The Annual Frequency of International Crises, 1918–2000

On 412 occasions, states confronted each other militarily between 1918 and 1994, in the hopes of forcing concessions. The frequency has varied over time, but its recurrence attests to states' compulsion to threaten each other with military force in the hope of getting their way.

SOURCE: Based on International Crisis Behavior (ICB) data, provided courtesy of Michael Brecher and Jonathan Wilkenfeld, and summarized in their book *A Study of Crisis* (Ann Arbor: University of Michigan, 1997), p. 44.

measured by the incidence of **militarized disputes**—"confrontations short of war characterized by the reciprocated threat, deployment, mobilization, or use of force" (Singer 1991; also Gochman and Maoz 1984).

Included in the category of militarized disputes is the practice of **gunboat diplomacy**—the high-profile sending of troops overseas to intimidate an enemy. Using the threat of force to persuade and compel is common, as many states believe that "actions speak louder than words" and that displaying one's military capabilities can convince the target to comply. The United States, for example, used shows of force 286 times between 1946 and 1984, an average of more than seven times a year (Blechman and Kaplan 1978, 547–53; Zelikow 1987, 34–36). Similarly, the former Soviet Union engaged in such behavior over 150 times between the mid-1940s and late 1970s (Kaplan 1981, 689–93). And in 1996 a bellicose China used this type of military intimidation when it conducted tests of its missiles by aiming them at a target area near a Taiwan port;

445

THE USE OF
COERCIVE DIPLOMACY
FOR DEFENSE,
DETERRENCE, AND
BARGAINING

In August 1997, the world held its breath as China and Taiwan squared off in a military showdown short of war. As democracy took root in Taiwan, it signaled its desire to officially declare its independence from China, and China interpreted this as a provocative act, despite nearly fifty years of separation and the uninterrupted respect for the unwritten "cease-fire" between China and its "rebel province." As China glared and threatened to invade, the threat of a military clash rose, with the danger compounded by the expectation that the United States could come to Taiwan's aid, assisted by Japanese troops because of the expanded defense pact in 1997 between Tokyo and Washington. Pictured here is an example of gunboat coercive diplomacy—new Taiwanese-made fighter jets poised for battle in August 1997 in the event of war.

in response, and to send China a warning, the United States sent two Navy aircraft carriers to the waters near the Taiwan Straits.

The evidence suggests a number of patterns. First, interstate crises have been recurrent in the twentieth century, and more than four hundred such situations threatened to escalate to war across *every* region and *every* decade since World War I. Second, the incidence has varied yearly, with many peaks of international tension followed by short troughs of relative calm. Third, many (in fact, most) states have either provoked or experienced these threats to peace, as the 412 crises involved as initiator or target more than 850 individual states, with more than 100 states triggering at least one crisis and 125 finding themselves the principal target of the threat that provoked one or more crises. Fourth, some states (especially great powers) have been the most prone to initiate crises. Finally, most crises in the twentieth century have been concentrated in the Global South's developing countries; two-thirds occurred in Africa, Asia, or the Middle East, while only one-fifth occurred in Europe (Brecher and Wilkenfeld, 1997).

The use of military threat for bargaining purposes between states and the crises that result are important because crises often trigger war. Examples of violence that were preceded by crisis include World War I (1914), Kashmir (1948), Suez (1956), Tibet (1959), the Bay of Pigs (1961), Goa (1961), and Kuwait (1990). More than 30 percent of all crises escalate to violence, with a large proportion (95 percent) of the most intense crises involving the major

446

THE USE OF
COERCIVE DIPLOMACY
FOR DEFENSE,
DETERRENCE, AND
BARGAINING

powers (Brecher 1993, 333, 576). The lesson, in short, is that militarized disputes often lead to full-scale war rather than its deterrence, even if the latter was the threatener's original intention. Coercive diplomacy with conventional weapons is clearly a dangerous game.

If past experience is a model, then the threat of war for bargaining is likely to continue in the future, and we can predict that

> the post-Cold War subsystems will retain an abundance of conflicts within which international crises are likely to erupt. . . . The ethnic/nationalist virus has created a context for other crises in the future. . . . The conclusion is disquieting: Most anticipated international crises in the coming years are likely to erupt in violence, though its severity will vary from minor clashes to full-scale war. (Brecher 1993, 546, 548)

The Future of Conventional Military Coercion

The sobering conclusion that international crises are likely to increase in the future raises concerns about the use of coercive bargaining by military means as a method of dispute management. Is this kind of bargaining a solution, or part of the security dilemma problem?

Policymakers today disagree about the appropriate place of coercive military bargaining in their strategic doctrines. Enthusiasts argue that the successful use of these strategies during the Cold War argues for applying the lessons of nuclear bargaining to situations requiring deterrence in the future. Skeptics disagree, maintaining that what may have worked in the realm of strategic deterrence is unlikely to work with respect to conventional deterrence, where in all probability most of the action will center. They feel that the kinds of armed conflicts and threats most in need of deterring will be most resistant to control through the strategies that help prevent nuclear attacks. Aggressors in the future—whether they are rough, outlaw states or criminal and terrorist organizations—very likely will employ advanced telecommunication networks to operate from dispersed locations, making the threat of massive retaliatory strikes against specific geographic regions ineffective.

It will clearly be much more difficult to deter the kinds of aggression that will employ conventional weapons than to deter aggression using nuclear weapons. The key elements of deterrence require three elements: (1) *capabilities*—the possession of military resources that can make threats of military retaliation plausible; (2) *credibility*—the belief that the actor is willing to militarily defend its declared position; and (3) *communication*—the actor's ability to send a potential aggressor the clear message that it is willing to carry out its threat. In today's world, it is difficult to combine these elements to make conventional deterrence work. As Richard Harknett (1994) cautions, deterrence of conventional warfare "will succeed if threatened costs can be communicated to the challenger, assessed by the challenger, and believed by the challenger." These requirements are difficult to satisfy with the diffuse conventional warfare raging throughout the world. "Unlike during the Cold War, interests deemed vital enough to fight for will be interests that probably will lead to actual fighting."

The prolonged difficulties that the United States and its NATO allies experienced in trying to deter the Bosnian Serbs from pursuing their expansionist war in the Balkans provide a graphic example of the ineffectiveness of conventional deterrence. Talk and threats were not believed and did not work. In des-

In September 1995, Operation Joint Endeavor sought to force the Bosnian Serbs to end their aggression in the Balkans. Shown here are British soldiers firing on Bosnian Serb artillery positions outside Sarajevo. This kind of coercive bargaining using conventional military force instead of ultimatums for deterrence and compellence is likely to be common in the future.

peration, the frustrated NATO countries under the leadership of the Clinton administration responded to Serbian atrocities with force, initiating in September 1995 a series of air strikes, under the auspices of the United Nations and through NATO, to compel an end to Serbian defiance. Operation Joint Endeavor, the NATO assault on strategic Serb targets, applied conventional force in order to relieve the cruel siege of Sarajevo and to persuade them through bombing to return to the bargaining table. As a U.S. State Department official explained, "Diplomacy was dead without the force" (Fedarko 1995). This episode could be an indication of how many future armed conflicts will be approached—through military coercion using conventional weapons.

However, bargaining by nonmilitary methods is also likely to be tried, and perhaps will be the method of choice, given the risks of military activities and the obstacles to their effective use. Economic sanctions will figure prominently among these alternative approaches.

● ● ●

BOYCOTTS, NOT BULLETS, AS WEAPONS: SANCTIONS AS INSTRUMENTS OF COERCION

When the Arab members of OPEC placed an embargo on the shipment of oil to the United States and the Netherlands in 1973, their purpose was to alter these countries' policies toward the Arab-Israeli conflict. When the UN Security Council decided in August 1990 that the world organization should cease trade with Iraq, its purpose was to accomplish the immediate and unconditional withdrawal of Iraqi forces from Kuwait. Both are examples of the use of **economic sanctions**—"deliberate government actions to inflict economic deprivation on a target state or society, through the limitation or cessation of customary economic relations" (Leyton-Brown 1987).

We will now look at the subcategory of economic sanctions, keeping in mind that sanctions may be defined more broadly to include acts "intended to convince or compel another state to desist from engaging" in some unacceptable behavior, by a wider range of methods than economic coercion; they may be military, involving the use of armed intervention; diplomatic or political (breaking formal relations); or cultural, aimed at undermining a deviant government's internal and international standing (Joyner 1995).

Economic sanctions are an increasingly popular choice from the broad array of instruments of economic statecraft available to governments. An alternative to applying military force, **sanctions** are enacted to express outrage and to change the target's behavior. Since World War I, there have been 120 observable episodes of foreign policy sanctions, 104 of which have been enacted since World War II (Hufbauer, Schott, and Elliott 1990). In the 1990s the use of **boycotts** instead of bullets as a strategy for exercising political influence became widespread. It was illustrated by the U.S. "dual containment" policy toward Iraq and Iran (alongside the continuation of sanctions against the North African "pariah state," Libya, that was accused of sponsoring terrorism), by the 1997 U.S. effort to sever economic ties with Burma for its human rights violations, and by the April 1997 Arab foreign ministers' plan to launch a business boycott of Israel in response to its decision to move forward with a housing project in East Jerusalem.

Despite their frequent use, most efforts to apply economic sanctions have failed. This fact has led many policy analysts to question their cost-effectiveness (Knorr 1977). Why is failure so prevalent? And why, then, have economic sanctions "become the weapon of choice in diplomatic confrontation in the wake of the Cold War" (Hoagland 1993b)? We can address these questions by looking at several prominent sanctions cases.

Superpower Sanctions: Three U.S. Failures

Between 1945 and 1990, when more than sixty cases of sanctions were undertaken, "a rate averaging better than one new action per year, more than two-thirds were initiated and maintained by the United States" (Lopez and Cortright 1995, 5). In 1998, half the world's population lived in countries that were under U.S. sanctions (*Harper's*, February 1998, 13). Three conspicuous cases in which the United States applied economic sanctions illustrate their shortcomings.

Cuba. The United States placed sanctions on the Castro regime shortly after it assumed power in 1960, beginning with a reduction in the amount of sugar permitted to enter the United States under its quota system. These sanctions later were extended to a full ban on all U.S. trade with Cuba, accompanied by pressure on other countries to follow suit. The U.S. goals were twofold: initially, to overthrow the Castro government; failing that, to contain the Castro revolution and Cuban interventionism in Central and South America and in Africa.

Through the late 1990s the United States remained unsuccessful in securing Castro's overthrow, and previously it had been only marginally successful in containing Cuba's promotion of revolution abroad. "The major accomplishment of the U.S. economic embargo . . . consisted of increasing the cost to Cuba of surviving and developing as a socialist country and of pursuing an international commitment" (Roca 1987). Several factors helped Cuba to withstand this pressure from the globe's foremost economic and military power for nearly forty years. Especially potent were the Soviet Union's prolonged subsidies of "as much as $2–3 billion annually" to Cuba (Elliott 1993, 35); U.S. in-

sanctions punitive actions by one state against another to retaliate for its previous objectionable behavior.

boycotts concerted efforts, often organized internationally, to prevent relations such as trade with a state, to express disapproval or to coerce acceptance of certain conditions.

ability to persuade its Western allies to curtail trade with and investment in Cuba; and Castro's charismatic leadership and popular support. Although the U.S. economic sanctions extracted a heavy burden on the target, they did not accomplish their political goals.

Not only did the United States fail to get its way, but it was snubbed by its key allies. In symbolic defiance, in October 1994 they voted 102 to 2 in favor of a UN resolution condemning the U.S. embargo, asserting that the embargo infringed on their sovereignty, free trade, and navigation rights; in 1995, a similar resolution passed by a vote of 117 to 3. With diminishing incentives in an era of globalization that was eroding the dividing line between domestic and international political interests, and with declining support and cooperation from others, the U.S. trade sanctions simply could not succeed. Latin America, once an obedient follower of the U.S. trade embargo against Cuba, saw that Castro was not likely to lose his grip on power in the face of outside pressure, and chose to ignore the U.S. effort to isolate Cuba and instead "to develop full economic and diplomatic relations with the Communist government. The United States is the only country in the Americas with a trade ban on Cuba and one of only five that do not have formal ties with it" (Brooke 1995), and Fidel Castro has survived the bullying of nine American presidents. The Cuban economy shows signs of recovering from the job cutbacks, low salaries, and food shortages brought on by the Soviet bloc's collapse, as reforms allowing Cubans to hold once-forbidden U.S. dollars and own small businesses have stimulated growth and removed many incentives to flee on boats and homemade rafts. In 1998, the verdict on the U.S. effort to isolate Cuba was in: The United States was isolated in its endeavors by most of the world. One by one, leaders, including the Pope, were meeting with President Fidel Castro and signing agreements for economic, cultural, and tourist exchanges in the hope that they can invest in the Cuban economy at the ground floor and benefit from Cuban development as it becomes a hemispheric economic force. The determined warming of relations, rooted in economics, flies in the face of the U.S. sanctions, and illustrates the extent to which states are willing to put their financial interests ahead of their compliance with powerful allies. St. Lucia's Prime Minister Kenny Anthony described his country's thinking in 1998 by stating "the world is closing in on us. We have to look for new economic opportunities." In the case of Cuba, geoeconomics overrides geopolitics. Twenty-one states meeting at the annual Ibero-American Summit signed a 1998 joint declaration restating a "firm condemnation" of the Helms-Burton law that seeks to punish countries doing business in Cuba. Against this multilateral pressure, in March 1998 the United States moved to relax its historic restrictive sanctions policy to improve Cuban–American relations by permitting travel to Cuba and humanitarian aid.

The Soviet Union and Afghanistan. After the Soviet Union's 1979 intervention in Afghanistan, the United States imposed a partial embargo on the sale of grain to the country and attempted to organize a boycott of the 1980 Moscow Summer Olympics. The sanctions also sought "to punish the Soviet Union while at the same time limiting the damage to the economic interests of important domestic groups" (Falkenheim 1987).

The grain embargo failed to stop the flow of agricultural produce to the Soviet Union, largely because other countries (principally Argentina) increased

449

THE USE OF
COERCIVE DIPLOMACY
FOR DEFENSE,
DETERRENCE, AND
BARGAINING

450

THE USE OF
COERCIVE DIPLOMACY
FOR DEFENSE,
DETERRENCE, AND
BARGAINING

their exports to make up the shortfall in U.S. exports. Although the U.S. sanctions produced suffering for Soviet citizens, it did not force their leaders to reverse their foreign policy. There were two reasons for this. First, the Soviet economy was largely self-sufficient, which lessened the impact of trade compression on its economy. Second, because Soviet leaders were determined to resist external pressures, the U.S. sanctions only increased their resolve (Falkenheim 1987).

The Soviet Union and Poland. Similar lessons apply to Poland. After the Polish government imposed martial law in 1981 to forestall continued labor unrest, the Reagan administration restricted U.S. government credits for Polish purchase of food and other commodities, banned high-technology exports to Poland, and suspended Poland's most-favored-nation trade status. To stiffen the sanctions' impact, the United States also targeted Poland's patron and primary trade partner, the Soviet Union. U.S. actions restricted the flow of Western goods and technology needed for the trans-Siberian gas pipeline to bring Soviet energy into Western European markets in the hope of increasing the economic strains under which both Poland and the Soviet system would have to operate (Marantz 1987).

The strategy failed to achieve these objectives, however, as the Reagan administration was forced to seek a face-saving compromise with its European allies permitting continued construction of the pipeline. The absence of consensus among the NATO allies contributed to the sanctions' failure. Other factors included the Soviet Union's ability and willingness to support its client, Poland. While the sanctions may have had some liberalizing influence on Poland, in the end the Soviet Union did not budge.

These three examples suggest that a superpower's successful use of economic sanctions faces substantial obstacles. The initiator often pays a high price (lost markets to exporters, increased costs to consumers) and receives a low payoff. In general, the more ambitious the goal, the less successful the efforts have been. "Sanctions are seldom effective in impairing the military potential of an important power, or in bringing about major changes in the policies of the target country" (Hufbauer, Schott, and Elliott 1990), and "have been absolutely ineffective in bringing about a change of government leadership within a target country" (Cortright and Lopez 1995).

Yet, as inventories of the use of economic sanctions indicate, states are increasingly prone to rely on them. In fact, as a high-profile, low-risk tactic of coercive diplomacy, sanctions may be the tool of choice for states seeking to make other states comply. The world may be entering "the sanctions era" (Cortright and Lopez 1995) in part because the growing volume of international commerce has made "trade-based diplomacy an increasingly prominent tool of statecraft." The advantages rationalizing the use of boycotts are suggested by cases that met with relatively greater success.

Relatively Successful Sanctions: Two Controversial Examples

The usefulness of economic sanctions as instruments of foreign policy has a checkered history at best. The case of South Africa illustrates the ability of sanctions to produce policy dividends. The case of Iraq illustrates the constraints on their use.

South Africa and Apartheid. For many years, the White leadership in South Africa practiced a punitive policy of racial separation known as **apartheid.** To force an end to this morally unjustifiable practice, in 1963 the United Nations, at the behest of Third World countries, imposed a voluntary arms and oil embargo against South Africa, which became mandatory in 1977.

451

THE USE OF
COERCIVE DIPLOMACY
FOR DEFENSE,
DETERRENCE, AND
BARGAINING

Because U.S. corporations held major investments in South Africa and the United States was a primary importer of the country's rich mineral reserves, the U.S. attitude toward South Africa was of special concern to opponents of apartheid. A frequent argument in the United States concerning an appropriate response to apartheid focused on who would be the victims of internationally applied sanctions: South African Blacks, already suffering under a policy of systematic racial discrimination, or the White minority regime who perpetuated apartheid. In 1981, the Reagan administration adopted a policy toward South Africa called *constructive engagement*, whose broad purpose was a soft diplomatic approach to the Pretoria regime. In 1985, however, in an unusual domestic political development, the U.S. Congress legislated, over a presidential veto, harsh mandatory sanctions against South Africa, hoping to change Reagan's policies, which Congress found objectionable.

In 1989, F. W. de Klerk, a reformer, came to power in South Africa and released Nelson Mandela, leader of the African National Congress (ANC), who had been a political prisoner for twenty-seven years. De Klerk also lifted the ban on the ANC and other anti-apartheid groups, opening the door to negotiations on political reforms between the South African government and the ANC. Thus the process of dismantling apartheid finally began and culminated in a historic agreement in 1993, which restored democracy for all South Africa's citizens and made possible Black majority rule. As trade restrictions were lifted, investors rushed into the vacuum and South Africa rejoined the community of nations. It was no longer an international pariah.

Were the sanctions responsible for setting South Africa on a path toward reform and majority rule? While the sanctions were being applied, analysts' evaluations differed, but now that apartheid has been officially lifted, most believe that the sanctions eventually paid off. Apartheid has been ended through the concerted cooperation and economic sanctions of many states in combination with the human rights activities of international institutions and nongovernmental organizations throughout the world.

Iraq after the Kuwait Crisis. Restraints on the long-term use of economic sanctions for political purposes are illustrated by the 1990 conflict in the Middle East. The first response of the international community to Iraq's invasion of Kuwait was to impose sanctions, including the prohibition of all exports to and imports from Iraq except for humanitarian shipments of medicine and some food. The embargo sought to compel the Iraqi government to withdraw from Kuwait and to foment enough discontent within Iraq to cause the ouster of the Hussein regime. In the months that followed, a vigorous debate took place at the United Nations and in various national capitals over the utility of the sanctions. Would they force Saddam Hussein from Kuwait? How long should they be applied before resorting to military power?

Iraq was especially vulnerable to a total embargo because it imported nearly three-fourths of its food and depended almost completely on oil exports for its foreign exchange. In addition, its oil could pass through only two routes, by ship through the Persian Gulf—which was easily blockaded—or overland through pipelines across other countries. In December 1990, the director of the U.S. Central Intelligence Agency reported that "more than 90 percent of imports and 97 percent of exports have been shut off." He also reported, however,

In a war of words that punctuated the weakness of economic sanctions as a tool of coercive diplomacy, the Iraqi government in January 1998 called on 1 million men and women of all ages to take part in a weapons training program. Pictured here are armed Iraqi women who joined a paramilitary group in response to a call to arms by Iraqi President Saddam Hussein, who claimed his state must be ready for a U.S. attack over the issue of UN arms inspections and economic sanctions.

that "we see no indication that Saddam is concerned at this point that domestic discontent is growing . . . or that problems resulting from the sanctions are causing him to rethink his policy on Kuwait. . . . There is no assurance or guarantee that economic hardships will compel Saddam to change his policies or lead to internal unrest that would threaten his regime." Little more than a month later, military power replaced economic sanctions to force Iraq from Kuwait.

During the debate over force and sanctions, two former chairmen of the U.S. Joint Chiefs of Staff urged that sanctions be given a year or more to work. "If in fact the sanctions will work in twelve to eighteen months instead of six months, the trade-off of avoiding war with its attendant sacrifices and uncertainties would, in my view, be worth it," Admiral William J. Crowe testified before the U.S. Congress. Historically, however, sanctions applied over long periods have seldom produced success, with the exceptions of the South African and Rhodesian situations:

> Sanctions imposed slowly or incrementally may simply strengthen the target government at home as it marshals the forces of nationalism. Moreover, such measures are likely to be undercut over time either by the sender's own firms or by foreign competitors. Sanctions are generally regarded as a short-term policy, with the anticipation that normal relations will be reestablished after the resolution of the crisis. Thus, even though popular opinion in the sender country may welcome the introduction of sanctions, the longer an episode drags on, the public support for sanctions dissipates. (Hufbauer, Schott, and Elliott 1990, 100-101)

Largely for these reasons, and because of growing concern for how long the coalition against Iraq would hold together, economic sanctions were abandoned in favor of the use of overwhelming military force. Whether this was wise or foolish remains debatable. The use of military force in the Gulf War did (at an estimated cost of $57 billion) drive Iraq from Kuwait, and arguably helped prevent Saddam Hussein from carrying out his crash program to build a nuclear weapon, and develop an arsenal of toxins for biological warfare, and it did contain his aggression (Hoaglund 1996). Nonetheless, the effort to topple the Iraqi dictator and demonize him in a **propaganda** campaign aimed at undermining his popularity failed, and his ruthless moves to retain power in Iraq succeeded. "Iraq was bombed into the Stone Age" with eighty-nine thousand tons of explosives killing more than forty-six thousand children (Al-Samarrai 1995), but the wrong party was targeted in operations "analogous to blowing up an aircraft with all passengers aboard to kill the hijacker." This case thus demonstrated at the time the uncertain payoff of military sanctions, and the limits of economic sanctions since. That latter component of the lesson was later punctuated when in 1997 and 1998 Saddam Hussein was still in power, being courted by major oil companies, making huge profits buying and selling oil futures after the United Nations in the Resolution 986 "oil for food" program partially lifted its oil embargo, and exporting oil on the black market through dummy companies to needy importers in order to buy illegal arms from foreign manufacturers to protect himself and his army from his own citizens. Sanctions failed to produce compliance or submission, as the Baghdad dictator prevented UN inspectors from determining whether Iraq had complied with Security Council's demands to scrap its long-range missiles and other chemical and biological weapons of mass destruction under the peace settlement that ended the 1991 Gulf War. The futility of the financially crippling UN embargo to drive Saddam Hussein out of office or to open his palaces to UN inspectors, and the repeated success of Saddam's stubborn brinkmanship bargaining, highlighted the impotence of sanctions as a method of modifying unacceptable behavior against a willful foe intent on thumbing his nose at the international community. In early 1998, the United States in frustration went on a military alert. The show of force was seen as an alternative option to sanctions. If that coercive warning is not heeded in Iraq, the jump from coercive diplomacy to violence will likely be made, and once again, as in so many instances throughout history, warfare will ignite from the tinderbox of failed diplomacy.

> **propaganda** communications used to manipulate people's thoughts, emotions, or actions.

Why Sanction?

The long and generally unsuccessful history of international economic sanctions has led many critics to conclude that sanctions are a weak tool in statecraft (Elliott 1993; Førland 1993; Haass 1997). They argue that:

- A typical response to economic coercion in the sanctioned society is a heightened sense of nationalism, a *laager* mentality (circle the wagons to face oncoming enemies), which stimulates resistance in the target state.

- Sanctions sometimes hurt the disempowered people they seek to help—the country's average citizens. "Sanctions substitute for military action against rulers who have total disregard for the economic hardships faced by their subjects. The logic of the policy [unrealistically] seems to be to make unarmed citizens desperate enough to rise up and throw off brutal regimes that . . . other powers are not willing to use the world's best armies to topple" (Hoagland 1993b).

- Governments often act covertly to support the sanctioned state even as they publicly profess their support of sanctions.

- "Midsized countries can thwart sanctions, when local dictators are able to quell dissent with a powerful military and divert pain to citizens with no influence" (Hufbauer 1994).

- The credibility of the state(s) imposing sanctions is often low, given their transparent costs and the fact that "economic sanctions always involve something lost for both sides" (Howell 1995).

- Widespread and collective sustained cooperation from the international community and international organizations seldom materializes, and unilateral sanctions seldom succeed in a globalized market with many competitive suppliers of embargoed goods.

The suitability of sanctions as instruments of persuasion is therefore customarily questioned whenever they are proposed or imposed. Recent examples of their use, amidst criticism, include the OAS embargo of Haiti to force the military junta to step down (and subsequent military intervention to fulfill the objective); the embargo of North Korea to dissuade it from building a nuclear bomb; the economic sanctions against the rebel army UNITA in Angola; the use of sanctions against the Serbs that led to their acceptance of the August 1995 Dayton agreement ending the fighting in Bosnia; and U.S. threats of trade sanctions against China in 1996 in response to its shipment of cruise missiles to Iran and its missile tests near Taiwan. Despite these modest successes, critics invariably argue that "the problem with economic sanctions is that they frequently contribute little to . . . foreign policy goals while being costly and even counterproductive" (Haass 1997) Futhermore,

> [p]olicymakers often have inflated expectations of what sanctions can and cannot accomplish. . . . At most there is a weak correlation between economic deprivation and political willingness to change. The *economic* impact of sanctions may be pronounced, both on the sender and the target country, but other factors in the situational context almost always overshadow the impact of sanctions in determining the *political* outcome. (Hufbauer, Schott, and Elliott 1990, 94)

If they usually encounter opposition and seldom prove effective, why have "sanctions become the main tool of coercive diplomacy" (Hoagland 1996) and now "the most favored tool of diplomats" (Pound and El-Tahri 1994) and the "tool of choice" for the United States, which between 1993 and 1996 targeted thirty-five countries with new American sanctions (Haass 1997, 74). One answer is that the chief alternative method of coercion, military force, is not very effective and is increasingly less popular. The threat of destruction is not very convincing because the target is unlikely to believe that it will be carried out. Moreover, if carried out, a military approach can easily backfire, taking soldiers' lives, draining government budgets, severing export earnings, and provoking public criticism at home and abroad. Simply put, military coercion to win contests with foreign foes is relatively unattractive, and the mandate for this strategy has waned except for those rare situations in which the use of force is likely to succeed in a short-term operation with few battle casualties. Hence, in comparison with military methods of coercion, economic sanctions look advantageous: "Sanctions have become a habit" because they look less costly and risky than the other options and, "once in place . . . create their own constituency" (Nathan 1997).

A second reason for the rising use of economic sanctions is a consequence of the **globalization** process that is unfolding at an accelerating rate. National

455

THE USE OF
COERCIVE DIPLOMACY
FOR DEFENSE,
DETERRENCE, AND
BARGAINING

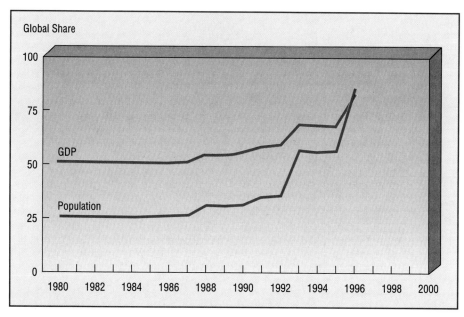

FIGURE 14.4

The Growing Percentage of Economies Linked by Trade in the Globalized Market since 1980: A New Context for Sanctions

Globalization has expanded the challenges many countries face as their economies have increasingly become dependent on exports. Because many states are more dependent on trade, and vulnerable to its disruption, the ability of economic sanctions to succeed against those states has grown, making sanctions a more frequently used method of coercive diplomacy.

SOURCE: *Economist,* June 14, 1997, 19, citing estimates generated by the Harvard Institute for International Development.

economies are increasingly integrated through trade (see Figure 14.4) and the exchange of ideas and information (review Chapter 9). Arguably, "for the first time in history, almost all of the world's people are bound together in a global capitalist system" (Sachs 1997). This transforms the calculus of choice regarding coercion and encourages leaders to regard economic sanctions more favorably. Because globalization is making most countries dependent on trade for their own prosperity, it makes sanctions that threaten targets with the loss of an export market more effective than in the past, when countries could better withstand a foreign embargo on the purchase of their products in the global marketplace.

Today, many states are highly dependent on exports for growth; they are increasingly trade dependent, and this condition of need makes it difficult to withstand an embargo (a government order prohibiting commerce) or a boycott (refusal to have commercial and other dealings with a state) that interrupts the target's export-generated income. Under these conditions, sanctions can better succeed against trade-dependent targets and countries that are highly dependent on imports of critical resources such as oil. This method draws on the commercial liberal logic of James Madison and Thomas Jefferson, who advocated "peaceable coercion" against those foreign governments that would have to yield to American pressure because U.S. goods were essential to their prosperity. Economic sanctions are also gaining proponents because the number of highly vulnerable "single-commodity-dependent economies," which

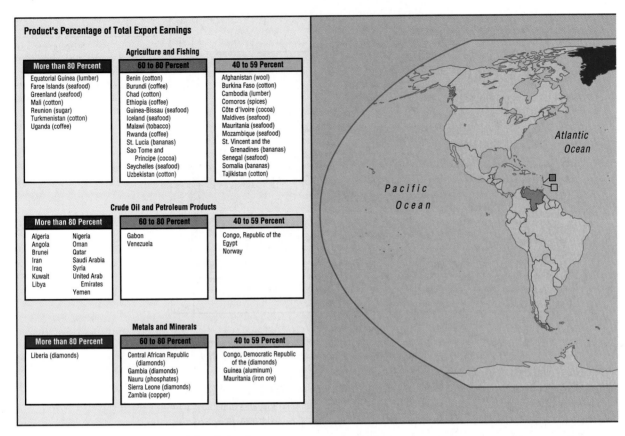

Product's Percentage of Total Export Earnings

Agriculture and Fishing

More than 80 Percent	60 to 80 Percent	40 to 59 Percent
Equatorial Guinea (lumber)	Benin (cotton)	Afghanistan (wool)
Faroe Islands (seafood)	Burundi (coffee)	Burkina Faso (cotton)
Greenland (seafood)	Chad (cotton)	Cambodia (lumber)
Mali (cotton)	Ethiopia (coffee)	Comoros (spices)
Reunion (sugar)	Guinea-Bissau (seafood)	Côte d'Ivoire (cocoa)
Turkmenistan (cotton)	Iceland (seafood)	Maldives (seafood)
Uganda (coffee)	Malawi (tobacco)	Mauritania (seafood)
	Rwanda (coffee)	Mozambique (seafood)
	St. Lucia (bananas)	St. Vincent and the
	Sao Tome and	Grenadines (bananas)
	Principe (cocoa)	Senegal (seafood)
	Seychelles (seafood)	Somalia (bananas)
	Uzbekistan (cotton)	Tajikistan (cotton)

Crude Oil and Petroleum Products

More than 80 Percent	60 to 80 Percent	40 to 59 Percent
Algeria — Nigeria	Gabon	Congo, Republic of the
Angola — Oman	Venezuela	Egypt
Brunei — Qatar		Norway
Iran — Saudi Arabia		
Iraq — Syria		
Kuwait — United Arab		
Libya — Emirates		
Yemen		

Metals and Minerals

More than 80 Percent	60 to 80 Percent	40 to 59 Percent
Liberia (diamonds)	Central African Republic (diamonds)	Congo, Democratic Republic of the (diamonds)
	Gambia (diamonds)	Guinea (aluminum)
	Nauru (phosphates)	Mauritania (iron ore)
	Sierra Leone (diamonds)	
	Zambia (copper)	

Atlantic Ocean

Pacific Ocean

MAP 14.1

Vulnerable Single-Commodity-Dependent Economies

Many states depend on a single commodity for exports, with 40–80 percent of their trade revenue derived from the willingness of people outside their borders to purchase these goods. Sanctions through boycotts and embargoes, undertaken to coerce a change in the trade-dependent country's policies, can be devastating. This vulnerability has made these states especially ripe targets; because they are usually developing countries, the Global South has been the locus for many acts of economic sanctions in the mid-1990s.

Note: The countries highlighted depend on a single commodity for 40 percent or more of their export earnings.
SOURCE: *Handbook of International Economic Statistics* (1997), 132–133.

derive at least 40 percent of their export revenues from foreign purchase of a single product, is large (see Map 14.1).

States pursue economic sanctions in pursuit of five major policy goals:

- *Compliance* ("to force the target to alter its behavior to conform with the initiator's preferences"), as in the case of the 1982 U.S. embargo of Libya designed to force it to end its support of terrorism.

- *Subversion* ("to remove the target's leaders . . . or overthrow the regime"), as in the case of the 1993–1994 U.S. trade embargo on Haiti.

- *Deterrence* ("to dissuade the target from repeating the disputed action in the future"), as in the case of the Soviet grain embargo by the United States.

457

THE USE OF
COERCIVE DIPLOMACY
FOR DEFENSE,
DETERRENCE, AND
BARGAINING

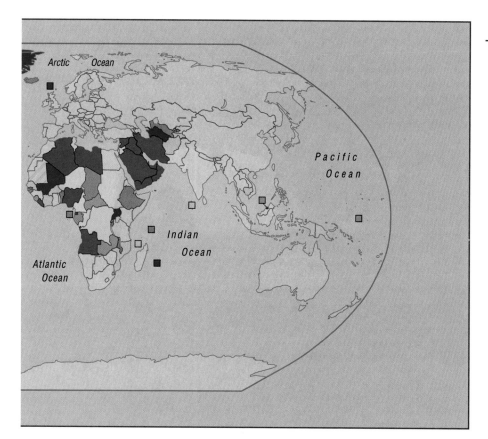

- *International symbolism* ("to send messages to other members of the world community"), as in the case of the British sanctions against Rhodesia after its unilateral declaration of independence in 1965.

- *Domestic symbolism* ("to increase its domestic support or thwart international criticism of its foreign policies by acting decisively"), as in the case of U.S. sanctions against Iran following its seizure of U.S. diplomats in 1979 (Lindsay 1986).

Past cases of sanctions suggest that *symbolism* is a primary motivation behind the impulse to use this tool. Sanctions enable a leader to show leadership without bearing the costs and dangers that other policy options, particularly military force, entail. "When military options are not feasible or desirable and the initiator wants to respond forcefully to the target's behavior, sanctions provide a means of 'doing something'" (Lindsay 1986).

It is disputable whether the "symbolic utility" of economic sanctions in the face of their otherwise "apparent disutility" is a cause for applause or concern. "Critics may deride the symbolic uses of trade sanctions as empty gestures, but symbols are important in politics. This is especially so when inaction can signal weakness and silence can mark complicity" (Lindsay 1986). Thus, economic sanctions are often used even though they sometimes fail to achieve the most visible aims for which they are implemented:

Although sanctions were successful . . . in 34 percent of 115 cases [between 1914 and 1989] (the overall U.S. success rate was 32 percent), success has

This photo shows a tanker carrying natural gas leaving Qatar for Japan. Qatar, with huge gas reserves, hopes exports will transform its economy; Japan badly needs natural gas to propel its consumer-rich economy. Japan's dependence on foreign suppliers of desperately needed energy sources reduces its willingness to use economic sanctions to influence the policies of suppliers. The use of economic sanctions is often influenced by the relationships between commodity-dependent importers and commodity-wealthy exporters.

become increasingly elusive in recent years. . . . The success rate among [forty-six] cases begun after 1973 was a little less than 26 percent. Even more striking is the decline in the effectiveness of sanctions imposed in pursuit of modest goals—mostly sought by the United States—which plummeted from 75 percent to 21 percent. (Elliott 1993, 34)

Nonetheless, sanctions serve important functions. They provide a policy alternative to the use of force to publicize and condemn unacceptable behavior and intolerable situations, thereby expressing outrage and making it appear that something is being done. In addition, under particular conditions, "sanctions work—if imposed by a major power against a much weaker, unstable, and economically dependent foe with no friends among the rival powers" (Elliott 1993). "Sanctions can be used to deter aggression, defend human rights, and discourage nuclear proliferation" (Lopez and Cortright 1993). For these reasons we can expect sanctions to remain popular.

● ● ●

DIPLOMATIC NEGOTIATION IN LIEU OF COERCION?

In today's globalized economy, sanctions are popular because they offer what appears to be a proportional response to challenges in which the interests at stake are less than vital (Haass 1997). To be sure, with the danger of warfare between states receding, most of the issues that divide countries and prompt them to take action to alter the unacceptable political behavior of their targets fall into this category. The use of **soft power** or "command power" (Nye 1998) as a means of bargaining to get other states to change their practices has gained increased recognition in international bargaining, since one country is more likely to follow another's lead because it seeks that country's markets and resources than because it fears its weapons. The National Conference of Catholic Bishops captures the growing sentiment by noting that "sanctions can offer a nonmilitary alternative to the terrible options of war or indifference when confronted with aggression or injustice."

There exists another alternative to either coercive diplomacy or sanctions as methods for states to exercise influence over other countries with whom they have disputes. This is through the tried and true method of **negotiation** to resolve differences and reach a mutually satisfactory settlement. Behind the scenes, every day, members of states' foreign policy bureaucracies (ranging from heads of state meeting at summits to representatives in embassies and at international organizations) regularly convene to exchange views, consult, and communicate their positions on specific issues. These highly institutionalized channels of communication are critical to the resolution of conflicts; they rely on established procedures at the negotiating table for states to identify mutually satisfactory options and choices that can eliminate the need for the use or threatened use of punishment or even war in order for either party to a disagreement to get its way. The **diplomatic process** provides a safety measure through which states can bargain to find common ground. In diplomatic dialogue we thus find the most widely used instrument through which crises are managed and peace is preserved in a system that otherwise encourages states to compete, clash, and confront one another.

Although (as with deterrence) it is difficult to identify those many cases in which diplomatic negotiation succeeds, in contemplating how states control their disagreements it is useful to remember that it may be the peacemakers convening in conferences who do the most to maintain the order we witness alongside international anarchy and ruthless violence. Diplomacy reduces international danger. Indeed, the peacemaking efforts of diplomatic negotiators may result in the positive outcome of what Dr. Martin Luther King, Jr. termed the "choice between chaos and community."

This chapter reviewed four basic approaches to controlling the behavior of others, concentrating especially on the use of force. Whether for deterrence or compellence, states will continue to rely on strategic weapons to prevent their own mass destruction. They will also continue to use conventional weapons and economic sanctions to defend themselves while bargaining to protect national interests. All three of these methods of coercive diplomacy place an emphasis on capabilities—both military and economic; all three are methods for bargaining that, when used, tell us that the fourth method, diplomatic negotiation, has failed or broken down. The next chapter evaluates how these approaches to the management of armed conflict are often complemented by still other strategies advocated by realism.

KEY TERMS

coercive diplomacy	neoliberal	commitment
politics	nuclear deterrence	brinkmanship
realist	conventional deterrence	massive retaliation
bargaining	signaling	countervalue targeting strategy
security dilemma	Cuban missile crisis	counterforce targeting strategy
spiral model	compellence	peaceful coexistence

peace enforcement	theater missile defense (TMD)	gunboat diplomacy
limited war	counterfactual arguments	economic sanctions
total war	conventional war	sanctions
extended deterrence	low-intensity conflict (LIC)	boycotts
second-strike capability	preventive diplomacy	apartheid
mutual assured destruction (MAD)	military intervention	propaganda
nuclear utilization theory (NUTs)	covert operations	globalization
Strategic Defense Initiative (SDI)	crisis	soft power
ballistic missile defense (BMD)	crisis decision	negotiation
	militarized disputes	diplomatic process

S U G G E S T E D   R E A D I N G

Berkowitz, Bruce D., and Allan E. Goodman. "The Logic of Covert Action," *The National Interest* 51 (Spring 1998): 38–46.

Brecher, Michael, and Jonathan Wilkenfeld, *A Study of Crisis*. Ann Arbor: University of Michigan Press, 1997.

Førland, Tor Egil. "The History of Economic Warfare: International Law, Effectiveness, Strategies," *Journal of Peace Research* 30 (May 1993): 151-62.

Glaser, Charles L. "The Security Dilemma Revisited," *World Politics* 50 (October 1997): 171-201.

Harvey, Frank P., and Ben D. Mor. *Conflict in World Politics: Advances in the Study of Crisis, War and Peace*. New York: St. Martin's, 1997.

Hoffmann, Stanley. *The Ethics and Politics of Humanitarian Intervention*. Chicago: University of Notre Dame Press, 1997.

Hopmann, P. Terrence. *The Negotiation Process and the Resolution of International Conflicts*. Columbia: University of South Carolina Press, 1996.

Hufbauer, Gary Clyde, Jeffrey J. Schott, and Kimberly Ann Elliott. *Economic Sanctions Reconsidered: History and Current Policy*, 2nd ed. Washington, D.C.: Institute for International Economics, 1990.

Lopez, George A., and Nancy J. Myers, eds. *Peace and Security: The Next Generation*. New York: Rowman and Littlefield, 1997.

Pape, Robert A. "Why Economic Sanctions Do Not Work," *International Security* 22 (Fall 1997): 90-136.

Stremlau, John. *Sharpening International Sanctions*. New York: Carnegie Corporation of New York, 1996.

Turner, Stansfield. *Caging the Nuclear Genie*. Boulder, Colo.: Westview, 1997.

W H E R E   O N   T H E   W O R L D   W I D E   W E B ?

http://ucsub.Colorado.EDU/~danielsm/PD/PD.html
The Prisoner's Dilemma Learn what the "Prisoner's Dilemma" is and play it online. After playing a few times, read the whole Web site and learn about the different game strategies. Actually, you'll be learning about human nature!

http://www.pbs.org/wgbh/pages/frontline/shows/nukes
Loose Nukes PBS's famous *Frontline* series is online with a look at "loose nukes" and the investigation of

the threat of nuclear smuggling from the former Soviet Union. *Frontline* chronicles the major nuclear smuggling incidents to date. The Web site includes a map that indicates declared and undeclared nuclear states and those states that have renounced or abstained from developing nuclear weapons. The site also provides a map of Russia's nuclear complex. Click on any of the sites and get the nuclear data and security status for each nuclear complex. Read interviews with policy experts, smugglers, scientists, analysts, and law enforcement agents, and analyze Russian and U.S. articles to get more facts. On the other hand, you may not want to look at this Web site at all: as a Russian proverb states, "The less you know the better you sleep."

http://www.csi.ad.jp/ABOMB/index.html

A-Bomb WWW Museum   Visit this Web site to obtain information concerning the impact that the first atomic bomb had on Hiroshima, Japan. While exploring this site, you will see pictures of what happened during the bombing and the devastation that was left behind. (For instance, a person was instantly vaporized at the moment of the bomb blast. All that remained of him was a silhouette imprint of his body on the stone where he had been sitting). You will hear stories from survivors and see some disturbing pictures—some of which are not for the faint of heart. The A-Bomb WWW Museum wants to make sure that the world does not forget about the horrors of the bombing.

http://www.peak.org/~danneng/decision/decision.html

Atomic Bomb: Decision   This Web site houses the available documents on the decision to use atomic bombs on the cities of Hiroshima and Nagasaki, Japan. Scan eyewitness accounts of the Trinity Test. Read what the individuals who were responsible for the bombings and the decision to drop the bombs had to say. See the official bombing order and hear the excerpt of President Truman's radio speech announcing the decision to drop the bomb. Then ask yourself: "Should the United States have dropped the bomb?"

http://www.exploratorium.edu/nagasaki/index.html

Remembering Nagasaki   An elegant and visually stunning Web site, "Remembering Nagasaki" presents the photographs of Japanese army photographer Yosuke Yamhata who took pictures the day after the bomb was dropped. Along with Yamhata's pictures is a public forum on issues related to the atomic age. This is a truly fascinating site that explores the issues of nuclear weapons from all sides of the debate.

CHAPTER 15

The Realist Road to Security through Alliances, the Balance of Power, and Arms Control

•••

It is necessary to put an end to the Cold War mentality and oppose bloc policy. We call for creation of a multipolar world that no one country can dominate.

—JOINT "NEW WORLD ORDER" STATEMENT OF BORIS YELTSIN AND JIANG ZEMIN, *presidents, Russia and China, 1997*

•••

I deplore both the Indian and the Pakistani [nuclear] tests . . . and call on both governments to sign the Comprehensive Test Ban Treaty [and] sign a no-first-use pledge with each other.

—KOFI ANNAN, *UN Secretary-General, 1998*

CHAPTER TOPICS AND THEMES

- Assumptions of realism about paths to peace
- Alliances and their impact on national and international security
- The balance of power
- Arms control agreements as instruments of national security policy
- Can the acquisition of allies and arms stabilize a twenty-first-century multipolar world?

Many countries have the military power to inflict enormous destruction on their enemies. As a consequence, national security remains, as ever, elusive. Due to the escalating dangers of modern weapons, most states' sense of security has decreased, rather than increased, during this century.

To defend themselves, states have several options. They may (1) arm themselves; (2) form (or sever) alliances with other countries; or (3) negotiate arms control and disarmament agreements to reduce the threat of adversaries' weapons. Although most leaders usually pursue various combinations of these strategies, each nonetheless represents a distinct military approach to security.

In focusing on world conflict and its management, our discussion has followed a logical progression. Chapter 12 began by exploring why the frequency of war makes preparations for it so necessary. Chapter 13 examined the search for national security through the acquisition of military capabilities. Chapter 14 assessed states' use of coercive diplomacy, both to realize their national goals abroad and to deter their rivals from aggression. We now concentrate on the other two military approaches to national security—the use of alliances and arms control to maintain a favorable balance of power and thereby enhance security. These approaches draw their inspiration primarily from the assumptions that realist theory makes about the most prudent paths to peace (see Table 15.1).

• • •

ALLIANCES AND THEIR IMPACT ON NATIONAL AND GLOBAL SECURITY

Alliances are formal agreements among states to coordinate their behavior in the event of military emergencies. Alliances thus are coalitions that heed realism's first rule of statecraft: to increase military capabilities. States can do this either by acquiring arms or by acquiring allies. Although alliances are more economical because they permit the defense burden to be shared, throughout history states have vigorously pursued both methods. While alliances appear to be the preferred method for increasing military capabilities, this solution has significant disadvantages. Making alliance choices has seldom been easy, as it requires weighing the military strength, goals, and reliability of allies and adversaries alike.

Allies offer a means to counterbalance threats in an international system that does not provide a world government to protect states. Throughout history many states involved in conflicts have forged alliances with others "even in advance, against [a] probable aggressor" (Morgenthau 1959).

Alliances are "typically against, and only derivatively for, someone or something" (Liska 1962). They tend to form when two or more states face a common threat, because a mutual defense alliance can reduce the probability of being attacked (deterrence), [provide each ally] greater strength in case of attack (defense), and prevent the ally's alliance with one's adversary (preclusion)" (G. Snyder 1991).

Alliances generally have not lasted long and have often dissolved when the common threat disappeared. For this reason, realists primarily see alliance formation as a strategy that includes both the recruitment and abandonment of allies. Recognizing that "alignment and dealignment are the main short-term

alliances coalitions that form when two or more states combine their military capabilities and promise to coordinate their policies to increase mutual security.

463

464

THE REALIST ROAD TO
SECURITY THROUGH
ALLIANCES, THE
BALANCE OF POWER,
AND ARMS CONTROL

TABLE 15.1 The Realist Road to Security: Assumptions and Policy Recommendations

The Realist Picture of the International Environment	
Primary global condition:	Anarchy
Probability of system change/reform:	Low
Prime actors:	States, and especially great powers
Principal actor goals:	Power over others, self-preservation, and physical security
Predominant pattern of actor interaction:	Competition and conflict
Pervasive concern:	National security
Prevalent state priorities:	Acquiring military capabilities
Popular state practice:	Use of armed force for coercive diplomacy
Realist Policy Prescriptions	
Preparations for war:	If you want peace, prepare for war.
Perpetual vigilance:	No state is to be trusted further than its national interest.
Persistent involvement and intervention:	Isolationism is not an alternative to active global involvement.
Preparedness with arms:	Strive to increase military capabilities, and fight rather than submit to subordination.
Preserve the balance of power:	Do not let any state or coalition of states become predominant.
Prevent arms races from resulting in military inferiority with rivals:	Negotiate agreements with competitors to maintain a favorable military balance.

strategies for increasing security," states have the choice of adding or expanding commitments to other states to increase their own state's security, as opposed to eliminating or reducing commitments to allies that are a drain on security (Scarborough and Bueno de Mesquita 1988). According to *realpolitik* logic, the best kind of alliance is one that can be dissolved easily when the threat to one's own security declines. As Britain's Lord Palmerston admonished in 1848, states "should have no eternal allies and no perpetual enemies." Their only duty, then, is to follow their interests, which may require abandoning an ally when it ceases to be useful.

The greatest risk to forming alliances is that they bind a state to a commitment that may later become disadvantageous. Throughout history, policymakers have been mindful of dangerous entanglements, because entrusting their security to the pledges of others reduces their future freedom of action. Consequently, many leaders are risk averse about making hasty commitments to a friendly government; indeed, "wise and experienced statesmen usually shy away from commitments likely to constitute limitations on a government's behavior at unknown dates in the future in the face of unpredictable situations" (Kennan 1984a). Although alliances provide some measure of protection, they also reduce a state's capacity to make accommodative realignments when conditions change. In fact, the usefulness of any alliance is destined to lessen once the common external threat that brought it together declines, as it inevitably will (Wolfers 1962). Policymakers are therefore often advised not to take a fixed position on temporary convergences of national interests and to forge alliances only to deal with immediate threats.

When considering whether a new alliance is a good idea—a **rational choice** in which the benefits outweigh the costs—most heads of state usually recognize that such decisions are hard. The payoffs and consequences of casting their fate with another state are difficult to foresee, and in the long run, allies can easily do more harm than good (see Focus 15.1).

In fact, many realists advise states to avoid alliances unless absolutely necessary for defense. They base their fears on five fundamental flaws:

- First, alliances enable aggressive states to combine military capabilities for aggression. This was the thinking of Adolf Hitler, who maintained that "Any alliance whose purpose is not the intention to wage war is senseless and useless." Alliances are to be feared because they allow expansionist states, counting on their allies' assistance, to act more aggressively than they otherwise would.

- Second, alliances threaten enemies and provoke them to form counteralliances. This results in reduced security for *both* coalitions.

  > Peacetime alliances may occur in order to reduce the insecurity of anarchy or reduce armament costs. If they do, they will tend to create relations of enmity as well as alignment. Even if the initial alliance is not directed at a specific opponent, other states will perceive it as a threat and begin to behave as enemies, perhaps by forming a counteralliance. (G. Snyder 1991, 88)

- Third, alliance formation may draw otherwise neutral parties into opposed coalitions. As Thomas Jefferson warned, alliances can be dangerously "entangling." They require members to come to one another's aid, involving members in the wars of their partners.

- Fourth, once states join forces, they must control the behavior of their own allies. Management of intra-alliance relations is necessary to discourage each member from reckless aggression against its enemies, threatening the security of the alliance's other members. In addition, allies must work to deter defection from the alliance and to ensure that allies' commitments to one another are faithfully honored.

- Finally, the possibility always exists that today's ally might become tomorrow's enemy. Realists believe that all states are natural enemies, that there are no permanent friends or adversaries. The historical record is noteworthy in this respect. In the period between the Congress of Vienna in 1815 and the 1960s, wars between allies were commonplace: "More than 25 percent of coalition partners eventually [went] to war against each other" (Russett and Starr 1996, 91). Thus, when alliances form, they can increase the prospects for and the scope of war.

In a 1917 address to the U.S. Senate, President Woodrow Wilson proposed that "all nations avoid entangling alliances which would draw them into . . . a net of intrigue and selfish rivalry." In taking this position, which reflected his liberal belief that alliances and secret diplomacy transform limited

What Can Help You Can Hurt You

Do Allies Weaken a State's Security?

States' alliance policies are usually shaped by an acute awareness of the many risks of sharing their fate with allies. While realists generally see alliances as a tool states can use for their own benefit, they caution that alliance formation is risky. A state making a defense pact with an ally, they warn, will also pay a heavy price. Creating alliances will also:

- Foreclose options.
- Reduce the state's capacity to adapt to changing circumstances.
- Weaken a state's capability to influence others by decreasing the number of additional partners with which it can align.
- Eliminate the advantages in bargaining that can be derived from deliberately fostering ambiguity about one's intentions.
- Provoke the fears of adversaries.
- Entangle states in disputes with their allies' enemies.
- Interfere with the negotiation of disputes involving an ally's enemy by precluding certain issues from being placed on the agenda.
- Preserve existing rivalries.
- Stimulate envy and resentment on the part of friends who are outside the alliance and are therefore not eligible to receive its advantages.

These potential dangers explain why opinions among policymakers about alliance decisions are so controversial, even when advocates enthusiastically propose that another state be sought as an ally for mutual defense. The posture of leaders about the advantage or disadvantage of alliances has depended on their personal philosophy and the country's cir-

cumstances. Pictured here, in 1796, is George Washington, the first President of the United States, expressing his policy preference on the topic to other American leaders in government. Washington advised that it should be the foreign policy of the United States to "steer clear of permanent alliances." He felt that whereas a state "may safely trust to temporary alliances for extraordinary emergencies" it is an "illusion . . . to expect or calculate upon real favors from nation to nation."

conflicts into global wars with many participants, Wilson underscored the difficulties and the dangers of making alliance decisions. Despite their uncertain usefulness, many states have chosen to ally throughout history, because despite the perceived risks, the benefits to security in a time of threat justified that decision.

To best picture how alliances affect global security, it is instructive to move from the state level of analysis, which views alliance decisions from the perspective of individual state's security, to the system level of analysis (recall Chapters 1 and 3) by looking at the impact of alliances on the frequency of interstate war. This view focuses attention on the possible contribution of alliance formation to maintaining the balance of power.

● ● ●

467

THE REALIST ROAD TO
SECURITY THROUGH
ALLIANCES, THE
BALANCE OF POWER,
AND ARMS CONTROL

THE BALANCE OF POWER

International anarchy makes each state responsible for its own national security. The seventeenth-century English realist philosopher Thomas Hobbes observed that this condition encourages among states a perpetual "war of all against all." Realists and neorealists argue that reforming this system is unrealistic because international anarchy is permanent, as is the selfish drive for power over rivals. Survival and world order rest on the proper functioning of a system of shifting military alignments commonly referred to as the "balance of power."

Assumptions of Balance-of-Power Theory

Balance of power is an ambiguous concept used in a variety of ways (see Claude 1962). At its core is the idea that peace will result when military power is distributed so that no one state is strong enough to dominate the others. If one state, or a combination of states, gains enough power to threaten others, compelling incentives will exist for those threatened to disregard their superficial differences and unite in a defensive alliance. The power resulting from such collaboration would, according to this conception, deter the would-be attacker from pursuing expansionism. Thus, from the laissez-faire competition of predatory and defensive rivals would emerge a balance of contending factions, which would maintain the status quo.

Balance-of-power theory is also founded on the realist premise that weakness invites attack and that countervailing power must be used to deter potential aggressors. Because realists assume that the drive for expanded power guides every state's actions, it follows that all countries are potential adversaries, and each must strengthen its military capability to protect itself. Invariably, this reasoning rationalizes the quest for military superiority because others pursue it as well.

On the surface, these realist assumptions appear dubious (especially to liberals). The arms races they justify can easily lead to the very outcome most feared—a destructive, global war. However, the realist policymakers in Europe who formulated classical balance-of-power theory after the Peace of Westphalia in 1648 were not irrational (Gulick 1955). They reasoned that a system founded on suspicion and competition, in which all states were independent and could make choices freely to advance their perceived national interests, would distribute power evenly through realignments. This, they believed, would curtail the temptation of any actor to seek to dominate others.

The Balance Process. In classic balance-of-power theory, fear of a third party would encourage **alignments**—shifts by neutrals to one coalition or the other—because those threatened would need help to offset the power of the mutual adversary. An alliance would add the ally's power to its own and deny the addition of that power to the enemy. As alliances combine power, the offsetting coalitions would give neither a clear advantage. Therefore, aggression would appear unattractive and would be averted.

To deter an aggressor, counteralliances were expected to form easily, because states sitting on the sidelines could not risk **nonalignment.** If they refused to ally, their own vulnerability would encourage the expansionist state to attack them at a later time. In theory, the result of these individual calculations would be the formation of coalitions approximately equal in power. This theory

balance of power the theory that peace and stability are most likely to be maintained when military power is distributed so that no single power or bloc can dominate the others.

balancer under a balance-of-power system, an influential global or regional great power that throws its support in decisive fashion to a defensive coalition. This role was often played by Great Britain in the eighteenth and nineteenth centuries.

presumes that state actors (agents) are rational and that they elect to make policies aimed at equalizing the power of competing coalitions because of their ability to recognize states' interest in stopping aggression. The so-called **size principle** accounts for the inclination of rational actors to form coalitions only sufficient in size to ensure victory and no larger, resulting in political coalitions that are roughly equal in size (see Riker 1962).

To maintain an even distribution of power, realists recommended certain *rules* be followed to promote fluid and rapidly shifting alliances. They recognized that a balance would develop only if states practiced certain behaviors. One requirement was that a great power not immediately threatened by the rise of another power or coalition would perform the role of a **balancer** by offsetting the new challenger's power. Since the modern state system began in the seventeenth century, Great Britain has often played this role by consistently supporting the weaker coalition to prevent an expansionist state and its allies from achieving dominance.

In addition to needing a balancer, all states had to obey the following "essential rules": "(1) increase capabilities but negotiate rather than fight; (2) fight rather than fail to increase capabilities; (3) stop fighting rather than eliminate an essential actor; (4) oppose any coalition or single actor which tends to assume a position of predominance within the system; (5) constrain actors who subscribe to supranational organizational principles; and (6) permit defeated or constrained essential national actors to reenter the system as acceptable role partners" (Kaplan 1957).

According to these rules, competition is proper because it leads to the equalization of capabilities among the major competitors. The balance-of-power approach deals with the problem of war in a way that preserves the problem. War is a way to measure national power as well as a means for changing the distribution of power in order to preserve the essential features of the system itself.

The successful operation of a balance-of-power system also presupposes some important preconditions for its successful operation. To maintain a balance, for example, Kenneth Waltz (1979) advances the neorealist thesis that "balance-of-power politics prevail whenever two, and only two, requirements are met: that the order be anarchic and that it be populated by units wishing to survive." Most other theorists hold a more complex view, and argue that the following conditions must exist:

- States must possess accurate information about others' capabilities and motives and react rationally to this information.
- There must be a sufficient number of independent states to make alliance formation and dissolution readily possible; stable balance-of-power systems usually require at least five great powers or blocs of states.
- There must be a limited geographic area.
- National leaders must have freedom of action.
- States' capabilities must be relatively equal.
- States must share a common political culture in which the rules of the security regime are recognized and respected.
- States in the system must have similar types of government and ideologies.
- States must have a weapons technology that inhibits **preemption**—quick mobilizations for war, first-strike attacks that defeat the enemy before it can organize a retaliatory response—and wars of annihilation.

The Balance of Power
A Precarious and Failed Security System?

Perhaps the foremost expert on the balance of power, the realist political scientist Inis L. Claude, came to this sobering conclusion:

> Balance-of-power theory is concerned mainly with the rivalries and clashes of great powers—above all—what we have come to describe as world wars, the massive military conflicts that engulf and threaten to destroy the entire multistate system. It is difficult to consider world wars as anything other than catastrophic failures, total collapses, of the balance-of-power system. They are hardly to be classed as stabilizing manoeuvres or equilibrating processes, and one cannot take seriously any claim of maintaining international stability that does not entail the prevention of such disasters as the Napoleonic wars or World War I. Mention of those and similar disasters, however, frequently evokes the reminder that the would-be universal emperor—be it Louis XIV or Napoleon or Hitler—was defeated; in accordance with balance of power principles, a coalition arose to put down the challenger and maintain or restore the independence of the various states. In short, the system worked. Or did it? Is the criterion of the effectiveness of the balance of power that Germany lose its bid for conquest, or that it be deterred from precipitating World War I? It is not easy to justify the contention that a system for the management of international relations that failed to prevent the events of 1914–1918 deserves high marks as a guardian of stability or order, or peace. If the balance-of-power system does not aim at the prevention of world war, then it aims too low; if it offers no hope of maintaining the general peace, then the quest for a better system is fully warranted. (Claude 1989, 78)

The question to be asked is whether the balance of power is a reliable mechanism to prevent global war or whether there is a better approach. If so, what is it? Is it collective security, as liberal idealists such as Woodrow Wilson believed, or some other approach?

- There must be no supranational institutions capable of interfering with states' alignments and realignments.

These preconditions characterized the environment of international politics during most periods before World War II. But do they exist today? Are the assumptions underlying classic balance-of-power theory still warranted?

The Breakdown of Power Balances. Is international order truly a product of alliance formation and power balances, as many realists (Liska 1968; Osgood 1968) believe? Or, when arms races and alliance formation combine power into contending blocs, do the aligned states find that their security actually declines and that major wars then usually erupt?

If the assumptions of the balance-of-power theory are correct, historical periods in which the basic preconditions listed above were in evidence should also have been periods in which war was less frequent. What does the historical record suggest?

The Eurocentric system that existed from the mid-seventeenth century until World War I is generally regarded as the "golden age" of balance-of-power politics. But even then the balance of power was always precarious at best (Dehio 1962). Indeed, the regularity of wars in Europe between the mid-1600s and the early twentieth century (the period when the necessary conditions for the "invisible hand" of the balance of power most clearly existed) attests to the repeated failure of its mechanisms to preserve peace (see Focus 15.2). Although

470

THE REALIST ROAD TO
SECURITY THROUGH
ALLIANCES, THE
BALANCE OF POWER,
AND ARMS CONTROL

hegemonic stability theory the argument that a dominant state is necessary to enforce international cooperation, maintain international rules and regimes, and keep the peace.

the classical systems may at times have prolonged the intervals of peace between conflicts and possibly limited wars' duration and damage when they occurred, a balancing of power has never kept the peace. Research shows that although during the nineteenth century alliance formation within the balance-of-power system was associated with the absence of war, throughout the first half of the twentieth century, this linkage no longer held; as many states became members of alliances, the international system became relatively more war-prone (Singer and Small 1968). However, this is not to argue that the pattern was entirely consistent in this time period. To be sure, several **long peaces**—long-lasting periods of great-power peace—occurred in Europe during the balance of power (between the Congress of Vienna in 1815 and the outbreak of war across Europe in 1848, and after the Franco-Prussian War in 1871 until 1914). An alternative explanation of the relative peace during several prolonged periods in nineteenth century Europe is offered by **hegemonic stability theory,** which postulates that the existence of a single, all-powerful military **hegemon** can safeguard system stability better than an equilibrium resulting from balance-of-power politics. At this time, it was the extraordinary dominance of power possessed and used by Great Britain, the world's hegemonic leader, that kept peace among its European rivals (Organski 1968). Whatever the causes of modern periods of peace followed by major wars, the most striking feature of the balance of power was the increasingly destructive general wars that erupted each time these balance-of-power systems collapsed.

In light of the previous repetitious breakdown of the balance of power, it is noteworthy that the pattern of recurrent general wars ended when the nuclear era began, after World War II. Since then, war among great powers has been virtually nonexistent. Another "long peace" (Gaddis 1991) has taken root. Could it be that the **balance of terror** created by nuclear weapons deterred great-power belligerence since 1945 more than the balance of power? Arguably, alliance formation and balance-of-power politics could not have caused this long peace. The rigid alliance blocs during the Cold War halted the rapid realignments necessary for the equilibrium that balance-of-power theory envisions. If that is so, then it seems likely that the annihilating destructiveness of nuclear weapons since the 1950s kept the peace—not the alliances and power balances that the great powers constructed.

Equally debatable is the realist assumption underlying balance-of-power theory that countries with dominant strength will be secure. Contrary evidence suggests that rapidly arming countries may actually invite attack. In five of the nine great-power wars that occurred in the 150 years following the 1815 Congress of Vienna, the countries attacked were stronger militarily than those initiating the war (Singer and Small 1974; see also Chapter 13). This belies the premise that seeking military advantages over others deters aggression. Instead, as liberal idealists warn, the growth of a state's military power may so terrify its adversaries that they are motivated to initiate a preemptive strike in order to prevent their defeat.

The Rise, Fall, and Revival of Collective Security as a Substitute for Power Balances

The outbreak of World War I, perhaps more than any other event, discredited balance-of-power politics and promoted the search for alternatives. The catastrophic proportions of that war led many, especially those attracted to the liberal theoretical interpretation of world politics, to view the balance-of-power mechanism as a *cause* of war instead of an instrument for its prevention. These critics cited the arms races, secret treaties, and cross-cutting alliances driving balance-of-power politics before the outbreak of the war as its immediate precipitants.

U.S. President Woodrow Wilson voiced the most vehement opposition to balance-of-power politics. He and other liberal reformers hoped to replace the alliances and counteralliances within the balance of power with the principle of **collective security,** a system of world order in which aggression by any state would be met by a collective response.

collective security a global or regional regime stipulating that any actor's aggression will be met by all other actors' combined military force.

The League of Nations embodied this belief, built on the assumption that peace-loving countries could collectively deter—and, if necessary, counteract—aggression. Instead of accepting war as a legitimate instrument of national policy, collective security advocates sought to inhibit war through the threat of collective action. The theory proposed: (1) to retaliate against *any* aggression or attempt to establish hegemony—not just those acts that threatened particular countries; (2) to involve the participation of *all* member states—not just a sufficient number to stop the aggressor; and (3) to create an international organization to identify acts of aggression and to organize a military response to them—not just to let individual states decide for themselves whether to undertake self-help measures. In essence, collective security may be defined as "collective self-regulation," occurring when "a group of states attempts to reduce security threats by agreeing to collectively punish any member state that violates the system's norms" (Downs 1994). As one realist authority impartially describes the concept,

> The rock bottom principle upon which collective security is founded provides that an attack on any one state will be regarded as an attack on all states. It finds its measure in the simple doctrine of one for all and all for one. War anywhere . . . is the concern of every state.
>
> Self-help and neutrality, it should be obvious, are the exact antithesis of such a theory. States under an order of neutrality are impartial when conflict breaks out, give their blessings to combatants to fight it out, and defer judgment regarding the justice or injustice of the cause involved. Self-help in the past was often "help yourself" so far as the great powers were concerned; they enforced their own rights and more besides. In the eighteenth and nineteenth centuries this system was fashionable, and wars, although not eliminated, were localized whenever possible. In a more integrated world environment, a conflict anywhere has some effect on conditions of peace everywhere. A disturbance at one point upsets the equilibrium at all other points, and the adjustment of a single conflict restores the foundations of harmony at other points throughout the world. (Thompson 1953, 755)

To the disappointment of its advocates, collective security was not endorsed by the very powers that after World War I had most championed it, such as the United States. Japan's aggression against Manchuria in 1931 (and China proper in 1937) and Italy's invasion of Ethiopia in 1935 were widely condemned. However, collective resistance was not forthcoming. Furthermore, Germany's encroachment on Czechoslovakia and other European countries in the late 1930s elicited no collective response. When World War II broke out, collective security was discredited, and balance-of-power politics regained favor as the most popular approach for preserving global peace. In the wake of

472

THE REALIST ROAD TO
SECURITY THROUGH
ALLIANCES, THE
BALANCE OF POWER,
AND ARMS CONTROL

that deadly, global war, realists convinced many people that national self-reliance was the only trustworthy safeguard of security. They loudly preached that peace must come through states' unilateral preparations for war and use of acquired military might, to confront a potential aggressor with an abundance of power to successfully deter its aggression. U.S. President Richard Nixon was one of many leaders who reaffirmed the balance-of-power approach and rejected multilateral collective peacekeeping; he argued "We must remember the only time in the history of the world that we have had any extended period of peace is when there has been a balance of power. . . . It will be a safer world . . . if we have a strong, healthy United States, Europe, Soviet Union, China, Japan, each balancing the other."

That *realpolitik* philosophy fell on receptive ears throughout the tense Cold War and helped to propel the worldwide arms race during it. It was only after the Cold War ended in 1991 that the world community began to once again consider collective security as the preferred method for letting the United Nations and regional defense organizations maintain world order (see Chapter 16). Changing times seemed to warrant a return to liberal approaches. At issue was which theory and approach, realism advocating the balance of power or liberalism advocating collective security, would be most preferred and practiced. Speaking to the relative strengths and weaknesses of either path to peace is the historical record. For lessons about the applicability of balance-of-power theory to today's realities, it is instructive to review the evolution of the international system's polarity structure in the post-World War II era (the world's longest period of great-power peace).

Post-World War II Models of the Balance of Power

Military power can be distributed in different ways. Historically, these have ranged from highly concentrated distributions on one end of the continuum to highly dispersed distributions on the other. The former have included regional empires (e.g., the Roman Empire), while an example of the latter is the approximate equality of power held by the European powers at the conclusion of the Napoleonic Wars in 1815. Following the conventional periodizations of analysts (e.g., Kaplan 1957; Kegley and Raymond 1994; Thompson 1988), we can identify three major distributions of international power since 1945, with a fourth probably emergent in the post-Cold War period.

Unipolarity. Most countries were devastated by World War II. The United States, however, was left in a clearly dominant position, its economy accounting for about half the world's combined gross national product. The United States was also the only country with an awesome new weapon, the atomic bomb, which it had already demonstrated its willingness to use. This underscored to others that it was without rival and incapable of being counterbalanced. The United States was not just stronger than anybody—it was stronger than *everybody*. This power configuration after World War II was unipolar, because power was concentrated in the hands of a single hegemon. This period, however, was short-lived.

Bipolarity. The recovery of the Soviet economy, the growth of its military capabilities, its maintenance of a large army, and growing Soviet-U.S. rivalry soon gave rise to a new distribution of world power. The Soviets broke the

U.S. monopoly on atomic weapons in 1949 and exploded a thermonuclear device in 1953, less than a year after the United States. This achievement symbolized the creation of a *bipolar* distribution, as military capabilities became concentrated in the hands of two competitive "superpowers," whose capacity to massively destroy anyone made comparisons with the other great powers meaningless.

The concentration of power (what scholars term **polarity**) in two dominant actors encouraged polarization. Power combined to form two opposing **blocs** or coalitions through **polarization** when states joined counterbalanced alliances. In interpreting these dynamics, it is important not to use the concepts of polarity and *polarization* interchangeably. They refer to two distinct dimensions of the primary ways in which military power is aggregated (or dispersed) at any point in time in the international system. When states independently build arms at home, their differential production rates change the system's *polarity*, or number of power centers (poles). In contrast, when states combine their arms through alliance formation, the aggregation of power through *polarization* changes the system's balance of power. A system with multiple power centers can be said to be moving toward a greater degree of polarization if its members form separate blocs whose external interactions are characterized by increasing levels of conflict while their internal interactions become more cooperative (Rapkin and Thompson with Christopherson 1989). Conversely, polarization decreases when the number of cross-cutting alignments expands. The concept of polarization is especially apt in this context because a *pole* is a fit metaphor for a magnet—it both repels and attracts.

The formation of the **North Atlantic Treaty Organization (NATO),** linking the United States to the defense of Western Europe, and the Warsaw Pact, linking the former Soviet Union in a formal alliance with its Eastern European clients, were produced by this polarization process. Through this process, states combined their military resources in two countercoalitions to reinforce a **bipolar** structure. The opposing blocs formed in part because the superpowers competed for allies and in part because the less-powerful states looked to one superpower or the other for protection. Correspondingly, each superpower's allies gave it forward bases from which to carry on the competition. In addition, the involvement of most other states in the superpowers' struggle globalized the East-West conflict. Few states remained outside the superpowers' rival alliance networks as neutral or nonaligned countries.

By grouping the system's states into two blocs, each led by a superpower, the Cold War's bipolar structure bred insecurity among all. The balance was constantly at stake. Each bloc leader, fearing that its adversary would attain hegemony, viewed every move, however defensive, as the first step toward world conquest. **Zero-sum** conflict was endemic as both sides viewed what one side gained as a loss for the other. Both the United States and the former Soviet Union therefore attached great importance to recruiting new allies. Fear that an old ally might desert the fold was everpresent. Bipolarity left little room for compromise or maneuver and worked against the normalization of superpower relations (Waltz 1993).

Bipolycentrism. The major Cold War coalitions associated with bipolarity began to disintegrate in the 1960s and early 1970s. As their internal cohesion eroded and new centers of power emerged, a bipolycentric system (Spanier 1975) came into being. **Bipolycentrism** described the continued military

474

THE REALIST ROAD TO
SECURITY THROUGH
ALLIANCES, THE
BALANCE OF POWER,
AND ARMS CONTROL

superiority of the two superpowers and their allies' continued reliance on their respective patrons for security. At the same time, the weaker alliance partners were afforded more room for maneuvering. Thus the term **polycentrism** was coined to describe the emergence of diverse relationships among the states subordinate to the superpowers at this second tier (e.g., the friendly relations between the United States and Romania, on the one hand, and those between France and the Soviet Union, on the other). The secondary powers also began to cultivate ties across alliance boundaries (e.g., between Poland and West Germany) to enhance their bargaining position within their own alliance. Although the superpowers remained dominant militarily, this less rigid system allowed other states to perform new foreign policy roles.

Rapid technological innovation in the superpowers' major weapons systems was a principal catalyst to the crumbling of the blocs. **Intercontinental ballistic missiles (ICBMs),** capable of delivering nuclear weapons through space from one continent to another, eroded the necessity of forward-base areas for striking at the heart of the adversary.

In addition, the narrowed differences in the superpowers' arsenals loosened the ties that had previously bound allies to one another. The European members of NATO in particular began to question whether the United States would, as it had pledged, protect Paris or Bonn by sacrificing New York. Under what conditions might Washington or Moscow be willing to risk a nuclear holocaust? The uncertainty became pronounced as the pledge to protect allies through **extended deterrence** by retaliating against their attacker seemed increasingly insincere. As former CIA director Stansfield Turner acknowledged in 1986, "It's not conceivable that any president would risk the very existence of [the United States] in order to defend [our] European allies from a conventional assault."

In partial response to the dilemma this posed, other states, particularly France, decided to protect themselves by developing their own nuclear capabilities. As a result, the diffusion of power already under way gathered momentum.

As these changes unfolded in the 1970s and 1980s, Cold War categories used to classify "free world" and communist countries' foreign policy alignments lost much of their relevance, as bipolycentrism implies. The acceptance of capitalism by many communist states in the late 1980s further eroded the adhesive bonds of ideology that had formerly helped these countries face their security problems from a common posture. Fissures in both blocs widened, as disputes arose in the Western alliance over strategic doctrine, arms control, U.S. military bases on allies' territory, and especially "out-of-area conflicts" (those beyond the traditional geographical boundaries of NATO). Not only decomposing blocs, but also declining support for the sanctity of alliance commitments in general became evident (Kegley and Raymond 1990). As fears of a new world war steadily lessened and the Cold War began to fade, leaders questioned whether defense alliances were still needed.

The 1989 dismantling of the Berlin Wall tore apart the post–World War II architecture of competing blocs. With the end of this division, and without a Soviet threat, the consistency of outlook and singularity of purpose that once bound NATO members together disappeared. To many critics, NATO and the Warsaw Pact had institutionalized antagonisms and perpetuated the Cold War—and were no longer needed.

Central to the unfolding debate was "the German question." According to Lord Ismay, the first Secretary General of NATO, the original purpose of the At-

extended deterrence the protection received by a weak ally when a heavily militarized great power pledges to "extend" its capabilities to it in a defense treaty.

475

THE REALIST ROAD TO
SECURITY THROUGH
ALLIANCES, THE
BALANCE OF POWER,
AND ARMS CONTROL

lantic alliance was "to keep the Russians out, the Americans in, and the Germans down." In 1990, although fearing a "Fourth Reich" (i.e., a united, powerful, and potentially expansionist German state), the Soviet Union reversed its long-standing opposition to German unification and agreed to withdraw its military forces from Europe. It did not make that dramatic concession without conditions, however. It insisted that unification be orchestrated through the active management of *all* the major World War II allies, that Germany reduce its armed forces, and that the United States keep a military presence in NATO on German soil.

Germany met all of these preconditions. In September 1990 the Four Powers (the United States, the Soviet Union, Great Britain, and France) and the two Germanys negotiated the **"Two Plus Four" Treaty** in Moscow, which terminated the Four Powers' rights over Germany. German leaders declared they had no territorial claims to make in Europe, including the territories in Poland that were annexed after World War II. Moreover, they pledged never to obtain nuclear weapons, and to reduce their 670,000-person armed forces to 370,000 troops (in exchange for the removal of 370,000 Soviet soldiers from Germany). Germany and the former Soviet Union also signed a bilateral treaty promising not to attack each other.

The West greeted these agreements (and Soviet concessions) with enthusiasm. The agreements symbolized at once the retreat of the Soviet Union from a region (east Europe) it had long regarded as central to its security. They also symbolized the geostrategic shift of NATO influence into the heartland of the Warsaw Pact, which formally dissolved early in 1991.

In the early 1990s many perceived the need to replace NATO and the defunct Warsaw Pact with a new security arrangement. However, most leaders maintained that some configuration of a European defense architecture was still necessary to cement relationships and stabilize the rush of cascading events. Presidents George Bush and Bill Clinton, for instance, were vocal advocates of the continuing need to anchor security in alliances, pledging to keep U.S. troops in Europe and promising that the United States would remain the backbone of NATO.

To others, a new *concert* system of conference diplomacy was needed, like the **Concert of Europe,** which the great powers created in 1815 in the wake of the Napoleonic Wars to keep the peace. Leaders in Moscow and some Western analysts recommended redefining NATO's purpose from the containment of enemies to the control of allies. For that, *all* the countries in Europe would be required to coordinate their defense policies. This would incorporate the east European and former Soviet republics pursuing democratization into a European-wide framework. It might also shift peacekeeping responsibilities from NATO to the larger Organization for Security and Cooperation in Europe (OSCE).

An alternative scenario was the conversion of NATO from a military alliance designed for defense against a predetermined enemy to a larger collective security community. The 1991 Rome Summit moved in this direction by creating a new **North Atlantic Cooperation Council (NACC)** "to build genuine partnership among the North Atlantic Alliance and the countries of Central and Eastern Europe." The next meeting of defense ministers months later witnessed the members of NATO sitting at the same table with the former Warsaw Pact states and newly independent Baltic republics, facing a request from Russia to become a member.

The goal was to keep NATO alive even though the Cold War had died. The old NATO was built on the joint will to resist Soviet aggression. The new NATO

Concert of Europe the security system with regular conferences among Europe's great powers, formed by the great powers in Europe at the 1816 Congress of Vienna to prevent war and revolts.

Realists argue that common interests are the only glue capable of holding alliances together. Others see convergent ideologies as important forces that can bind states together in alliances. In 1998 only five countries (China, Cuba, Laos, North Korea, and Vietnam) remained members of the "communist bloc." In 1988, before the Cold War ended, that coalition consisted of fifteen countries. Pictured here is Cuba's Fidel Castro being assisted by Vietnam's General Secretary Do Muoi and a Vietnamese soldier at farewell ceremonies to a 1995 summit in Hanoi. The Cuban leader visited both China and Vietnam to observe how they had adapted Marxism to market economies. The meeting raises the question of whether communist ideology can still unify what remains of the communist bloc in a common coalition.

sought to survive by preparing to contain ethnonational civil wars, foster disarmament, and preserve U.S. involvement in European security.

In January 1994 the historic dynamics of balance-of-power realignments again were exhibited when the four most advanced democracies in the former communist bloc (Poland, the Czech Republic, Slovakia, and Hungary) lobbied aggressively for full NATO membership. Rather than accept this effort to **bandwagon** by permitting states to abandon one alliance and join the stronger one, under U.S. advocacy NATO cut a compromise deal by offering them participation and a measure of protection by becoming "peace partners" under the **Partnership for Peace (PFP)** plan. The PFP did not give the new affiliates the same security guarantee of aid in the event of an attack that the sixteen existing full members enjoyed. But it became a pivotal step in the enlargement process to broaden NATO's membership and geographical stretch to the east—a strategy to help create a peaceful, united, and democratic Europe. The PFP states were allowed to participate and train with NATO troops for peacekeeping and crisis-management operations (as they did in Operation Joint Endeavor in Bosnia). Seeking to avoid excluding any states and creating

bandwagon the tendency for weak states to seek alliance with the strongest power, irrespective of that power's ideology or form of government, in order to increase security.

another interbloc confrontation, the PFP redesigned itself for a single common defense without specifying a single common enemy. By 1997 at the Madrid Summit, twenty-one states from the former Warsaw Pact, including Russia, had become Partners for Peace, and three (the Czech Republic, Hungary, and Poland) were invited to become full legal members by 1999 (at NATO's fiftieth anniversary). Other states are awaiting permission to apply, and in a series of steps, NATO could expand to thirty members (see Map 15.1). **Enlargement** has shifted the balance of power to the east and given NATO an enlarged agenda. Under the new **Planning and Review Process (PARP)** and wider **Euro-Atlantic Partnership Council (EAPC),** twenty-five PFP partners now address the full range of political, military, financial, and security issues facing all of Europe in the twenty-first century, including the management of crises arising from internal rebellion. A new chapter in NATO's history was opened. Revitalized with a larger membership and, territorial reach, NATO seeks to orchestrate a cooperative approach to security among liberal democracies across the new Europe.

477

THE REALIST ROAD TO
SECURITY THROUGH
ALLIANCES, THE
BALANCE OF POWER,
AND ARMS CONTROL

Critics of NATO's enlargement complain that NATO's expansion could backfire, undermining the security of those states it excludes. This, indeed, has been the threat perceived by Russian nationalists, who see enlargement as a new effort to contain Russia's future revival and potential military recovery of its lost Cold War empire. China, Japan, and other powers likewise have charged that the creation of a solidified military alliance in Europe without other strong military alliances to balance it poses a threat to global security. NATO asserts that these charges are unjustified because its new decision rules, giving every full member a veto over decisions regarding coercive military operations, removes the threat of a NATO preemptive strike. Other proponents of NATO and European Union enlargement claim that the maze of overlapping European security organizations (including the Organization for Security and Cooperation in Europe [OSCE], the Western European Union [WEU], and the Council of Europe) are too cumbersome and slow to permit any of them to take decisive military actions outside their sphere of influence, and that these liberal democracies, moreover, are inherently pacific in values and goals. Whatever the ultimate consequences, the innovative redesign of NATO and its expansion have created a far different distribution of military power than that which existed in the bipolycentric system of the 1970s and 1980s and the bipolar system that preceded it in the 1950s and 1960s. The changes that have unfolded foretell the beginning of a new multipolar system.

Multipolarity. U.S. Secretary of State Lawrence Eagleburger proclaimed in 1989 that "we are now moving into . . . a world in which power and influence [are] diffused among a multiplicity of states—[a] multipolar world." A *multipolar* system of relatively equal powers, similar to the classical European balance-of-power system, may indeed best describe the emerging distribution of power. Such a multipolar system is likely to consist of the United States, China, Germany, Japan, and Russia. To these might someday be added an integrated European Union with a common defense policy (see Chapter 16).

What will be the likely character of such a multipolar world? As shown, when power has been relatively evenly distributed in the past, each player has been assertive, independent, and competitive; diplomacy has displayed a nonideological, chesslike character; and conflict has been intense as each contender has feared the power of its rivals.

The Enlarged NATO and the New Geostrategic Balance of Power

The geostrategic landscape has been transformed in the closing days of the twentieth century by NATO's enlargement process. NATO now casts its security umbrella across (and beyond) the continent, consolidating former enemies to the east in a common collective security regime. Enlargement of membership and mission demonstrates NATO's resolve not to dissolve in the absence of a Cold War threat, in order to solidify the alliance of liberal democracies. If NATO succeeds by surviving, it will defy the historic tendency of Europe's past alliances to collapse after the defeat of a common foe.

SOURCE: *U.S. News & World Report,* July 14, 1997, p. 36.

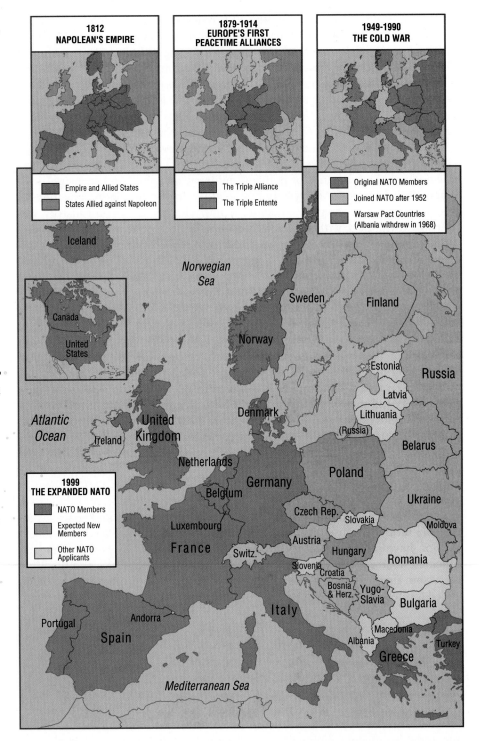

1812 NAPOLEAN'S EMPIRE

- Empire and Allied States
- States Allied against Napoleon

1879-1914 EUROPE'S FIRST PEACETIME ALLIANCES

- The Triple Alliance
- The Triple Entente

1949-1990 THE COLD WAR

- Original NATO Members
- Joined NATO after 1952
- Warsaw Pact Countries (Albania withdrew in 1968)

1999 THE EXPANDED NATO

- NATO Members
- Expected New Members
- Other NATO Applicants

If a truly multipolar world develops, it is difficult to foresee how each great power's relationship with the others will evolve. Realignments—sometimes rapid—are to be expected. With the probable expansion of the number of great powers to as many as five, realist theory predicts that new cleavages will inevitably develop. It also predicts that rivalry will likely intensify as each jockeys for privilege, position, and power.

A world consisting of five or more independent and approximately equal centers of power will create an enlarged global chessboard of multiple bilateral geostrategic relationships. Such a congested landscape will be fraught with potential for conflict and confusion about the identity of friends and foes. To make the setting even more confusing, the interplay is likely to take place simultaneously on two playing fields—the first economic and the second military (recall Table 4.2).

In a new multipolar system, we can expect the major powers to align together against others on particular issues, as interests dictate. Behind the diplomatic smiles and handshakes, one-time friends and allies are likely to grow apart, and formally "specialized" relations are likely to dissolve. Consider the already heated U.S.-Japan-EU trade-bloc rivalry on the economic battlefield (see Chapter 8).

Multipolarity also foretells the potential alignment of former adversaries. The United States and Russia, allied victors in World War II, are now both apprehensive about the powers they defeated: Japan and Germany. Therefore, as balance-of-power theory would predict and as Russian strategist Peter Gladkov foresaw in 1992, the United States and Russia have been given incentives to someday become true allies. But other realignments are also likely, as suggested by Russia's determination to restore its troubled relationship with China while at the same time seeking full NATO membership in order to deter potential Chinese expansionism.

Contemplating a Multipolar Future

As the fundamental trend toward the dispersion of global power continues, the prospects for peace will undoubtedly be affected. The emergence of a multipolar international system appears very likely, but the probable consequences are not clear, as the three different schools of thought on the relationship between polarity and global stability suggest (see Focus 15.3). Because there is no real consensus on whether systems with a certain number of poles are more war-prone than others (Russett and Starr 1996; see also Levy 1999), it would be imprudent to conclude that a new multipolar system will necessarily produce another period of warfare or of peace.

Different types of multipolar systems can emerge, involving variant armament ratios and alliance networks. These combinations can lead to very different conditions. It is possible to imagine a wide diversity of plausible but possible geopolitical relationships in the twenty-first century (see Brzezinski 1998), and the presence or absence of a particular polarity balance by itself is unlikely to solely determine whether war clouds will gather or dissipate. For example, a new era of unipolarity could arise like that after World War II with the resurgence of the United States and its reascendence as the globe's only superpower: To hegemonic stability theorists, this age of unrivaled dominance would provide a leader to police chaos, but to many Germans, Chinese and Japanese, the growing accumulation of so much political, military,

480

THE REALIST ROAD TO
SECURITY THROUGH
ALLIANCES, THE
BALANCE OF POWER,
AND ARMS CONTROL

When NATO approved formal enlargement in 1997, both Russia's and China's sense of security plummeted. In reaction, the old rivals, feeling excluded, repaired their broken alliance ties by agreeing to a new "strategic partnership" aimed at rearranging the global geostrategic chessboard. Shown here are Russian Premier Vickor Cheknomyrdin (right) and Chinese President Jiang Zemin on his Moscow arrival in April 1997 to negotiate the "new world order" joint statement, which called for creation of a new "multipolar" system cemented by a new Sino-Russian axis to counter the threat of global domination by the U.S. hegemonic superpower. The logic of balance-of-power politics rationalizes the formation of these kinds of strategic unions to check the growing influence of a rising great-power rival. The same thinking inspired the August 1997 new common defense treaty between Japan and the United States to offset the expanding military power of China.

economic, and cultural clout by the United States is breeding an alarming ar-
rogance and a dangerous impulse to bully the rest of the world. Without a
check on American interference, some of America's closest allies fear that
U.S. dominance will lead to a heavy-handed U.S. imperialism that threatens
global stability (Drozdiak 1997). Likewise, others picture the likely return of
coalition politics, with a new bipolar or bipolycentric but unstable configuration emerging from the formation of a new Sino-Russian bloc, European-
Russian entente, or Sino-Japanese alliance to counter an alliance spearheaded by the United States (Brzezinski 1998). Here it is possible to visualize
turmoil as various states join together to restrain the American behemoth or
another great-power bloc from harming others with their power. And others
picture a new world order and/or disorder developing from a new multipolar
division of competing systems, or, alternatively, a system breakdown because
"when the Cold War ended in 1989, so did the balance of power systems . . .
and the centuries-old way of looking at the world" (*Economist*, December 20,
1997, 41). It is, indeed, very difficult to predict what the twenty-first-century
geostrategic chessboard will look like, and whether it will be chaotic or sta-

Polarity and Peace?
Three Schools of Thought

In the wake of the Cold War and the disintegration of its bipolar structure, the long-standing debate has intensified about which type of polarity distribution—unipolar, bipolar, or multipolar—is the most stable.

One interpretation holds that "There were periods when an equal distribution of power between contenders actually existed . . . but these . . . were the exception rather than the rule. . . . Closer examination reveals that they were periods of war, not peace" (Organski 1968). If this view is accurate, then peace will occur when one hegemonic state acquires enough power to deter others' expansionist ambitions. If we think of the United States as the hegemonic power in the post-World War II system, this seemingly plausible conclusion about the stability of unipolar systems does not bode well for peace in the future. If present trends continue, the so-called "unipolar moment" of unchallenged U.S. hegemony (Krauthammer 1991) will pass and, without a dominant global leader, the twenty-first century will be increasingly disorderly.

In contrast, a second school of thought (e.g., Waltz 1964) maintains that bipolar systems are the most stable. According to this line of reasoning, stability, ironically, results from "the division of all nations into two camps [because it] raises the costs of war to such a high level that all but the most fundamental conflicts are resolved without resort to violence" (Bueno de Mesquita 1975). Under such stark simplicities and balanced symmetries, the two leading rivals have incentives to manage crises so that they do not escalate to war.

Those who believe that a bipolar world is inherently more stable than either its unipolar or multipolar counterparts draw support from the fact that in the bipolar environment of the 1950s, when the threat of war was endemic, major war did not occur. Extrapolating, these observers (e.g., Mearsheimer 1990) reason that because now a new multipolar distribution of global power makes it impossible to run the world from one or two centers, disorder will result:

> It is rather basic. So long as there were only two great powers, like two big battleships clumsily and cautiously circling each other, confrontations—or accidents—were easier to avoid. Now, with the global lake more crowded with ships of varying sizes, fueled by different ambitions and piloted with different degrees of navigational skill, the odds of collisions become far greater. (House 1989, A10)

A third school of thought argues that multipolar systems are the least war-prone. While the reasons differ, advocates share the belief that polarized systems that either concentrate power, as in a unipolar system, or that divide the world into two antagonistic blocs, as in a bipolar system, promote struggles for dominance (see Thompson 1988; Morgenthau 1985). The peace-through-multipolarity school perceives multipolar systems as stable because they encompass a larger number of autonomous actors, giving rise to more potential alliance partners. This is seen as pacifying because it is essential to counterbalancing a would-be aggressor, as shifting alliances can occur only when there are multiple power centers (Deutsch and Singer 1964).

Abstract deductions and historical analogies can lead to contradictory conclusions, as the logic underlying these three inconsistent interpretations illustrates. The future will determine which of these rival theories is the most accurate.

ble. But if the past truly is a guide to the future, the distribution of global power will exert a strong influence on the kind of global system the world will experience.

The preservation of peace by states aggregating power in order to balance power has a rather checkered history. In the long run, the resulting alliances and distributions of power have failed to avert a breakdown of world order. The great powers have persistently been drawn into wars this century by the collapse of the balance of power in either Europe or East Asia or both. Yet history also suggests that the prospects for peace in unipolar, bipolar, and multipolar systems depend on other factors as well. Negotiated arms agreements designed to change the existing balance of power are a critical component that could alter the tendency of multipolar systems to culminate in widespread warfare.

482

THE REALIST ROAD TO
SECURITY THROUGH
ALLIANCES, THE
BALANCE OF POWER,
AND ARMS CONTROL

● ● ●

CONTROLLING MILITARY POWER THROUGH ARMS AGREEMENTS

Liberal reformers have often attacked the theory that power can be balanced with power to preserve world order. They have advocated instead the biblical prescription that nations should beat their swords into plowshares. The destructiveness and dispersion of today's weapons have inspired many people once again to take this tenet of liberal theory seriously. But this approach is not solely a liberal preserve. Most realists also see arms control as a way of influencing the international distribution of military power in ways that promote peace and individual states' national security. In fact, most policymakers who have negotiated arms control agreements have been realists who perceived these treaties as a prudent tool to promote their countries' security. At times, they have been the leading advocates of arms control to adjust their states' military power relative to the rivals', and to help maintain the balance of power.

Controlling Weapons: Approaches

It will be useful to review the historical record of negotiators' efforts to preserve the global distribution of weapons and their uses. This will allow us to assess the implications of such negotiations for peace. However, two concepts must first be distinguished. Many people incorrectly assume that the terms "arms control" and "disarmament" are synonymous. **Arms control** refers to agreements designed to regulate arms levels either by limiting their growth or by restricting how they may be used. This is a far less ambitious endeavor than **disarmament,** which seeks to reduce or eliminate weapons.

arms control multilateral or bilateral agreements to contain arms races by setting limits on the number and types of weapons states are permitted.

> Arms control can be implicit or explicit, formal or informal, and unilateral, bilateral, or multilateral. It is a process of jointly managing the weapons-acquisition processes of the participant states in the hope of reducing the risk of war. . . . Arms control [refers] to formal agreements imposing significant restrictions or limitations on the weapons or security policies of the signatories.
>
> Disarmament rests on a fundamentally different philosophical premise than arms control. It envisions the drastic reduction or elimination of all weapons, looking toward the eradication of war itself. Disarmament is based on the notion that if there were no more weapons there would be no more war. This is a compelling proposition, with enough truth to give it a very long life in the history of thought about war and peace. Arms control, on the other hand, accepts the existence of weapons and the possibility of conflict. Contrary to popular impression, it is not necessarily about reducing arms levels. Arms control attempts to stabilize the status quo and to manage conflict, to encourage peaceful resolution of disputes, and limit the resort to military force. Although many visceral opponents would be shocked at the thought, arms control is fundamentally a conservative enterprise. Disarmament, by contrast, is a radical one. Disarmament seeks to overturn the status quo; arms control works to perpetuate it. (Kruzel 1991, 249)

Bilateral agreements should also be differentiated from **multilateral agreements.** Because the former are agreements between only two countries, they are often easier to negotiate and to enforce than are the latter, which are agreements among three or more countries. Negotiating a multilateral agreement, simultaneously binding on many states, poses many obstacles because states' security interests are very different, as are the domestic processes by which governments approve international agreements. As a result, the record of bilateral agreements differs from that of multilateral agreements with respect to both arms control and disarmament.

Multilateral Diplomacy: The Disarmament and Arms Control Record

It is hardly a novel idea that it is possible to control war by reducing the world's arsenals. Yet until very recently, one of the few constants in the changing international system has been the repetition with which states had advocated disarmament but failed to implement it. True, some countries in the past did reach agreements to reduce their armaments levels. For example, the Chinese states in 600 B.C.E. formed a disarmament league that produced a peaceful century for the league's members, and in the Rush-Bagot Agreement of 1818 Canada and the United States disarmed the Great Lakes. Disarmament proposals also figured prominently in the League of Nations' abortive World Disarmament Conference of 1932 and rather continuously in the United Nations since 1946 (especially in its many "special sessions" on disarmament). Nonetheless, these kinds of achievements have been relatively rare in history. Many more countries have raced to expand their arsenals than have tried to cut them. Most disarmament is involuntary, the product of reductions imposed by the victors in the immediate aftermath of a war, as when the Allied powers attempted (unsuccessfully) to permanently disarm a defeated Germany after World War I.

In contrast with disarmament, there are many historical examples of arms control efforts. As early as the eleventh century, the Second Lateran Council prohibited the use of crossbows in fighting. The 1868 St. Petersburg Declaration prohibited the use of explosive bullets. In 1899 and 1907, International Peace Conferences at the Hague restricted the use of some weapons and prohibited others. The leaders of the United States, Britain, Japan, France, and Italy signed treaties at the Washington Naval Conferences (1921–1922) agreeing to adjust the relative tonnage of their fleets.

The post–World War II period saw a variety of new arms control proposals. The **Baruch Plan** (1946) called for the creation of a United Nations Atomic Development Authority, which would have placed atomic energy under an international authority to ensure its use for only peaceful purposes. However, the great powers never approved the proposal. The **Rapacki Plan** (1957) to prevent the deployment of nuclear weapons in Central Europe also failed.

Nonetheless, leaders have made recurrent efforts to resolve differences so formal arms control agreements might be realized. Prominent among them were the arms control summit meetings of the great powers, of which those between the United States and former Soviet Union—the world's nuclear superpowers—were the most frequent. Summit talks between the Cold War antagonists began in July 1955, when U.S. President Eisenhower and Soviet leader Nikita Khrushchev met in Geneva. Among other things, these summits sought and often resulted in an improved atmosphere for serious arms control negotiations. In addition, they paved the way for the ambitious agreements that were reached as the Cold War ended to cement a new world order based on a reduced and stable military power balance.

484

THE REALIST ROAD TO
SECURITY THROUGH
ALLIANCES, THE
BALANCE OF POWER,
AND ARMS CONTROL

verification processes
through which signatories'
adherence to arms control
and disarmament
agreements is confirmed.

Multilateral negotiations on particular issues have also taken on the character of institutionalized efforts to reach arms control agreements. Nine examples illustrate their range and breadth:

- The **Mutual and Balanced Force Reductions (MBFR)** talks were conducted from 1973 to 1988 in an effort to realize force reductions between the blocs dividing Europe. Although they did not produce a treaty, during the Cold War they sustained a "consensus that arms control negotiations are a necessary component of alliance defense strategy" and "were helpful in preparing for the negotiations on Conventional Armed Forces in Europe (CFE)" (Hallenbeck and Shaver 1991).

- The **Comprehensive Test Ban (CTB)** negotiations have been held periodically since the late 1950s in an effort to reach agreement on a treaty banning all nuclear explosions. The Reagan administration broke off negotiations in 1982, citing **verification** obstacles to public inspection of tests and the need to test nuclear weapons as long as deterrence rested on them. Nonetheless, negotiations on verification protocols resumed in November 1987, and new protocols were added to the existing Threshold Test Ban Treaty and the Peaceful Nuclear Explosions Treaty. In September 1996 the new draft Comprehensive Test Ban Treaty (CTBT) banned all nuclear explosions was opened for signature, but India and Pakistan refused to sign it and conducted nuclear tests in May 1998.

- The Conventional Force Reductions in Europe negotiations, which began in 1989, produced the **Conventional Forces in Europe (CFE)** treaty, which entered into force in late 1992. The CFE set ceilings on five categories of conventional arms (battle tanks, armored combat vehicles, artillery pieces, combat aircraft, and attack helicopters) for the thirty countries in an area stretching from the Atlantic to the Urals (the ATTU zone). Inspections in 1995 and 1996 ensured that the ceilings agreed to were not exceeded, which prepared the way for the subsequent 1997 "Basic Elements" document. This document is a "cornerstone" for reducing arms and increasing security and transparency in Europe, and for formally welcoming the new members of the enlarged NATO in 1999.

- The **Organization for Security and Cooperation in Europe (OSCE)** emerged from the Conference on Security and Cooperation in Europe (CSCE), which began in Helsinki in 1973. Soon after, it became the leading multilateral institution for managing the transformation of Europe from a system of counterpoised alliances (NATO and the Warsaw Pact) to one based on common principles stretching across the entire continent and North America. Formalized in 1995, the fifty-three-member OSCE administers a Conflict Prevention Center and aims at a leadership role in preventive diplomacy, post-conflict rehabilitation, and regional cooperation to expand the military, economic, democratization, and human rights provisions of the 1975 Helsinki accords. In 1996 missions were undertaken in eleven countries.

- The signatories of the historic 1968 **Nuclear Nonproliferation Treaty (NPT)** have held Review Conferences every five years to discuss compliance and enforcement programs. In 1995 twenty-five years after the NPT entered into force, the review conference agreed to continue the treaty indefinitely; the 186 parties identified objectives on seven issues (universality,

nonproliferation, nuclear disarmament, nuclear-weapon-free zones, security assurances, safeguards, and peaceful uses of nuclear energy). Yet doubts remain about the NPT's ability to contain the future spread of nuclear weapons, especially in light of the May 1998 nuclear testing by India and Pakistan (see Chapter 13).

nonproliferation the absence of the development of nuclear weapons or technology by countries that do not already possess them.

- The **Conference on Disarmament (CD)** emerged from the bilateral U.S.–Soviet negotiations that began in 1976 to ban the production, stockpiling, and use of chemical weapons. In 1981 those closed negotiations became a part of the UN's arms control forum in Geneva. The sixty-one-member CD can be given credit for producing the 1990 U.S.-Soviet Chemical Weapons Destruction Agreement, for starting negotiations on the 1996 Comprehensive Test Ban Treaty (CTBT), and for lobbying on behalf of a comprehensive and worldwide multilateral chemical weapons disarmament convention and a worldwide ban on the production of fissile materials for use in nuclear weapons (the Fissile Material Cut-Off Treaty [FMCT]).

- The Review Conferences of the **Biological Weapons Convention (BWC)** have convened periodically since the 1972 Bacteriological (Biological) and Toxin Weapons Convention (TWC) was ratified in 1972. The TWC was the first multilateral arms control agreement aimed at prohibiting the development of an entire category of weapons of mass destruction. It banned the development, production, stockpiling, acquisition, or retention of biological and toxin weapons but did not specifically ban their use. That had already been done by the 1925 Geneva Protocol for the Prohibition of the Use in War of Asphyxiating, Poisonous, or Other Gases and of Bacteriological Methods of Warfare. The two instruments were seen as complementing each other. From these emanated the 1993 **Chemical Weapons Convention (CWC).** Signed by 164 countries as of January 1998, the CWC calls for the destruction of all chemical weapons by the year 2003. It is administered by the Organization for the Prevention of Chemical Weapons (OPCU) in the Hague.

Some states see their security improved by voluntary reductions in their arsenals of weapons, as Russia and most NATO countries did in the 1990s when they chose to make deep disarmament cuts. More often, disarmament is forced and enforced by external powers' interventions and sanctions. Pictured here are the remains of some of Iraq's pre-Gulf War chemical weapons arsenal. The mustard gas bombs at Muthanna, Iraq, were uncovered and destroyed by a United Nations inspection team. The Chemical Weapons Convention (CWC), signed by 164 states in early 1998, requires existing stockpiles of these lethal weapons to be destroyed by 2003.

486

THE REALIST ROAD TO
SECURITY THROUGH
ALLIANCES, THE
BALANCE OF POWER,
AND ARMS CONTROL

- The **Missile Technology Control Regime (MTCR)** is an informal arrangement among the world's most advanced suppliers of missile-related equipment to control the export of ballistic and cruise missiles and missile-related technologies. Initially designed to deter the spread of nuclear-capable missiles, the MTCR was expanded in 1993 to prevent the diffusion of missile systems for delivering chemical and biological weapons. The regime, created by seven founding countries in 1987, has since expanded to include twenty-five additional states. Following U.S. President Bill Clinton's advocacy in 1993, the 1994 Stockholm MTCR plenary meeting sought to transform the export regime into a set of rules commanding universal adherence. However, the MTCR currently relies on voluntary compliance and is neither an international treaty nor a legally binding agreement. Its weaknesses were illustrated in 1993 when the United States determined that China, which had earlier pledged to abide by the terms of the MTCR had transferred missile components to Pakistan in violation of its provisions.

- The **United Nations Register of Conventional Arms** is the first international effort to gather official information on the weapons trade since the League of Nations attempted to compile a similar list. Implemented in 1992, the register invites states to submit information voluntarily about their trade in various categories of major weapons. Each of the world's top suppliers has submitted reports. However, the UN's members regularly submit yearly reports.

Table 15.2 (pages 488–489) summarizes the major multilateral arms control agreements reached since World War II. These agreements limit the range of permissible actions and weapons systems available to states. They have also helped to slow the global arms race and paved the way for still more ambitious proposals. In addition, they contribute important confidence-building measures that reduce the political tensions underlying the urge to arm.

Bilateral Diplomacy and the Control of Nuclear Arms: Superpower Agreements

Throughout the Cold War, Soviet and U.S. arms control efforts understandably focused on ways to lessen the threat of nuclear war. These efforts intensified with the disintegration of the Soviet Union. Table 15.3 (pages 490–491) summarizes the results of these negotiations, listing the major bilateral arms control agreements between the two superpowers since 1960.

To these we might add an indeterminate number of tacit understandings about the level and use of weapons to which the two powers agreed. These understandings did not achieve the status of formal agreements but were observed by the two superpowers nonetheless. They included occasional pledges to refrain from the offensive use of nuclear arsenals, as indicated by President Carter's and Soviet Foreign Minister Andrei Gromyko's promise that their states would never be the first to use nuclear weapons in any conflict. Such commitments were not legally binding. Indeed, NATO based its "flexible response" strategy on the right to retaliate with nuclear weapons against an attack. More recently, in 1993, Russia's new strategic doctrine reserved the right to use nuclear weapons in the event of an attack. Nonetheless, these understandings undeniably help enforce great-power respect for the "no-first-use doctrine" (as do China's vocal support for the same principle and the 1995 agreement between

China and Russia to stop aiming nuclear weapons at each other). Such informal rules have paved the way to creating greater institutional controls over the use of strategic weapons.

SALT. Of the superpowers' explicit, formal arms control agreements, the two so-called **Strategic Arms Limitation Talks (SALT)** agreements were precedent-setting. SALT I, signed in 1972, consisted of: (1) a treaty restricting the deployment of antiballistic missile defense systems to equal and very low levels, and (2) a five-year interim accord on strategic offensive arms that restricted intercontinental ballistic missile (ICBM) and submarine-launched ballistic missile (SLBM) launchers. The SALT I agreement was essentially a confidence-building, "stopgap" step toward a longer-term, more comprehensive treaty. The 1979 SALT II agreement, then the most extensive arms control agreement ever negotiated, sought to realize that aim. The agreement called for placing an eventual overall ceiling for each superpower of 2,250 on the number of ICBM launchers, SLBM launchers, heavy bombers, and air-to-surface ballistic missiles (ASBMs) with ranges over six hundred kilometers. These limitations reduced by as many as 8,500 the total number of strategic nuclear weapons that the United States and the Soviet Union would have possessed by 1985 without the agreement.

The obstacles to arms control were illustrated by the problems that SALT II encountered. The U.S. Senate deferred ratification of the SALT II treaty indefinitely following the 1979 Soviet invasion of Afghanistan. Although both superpowers continued to abide by the basic terms of SALT II through the early 1980s, the "final result as embodied in SALT II was a clear disappointment to the hopes generated in the early 1970s. In essence, SALT II failed to achieve actual arms reductions. Its basic fault was that it would have permitted substantial growth in the strategic forces of both sides" (U.S. Department of State 1983).

START. Against the background of what they labeled "the failed promise of SALT," U.S. leaders set the agenda for new approaches to strategic arms control. At this time, the fear inspired by the relentless arms race and frustration with the lack of progress in the arms control process gave the idea of a nuclear freeze on the testing, production, and deployment of nuclear weapons increased momentum on both sides of the Atlantic. Freeze advocates were motivated by the view, expressed by one realist U.S. policymaker, that it was a "delusion" to see "nuclear weapons as just one more weapon, like any other weapon, only more destructive" (Kennan 1982). To help dispel this delusion, the American Catholic bishops composed a widely read Pastoral Letter that called for an immediate end to the arms race. It also asserted that the deliberate initiation of nuclear warfare, on however restricted a scale, could not be morally justified. As a policy proposal, a total freeze envisioned a path to disarmament that would first stop production of new weapons systems before starting to reduce the existing ones. This vision was premised on the belief that both sides' deterrent capabilities were invulnerable and that a freeze would keep them that way. Once the arms race was curtailed, it was reasoned, arms reductions could then be considered.

The **nuclear freeze movement** in the early 1980s helped set the stage for the progress that occurred in the early 1990s when the Cold War no longer constrained negotiations. In June 1982 the Reagan administration initiated a new

TABLE 15.2 Major Multilateral Arms Control Treaties since 1945

Date	Agreement	Number of Parties (1998)	Principal Objectives
1959	Antarctic Treaty	43	Prevents the military use of the Antarctic, including the testing of nuclear weapons
1963	Limited Test Ban Treaty	124	Prohibits nuclear weapons in the atmosphere, outer space, and under water
1967	Outer Space Treaty	100	Outlaws the use of outer space for testing or stationing any weapons, as well as for military maneuvers
1967	Treaty of Tlatelolco	33	Creates the Latin America Nuclear Free Zone by prohibiting the testing and possession of nuclear facilities for military purposes
1968	Nuclear Nonproliferation Treaty	186	Prevents the transfer of nuclear weapons and nuclear-weapons-production technologies to nonnuclear-weapon states
1971	Seabed Treaty	93	Prohibits the deployment of weapons of mass destruction and nuclear weapons on the seabed beyond a twelve-mile coastal limit
1972	Biological Weapons Convention	140	Prohibits the production and storage of biological toxins; calls for the destruction of biological weapons stocks
1977	Environmental Modifications Convention (Enmod Convention)	64	Bans the use of technologies that could alter the earth's weather patterns, ocean currents, ozone layer, or ecology
1980	Protection of Nuclear Material Convention	57	Obligates protection of peaceful nuclear material during transport on ships or aircraft
1981	Inhumane Weapons Convention	63	Prohibits the use of such weapons as fragmentation bombs, incendiary weapons, booby traps, and mines to which civilians could be exposed
1985	South Pacific Nuclear Free Zone (Roratonga) Treaty	12	Prohibits the testing, acquisition, or deployment of nuclear weapons in the South Pacific

round of arms talks aimed at significantly reducing both superpowers' strategic arsenals. Termed the **Strategic Arms Reduction Talks (START),** the initiative resumed the SALT process, but expanded its agenda by seeking to remove inequalities that had developed in the superpowers' weapons systems.

The Post-Cold War Disarmament Race. In September 1991, responding to widespread complaints that the START treaty barely initiated the arms reductions possible now that the threat of a Soviet attack had vanished, President Bush declared that the United States must seize "the historic opportunity now before us." Describing the Soviet Union as "no longer a realistic threat," he called

TABLE 15.2 *Continued*

Date	Agreement	Number of Parties (1998)	Principal Objectives
1986	Confidence-Building and Security-Building Measures and Disarmament in Europe (CDE) Agreement (Stockholm Accord)	29	Requires prior notification and mandatory on-site inspection of conventional military exercises in Europe
1987	Missile Technology Control Regime (MTCR)	32	Restricts export of ballistic missiles and production facilities
1990 1992	Conventional Forces in Europe (CFE)	30	Places limits on five categories of weapons in Europe and lowers force levels
1990	Confidence- and Security-Building Measures (CSBM) Agreement	53	Improves measures for exchanging detailed information on weapons, forces, and military exercises
1991	UN Register of Conventional Arms	88	Calls on all states to submit information on seven categories of major weapons exported or imported during the previous year
1992	Open Skies Treaty	27	Permits flights by unarmed surveillance aircraft over the territory of the signatory states
1993	Chemical Weapons Convention (CWC)	164	Requires all stockpiles of chemical weapons to be destroyed within ten years
1995	Protocol to the Inhumane Weapons Convention	135	Bans some types of laser weapons that cause permanent loss of eyesight
1995	Wassenaar Export-Control Treaty	28	Regulates transfers of sensitive dual-use technologies to nonparticipating countries
1996	ASEAN Nuclear Free Zone Treaty	10	Prevents signatories in Southeast Asia from making, possessing, storing, or testing nuclear weapons
1996	Comprehensive Test Ban Treaty (CTBT)	45	Bans all testing of nuclear weapons
1996	Treaty of Pelindaba	48	Creates an African nuclear-weapon-free zone
1997	Treaty of Bangkok	10	Creates a nuclear-weapon-free zone in Southeast Asia
1998	Antipersonnel Landmines Treaty (APLT)	100	Bans the production and export of landmines and pledges plans to remove them

SOURCE: Stockholm International Peace Research Institute, *SIPRI Yearbooks;* Arms Control Association Fact files.

long-range bombers off twenty-four-hour alert, canceled plans to deploy the long-range MX on rail cars, and offered to negotiate sharp reductions in the most dangerous kinds of globe-spanning missiles with the Soviets. Bush also proposed removing short-range nuclear weapons from U.S. bases in Europe and Asia and from U.S. Navy vessels around the world. However, Bush warned that the proposed U.S. cuts might not be made if the Soviet Union did not respond in kind. This set the stage for a showdown on a new race to *dis*arm.

The fragmentation of the Soviet Union shortly thereafter and the improved political relationship between Russia and the United States removed the major barriers to disarmament. Instructively, the disarmament process began first

TABLE 15.3 Major Bilateral Arms Control Agreements between the United States and the Soviet Union/Russia

Date	Agreement	Principal Objectives
1963	Hot Line Agreement	Establishes a direct radio and telegraph communication system between the governments to be used in times of crisis
1971	Hot Line Modernization Agreement	Puts a hot line satellite communication system into operation
1971	Nuclear Accidents Agreement	Creates a process for notification of accidental or unauthorized detonation of a nuclear weapon; creates safeguards to prevent accidents
1972	Antiballistic Missile (ABM) Treaty (SALT I)	Restricts the deployment of antiballistic missile defense systems to one area and prohibits the development of a space-based ABM system
1972	SALT I Interim Agreement on Offensive Strategic Arms	Freezes the superpowers' total number of ballistic missile launchers for a five-year period
1972	Protocol to the Interim Agreement	Clarifies and strengthens prior limits on strategic arms
1972	High Seas Agreement	Creates procedures to prevent crisis-provoking incidents on the oceans
1973	Agreement on the Prevention of Nuclear War	Requires superpowers to consult if a threat of nuclear war emerges
1974	Threshold Test Ban Treaty with Protocol	Restricts the underground testing of nuclear weapons above a yield of 150 kilotons
1974	Protocol to the ABM Treaty	Reduces permitted ABMs to one site
1976	Treaty on the Limitation of Underground Explosions for Peaceful Purposes	Broadens the ban on underground nuclear testing stipulated in the 1974 Threshold Test Ban Treaty; requires on-site observers of tests with yields exceeding 150 kilotons
1977	Convention on the Prohibition of Military or Any Other Hostile Use of Environmental Modification Techniques	Bans weapons that threaten to modify the planetary ecology

through unilateral proposals and gained momentum only later through incremental accords painstakingly negotiated at the bargaining table. But when disarmament agreements finally came, they did so rapidly.

On January 25, 1992, new Russian President Boris Yeltsin declared that his country "no longer consider[ed] the United States our potential adversary." He then announced the decision to stop targeting U.S. cities with nuclear missiles, clearing the way for another U.S. response. Four days later, in his State of the Union Address, President Bush announced a series of unilateral arms cuts. Among them were the decision to suspend production of the B-2 bomber, halt development of the Midgetman mobile nuclear missile, and cease purchases of advanced cruise missiles. In addition, Bush canceled production of warheads used aboard Trident submarine missiles.

Yeltsin did not wait for his scheduled summit meeting with Bush at Camp David to reply to this initiative. Within hours, he recommended that the two powers reduce their nuclear arsenals to only two thousand to twenty-five hundred warheads each—far below the cuts called for in the START agreement and almost 50 percent greater than the reductions Bush had earlier proposed. In other statements, Yeltsin announced his intention to reduce Russian military

TABLE 15.3 *Continued*

Date	Agreement	Principal Objectives
1979	SALT II Treaty (never ratified)	Places ceilings on the number of strategic delivery vehicles, MIRVed missiles, long-range bombers, cruise missiles, ICBMs, and other weapons; restrains testing
1987	Nuclear Risk Reduction Centers Agreement	Creates facilities in each national capital to manage a nuclear crisis
1987	Intermediate-Range Nuclear Force (INF) Treaty	Eliminates U.S. and USSR ground-level intermediate-and shorter-range nuclear weapons in Europe and permits on-site inspection to verify compliance
1990	Chemical Weapons Destruction Agreement	Ends production of chemical weapons; commits cutting inventories of chemical weapons in half by the end of 1999 and to five thousand metric tons by the end of 2002
1990	Nuclear Testing Talks	New protocol improves verification procedures of prior treaties
1991	START (Strategic Arms Reduction Treaty)	Reduces arsenals of strategic nuclear weapons by about 30 percent
1992	START I Protocol	Holds Russia, Belarus, Ukraine, and Kazakhstan to strategic weapons reductions agreed to in START by the former USSR
1992	Open Skies Agreement	Permits unarmed surveillance aircraft to fly over the United States, Russia, and their allies
1993	START II	Cuts the deployed U.S. and Russian strategic nuclear warheads on each side to between 3,000 and 3,500 by the year 2003; bans multiple-warhead land-based missiles
1995	HEU Agreement	Reduces risk of diversion or theft of nuclear-weapon-grade highly enriched uranium (HEU) recovered from dismantled nuclear warheads through government purchase and use as civilian reactor fuel
1997	Fissile Material Cut-Off Treaty (FMCT)	Bans production of fissile material for nuclear weapons or other nuclear explosive devices

spending to less than one-seventh of the previous year's allocation and to trim the Russian army in half. To emphasize the new climate of Russian–American friendship, Yeltsin proposed creating a joint U.S.–Russian global defense system and a new international agency to oversee the orderly reduction of nuclear weapons. He also proposed eliminating strategic nuclear weapons entirely by the year 2000.

Even in this hopeful climate of reciprocated reductions, obstacles remained to dismantling the weapons with which each superpower had threatened the existence of the other. The differences centered on where the cuts should be made. Bush called for the elimination of all land-based strategic missiles with multiple warheads **(MIRVs),** the category in which Russia was strongest. But on submarine-launched missiles (SLBMs), where the United States had the advantage, Bush refused to accept reductions beyond one-third and fought the Russian quest for across-the-board cuts.

The uncertain future of Russia's government further impeded progress. Even more problematic were the nuclear arsenals of other former Soviet republics. Although Ukraine, Kazakhstan, and Belarus signed the May 1992 Lisbon protocol to the START agreement, pledging their elimination of all nuclear

MIRVs an acronym for Multiple Independently Targeted Reentry Vehicles, which make it possible to attack many targets with nuclear warheads from a single ballistic missile.

492

THE REALIST ROAD TO
SECURITY THROUGH
ALLIANCES, THE
BALANCE OF POWER,
AND ARMS CONTROL

weapons on their territory by 1999 and their willingness to join the NPT as nonnuclear states, that full cooperation remained much in doubt. In fact, it was not forthcoming until several years later when they began to dismantle their strategic weapons in compliance with START.

However, even while this progress was occurring, the superpowers continued their efforts to modernize their arsenals. The former Cold War enemies planned to be heavily armed after their cuts were complete. The lack of realistic targets and the technological breakthrough of miniaturization made most of the discarded weapons obsolete. The former adversaries continued their armament modernization programs and were still militarily preparing to project power in the global arena, even with the planned cuts and while the United States was assisting the Russians in destroying their strategic arsenals.

Yet, just when it appeared that the disarmament process might lose momentum, a new breakthrough was achieved. At the June 1992 Washington summit, Presidents Yeltsin and Bush made the surprise announcement that Russia and the United States would make additional deep cuts in their strategic arsenals. The formal Joint Understanding accord to the START agreement called for a 60 percent reduction of the two powers' combined total nuclear arsenals from about fifteen thousand warheads to sixty-five hundred by the year 2003 (see Figure 15.1). Even more dramatically, this so-called "Follow-on" treaty to START reshaped the strategic landscape. Signed in January 1993, START II not only cut by three-fifths the number of actual warheads in each side's strategic arsenal that had been projected under START, but it also altered drastically the kinds of weapons in each country's arsenal. Under the agreement, Russia and the United States would give up all the multiple warheads on their land-based ICBM missiles. Specifically, by banning all MIRVed ICBMs and reducing SLBM warheads to no more than 1,750, the new agreement "promised a significant enhancement of U.S.-Russian strategic stability since these missiles have long been seen as the most threatening because of their preemptive capabilities" (Keeny 1993).

If adhered to, the Follow-on START agreement could reduce the chances of a war of annihilation by banning the nuclear weapons that both powers would be most likely to use in a preemptive strike, with the U.S. inventory reduced by the year 2003 to 3,500 strategic warheads and Russia's to 3,296. The agreement would leave them with only those weapons they would be likely to use in a retaliatory strike. By reducing the probability of a nuclear war, the agreement thus signals the potential dawning of a new era. As President Bush put it, "With this agreement the nuclear nightmare recedes more and more for ourselves, for our children, and for our grandchildren." President Yeltsin concurred, noting that, "we are departing from the ominous parity where each country was exerting every effort to keep up."

The Problematic Future of Arms Control

As promising as some of the great powers' recent arms control agreements might appear, the history of their past negotiations testifies to the many obstacles to arms control agreements that exist. It also attests to the extent to which they are dependent on prior improvement in adversaries' political relations. That history raises questions as to whether arms control agreements can restrain the arms race in the long run. After all, these obstacles could resurface in a new multipolar system characterized by rivalry among five or more great powers and a potentially large number of new nuclear-weapon states.

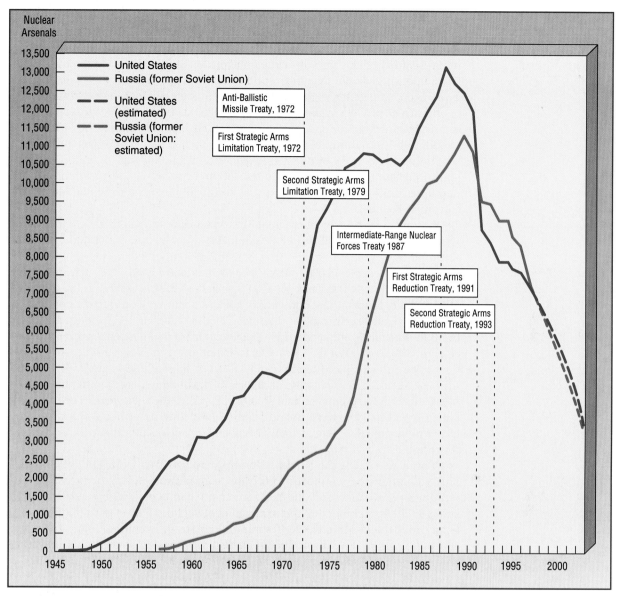

FIGURE 15.1

Countdown to Strategic Parity: The Negotiated End of the U.S.-Russian Arms Race

After years of rapid buildup of their nuclear weapons, the United States and (now) Russia have agreed to cut dramatically the size of their nuclear arsenals (warheads in their stockpiles).

SOURCE: Based on data from Worldwatch data diskette, Arms Control Association Fact Files and *SIPRI Yearbooks*.

Until recently, international agreements controlled only obsolete armaments or ones that the parties to the agreements had little incentive for developing in the first place. Do states purposely leave the most threatening problems outside negotiations and seek only to control the weapons they no longer deem necessary to their national security? Indeed, does the record demonstrate that states rarely take arms control seriously when they perceive their survival

494

THE REALIST ROAD TO
SECURITY THROUGH
ALLIANCES, THE
BALANCE OF POWER,
AND ARMS CONTROL

to be at stake? Many trends point to the tendency for more states to cling tenaciously to the realist belief that preparations for war are required than to accept the liberal belief that armament *reductions* can increase national and international security. The limits to arms control are illustrated by several activities that undermine confidence in the ability of arms control to lower states' capacities for causing death in the twenty-first century. Consider first that states disregard arms control conventions, even some states that were signatories to the treaties banning the weapons they later either illegally developed or used in war. In 1997, for example, the United States stockpiled 31,500 tons and Russia stockpiled 40,000 tons of chemical weapons, and additional chemical and biological production programs were secretly under way in Iran, Iraq, Libya and perhaps twenty other countries—despite the global ban on their manufacture (Sivard 1996, 26–27).

Second, the testing of nuclear weapons also speaks to the tendency of states to make improving their weaponry a priority over controlling it. The seven known nuclear states conducted 2,058 nuclear explosions between 1945 and May 1998 *(SIPRI Yearbooks)*, an average of one test almost every nine days. The pace did not slow as a result of the partial test ban treaty of 1963, which prohibited atmospheric and underwater testing but not underground explosions. In fact, three-fourths of all nuclear tests took place after the ban went into effect in 1963. Disclosures by the U.S. government in December 1993 revealed 204 previously unannounced secret nuclear-weapons tests above the 1,030 officially reported tests between 1945 and 1994. Some of these resulted in accidental releases of radioactive gases into the atmosphere. Energy Secretary Hazel R. O'Leary described the arms race cult by lamenting that "[w]e were shrouded and clouded in an atmosphere of secrecy that compromised safety and environmental considerations. . . . I would call it repression."

Third, recall that the Nuclear Nonproliferation Treaty (NPT) of 1968 obligates the nonnuclear countries to refrain from manufacturing or acquiring nuclear weapons. Adherence to the agreement has been widespread, with 186 states in 1998 members of the arms control regime. However, India and Pakistan broke the barriers the NPT sought to create by becoming nuclear-weapon states, Israelis capable of producing nuclear weapons on short notice, and Iraq, Iran, Libya and North Korea remain outside the treaty and are seeking to become nuclear-weapon states. In addition, even the existing nuclear states have sought to develop ever more imposing arsenals at the same time they were reducing the size of their arsenals, as indicated by the fact that while the United States began eliminating some of its warheads, since 1990 it increased the number of Trident II warheads by 960 (*Harper's,* March 1996, 13). What is more, it is transparent that the superpowers have pursued invention of new technologies to create substitute deterrence forces for the previous generation of banned weapons. For example, the START agreements would leave the United States and Russia defenseless against a handful of nuclear missiles launched in an accidental or unauthorized strike or by a radical regime such as Iran, Iraq, North Korea, or Libya. Because the menace of nuclear proliferation is still very real and the capacity to use these weapons could easily be acquired by ruthless terrorist groups, states' efforts to guarantee their citizens safety from such attacks have persisted: U.S. ballistic-missile defense programs to provide a shield with hit-and-destroy lasers in space are being pursued, despite the fact that these violate the ABM treaty (Lewis and Postol 1997). Given their historic appetite for expanded strategic inventories, it is understandable that the nonnuclear members of the NPT question why they should remain restrained while the existing nuclear states refuse to destroy their nuclear arsenals.

Fourth, consider the sobering lessons suggested by the SALT agreements. SALT I did freeze the number of strategic launchers in operation or under construction but did not cover strategic bombers or prevent the kinds of qualitative improvements that would make quantitative thresholds meaningless. For instance, the superpowers deployed four times as many MIRVs on missiles in 1977 as when the SALT talks began, even though SALT I froze the number of delivery vehicles at the superpowers' disposal. Perhaps this troublesome outcome led Herbert Scoville, a former deputy director of the U.S. Central Intelligence Agency, to note at the time of the signing of SALT I that "arms control negotiations [were] rapidly becoming the best excuse for escalating rather than toning down the arms race." The pattern revealed in this and other developments prompted one former U.S. policymaker to conclude that "three decades of U.S.-Soviet negotiations to limit arms competition have done little more than to codify the arms race" (Gelb 1979). This grim conclusion is validated by the existence in 1996 of eight nuclear powers whose combined strategic and tactical nuclear inventories numbered "at least 40,000 weapons" (Burroughs and Cabasso 1996, 41).

Fifth, some types of weapons have been globally recognized as counterproductive and dangerous, yet the international community has proven weak, slow, and in effective in mobilizing sufficient clout to ban them. Consider the case of **antipersonnel landmines (APLs).** In 1994, not a single state would endorse a prohibition on these deadly weapons. Over 100 to 300 million are believed to be scattered on the territory of more than seventy countries (with another 100 million in stockpiles). These are weapons of mass destruction that cannot discriminate between combatant soldiers and civilians. In the mid-1990s there was about one mine for every 50 humans on earth, and each year they killed or maimed more than twenty-six thosand people—almost all of them civilians (see Map 15.2). It took a peace activist, Jody Williams, to organize the International Campaign to Ban Land Mines that proposed a 1997 treaty, signed by more than one hundred countries in Geneva, that requires the removal of those landmines and bans the production of new ones. For her efforts, Williams was awarded the Nobel Peace Prize. But the Oslo treaty was stubbornly revisited by the United States, Russia, and other great powers until the coalition of NGO peace groups mounted sufficient pressure in world public opinion to coerce their consent to this epic convention. If adhered to, the challenge of enforcing the ban and the removal of APLs could prove staggering (the United Nations estimates they cost less than one dollar to produce but $700-3000 each to remove, so the global cleanup bill could exceed $30 billion and one thousand years at current work rates. Hence, as with other arms control and disarmament programs, delay, disregard, and inaction seem to be part and parcel of crusades to outlaw inhumane weapons that defense planners claim are necessary for national security. And it appears that the smaller and more transportable the weapon, the tougher the task of implementing controls. The example of biological weapons illustrates the principle: the low cost and ease of secretly producing lethal bacteria, viruses, and other microbes (a kitchen lab can make enough to wipe out a city) accounts for the world's inability to stop the thirteen countries suspected of trying to develop biological arsenals (*Christian Science Monitor,* May 21, 1997, 3).

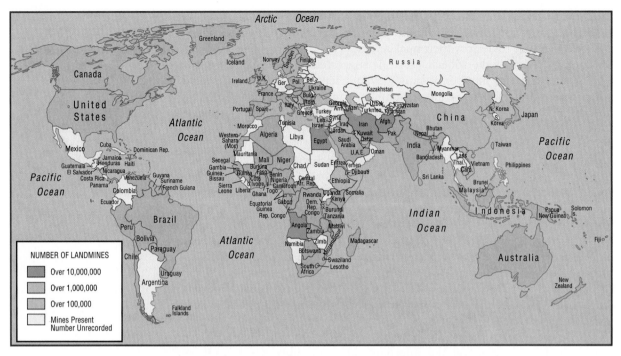

MAP 15.2

Can Conventions Police the Global Plague of Landmines?

The world is littered with 100 to 300 million antipersonnel landmines (APLs) planted in the soil of seventy countries, according to UN estimates. These weapons are lethal: in Cambodia 10 million landmines cause the amputation of three hundred limbs each month, and in Afghanistan they left sixty thousand children in need of artificial limbs (D. Smith, 1997, 29). The International Red Cross estimated that in Vietnam one of every 334 inhabitants were amputees. Militaries insist that landmines are necessary for defense, even though the victims are nearly all civilians. In 1997, over staunch opposition at first from the United States, more than one hundred countries joined the negotiations for a new treaty banning these inhumane weapons. The obstacles to enforcement are high, however.

SOURCE: Sivard (1996), 15.

arms control regimes rules accepted by the parties to treaties to prohibit the production, deployment, sale, or use of particular categories of weapons.

Finally, note that the various **arms control regimes** established to control the *export* of particular categories of weapons (such as the 1978 Nuclear Suppliers Group, the 1987 Missile Technology Control Regime [MTCR], and the 1998 European Union Dual-Use Regulation regime) are simply not very effective. The arms trade in illegal weapons is active and growing despite the barriers posed to this traffic. In 1997, for example, it was discovered that China had sold Pakistan the illegal material to build a missile plant; export controls slowed but failed to stop Iran's push for nuclear weapons capability; and Iraq's import of materials for making weapons of mass destruction showed that blocking arms trade to prevent proliferation "will be difficult if not impossible" (*Economist*, April 12, 1997, 79–82). The globalization of weapons systems throughout the world, making states' capabilities increasingly sophisticated and similar, has continued apace in the so-called new arms control era, because the globalized arms trade has few barriers to dispersion.

The past half century of arms control does not create confidence in the ability of arms control agreements to reduce the number of weapons or to con-

Can Arms Agreements Control the Next Generation of Weapons?

Although the 1991 Persian Gulf War involved six hundred thousand troops with new high-tech weapons, the conflict ended with a victory that involved only 148 combat deaths. This has instilled confidence that future wars will involve "clean combat," which—like a video-arcade game—will convey the impression that war is not dirty. Nonetheless, General John Shalikashvili, then Chairman of the U.S. Joint Chiefs of Staff, warned in 1995 that the hope of a new generation of "nonlethal weapons" is an illusion: "It is that somehow you can make combat surgical and clean and pristine. And you cannot. Combat . . . is dirty and painful, and casualties are almost a natural by-product."

War might be made to appear more acceptable in the public eye as stealth technology, pilotless combat airplanes, and electronic warfare keep killing from view. The new robotic and laser weapons offer little protection to innocent noncombatants (e.g., civilians, clergy, children) who can easily become the targets. In 1995 the United States had plans to develop an antipersonnel weapon known as the Laser Countermeasure, based on a secret technology that was "cruel and inhumane even by the standards of war. It is a forty-pound portable gun that fires a beam powerful enough to burn out human retinas from up to three thousand feet away" (Arkin 1995). By blinding people—so the rationale for the construction of this and other equally awesome new weapons goes—war could be made safe for the attacker.

Is the rationale sound? Who will protect us all from ruthless aggressors using such weapons as these instruments of violence spread to terrorists and governments unrestrained by moral compassions (as they surely will on the covert arms market)? Concerns such as these reduce confidence in the ability of the world to control the armament innovations that advanced technology makes possible, despite the "surprising" 1996 agreement to ban the use (but not the production) of some types of blinding laser weapons (Wurst 1996).

tain their dispersion in the next fifty years. Technology has increased the problem. Its constant movement has led to the birth of an ever-widening range of novel new weapons—increasingly smaller, deadlier, easier to conceal, and capable of destroying by means unimaginable until recently. The next generation of lethal and **nonlethal weapons** on the drawing boards will revolutionize warfare in the twenty-first century (see Focus 15.4). And their production, stockpiling, and sale across borders in the borderless globalized world will be ever more difficult to control. How can the international community be expected to police deadly microbes and other "poor states' nukes" such as chemical poisonous gases and contagious biological viruses that cannot be seen? Detecting an attack is the first challenge; detecting the presence of such weapons is another, much bigger problem. These will be the weapons of choice for rogue governments and terrorist groups and they are highly resistant to control. Many countries have **dual-use production technologies** such as "chemical manufacturing and processing plants and pharmaceutical laboratories which could produce deadly agents, possibly on very short notice, for use in warfare" (Sivard 1996, 27). The banning of such indiscriminate weapons of mass destruction and creation of dependable enforcement and verification procedures could pose the globe's greatest security challenge.

The primary reason for skepticism is that arms control will not be implemented without sufficient *political will*. And here again, the past record of low expectations and low arms control performance fails to inspire much confidence about the prospects for meaningful arms control of the next century's array of invisible, precise, and deadly killing systems. Recall the experience during the hopeful time for arms control when the superpowers' incentives for disarmament were great. Then, with "the case for cutting nuclear weapons as strong as ever," and with acceptance of the fact during the Cold War "that the nuclear balance would be firmer and cheaper to maintain with fewer weapons, not more," why is it that START II did not go further? Why couldn't the superpowers "finish what they STARTED"? (*Economist*, January 27, 1996, 17). Why do states often make decisions to arm that apparently imprison them in the grip of perpetual insecurity? On the surface, the incentives for meaningful arms control seem numerous. Significant controls would save money, reduce tension and hence the dangers of war, symbolize leaders' desire for peace, lessen health hazards, reduce the environmental hazards of nuclear waste, diminish the potential destructiveness of war, dampen the incentive for one state to seek a power advantage over others, reduce the possibility of being the target of a preemptive attack, and achieve a propaganda advantage for those advocating peace. To these we can add moral satisfaction and the opportunity to live in a less threatening global environment.

However, states did not—and perhaps still do not—significantly control the growth of arms. There are many reasons to rely on military preparedness as a path to peace; they stem from the fear that is endemic to international anarchy. Most countries are reluctant to engage in arms limitations in a self-help system that requires each state to protect itself. Thus states find themselves caught in a vicious cycle of fear. This creates the **security dilemma**—a condition that is in no actor's best interest but that permits no easy escape. Its influence on behavior is potent and helps explain why military establishments often subscribe to two basic principles: "(1) `Don't negotiate when you are behind. Why accept a permanent position of number two?' and (2) `Don't negotiate when you are ahead. Why accept a freeze in an area of military competition when the other side has not kept up with you?'" (Barnet 1977).

Arms bargaining is a game of give and take, but all participants typically want to take much and give little. As a result, with the powerful restraining impact of domestic politics on the negotiation process, it is little wonder that meaningful agreements are so hard to achieve and that states develop weapons systems as bargaining chips for future negotiations. Compounding the problem is the fact that many people benefit financially from arms races and lobby against arms agreements because they could lose their jobs if military spending is cut. **Military-industrial complexes** (see Rosen 1973; Paget 1995) exist in all societies whose influence is tied to high defense spending. The resistance of military planners and defense specialists to reductions in arsenals, even in the wake of the Cold War, attests to the continuing penchant of defense experts and arms manufacturers to insist that "prudence" dictates preparing for the worst contingency by retaining military preparedness at as high a level as possible. "The business of defense is defending business" is the way one analyst summarized the problem (Mulhollin 1994).

Arms control still remains a murky policy area, and the past record suggests that we should not expect too much of arms control or exaggerate its potential.

> The history of the postwar era proves that arms control, if pursued wisely and properly, can reduce the threat; it can never eliminate the risk of war altogether. Arms control is not a substitute for weapons but a complement to them. Arms and arms control, one by creating the means to inflict unacceptable damage on a potential enemy and the other by protecting that ca-

security dilemma the reduction in national security experienced by two or more states competing in an arms race.

pability from enemy attack, are both necessary for national security. A defense policy that fails to pursue the two together, that emphasizes one approach to the exclusion of the other, is dangerous and incomplete. . . .

True international security depends not as much on arms or arms control as on reducing as much as possible the sources of conflict in international relations and on finding effective nonviolent means of resolving the conflicts that remain. (Kruzel 1991, 268)

499

THE REALIST ROAD TO
SECURITY THROUGH
ALLIANCES, THE
BALANCE OF POWER,
AND ARMS CONTROL

• • •

MILITARY POWER AND THE SEARCH FOR A TWENTY-FIRST-CENTURY PEACE

The obstacles to arms control are formidable. The idea that a disarmed world would be a more secure one does not have the force of history behind it, whereas the realist idea that military preparedness produces security does. As long as aggressive states exist, it would be imprudent to disarm. Arms control does not solve the basic problem of rivalry between states, because as long as states have and can use weapons, such agreements are little more than cooperative arrangements between adversaries. They define the competition and confine the potential destruction that war brings but do not remove the *source* of the conflict.

Alternatively, managing political conflicts without violence may be the key to arms control. Arms, after all, are less causes of war than symptoms of political tension: People "do not fight because they have arms. They have arms because [they are afraid and] they deem it necessary to fight" (Morgenthau 1985). From this perspective, controlling arms is contingent on removing the fears that underlie states' conflicts. The quest for national security in an anarchical world springs from states' fear of one another. Yet, because one country's security makes others insecure, nearly all states prepare for war to defend themselves. In this sense the realists' military paths to peace discussed in this chapter are intimately related to the widespread quest for armaments described in Chapter 13.

Still at issue, however, is whether world security is served by states' military search for their own national security. Perhaps the forces that propel the pursuit of peace and security through military might have sown the seeds of the world's destruction. Nothing makes the search for peace through political means more compelling. Hope may be inspired by the observations of former U.S. Secretary of Defense Robert McNamara: "We have reached the present dangerous and absurd confrontation by a long series of steps, many of which seemed rational in their time. Step by step we can undo much of the damage."

Chapter 16 examines some proposals recommended especially by liberal theorists for preventing the damage caused by arms races, power transitions, and the wars they ignite.

K E Y   T E R M S

alliances	nonalignment	long peace(s)
rational choice	size principle	hegemonic stability theory
balance of power	balancer	hegemon
alignments	preemption	balance of terror

collective security
polarity
blocs
polarization
North Atlantic Treaty
   Organization (NATO)
bipolar
zero-sum
bipolycentrism
polycentrism
intercontinental ballistic missiles
   (ICBMs)
extended deterrence
"Two Plus Four" treaty
Concert of Europe
North Atlantic Cooperation
   Council (NACC)
bandwagon
Partnership for Peace (PFP)
enlargement
Planning and Review Process
   (PARP)

Euro-Atlantic Partnership Council
   (EAPC)
multipolarity
arms control
disarmament
bilateral agreements
multilateral agreements
Baruch Plan
Rapacki Plan
Mutual and Balanced Force
   Reductions (MBFR)
Comprehensive Test Ban (CTB)
verification
Conventional Forces in Europe
   (CFE)
Organization for Security and
   Cooperation in Europe (OSCE)
Nuclear Nonproliferation Treaty
   (NPT)
nonproliferation
Conference on Disarmament (CD)

Biological Weapons Convention
   (BWC)
Chemical Weapons Convention
   (CWC)
Missile Technology Control
   Regime (MTCR)
United Nations Register of
   Conventional Arms
Strategic Arms Limitation Talks
   (SALT)
nuclear freeze movement
Strategic Arms Reduction Talks
   (START)
MIRVs
antipersonnel landmines (APLs)
arms control regimes
nonlethal weapons
dual-use production technologies
security dilemma
military-industrial complexes

S U G G E S T E D   R E A D I N G

Betts, Richard K. "The New Threat of Mass Destruction," *Foreign Affairs* 77 (January/February 1998): 26–41.

Brzezinski, Zbigniew. *The Grand Chessboard: American Primary and Geostrategic Imperatives*. New York: Basic Books, 1997.

Bueno de Mesquita, Bruce. *The War Trap*. New Haven, Conn.: Yale University Press, 1981.

Burstein, Daniel, and Arne Keijzer. *Big Dragon: China's Future*. New York: Simon and Schuster, 1998.

Claude, Inis L., Jr. *Power and International Relations*. New York: Random House, 1962.

Coker, Christopher. *Twilight of the West*. Boulder, Colo.: Westview, 1998.

The Editors of *The Economist*. "The Next Balance of Power," *Economist*, Vol. 346 (January 3, 1998): 17–19.

Friedman, Gil, and Harvey Starr. *Agency, Structure and International Politics*. London: Routledge, 1998.

Kegley, Charles W., Jr., and Gregory A. Raymond. *A Multipolar Peace? Great-Power Politics in the Twenty-First Century*. New York: St. Martin's Press, 1994.

Klare, Michael, and Yogesh Chandrani, eds. *World Security: Challenges for a New Century*, 3rd ed. New York: St. Martin's Press, 1998.

Pierre, Andrew. *Cascade of Arms: Managing Conventional Arms Proliferation*. Washington, D.C.: Brookings, 1998.

Rusi, Alpo M. *Dangerous Peace: New Rivalry in World Politics*. Boulder, Colo.: Westview, 1997.

Sabrosky, Alan Ned, ed. *Polarity and War: The Changing Structure of International Conflict*. Boulder, Colo.: Westview Press, 1985.

http://www.bullatomsci.org/

The Bulletin of the Atomic Scientists   After World War II, many of the scientists who were responsible for the production of the atomic bomb formed a movement to control nuclear energy. In 1945, these scientists first published the *Bulletin* to help establish the international control of nuclear energy. The *Bulletin* now appears online. While exploring this site, click on the "Doomsday Clock" to see how international tensions and nuclear developments have brought us closer and closer to "midnight" and, consequently, doomsday. Read either a short or long history of nuclear energy development and tensions among nations.

http://www.nato.int/

NATO   The North Atlantic Treaty Organization's (NATO) Web site contains information on NATO expansion as well as the Partnership for Peace (PFP) initiative. Click on the "Partnership" link to get a list of the countries that are part of the PFP, read speeches from the respective countries, and get country-specific information. Also, read the study on NATO expansion. Are you convinced by the rationale for expansion?

http://www.unog.ch/frames/disarm/disdoc.htm

United Nations Conference on Disarmament   The United Nations Conference on Disarmament Web page provides links to all the major international disarmament documents starting with the Geneva Convention and ending with the Comprehensive Test Ban Treaty. Read the texts of some of the most influential international agreements that control or eliminate weapons of mass destruction.

http://www.un.org/Depts/Landmine/index.html

United Nations Demining Database   This comprehensive site explores the issues involved with demining. Click on the "Country Overview" and read about specific countries' problems and the origins of landmines found within their borders. See how many landmines various countries have, the area contaminated, and the number of landmine blast victims. Which countries have the greatest number of landmines? Why do you think this is so? Who are the biggest suppliers of landmines?

The Liberal Institutional Paths to Peace through Law, Integration, and Democratization

•••
My first axiom: The quest for international security involves the unconditional surrender by every nation, in a certain measure, of its liberty of action, its sovereignty that is to say, and it is clear beyond all doubt that no other road can lead to such security.

—ALBERT EINSTEIN,
German-born Swiss-American scientist, 1932

•••
Liberal internationalists see a need for international rules and institutions to solve states' problems, proclaim the end of the nation-state, [and see] transgovernmentalism rapidly becoming the most widespread and effective mode of international governance. [However], a gain in power in nonstate actors does not necessarily translate into a loss of power for the state.

—ANNE-MARIE SLAUGHTER,
Harvard Law School professor, 1997

CHAPTER TOPICS AND THEMES

■ Neoliberal institutionalists' approaches to twenty-first-century global security

■ International law and world order

■ Human rights and the protection of humans' freedom and security

■ International organization and world order

■ The United Nations in a globalizing world of united and disunited states

■ Political integration: Functional and neofunctional paths to peace

■ Failed states, fragmentation, and the danger of political disintegration

■ A democratic peace?

■ Liberal institutions and world order

Since antiquity, the world has pursued two primary paths to peace. The realist road emphasizes *military* solutions; the liberal road emphasizes *political* solutions. This chapter examines four principal approaches to the control of armed conflict from the liberal theoretical tradition: international law, organization, integration, and democratization (see Table 16.1). Because all four stress institutions, the new advocates of these liberal paths are sometimes referred to collectively as **neoliberal institutionalists** (Grieco 1995). While they differ in their approach to preserving twenty-first-century security, they share a fear of the historic tendency of states to make war. They are also concerned that because there is as yet "no universal international law, no global sovereign, or an effective enforcement mechanism accepted by all, change in the international system is condoned or rejected by individual states," war will continue to erupt (Hammond 1996).

neoliberal institutionalism
adherents to the recent theoretical effort to explain how peace and prosperity instead of war might be created through law, global governance, and liberal democracies' cooperation to engineer international change.

• • •

INTERNATIONAL LAW AND WORLD ORDER

In 1984, the United States announced that it would unilaterally withdraw from the World Court's jurisdiction. This followed disputes with several Central American countries after Nicaragua's accusation that the U.S. Central Intelligence Agency had illegally attempted to "overthrow and destabilize" the elected Sandinista government. Nicaragua charged that the United States had illegally mined its ports and supplied money, military assistance, and training to the rebel *contra* forces. The United States denied the tribunal's authority. In so doing, however, it was not acting without precedent; others had done so previously. Nonetheless, by thumbing its nose at the court and the rule of law it represents, had it, as some claimed, become an "international outlaw?" Or, as others asserted, had it acted within its rights?

The World Court supported the former view. In 1984, the court ruled as follows:

> The right to sovereignty and to political independence possessed by the Republic of Nicaragua, like any other state of the region or of the world, should be fully respected and should not in any way be jeopardized by any military and paramilitary activities which are prohibited by the principles of international law, in particular the principle that states should refrain in their international relations from the threat or the use of force against the territorial integrity or the political independence of any state, and the principle concerning the duty not to intervene in matters within the domestic jurisdiction of a state. (*New York Times*, May 11, 1984, 8)

Yet this ruling had little effect, as neither the court nor Nicaragua had anyone to enforce it. Events such as this have led many critics to conclude that international law is "weak and defenseless" (Fried 1971). Indeed, many experts—whether they are realists or liberal idealists—skeptically ask whether international law is really law.

There are many reasons to answer this question affirmatively. Although international law is imperfect, actors regularly rely on it to redress grievances (see Joyner 1998; von Glahn 1996). Most of this activity falls within the realm of **private international law**—the regulation of routine transnational activities in such areas as commerce, communications, and travel. While largely invisible

504

THE LIBERAL
INSTITUTIONAL PATHS
TO PEACE THROUGH
LAW, INTEGRATION,
AND DEMOCRATIZATION

TABLE 16.1   Some Liberal Paths to International Security

Prescription	Premise
Provide states rules of international law to regulate competition.	Interstate cooperation can be encouraged by creating rules for peaceful interaction.
Participate in the creation of international organizations.	If you want peace, prepare global institutions to keep it.
Practice collaboration to bind independent states together in integrated security communities.	Interdependence makes imperative the amalgamation of states, not their division.
Promote the spread of democratic governance.	Countries that protect their own citizens' civil liberties do not wage war against other governments that also protect their citizens' human rights.
Prepare rules to facilitate free trade.	Trade protectionism is counterproductive to prosperity and peace.
Produce agreements to reduce armaments to levels that discourage war.	States get what they plan for—beat swords into plowshares.
Provide humanitarian assistance to the impoverished.	Rich states can only help themselves by helping poor people also.
Principles are more important than power.	Recognize the rewards of higher principles to one's self, such as *reciprocity*, or the Golden Rule to do unto others as you would have them do unto you.

to the public, private international law is the locus for all but a small fraction of international legal activities. It is where the majority of transnational disputes are regularly settled and where the record of compliance compares favorably with that achieved in domestic legal systems (Brownlie 1990).

In contrast, **public international law** covers issues of public order, including relations between governments and the interactions of governments with intergovernmental organizations (IGOs) and nongovernmental organizations (NGOs) such as multinational corporations. Some believe that we should use the phrase *world law* to describe the mixture of public and private, domestic and international transactions that public international law seeks to regulate in an increasingly globalized world. However, it is the regulation of government-to-government relations that dominates the headlines in discussion of public international law. This area of activity also captures most of the criticism; for here, failures—when they occur—are quite conspicuous. This is especially true with respect to the breakdown of peace and security. When states engage in armed conflict, criticism of its shortcomings escalates. Consider Israeli Ambassador Abba Eban's lament that "international law is that law which the wicked do not obey and the righteous do not enforce."

Because this chapter examines the capacity of public international law to control war, our discussion will address only the laws and institutional machinery created to manage armed conflict between states. That is, it will explore that segment of public international law popularly regarded as the most deficient.

Enraged by the inhumane international conditions he witnessed during his lifetime, Dutch reformer Hugo Grotius (1583–1645) wrote *De Jure Belli et Pacis (On the Law of War and Peace)* in 1625. His treatise called on the great powers to resolve their conflicts by judicial procedures rather than on the battlefield, and specified the legal principles he felt could encourage cooperation, peace, and more humane treatment of people. Grotius consequently became known as the "founder of international law."

Law at the International Level: Core Principles

Public international law is usually defined as rules that govern the conduct of states in their relations with one another. The *corpus juris gentium* (the body of the law of nations) has grown considerably over the past three centuries, changing in response to transformations in international politics (Kaplan and Katzenbach 1961). An inventory of the basic legal principles relevant to the control of war clarifies the international system's character (for authoritative texts, see Higgins 1994; von Glahn 1996).

The Rules of International Law. No principle of international law is more critical than state sovereignty. **Sovereignty** means that no authority is legally above the state, except that which the state voluntarily confers on the international organizations it joins. In fact, as conceived by **realists** in the seventeenth century, the rules of international law were written to protect states, and permitted states "a complete freedom of action" (Parry 1968) to preserve their sovereign independence.

Nearly every legal doctrine supports and extends the cardinal principle that states are the primary subjects of international law. Although the Universal Declaration of Human Rights in 1948 expanded concern about states' treatment of individual people, states remain supreme. "Laws are made to protect the state from the individual and not the individual from the state" (Gottlieb 1982). Accordingly, the vast majority of rules address the rights and duties of states, not people. For instance, the principle of **sovereign equality** entitles each state to full respect by other states as well as equal protection by the system's legal rules. The right of independence also guarantees states' autonomy in their domestic affairs and external relations, under the logic that the independence of

sovereignty the legal doctrine that states have supreme authority to govern their internal affairs and manage their foreign relations with other states and IGOs.

realists adherents to the theoretical tradition that defines sovereign states as the most important global actors that should be unrestrained by law, principles of justice, or supranational organizations when making decisions regarding war and peace.

506

THE LIBERAL
INSTITUTIONAL PATHS
TO PEACE THROUGH
LAW, INTEGRATION,
AND DEMOCRATIZATION

each presumes that of all. Similarly, the doctrine of **neutrality** permits states to avoid involvement in others' conflicts and coalitions.

Furthermore, the noninterference principle forms the basis for **nonintervention**—that is, states' duty to refrain from uninvited involvement in another's internal affairs. This sometimes abused classic rule gives governments the right to exercise jurisdiction over practically all things on, under, or above their bounded territory. (There are exceptions, however, such as **diplomatic immunity** for states' ambassadors from the domestic laws of the country where their embassies are located, and **extraterritoriality,** which allows control of embassies on other states' terrain.)

In practice, domestic jurisdiction permits a state to enact and enforce whatever laws it wishes for its own citizens. In fact, international law was so permissive toward the state's control of its domestic affairs that, prior to 1952, "there was no precedent in international law for a . . . state to assume responsibility for the crimes it committed against a minority within its jurisdiction" (Wise 1993). A citizen was not protected against the state's abuse of human rights or **crimes against humanity.** Note also that international law permits states to set their own rules for citizenship. Two basic principles govern the way nationality and citizenship are conferred: under *jus soli*, citizenship is determined by the state on whose territory the birth took place; under *jus sanguinis*, nationality is acquired by descent from a parent who is a national.

In addition, from the earlier periods of modern international law, states were permitted to create whatever form of government they desired without regard to its acceptability to other states. This principle was expressed in the *realpolitik* language of the Treaty of Augsburg (1515) and the Westphalian Treaties (1648), which made states all-powerful by recognizing the **divine right of kings.** This doctrine was reaffirmed in the 1943 Atlantic Charter's pledge of "the right of all people to choose the form of government under which they will live." However, this rule has recently undergone an erosion, and the right of people to live under the liberties of democracy is increasingly being defined as an "entitlement" or a basic human right (Franck 1994; also von Glahn 1996). Moreover, international law gives states the freedom to regulate economic transactions within their boundaries and empowers the state to draft those living on its soil into its armed forces to fight—and die, if necessary—to defend the state.

The Montevideo Convention of 1933 on the Rights and Duties of States summarizes the major components of **statehood.** A state must possess a permanent population, a well-defined territory, and a government capable of ruling its citizens and of managing formal diplomatic relations with other states. Other rules specify how and when these conditions are satisfied. Essentially, the acquisition of statehood depends on a political entity's recognition as such by other states. Whether a state exists thus rests in the hands of other states; that is, preexisting states are entitled to extend **diplomatic recognition** to another entity. **De facto recognition** is provisional and capable of being withdrawn in the event that the recognized government is superseded by another. It does not carry with it the exchange of diplomatic representatives or other legal benefits and responsibilities. **De jure recognition,** on the other hand, extends full legal and diplomatic privileges from the granting state. This distinction emphasizes that recognition is a political tool of international law, through which approval or disapproval of a government can be expressed.

crimes against humanity a category of activities, made illegal at the Nuremberg war crime trials, condemning states which abuse the human rights of their citizens.

divine rights of kings the realist doctrine that because kings are sovereign they have the right to rule their subjects authoritatively and are not accountable to the public because their rule is ordained by God.

de facto recognition a government's acknowledgment of the factual existence of another state or government short of full recognition.

de jure recognition one government's formal, legal recognition of another government or state.

Today, with the exception of Antarctica, which is administered jointly by several states and is outside the jurisdiction of any one of them, no significant land mass remains *terra nullius* (territory belonging legally to no one). Consequently, the birth of a new state must be at the expense of an existing one. Thus, the recognition of a new state almost always means the recognition of a new government's control over a particular territory. Because recognition is a voluntary political act, **nonrecognition** is a legally institutionalized form of public insult to a government aspiring to be accepted as legitimate. It may be seen as a form of sanction against an unwanted political regime.

States are free to enter into treaty arrangements with other states. Rules specify how treaties are to be activated, interpreted, and abrogated. International law holds that treaties voluntarily entered into are binding *(pacta sunt servanda)*. However, it also reserves for states the right to unilaterally terminate treaties previously agreed to, by reference to the escape clause known as *rebus sic stantibus*. This is the principle that a treaty is binding only as long as no fundamental change occurs in the circumstances that existed when it was concluded.

Procedures for Dispute Settlement. In addition to these general principles, international law provides a wide variety of legal methods for states to resolve their conflicts. The laws of negotiation do not obligate states to reach agreement or to settle their disputes peacefully. They do, however, provide rules for several conflict resolution procedures, including:

- **Mediation:** when a third party proposes a nonbinding solution to a controversy between two other states, as illustrated by U.S. President Carter's historic mediation at the 1978 Camp David meeting between Egypt and Israel.

- **Good offices:** when a third party offers a location for discussions among disputants but does not participate in the actual negotiations, as Switzerland often does.

- **Conciliation:** when a third party assists both sides but does not offer any solution.

- **Arbitration:** when a third party gives a binding decision through an ad hoc forum.

- **Adjudication:** when a third party offers a binding decision through an institutionalized tribunal, such as a court.

The Institutional Limitations of the International Legal System

Sovereignty and the legal principles derived from it shape and reinforce international anarchy. The nature of world politics is legally dependent on what governments choose to do with one another and the kinds of rules they voluntarily support. It is a legal system by and for states, which is often seen by liberal reformers as a serious flaw undermining the effectiveness of international law (see Focus 16.1).

Beyond the barriers to legal institutions that sovereignty poses, still other weaknesses reduce confidence in international law. Critics and reformers usually cite these alleged deficiencies:

- *International law lacks universality*. An effective legal system must represent the norms shared by those it governs. According to the precept of

The Institutional Deficiencies of International Law

Many theorists consider the international legal system institutionally defective due to its dependence on the attitudes and behaviors of those it governs. Because formal legal institutions (like those within states) are weak at the international level, critics make the following points.

First, in world politics no legislative body capable of making binding laws exists. Rules are made only when states willingly observe or embrace them in the treaties to which they voluntarily subscribe. There is no systematic method of amending or revoking them. Article 38 of the Statute of the International Court of Justice (or World Court) affirms this. Generally accepted as the authoritative definition of the "sources of international law," it states that international law derives from (1) custom, (2) international treaties and agreements, (3) national and international court decisions, (4) the writings of legal authorities and specialists, and (5) the "general principles" of law recognized since the Roman Empire as part of "natural law" and "right reason."

Second, in world politics no judicial body exists to authoritatively identify the rules accepted by states, record the substantive precepts reached, interpret when and how the rules apply, and identify violations. Instead, states are responsible for performing these tasks themselves. The World Court does not have the power to perform these functions without states' consent, and the UN Security Council cannot speak on judicial matters for the whole global community (even though it has recently defined a new scope for Chapter VII of the UN Charter that claims the right to make quasi-judicial authoritative interpretations of global laws).

Finally, in world politics there is no executive body capable of enforcing the rules. Rule enforcement usually occurs through the self-help actions of the victims of a transgression or with the assistance of their allies or other interested parties. No centralized enforcement procedures exist, and compliance is voluntary. The whole system rests, therefore, on states' willingness to abide by the rules to which they consent and on the ability of each to enforce through retaliatory measures the norms of behavior they value.

Consequently, states themselves—not a higher authority—determine what the rules are, when they apply, and how they should be enforced. This raises the question: When everyone is above the law, is anyone ruled by it?

Roman law, *ubi societas, ibi jus* (where there is society, there is law), shared community values are a minimal precondition for forming a legal system. Yet the contemporary international order is culturally and ideologically pluralistic and lacks consensus on common values. Although some claim the Western-based international legal order approximates universality, state practice and the simultaneous operation of often incompatible legal traditions throughout the world contradict this claim (Bozeman 1994).

- *International law justifies the competitive pursuit of national advantage without regard to morality or justice.* As in any legal system, in international politics what is legal is not necessarily moral (see Nardin 1983). In fact, international law legitimizes the drive for hegemony and contributes to conflict (Lissitzyn 1963). Self-help does not control power; it is a concession to power. By accepting the view that the unbridled autonomy of sovereign independence is sacrosanct, international law follows the realists' "iron law of politics"—that legal obligations must yield to the national interest (Morgenthau 1985).

- *International law is an instrument of the powerful to oppress the weak.* In a voluntary consent system, the rules to which the powerful willingly agree are those that serve their interests. These rules therefore preserve the existing hierarchy (Friedheim 1965). For this reason, some liberal theorists claim that international law has bred the so-called **structural violence** resulting from the hierarchical organization of world politics in which the strong benefit at the expense of the weak (Galtung 1969). Enforcement is left "to the vicissitudes of the distribution of power between the violator of the law and the victim of the violation." Therefore, political scientist Hans J. Morgenthau (1985) concedes, "it makes it easy for the strong both to violate the law and to enforce it, and consequently puts the rights of the weak in jeopardy. A great power can violate the rights of a small nation without having to fear effective sanctions on the latter's part."

- *International law is little more than a justification of existing practices.* When a particular behavior pattern becomes widespread, it becomes legally obligatory; rules *of* behavior become rules *for* behavior (Hoffmann 1971). The eminent legal scholar Hans Kelsen's contention that states ought to behave as they have customarily behaved (see Onuf 1982) and E. Adamson Hoebel's (1961) dictum that "what the most do, others should do" reflect the **positivist legal theory** that when a type of behavior occurs frequently, it becomes legal. In fact, the highly regarded positivist legal theorists stress states' customary practices as the most important source from which laws derive. In the absence of formal machinery for creating international rules, for evidence of what the law is, positivists observe leaders' foreign policy pronouncements, repeated usage in conventions voluntarily accepted by states, general practices (by an overwhelmingly large number of states), the judicial decisions of national and international tribunals, and legal principles stated in the resolutions of multinational assemblies such as the UN General Assembly. When the sources of international law are interpreted in this way, the actions of states shape law, not vice versa.

- *International law's ambiguity reduces law to a policy tool for propaganda purposes.* The vague, elastic wording of international law makes it easy for states to define and interpret almost any action as legitimate. "The problem here," observes Samuel S. Kim (1991), "is the lack of clarity and coherence [that enables] international law [to be] easily stretched, . . . to be a flexible fig leaf or a propaganda instrument." This ambivalence makes it possible for states to exploit international law to get what they can and to justify what they have obtained (Wright 1953).

These deficiencies illustrate but do not exhaust the international legal order's alleged inadequacies. Critics conclude that international law is least developed in the state system's most critical realm: where national security is at stake when the threat of armed conflict arises.

The Relevance of International Law

International law is fraught with deficiencies. Still, we can question the proposition that it is irrelevant to contemporary international politics. States themselves do not deem public international law irrelevant. They attach considerable importance to it and expend considerable time and energy fighting over its interpretation while attempting to shape its evolution. If law were meaningless, we would not be able to point to the existence of a systematic code of rules repeatedly affirmed by states in multilateral agreements, resolutions, and declarations (Jones 1991). These instrumentalities reflect state opinion and show that there *are* basic principles that states formally recognize and agree to respect.

"The reality as demonstrated through their behavior," legal scholar Christopher Joyner (1998) observes, "is that states do accept international law as law and, even more significant, in the vast majority of instances they . . . obey it." The major reason states practice self-restraint is because even the most powerful states appreciate its benefits. International reputations are important. Those who play the game of international politics by recognized rules receive rewards, whereas states that ignore international law or opportunistically break customary norms pay costs for doing as they please. For instance, other countries will be reluctant to cooperate with them. They must also fear reprisals and retaliation by those victimized, as well as the loss of prestige. For this reason, only the most ambitious or reckless state is apt to flagrantly disregard accepted standards of conduct.

A primary reason why states value international law and affirm their commitment to it is that they need a common understanding of the "rules of the game." International law is an "institutional device for communicating to the policymakers of various states a consensus on the nature of the international system" (Coplin 1965). Law helps shape expectations, and rules reduce uncertainty and enhance predictability in international affairs. These communication functions serve every member of the international system.

While the members of the state system usually agree on certain general values, they often fail to recognize the responsibilities these values create for them (Coplin 1966). Thus it is tempting to agree with critics who assert that the lack of supranational sanctioning powers makes international law useless for its most important function—controlling violence. This conclusion is questionable, however, as it stems from the misleading comparison critics often draw between the international legal order's primitive institutions and states' highly centralized domestic legal systems. Comparison invites the mistaken conclusion that a formal legal structure (a centralized, "vertical system of law") is automatically superior to a decentralized, self-help, "horizontal system of law." The organizational differences between domestic (municipal) and international legal systems hide similarities and obscure the key question: Which type of legal order is more effective?

Evidence shows that unorganized or primitive legal systems succeed in containing violence and ensuring compliance with rules (see Masters 1969). Even in systems without the kinds of institutionalized procedures typically found in municipal legal systems for punishing rule violation (such as tribal societies without formal governments), sanctions often operate effectively (Barkun 1968). Thus we should not be surprised to learn that "international law is not violated more often, or to a higher degree, than the law of other systems" (Joyner 1998). The historical record demonstrates that states have regularly resolved their differences through legal procedures. In 97 interstate conflicts between 1919 and 1986, 168 attempts were made by the contending parties to negotiate, mediate, adjudicate, or otherwise settle their disputes through formal procedures of conflict resolution. More impressively, 68 of these attempts were successful (Holsti 1988, 420). In other words, since World War I states have been able to resolve their differences 70 percent of the time by using pacific settlement procedures.

It is also clear that formal institutions for rule enforcement do not guarantee compliance. No legal system can deter all of its members from breaking existing laws. Consequently it is a mistake to expect a legal system to prevent all criminal behavior or to assert that any violation of the law proves the inadequacy of the legal structure. Law is designed to deter crime, but it is unreasonable to expect it to prevent it.

Similarly, we should not view every breakdown of international law as confirming general lawlessness. Conditions of crisis strain all legal systems, and few, when tested severely, can contain all violence. Since 1500, more people have died from civil wars than from wars between sovereign states (Sivard 1991). Today, with street crime in cities worldwide at epidemic proportions and ethnopolitical warfare within countries exacting a deadly toll against hundreds of minority groups (Gurr 1998), states' domestic legal systems are patently failing to prevent killing. Thus, the allegedly "deficient" international legal system performs its primary job—inhibiting violence—more effectively than the supposedly more sophisticated domestic systems. Perhaps, then, the usual criteria by which critics assess legal systems are dubious. Should they be less concerned with structures and institutions, and more concerned with performance?

Even the most skeptical of theorists who claim that leaders act without consideration of the rules must acknowledge that legal norms help to order the process of bargaining and the formation of **security regimes**—sets of rules to contain armed conflict (see Jervis 1982; Stein 1993). At the onset of militarized disputes, law "serves as a sort of signal to tell states which of these clashes are acceptable and which are deserving of retaliation" (D'Amato 1982). Once a crisis erupts, rules eliminate the need to decide on a procedure for deciding.

At another level, public international law makes possible the routine transactions otherwise governed by private international law in such activities as international trade, foreign travel, mail flows, currency exchange, environmental protection, and debt obligations. Parties to the *regimes*, or rules for cooperative exchanges, in these areas regard them as binding and abide by their provisions (Kim 1991; Soroos 1986). Arguably, by removing disputes from possible resolution by armed force, international law reduces the sources of aggression. This helps make an anarchical world more orderly.

The Legal Control of Warfare

Liberal reformers often complain that law clearly fails in the realm of behavior most resistant to legal control—conflict management. If under international law, as fashioned by realist leaders, states are "legally bound to respect each other's independence and other rights, and yet free to attack each other at will" (Brierly 1944), international law may actually encourage war. The ethical and jurisprudential **just war doctrine** from which the laws of war stem shapes discussions of contemporary public international law (see Focus 16.2).

Throughout history, international law has evolved in response to changing global conditions. This can be illustrated by reviewing changes in the rules for war's initiation and the means for waging it.

The Use of Force. Especially since World War I, the international community's tolerance of war has declined. As Figure 16.1 shows, international law has increasingly rejected the traditional legal right of states to employ force to achieve their foreign policy objectives.

This is not to suggest that the right to use force to punish wrongdoers in just war theory has been repudiated. The "neo-just war doctrine . . . no longer seriously purports to accept the view that peace is unconditionally a higher view than justice. We have returned to the medieval view that it is permissible

511

THE LIBERAL
INSTITUTIONAL PATHS
TO PEACE THROUGH
LAW, INTEGRATION,
AND DEMOCRATIZATION

The Just War Doctrine
Ethical Perspectives on Violence

Many people are confused by international law because it both prohibits and justifies the use of force. The confusion derives from the just war tradition in "Christian realism," in which the rules of war are philosophically based on **morals** (principles or rules of behavior) and **ethics** (principles rationalizing why these rules are proper). In the fourth century, St. Augustine questioned the strict view that those who take another's life to defend the state necessarily violate the commandment "Thou shalt not kill." He counseled that "it is the wrong-doing of the opposing party which compels the wise man to wage just wars." The Christian was obligated, he felt, to fight against evil and wickedness. To St. Augustine, the City of Man was sinful, in contrast to the City of God; in the secular world it was sometimes permissible to kill—to punish a sin by an enemy (while still loving the sinner) to achieve a "just peace." This realist logic was extended by Pope Nicholas I, who in 866 proclaimed that *any* defensive war was just.

From this perspective evolved the modern just war doctrine as developed by such medieval secularists as Hugo Grotius, who challenged the warring Catholic and Protestant Christian powers in the Thirty Years' War (1618–1648) to abide by humane standards of conduct, and sought to replace the two cities or ethical realms of Augustine (and Luther) with a single global society under rational law. For Grotius, a just war was one of self-defense or punishment for inflicted damages; he wrote that "No other just cause for undertaking war can there be excepting injury received," and for war to be moral it must be fought by just means without harm to innocent noncombatants. From this distinction evolved the modern version of just war doctrine, consisting of two categories of argumentation, *jus ad bellum* (the justice of a war) and *jus in bello* (justice in a war). The former sets the criteria by which a political leader may determine whether a war should be waged. The latter specifies restraints on the range of permissible tactics to be used in fighting a just war.

These distinctions have been hotly debated since their inception. Drawing the line between murder and just war is a controversial task. Yet just war theory seeks to define these boundaries. According to this legal tradition, some circumstances in which lethal force may be justifiable are recognized under international law, which also provides guidelines for sanctioned methods.

At the core of the just war tradition is the conviction that the taking of human life may be sanctioned as the "lesser evil" when necessary to prevent life-threatening aggression. St. Thomas More contended that the assassination of an evil leader responsible for starting a war was justified if it would prevent the taking of innocent lives. From this premise, a number of other principles follow. The criteria today include ten key ideas:

1. That all other means to a morally just solution of conflict must be exhausted before a resort to arms can be justified.
2. That war can be just only if employed (a) to defend a stable political order or a morally preferable cause against a real threat or (b) to restore justice after a real injury has been sustained.
3. That war must be waged with the attitude of magisterial correction rather than malicious revenge.
4. That a just war must be explicitly declared by a legitimate authority.
5. That a war have a reasonable chance of success.
6. That certain parts of the population, especially noncombatants, be immune from intentional attack.
7. That the damage likely to be incurred by the war may not be disproportionate to the injury suffered.
8. That only legitimate and moral means may be employed in prosecuting the war.
9. That the final goal of the war must be the reestablishment of peace and justice.
10. That negotiations to end the war be in continuous process as long as fighting continues. (Brinsfield 1990)

These ethical criteria continue to color thinking about the rules of warfare and the circumstances under which the use of armed force is legally permissible. However, the advent of nuclear and other (chemical or biological) weapons of mass destruction have created a crisis of relevance in just war doctrine, as many of these moral and ethical principles do not clearly apply to the fuzzy circumstances that have materialized with innovations in military technology. As containment and prevention of violence has become the chief purpose of arms and armies today, leaders and scholars are wrestling with developing a revised just war code of conduct to deal with the new strategic realities of the twenty-first century.

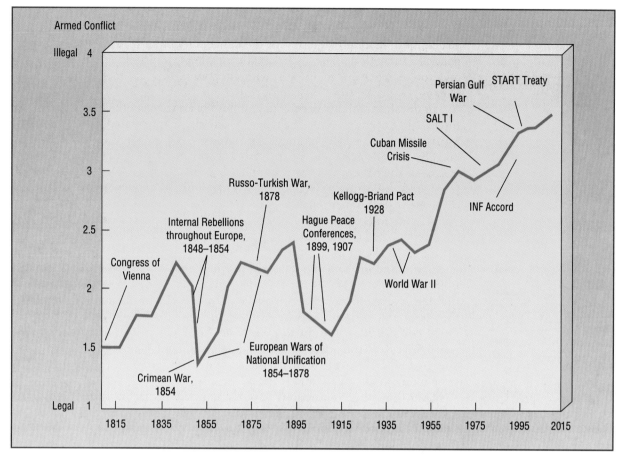

FIGURE 16.1

The Legal Prohibition of War of Aggression since 1815

Legal restraints on the historic right of states to start a war *(jus ad bellum)* have grown over time, but only steadily since World War I. The experience of past wars has significantly influenced the legal interpretation of prohibitions against the initiation of wars of conquest. Transitions in the legal status of initiating war have also been influenced both by international crises and by international conventions.

SOURCE: Transnational Rules Indicators Project (TRIP), as described by Kegley and Raymond (1990).

. . . to fight to promote justice, broadly conceived. Evil ought to be overturned, and good ought to be achieved, by force if necessary" (Claude 1988). Indeed, some interpret just war theory to condone savage behavior to end a war quickly and coerce surrender. As the Prussian military theorist Karl von Clausewitz (1976) argued in his 1832 treatise, *On War*, it is necessary to use "force unsparingly, without deference against the bloodshed involved. . . . To introduce into a philosophy of war a principle of moderation would be an absurdity. War is an act of violence pushed to its utmost bounds." Yet, the modern revival of just war theory reflects the continuing quest to place legal and moral constraints on the use of armed force in order to create a moral consensus about the conditions under which ends justify means, even though "today there is a sharp difference of opinion about the criteria that should be accepted" (von Glahn 1996).

514

THE LIBERAL
INSTITUTIONAL PATHS
TO PEACE THROUGH
LAW, INTEGRATION,
AND DEMOCRATIZATION

The Hague conferences of 1899 and 1907 were early developments in shaping new attitudes toward the start of armed conflict. World War I, however, revealed more than any other event the dangers inherent in the fact that "under general international law, as it stood up to 1914, any state could at any time and for any reason go to war without committing an international delinquency" (Kunz 1960).

In the aftermath of World War I, states began to reject the legal right to use force. The Covenant of the League of Nations, incorporated as Part I of the Treaty of Versailles in 1919, implemented a new regime. Articles 11 to 17 stipulated that in no case could a state resort to war until three months after a judicial determination by the League had elapsed. These articles also contained provisions subjecting any member "who committed an act of war against another member to sanctions."

Another important step was taken in 1928 in the *Treaty Providing for the Renunciation of War as an Instrument of National Policy,* known as the Kellogg-Briand Pact. The prohibition was reaffirmed in the 1933 Anti-War Treaty of Rio de Janeiro and in the Nuremberg war crimes trials at the end of World War II. Both spoke of war as "the supreme international crime." The United Nations Charter (Article 2) expanded the prohibition by unequivocally outlawing both the threat and initiation of war. At the same time, Article 39 gave the international community the right to determine "the existence of any threat to the peace, breach of the peace or act of aggression," and Article 42 authorized the Security Council "to take such action . . . as may be necessary to maintain or restore international peace and security."

Over time, legal injunctions have increasingly restricted states' right to resort to war. The doctrine of **military necessity** clarifies international law's position by restricting the justifiable use of military force to a last recourse for defense (Claude 1988). The modern legal conception of just war thus still embraces the traditional *jus ad bellum.* Now, however, it confines the right to wage a war to the purposes of punishing aggression, deterring attack, protecting innocents' human rights, and generally defending "the system's rules" (Kelsen 1945). This change modifies the political culture in which states compete: "The willingness of nations to subscribe, even in principle, to the renunciation of their rights to use force (except in self-defense) is a significant step, an expression of willingness to move in one direction rather than the other, and a disclosure of consensus on the most important aspect of political order in world affairs" (Falk 1965).

Although acceptance of the right of states to start a war has waned, until the Cold War ended in 1989, the frequency of wars between states did not decline. In the period between World War II and 1989, in fact, the prohibition of initiating war did not prevent its initiation. True, the great powers did not take up arms against each other; however, they often used armed force against other states, and wars between Global South countries were common (see Chapter 12). Many of these actions were conducted in ways arguably prohibited by international law, despite the attacking states' claims that international law sanctioned their behavior (Tillema and Van Wingen 1982).

Still, because war is no longer licensed, the intention to make war is a crime, and those who start a war are now criminals. That consensus may be an important psychological restraint on future policymakers' choices. (Some realists, however, would undoubtedly disagree, arguing that aggressive leaders will not be restrained by the mere delegitimization of violence.)

In addition to this prohibition, contemporary international law has sought to grapple with newer forms of armed conflict, though this has proven difficult. Consider three examples.

515

THE LIBERAL
INSTITUTIONAL PATHS
TO PEACE THROUGH
LAW, INTEGRATION,
AND DEMOCRATIZATION

First, international law advances guidelines for states' permissible military response to terrorism. It restricts that response to cases where another state's responsibility for the act of terrorism is beyond all doubt. Moreover, "this right does not allow retaliation for past attacks. The response in self-defense to an armed [terrorist] attack must be necessary and proportional . . . and the victim of an act of terrorism will have to pursue other remedies against states it believes responsible and against the states that encourage, promote, condone, or tolerate terrorism or provide a haven to terrorists" (Henkin 1991).

Second, consider the rise of military intervention and arms sales as policy instruments in world affairs alongside the decay since 1945 of the distinction between internal and international situations:

> International law does not forbid one state to sell arms to another state, and upon authentic invitation, a state may introduce military forces into the territory of another to assist the government for various purposes, including maintaining internal order. On the other hand, a state may not introduce arms or armed forces into a country without the consent of its government, surely not to support any groups hostile to the government. (Henkin 1991, 63)

Yet here we note that the traditional prohibition against external intervention in a sovereign state's territory has eroded since the mid-1970s. As Figure 16.2 shows, the nonintervention rule is increasingly challenged, and "the belief that governments have a right, even obligation, to intervene in the affairs of other states seems to have gained great currency in recent years" (Blechman 1995). Rising global interdependence has made the concepts of defined borders, external penetration, and sovereign territoriality less and less meaningful. In an age of instantaneous global communications; the unprecedented movement of people, goods, and money across national borders; and the heavy involvement of "foreigners" in the internal affairs of states everywhere, international law has broadened the definition of the conditions under which intervention is legally permissible, accepting the right of states to intervene for humanitarian purposes.

Third, international law has had great difficulty keeping pace with the rapid technological innovations in weapons systems. The recent creation of a whole category of nonlethal weapons, for example, has raised serious questions about the ethics and legality of their use and the conditions under which they might be deployed. The slow pace of the movement to ban antipersonnel land mines illustrates the problems of legal reform. Today's technological advances in weapons are moving so fast that international law has been unable to construct rules to regulate the types of military activities now possible. This problem prompts taking a closer look at the evolving legal rules for the conduct of armed conflict.

The Rules for War's Conduct and the Expansion of Human Rights Legislation.
Laws regulating the methods that states may use in war *(jus in bello)* have also grown. These restraints include the principles of discrimination and **noncombatant immunity,** which attempt to protect innocent civilians by restricting military targets to soldiers and supplies. The laws of retaliation specify conditions under which certain practices are legitimate. One category,

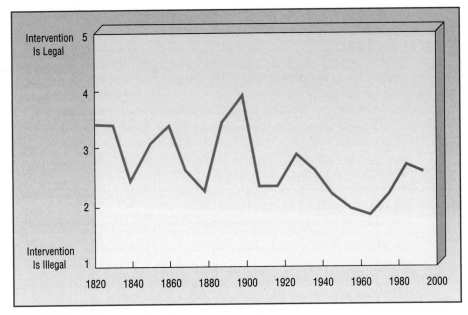

FIGURE 16.2

The Changing Status of the Nonintervention Rule in International Law since 1820

Over time, the illegality of intervening in sovereign states has changed. Since 1960, international law has adopted an increasingly permissive posture toward this form of coercive diplomacy for a variety of purposes including humanitarian aid, preventing genocide, protecting civil liberties, and promoting democracy through "reform interventions."

SOURCE: Transnational Rules Indicators Project (TRIP), as measured in Kegley, Raymond, and Hermann (1998).

reprisals (hostile and illegal acts permitted only if made in proportionate response to a prior hostile and illegal act), stipulates procedures for military occupations, blockades, shows of force, and bombardments. Another category, **retorsion** (hostile but legal retaliatory acts made in response to similar legal acts initiated by other states), provides rules for embargoes, boycotts, import quotas, tariffs, and travel restrictions to redress grievances.

While the cynic may conclude that the laws of retaliation (particularly reprisals) are really instructions for killing, that conclusion is unwarranted. Restrictions on the weapons that can be used and the permissible methods of fighting reduce killing in warfare. The widening scope of acts now classified as **war crimes** (the abuse of, and atrocities committed on, enemy soldiers, prisoners of war, and civilians during an armed conflict) also promises to limit the violence, savagery, and genocide that have been practiced in many recent civil wars. Consider the following examples from among more than thirty recognized rules (from von Glahn 1996), which suggest the impressive degree to which international humanitarian law (sometimes called the law for **human rights** in war) has expanded for protection of and assistance to victims of armed conflicts.

human rights the innate freedoms and dignity of all individuals because of their humanness, which in principle some states violate when they mistreat innocent minority populations.

- No attacking of unarmed enemies.

- No use of forbidden arms or munitions.

517

THE LIBERAL
INSTITUTIONAL PATHS
TO PEACE THROUGH
LAW, INTEGRATION,
AND DEMOCRATIZATION

How a state treats its own citizens was, until very recently, its own business under the nonintervention rule in international law protecting states from external interference in their domestic affairs. Now the global community has defined the humane treatment of people as a fundamental *human right,* and the UN Security Council has stretched the traditional definiton of threats to international peace in order to authorize various kinds of intervention to protect the universal human rights of people within states. This enlarged definition has infuriated some states who complain that their sovereign rights have been compromised. Shown here is an example of the kind of state behavior at the center of the debate: to deter crime, China's leaders have ordered the execution of hundreds of alleged criminals, and many other states have complained that this gross violation of civil liberties without fair trial warrants reprisals.

- No firing on undefended localities without military significance.
- No improper use or destruction of privileged (i.e., exempt, immune) buildings for military purposes.
- No poisoning streams or wells.
- No pillaging.
- No killing or wounding military personnel who have surrendered or are disabled by wounds or sickness.
- No assassinating and hiring of assassins.
- No ill-treating prisoners of war.
- No compelling the inhabitants of occupied enemy territory to furnish information about the armed forces of the enemy or its means of defense.
- No bombarding from the air to terrorize or attack civilian populations.
- No attacking enemy vessels that have indicated their surrender by lowering their flag.
- No destroying civilian cultural objects and places of worship.

518

THE LIBERAL
INSTITUTIONAL PATHS
TO PEACE THROUGH
LAW, INTEGRATION,
AND DEMOCRATIZATION

These illustrative objections to practices once condoned move warfare away from barbarism, providing that courts and legal tribunals are willing and able to enforce humanitarian laws (see Focus 16.3). This is underscored by the international community's impressive expansion of the legal human rights protections it grants (see Table 16.2, page 520).

Law's Contribution to Peace. Cynics who contend that international law is irrelevant to the control of war overlook several dimensions of law's character. First, international law is not intended to prevent all warfare. Aggressive war is illegal, but defensive war is not. It is a mistake, therefore, to claim that international law has broken down whenever war breaks out.

Second, instead of doing away with war, international law preserves it as a sanction against the breaking of rules. Thus war is a device of last resort to punish aggressors and thereby maintain the system's legal framework.

Third, international law is an institutional substitute for war. Legal procedures exist to resolve conflicts before they erupt into open hostilities. Although they cannot prevent war, they sometimes make recourse to violence unnecessary by resolving disputes that might otherwise escalate to war.

The demonstrable capacity of pacific methods to reduce the frequency of war does not mean that international adjudicative machinery is well developed or functionally effective. Nowhere is this more evident than with the **International Court of Justice (ICJ),** known as the World Court, that was created after World War II as the highest judicial body on earth. The World Court was an inactive judicial institution until very recently. Between 1946 and 1991 it heard only sixty-four contentious cases between states, rendered judgments on less than half of these, and handed down only nineteen advisory opinions, and over the last century has averaged only about three cases per year. Since 1991, however, the ICJ has expanded its workload, and considered cases dealing with many new issues (see Map 16.1). Even though only governments of states may apply for an appearance before the Court (and are hesitant to do so because ICJ decisions are final, without a possibility of appeal), an increasing number have done so: between 1992 and 1995, the ICJ heard twenty-four cases, and the judicial activity jumped to an average of fourteen cases each year between 1996 and 1998. The Court also became increasingly active in responding to requests for advisory opinions; for example, in 1996 the ICJ dealt with two such issues, and rendered an advisory opinion on the highly controversial question of whether the use or threat of nuclear weapons could be declared illegal (answering that for the most part it should be). Thus, although there has been a "slight upswing in the number of cases on the ICJ's docket," the World Court remains underutilized, because "states do not like to litigate against other states," and "the increased number of cases per annum from two or three to something like ten only indicates a relative but minor change in the Court's utility" (Forsythe 1997).

The World Court's past impact has been marginal, partly because most judicial conflict settlements take place in the domestic courts of one of the contestants or in other international tribunals, where there is stronger evidence of compliance with court decisions (Falk 1964; von Glahn 1996). Still other controversies are settled through ad hoc arbitration and mediation proceedings, and the idea of allowing international law to become less state-centric by encompassing nonstate parties (as was the case in the eighteenth century) has not gained sufficient support to begin to give nonstate parties (such as victims of

Can Courts Stop War Crimes?

When armed conflict erupts, international law requires the participants to refrain from activities that violate certain principles accepted by the international community. One of these rules is the protection of innocent noncombatants. But what can international judicial bodies do when violations occur? They can condemn the actions and the criminals who commit such crimes, as they have been especially prone to do in the late 1990s. However, courts and international tribunals cannot prevent the crime.

This powerlessness was illustrated in Bosnia-Herzegovina on July 25, 1995, when Bosnian Serb rebels, seizing their second United Nations "safe area" in two weeks, marched into Zepa and began to methodically slaughter thousands of Muslims. On the same day, their leaders were called before a UN court on charges of genocide and crimes against humanity for committing atrocities against civilians and captured soldiers. In the Hague, the Prosecutor's Office of the Yugoslav War Crimes Tribunal (created in 1993 by the UN Security Council) indicted Bosnian Serb General Ratko Mladic and the nationalist rebels' political leader, Radovan Karadzic, as war criminals. Mladic—a hero to his troops—personally oversaw the capture of the "safe area" Srebrenica, where UN officials said Muslims were then killed, raped, or taken captive. Up to seven thousand people remained missing. As the indictment was announced, Mladic was meeting with the UN commander for Bosnia, Lieutenant General Rupert Smith. Officials at UN headquarters in New York defended the decision to negotiate with the Serb nationalists despite the indictments.

The international community often finds itself facing ethical dilemmas in situations of this sort. Although it sets standards for individuals and states to follow, those who flout these rules are the ones with whom the global community must negotiate to settle the conflicts that have led to the illegal behavior. Although the criminals are outlaws (outside the law), they are often treated as respected leaders with whom bargaining must occur if the conflict is to be resolved. They are the only people who can make binding decisions for the groups they lead.

While many people and states still commit war crimes without facing punishment, the resumption of war crime tribunals in 1993 signaled to would-be perpetrators the global community's intolerance for these atrocities. The Prosecutor's office of the UN's **International Criminal Tribunal** had indicted seventy-seven people and arrested seven for crimes in Bosnia by October 1997. Only ten suspects were in custody, and it is unlikely that all of the accused will face trial. Nonetheless, the indicted "are not subject to any statute of limitations, and until the day they die, even if the tribunal has long since gone out of existence, they will be subject to prosecution and punishment anywhere in the world" (Neier 1995). Many Nazi war criminals even today face that haunting reality.

The Balkan War Crimes investigation conducted by the antecedent Commission in the Hague faced many problems in its efforts to force alleged war criminals to face charges of genocide and crimes against humanity (as did the 1992 UN war crimes tribunal for Rwanda). It was difficult to find ways to persuade the leaders of Serbia and Croatia, obligated under the Dayton Accord to cooperate with the tribunal, to send the indicted war criminals they harbored to the Hague, or to find a legal way for NATO peacekeeping forces to arrest the suspects. Nonetheless, the obstacles have not slowed the global community's efforts to create a **permanent world criminal court.** The establishment of a standing international court to judge the most terrible of mass crimes—including especially acts of **genocide** (the massacre of ethnic, religious, or political populations) such as those occurring in the ethnopolitical conflicts in recent years—is a goal the UN has pursued for half a century. It is now on the verge of becoming a reality, providing states' wariness of a global criminal court with jurisdiction inside their borders can be overcome. A consensus has not been reached on the kinds of crimes such a court would consider, the procedures for bringing an accused criminal to trial, and the authority of a chief prosecutor. But many human rights experts were confident that the Rome treaty conference in June 1998 would create a new international legal organization to take sanctions against this kind of crime, because in August 1997 virtually all governments had voiced support for the idea of creating a standing war crimes court (Crossette 1997). Whether this institutional innovation will actually be implemented nonetheless remains uncertain because the United States has taken the position that it will not become a party to such a treaty unless the UN Security Council can control the cases such a war crimes court can hear.

520

THE LIBERAL
INSTITUTIONAL PATHS
TO PEACE THROUGH
LAW, INTEGRATION,
AND DEMOCRATIZATION

TABLE 16.2 Legal Steps in the Development of Human Rights: Some Major Conventions

Year	Convention
1948	Universal Declaration of Human Rights
1949	Convention on the Prevention and the Punishment of the Crime of Genocide
1950	European Convention for the Protection of Human Rights and Fundamental Freedoms
1950	Convention for the Suppression of the Traffic of Persons and the Exploitation of the Prostitution of Others
1951	Convention Relating to the Status of Refugees
1953	Convention on the Political Rights of Women
1956	Supplementary Convention on the Abolition of Slavery, the Slave Trade, and Institutions and Practices Similar to Slavery
1957	Convention on the Nationality of Married Women
1961	Convention on the Reduction of Statelessness
1965	International Convention on the Elimination of All Forms of Racial Discrimination
1966	International Covenant on Civil and Political Rights
1966	Optional Protocol to the International Covenant on Civil and Political Rights
1967	Convention on the Elimination of All Forms of Discrimination against Women
1967	Declaration on Territorial Asylum
1967	Protocol Relating to the Status of Refugees
1969	Inter-American Convention on Human Rights
1976	International Covenant on Economic, Social, and Cultural Rights
1977	Protocols on Humanitarian Law for International Armed Conflicts and Noninternational Armed Conflicts
1981	Covenant of Civil and Political Rights
1981	Convention of the Elimination of All Forms of Discrimination Against Women
1981	Declaration on the Elimination of All Forms of Intolerance and of Discrimination Based on Religion or Belief
1983	Inhumane Weapons Convention
1984	Convention against Torture and Other Cruel, Inhuman, or Degrading Treatment or Punishment
1989	Convention on the Rights of the Child
1989	Second Optional Protocol to the International Covenant on Civil and Political Rights, Aiming at the Abolition of the Death Penalty
1991	Convention on the Elimination of Political, Economic, Social, Cultural, and Civil Discrimination against Women
1991	Convention on the Prevention and Suppression of Genocide
1992	Declaration of Principles of International Law on Compensation to Refugees
1993	Vienna Convention on Human Rights
1994	African Convention on Human and Peoples Rights

521

THE LIBERAL
INSTITUTIONAL PATHS
TO PEACE THROUGH
LAW, INTEGRATION,
AND DEMOCRATIZATION

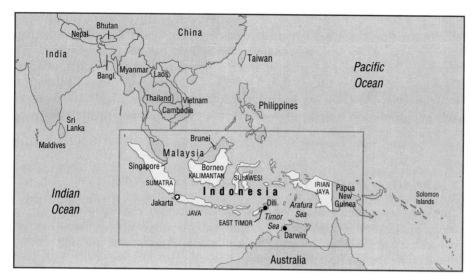

MAP 16.1

The Legal Battle over East Timor

Indonesia militarily took over East Timor after Portugal abandoned it as a colony in 1975. In 1995, Portugal took its case to the World Court in the Hague, challenging the Timor Gap Agreement between Indonesia and Australia, which established a 38,125 square-mile zone in the sea, as shown in this map. Portugal argued before the World Court that Indonesia and Australia had granted oil concessions in the territory that did not belong to them. This is the type of dispute that the World Court was created to resolve peacefully.

war crimes) legal standing before the ICJ (Forsythe 1997). The most important reason, however, is that the World Court's jurisdiction is not compulsory. Although all UN members are members of the Court, only one-third have accepted the ICJ's compulsory jurisdiction in conflicts involving them. All but a handful of these have stipulated reservations to their acceptance, and thereby excluded the automatic jurisdiction through treaties under Article 36 (1). The United States, for example, has undermined the drive to strengthen the World Court by adhering to the so-called Connally amendment, which reserves the U.S. right to determine the cases in which it will allow the court jurisdiction; the Reagan administration withdrew from a qualified grant of compulsory ICJ jurisdiction, and "neither the Bush nor Clinton administrations" since then "saw fit to return to the axiom articulated by President Eisenhower: '[i]t is better to lose a point now and then in an international tribunal and gain a world in which everyone lives at peace under the rule of law.' States for the most part still tend to opt for freedom over order, and to reject the notion that the most meaningful freedom is found precisely within a workable system of order" (Forsythe 1997). Exceptions to this occur at the regional level. For example, the **European Court of Justice (ECJ)** has authority over state members and acts as a legal engine for the integration of the European Union, and the European Court on Human Rights, under the Council of Europe, exercises authoritative jurisdiction; in South America, the Inter-American Court on Human Rights has also considered cases.

World order in the twenty-first century will depend to a considerable extent on the uses to which states put international law. Its alleged shortcomings lie not with the laws but with their creators—states and their addiction to sover-

522

THE LIBERAL
INSTITUTIONAL PATHS
TO PEACE THROUGH
LAW, INTEGRATION,
AND DEMOCRATIZATION

eignty as a legal right. The intentions of states acting individually or in concert, and not the slow processes by which legal development grows, will be decisive. The international community could, in principle, strengthen international law's capacity to curtail aggression. Still, many barriers remain to creating, as John F. Kennedy expressed liberal theory's hope, "a new world of law, where the strong are just and the weak secure and the peace preserved." That conclusion leads naturally to a consideration of the role of international organizations in maintaining world peace.

• • •

INTERNATIONAL ORGANIZATION AND WORLD ORDER

Liberal theorists recommend the creation of international organizations as a second political path to peace. To understand this approach, we must also understand its theoretical underpinnings. The expectations about and performance of the United Nations exemplify those theoretical premises.

The United Nations and the Preservation of Peace

Like its predecessor, the League of Nations, the UN's primary mission—as its charter states—is the "maintenance of international peace and security." The stipulation that membership is open to all "peace-loving" countries reaffirms this purpose, as does the charter's requirement that members "settle their international disputes by peaceful means."

Collective Security. Collective security is often viewed as a liberal alternative to the competitive balanced alliances that realists recommend. In a balance-of-power system, it is assumed that each state, acting in its own self-interest for its individual protection, will form coalitions offsetting others and that the resulting equilibrium will prevent war. In contrast, collective security asks each state to share responsibility for every other states' security. It "assumes that every nation perceives every challenge to the international order in the same way, and is prepared to run the same risks to preserve it" (Kissinger 1992). All states are to take joint action against *any* transgressor, and *all* are to act in concert. This presumes that the superior power of the entire community will deter those contemplating aggression or, failing this, that collective action will defeat any violator of the peace.

Faced with the League's inability to put collective security into practice, realist critics attacked what they regarded as the illusory expectations on which liberal proponents had built the model. The League's failures stemmed from the U.S. refusal to join the organization; the other great powers' fear that the League's collective strength might be used against them; disagreement over objectively defining an instance of aggression in which all concurred; states' pervasive dread of inequities in sharing the risks and costs of mounting an organized response to aggression; and their tendency to voice approval of the value of general peace but to be unwilling to organize resistance except when their own security was threatened. In the final analysis, the theory's central fallacy was that it expected a state to be as anxious to see others protected as it was to protect itself. That assumption was not upheld in the period between World War I and World War II. As a result, the League of Nations never became a true collective security system.

The architects of the United Nations were painfully aware of the League's disappointing experience. While they voiced support for collective security, their design restored the balance of power to maintain peace. The United Nations Charter, signed June 26, 1945, permitted any of the Security Council's five permanent members (the United States, the Soviet Union, Great Britain, France, and China) to veto and thereby block any proposed enforcement action that any of them disapproved. Because the Security Council could act in concert only when the permanent members fully agreed, the UN Charter was a concession to states' sovereign freedom:

523

THE LIBERAL
INSTITUTIONAL PATHS
TO PEACE THROUGH
LAW, INTEGRATION,
AND DEMOCRATIZATION

> In the final analysis, the San Francisco Conference must be described as having repudiated the doctrine of collective security as the foundation for a general, universally applicable system for the management of power in international relations. The doctrine was given ideological lip service, and a scheme was contrived for making it effective in cases of relatively minor importance. But the new organization reflected the conviction that the concept of collective security had no realistic relevance to the problems posed by conflict among the major powers. (Claude 1962, 164–65)

To further enhance the great powers' authority relative to the United Nations, the charter severely restricted the capacity of the General Assembly to mount collective action. The charter authorized it only to initiate studies of conflict situations, bring perceived hostilities to the attention of the Security Council, and make recommendations for initiatives to keep the peace. Moreover, it restricted the role of the secretary general to that of chief administrative officer. Article 99 confined the secretary general, and the working staff of the Secretariat created to aid that person, to alerting the Security Council to peace-threatening situations and to providing administrative support for the operations that the Security Council authorized.

Although the UN's structure compromises the organization's security mission, it is still much more than a mere debating society. It is also more than an arena for the conduct of power politics. During the Cold War the United Nations fell short of many of the ideals its more ambitious founders envisioned, principally because its two most powerful members (the United States and the Soviet Union) in the Security Council did not cooperate (see Chapter 6). Nevertheless, like any adaptive institution, it found ways to overcome the compromising legal restrictions that inhibited its capacity to preserve world order.

From Collective Security to Peacekeeping. The Korean police action in 1950 provided a glimmer of hope that the United Nations might overcome its institutional barriers to preserving world order. However, that episode was an intervention sponsored and fought by the United States under UN auspices and did not set a precedent for equally ambitious initiatives in later conflicts. After the disillusioning Korean experience, the UN did not undertake another "enforcement" mission to defeat an aggressor for another forty years, until it mounted a collective response to Iraq's invasion of Kuwait.

During the long period between Korea and Kuwait, the UN adaptively sought to overcome the political obstacles posed by superpower discord. Its experiments with monitoring explosive situations began during its formative period. In 1948, for example, it created the United Nations Truce Supervision

524

THE LIBERAL
INSTITUTIONAL PATHS
TO PEACE THROUGH
LAW, INTEGRATION,
AND DEMOCRATIZATION

Organization (UNTSO) to monitor the cease-fire between Israel and neighboring countries. It also created the United Nations Military Observer Group in India and Pakistan (UNMOGIP) to protect a cease-fire zone in Kashmir. After the Korean War, these initiatives became precedents for a new approach, called peacekeeping. In contrast to peace enforcement, as in Korea, peacekeeping means separating antagonists. Acting in response to the Suez crisis under the Uniting for Peace resolution, in 1956 the General Assembly created the United Nations Emergency Force (UNEF). It also charged the secretary general with primary responsibility for managing this, the UN's first peacekeeping operation, to prevent the combatants from resuming fighting.

The General Assembly designed UNEF to forestall the superpowers' competitive intrusion into a potentially explosive situation and to overcome the Security Council's inaction. This innovative approach went beyond prior UN fact-finding commissions and observer forces. It was largely improvisational, since the charter had not provided for peacekeeping activities authorized by the General Assembly and managed by the secretary general. The principles underlying UNEF were different from collective security. The latter emphasized checking aggression through collective enforcement. UNEF, by contrast, emphasized noncoercive activities aimed at placing the UN's neutral "thin blue line" between the clashing armies to permit time for negotiations to resolve the conflict.

Success can be infectious. Following UNEF, the UN sprang into action to authorize other operations designed to prevent conflicts from reigniting. These missions have since become closely identified with the process of peacekeeping. For example, in 1958 the UN Observer Group helped to defuse the crisis in Lebanon. And in 1960 the largest UN peacekeeping force ever entered the Congo to stabilize that newly independent country. In 1964, the UN sent the UNFICYP peacekeeping force to Cyprus. Other increasingly diverse and ambitious UN peace missions followed from these precedents (see Ratner 1997 for descriptions of these operations). Map 16.2 displays the worldwide location of more than sixty-five of the UN's best-known operations.

Of these operations, nearly all have successfully fulfilled their goals. UN missions have usually succeeded in creating buffers between the warring disputants, providing time for negotiating cease-fires and ensuring compliance with agreements. On many occasions they have also helped to contain conflicts that threatened to escalate to large-scale wars with additional participants. Over time, the roles associated with UN peacekeeping have evolved. Traditional or first-generation peacekeeping activities were designed to handle military matters between states; second-generation peacekeeping activities are more complex, and include a broader range of programs that have taken the UN from managing crises "during incipiency" to bolder security- and confidence-building measures, verification, legal assistance in civil wars, combating terrorism, humanitarian aid, drug interdiction, election monitoring, naval peacekeeping, and other operations beyond the activities originally envisioned.

The Changing Role of the Secretary General. Drawing on the UN's experience with UNEF, in 1960 Secretary General Dag Hammarskjöld of Sweden articulated his vision for a new UN role in managing peace and security, which he termed **preventive diplomacy.** Perceiving the need for the United Nations to take bolder conflict-avoidance measures, Hammarskjöld practiced preventive diplomacy to resolve conflicts before they reached the crisis stage (in

preventive diplomacy
diplomatic actions taken in advance of a predictable crisis to prevent or limit violence.

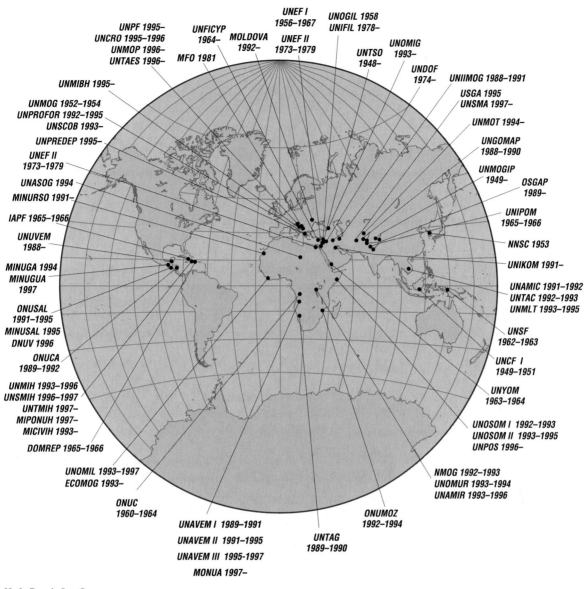

UNPF 1995–
UNCRO 1995–1996
UNMOP 1996–
UNTAES 1996–

UNFICYP 1964–

MOLDOVA 1992–

MFO 1981

UNEF I 1956–1967

UNEF II 1973–1979

UNOGIL 1958
UNIFIL 1978–

UNTSO 1948–

UNOMIG 1993–

UNDOF 1974–

UNIIMOG 1988–1991

USGA 1995
UNSMA 1997–

UNMOT 1994–

UNGOMAP 1988–1990

UNMOGIP 1949–

OSGAP 1989–

UNIPOM 1965–1966

NNSC 1953

UNIKOM 1991–

UNAMIC 1991–1992
UNTAC 1992–1993
UNMLT 1993–1995

UNSF 1962–1963

UNCF I 1949–1951

UNYOM 1963–1964

UNOSOM I 1992–1993
UNOSOM II 1993–1995
UNPOS 1996–

NMOG 1992–1993
UNOMUR 1993–1994
UNAMIR 1993–1996

ONUMOZ 1992–1994

UNTAG 1989–1990

UNAVEM I 1989–1991
UNAVEM II 1991–1995
UNAVEM III 1995–1997
MONUA 1997–

ONUC 1960–1964

DOMREP 1965–1966

UNOMIL 1993–1997
ECOMOG 1993–

UNMIH 1993–1996
UNSMIH 1996–1997
UNTMIH 1997–
MIPONUH 1997–
MICIVIH 1993–

ONUCA 1989–1992

ONUSAL 1991–1995
MINUSAL 1995
DNUV 1996

MINUGA 1994
MINUGUA 1997

UNUVEM 1988–

IAPF 1965–1966

MINURSO 1991–

UNASOG 1994

UNEF II 1973–1979

UNPREDEP 1995–

UNMOG 1952–1954
UNPROFOR 1992–1995
UNSCOB 1993–

UNMIBH 1995–

MAP 16.2

UN Peace Missions since 1948

From its origin through 1998, the United Nations has undertaken more than sixty-five peace missions worldwide. The UN's Blue Helmets have been dispatched to nearly ninety countries, with the UN personnel drawn from the armed forces of more than seventy-five UN members.

SOURCE: United Nations Information Center.

contrast to ending wars once they erupted). His efforts were greatly inspired by his frustration with Security Council inaction.

More than his unobtrusive predecessor, Trygve Lie of Norway (who resigned under pressure in November 1952), Hammarskjöld saw the secretary general's role as that of an active crisis manager. He independently enlarged the

525

526

THE LIBERAL
INSTITUTIONAL PATHS
TO PEACE THROUGH
LAW, INTEGRATION,
AND DEMOCRATIZATION

defined responsibilities of the executive organ of the United Nations by using his "good offices" to mediate international disputes and by strengthening the UN's administrative support for peacekeeping operations.

After Hammarskjöld met an untimely tragic death in the line of duty in September 1961, his successor, U Thant of Burma, pursued a much less activist program in his two terms of office, which ended in 1971. Constrained by increasing U.S. and Soviet pressure, U Thant concentrated on "quiet diplomacy" to manage crises that not he but the Security Council or the General Assembly identified. This approach was more akin to that which had prevailed in the early 1950s, stressing crisis response rather than crisis prevention.

The next secretary general, Kurt Waldheim of Austria, shared U Thant's preference for avoiding offending the great powers. Waldheim did seek to resolve some interstate disputes; for example, he made efforts to obtain the release of U.S. hostages seized in Iran in 1979. His initiatives were restrained, however. In his first public statement as secretary general, Waldheim stressed that "in this position one has to know the limits." This passivity endeared Waldheim to the superpowers, who rewarded his submissiveness by supporting his reappointment in 1976 and by promoting his reelection to a third term in 1981. But by this time, China—insisting on the election of a candidate from the developing countries and vowing to use its veto to prevent Waldheim's reelection—paved the way for the election of a more experienced diplomat with greater ambitions (Jakobson 1991).

Waldheim's successor, Javier Pérez de Cuéllar of Peru, also held "quiet diplomacy" in respect. Yet Pérez de Cuéllar was outspokenly critical of the "alarming succession of international crises" in which the United Nations was "unable to play as effective and decisive a role as the Charter certainly envisaged for it." To rectify its impotence, he called for renewed use of the Security Council that "too often [found] itself on the sidelines" because of alleged "partisanship, indecisiveness or incapacity arising from divisions among member states." He felt the Security Council should "keep an active watch on dangerous situations and, if necessary, initiate discussions with the parties" to defuse them "at an early stage before they degenerate into violence." Lamenting the fact that "the power of exposure" was the secretary general's only authorized power under the charter, in May 1989 Pérez de Cuéllar declared, "I cannot accept that, in each and every case, we need agreement by the two great powers before we can advance." Acting on this principle, he aggressively pursued both **peacemaking** and **peacekeeping** initiatives. He explained his approach in these terms:

> I have tried to simplify the procedures for finding peaceful solutions to international conflicts. The sequence of events is always the same. First you have to get a truce—end the hostilities. That is what we call "peacemaking" in diplomatic parlance. Once that is achieved and approved by the UN Security Council, we set up operations to keep the peace. That is what we call "peacekeeping."

On January 1, 1997, Kofi Annan of Ghana, formerly Under-Secretary for Peacekeeping Operations, took office as secretary general for a five-year term. Understandably, he approached the problem of managing the UN's **peace operations** enthusiastically, but he was highly aware of the administrative and budgetary constraints that limited the capacity to respond to every serious threat to peace. Using his personal humility and diplomatic charm to woo the support of

peacemaking the process of diplomacy, mediation, negotiation, or other forms of peaceful settlement that arranges an end to a dispute, and resolves issues that led to conflict.

peacekeeping military operations undertaken with the consent of all major parties to a dispute, designed to monitor and facilitate implementation of an agreement (cease-fire, truce, or other such agreement) and support diplomatic efforts to reach a long-term political settlement.

peace operations a general category encompassing both peacekeeping and peace enforcement operations undertaken to establish and maintain peace between disputants.

the major powers, Annan concentrated his efforts on massive administrative and organizational reforms to make the UN more efficient and cost-conscious (see Chapter 6). These reforms required a more selective peacekeeping policy, and resulted in the streamlining and downsizing of existing missions and a reluctance on the part of the Security Council to launch new missions. The number of missions in 1997 remained active in sixteen locations, but financial restraints reduced troop levels from thirty-one thousand at the start of 1996 to twenty-five thousand at the start of 1997, as the peacekeeping budget was cut in half. Nonetheless, Secretary General Annan continued to pursue plans to establish a **Rapidly Deployable Mission Headquarters (RDMH)** to accelerate the dispatch of UN Blue Helmets in future peace operations.

527

THE LIBERAL
INSTITUTIONAL PATHS
TO PEACE THROUGH
LAW, INTEGRATION,
AND DEMOCRATIZATION

Cold War Obstacles to Conflict Prevention. Pérez de Cuéllar's ambitious efforts strengthened the UN's capacity to preserve world peace (Skjelsbaek 1991). Still, until the closing days of the Cold War, the UN's record of preventing and settling conflicts attested to the barriers that then existed, for "only about two out of five" of the UN's attempts to mediate conflicts succeeded (Holsti 1988, 423). Similarly, of 319 international disputes in which some fighting occurred between 1945 and 1984, only 137, or 43 percent, were referred to the UN for management. Moreover, the United Nations failed to control nearly half of these disputes and failed to fully settle 75 percent of them (Haas 1986, 17). Hence, the UN's *peacemaking* achievements during the Cold War were modest at best.

Yet the achievements that were recorded demonstrate that the United Nations was, to some extent, able to transcend the substantial barriers symbolized by 264 vetoes, on one-third of its resolutions, in the Security Council between 1945 and 1991 (Riggs and Plano 1994, 58). This mixed record of success and impotence suggests that the UN's usefulness as an instrument of conflict management in the Cold War's inauspicious climate was greatest when a conflict:

- Did not involve the superpowers.
- Was outside the context of the East-West rivalry.
- Was important to the Security Council.
- Was intense and in danger of spreading geographically.
- Entailed fighting (albeit at a limited level).
- Centered on a decolonization dispute.
- Involved middle-sized and small states, comparatively unprepared militarily.
- Was identified as a threat to peace by the secretary general, who led efforts to organize UN resistance to its continuation.

The record underscores the extent to which, as Trygve Lie noted in 1946, "the United Nations is no stronger than the collective will of the nations that support it. Of itself it can do nothing. It is a machinery through which nations can cooperate. It can be used and developed . . . or it can be discarded and broken."

Given this reality, it is understandable why, while the United Nations was a captive of Cold War competition, it directed its activities primarily toward addressing the deep-seated structural causes of war, where it could make a difference. This is seen in its "rear door" efforts to alleviate the conditions of poverty, inequality, frustration, and despair that provoke violence. The UN's greatest effort is geared toward **peacebuilding** (creating conditions that make war unlikely) rather than peacemaking (ending fighting already under way). These programs are inspired by the liberal principle that improving the quality of people's lives can reduce the need for military arsenals. The conviction is expressed in the UN's work on human rights, technical assistance, refugees, decolonization, world trade, protection of children, world hunger, social discrimination, the equality of women, agricultural development, religious discrimination, disaster relief, environmental protection, and a host of other world problems that influence the quality of life and serve as potential wellsprings for aggression.

Despite its weaknesses, the United Nations is in many respects, as U.S. President John F. Kennedy (a realist who described himself as an "idealist without illusions") put it, "our last hope in an age where the instruments of war have far outpaced the instruments of peace." This fulfillment of promise gained new momentum when the end of the Cold War opened a new chapter on the UN's quest for world order.

The UN's Blue Helmets and Multilateral Peacekeeping. The United Nations was a victim of superpower rivalry for more than four decades. But the end of the Cold War removed impediments to the organization's ability to fulfill its security-preserving mission. That possibility was made clear in 1990, when Iraq invaded Kuwait. The Security Council promptly passed Resolution 678, authorizing member states "to use all necessary means" to coerce Iraq's withdrawal from Kuwait. Under the authority of this resolution, on January 16, 1991, U.S. President Bush ordered an air war against Iraq's military machine, the fourth largest in the world. Forty-three days later, Iraq agreed to a cease-fire and to withdraw from Kuwait.

Bolstered by this success at collective security, optimism about the UN's capacity to take the lead in peacemaking started to grow. This optimism was facilitated by the shift of power from the General Assembly back to the Security Council. Acting in concert, it authorized the United Nations to launch nearly twice the peacekeeping missions between 1988 and 1994 than it had in the previous forty-three years of its existence (see Table 16.3). That activity has remained high, with the UN managing seventeen peacekeeping operations in 1995, sixteen in 1996, fifteen in 1997, and fifteen in 1998.

In 1992, when Boutros Boutros-Ghali became Secretary General, the United Nations greatly expanded its profile and agenda. Under his lobbying, the UN peacekeepers—its so-called "Blue Helmets"—increased from four thousand to more than seventy thousand by 1995. Boutros-Ghali's bold "Agenda for Peace" proposed creation of a standing UN "peace enforcement force" to quickly "enforce a cease-fire by taking coercive action against either party, or both, if they violate it." Under this innovation, which set the stage for **peace enforcement** operations, UN rapid deployment units would be established by the voluntary contribution of member states, go into action when authorized by the Security Council, and serve under the command of the secretary general. Unlike traditional peacekeeping operations, however, their use could be ordered without the express consent of the disputants, and they would be trained and equipped to use force if necessary. This would enable UN forces, "by presenting a credible military threat, . . . to convince all conflictual parties that violence will not succeed. . . . The military objective of the strategy, then, is to deter, dissuade, and deny (D^3)" (Ruggie 1993).

TABLE 16.3 The Rise and Decline of the UN's Peacekeeping Role, 1988, 1994, 1997			
	1988	**1994**	**1997**
Security Council peacekeeping resolutions for new operations adopted	15	78	3
Disputes and conflicts in which the UN was actively involved in preventive diplomacy or peacemaking	11	28	26
Peacekeeping operations deployed	5	17	19
Military personnel under UN flag	9,600	73,000	25,000
Civilian police deployed	35	2,130	2,739
Countries contributing military and police personnel	26	76	71
UN annual budget for peacekeeping operations	$230,000,000	$3,610,000,000	$1,300,000,000
Countries in which the United Nations undertook electoral activities	0	21	11
Sanctions administered by the Security Council	1	7	8

SOURCE: United Nations Information Center, SIPRI (1998).

A number of barriers to these ambitious security goals exist. The first is political—the expanded size of the UN complicates decision making. Between March 1992 and March 1995, twenty countries joined the United Nations. This swelled the UN to 185 members, ranging in size from geographic giants such as Russia and China to microstates such as Andorra, Palau, and Eritrea. In addition, the 1996 proposals to expand the Security Council to eight or ten members (a move to make it more representative by bringing in Germany, Japan, and perhaps leading Global South countries) would make agreements about new peacekeeping ventures difficult, because great powers' interests are often

The job of "superclerk," running the United Nations as secretary general is perhaps the most challenging in the world. In 1997 that position changed hands, as Kofi Annan of Ghana (at right) replaced Boutros Boutros-Ghali. Annan undertook massive reforms while seeking, with reduced finances, "to maintain the organization's capacity to manage existing operations and, if necessary, to launch new operations." As a key element in his organizational reform package, Annan won approval for the appointment of Louise Frechette (at left) as the UNs first deputy secretary general.

529

530

THE LIBERAL
INSTITUTIONAL PATHS
TO PEACE THROUGH
LAW, INTEGRATION,
AND DEMOCRATIZATION

incompatible and the prospect for reaching a consensus declines as the size of a group increases. Even if the post-Cold War environment is more hospitable to global security enforcement than in the past, implementing collective security through the United Nations will not be easy.

As in the past, there remains the temptation for members to support only those peacekeeping efforts that affect their own immediate security interests. For example, the September 1993 U.S. Presidential Decision Directive 13 prohibited contributing U.S. military units to a permanent standby force such as that authorized by Article 43 of the UN Charter. This prohibition was made despite more than fifteen other UN members having earlier agreed to provide fifty-four thousand troops. The decision by the United States thus increased the gap between the UN's aspirations for maintaining peace and its capabilities, since "[w]ithout U.S. leadership and power, the United Nations lacks muscle," but with it, ironically, "the United Nations loses its independent identity" (Gelb 1993).

The second constraint to realizing the UN's security goals is organizational. The United Nations remains poorly designed to carry out a full-fledged peace and security program. Its goals have exceeded the institutional apparatus. UN troops no longer just patrol truce lines. Now they also monitor elections, promote democratic reforms, protect human rights, train local police, guard humanitarian relief deliveries, and take up arms against those who get in their way—all without sufficient technical and logistical support.

The danger of becoming overwhelmed by this ambitious agenda was illustrated in the UNPROFUR mission in the former Yugoslavia. In 1992 forty-thousand Blue Helmets were sent to stop the carnage threatening to kill millions. They were unprepared in training and did not have the authorization required to get the job done. It was only after NATO's September 1995 air strikes and the alliance's Operation Joint Endeavor got under way in January 1996 that the prospects for peace brightened. UNPROFUR showed that UN peacemaking initiatives are destined to fail unless the great powers provide the needed resources.

The third barrier is financial. The UN's peacekeeping budget is less than the amount it takes to run the New York City police, fire department, and prisons (Evans 1995, 8). This lack of funds works against a managerial security role for the United Nations. Indeed, the United Nations cannot pay for its expanded list of expensive peace missions, let alone assume responsibility for new initiatives. In 1987 peacekeeping cost UN members $240 million in assessments; by 1996 the bill had risen to $3.6 billion, and at that time eighty UN members were in arrears. The United States owed 69 percent of the UN debt in January 1997 (*SIPRI 1997*, 49), and in late 1997 requested that its assessment be reduced to 20 percent (from 25 percent) and that China increase its contribution from 0.7 to 4 percent to help cover the gap. Although half the peacekeeping missions the United Nations had ever undertaken occurred between 1993 and 1997, the organization was budgetarily crippled and nearing bankruptcy, and unable to find the funds to carry out the peacekeeping function the Security Council had asked of it. In this climate, the retrenchment in peace operation activities that began in 1997 under Secretary General Kofi Annan's reforms is likely to continue, with the prospects for the presence of the Blue Helmets in many future global hot spots becoming more remote.

The UN's problems raise concerns about its future ability to police the many ethnic conflicts and potential civil and interstate wars on the horizon. The United Nations is not yet a true collective security organization. Its blueprint for global involvement is just that—a blueprint. It is a design without a realistic structure, and the United Nations is not yet empowered for the high purposes it has been asked to perform. Currently, its advocates' expectations exceed its capabilities.

Impeding the United Nations' success are the same forces that have eroded past collective security mechanisms. In the face of aggression, many states have sought to "free ride" on the defense efforts of others, and have only supported collective efforts when their own immediate security was at stake. If countries do not act on the perception that violence and injustice anywhere are threats everywhere, the prospects for collective responses are poor. Still, it is likely that powerful members of the international community will, at times, respond to the threats and human suffering that aggression causes.

531

THE LIBERAL
INSTITUTIONAL PATHS
TO PEACE THROUGH
LAW, INTEGRATION,
AND DEMOCRATIZATION

> In the great uncertainties and disorders that lie ahead, the United Nations, for all its shortcomings, will be called on again and again, because there is no other global institution, because there is a severe limit to what even the strongest powers wish to take on themselves. . . . Either the UN is vital to a more stable and equitable world and should be given the means to do its job, or peoples and governments should be encouraged to look elsewhere. But is there really an alternative? (Urquhart 1994, 33)

Actually, there *is* a conspicuous alternative. The great powers' reluctance to equip the United Nations to contain civil wars lends credence to the 1995 prophecy of Karel Kovanda (the Czech Republic's UN ambassador), that "[t]he important issues are going to be taken care of by regional organizations . . . with the United Nations giving its blessings."

Regional Security Organizations and Conflict Management

If the United Nations reflects the lack of shared values and common purpose characteristic of a global community, perhaps regional organizations, whose members already share some interests and cultural traditions, offer better prospects. The kinds of wars raging today do not lend themselves to control by a worldwide body, because these conflicts are now almost entirely civil wars. The UN was designed to manage only interstate wars; it was not organized or legally authorized to intervene in battles *within* sovereign borders. This, however, is not the case for regional institutions; regional IGOs see their security interests vitally affected by armed conflicts within countries in their area or adjacent to it, and historically have shown the determination and discipline to police bitter civil conflicts "in their backyards." Hence, regional security organizations can be expected to play an increasingly larger role in the future security affairs of their regions.

During the Cold War, the North Atlantic Treaty Organization (NATO) and the Warsaw Pact were the best-known regional security organizations. Others now include the Organization for Security and Cooperation in Europe (OSCE), the Western European Union (WEU), the ANZUS pact (Australia, New Zealand, and the United States), the Southeast Asia Treaty Organization (SEATO), and the Commonwealth of Independent States (CIS) made up of the former members of the Soviet Union. Regional organizations with somewhat broader political mandates beyond defense include the Organization of American States (OAS), the League of Arab States, the Organization of African Unity (OAU), the Nordic Council, the Association of Southeast Asian Nations (ASEAN), and the Gulf Cooperation Council.

532

THE LIBERAL
INSTITUTIONAL PATHS
TO PEACE THROUGH
LAW, INTEGRATION,
AND DEMOCRATIZATION

Although Article 51 of the United Nations Charter encourages the creation of regional organizations for collective self-defense, it would be misleading to describe NATO and the other regional organizations as a substitute collective security instrument for the UN. They are not. More accurately, **regional collective defense** systems are designed to deter a potential common threat to the region's peace (one typically identified in advance).

Many of today's regional security organizations are influenced by reductions in their members' perception of a clearly identifiable external enemy or common threat. A sign of the times was NATO's response to the virtual disappearance of the Soviet threat it was created to prevent, and confusion over how to deal with domestic instability within individual countries. NATO's enlargement through the Partnership for Peace (PFP) program (see Chapter 15), did not strengthen NATO's capacity to act as a regional alliance for collective security. The new "peace partners" were not offered the security guarantee that NATO's full members enjoy—that an attack on one would be considered an attack on all. Thus NATO's security-protecting capacity remains in doubt, and skeptics ask what the military alliance's purposes are without an agreed-upon *external* enemy.

The ambiguous European security setting after the Cold War is marked by numerous ethnopolitical conflicts and separatist revolts, as in Bosnia and other areas of Europe. NATO was not designed to deal with this kind of vague internal threat. Its original charter envisioned only one purpose—mutual self-protection from external attack; it never defined policing civil wars as a goal. Consequently, it was not surprising that the nineteen full-member states and the now eighteen associated "partners for peace" were reluctant to call on NATO to intervene to contain ethnic warfare. However, they eventually overcame that reluctance in December 1995, when NATO took charge of all military operations in Bosnia-Herzegovina from the UN. The redefinition of NATO's mission adapted the alliance to a new purpose and gave it a new lease on life. Operation Joint Endeavor demonstrated that NATO had a positive role to play, as described by President Clinton in January 1996, in making "the difference between a war that starts again and peace that takes hold." Nonetheless, doubt remains as to whether NATO will be willing to undertake similar interventions to contain ethnic violence *within* other countries, especially if enlargement in NATO's memberships progresses any further (see Chapter 15). In the late 1990s, NATO is seeking to become both an alliance of security and an alliance for promoting the liberal democratic values of the region's countries. NATO's current goals are to expand its capabilities for new missions, to embrace Europe's emerging democracies as members, and to build a collaborative relationship with Russia.

Likewise, in other regional mutual security systems, controversies among the coalition partners about the identity of "the enemy" and the conditions warranting intervention raise doubts about their capacity to engineer collective defense projects. These doubts are fueled by the history of regional organizations in peacemaking efforts. Between 1945 and 1984, of 291 armed conflicts involving military units, only 68 (or 23 percent) were handled by regional organizations; regional organizations were unable to halt 77 percent of these high-intensity armed conflicts (Holsti 1992, 353). This record suggests that although regional collective defense institutions were, to some extent, created to overcome the deficiencies of global institutions, they may not be able to perform that task any better than global institutions.

533

THE LIBERAL
INSTITUTIONAL PATHS
TO PEACE THROUGH
LAW, INTEGRATION,
AND DEMOCRATIZATION

The chaos and killing in many Global South countries has provoked widespread dismay, but many states and institutions have been reluctant to intervene to keep the peace in civil wars outside their sphere of influence. There are exceptions. Pictured here, as part of the U.S. African Crisis Response Initiative (ACRI) budgeted at $15 million yearly, is one of 120 U.S. Army Special Forces soldiers demonstrating mine detonation techniques to Ugandan peacekeeping troops in strife-torn Africa.

The crisis in Bosnia again exemplified the obstacles that regional organizations often face. Recall that when the civil war broke out in June 1991 and Croatia declared its independence, neither NATO nor the European Union was able to agree on action to preserve peace. Both initially relied on the United Nations to enforce a cease-fire and orchestrate a peace plan. Only reluctantly did they succumb in 1995 to UN pressure to participate militarily. This case and others suggest that regional organizations have the capacity to bring armed conflict within their territory (or in close proximity) under control when their members are in agreement. However, it also indicates that they often lack the consensus and political will to control controversial conflicts, and require pressure from world public opinion mobilized in global organizations such as the United Nations to take action. The future of peacekeeping in regional settings may best be predicted by the recent experience in Africa—the scene of widespread violence within **failed states** in the 1990s. Here, a combination of unilateral interventions by a single power (for example, the 1997 African Crisis Response Initiative [ACRI] by the United States), alongside UN and other regionally organized peacekeeping forces, smothered the wars and crises erupting on the continent in the wake of the genocidal massacres in the 1994 Rwandan civil war (see Map 16.3).

In the twenty-first century, regional collective defense institutions, assisted by unilateral peacekeeping forces from particular interested states, may help to build a global security community in which the expectation of peace exceeds the expectation of war. The processes through which such metamorphoses might occur are addressed by the functional and neofunctional approaches to peace within the liberal paradigm.

failed states countries whose governments have collapsed in corruption and incompetence, resulting in anarchy and civil war among rival groups without effective institutions to govern.

MAP 16.3

Peacekeeping Operations in Strife-Torn Africa

The wave of violence that swept Africa in the 1990s was met with humanitarian intervention by a number of individual states as well as multilateral, global, and regional peacekeeping forces. Shown here are the key peacekeeping missions undertaken or planned as of late 1997. Other violence-prone regions could prompt similar kinds of peacekeeping responses.

SOURCE: *U.S. News & World Report,* September 29, 1997, p. 36, citing as its sources the United Nations and the U.S. State Department.

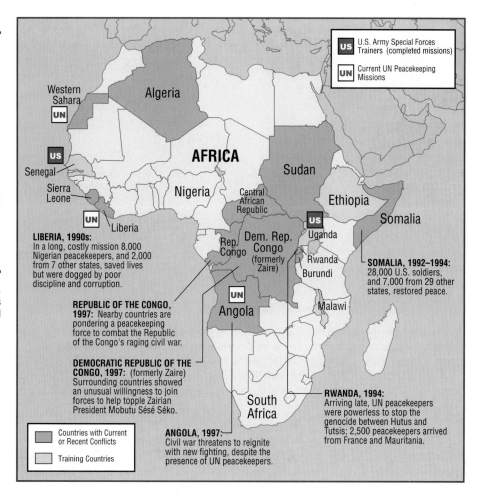

US U.S. Army Special Forces Trainers (completed missions)

UN Current UN Peacekeeping Missions

AFRICA

Western Sahara **UN**

Algeria

US Senegal

Sierra Leone

UN Liberia

Nigeria

Sudan

Central African Republic

Ethiopia

US Uganda

Somalia

Rep. Congo

Dem. Rep. Congo (formerly Zaire)

Rwanda

Burundi

UN Angola

Malawi

South Africa

LIBERIA, 1990s: In a long, costly mission 8,000 Nigerian peacekeepers, and 2,000 from 7 other states, saved lives but were dogged by poor discipline and corruption.

REPUBLIC OF THE CONGO, 1997: Nearby countries are pondering a peacekeeping force to combat the Republic of the Congo's raging civil war.

DEMOCRATIC REPUBLIC OF THE CONGO, 1997: (formerly Zaire) Surrounding countries showed an unusual willingness to join forces to help topple Zairian President Mobutu Sésé Séko.

SOMALIA, 1992–1994: 28,000 U.S. soldiers, and 7,000 from 29 other states, restored peace.

RWANDA, 1994: Arriving late, UN peacekeepers were powerless to stop the genocide between Hutus and Tutsis; 2,500 peacekeepers arrived from France and Mauritania.

Countries with Current or Recent Conflicts

Training Countries

ANGOLA, 1997: Civil war threatens to reignite with new fighting, despite the presence of UN peacekeepers.

• • •

POLITICAL INTEGRATION: THE FUNCTIONAL AND NEOFUNCTIONAL PATHS TO PEACE

political integration the processes and activities by which the populations of two or more states transfer their loyalties to a merged political and economic unit.

Political integration refers to either the process or the product of efforts to build new political communities and supranational institutions that transcend the state. Their purposes are to remove states' incentives for war and to engineer reform programs to transform international institutions from instruments *of* states to structures *over* them.

World Federalism

Functionalism in its various forms does not represent a frontal attack on the state by proposing to replace it with some central authority. That radical remedy is represented by **world federalism,** an approach to integration based on the merger of previously sovereign states into a single federal union. Federalists follow the liberal physicist Albert Einstein's conviction that "there is no salvation for civilization, or even the human race, other than the creation of a world government."

Federalists reason that if people value survival more highly than relative national advantage, they will willingly transfer their loyalty to a supranational authority to dismantle the system of competitive territorial states that produces war. "World government," they believe, "is not only possible, it is inevitable," because it appeals to the patriotism of people who "love their national heritages so deeply that they wish to preserve them in safety for the common good" (Ferencz and Keyes 1991).

It is not surprising that ardent adherents to **nationalism** have vehemently attacked the revolutionary federalist "top-down" peace plan. Because it seeks to subvert the system of sovereign states, the plan threatens many entrenched interests. More abstractly, other critics reject the world federalists' proposition that governments are bad but people are good, wise, and enlightened (see Claude 1971). Likewise, they challenge the assumption that the need for changes will automatically lead to global institutional innovation.

The United World Federalists (an international nongovernmental pressure group) still actively promotes a world government. Nevertheless, aversion to war and raised consciousness of its dangers have not mobilized widespread grassroots enthusiasm for this radical step. Other approaches to reforming the world political system have attracted more adherents.

nationalism the feeling of loyalty to a particular state and/or nationality or ethnic group, to the exclusion of attachment to other states, universal religious values, or the collective welfare of all people.

Functionalism

Classical functionalism is a rival but complementary reform movement associated with liberalism. In contrast to federalism, **functionalism** is not directed toward creating a world federal structure with all its constitutional paraphernalia. Rather, it seeks to build "peace by pieces" through transnational organizations that emphasize the "sharing of sovereignty" instead of its surrender. Functionalism advocates a "bottom-up," evolutionary strategy for building cooperative ties among states.

According to functionalists, technical experts, rather than professional diplomats, are the best agents for building collaborative links across national borders. They see diplomats as being overly protective of their country's national interests at the expense of collective human interests. Rather than addressing the immediate sources of national insecurity, the functionalists' peace plan calls for transnational cooperation in technical (primarily social and economic) areas as a first step. Habits of cooperation learned in one technical area (e.g., telecommunications or medicine), they assume, will "spill over" into others—especially if the experience is mutually beneficial and demonstrates the potential advantages of cooperation in other areas (e.g., transportation and communication).

To enhance the probability that cooperative endeavors will prove rewarding, the functionalist plan recommends that less difficult tasks be tackled first. It assumes that successful mastering of one problem will encourage attacking other problems collaboratively. If the process continues unabated, the bonds among countries will multiply, because no government would oppose a web of functional organizations that provide such clear-cut benefits to its citizens. Thus, "the mission of functionalism is to make peace possible by organizing particular layers of human social life in accordance with their particular requirements, breaking down the artificialities of the zoning arrangements associated with the principle of sovereignty" (Claude 1971). Its intellectual parent, David Mitrany (1966), argued in *A Working Peace System* (first published in 1943) that functionalism is based on self-interest.

functionalism the theory advanced by David Mitrany and others explaining how people came to value transnational institutions (IGOs, integrated or merged states) and why they give those institutions authority to provide the public goods (for example, security) previously supplied by their state.

> Functionalism proposes not to squelch but to utilize national selfishness;
> it asks governments not to give up sovereignty which belongs to their peo-

ples but to acquire benefits for their peoples which were hitherto unavailable, not to reduce their power to defend their citizens but to expand their competence to serve them. It intimates that the basic requirement for peace is that states have the wit to cooperate in pursuit of national interests that coincide with those of other states rather than the will to compromise national interests that conflict with those of others. (Claude 1971, 386)

Persuaded by the logic of this argument, far-sighted liberals such as Jean Monnet applied functionalist theory to begin the process by which war-prone Europe began to form an integrated "security community" after World War II (Deutsch et al. 1999).

The permanent problem-solving organizations created in the 1800s, such as the Rhine River Commission (1804), the Danube River Commission (1857), the International Telegraphic Union (1865), and the Universal Post Union (1874), suggested a process by which states might cooperate to enjoy mutual benefits and hence to launch the more ambitious experiments that functionalists anticipated. Their lessons informed the early organizational ideology that also inspired the missions assigned to the UN's specialized agencies (such as the World Health Organization) and the growth of intergovernmental organizations (IGOs) and **nongovernmental organizations (NGOs)** generally.

nongovernmental organizations
NGOs are transnational organizations of private citizens from different states working together on international problems, which maintain a consultative status with the United Nations.

Functionalism, as originally formulated, did not pertain to multinational corporations (MNCs)—to some, the "dominant governance institutions on the planet" (Korten 1995). However, many now believe that multinational corporations are powerful agents in the integration of states' economies and the globalization of world politics, in ways consistent with functionalist logic. Individuals who manage global corporations often think and speak of themselves as a "revolutionary class," possessing a holistic, cosmopolitan, or supranational vision of the earth that challenges traditional nationalism (Barnet and Müller 1974). This ideology and the corresponding slogan "Down with borders" are based on the assumption that the world can be managed as a single, integrated market. From it flows an interpretation that sees global corporations as the primary catalysts to a borderless world opposed to governments that interfere unnecessarily with the free flow of capital and technology. According to this perspective, MNCs' investments and trade promote the growing level of cooperation and compromise exhibited between otherwise competitive states that is creating the emerging global culture—a culture that is eroding state sovereignty as states' economies become interdependent and states' politics become increasingly intermestic (simultaneously international and domestic).

As a theory of peace and world order, though, critics charge that functionalism does not take into account some important political realities. First, they question its assumption about the causes of war. Do poverty and despair cause war, or does war cause poverty and despair? Indeed, may not material deprivation sometimes breed not aggression, but rather apathy, hopelessness, and hostility without recourse to violence? Why should we assume that the functionalist theory of the causes of war is more accurate than others?

Second, functionalism assumes that political differences among countries will be dissolved by the habits of cooperation learned by experts organized transnationally to cope with technical problems such as global warming, environmental deterioration, or contagious disease. The reality, say critics, is that technical cooperation is often more strongly influenced by politics than the other way around. The U.S. withdrawal from the International Labor Organization (ILO) and the United Nations Educational, Scientific, and Cultural Organization (UNESCO) because of their politicized nature illustrates the entrenched primacy of political competition.

537

THE LIBERAL
INSTITUTIONAL PATHS
TO PEACE THROUGH
LAW, INTEGRATION,
AND DEMOCRATIZATION

As skeptics conclude, functionalists are naive to argue that technical (functional) undertakings and political affairs can be separated, because they cannot. If technical cooperation becomes as important to state welfare as the functionalists argue that it will, states will not step aside. Welfare and power cannot be separated, because the solution of economic and social problems cannot be divorced from political considerations. The expansion of transnational institutions' authority and competency at the expense of national governments and state sovereignty is, therefore, unlikely. Functionalism, in short, is an idea whose time has passed.

Neofunctionalism

A new, albeit derivative, theory arose in the 1950s to question the assumption that ever-expanding functional needs for joint action to address property rights, health, technological change, and other shared problems would force the resolution of political disputes. Termed **neofunctionalism,** the reconstructed liberal theory sought to directly address the political factors that dominate the process of merging formerly independent states.

> *Neofunctionalism* holds that political institutions and policies should be crafted so that they lead to further integration through the process of . . . "the expansive logic of sector integration." For example, [the first] president of the ECSC [European Coal and Steel Community], [Jean] Monnet, sought to use the integration of the coal and steel markets of the six member countries as a lever to promote the integration of their social security and transport policies, arguing that such action was essential to eliminate distortions in coal and steel prices. [The] neofunctionalism of Monnet and others [had] as its ultimate goal . . . the creation of a federal state. (Jacobson 1984, 66)

neofunctionalism the revised functional theory that explains that the IGOs states create to manage common problems exert new pressures to expand the benefits further, and that this leads to states' political integration, the creation of additional IGOs, and the globalization of international relations in an expanding network of interdependence that reduces state's incentives to wage war.

Neofunctionalism thus proposes to accelerate the processes leading to new supranational communities by purposely pushing for cooperation in politically controversial areas, rather than by avoiding them. It advocates bringing political pressure to bear at crucial decision points to persuade opponents of the greater benefits of forming a larger community among formerly independent national members.

The European Experience. Western Europe is the preeminent example of the application of neofunctionalist principles to the development of an integrated political community (see Deutsch et al. 1999). Within a single generation, cooperation across European borders progressed toward a single European economic market with a single currency and toward the promise of a politically integrated Europe in the formal regional institution known as the **European Union (EU)** (see Chapter 6). The 1992 Maastricht Treaty on European Union set the stage for EU "enlargement." In 1995 Austria, Finland, and Sweden joined the European Union, swelling its membership to fifteen countries, and in 1998 the EU took the next step in its ambitious enlargement goals when, in a historic milestone, the EU agreed to a two-tier approach to admitting eleven new states in the next decade into the community of EU liberal democracies

MAP 16.4

A European Union on the Verge of Enlargement

The European Union is a premier example of a supranational regional organization. It has grown from the six states that formed the European Economic Community in 1957 to twenty-one countries designated for inclusion, and in the aftermath of the October 1997 Amsterdam summit, no less than five other applicants are seeking membership. The package for enlargement, known as *Agenda 2000*, sets goals for the European Union's growth well into the next century.

SOURCE: *Economist,* May 31, 1997, p. 5, citing the European Commission.

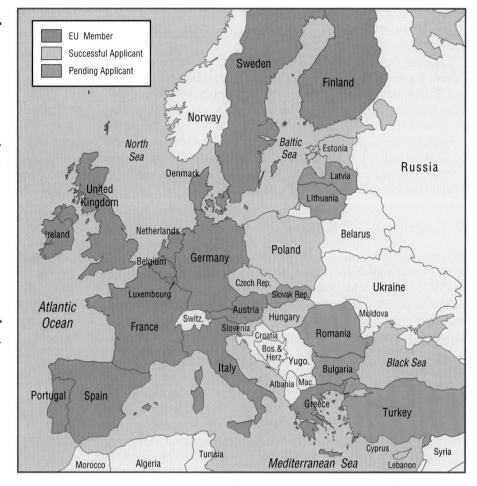

EU Member
Successful Applicant
Pending Applicant

(providing they can meet the conditions for democratic and free-market reforms that the EU set for inclusion). And still other applicants are seeking membership (see Map 16.4).

Yet despite EU enlargement and the opportunities that this movement symbolizes for writing a new chapter of European history, obstacles remain. These were made evident in the wake of the Maastricht Treaty, which entered into force in November 1993 and created the EU as the umbrella term for the European Community's diverse institutions. The treaty provided a timetable for completing a single-market Economic and Monetary Union (EMU) that created the single "euro" currency in 1999—the most potent symbol of Europe's new dynamism, making the euro competitive as a reserve currency in the global monetary system, alongside the U.S. dollar. In addition, the EU states pledged to cooperate not only in finance and economics but also in defense and foreign policy, with endorsement of the Common Foreign and Security Policy (CFSP).

These ambitious goals notwithstanding, progress toward full integration has proven difficult. As Jacques Delors, former President of the European Commission, lamented in December 1995, "Building Europe has never been a long, calm river. There are moments of stagnation, of crises." It is unclear whether the dream of true European unity in a much wider confederation to include eastern Europe and to encompass twenty-six states by 2010 will become a reality. Contributing to the pessimism are chronic suspicion, selfishness, and tenacious national memories of the dark side of Europe's twentieth-century history. Furthermore, EU states are aware of the potential for interdependence to provoke competition and struggles for advantage and disagreement about the desirability of true political unification remains. For the next large, courageous, and integrative steps to be taken, the fifteen EU legislatures will have to ratify the epic October 1997 Amsterdam treaty—and this will take years (a limitation that prompted the treaty's advocates to call it a "foundation document"). "The treaty of Amsterdam will not be the last treaty on European cooperation," the Dutch Prime Minister, Wim Kok, predicted. "It provides a firm basis for the construction of a strong and enlarged Europe that can face the challenges of the twenty-first century."

Even if Europeans do not soon realize their aspiration of political union, Europe has already constructed a **security community** in which the expectation of war between states has vanished from one of the historically most violence-prone regions of the world (Deutsch et al. 1957; 1999). The onset of armed conflict between the EU's democracies is *very* unlikely. Still, how deep and geographically wide this integrative process will go is highly uncertain (see Chapter 6). In addition, the uncertain membership of this "common European home" is likely to prove consequential for European security because there is a danger that the "one Europe" proponents envisioned will in fact be two Europes, one rich and stable and the other poor and unstable. That could create future conflicts not unlike those of the past.

The Preconditions for Regional Integration. The record of previous integrative experiments demonstrates that the factors promoting (or inhibiting) successful integration efforts are many and their mixture complex. It is not enough that two or more countries choose to interact cooperatively. Research indicates that the probability of such cooperative behavior resulting in integration is remote without geographical proximity, steady economic growth, similar political systems, supportive public opinion led by enthusiastic leaders, cultural homogeneity, internal political stability, similar experiences in historical and internal social development, compatible forms of government and economic systems, similar levels of military preparedness and economic resources, a shared perception of a common external threat, bureaucratic compatibilities, and previous collaborative efforts (Cobb and Elder 1970; Deutsch et al. 1953). While not all of these conditions must be present for integration to occur, the absence of more than a few considerably reduces the chances of success. The integration of two or more societies—let alone entire world regions—is, in short, not easily accomplished.

European institution building nonetheless has served as a model for the application of the neofunctionalist approach to integration in other regions, including Africa, Asia, and Latin America. However, current evidence suggests that political integration may be peculiarly relevant to the Global North's advanced industrial democracies but of doubtful applicability to the developing countries of the Global South. The record, moreover, indicates that even where conditions are favorable there is no guarantee that integration will proceed automatically. As noted, even in Europe high hopes have alternated with periods of disillusionment. When momentum has occurred, **spillover**—involving either

539

THE LIBERAL
INSTITUTIONAL PATHS
TO PEACE THROUGH
LAW, INTEGRATION,
AND DEMOCRATIZATION

540

THE LIBERAL
INSTITUTIONAL PATHS
TO PEACE THROUGH
LAW, INTEGRATION,
AND DEMOCRATIZATION

the deepening of ties in one functional area or their expansion to another to en-sure the members' satisfaction with the integrative process—has led to further integration. But there is no inherent expansive momentum in integration schemes. Thus, **spillback** (when a regional integration scheme fails, as in the case of the East African Community) and **spillaround** (when a regional inte-gration scheme stagnates or its activities in one area work against integration in another) are also possible.

Political Disintegration

The substantial difficulty that most regions have experienced in achieving a level of institution building similar to that of the EU suggests the magnitude of existing barriers to creating new political communities out of previously di-vided ones. Furthermore, the paradox that the planet is falling apart precipi-tately *and* coming together reluctantly at the very same moment confounds pre-dictions. We are witnessing a convulsive splintering of states, as hundreds of ethnic nationalities are currently seeking autonomy. Consider Europe, where in 1991 hypernationalism led to the creation of fifteen newly independent coun-tries. Since then four new states achieved independence at precisely the time when important steps toward economic and political integration were being un-dertaken elsewhere, as illustrated by the historic reconsolidation of Hong Kong into China on July 1, 1997 (after 156 years of forced separation by imperial/colonial conquest).

The surge of ethnic and religious tensions tearing countries apart is not confined to Europe. Equally sobering is the UN prediction that the world could fracture into five hundred states from the current two hundred. Be-tween 1989 and 1991, fifty regions worldwide declared themselves auton-omous (*Harper's,* December 1991, 17). And in a world in which "few modern states—probably fewer than 20—are ethnically homogenous" and in which 268 minorities were at risk of extermination and ripe for rebellion in 114 countries in 1995 (Gurr 1990, 85; 1997, 14), the prospects are high that **polit-ical disintegration** will continue, alongside the continuing willingness of states to accept devolution (the granting of greater governing power to quasi-autonomous regions) in the hope of containing separatist revolts. Where de-volution is not being pursued, the hypernationalist quest for independence under the banner of the **self-determination** principle threatens to dismem-ber some formerly integrated sovereign states, including such widely dissimi-lar states as Canada, Russia, Spain, South Africa, and the United Kingdom, where **minorities** (the proportion of a state's population made up by different ethnic, nationality, or racial groups) are often a repressed subclass ripe for revolution. This is the case in a world in which 40 to 50 percent of nearly twenty countries have dissatisfied, politically repressed minorities struggling for human rights and independence (see D. Smith 1997, 20–21, which esti-mates that at least 20 percent of the existing countries are in this category). Such developments are not new, of course, as witnessed by the U.S. Civil War in 1861 and by the thirty-year civil war in Ethiopia, which enabled Eritrea to gain independence in 1991. These counterintegrative tendencies remind us that states may either merge or fragment. There is little reason to expect in-tegrative processes, once under way, to continue by the force of their own momentum.

self-determination the standard advocated strenuously in U.S. President Woodrow Wilson's "14 Points" address that national and ethnic groups have a right to statehood so they can govern themselves as independent countries.

A DEMOCRATIC PEACE

The liberal path to peace historically has focused on the global or structural characteristics of international society, such as anarchy, as most in need of institutional reform. For this reason liberalism is closely associated with international law, organization, and integration. But a fourth institutional approach is also central to the liberal tradition: that the types of governments in the world predict the probability of armed conflict. It matters—and matters greatly—whether states are ruled democratically, because if so, the world will become peaceful. (This liberal thesis, of course, runs directly counter to the realist and especially the neorealist assumption that states' forms of government do not have much influence on their foreign relations. They believe that governments—whether democratic or autocratic—respond similarly to similar security threats.)

The liberal ideas underlying expectations about a **democratic peace** spring from convictions that first were popularized in the late eighteenth century, the age of democratic revolution against absolute monarchy. Then—when only the fledgling United States, Switzerland, and Republican France could reasonably be counted as democratic—liberal enthusiasts voiced their belief about the impact that the spread of democratic institutions might have on international security. German philosopher Immanuel Kant predicted in 1795 that republican governments ruled by the consent of the governed would likely maintain friendly relations with one another, and would resolve any disputes at the bargaining table instead of the battlefield. This core idea had been advanced three years earlier, when a future American President, James Madison, argued that "in the advent of republican governments [would be found] not only the prospect of a radical decline in the role played by war but the prospect as well of a virtual revolution in the conduct of diplomacy" (Tucker and Hendrickson 1990).

Liberal and now neoliberal policymakers have taken heart in the spread of democracy as the preferred and now most popular kind of institution for governing states throughout the world. Since the mid-1970s freedom and civil liberties have grown, in a series of transitions, and today the enlarged community of liberal democracies makes up a healthy majority with nearly three-quarters of the globe's governments ruling with free or partially free institutions (see Figure 16.3).

This enlargement of the percentage of free and partially free countries has made liberal institutionalists especially hopeful that a democratic peace can be a reliable anchor for global security in the twenty-first century. States that base their security policies on this expectation have been inspired by research that demonstrates convincingly that "wars between democracies are extremely rare events" (Russett 1995), as "stable democracies sharing common concepts of democratic legitimacy have . . . a remarkable record in not fighting one another" (Fukuyama 1994). There is much evidence to suggest that liberal expectations are not wishful thinking. "Well-established democracies have never made war on one another [and] republics and only republics have tended to form durable, peaceful leagues" (Weart 1994). Democracies not only routinely refrain from using armed conflict to settle disputes with one another, but they are also far less likely to be attacked by other governments, whether democratic or dictatorial (Kegley and Hermann 1996). Democratization *does*, as Woodrow

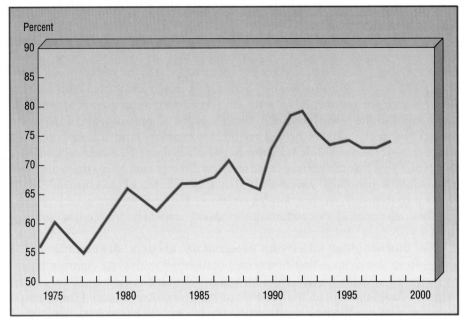

FIGURE 16.3

The Growth of Democratic Governance throughout the Globe since 1974

According to Freedom House, the number of free and partly free countries that are members of the community of democracies has increased as a percent of the world's state governments since 1973, in fits and starts. The human rights and civil liberties of populations living in relatively liberal states are protected (although some "illiberal" democratically ruled countries, such as Iran, Croatia, and Georgia, do not protect the civil rights of their minority populations). Countries with free and fair elections benefit from the strong tendency for foreign relations among them to be pacific.

SOURCE: Annual Surveys of Freedom House, as scaled by Harvey Starr.

Wilson and other post-World War I idealists hoped, demonstrably help to make democratic states secure. Thus the spread of democracy portends that a world made up exclusively of democracies *would* be a much safer world (see Chapter 12).

This lesson has not been lost on leaders in democratic states seeking to find a principle on which to ground their twenty-first-century national security strategies. The United States under President Clinton embraced the thesis of democratic peace advocates enthusiastically. In his 1994 State of the Union Address, Clinton declared, "Democracies don't attack each other," and argued that because of this empirical law, "ultimately the best strategy to insure our security and to build a durable peace is to support the advance of democracy elsewhere." The 1994 *U.S. National Strategy of Engagement and Enlargement* defined the promotion of democracy as a pillar of America's post-Cold War foreign policy. Clinton's goal was to enlarge the existing community of liberal democracies, and he was joined enthusiastically and officially by the other major EU and NATO liberal democracies whose members insist on states being democratically ruled as a condition for their inclusion as applicant-members or as beneficiaries of their political support (refer again to Chapters 3 and 12).

543

THE LIBERAL
INSTITUTIONAL PATHS
TO PEACE THROUGH
LAW, INTEGRATION,
AND DEMOCRATIZATION

As the United States has pushed its democratization agenda to the forefront, many other democracies and international organizations have also embraced the aspiration. For example, the Group of Seven (G-7) has endorsed the promotion of democracy as a priority foreign policy goal. So, too, have the World Bank, the IMF, and the OECD—all of which have designated democratic reform as a condition for receipt of loans and development assistance. The Organization of American States (OAS) has similarly accepted the principle that it is permissible to export democracy. Its June 1991 *Santiago Commitment to Democracy and Renewal of the Inter-American System* established an OAS intervention policy to guarantee hemispheric democracy. Following suit, the United Nations has affirmed democratization as a human-rights entitlement in many of its recent resolutions. Thus, the United States and the democratic majority have the numbers to seek revision of international law. They are exercising their influence multilaterally to permit intervention on behalf of democratic reforms (von Glahn 1996).

Some skeptics question whether democratic states' relations are really peaceful. Citing the Boer War, the American Civil War, and the wars waged by Imperial Germany against other democracies in World War I despite its elected parliament, and taking into consideration other factors (extensive trade and alliances, for example), they doubt if the relationship between democratization and peace is as solid as democratic peace proponents argue. However, the weight of the evidence is strongly on the side of the democratic peace proposition (Russett 1998). Hence, existing liberal democracies' efforts to enlarge their community could, potentially, usher in a major transformation of world politics—providing that they continue to abide by their past record of dealing with conflicts by compromise through negotiation, mediation, arbitration, and adjudication. If so, and if "the worldwide democratic revolution" does not begin to "cool off around the globe" as some predict (Carothers 1997), liberalism will be vindicated; the future will witness less bloodshed, and the 1995 hopes Pope John Paul II expressed could make an ancient dream a reality: "No more war, war never again."

However, promise dictates neither performance nor destiny. As Prime Minister Ingvar Caarlsson of Sweden warned in 1995, "If we fail to nurture democracy—the most fundamental political project of this century—we will never be able to realize our goals and the responsibilities which the future will call for."

• • •

LIBERAL INSTITUTIONS AND WORLD ORDER: FROM SECURITY TO STABILITY?

Liberal and neoliberal theories that focus on international law, organization, integration, and democratization see armed conflict as deriving from prevailing and deeply rooted institutional deficiencies. Neoliberal reformers believe that the current anarchical system is the problem, not the solution, because weak institutions make security dear and global welfare subservient to national welfare. To change this, they advocate legal and institutional methods to pool sovereignty and reform the character of nondemocratic governments. Seeing the international system as underdeveloped and unstructured, advocates of these reforms believe that a rebuilt state system can best eliminate the roots of war. As one liberal scholar argues, global change requires innovation because "During the coming decades global challenges will continue and may increase. . . .

544

THE LIBERAL
INSTITUTIONAL PATHS
TO PEACE THROUGH
LAW, INTEGRATION,
AND DEMOCRATIZATION

There is more and more of an overlap between national interests and global responsibilities. The task of multilateral diplomacy is to cope with new issues, new demands and new situations [through] 'shared responsibilities' and 'strengthened partnership'" (Kinnas 1992).

To liberal advocates, the big problems on the global agenda are ones that simultaneously affect many states. They cannot be meaningfully managed unilaterally; they are transnational and cannot be met effectively with a national response. In such areas as trade, the environment, the control of AIDS, or even armed conflict, arguably a multilateral cooperative approach is required under conditions of interdependence and globalization. In this context, Bill Clinton claimed that "multilateral action holds promise as never before" and pledged that his administration would therefore seek "collective stands against aggression," providing that multilateral institutions such as the United Nations "reinvent" the way they operate.

The contributions of the expanding number of international institutions created in the twentieth century to this grand purpose have, until recently, been rather modest. Despite some promising developments, armed conflict has been frequent. This is not surprising in a system in which, during the mid-1990s, states allocated less than $2 for every man, woman, and child to the United Nations for humanitarian and security emergencies, while at the same time their combined annual defense expenditures exceeded $960 billion (Laurenti 1995, 11; Evans 1995, 8). However, the impact of multilateral management of strife-torn areas should not be minimized. As Inis L. Claude maintains,

> Particular *organizations* may be nothing more than playthings of power politics and handmaidens of national ambitions. But international *organization*, considered as an historical process, represents a secular trend toward the systematic development of an enterprising quest for political means of making the world safe for human habitation. It may fail, and peter out ignominiously. But if it maintains the momentum that it has built up in the twentieth century, it may yet effect a transformation of human relationships on this planet which will at some indeterminate point justify the assertion that the world has come to be governed—that mankind has become a community capable of sustaining order, promoting justice, and establishing the conditions of that good life which Aristotle took to be the supreme aim of politics. (Claude 1971, 447–48, emphasis added)

As the twenty-first century nears, liberal institutionalists ponder the fate of states. Sovereign states do not manage their affairs very well; they have historically been instruments for making war with other states, and recently national governments have proven inefficient at either preventing civil wars or commanding widespread loyalty and respect from their constituents. The global "crisis of confidence" in governments has resulted in the disintegration of failing states at the same time that these fragile states have become tied together in an interdependent global community. States are uniting — forming global institutions to protect themselves against the many common problems they face. Borders and oceans cannot isolate or insulate states from these threats to security; they can only be controlled in the global commons by a collective effort. It is for this reason that many intergovernmental organizations (IGOs) originally came into being, and it is the persistence of collective threats produced by an increasingly globalized world that makes IGOs durable (Culpitt, Whitlock, and Whitlock 1996). As the globe shrinks and borders become even more porous, we can predict that liberal paths to peace and prosperity will continue to find favor. Will the liberal approaches to the control of armed conflict, if pursued, create a different pattern? The world awaits an answer.

KEY TERMS

neoliberal institutionalists
private international law
public international law
sovereignty
realists
sovereign equality
neutrality
nonintervention
diplomatic immunity
extraterritoriality
crimes against humanity
divine right of kings
statehood
diplomatic recognition
de facto recognition
de jure recognition
nonrecognition
mediation
good offices
conciliation
arbitration
adjudication
structural violence

positivist legal theory
security regimes
just war doctrine
morals
ethics
jus ad bellum
jus in bello
military necessity
noncombatant immunity
reprisal
retorsion
war crimes
human rights
International Court of Justice (ICJ)
International Criminal Tribunal
permanent world criminal court
genocide
European Court of Justice (ECJ)
collective security
preventive diplomacy
peacemaking
peacekeeping

peace operations
Rapidly Deployable Mission Headquarters (RDMH)
peacebuilding
peace enforcement
regional collective defense
failed states
political integration
world federalism
nationalism
functionalism
nongovernmental organizations (NGOs)
neofunctionalism
European Union (EU)
security community
spillover
spillback
spillaround
political disintegration
self-determination
minorities
democratic peace

SUGGESTED READING

Brown, Michael E., Sean M. Lynn-Jones, and Steven E. Miller, eds. *Debating the Democratic Peace.* Cambridge, Mass.: MIT Press, 1998.

Coate, Roger, and Craig Murphy, eds. *Global Governance: A Review of Multilateralism and International Organizations.* Boulder, Colo.: A quarterly journal published by Lynne Rienner.

Donnelly, Jack. *International Human Rights.* Boulder, Colo.: Westview Press, 1997.

Doyle, Michael W. *Ways of War and Peace.* New York: Norton, 1997.

Finnemore, Martha. *National Interests in International Society.* Ithica, N.Y.: Cornell University Press, 1998.

Hsiung, James C. *Anarchy and Order: The Interplay of Politics and Law in International Relations.* Boulder, Colo.: Lynne Rienner, 1997.

Joyner, Christopher C. *The United Nations and International Law.* New York: Cambridge University Press, 1997.

Latham, Robert. *The Liberal Moment: Modernity, Security, and the Making of Postwar International Order.* New York: Columbia University Press, 1997.

Mapel, David R. and Terry Nardin. *International Society: Diverse Ethical Perspectives.* Princeton, N.J.: Princeton University Press, 1998.

Otunnu, Olara A., and Michael W. Doyle, eds. *Peacemaking and Peacekeeping for the New Century.* Lanham, Md.: Rowman and Littlefield, 1998.

Peck, Connie. *Sustainable Peace: The Role of the World Regional Organizations in Preventing Conflict.* Lanham, Md.: Rowman & Littlefield, 1998.

Ruggie, John Gerald. *Constructing the World Polity: Essays on International Institutionalization.* New York: Routledge, 1998.

Starr, Harvey. *Anarchy, Order and Integration.* Ann Arbor: University of Michigan Press, 1997.

Woodhouse, Tom, Robert, Bruce, and Malcolm Dando, eds. *Peacekeeping and Peacemaking.* London: Macmillan, 1998.

http://www.un.org/Depts/dpko/
United Nations Peacekeeping Operations The United Nations has deployed numerous international military and civilian personnel to conflict areas to stop or contain hostilities and supervise peace agreements. View the "World Map of All Missions" on the home page. Click on an ongoing mission and read about the profile, background, and figures concerning the mission. Do the same thing for another, older mission. What are the similarities or differences between the missions?

http://www.lib.uchicago.edu/LibInfo/Law/intl.html
LibInfo Foreign and International Law The University of Chicago Library Information System brings you a Web site that has links to virtually every legal document on the Internet. If you want information on the European Union, the United Nations, war crimes, human rights, intellectual property, or international law journals, this site has it all.

http://www.icj-cij.org/
The International Court of Justice The International Court of Justice (ICJ) is the principal judicial wing of the United Nations. Examine the Court's statute to find out who can bring cases to the Court. Then, read the biographies of the court's fifteen members. Finally, access the "Decisions" link to examine some of the Court's contentious cases. Scanning the listings, which countries have brought the United States before the Court? What was the Court's rulings?

http://www.tufts.edu/fletcher/multilaterals.html
Multilaterals Project The Fletcher School of Law and Diplomacy makes the texts of international multilateral conventions and other instruments available to readers. The Web site has a searchable database as well as conventions that are organized by subject. For instance, you can access covenants pertaining to the rules of warfare, the environment, cultural protection, or biodiversity. You can also view the Treaty of Westphalia as well as the Covenant of the League of Nations. Try reading the documents chronologically.

http://oz.uc.edu/thro/genocide/index.html
The International Court of Justice Considers Genocide Professor Howard Tolley at the University of Cincinnati has created an interactive Web site where you can play the judge at the International Court of Justice when Bosnia brought charges against Yugoslavia in 1993. You can explore the facts, research the law, consider opposing arguments that support one side or the other, and then make your judgment.

CHAPTER 17

Ten Questions about Global Prospects on the Cusp of a New Century

•••

Trend is not destiny.

—RENÉ DUBOS,
French author, 1975

•••

The . . . challenge for the next millennium is different from anything in our previous experience. . . . In the period ahead our biggest challenge will be to help construct a system in which the rewards and penalties are conducive to a broader sense of global well-being.

—HENRY A. KISSINGER,
former U.S. Secretary of State, 1997

CHAPTER TOPICS AND THEMES

- What is the national interest?

- Of what value is military power?

- Is war between states obsolete?

- Can cultural conflict be controlled?

- Has the quest of empire ended?

- Who will cope with globalization?

- Is "realism" still realistic?

- Is the world preparing for the wrong war?

- Is this the "end of history"?

- Is there a recognized global agenda?

The opposing global trends toward globalization and fragmentation in the twilight of the twentieth century point toward a new international system—one whose character has yet to develop definition and coloration. Uncertainty and unpredictability thus define the current mood toward the approaching historic juncture. But one thing is certain: The seismic shifts under way will challenge the wisdom of old beliefs and orthodox visions. Because turmoil and turbulence govern contemporary international affairs, they require that we ask unconventional questions about conventional ideas. They push us to try to think four-dimensionally in order to perceive how political, military, market, and environmental pressures—intensified through globalization—are increasingly being brought to bear on the countries of the world, the people who reside in them, and their interactions.

Chapter 1 suggested that the investigative challenge to interpreting the future of world affairs would require the consideration of five controversial questions:

1. Are states becoming obsolete and losing their power and sovereign control?

2. Is global interdependence a cure or a curse?

3. Is technological innovation a blessing or a burden?

4. Will geo-economics replace geopolitics as transnational economic forces become more important relative to interstate armed conflict over territory?

5. What constitutes human well-being on an ecologically fragile planet?

Answers to these questions are elusive. The conclusions boldly asserted by would-be prophets are not likely to prove definitive, because, as former UN Secretary General Boutros Boutros-Ghali warned in 1996, "those caught up in revolutionary change rarely understand its ultimate significance." It is hard to recognize, and to describe, the bewildering array of problems that we carry into the new millennium. As President Bill Clinton lamented in his 1997 National Security Strategy of the United States,

> The dangers we face are unprecedented in their complexity. Ethnic conflict and outlaw states threaten regional stability; terrorism, drugs, organized crime and proliferation of weapons of mass destruction are global concerns that transcend national borders; and environmental damage and rapid population growth undermine economic prosperity and political stability in many countries.

Given this complex and dangerous environment, it is important to weigh plausible answers to these same five key questions as we attempt to prepare ourselves intellectually for understanding twenty-first-century world politics.

This final chapter addresses ten additional questions about the future, based on the preceding discussion of the major trends currently unfolding in world politics.

• • •

TOWARD THE FUTURE: MORE CRITICAL QUESTIONS AT THE DAWN OF THE NEW MILLENNIUM

Leaders and policy analysts worldwide are debating a number of controversial issues that require policy choices. How these and other questions are answered will significantly shape world politics in the twenty-first century.

1. What Is the "National Interest"?

What goals should states pursue? In earlier times, the answer was easy: The state should promote the internal welfare of its citizens, provide for defense against external aggression, and preserve the state's values and way of life.

Leaders pursue the same goals today, but their domestic and foreign policy options are increasingly limited. In an age of tradeoffs, many problems can be resolved only at the risk of worsening others. Under such conditions, the quest for narrow self-advantage often carries prohibitively high costs. The historic tendency toward **chauvinism** (my country, right or wrong) in defining national interests can be counterproductive domestically as well as internationally. No country can long afford to pursue its own welfare in ways that reduce the security and welfare of its competitors.

Those who questioned orthodox definitions of the national interest in the past seldom found support, but this is changing. As the eminent anthropologist Margaret Mead mused, "Substantially we all share the same atmosphere today, and we can only save ourselves by saving other people also. There is no longer a contradiction between patriotism and concern for the world." Former U.S. Secretary of State Cyrus Vance voiced a similar idea when he observed that "more than ever cooperative endeavors among nations are a matter not only of idealism but of direct self-interest."

E. H. Carr (1939), a British pioneer of **realism,** was convinced of the realism of idealism, maintaining that opposing the general interests of humankind does not serve a country's self-interest. Failing to recognize the plight of others can ultimately threaten one's own well-being—a view underscored by Martin Luther King, Jr., who urged that "injustice anywhere is a threat to justice everywhere." If these ideas, largely rooted in the legacy of **liberalism,** gain a large following, will the collective concerns of all humanity begin to compete for attention with states' traditional preoccupation with their own narrow national interests?

realism the orthodox theory of world politics based on the assumption that because humans are born to seek self-advantage, international politics is doomed to be a struggle for power involving war.

liberalism the optimistic view that because humans are capable of compassion, cooperation, and self-sacrifice for collective gain, it is possible for world politics to progress beyond narrow competition and war.

2. Of What Value Is Military Power?

In the past, military might enabled states to project power, exercise influence, and dominate others. Today nuclear and advanced (biological and chemical) weapons of mass destruction make the use of military might risky. Continuing arms proliferation raises new questions. Does the acquisition of more weapons increase security—a psychological phenomenon? Or are preparations for war and defense responsible for the **security dilemma** that all countries face?

To be sure, most leaders agree with the ancient Greek philosopher Aristotle, who argued that "a people without walls is a people without choice." Thus most accept the realist premise that preparing for war is necessary for peace. Yet the capacity to destroy does not always make for a convincing threat, even against countries without the capacity to retaliate. Today, the threat of force often lacks credibility. Military power has become impotent by its very strength. And when military might no longer compels others' compliance, then weapons will have lost their primary role as a basis, or substitute, for diplomacy.

No level of military might can guarantee a state's invulnerability. And states' primary security problem today is internal, not external, aggression. Therefore, preparations for war can be assessed only in terms of other consequences. Thresholds may exist beyond which the addition of greater destructive power or the discovery of technologically revolutionary new kinds of lethal and nonlethal weapons is meaningless. Furthermore, excessive preparations for war may leave a country heavily fortified with little left to defend, as U.S. President Eisenhower warned in 1961.

Although the end of the Cold War has further eroded justifications for the pursuit of military power, states' traditional quest for military superiority has not entirely lost its appeal. Arms trading is the world's largest industry (*Harper's,* December 1996, 13). Nonetheless, the allure of weapons has declined in many national capitals, where governments facing economic crises have slashed military budgets and reduced the size of their armies and arsenals. Perhaps this is because leaders in these states have begun to recognize that in the long run high military spending can reduce a state's industrial growth, weaken its global economic competitiveness, and ultimately undermine its ability to pursue and preserve dominance (Kennedy 1987). And when a government cannot satisfy citizens' cravings for a promising financial future and a standard of living comparable to that of people living abroad, revolt from within can be expected, followed, potentially, by political disintegration and civil war.

However, as India's and Pakistan's quest for prestige through nuclear weapons suggest, many leaders will not take this lesson seriously. Moreover, as the one predicament that nearly every state finds unacceptable is being vulnerable to foreign aggression or subject to other states' dictates. Consequently, the pursuit of military power is likely to continue at the same time that concerns about the social and economic costs of preparations for war are likely to rise.

3. Is War between States Obsolete?

Prevalent practices tend to wither away when they cease to serve their intended purpose, as the examples of slavery, dueling, and colonialism illustrate. Is war between states subject to these same forces? Since World War II, legal prohibitions against military aggression have expanded, and war has occurred almost exclusively in the Global South. The period since 1945 has been the longest span of great-power peace since the seventeenth century, raising expectations that the major powers have "retreated from doomsday" (Mueller 1989) and that large-scale wars between states will continue to decline and perhaps cease altogether. (This hope exists even as internal or civil wars are on the rise, and humanitarian concerns about genocide and war crimes increasingly require interventionary peacekeeping.) "For modern states the anticipated costs [of waging war], political and economic as well as human, generally exceed the benefits" (Mack 1996).

It is, of course, debatable whether the disincentives and dangers of using today's destructive weapons are truly making war between states obsolete. Instead, this kind of war may eventually disappear in another, far more frightening way—because resort to weapons of mass destruction will obliterate humankind. The puzzle, then, is when and by what means war will become obsolete. As Martin Luther King, Jr., put it, "The choice is either nonviolence or nonexistence."

4. Can Cultural Conflict Be Controlled?

Throughout the world's history, when distinct cultures have come into contact, either the collisions have sparked communication and a healthy respect for diversity or familiarity has bred contempt. When followers have embraced **eth-**

In the 1990s wars between states have almost ceased entirely, but this does not mean that guns have fallen silent. Civil wars have grown in frequency and destructiveness in many Global South countries, taking the lives of civilians caught in the crossfire. This epidemic of chaos has demanded external intervention to alleviate the suffering of the innocent victims. Shown here are French soldiers conducting a 1997 airlift of civilians from Brazzaville, Congo Republic's capital, where fighting between the Central African Army and rebel soldiers put the lives of thousands in peril.

nocentrism, the view that their own group's values are inherently superior, animosity and disrespect for differences have been especially characteristic, and persecution and killing have often followed.

The fading of the Cold War's divisive ideological contest between communism and capitalism has been replaced by the reappearance of another kind of major divisive conflict—cultural cleavages and hatreds. Tribalism, religious fanaticism, and hypernational ethnicity are again on the rise, leading to large-scale violence and repression. Conflicts between "cultures"—ethnic groups who share a language, religion, or history that binds them together and makes them feel different from others—have resulted in **ethnic cleansing**—genocidal efforts to destroy unprotected members of other ethnic groups. Hypernationalistic movements respect neither liberty nor life, as shown by the civil wars that followed the internal collapse of Albania, Bosnia, Burundi, Cambodia, Chechnya, Rwanda, and Somalia in the 1990s.

Hundreds of minority groups are at risk worldwide. They have been denied basic human rights, and prejudice has made them the victims of aggression and persecution. Minorities have consistently become refugees, fleeing across borders to survive. According to the UN High Commissioner on Refugees, in 1998 more than 80 million displaced people were forced from their homes, causing them to seek sanctuary elsewhere. "Peace is not only the absence of conflict," observed Juan Somavia, Chile's representative at the United Nations, in 1997. "It is the presence of human security—at the individual level, the family, the community. Peace is also positive things happening within a society. The two peaces are necessary. The problem today is that, yes, you have less major conflict, but you also have more human insecurity worldwide. The real security threat of the future is that people feel insecure in their own societies."

National armies are neither well prepared nor well trained to defend these victims. (Indeed, in many cases, the armies perpetrate violence against displaced people in their own countries.) Likewise, few international organizations are empowered through widespread multilateral cooperation to stop the

551

carnage. The fact that the weak, the poor, and the exploited have no power contributes to their victimization.

Most states are multiethnic societies, and many people give primary loyalty to their ethnic group rather than their country. Therefore, the predictable consequence of ethnonationalism is the disintegration of **failed states** into smaller and smaller units, incapable of preserving their sovereignty. Cultures pitted against cultures and the mobilization of protesting cultural groups threaten to balkanize states into divided units (Barber 1995). If this happens, the United Nations predicts the twenty-first century will see the creation of as many as another three-hundred new states beyond the nearly two hundred that presently exist. What is more, there will be reason to worry that a **clash of civilizations** will occur between groups of people belonging to "cultural areas" who share similar religious or philosophical beliefs and a common historical experience (Huntington 1996). Such competition between cultures or civilizations that refuse to surrender their separate identities will prevent people coming together in unity in a globalized system; it will tear them apart and could spark a new era of mass violence.

Of great concern, therefore, is whether the moral outrage of the world's states is sufficient to end, through concerted action, the ethnic and cultural conflicts that now rage out of control. Will a humanitarian concern for the victims of ethnic conflicts and cultural clashes crystallize in collaborative responses? Or will the victims perish in a sea of indifference?

5. Has the Quest for Empire Ended?

Much of world history is written in terms of dreams of world conquest—the quest of rulers for world domination, and the efforts of others to prevent it. Some leaders continue to think and act as though they believe others still ac-

Although its quest for empire has ostensibly ended, Russia engaged in a brutal ongoing internal conflict against the secessionist movement in Chechnya in the mid-1990s. No less than its survival as a single country was at stake, as a successful bid for independence by the Chechen rebels could have encouraged similar secessionist movements in other dissatisfied governments in the Russian Federation. Pictured here, Chechnya's national colors are waved from the roof of the destroyed presidential palace in the capital city of Grozny.

tively plan territorial conquest. However, the past five decades have witnessed the great powers' race to relinquish their overseas empires, not expand them. Even the Soviet Union, the last world empire of any size, has now disintegrated—by choice, not by coercion from abroad.

Why has the quest for empire seemingly ended? A plausible explanation is that empire did not benefit the imperial powers materially (Boulding 1978). Writing in the early 1960s, the height of the decolonization period, William Langer argued similarly:

> It is highly unlikely that the modern world will revert to the imperialism of the past. History has shown that the nameless fears which in the late nineteeth century led to the most violent outburst of expansionism were largely unwarranted. The Scandinavian states and Germany since Versailles have demonstrated that economic prosperity and social well-being are not dependent on the exploitation of other peoples, while better distribution of wealth in the advanced countries has reduced if not obviated whatever need there may have been to seek abroad a safety-valve for the pressures building up at home. Even in the field of defense, the old need for overseas bases or for the control of adjacent territories is rapidly being outrun. (Langer 1962, 129)

If imperialism, empire building, and territorial acquisition are no longer in a state's self-interest, why continue to prepare for military defense against the expansionist aims of others?

6. Who Will Cope with Globalization?

In 1517 Martin Luther nailed his ninety-five theses to the door of a church in Wittenberg, Germany, and ignited the Protestant Reformation. To his surprise, his effort at religious reform undermined the Catholic church's authority over states. Ever since then, sovereign states have assumed primary responsibility for controlling affairs within their territorial borders and managing foreign relations with other, similarly empowered, secular state actors.

This system put sovereign states in charge of world affairs, without serious challenge. "People did what they were told to do because that is what one did. As a result, authority structures remained in place for decades, even centuries, as people tended to yield unquestionably to the dictates of governments" (Rosenau 1995).

That has begun to change. The power of sovereign states to control their internal affairs and external relations has eroded precipitously. As Bill Clinton observed on the eve of the 1997 Denver summit of the world's eight industrial giants (the G-7 and Russia), "globalization is irreversible" and "computers and modems, faxes and photocopiers, increased contacts and binding contracts carry with them the seeds of change" that are destroying the distinction between domestic and foreign affairs. In this borderless globe, there are no more oceans. There is only next door. With the demise of distance and the rise of states' vulnerability to external pressures, doubt has climbed about the capacity of governments to exercise control over behavior within their territories. The very concept of governmental authority is being challenged by public opinion, which no longer automatically accepts leaders' decisions as legitimate. And in

globalization the integration of states through increasing contact, communication, and trade to create a holistic, single global system in which the process of change increasingly binds people together in a common fate.

the realm of foreign relations, the forces of **globalization** are undermining the political underpinnings of the past legal and political system of independent states. New technologies can propel huge sums of money halfway round the world in seconds and capital mobility has been facilitated by the sweeping deregulation of financial markets in the leading industrial countries since the 1980s. The lightning speed with which information, communication, labor, and trade also now move across borders, along with the accelerating spread of technological innovation internationally and the growing interdependent integration of states' markets and economies, are creating pressures that states are not well organized to address. The globalization process "has noticeably tamed the state's old feelings of confident independence. . . . These basic units have all, big and small, become less dominant, less independent, and, in a way, less separate than they were in their prime" (*Economist* 1998). States are less and less capable of coping with the "increasingly interconnected" international system, which shrinks distances and heightens the probability and impact of future financial crises.

To some, "globalization is the world's long-term problem" (Boutros-Ghali 1996). It threatens to reduce control over the future, and disintegrate states as governments lose their capacity to govern. To others, "the only practical prospect for universal peace [and prosperity] must be more civilization" through globalization, and that to attain this goal "we should strive to create the largest social, economic, and political units possible, ideally one encompassing the whole world" (Keeley 1996). These optimists see globalization as an unstoppable engine of unity and progress. People who trade have shared interests and fewer incentives to fight; by integrating countries' investments and consumers in the global economy, the capacity for troublemaking and warmaking among countries will be reduced.

There are, in actuality, serious questions about whence the power to address future domestic and international problems will come in such a globalized world without organized global governance. These questions are prompted by the challenge of minority groups' quest for autonomy from within, and by the challenge of nongovernmental organizations (such as Doctors without Borders and multinational corporations such as McDonald's from outside). Many observers have blamed the absence of identifiable enemies since the Cold War for world leaders' confusion as to how to react, but the crisis of understanding may be deeper. It may be embedded in the problem of determining whether any actor is, or can be, in charge of globalizing processes driven by their own unmanaged momentum.

However, although internal fragmentation and globalization are undermining the state, "the emasculated state is a myth" (*Economist* 1998). Despite the state's loss of control, it remains the most powerful instrument for managing global change. If states cannot respond to the challenge, can the world count on supranational global institutions? This may be the most important issue facing the world in the twenty-first century. For if states will not take charge, can the global community count on other actors to assume responsibility?

7. Is "Realism" Still Realistic?

Since the eve of the Second World War, leaders and scholars alike have organized their thoughts and images almost exclusively from the perspective of realism. Their reliance on realism to explain and predict international developments was understandable. Finding a fertile ground in which to flourish during the conflict-ridden fifty-year period between 1939 and 1989, realism accounted for the prevailing lust for power, the appetite for imperial expansion and struggle for hegemony, the all-consuming arms race, and the obsession with military security better than did any other theoretical perspective.

Now, however, on the cusp of the twenty-first century, a window has opened to expose quite different dimensions of world politics heretofore largely neglected. The global agenda has shifted as new issues and problems have risen to prominence. "The problem . . . today is not new challengers for hegemony; it is the new challenge of transnational interdependence" (Nye 1998). As one analyst predicts, "Welfare, not warfare, will shape the rules [and] global threats like ozone holes and pollution will dictate the agenda" (Joffe 1990). As a consequence of these changing issues commanding the world's concern, the realist image of states as unitary rational actors has looked increasingly archaic. In the borderless global village, nongovernmental organizations (NGOs) composed of private citizen groups have flexed their muscles and raised their voices, and they are being heard and orchestrating changes in people's values. "More and more," observed Espen Barth Eide of the Norwegian Foreign Policy Institute in 1997, "the global agenda is being set by others . . . rather than superpowers and governments."

To a number of theorists, the broadened and transformed global agenda goes beyond what realism can be expected to address accurately. To their minds, realist preoccupations threaten to mask the deeper political, economic, and social challenges in international affairs. Many critics are disturbed by realism's failure to anticipate the democratic revolutions that accompanied the Cold War's end, the voluntary retreat of the Soviet Union, and global change and cooperation generally. "The wisdom [that] calls itself 'realism'," scolded Harvard political scientist Stanley Hoffmann (in Friedman 1993), "is utter nonsense today." Realism *was* predictively weak. Moreover, critics charge that realism is scientifically inaccurate and fails to provide

> an adequate understanding of the dynamics of peace and war [which are at the heart of the paradigm, the topics that realism claims to provide the best answers]. An entirely new theoretical approach may be needed, one that will put both existing findings and unresolved questions into a perspective that makes sense of both. (Vasquez 1993, 4, 10)

If these critics of realism's receding accuracy and relevance are correct, then pressure will mount for a new theoretical approach to replace orthodox realism and its more recent neorealist variant.

What a new theory will or should look like is not presently obvious, as challengers to realism differ in their prescriptions. Yet many agree with the general view that "[i]t is time for a new, more rigorous idealist alternative to realism" (Kober 1990) and that "there are good reasons for examining aspects of the liberal international legacy once again" (Fukuyama 1992a) by giving Woodrow Wilson's liberal vision "the fair test it has never received" (Gaddis 1990). Will a reconstructed theory that fuses the best properties of realism and emerging (neo)liberal theories provide the intellectual framework needed to understand world politics in the twenty-first century?

8. Is the World Preparing for the Wrong War?

To preserve peace, one must prepare for war. That remains the classical realist formula for national security. But would states not be wiser to prepare to conquer the conditions that undermine prosperity, freedom, and welfare? "War for survival is the destiny of all species," observes philosopher Martin J. Siegel (1983). "In our case, we are courting suicide [by waging war against one another]. The world powers should declare war against their common enemy—the catastrophic and survival-of-the-fittest forces that destroyed most of the species of life that came before us."

Increasingly, fewer world leaders are succumbing to the single-mindedness of preparing to compete with other states. President François Mitterrand of France warned in 1983 that "together we must urgently find the solutions to the real problems at hand—especially unemployment and underdevelopment. This is the battlefield where the outlines of the year 2000 will be drawn." India's Prime Minister Indira Gandhi predicted that "either nuclear war will annihilate the human race and destroy the earth, thus disposing of any future, or men and women all over must raise their voices for peace and for an urgent attempt to combine the insights of different civilizations with contemporary knowledge. We can survive in peace and goodwill only by viewing the human race as one, and by looking at global problems in their totality." These prescriptions adhere to a fundamental premise, as expressed in 1995 by Martti Ahtisaari, President of Finland: "To deal with the great security challenges of our time, including population growth, the spread of weapons of mass destruction, crime, environmental degradation and ethnic conflicts, we must resolutely adopt new methods of managing change and building global security."

These rhetorical positions doubtless reflect the problems and self-interests the leaders faced at home and abroad. Nonetheless, they reveal a minority view. The war of people against people goes on. Humankind may consequently self-destruct, not because it lacks opportunities, but because of its collective inability to see and to seize them. "Perhaps we will destroy ourselves. Perhaps the common enemy within us will be too strong for us to recognize and overcome," the eminent astronomer Carl Sagan (1988) lamented. "But," he continued, "I have hope. . . . Is it possible that we humans are at last coming to our senses and beginning to work together on behalf of the species and the planet?"

9. Is This the "End of History"?

To many observers, the history of world affairs is the struggle between tyranny and liberty. The contest has taken various forms since antiquity: between kings and mass publics; authoritarianism and republicanism; despotism and democracy; ideological principle and pragmatic politics. Labels are misleading and sometimes dangerous. However, they form the vocabulary of diplomacy and inform theoretical discourse about governance and statecraft. History, in this image, is a battle for the hearts and minds of civilizations. It is an ideological contest for the allegiance of humankind to a particular form of political, social, and economic organization.

Since the Bolshevik revolution in 1917 brought socialism to power in Russia and made Marxism a force in international affairs, the fight for allegiance in the twentieth century has been dominated by the contests between communism, fascism, and democratic capitalism. With the defeat of fascism in World

War II and the collapse of the international communist movement a generation later, it has become fashionable to argue that we have witnessed the end of a historic contest of epic proportions—and thus the triumph of liberalism and the **end of history:**

> The twentieth century saw the developed world descend into a paroxysm of ideological violence, as liberalism contended first with the remnants of absolutism, then bolshevism and fascism, and finally an updated Marxism that threatened to lead to the ultimate apocalypse of nuclear war. But the century that began full of self-confidence in the ultimate triumph of Western liberal democracy seems at its close to be returning full circle to where it started: not to an "end of ideology" of a convergence between capitalism and socialism, as earlier predicted, but to the unabashed victory of economic and political liberalism. (Fukuyama 1989, 3)

The abrupt repudiation of communism in Moscow and eastern Europe and China's embrace of a free-market economy have raised expectations that history has indeed "ended," in the sense that liberal democratic capitalism has triumphed throughout much of the world. Liberals are heartened by the doubling since the mid–1980s of the number of countries practicing multiparty elections and capitalism at home and in foreign trade. World order, they believe, can best be created by free governments practicing free trade. As Woodrow Wilson argued, making the world "safe for democracy" would make the world itself safe. From this liberal perspective, the diffusion of democratic capitalism bodes well for the future of world politics in the next millennium. This is why such a hard-core realist as former U.S. Secretary of State Henry Kissinger was driven in 1997 to conclude that he considered "it essential to promote the democratic ideal by fostering close cooperation where it already exists [because] military conflict among these nations is nearly inconceivable."

A less reassuring possibility is that history has not "ended" and that the battle between totalitarian and democratic governance is not truly over. There remain many democracies ruled by one-party despots who, although elected, disregard constitutional limits on their power and deny their citizens basic civil, religious, and economic human rights. Fundamental civil liberties and freedoms continue to be ignored by many governments. This persistence of leaders not accountable to the electorate suggests that with the end of the ideological dimension to the Cold War we may be witnessing not history's end, but a watershed. Like previous turning points in history, tomorrow may signal history's resumption: the return to the ageless search for barriers against the resurgence of tyranny, nationalism, and war. Especially to followers of *realpolitik*, the most salient feature of world politics—the relentless competitive struggle for power under international anarchy—is permanent. The end of the Cold War does not assure that the international community has moved beyond tyranny or interstate competition and war. As former Soviet President Mikhail Gorbachev noted in 1992, "In the major centers of world politics, the choice, it would seem, has today been made in favor of peace, cooperation, interaction, and overall security." However, he warned, "A major international effort will be needed to render irreversible the shift in favor of a democratic world—and democratic for the whole of humanity, not just half of it."

10. Is There a Reordered Global Agenda?

The paradox of contemporary world politics is that a world liberated from the paralyzing grip of the Cold War must now face a series of challenges every bit as threatening and as potentially unmanageable. Globalization has simultaneously enlarged the responsibilities and expanded the issues to be confronted. As Bill Clinton observed in 1993, "Profound and powerful forces are shaking and remaking our world. And the urgent question of our time is whether we can make change our friend and not our enemy."

The changes in recent years have spawned threats to world order, other than the resurgence of nationalism, ethnic conflict, and separatist revolts. These include acid rain, AIDS and other transnationally contagious diseases, drug trafficking, international organized crime, ozone depletion, climate change, obstacles to gender equality, energy and food insecurity, desertification and deforestation, financial crises and collapsing economies, and neomercantile trade protectionism.

The potential impact of these additional threats is formidable, as emerging trends suggest that nonmilitary dangers will multiply alongside the continuing threat of arms and ethnic and regional conflict. Accordingly, the distinction between **high politics** (war and peace) and **low politics** (economic and other issues of human welfare) may disappear. "In the post-Cold War world, low politics is becoming high politics" as distance ceases to act as a barrier between people in a "global village" (Moran 1991).

● ● ●

A NEW WORLD ORDER?

From our vantage point on the eve of the twenty-first century, the world appears to have undergone a fundamental transformation. Previously established patterns and relationships have been obliterated. Something revolutionary, not simply new, has unfolded.

Juxtaposed against the revolutionary is the persistent—the durability of accepted rituals, existing rules, established institutions, and entrenched customs that resist the pull of the momentous recent changes in world politics. Persistence and change coexist uneasily, and it is this mixture that makes the future so uncertain. The twin forces of integration and disintegration, continuity and change, create a mood of both confidence and disorientation. As Australia's Prime Minister John Howard put it in 1997, "In one sense, you are a remarkably lucky generation, but in another sense you have been born into a period of social and technological change and economic change and economic evolution."

The outcomes of two races will determine the difference between the world that is and the world that will be. The first is the race between knowledge and oblivion. Ignorance stands in the way of global progress and justice. Advances in science and technology far outpace resolution of the social and political problems they generate. Building the knowledge to confront these problems may therefore present the ultimate challenge. "The splitting of the atom," Albert Einstein warned, "has changed everything save our modes of thinking, and thus we drift toward unparalleled catastrophe. Unless there is a fundamental change in [our] attitudes toward one another as well as [our] concept of the future, the world will face unprecedented disaster."

Globalization "implies a holistic worldview and a rejection of the traditional realist paradigm. A globalist perspective embraces a much wider range of important international actors than realism does and addresses a much broader range of issues, as well as expanding the definition of existing concepts such as security" (Sheehan 1996). This view of a globe without borders is captured by this photo taken of the eastern Mediterranean from the Earth-orbiting space shuttle *Columbia*. It pictures an integrated world community, in which humanity shares a common destiny. It also captures the kinds of threats confronting humanity in a globalized world, where problems do not stop at borders. According to scientists studying this photo, the difference in visibility in this panorama suggests that a pollution event near the Black Sea contaminated the atmosphere.

"Knowledge is our destiny," philosopher Jacob Bronowski declared. If the world is to forge a promising future, it must develop more sophisticated knowledge. Sophistication demands that we see the world as a whole, as well as in terms of its individual parts. We must overcome the temptation to picture others according to our images of ourselves and to project onto them our own aims and values. We must discard the belief in a simple formula for a better tomorrow and resist single-issue approaches to reform. Toleration of ambiguity, even the pursuit of it, is essential.

The future of world politics also rests on the outcome of a race between states' ability to cooperatively act in concert and their historic tendency to compete and fight. As U.S. National Security Advisor Samuel Berger, paraphrasing a line from William Shakespeare's *Julius Caesar*, said in 1997, it is time for the international community to get beyond settling conflicts by force: "I come not only to praise the post-Cold War era, but to bury it." Only concerted international cooperation can avert slipping back into regional conflicts guided by the belief that "might alone makes right." The world's political will to implement the reforms necessary to meet global challenges is being tested.

The world's future is uncertain, but it is our future. The moving words of President Kennedy thus describe a posture we might well assume: "However close we sometimes seem to that dark and final abyss, let no man of peace and freedom despair. For he does not stand alone. . . . Together we shall save our planet or together we shall perish in its flames. Save it we can, and save it we must, and then shall we earn the eternal thanks of mankind."

KEY TERMS

chauvinism
realism
liberalism
security dilemma

ethnocentrism
ethnic cleansing
failed states
clash of civilizations

globalization
end of history
high politics
low politics

SUGGESTED READING

Burtloss, Gary, Robert Z. Lawrence, Robert E. Litan, and Robert J, Shapiro. *Globaphobia: Confronting Fears about Open Trade.* Washington, D.C.: Brookings Institution Press, 1998.

Buzan, Barry, and Gerald Segal. *Anticipating the Future: Twenty Millennia of Human Progress.* London: Simon & Schuster, 1998.

Cohen, Joshua, ed. *Debating the Limits of Patriotism.* Boston: Beacon Press, 1996.

Eban, Abba. *Diplomacy for the Next Century.* New Haven, Conn.: Yale University Press, 1998.

Fukuyama, Francis. *The End of History and the Last Man.* New York: Free Press, 1992.

Heilbroner, Robert. *Visions of the Future: The Distant Past, Yesterday, Today, and Tomorrow.* New York: Oxford University Press, 1995.

Hopkins, Terence K., and Immanuel Wallerstein. *The Age of Transition: Trajectory of the World-System, 1945–2025.* London: Zed Books, 1996.

Hughes, Barry B. *International Futures: Choices in the Creation of a New World Order*, 2nd ed. Boulder, Colo.: Westview, 1996.

Iriye, Akira. *Cultural Internationalism and World Order.* Baltimore: Johns Hopkins University Press, 1997.

Kennedy, Paul. *Preparing for the Twenty-First Century.* New York: Random House, 1993.

Maoz, Zeev. "Realist and Cultural Critiques of the Democratic Peace: A Theoretical and Empirical Re-Assessment," *International Interactions* 24 (No. 1, 1998): 3–89.

Martin, Hans-Peter, and Harald Schumann. *The Global Trap: Globalization and the Assault on Prosperity and Democracy.* New York: St. Martin's Press, 1998.

Mathews, Jessica. "Power Shift: The Rise of Global Civil Society," *Foreign Affairs* 76 (January/February 1997): 50–66.

Rosenau, James N. "Disorder and Order in a Turbulent World: The Evolution of Globalized Space," pp. 145–69 in Charles W. Kegley, Jr. and Eugene R. Wittkopf, eds., *The Global Agenda*, 5th ed. New York: McGraw Hill, 1998.

http://www.oecd.org/sge/au/oecdifp.htm
International Futures Programme The Organization for Economic Cooperation and Development (OECD) has designed a program to help decisionmakers in government and industry come to grips with the formidable challenge of assessing the long-term trends that shape our global future. Scan the Web site and read about the conferences and the projects that are underway. Do you think this program is a good model for other organizations that strive to understand the changes that are underway in the international system? What suggestions can you give?

http://www.worldcitizen.org/
World Citizen Web As a student of international relations, you may wonder if there is a better way of or-ganizing international relations than relying on the state system. The World Citizen Web site allows you to think about your world citizenship. This site asks "How can we, as sovereign world citizens, govern our world?" This organization believes that the Internet can help serve as a communications tool whereby the citizens of the world can finally vote on common global issues. Click on the "World Citizen Referendum." Take the world citizen referendum ballot and then give your world voter information. Then, read about the organization's "World Syntegrity Project." Do you think the organization's type of initiative is "pie in the sky" or do you believe that one day soon we may be able to vote on world issues like we vote on national issues? Is it possible to form a world government?

Glossary

absolute gains: a condition in which all participants in exchanges become better off.

absolute poverty: severe economic deprivation that so reduces poor people's standard of living that they struggle to survive without access to safe drinking water, food, housing, and other basic human needs.

acid rain: precipitation that has been made acidic through contact with sulfur dioxide and nitrogen oxides.

ACP states: African, Caribbean, and Pacific developing countries linked to the European Union through treaties of cooperation.

adjudication: a conflict resolution procedure in which a third party makes a binding decision through an institutionalized tribunal.

agenda setting: the thesis that by their ability to identify issues, the communications media determine the problems that receive attention by governments and international organizations.

aid burden: the ratio between aid and a donor's income as measured by gross national product.

AIDS: acquired immune deficiency syndrome, a deadly infectious disease resulting from the human immunodeficiency virus (HIV).

Algiers Summit Conference (1973): the international meeting that resulted in the Group of 77 joining forces with the Nonaligned Movement (NAM).

alignments: the acceptance by a neutral state threatened by foreign enemies of a special relationship short of formal alliance with a stronger power able to protect it from attack.

alliances: coalitions that form when two or more states combine their military capabilities and promise to coordinate their policies to increase mutual security.

anarchy: an absence of governmental authority.

antipersonnel landmines (APLs): weapons buried below the surface of the soil that explode on contact with any person—soldier or citizen—stepping on them.

apartheid: the South African policy of racial separation.

appeasement: a strategy of making concessions to an aggressor state without retaliation in the hope that, satisfied, it will not make additional claims on the territory of its neighbors.

arbitrage: the selling of one currency (or product) and purchase of another to make a profit on the changing exchange rates; traders ("arbitragers") help to keep states' currencies in balance through their speculative efforts to buy large quantities of devalued currencies and sell them in countries where they are valued more highly.

arbitration: a conflict resolution procedure in which a third party makes a binding decision through an ad hoc forum.

armed force: combat between the military forces of two or more states or groups.

arms control: multilateral or bilateral agreements to contain arms races by setting limits on the number and types of weapons states are permitted.

arms control regimes: rules accepted by the parties to treaties to prohibit the production, deployment, sale, or use of particular categories of weapons.

arms race: the buildup of weapons and armed forces by two or more states that threaten each other, with the competition driven by the conviction that gaining a lead is necessary for security.

ASAT weapon: antisatellite weapon.

Asian Tigers: the four Asian NIEs (Hong Kong, South Korea, Singapore, and Taiwan) that experienced far greater rates of economic growth during the 1980s than the more advanced industrial societies of the First World; Hong Kong is now a part of China.

asylum: the provision of sanctuary to safeguard refugees escaping from the threat of persecution in the country where they hold citizenship.

Atlantic Charter: a declaration issued in 1941 by U.S. President Franklin D. Roosevelt and British Prime Minister Winston Churchill outlining the principles that would guide the construction of a postwar general security system.

atrocities: brutal and savage acts against targeted citizen groups or prisoners of war, defined as illegal under international law.

autocratic rule: a system of authoritarian or totalitarian government where unlimited power is concentrated in a single person.

Baker initiative: a proposal to resolve the Third World debt problem by encouraging domestic economic reforms and seeking new loans from private banks.

balance of payments: a summary statement of a state's financial transactions with the rest of the world, including such items as foreign aid transfers and the income of citizens employed abroad who send their paychecks home.

balance of power: the theory that peace and stability are most likely to be maintained when military power is distributed so that no single power or bloc can dominate the others.

balance of terror: a concept used to describe situations of mutual nuclear deterrence.

balance of trade: a state's net trade surplus or deficit, based on the difference in the value of its imports and exports.

balancer: a role played by an influential global or regional great power that gives its support to the weaker side of a dispute to ensure that the balance of power is preserved so that the stronger state does not achieve preponderance.

ballistic missile defense (BMD): a system to defend against an attack by incoming ballistic missiles.

Bandung Conference (1955): a meeting of twenty-nine Asian and African nations that was held in Bandung, Indonesia to devise a strategy to combat colonialism.

bandwagon: the tendency for weak states to seek alliance with the strongest power, irrespective of that power's ideology or form of government, in order to increase security.

bargaining: negotiation by states to try to settle their disputes without actually resorting to armed force.

barter: the exchange of one good for another rather than the use of currency to buy and sell items.

Baruch Plan (1946): a call for the creation of a UN Atomic Development Authority that would place atomic energy under international authority.

basic human needs: adequate food intake (in terms of calories, proteins, and vitamins), safe drinking water, sufficient clothing and shelter, literacy, sanitation, health care, employment, and dignity.

beggar-thy-neighbor policy: efforts to promote domestic welfare by promoting trade surpluses that can be realized only at other countries' expense.

behavioralism: an approach to the study of international relations that emphasizes the application of scientific methods.

bilateral: relationships between two states.

bilateral agreements: arms control agreements negotiated between two states.

bilateral aid: aid that flows directly from one country to another.

billiard ball model: a metaphor that compares world politics to a game in which billiard balls (states) continuously clash and collide with one another. The actions of each are determined by their interactions with the others, not by what occurs within them.

biodiversity: the variety of life on earth.

Biological Weapons Convention (BWC): a 1972 agreement prohibiting the development, production, and stockpiling of biological weapons.

bipolarity: a condition in which an international system has two dominant power centers.

bipolarity, bipolar distribution of power: the division of the balance of power into two coalitions headed by rival military powers, each seeking to contain the other's expansion.

bipolarization: the clustering of smaller states in alliances around the two dominant power centers.

bipolycentrism: the existence of military bipolarity between the United States and Soviet Union, coupled with multiple political centers of independent foreign policy decisions.

bloc: a rigid, highly cohesive alliance among a group of states.

Bottom Up Review (BUR): the 1993 redefinition of U.S. military strategy and defense policy resulting from a reassessment of the global situation.

bounded rationality: a concept that decision makers' capacity to choose the best option is often constrained by many human and organizational factors.

boycotts: concerted efforts, often organized internationally, to prevent relations such as trade with a state, to express disapproval or to coerce acceptance of certain conditions.

Brady initiative: an approach to resolving the Third World debt crisis by reducing the debt of all debtor nations.

Bretton Woods system: the rules, institutions, and decision-making procedures devised during World War II to govern international economic relations in the postwar era.

Brezhnev Doctrine: the assertion by Leonid Brezhnev following the 1968 Soviet invasion of Czechoslovakia that the USSR had the right to intervene to preserve communist party rule in any state within the Soviet bloc.

brinkmanship: the threat of nuclear escalation in a confrontation to compel submission.

Brundtland Commission: the 1987 World Commission on Environment and Development that called for sustainable development.

bureaucracies: the agencies, regulatory commissions, and departments that conduct the functions of a central government.

bureaucratic politics model: an interpretation of policy making that stresses the bargaining and compromises among the contending governmental organizations that exert influence on the foreign policy choices of political leaders.

Camp David Declaration on New Relations (1992): a joint statement by Russian President Boris Yeltsin and U.S. President George Bush that asserts the relationship between Russia and the United States will be characterized by friendship and partnership.

capital mobility hypothesis: the proposition that MNCs' movement of investment capital has led to the globalization of finance.

carrying capacity: the maximum biomass that can be supported by a given territory.

cartel: an organization of the producers of a commodity that seeks to regulate the pricing and production of the commodity.

Carter Doctrine: President Jimmy Carter's declaration of

U.S. willingness to use military force to protect its interests in the Persian Gulf.

caucuses: informal groups that individuals in government join to promote their common interests.

chain reaction arms race cycle: arms races propelled when states increase their military capabilities to offset the expected growth of their adversaries' capabilities, which prompts other states to increase their capabilities in self-defense—an interaction that produces an upward spiral in weaponry but reduces every state's security.

chaos theory: the application of mathematical methods to identify in rapidly changing and seemingly unconnected relationships (such as many global phenomena appear) underlying and episodically recurring patterns, in order to better interpret complex reality.

chauvinism: the nationalistic belief in the inherent morality and virtue of one's country, which, extending the meaning of patriotism, accepts the maxim "my country, right or wrong."

Chemical Weapons Convention (CWC): an agreement, signed by 164 states, requiring the destruction of existing stocks of chemical weapons by the year 2003.

Chernobyl nuclear accident: a nuclear catastrophe that occurred at a power plant in the Ukraine during 1986.

civil war: war between factions within the same country.

clash of civilizations: political scientist Samuel Huntington's controversial thesis that in the twenty-first century the globe's major civilizations will conflict with one another, leading to anarchy and warfare similar to that resulting from conflicts between states over the past five hundred years.

classical imperialism: the first wave of European empire building that began during the fifteenth century, as the English, French, Dutch, Portuguese, and Spanish used their military power to achieve commercial advantages overseas.

classical liberal economic theory: a body of thought based on Adam Smith's ideas about the forces of supply and demand in the marketplace, emphasizing the benefits of minimal government regulation of the economy and trade.

classical realism: see political realism.

Clinton Doctrine: a policy of active engagement in world affairs, pledging the United States to seek the enlargement of the peaceful liberal democratic community.

closed economic system: a system based on a centrally planned or command economy.

Club of Rome: a private group that has popularized a neo-Malthusian interpretation of growth.

coercive diplomacy: the use of threats or limited force to persuade an adversary to call off or undo an encroachment.

cognitive dissonance: people's psychological reaction to discrepancies between their existing beliefs and new information.

collective goods: goods such as safe drinking water from which everyone benefits.

collective security: a security regime agreed to by the great powers setting rules for keeping peace, guided by the principle that an act of aggression by any state will be met by a collective response from the rest.

colonialism: the rule of a region by an external sovereign power.

Cominform (Communist Information Bureau): a Soviet organization created during the Cold War to coordinate the activities of communist parties worldwide.

commercial liberalism: an economic theory advocating free markets and the removal of barriers to the flow of trade and capital as a locomotive for prosperity.

commitment: negotiator's promise during bargaining, designed to change the target's expectations about the negotiator's future behavior.

common foreign and security policy (CFSP): the agreement reached by the European Union defining the goals in foreign and defense policy the EU pledges to jointly pursue.

common market: a form of economic integration where restrictions on the free movement of commodities, capital, and labor among member states are abolished and a common external tariff is established.

common security: a concept advocating replacing the nation of states competing with one another for their own national security with collective security to promote the security of all states.

Commonwealth of Independent States (CIS): the political entity that replaced the Soviet Union on January 1, 1992.

communist theory of imperialism: the Marxist-Leninist economic interpretation of imperial wars of conquest as driven by capitalism's need for foreign monies to generate capital.

comparative advantage: a concept in liberal economics assuming that a nation will benefit if it specializes in those goods it produces comparatively cheaply and acquires through trade goods that it can only produce at a higher cost.

comparative foreign policy: research method seeking to test rival hypotheses about the determinants of states' interactions and their positions toward the issues on the global agenda.

compellence: the use of nuclear weapons as instruments of coercive diplomacy.

complex interdependence: a theory stressing the complex ways in which the growing ties among transnational actors make them vulnerable to each other's actions and sensitive to each other's needs.

comprehensive test ban (CTB): negotiations held periodically since the 1950s aimed at banning all nuclear testing.

concert: a cooperative agreement among great powers to manage jointly the international system.

concert of Europe: a system of great-power conference diplomacy organized in Europe after the Napoleonic Wars.

conciliation: a conflict resolution procedure in which a third party assists both sides but offers no solution.

Conference on Disarmament (CD): a multilateral arms reduction conference held in Geneva, beginning in 1981, which produced the U.S.-Soviet Chemical Weapons Destruction Agreement of 1990.

conflict: discord, often arising in international relations over perceived incompatibilities of interest.

consensus decision making: voting by voice without a record of individual members' formal positions, in order to reach agreement without generating criticism from opponents within the members' domestic systems.

constitutional democracy: government processes that allow people or their elected representatives to exercise power and influence the state's policies.

containment: a term coined by U.S. policymaker George F. Kennan for deterring Soviet Russia's expansionist aims by counterpressures, which has since become a general term used by strategists to describe the methods used to prevent an expanding great power from flexing its military muscles.

continuity: persistence of a trend without a fundamental change.

Convention on Biodiversity: a 1993 treaty obligating ratifying states that adhere to the agreement's rules for sharing the profits of biotechnological research discoveries and for protecting endangered species and habitats.

Conventional Forces in Europe (CFE) Treaty: a 1992 treaty that set ceilings on five categories of conventional arms.

conventional deterrence: dissuading an adversary from attacking by means of nonnuclear weapons.

conventional (liberal) theory of economic development: a theory that emphasized indigenous impediments to Third World development. Based on the assumption that growth meant increasing increments of per-capita GNP, the task was to identify and remove obstacles to growth and supply missing components, such as investment capital.

conventional war: armed conflicts waged with nonnuclear naval, air, and ground weapons.

cornucopians: optimists who question limits-to-growth analyses and contend that markets effectively maintain a balance between population, resources, and the environment.

Council of Europe: an organization founded in 1949, whose members now include forty states, for the purpose of promoting unity and preserving Europe's cultural heritage.

Council for Mutual Economic Assistance (CMEA): an international economic organization created in 1949 containing the Soviet Union and the countries of Eastern Europe.

counterfactual arguments: thought experiments to consider the consequences that probably would have resulted had something happened that actually did not, such as speculating "what if Adolf Hitler had invaded Britain" or "what if John F. Kennedy had not been assassinated."

counterforce: the targeting of strategic nuclear weapons on particular military capabilities of an enemy's armed forces and arsenals.

counterforce targeting strategy: the targeting of strategic nuclear weapons on particular military capabilities of an enemy's armed forces and arsenals.

counterinsurgency: combat against revolutionary guerrillas.

countervalue targeting strategy: targeting an opponent's industrial and population centers.

countries in transition: the remnant states of the former communist countries (Second World) in Central and Eastern Europe that are undertaking economic reforms to introduce capitalism.

covert operations: secret activities performed through clandestine means to realize specific political or military goals.

crimes against humanity: a category of activities, made illegal at the Nuremberg war crime trials, that involve a state's abuse of the human rights of its citizens.

crisis: a situation that threatens high-priority goals, restricts the time available for response, and surprises decision makers.

crisis decision: a choice made in highly threatening and potentially grave situations, involving elements of surprise and restricted response time, by the highest level of authoritative decision makers.

Cuban missile crisis: the U.S. naval blockade of Cuba in October 1962 to force Soviet withdrawal of offensive missiles after the discovery of the Soviet's plan to deploy them.

cultural conditioning: the impact of national traditions and moral principle on the behavior of states, under the assumption that culture affects national decision making about issues such as the acceptability of aggression.

cultural domains: groups that share a common intellectual heritage and values and recognize no national borders.

cultural imperialism: imposing one country's value system on another people who do not welcome such foreign influence.

current history approach: a view of the purpose of inquiry which maintains that, to understand international relations, scholars should focus on the description of events, not theoretical explanations of their causes.

customs union: a market in which sovereign states agree

to remove taxes on goods exported across the borders of the union's members.

cyberspace: metaphorical term used to describe the global electronic web of people, ideas, and interactions on the Internet, which is unencumbered by the borders of a geopolitical world.

cycles: successions of periodically recurring events or phenomena.

de facto **recognition:** a government's acknowledgment of the factual existence of another state or government short of full recognition.

de jure **recognition:** a government's formal, legal recognition of another government or state.

debt decade: a prolonged financial crisis that began in 1982 when it appeared that Third World debtor nations might default on their loans.

debtor's cartel: a proposal that Third World debtor states confront the creditor states with a coalition when pressing for a solution to the debt crisis.

decision-making theory: an analytic approach to the determinants of states' foreign policy that focuses on the settings and situations in which leaders find themselves when they make decisions.

Declaration on the Granting of Independence to Colonial Countries and Peoples (1960): a declaration passed by the UN General Assembly that proclaimed the subjection of any people to colonial domination was a denial of human rights.

decolonization: the political process freeing colonial peoples from their dependent status.

defense conversion: the process of shifting resources from the production of military-related goods to civilian products.

deforestation: the destruction of forests.

democracy: government processes which allow people or their elected representatives to exercise power and influence the state's policies.

democratic peace: the theory that, because democratic states do not fight each other, the diffusion of democratic sovernance throughout the world will reduce the probability of war.

demographic transition: an explanation of population changes over time that highlights the causes of declines in birth and death rates.

demography: the study of population changes, their sources, and their impact.

dependence theory: a theory that claims the relationship between advanced capitalist societies and those at the periphery of the world economy is exploitative. According to this view, capitalism's need for external sources of demand and profitable investment outlets led to the penetration of virtually every part of the Third World and the establishment of a dominance-dependence relationship between North and South.

dependency theory: perspective that perceives the international economic system as responsible for the less developed Third World countries' dependence on, and exploitation by, the wealthy countries.

dependent development: the industrialization of peripheral areas within the confines of the dominance-dependence relationship between North and South.

desertification: the creation of deserts due to soil erosion, overfarming, and deforestation, which converts cropland to nonproductive, arid sand.

détente: in general, a strategy seeking to relax tensions between adversaries.

deterrence: a preventive strategy designed to dissuade an adversary from doing what it would otherwise do.

developed countries: a category used by the World Bank to designate those countries with a GNP per capita (in 1995) above $765 annually.

developing countries: a category used by the World bank to designate those countries with a GNP per capita (in 1995) equal to or below $765 annually.

development: the processes through which a country increases its capacity to meet its citizens' basic human needs and raise their standard of living.

devolution: states' granting of political power to ethnopolitical national groups and indigenous people under the expectation that greater autonomy will curtail their quest for independence as a new state.

diasporas: dispersed emigrant communities residing outside their homelands while preserving their identification with their country of origin.

digital world economy: a system based largely on globalized electronic debt and credit systems.

diplomatic immunity: the legal doctrine that gives ambassadors immunity from the domestic laws of the countries where their embassies are located.

diplomatic process: the practice of diplomacy through which states reach bargains about agreements.

diplomatic recognition: the formal legal acceptance of a state's official status as an independent country.

disarmament: agreements designed to reduce or eliminate weapons.

displaced people: people involuntarily uprooted from their homes but still living in their own countries.

diversionary theory of war: the contention that leaders initiate conflict abroad as a way of increasing national cohesion at home.

divine right of kings: the realist doctrine that because kings are sovereign, they have the right to rule their subjects authoritatively and are not accountable to the public because their rule is ordained by God.

dollar convertibility: a commitment by the U.S. government to exchange dollars for gold.

domestic policy: that set of issues within a state that governments seek to manage, as distinct from foreign policy problems beyond state borders.

domino theory: a metaphor that predicts that if one state falls to communism, its neighbors will also fall in a chain reaction, like a row of dominoes.

dualism: the existence of a rural, impoverished, and neglected sector of society alongside an urban, developing, or modernizing sector, with little interaction between the two.

dual-use technology: technology that has both commercial and military uses.

Earth Summit: an international meeting held in 1992 in Rio de Janeiro, Brazil, aimed at creating a program of action to address a broad range of environmental and developmental issues.

ecological overshoot: the exploitation of natural resources that exceeds the earth's carrying capacity.

ecological transition: a process in situations of high population growth where human demands come to exceed sustainable yield.

economic sanctions: government actions aimed at inflicting deprivation on a target state through the limitation or termination of economic relations.

ecopolitics: how political actors influence perceptions of, and policy responses to, their environments.

electromagnetic-pulse (EMP) bomb: a futuristic weapon that could disable the communications and computer networks of an entire city.

electronic cash: the instantaneous transfer of money for transnational purchases by computers and electronic telecommunications that, unregulated, leads to global financial crises, corruption, and crime because these exchanges cannot be easily detected by traditional accounting methods.

elitist decision making: a model of the policy-making process that ascribes disproportionate control over foreign policy making to a small ruling group.

elitism: the argument that because a "power elite" really controls democratic governments for their own interests, ordinary citizens are given participation without power, involvement without influence.

embargo: a government order prohibiting commerce with a target state.

emerging markets: the Global South states whose domestic political economies have rapidly grown as a result of liberal economic reforms and foreign investment.

enclosure movement: the claiming of common properties by states or private interests.

end of history: the thesis that economic and political liberalism have triumphed as an accepted philosophy throughout the world, ending the contest between market democracies and centrally planned governance.

engagement and enlargement strategy: the Clinton administration's strategy that commits U.S. power to help manage conflicts throughout the world and to enlarge the community of liberal democracies.

Engel's law: poorer families spend a greater percentage of their budget on food than do higher-income families.

entente: an agreement between states to consult if one is attacked by another party.

Entente Cordiale: an alliance between Britain and France that was established in 1902.

environmental refugee: a person who abandons land no longer fit for human habitation due to environmental degradation.

environmental security: a concept that recognizes that threats to global life systems are as important as the threat of armed conflicts.

epistemic community: a group of experts from around the world who, based on their knowledge, develop a shared understanding of a problem on the global agenda and a set of preferences for responding to it.

ethics: the criteria by which right and wrong behavior and motives are distinguished.

ethnic cleansing: the extermination of an ethnic minority group by the state, in violation of international law.

ethnic group: a group of people of the same nationality who share a common culture, set of ancestors, or language.

ethnic nationalism: devotion to a cultural, ethnic, or linguistic community within an existing state.

ethnicity: perceptions of likeness among members of a particular racial or linguistic grouping leading them to act prejudicially toward outsiders in other kinship or cultural groups.

ethnocentrism: the belief that one's nationality is special and superior, and that others are secondary and inferior.

ethnopolitical groups: people whose identity is defined by their sense of sharing a common nationality, language, cultural heritage and kinship ties.

ethologists: scholars who study animals in order to understand human behavior.

Euro-Atlantic Partnership Council (EAPC): a coordinating institution within NATO created in 1998 to manage the common political, military, financial, and security issues confronting Europe.

eurocrat: a member of the professional staff who assist the Executive Commission of the European Union.

European Community (EC)/European Union (EU): a regional organization created by the merger of the European Coal and Steel Community, the European Atomic Energy Community, and the European Economic Community; known as the European Union after November 1993.

European Court Justice (ECJ): a court created by the European Union and given jurisdiction by it to settle disputes between EU members.

European Free Trade Association (EFTA): an organization created in 1960 as a counterpoint to the European Economic Community.

European Monetary System (EMS): an arrangement designed to stabilize the currency values of EU member's against one another and against the dollar.

European Political Cooperation (EPC): the ongoing effort of European Union members to devise a common position on foreign policy issues through regular meetings among EU foreign ministers.

export-led industrialization: a strategy that involves developing domestic export industries capable of competing in overseas markets.

export quotas: a barrier to free trade imposed pursuant to negotiated agreements between producers and consumers.

extended deterrence: a strategy that seeks to deter an adversary from attacking one's allies.

externalities: the side effects produced by economic activities, especially costs such as pollution.

extraterritoriality: the legal doctrine that allows a state to maintain jurisdiction over its embassies in other states.

extreme militant religious movements: politically active organizations based on strong religious convictions whose members are fanatically devoted to the global promotion of their religious beliefs.

failed states: countries whose governments have so mismanaged policy that they have lost the loyalty of their citizens who, in rebellion, threaten to disintegrate the state.

failing states: those governments that are in danger of losing the loyalty of their citizens, who are rebelling against corruption and administrative failure, and in the process tearing the country into separate political parts.

fascism: a far-right ideology that promotes extreme nationalism and the establishment of an authoritarian society built around a single party with dictatorial leadership.

fast-track negotiating authority: a concession by the U.S. Congress permitting the president to negotiate reciprocal tariff-reduction agreements with other countries which, when granted, enables the United States to reach bilateral trade treaties more easily.

feminist theory: a body of scholarship that emphasizes gender in the study of world politics.

fertility rate: the average number of children born to a woman (or group of women) during her lifetime.

financial veto: withholding payment selectively from certain UN programs as a way to register resentment of the organization's activities and to change them.

firebreak: the psychological barrier between conventional and nuclear war.

First World: countries that share a commitment to varying forms of democratic political institutions and developed market economies, including the United States, Japan, Canada, Australia, New Zealand, Israel, Malta, South Africa, and the countries of Western Europe.

fixed exchange rates: a system under which states establish the parity of their currencies and commit to keeping fluctuations in their exchange rates within narrow limits.

floating exchange rates: a system where market forces rather than government intervention determine the value of currencies.

food ladder: a conceptualization based on the biological food chain. As personal income increases, individuals move up the ladder, consuming grains indirectly as meat rather than directly.

food security: access by all people at all times to enough food for an active, healthy life.

foreign aid: economic assistance in the form of loans and grants provided by a donor country to a recipient country for a variety of purposes.

foreign direct investment (FDI): according to the United Nations, like plant and equipment, FDI also implies "a lasting involvement in the management of enterprises in the recipient economy." In contrast, *equity investment* flows such as stock ownership are typically more speculative in nature and respond quickly to changing perceptions of risk and reward.

foreign policy: the decisions governing authorities make in the name of the state to realize international goals.

fossil fuels: fuels such as coal, petroleum, and natural gas that are formed from organic remains.

Fourteen Points speech (1918): a speech delivered by U.S. President Woodrow Wilson that called for open diplomacy, self-determination, free trade, freedom of the seas, disarmament, and collective security.

Fourth World: indigenous people who often live in poverty and deprivation within a state that occupies the land from which they originate. Sometimes used to refer to the least developed of the less developed countries.

free-floating exchange rates: a system in which market forces determine currency values.

free riders: those who enjoy the benefits of collective goods but pay little or nothing for them.

Free Trade Area of the Americas (FTAA): a set of rules to promote free trade among thirty-four democracies in North and South America.

functionalism: a bottom-up approach to fostering political integration through transnational organizations that emphasize pooling sovereignty.

gender empowerment index: the UN Development Program's attempt to measure the extent of gender equality across the globe's countries, based on estimates of women's relative economic income, high-paying positions, and access to professional and parliamentary positions.

gender inequalities: differences between men and women in opportunity and reward that are determined by the values that guide states' foreign and domestic policies.

General Agreement on Tariffs and Trade (GATT): an international organization that seeks to promote and protect the most-favored-nation principle as the basis for international trade.

General Assembly: one of six principal organs established by the UN Charter. It is the only body representing all the member states. Decision making follows the principle of majority rule, with no state given a veto.

Generalized System of Preferences (GSP): a scheme that permits First World states to grant preferences to developing states without violating the WTO's nondiscrimination principle.

genetic engineering: research geared to discover seeds for new types of plant and human life for sale and use as substitutes for those produced naturally.

genocide: the deliberate extermination of an ethnic or minority group.

geo-economics: the relationship between geography and the economic conditions and behavior of states that define their levels of production, trade, and consumption of goods and services.

geopolitics: the relationship between geography and politics and their consequences for states' national interests and relative power.

glasnost: the Russian word for Mikhail Gorbachev's policy of openness.

global agenda: the primary issues, problems, and controversies on which states and humanity concentrate their attention and allocate resources to address.

global commons: the entire environment considered to be the common heritage and property of the human race on the planet Earth, including the ocean floor under international waters, the Antarctic, and the celestial bodies in outer space.

Global Environment Facility (GEF): an instrument for resource transfers from North to South, as spelled out in the biodiversity convention.

globalization: the integration of states through increasing contact, communication and trade to create a holistic, single global system in which the process of change increasingly binds people together in a common fate.

globalization of finance: the increasing transnationalization of financial markets.

global level of analysis: an analytical approach to world politics that emphasizes the impact of global conditions on foreign policy behavior.

global migration crisis: the growing number of people moving from their home country to another country that has created a crisis because the sheer volume exceeds the ability of host countries to absorb the foreign migrants.

Global North: a term used to refer to the world's wealthy, industrialized countries located primarily in the Northern Hemisphere.

Global South: a term now often used instead of "Third World" to designate the less developed countries located primarily in the Southern Hemisphere.

global village: popular image used to describe the growth of awareness that all people share a common fate, stemming from a macro perspective that views the world as an integrated and interdependent whole.

global warming: the gradual rise in world temperature, a suspected consequence of greenhouse gases trapping heat remitted from earth that would otherwise escape into outer space.

good offices: the third-party offering of a location for discussions among disputants.

great powers: the most powerful countries, militarily and economically, in the international system.

greenhouse gases: carbon dioxide, methane, nitrous oxide, chloroflourocarbons, and other gas molecules that tend to trap heat remitted from the earth that would otherwise escape into outer space.

green revolution: the introduction of new high-yield grains to Third World countries.

gross national product (GNP) and gross domestic product (GDP): measures of the production of goods and services within a given time period, which differ only in whether nationality (GNP) or residency (GDP) is used to delimit the geographic scope of production. GNP measures production by a state's citizens or companies, regardless of where the production occurs. GDP measures production occurring within the territory of a state, regardless of the national identity of the producers.

Group of Five (G-5): a group composed of the United States, Britain, France, Japan, and West Germany that periodically meets to negotiate international monetary policy and other issues.

Group of Seven (G-7): a group composed of the United States, Britain, France, Japan, Germany, Canada, and Italy that meets in regular economic summit conferences.

Group of 77 (G-77): a coalition of the world's poor countries formed during the 1964 United Nations Conference on Trade and Development (UNCTAD) in Geneva. Originally composed of seventy-seven states, the coalition now numbers over one hundred twenty developing countries and continues to press for concessions from the wealthy nations.

groupthink: the propensity for members of a group to accept and agree with the group's prevailing attitudes, rather than speaking out for what they believe.

gunboat diplomacy: a show of military force, historically called naval force.

guns-versus-growth: the trade off that exists between military spending and economic development, and controversy over the extent to which spending on weapons reduces the rate of growth of a state's GNP.

Hague Peace Conferences (1899, 1907): international meetings that restricted the use of certain weapons and sought to promote peaceful methods of dispute resolution.

hard power: the ability to exercise influence in world politics because of tangible resources such as military and economic strength.

hegemon: a single dominant military and economic state that uses its unrivaled power to create and enforce rules aimed at preserving the existing world order and its own position in that order.

hegemonic stability theory: the argument that a dominant state is necessary to enforce international cooperation, maintain international rules and regimes, and keep the peace.

hegemony: the ability of one state to dominate the rules and arrangements governing international economics and politics.

Helsinki Accord (1975): an agreement signed by NATO, Warsaw Pact, and thirteen neutral and nonaligned European countries that sought to establish peace in Europe by calling for the implementation of confidence-building measures, economic, environmental, and scientific cooperation, and the free flow of people, ideas, and information.

hidden veto: the ability of the United States during the formative period of the United Nations to persuade a sufficient majority of other UN Security Council members to vote negatively on an issue so as to avoid the stigma of having to cast the single blocking vote.

hierarchy: a division of entities (such as nation-states) into ordered ranks.

high politics: geostrategic issues of national and international security that pertain to matters of war and peace.

history-making-individuals model: an interpretation of foreign policy behavior that equates states' actions with the preferences and initiatives of the highest government officials.

HIV: human immunodeficiency virus, a contagious disease that causes the fatal infection AIDS.

horizontal nuclear proliferation: an increase in the number of states that possess nuclear weapons.

horizontal system of law: a decentralized, self-help system of law.

host country: the country where a corporation headquartered in another country conducts its business activities.

hot line: a teletype communications link between Moscow and Washington that would permit national leaders to communicate directly during a crisis.

human development index (HDI): an index that uses life expectancy, literacy, average number of years of schooling, and income to assess a country's human development performance.

human rights: the political rights and civil liberties recognized by the international community as inalienable and valid for individuals in all countries by virtue of their humanness.

ICBM: intercontinental ballistic missile.

ideology: a set of core philosophical principles that leaders and citizens collectively hold about politics, the interests of political actors, and the ways people ought to ethically behave.

imperial overstretch: a condition where commitments exceed a state's ability to fulfill them.

imperialism: intentional imposition of one state's power over another, usually through territorial conquest and denial of the victim population's freedom to have a voice in the conquering regime's decisions.

import quotas: a nontariff barrier to free trade that involves limits on the quantity of a particular product that can be imported.

import-substitution industrialization: a strategy that involves encouraging domestic entrepreneurs to manufacture products traditionally imported from abroad.

inadvertent war: a war that is not the result of anyone's master plan; rather it occurs due to uncertainty, confusion, and circumstances beyond the control of those involved.

independents (oil companies): competitors of the major oil companies who historically stood outside of the international oil regime controlled by the majors.

indigenous peoples: the native ethnic and cultural inhabitant populations within countries ruled by a government controlled by others, referred to as the "Fourth World."

individual level of analysis: an analytical approach to the study of world politics that emphasizes the psychological and perceptual origins of states' foreign policy behaviors, with special attention to leaders.

infant industry: a newly established industry that is not yet strong enough to compete effectively in the global marketplace.

information warfare (IW) or infowar tactics: attacks on an adversary's telecommunications and computer networks to penetrate and degradate an enemy whose defense capabilities depend heavily on these technological systems.

instrumental rationality: a conceptualization of rationality asserting that individuals have preferences, and when faced with two or more alternatives, they will choose the one that yields the preferred outcome.

integration: the processes and activities by which the populations of two or more states transfer their loyalties to a merged political and economic unit.

intercontinental ballistic missiles (ICBMs): rockets capable of carrying weapons from one continent to another.

interdependence: a situation arising when the behavior of international actors greatly affects others with whom they have contact, so that the parties to the exchange become mutually sensitive and vulnerable to the others' actions.

interethnic competition: a struggle for supremacy within a geographic area between two or more ethnic groups.

571

intergovernment organizations: Intergovernmental organizations or IGOs are institutions created and joined by governments, which give them authority to make collective decisions to manage particular problem(s) on the global agenda.

intergovernmental organization (IGO): an international organization whose members are states.

intergovernmental panel on climate change (IPCC): a large group of scientists from around the world sponsored by UN agencies to study global climate change.

intermediate-range nuclear forces (INF) disarmament agreement (1987): an agreement between the United States and the Soviet Union to remove intermediate-range nuclear forces from Europe.

intermestic politics: those issues confronting a state that are simultaneously international and domestic.

internally displaced people: people who live in a refugee-like situation in their own countries.

International Criminal Tribunal: a UN court established by the United Nations for indicting and administering justice to people in Bosnia committing war crimes.

International Court of Justice: the primary judicial organ of the United Nations; also known as the World Court.

International Labor Organization: a UN Specialized Agency responsible for improving working conditions in member countries.

international liquidity: reserve assets used to settle international accounts.

International Monetary Fund (IMF): a specialized agency of the United Nations that seeks to maintain monetary stability and assist member states in funding balance of payments deficits.

international monetary system: the set of procedures used to calculate the value of foreign currencies and credits when capital is transferred across borders through trade, investments, and loans.

international nongovernmental organization (INGO): an international organization whose members are private individuals and groups.

international organized crime (IOC): organized crime syndicates that use technology to cooperatively network with each other throughout the world.

international political economy: According to Robert Isaak, "the study of the inequality in power and wealth between peoples and nations and the patterns of collective power and learning that change this inequality."

international political system: a pattern of interactions among world political actors who have sufficient regular contact to make the behavior of each a central part of the calculations of the others.

international regime: the set of rules, norms, and decision-making procedures that coordinates state behavior within a given issue area.

international terrorism: the use of terrorism against targets in other countries.

International Tropical Timber Association (ITTA): the principal international forum for addressing transnational issues in timber products, dominated by forestry interests.

interspecific aggression: killing members of species other than one's own.

intervention, military: an overt or covert use of force by one or more countries that crosses the border of another country in order to effect the authority structure of the target country.

intraspecific aggression: killing members of one's own species.

irredentism: movement by an ethnonational group to regain control of territory by force so that existing state boundaries will no longer separate the group.

irreversible conservation measures: permanent steps taken toward conserving a resource.

isolationism: a policy of withdrawing from active participation with other actors in world affairs and instead concentrating state efforts on managing internal affairs.

jus ad bellum: the justice of a war; criteria by which a political leader decides whether to wage a war.

jus in bello: justice in war; specifies permissible tactics in fighting a just war.

just war doctrine: a doctrine that pertains to the moral considerations under which war may be undertaken and how it should be fought once it begins.

Kellogg-Briand Pact (Pact of Paris, 1928): a multilateral treaty negotiated in 1928 that outlawed war as a method for settling interstate conflicts.

Kyoto protocol: a treaty signed in 1997 in Kyoto, Japan, pledging the parties to it to reduce their levels of greenhouse gas emissions in order to alleviate the danger of global warming and climate change.

laissez-faire economies: the philosophical principle of free markets with little governmental regulation of the marketplace.

League of Nations mandate system: the placement of colonies previously held by the Central Powers of World War I under the administration of certain Allied nations. Implicit in the system was the idea that colonies were a trust rather than a territory to be exploited.

League of Nations: a global intergovernmental organization established after World War I.

least-developed of the less-developed countries (LLDCs): the most impoverished members of the Third World in the Global South.

levels of analysis: alternative perspectives on world politics that may focus on the personal characteristics of individual decision makers, the attributes of states, or the structure of the global system.

liberalism: a paradigm predicated on the hope that the application of reason and universal ethics to international relations can lead to a more orderly, just, and cooperative world, and that international anarchy and war can be policed by institutional reforms that empower international organizations and laws.

liberal institutionalism: the so-called neoliberal theory in international relations that advocates creating global institutions to promote peace and security among states.

liberal international economic order (LIEO): the set of regimes created after World War II, designed to promote monetary stability and reduce barriers to the free flow of trade and capital.

limited war: the restrained use of armed force, short of full-scale warfare, fought for limited objectives.

limits-to-growth proposition: the theory that the earth's capacity to support life has natural limits and that if important resources such as fresh water are depleted, many will perish.

linkage strategy: a set of assertions that claims leaders should take into account another country's overall behavior when deciding whether to reach agreement on any one specific issue.

Lomé Convention (1975): the series of agreements inspired by the NIEO movement that links forty-six developing countries to Europe help the African, Caribbean, and Pacific (ACP) countries to stabilize their export earnings and to provide them financial and technical assistance.

long-cycle theory: a theory that focuses on the rise and fall of the leading global power as the central political process of the modern world system.

long peace(s): long-lasting periods of great-power peace.

low-intensity conflict: fighting that falls below the threshold of full-scale military combat between modern armies.

low politics: the category of global issues related to the economic, social, demographic and environmental aspects of relations between governments and people.

Maastricht summit (1991): a meeting of European Community members in The Netherlands that set forth a framework for achieving greater European unity.

machtpolitik: power politics.

macroeconomic policies: states' economic plans that emphasize aggregate economic indicators such as GDP, the money supply, and the balance of trade that governments monitor to measure changes in the state's national economy.

macropolitical perspective: an approach to the study of international affairs that looks at world politics as a system, with general global patterns of interaction among parts.

majors (oil companies): Exxon, Gulf, Mobil, Standard Oil of California, Texaco, British Petroleum, Royal Dutch Shell, and Compagnie Francaise des Petroles.

Malthusian projection: the prediction that population when unchecked increases in a geometric ratio, whereas subsistence increases in only an arithmetic ratio.

Marshall Plan: a program of grants and loans established by the United States to assist the recovery of Western Europe after World War II.

Marxism-Leninism: communist theory as derived from the writings of Karl Marx, V. I. Lenin, and their successors, which criticizes capitalism as a cause of class struggle, the exploitation of workers, colonialism, and war.

massive retaliation: the strategic posture of the United States during the Eisenhower administration, which advocated the use of nuclear weapons to contain communism and Soviet expansionism.

mechanical majority: a complaint voiced by the Soviet Union during the early history of the United Nations that the United States enjoyed a commanding position in the General Assembly due to the fact that its allies constituted a majority of the United Nations membership on whose support the United States could always depend.

mediation: a conflict resolution procedure in which a third party offers a nonbinding solution to the disputants.

mercantilism: a government trade strategy for accumulating state wealth and power by encouraging exports and discouraging imports.

mid-intensity conflict (MIC): U.S. military classification of regionalized trouble spots where the threat of armed conflict short of large-scale warfare is probable.

migration: movement from one place of abode to another.

militarized disputes: confrontations short of war, characterized by the reciprocated threat, deployment, mobilization, or use of force.

military-industrial complex: the term coined by U.S. President Eisenhower to describe the coalition among arms manufacturers, military bureaucracies, and top government officials, that promotes unnecessary defense expenditures for their own profit and power.

military intervention: an overt or covert use of force by one or more countries that crosses the borders of another country in order to affect the government and policies of the target country.

military necessity: the legal doctrine asserting that violation of the rules of warfare may be excused during periods of extreme emergency.

military-technical revolution (MTR): the new generation of weapons systems created by the application of microprocessing and precision-guided technologies to fight wars with a minimum of civilian causalities.

minorities: groups within a state's population that on the basis of ethnic, nationality, language or religion are often the targets of human rights violations by the states' majority population.

mirror images: the tendency of states and people in competitive interaction to perceive each other similarly—to see others the same way they see us.

missile technology control regime (MTCR): an informal arrangement among the most advanced suppliers of missile-related equipment to control the export of ballistic and cruise missiles and associated technologies.

monetary system: a stable and predictable method for calculating the value of sales and foreign investments.

Montevideo Convention (1933): an agreement that summarizes the major components of statehood and the rights and duties of states.

morals: principles or rules for behavior that differentiate right from wrong.

mortality rate: crude death-rate is the most common measure of mortality. The age-adjusted death rate is often used in its place because it is free of distortions due to differences in age composition.

most-favored-nation (MFN) principle: tariff preferences granted to one nation must be granted to all others exporting the same product.

muddling through: the tendency for leaders to make foreign policy decisions that produce incremental policy changes through small steps.

multilateral: relationships among many states for the purpose of collective action.

multilateral agreements: arms control agreements negotiated among more than two states.

multilateral aid: aid that is channeled through international institutions.

multinational corporations (MNCs): business enterprises headquartered in one state that invest and operate extensively in other states.

multiple independently targetable reentry vehicle (MIRV): a technological innovation permitting many weapons to be delivered from a single missile.

multipolar: an international system with more than two dominant power centers.

multipolarity: a global distribution of power with three or more great powers or poles attaining a disproportionate position of strength relative to all others, but with each pole or center of power approximately equal to the others.

Munich Conference (1938): the conference at which Britain and France accepted Adolf Hitler's demand to annex the German-populated area of the Sudetenland in Czechoslovakia.

mutual and balanced force reductions (MBFR): a series of discussions held between 1973 and 1988 that attempted to reduce the military forces of the East and West blocs.

mutual assured destruction (MAD): a system of mutual deterrence in which both sides possess the ability to survive a first strike and launch a devastating retaliatory attack.

mutual security: a belief that a diminution of the national security of one's adversary reduces one's own security.

mutual sensitivity: liability of states to costs imposed by external events before policies are changed to deal with the situation.

mutual vulnerability: liability of states to costs imposed by external events even after policies have been changed to deal with the situation.

nation: a collection of people who, on the basis of ethnic, linguistic, or cultural affinity, perceive themselves to be members of the same group.

national attributes: characteristics of nation-states (such as level of economic development or extent of military capability) that may influence their foreign policy behavior.

national character: the collective characteristics ascribed to the people within a state.

national interest: the goals that states pursue to maximize what is selfishly best for their country.

nationalism: a mindset glorifying the nationalities of a people living in a state that assigns loyalty to the state's national interests as a supreme value.

national security: a country's psychological freedom from fear of foreign attack.

nation-state: a polity (system of government) controlled by members of some nationality recognizing no higher authority.

nature-nurture: the controversy over whether human behavior is caused by human's biological traits or by the cultural conditions that influence human behavior.

negotiation: the process and art of discussing and debating issues when a conflict arises, in order for the disputing parties to reach a mutually satisfactory compromise agreement to resolve the issue.

neocolonialism (neoimperialism): the economic rather than military domination of foreign countries.

neofunctionalism: the revised functional theory that explains that the IGOs states create to manage common problems exert new pressures to expand the benefits further, and that this leads to states' political integration, the creation of additional IGOs, and the globalization of international relations in an expanding network of interdependence that reduces state's intentions to wage war.

neoliberal institutionalists: adherents to the recent theoretical effort to explain how peace and prosperity instead of war might be created through law, global governance, and liberal democracies' cooperation to engineer international change.

neoliberal theory: a philosophy that maintains that peaceful change with prosperity can be encouraged through cooperation in institutions that knit the states and peoples of the world together into a true global community.

neoliberalism: a perspective that accounts for the way international institutions promote global change, cooperation, peace, and prosperity through collective reform approaches.

neo-Malthusians: pessimists who warn of the global ecopolitical implications of uncontrolled growth.

neomercantilism: a state trade policy that seeks to maintain a balance-of-trade surplus by reducing imports, stimulating domestic production, and promoting exports.

neonationalism: the expression of communal or ethnic aspirations of a dissatisfied group within a given state.

neorealism: a theoretical account of states' behavior that explains it as determined by differences in their relative power instead of by other factors, such as their values, types of government, or domestic circumstances.

neorealist theory: the new realist theory that the behavior of competitive states is shaped by changes in the distribution of global power more than by changes in their domestic systems.

neutrality: the legal doctrine that provides rights and duties for states who remain nonaligned with adversaries during wartime.

new imperialism: the second wave of European empire building that began in the 1870s and extended until the outbreak of World War I. In contrast with classical imperialism, extraordinary competition among the imperial powers marked the new imperialism as colonies became an important symbol of national power and prestige.

new international division of labor: a projection that developing nations will provide the First World with manufactured and processed goods, while the latter will provide developing nations with raw materials and agricultural products.

new international economic order (NIEO): a policy resolution backed by the Global South to replace the U.S.-sponsored Liberal International Economic Order (LIEO) with an international economic regime more favorable to the interests of developing countries.

newly industrialized countries (NICs): a group of upper-middle-income countries that have become important exporters of manufactured goods, as well as important markets for the major industrialized countries that export capital goods. Included within this group are Brazil, Mexico, Singapore, South Korea, and Taiwan.

New World Information and Communication Order (NWICO): a new regime demanded by the Third World for covering the flow of information between North and South due to dissatisfaction with the media coverage provided by news agencies from the developed countries.

1997 "Rio Plus Five" UN Earth Summit: a meeting where attendees affirmed the proposition that protecting the environment is a primary national security issue.

Nixon Doctrine: the position taken by President Richard Nixon that U.S. allies should bear a greater share of the burden for their own defense.

nomothetic generalizations: lawlike statements that are presumed to hold across time and space.

nonaligned movement (NAM): a group of more than one hundred newly independent, mostly less-developed states that joined together as a group of neutrals to avoid entanglement with the superpowers' competing alliances and to advance the Third World's common interests in economic cooperation and growth.

nonaligned states: countries that do not participate in military alliances with rival blocs because of a fear that formal alliance will lead to involvement in an unnecessary war.

nonalignment: a foreign policy posture in which states do not participate in military alliances with either the East or West for fear that one form of domination might simply be replaced by another.

noncombatant immunity: the legal principle that military force should not be used against innocent civilians.

nondiscrimination: a principle for trade that proclaims that goods produced at home and abroad are to be treated the same for import and export agreements.

no-first use: the doctrine adhering to the principles that a nuclear-weapon state would not use its strategic weapons in the event of an attack on it with conventional weapons by another state.

nongovernmental organizations: NGOs are transnational organizations of private citizens maintaining consultative status with the United Nations; they include professional associations, foundations, multinational corporations, or simply internationally active groups in different states joined together to work toward common interests.

nonintervention, noninterference principle: the duty of states to refrain from uninvited involvement in another's internal affairs.

nonlethal weapons: the wide array of "soft-kill," low-intensity methods of incapacitating an enemy's people, vehicles, communications systems, or entire cities without killing either combatants or noncombatants.

nonproliferation: the absence of the development of nuclear weapons or technology by countries that do not already possess them.

nonrecognition: withholding official legal acceptance as a form of sanction against another established government recognized as an independent state by others.

nonstate actors: all transnationally active groups other than states, such as organizations whose members are states and nongovernmental organizations whose members are individuals and private groups from more than one state.

nonstate entities: associations of individuals or groups, such as multinational corporations and nongovernmental organizations, created without agreements by states.

nonstate nations: national or ethnic groups struggling to obtain power and/or statehood.

nontariff barriers (NTBs): measures that discriminate

against imports without direct tax levies and beyond the scope of international regulation.

normalization of diplomatic relations: the restoration of peaceful and cooperative relations following a period of hostility between two states, during which their communication and contact were ruptured.

North American Free Trade Agreement (NAFTA): an agreement designed to bring Mexico into the free-trade zone that already linked Canada and the United States.

North Atlantic Cooperation Council (NACC): a NATO council that was proposed in 1991 to build a partnership between NATO and the countries of Central and Eastern Europe.

North Atlantic Treaty Organization (NATO): a military alliance created in 1949 to deter a Soviet attack on Western Europe.

Nth country problem: the addition of new nuclear states.

nuclear deterrence: dissuading an adversary from attacking by threatening retaliation with nuclear weapons.

nuclear freeze movement: a popular revolt against the escalating strategic arms race in the 1980s that called for a suspension or freeze in building more nuclear warheads in the hopes that the threat of nuclear annihilation would be reduced.

Nuclear Nonproliferation Treaty (NPT): an international agreement that seeks to prevent horizontal proliferation by prohibiting nuclear weapons sales, acquisitions, or production.

nuclear utilization theory (NUTs): a body of strategic thought that claims deterrent threats would be more credible if nuclear weapons were made more usable.

oil shocks: the rapid increases in oil prices in the aftermath of Yom Kippur War, the revolution in Iran, and the invasion of Kuwait.

OPEC: Organization of Petroleum Exporting Countries.

OPEC decade: the period between October 1973 and March 1983, which saw the rise and decline of OPEC's power in the world political economy.

open economic system: a system based on a market economy.

open skies proposal (1955): a call for allowing aerial reconnaissance to monitor military maneuvers.

Operations Plan 90-1002: a plan devised in the early 1980s that called for a massive air- and sea-lift of U.S. military personnel and equipment in the event of conflict in a distant region where the U.S. had no military bases.

opportunity costs: a concept in decision-making theories referring to the fact that when resources are held and the opportunity arises to use them, what is gained for one purpose is lost for other purposes, so that every choice entails the "cost" of some lost opportunity.

orderly market arrangements (OMAs): voluntary export restrictions that involve a government-to-government agreement and often specific rules of management.

Organization for the Prevention of Chemical Weapons (OPCW): an international organization headquartered in The Hague that is designed to control chemical weapons.

Organization for Security and Cooperation in Europe (OSCE): a multilateral institution that led in the transformation of Europe from a system of counterpoised military alliances to one based on common principles for maintaining security in the post-Cold War World.

ozone depletion: the thinning of the ozone layer in the upper atmosphere due to the release of chlorofluorocarbons.

ozone layer: the protective layer of the upper atmosphere over the earth's surface that shields the planet from the sun's harmful impact on living organism's on the planet.

pacifism: a philosophy that rejects the right of people or states to kill, no matter what the provocation, and searches for non-violent methods of resolving disputes, such as negotiation.

pacta sunt servanda: the norm that treaties are binding.

paradigm: derived from the Greek *paradeigma* meaning an example, a model, or an essential pattern, a paradigm structures thoughts about an area of inquiry.

parallel currency: the universal acceptance of the dollar in the immediate postwar period as the currency against which every other country sold or redeemed its own national currency in the exchange markets.

Partnership for Peace (PFP): a plan proposed in 1993 by the United States that established limited military partnerships between NATO and the former Warsaw Pact countries.

pax atomica: the notion that nuclear weapons have preserved peace.

peace dividend: the global savings from arms expenditure reductions made possible by the end of the Cold War.

peace enforcement: military actions undertaken to impose a peace settlement, truce, or agreement to surrender by a warring party, or to prevent the resumption of fighting by the participants in a past war.

peace operations: a general category encompassing both peacekeeping and peace enforcement operations undertaken to support diplomatic efforts to establish and maintain peace between disputants.

peacebuilding: creating conditions that make war unlikely.

peaceful coexistence: Soviet leader Nikita Khruschev's 1956 doctrine that war between capitalist and communist states was not inevitable and that inter-bloc competition could be peaceful.

peacekeeping: the use of a United Nations military force to function as a buffer between disputants in order to prevent fighting.

peacemaking: the process of diplomacy, mediation, negotiation, or other forms of peaceful settlement that arranges an end to a dispute, and resolves issues that led to conflict.

perestroika: the Russian word for Mikhail Gorbachev's policy of economic restructuring.

permanent world criminal court: a standing international court to judge mass crimes such as genocide.

photovoltaic (PV) cells: semiconductors that convert sunlight into electricity.

Physical Quality of Life Index (PQLI): an index that uses life expectancy, infant mortality, and literacy rates to assess progress in meeting basic human needs.

Planning and Review Process (PARP): a program undertaken by the twenty-five Partnership for Peace members to address the political, military, financial, and security issues facing Europe in the twenty-first century.

plaza agreement (1985): an arrangement by the major industrialized nations to coordinate efforts at managing exchange rates internationally and interest rates domestically.

pluralism: a model of the policy-making process that highlights the impact of competitive domestic groups in pressuring the government for policies responsive to their interests and needs.

polarity: the degree to which power is concentrated among the major powers in the state system.

polarization: the degree to which states cluster in alliances around the most powerful members of the state system.

policy agenda: the changing list of problems or issues to which governments pay special attention at any given moment.

policy networks: leaders and organized interests (such as lobbies) that form temporary alliances to influence a particular foreign policy decision.

political disintegration: the political fragmentation of a state.

political economy: a field of study that focuses on the intersection of politics and economics in international relations.

political efficacy: a leader's belief in his or her power to control events politically.

political idealism: an approach to international relations that assumes people are not by nature sinful or wicked, and that harmful behavior is the result of structural arrangements that motivate people to act selfishly.

political integration: the process or the product of efforts to build new political communities and supranational institutions that transcend the state.

political realism: an approach to international relations that assumes people by nature are sinful or wicked, and that the purpose of statecraft is to acquire the power needed to survive in a hostile environment.

politics: the exercise of influence.

polycentrism: a concept used to describe the emergence of new centers of independent power within the polarized bloc structure of the Cold War.

pooled sovereignty: the sharing of decision-making responsibility among several governments and between them and international institutions.

population momentum: the concept that population growth will continue for several decades after replacement-level fertility is achieved.

positivism: an approach based on the scientific method and concerned with empirically based phenomena and facts that excludes speculation about ultimate causes or origins.

positivist legal theory: a theory that stresses state's customs as the most important source of law.

postbehavioral movement: an approach to the study of international relations that calls for increased attention to the policy relevance of research.

postmodern deconstructionists: theorists who believe the complexity of the world system renders precise description impossible, and that the purpose of scholarship is to understand actors' motives by deconstructing their textual statements.

postmodern terrorism: the prediction that in the twenty-first century technology has improved the prospects for terrorists to use new weapons to threaten their adversaries for political purposes.

postmodernism: an approach to the study of international relations that emphasizes the study of texts, hidden meanings, and discourse in the writing and speeches of those policymakers and analysts who interpret world affairs.

power: the factors that enable one actor to manipulate another actor's behavior against its preferences.

power potential: the relative amount of capabilities or resources that are presumed necessary for a state to achieve influence over others.

power transition: a circumstance that occurs when the military capabilities of one great power climb to challenge those of its nearest rival, often resulting in a war breaking out due to the escalating fears this transition tends to provoke.

power transition theory: the contention that war is most likely when the differentials between the capabilities of rival states narrow.

preemption: a quick first-strike attack that seeks to defeat an adversary before it can organize a retaliatory response.

preferential trade: the granting of special trade treatment to certain states.

preventive diplomacy: diplomatic actions taken in advance of a predictable crisis to prevent or limit violence.

price inelasticity of demand: a condition where price in-

577

creases have little impact on the amount of a commodity that is consumed.

price inelasticity of supply: a condition where new producers of a commodity cannot enter a market to take advantage of higher rates of return.

primary products: raw materials and agricultural products.

private international law: law pertaining to routinized transnational intercourse between or among nongovernmental actors.

procedural rationality: a method of decision making based on having perfect information and carefully weighing all possible courses of action.

product cycle theory: a hypothesis that maintains that overseas expansion is a defensive maneuver designed to forestall foreign competitors and thereby reinforce the global competitiveness of domestically-based industries.

proliferation: the spread of weapon capabilities from a few to many states in a chain reaction, so that an increasing number of states gain the ability to launch an attack on other states with devastating (e.g., nuclear) weapons.

pronatalist policy: a conscious governmental attempt to increase fertility.

propaganda: communications used to manipulate people's thoughts, emotions, or actions.

prospect theory: the idea that an individual's decision making is constrained by formed opinions and tendencies to overreact in crises, and that decisions will be made based on the perceived prospects of choices to fulfill objectives.

protectionism: barriers to foreign trade, such as tariffs and quotas, that protect local industries from competition.

public international law: law pertaining to government-to-government relations.

Rapacki Plan (1957): a call for the denuclearization of Central Europe.

rapidly deployable mission headquarters (ROMH): a proposed new administrative unit designed to enable the United Nations to carry out future peacekeeping operations on short notice when crises erupt.

rapprochement: in diplomacy, a policy seeking to reestablish normal relations between enemies.

rationality or rational choice: decision-making procedures guided by careful definition of situations, weighing of goals, consideration of all alternatives, and selection of the options most likely to achieve the highest goals.

rational decision-making model: an idealized portrayal of decision making according to which the individual uses the best information available to choose from the set of possible responses that are most likely to maximize his or her goals.

Reagan Doctrine: a pledge of U.S. support for anticommunist insurgents who sought to overthrow Soviet-supported governments.

realism: a paradigm based on the premise that world politics is essentially and unchangeably a struggle among self-interested states for power and position under anarchy, with each competing state pursuing its own national interests.

realist theory: the view that states are unitary global actors in relentless competition with each other for position and prosperity in the international hierarchy, dedicated to the promotion of their own interests at the expense of other states.

realpolitik: the theoretical outlook prescribing that countries should prepare for war in order to preserve peace.

rebus sic stantibus: the norm that reserves the right of states to terminate treaties unilaterally if conditions at the time of the signing have since changed.

reciprocity: a principle that requires countries to reduce their own tariffs in return for another's reductions.

refugees: people who flee for safety to another country because of a well-founded fear of persecution.

regional collective defense: organizations and military alliances within a specific region created to collectively preserve peace and security for their members.

relative burden of military spending: the ratio of defense spending to gross national product.

relative deprivation: the belief that one is unfairly deprived, in comparison to others, of the wealth and status that one deserves.

relative gains: a condition in which some participants benefit more than others.

religious movements: politically active organizations based on strong religious convictions.

reparations: compensation paid by a defeated state for damages or expenditures sustained by the victor during hostilities.

replacement-level fertility: one couple replacing themselves with two children.

reprisal: hostile and illegal retaliatory acts.

retorsion: hostile but legal retaliatory acts.

returnees: former refugees who have moved back home.

reversible conservation measures: non-permanent conservation measures that often derive from behavioral changes.

revolution in military affairs (RMA): the goal of seeking to increase military capabilities and effectiveness with new technology that does not rely on weapons of mass destruction.

revolution in military technology (RMT): the sophisticated new weapons technologies that make fighting without mass armies possible.

sanctions: punitive actions by one state against another to retaliate for its previous objectionable behavior.

satisficing behavior: the tendency for decision makers to choose the first available alternative that meets minimally acceptable standards.

schema: the process of reasoning by which new information is interpreted according to a memory structure that contains a network of genetic scripts, metaphors, and stereotypical characters.

secession or separative revolts: the attempt by a religious (or ethnic) minority to break away from an internationally recognized state.

second-strike capability: a state's capacity to retaliate after absorbing a first-strike attack with weapons of mass destruction.

Second World: a group of countries with centrally planned economies. It consisted of the Soviet Union and its allies in Eastern Europe during the Cold War.

Secretary General: the chief administrative officer of the United Nations and the head of the Secretariat, one of the six principal organs established by the United Nations Charter.

security community: a group of states whose high level of noninstitutionalized collaboration results in the settlement of disputes by compromise rather than by force.

security council: one of six principal organs established by the UN Charter. Its primary responsibility is the maintenance of international peace and security.

security dilemma: the propensity of armaments undertaken by one state for ostensibly defensive purposes to be perceived by others as threatening.

security regime: norms and rules for interaction agreed to by a set of states to increase their security.

self-determination: the doctrine that asserts nationalities have the right to determine what political authority will represent and rule them.

self-fulfilling prophecy: the tendency for one's expectations to evoke behavior that confirms the expectations.

self-help: the principle that in anarchy actors must rely on themselves.

signaling: in conflict situations, either explicit or implicit communication by states to reveal both their intentions and their capabilities.

size principle: the propensity for competitors to form coalitions only sufficient in enough size to ensure victory, even if by a narrow margin, with the result that over time opposed alliances tend to remain roughly equal to one another.

SLBM: submarine-launched ballistic missile.

smart bombs: precision guided military technology that enables a bomb to search for its target and detonate at the precise time it can do the most damage.

social constructivism: a liberal-realist theoretical approach advocated by Alexander Wendt that sees self-interested states as the key actors in world politics; their actions are determined not by anarchy but by the ways states socially "construct" and then respond to the meanings they give to power politics so that as their definitions change, cooperative practices can evolve.

socialization: the processes by which people learn the beliefs, values, and behaviors that are acceptable in a given society.

soft power: the ability to exercise influence in world politics due to intangible resources such as culture and ideas.

sovereign equality: the principle that states, as legally equals, are entitled to equal protection under international law.

sovereignty, or state sovereignty: the legal doctrine that states have supreme authority to govern their internal affairs and manage their foreign relations with other states and IGOs.

special drawing rights (SDRs): reserves created and held by the International Monetary Fund (IMF) that member states can draw upon to help manage the values of their currencies.

sphere of influence: a region dominated by the power of a foreign state.

spillaround: the stagnation or encapsulation of regional integration activities.

spillback: the failure of regional integration.

spillover: within the process of international integration, the deepening of ties among states in one sector or expansion of ties to another sector.

spiral model: a metaphor used to describe the tendency of efforts to enhance defense to result in escalating arms races.

stagflation: a situation in which economic stagnation and high inflation occur at the same time and the usual tendency for an economic downturn to drive down prices does not occur.

standard operating procedures (SOPs): established methods to be followed for the performance of designated tasks.

state: a legal entity with a permanent population, a well-defined territory, and a government capable of exercising sovereignty.

statehood: as outlined by the Montevideo Convention of 1933, a state must possess a permanent population, a well-defined territory, and a government capable of ruling its citizens and managing diplomatic relations with other states.

state level of analysis: an analytical approach to the study of world politics that emphasizes how the internal attributes of states explain their foreign policy behaviors.

state-sponsored terrorism: formal assistance, training, and arming of foreign terrorists by a state in order to achieve foreign policy goals.

state system: a pattern of interaction among sovereign states that are in contact with one another.

state terrorism: the support of terrorist groups by government authorities.

state sovereignty: under international law, the status of states as equals in that they are within their territory and subject to no higher external authority.

states' attributes: state characteristics that shape foreign policy behavior, such as military capabilities or type of government.

Strategic Arms Limitations Talks (SALT): two sets of agreements reached during the 1970s between the United States and the Soviet Union that established limits on strategic nuclear delivery systems.

Strategic Arms Reduction Talks (START): a series of negotiations that led to a 1991 treaty to reduce U.S. and Soviet strategic forces.

strategic corporate alliances: cooperation between MNCs and foreign companies in the same industry, driven by the movement of MNC manufacturing overseas.

strategic defense initiative (SDI): a ballistic missile defense system using space-based laser technology.

strategic stockpile: the inventory of nuclear warheads deployed for waging wars of mass destruction.

strategic trade policy: an industrial policy that targets government subsidies toward particular industries so as to gain a competitive advantage over foreign producers.

strategic weapons: weapons of mass destruction carried on either intercontinental ballistic missiles (ICBMs), submarine-launched ballistic missiles (SLBMs), or long-range bombers capable of annihilating an enemy state.

structural realism: a theory that emphasizes the influence of the structure of world power on the behavior of the states within it.

structural violence: oppression resulting from the hierarchical structure of world politics, which makes it difficult for weak states to impose effective sanctions on the powerful.

structuralism: a neorealist theory that sees the changing distribution of power within the global system as the primary determinant of states' behavior and of whether coalitions will form and peace will prevail.

summit conference: personal diplomatic negotiations between national leaders.

supranational authority: the power of an international institution to make decisions binding on its national members without being subject to their individual approval.

supranational entities: an organization that supersedes the individual countries that comprise it.

survival of the fittest: a realist concept derived from Charles Darwin's theory of evolution that advises that ruthless competition is ethically acceptable to survive, even if the actions violate moral commands not to kill.

sustainable development: economic growth that does not deplete the resources needed to maintain growth.

suzerainty: the claim by a powerful state of the right to exercise influence over its neighbors.

system transformation: profound changes in the units that make up the international system, the predominant foreign policy goals that the units seek, or what the units can do to each other with their military and economic capabilities.

terms of trade: the ratio of export prices to import prices. Developing nations believe that the prices they receive for their exports fall in the long run, while the prices of the manufactured goods they import increase steadily.

terrorism: criminal acts and threats against a targeted actor for the purpose of arousing fear in order to get the target to accept the terrorists' demands.

theater missile defense (TMD): high-altitude defense systems to prevent strategic ballistic missiles from reaching their targets on land.

theory: a set of hypotheses postulating the relationship between variables or conditions, advanced to describe, explain, or predict phenomena, and make prescriptions about how positive changes ought to be engineered to realize particular principles.

Third World: a term commonly used to refer to the world's poorer, economically less developed countries. It includes all of Asia, the Middle East, and Oceania except Israel, Japan, Turkey, Australia, and New Zealand; all of Africa except South Africa; and all of the Western Hemisphere except Canada and the United States.

Three Mile Island nuclear accident: an accident in Pennsylvania during 1979 that resulted in the largest-ever level of radioactive contamination by the U.S. commercial nuclear industry.

tied aid: the existence of conditions or "strings" attached to foreign aid.

Tokyo Round of GATT: multilateral of trade negotiations held between 1973 and 1979.

total war: battle against an enemy state's civilian population and economic resources to drive it to surrender.

trade integration: the difference between growth rates in trade and gross domestic product.

tragedy of the commons: a metaphor widely used to explain the impact of human behavior on ecological systems. Rational self-interested behavior by individuals may have a destructive collective impact.

transfer-pricing mechanism: the trading of commodities between a parent company's subsidiaries in different countries in order to record profits in jurisdictions where taxes are low.

transformation: a change in the characteristic pattern of interaction among the most active participants in world politics of such magnitude that it appears that one "international system" has replaced another.

transnational banks (TNBs): the globe's top banking firms, whose financial activities are concentrated in transactions that cross state borders.

Treaty of Rome (1957): the agreement that created the European Economic Community, popularly known for many years as the European Common Market.

Truman Doctrine: the declaration by U.S. President Harry S Truman that the policy of the United States must be to support "free peoples who are resisting attempted subjugation by armed minorities or by outside pressures."

two-level games: a concept referring to the growing need for national policymakers to make decisions that will meet both domestic and foreign goals.

Two Plus Four Treaty: the 1990 agreement between four powers (the United States, the Soviet Union, Great Britain and France) and the two Germany's (East and West) that ended the Four Powers' rights of occupation and enabled German reunification.

UN environment program: a program created after the 1972 Stockholm Conference that sought regulatory action on environmental problems.

UN framework convention on climate change: a statement signed by 160 states that pledges the signees to contain greenhouse gasses at levels that will avoid threatening climate change.

underemployment: a condition critics trace to trade globalization in which a large portion of the labor force works short hours at low pay in occupations below their skill level.

unilateral: a go-it-alone, self-reliant strategy for dealing with threats from another actor or global problem, as opposed to multilateral approaches, which involve working with allies or collective problem-solving institutions.

unipolarity: a condition in which an international system has a single dominant power center.

unitary actor: a conceptualization based on the assumption that all states and the individuals responsible for their foreign policies confront the problem of national survival in similar ways.

United Nations: a global, multipurpose international, intergovernmental organization established in 1945, consisting of six major organs and numerous specialized agencies, conferences, and commissions.

United Nations Conference on Trade and Development (UNCTAD): a special trade conference held in Geneva during 1964 that has become a regular forum for developing world trade policies.

United Nations Educational, Scientific and Cultural Organization (UNESCO): the UN Specialized Agency responsible for promoting cooperation in the fields of education, science, and culture.

United Nations Emergency Force (UNEF): authorized by the General Assembly in 1956 under the Uniting for Peace procedures to attempt to restore peace in the Middle East following the outbreak of war between Egypt and a coalition of Israel, Britain, and France.

United Nations Environment Programme (UNEP): a UN agency created in 1972 to study environmental deterioration and propose regulations to protect the global environment.

United Nations Register of Conventional Arms: an effort begun in 1992 to have states submit information on their trade in various categories of weapons.

uniting for peace resolution: a device which empowered the United Nations General Assembly to meet in emergency sessions to deal with threats to peace and acts of aggression.

unity actor: a transnational actor whose internal differences do not influence its international behavior.

Uruguay Round: the multilateral trade negotiations of GATT that began in 1986 and concluded in 1994 with creation of the World Trade Organization.

verification: processes through which signatories' adherence to arms control and disarmament agreements is confirmed.

vertical nuclear proliferation: an increase in the capabilities of existing nuclear powers.

vertical legal system of law: a centralized, hierarchical legal system.

virtual corporations: links between MNCs that involve co-ownership and coproduction.

virtual nuclear arsenals: the next generation of "near-nuclear" military capabilities produced by the revolution in military technology that would put strategic nuclear weapons of mass destruction at the margins of national security strategies by removing dependence on them for deterrence.

virtuality: the imagery created by computer technology of objects and phenomena that produces a fictitious picture of actual things, people, and experiences.

voluntary export restrictions (VERs): a generic term for all bilaterally agreed-to restraints on trade.

war: the use of states to resolve disputes by armed force—a condition under international law with rules for its initiation and conduct.

war contagion: a metaphor that likens the diffusion of war to the spread of disease.

war crimes: acts performed during war that the international community defines as illegal crimes against humanity, such as atrocities committed on an enemy's prisoners of war and civilians or the state's own minority population.

war weariness hypothesis: the contention that a state at war will become exhausted and lose its enthusiasm for another war, but only for a time.

Warsaw Pact: a military alliance created by the Soviet Union in 1955 that included communist regimes in Eastern Europe; disbanded in 1991.

Washington Naval Conferences (1921–1922): arms control meetings that resulted in an agreement among the U.S., Britain, France, Japan, and Italy to adjust relative tonnage of their fleets.

weighted voting: a system in which votes are distributed among states in proportion to their financial contribution to an organization.

Western European Union (WEU): a military pact composed of ten European countries.

World Bank: also known as the International Bank of Reconstruction and Development (IBRD), the World Bank is the globe's major IGO for financing economic growth in the Global South.

world federalism: an approach to integration based on the merger of previously sovereign states into a single federal union.

world-system theory: a theory that claims there is an international division of labor in which core states specialize in the capital-intensive production of sophisticated manufactured goods and peripheral states concentrate on the labor-intensive production of raw materials and agricultural commodities.

World Trade Organization (WTO): a multilateral agency established as part of the trade reform pact signed by GATT negotiators in Morocco during 1994 that monitors the implementation of trade agreements and settles disputes among trade partners.

xenophobia: the suspicious dislike, disrespect, and disregard for members of a foreign nationality, ethnic, or linguistic group.

Yalta Conference (1945): 1945 summit meeting among Franklin D. Roosevelt, Joseph Stalin, and Winston Churchill to resolve postwar territorial issues and voting procedures in the United Nations.

Yoshida Doctrine: a security policy proposing that Japan should avoid international disputes, keep a low profile on divisive global issues, and concentrate on economic pursuits.

zeitgeist: "the spirit of the times" or the dominant cultural norms assumed to influence the behavior of people living in particular periods.

zero-sum: the perception in a rivalry that if one side gains, the other side loses.

References

Adelman, Kenneth L., and Norman R. Augustine. (1992) "Defense Conversion," *Foreign Affairs* 71 (Spring): 26–47.

Albright, David. (1993) "A Proliferation Primer," *Bulletin of the Atomic Scientists* 49 (June): 14–23.

Allison, Graham T. (1971) *Essence of Decision: Explaining the Cuban Missile Crisis.* Boston: Little, Brown.

Al-Sammarrai, Bashir. (1995) "Economic Sanctions against Iraq," pp. 133–39 in David Cortright and George A. Lopez (eds.), *Economic Sanctions.* Boulder, Colo.: Westview.

Ambrose, Stephen E. (1995) "The Bomb: It Was More Than Death," *New York Times* (August 5): A15.

Amoore, Louise, et al. (1997) "Overturning 'Globalisation'," *New Political Economy* 2 (No. 1): 179–95.

Angell, Norman. (1910) *The Great Illusion: A Study of the Relationship of Military Power in Nations to Their Economic and Social Advantage.* London: Weidenfeld and Nicholson.

Apter, David E., and Louis W. Goodman (eds.). (1976) *The Multinational Corporation and Social Change.* New York: Praeger.

Arat, Zehra F. (1995) "Women under Layers of Oppression: The (Un)Changing Political Economy of Gender," pp. 265–93 in Manochehr Dorraj (ed.), *The Changing Political Economy of the Third World.* Boulder, Colo.: Lynne Rienner.

Arkin, William M. (1997) "What's 'New'," *Bulletin of the Atomic Scientists* 53 (November/December): 21–27.

———. (1995) "The Pentagon's Blind Ambition," *New York Times* (May 10): A19.

Ashley, Richard K., and R. B. J. Walker (eds.). (1990) "Speaking the Language of Exile: Dissident Thought in International Studies," Special issue, *International Studies Quarterly* 34 (September): 259–417.

Avery, Dennis. (1995) "Saving the Planet with Pesticides," pp. 49–82 in Ronald Bailey (ed.), *The True State of the Planet.* New York: Free Press.

Ayoob, Mohammed. (1995) *The Third World Security Predicament.* Boulder, Colo.: Lynne Rienner.

Babai, Don. (1993) "General Agreement on Tariffs and Trade," pp. 342–48 in Joel Krieger (ed.), *The Oxford Companion to Politics of the World.* New York: Oxford University Press.

Bagdikian, Ben H. (1992) *The Media Monopoly.* Boston: Beacon Press.

Balaam, David N., and Michael Veseth. (1996) *Introduction to International Political Economy.* Upper Saddle River, N.J.: Prentice Hall.

Baldwin, David A. (ed.). (1993) *Neorealism and Neoliberalism: The Contemporary Debate.* New York: Columbia University Press.

———. (1989) *Paradoxes of Power.* New York: Basil Blackwell.

Ball, Nicole. (1991) *Briefing Book on Conventional Arms Transfers.* Boston: Council for a Livable World Education Fund.

Barber, Benjamin R. (1995) *Jihad vs. McWorld.* New York: Random House.

Barkun, Michael. (1968) *Law without Sanctions: Order in Primitive Societies and the World Community.* New Haven, Conn.: Yale University Press.

Barnet, Richard J. (1990) "U.S. Intervention: Low-Intensity Thinking," *Bulletin of the Atomic Scientists* 46 (May): 34–37.

———. (1980) *The Lean Years.* New York: Simon & Schuster.

———. (1977) *The Giants: Russia and America.* New York: Simon & Schuster.

Barnet, Richard J., and John Cavanagh. (1994) *Global Dreams: Imperial Corporations and the New World Order.* New York: Simon & Schuster.

Barnet, Richard J., and Ronald E. Müller. (1974) *Global Reach: The Power of the Multinational Corporations.* New York: Simon & Schuster.

Baron, Samuel H., and Carl Pletsch (eds.). (1985) *Introspection in Biography: The Biographer's Quest for Self-Awareness.* Hillsdale, N.J.: Analytic Press.

Bayard, Thomas O., and Kimberly Ann Elliott. (1994) *Reciprocity and Retaliation in U.S. Trade Policy.* Washington, D.C.: Institute for International Economics.

Beckman, Peter R., and Francine D'Amico (eds.). (1994) *Women, Gender, and World Politics.* Westport, Conn.: Bergin & Garvey.

Beer, Francis A. (1981) *Peace against War: The Ecology of International Violence.* San Francisco: Freeman.

Bell, Coral. (1995) "The Future of Power in World Affairs," *Quadrant* 39 (September): 49–56.

Bendor, Jonathan. (1995) "A Model of Muddling Through," *American Political Science Review* 89 (December): 819–40.

Bendor, Jonathan, and Thomas H. Hammond. (1992) "Rethinking Allison's Models," *American Political Science Review* 86 (June): 301–22.

Benedick, Richard Elliot. (1991) "Protecting the Ozone Layer: New Directions in Diplomacy," pp. 112–53 in Jessica Tuchman Mathews (ed.), *Preserving the Global Environment.* New York: Norton.

Bennett, A. Leroy. (1988) *International Organizations,* 4th ed. Englewood Cliffs, N.J.: Prentice Hall.

Bergesen, Albert, and Ronald Schoenberg. (1980) "Long Waves of Colonial Expansion and Contraction, 1415–1969," pp. 231–77 in Albert Bergesen (ed.), *Studies of the Modern World-System.* New York: Academic Press.

Berghahn, Volker R. (1995) *Imperial Germany, 1871–1914.* Providence, R.I.: Berghahn Books.

Bergsten, C. Fred. (1997) "American Politics, Global Trade," *Economist* 344 (September 27): 23–26.

Bertelsen, Judy S. (ed.). (1977) *Nonstate Nations in International Politics.* New York: Praeger.

Bhagwati, Jagdish. (1993) "The Case for Free Trade," *Scientific American* 269 (November): 41–49.

Bienefeld, Manfred. (1994) "The New World Order: Echoes of a New Imperialism," *Third World Quarterly* 15 (March): 31–48.

Blainey, Geoffrey. (1988) *The Causes of War,* 3rd ed. New York: Free Press.

Blanton, Shannon Lindsey, and Charles W. Kegley, Jr. (1997) "Reconciling U.S. Arms Sales with America's Interests and Ideals," *Futures Research Quarterly* 13 (Spring): 85–101.

Blechman, Barry M. (1995) "The Intervention Dilemma," *Washington Quarterly* 18 (Summer): 63–73.

Blechman, Barry M., and Stephen S. Kaplan, with David K. Hall, William B. Quandt, Jerome N. Slater, Robert M. Slusser, and Philip Windsor. (1978) *Force without War*. Washington, D.C.: Brookings Institution.

Block, Fred L. (1977) *The Origins of International Economic Disorder*. Berkeley: University of California Press.

Blumenthal, W. Michael. (1988) "The World Economy and Technological Change," *Foreign Affairs* 66 (No. 3): 529–50.

Borrus, Michael, Steve Weber, John Zysman, and Joseph Willihnganz. (1992) "Mercantilism and Global Security," *The National Interest* 29 (Fall): 21–29.

Bostdorff, Denise M. (1993) *The Presidency and the Rhetoric of Foreign Crisis*. Columbia: University of South Carolina Press.

Boswell, Terry. (1989) "Colonial Empires and the Capitalist World-Economy: A Time Series Analysis of Colonization, 1640–1960," *American Sociological Review* 54 (April): 180–96.

Boulding, Kenneth E. (1978) *Stable Peace*. Austin: University of Texas Press.

Boutros-Ghali, Boutros. (1996) "Global Leadership after the Cold War," *Foreign Affairs* 75 (March/April): 86–98.

———. (1995) "Ways to Improve the United Nations," *International Herald Tribune* (August 17): 8.

Bozeman, Adda B. (1994) *Politics and Culture in International History*. New Brunswick, N.J.: Transaction.

BP Statistical Review of World Energy. (1995). London: British Petroleum Company.

Brecher, Michael. (1993) *Crises in World Politics: Theory and Reality*. Oxford, Eng.: Pergamon.

Brecher, Michael, and Johnathan Wilkenfeld. (1997) *A Study of Crisis*. Ann Arbor: University of Michigan Press.

Brierly, James L. (1944) *The Outlook for International Law*. Oxford, Eng.: Clarendon Press.

Brinsfield, John W. (1990) "From Plato to NATO: The Ethics of Warfare; Reflections on the Just War Theory," *Military Chaplains' Review* 19 (Winter): 21–36.

Bronfenbrenner, Urie. (1971) "The Mirror Image in Soviet–American Relations," *Journal of Social Issues* 27 (No. 1): 46–51.

Brooke, James. (1995) "Latin America Now Ignores U.S. Lead in Isolating Cuba," *New York Times* (July 8): 1, 5.

Brooks, Stephen G. (1997) "Dueling Realisms," *International Organization* 51 (Summer): 445–77.

Brown, Eugene. (1993) *Japan's Search for Strategic Vision*. Carlisle Barrocks, Penn.: U. S. Army War College.

Brown, Lester R. (1995) *Who Will Feed China? Wake-Up Call for a Small Planet*. New York: Norton.

———. (1994) "The Cairo Plan," *World Watch* 7 (November/December): 2.

———. (1979) *Resource Trends and Population Policy: A Time for Reassessment*. Washington, D.C.: Worldwatch Institute.

Brown, Lester R., et al. (1998) *State of the World 1998*. New York: Norton.

———. (1997) *State of the World 1997*. New York: Norton.

———. (1996) *State of the World 1996*. New York: Norton.

Brown, Lester R., and Hal Kane. (1994) *Full House: Reassessing the Earth's Population Carrying Capacity*. New York: Norton.

Brown, Lester R., Michael Renner, Christopher Flavin et al. (eds.). (1997) *Vital Signs 1997*. New York: Norton.

Brown, Lester R., Nicholas Lenssen, and Hal Kane. (1995) *Vital Signs 1995*. New York: Norton.

Brownlie, Ian. (1990) *Principles of Public International Law*, 4th ed. New York: Oxford University Press.

Brzezinski, Zbigniew. (1998) "The Grand Chessboard," *Harvard International Review* 20 (Winter): 48–53.

Bueno de Mesquita, Bruce. (1981) *The War Trap*. New Haven, Conn.: Yale University Press.

———. (1975) "Measuring Systemic Polarity," *Journal of Conflict Resolution* 22 (June): 187–216.

Bueno de Mesquita, Bruce, and David Lalman. (1992) *War and Reason: Domestic and International Imperatives*. New Haven, Conn.: Yale University Press.

Bull, Hedley. (1977) *The Anarchical Society: A Study of Order in World Politics*. New York: Columbia University Press.

Bundy, McGeorge. (1990) "From Cold War to Trusting Peace," *Foreign Affairs* 69 (no. 1): 197–212.

Burkhart, Ross E., and Michael S. Lewis-Beck. (1994) "Comparative Democracy: The Economic Development Thesis," *American Political Science Review* 88 (December): 903–10.

Burroughs, John, and Jacqueline Cabasso. (1996) "Nukes on Trial," *Bulletin of the Atomic Scientists* 52 (March/April): 41–45.

Cahn, Anne H. (1995) "Does the Defense Industry Really Need Welfare?" *Christian Science Monitor* 87 (May 15): 19.

Cairncross, Frances. (1994) "Environmental Pragmatism," *Foreign Policy* 95 (Summer): 35–52.

Caldwell, Dan. (1977) "Bureaucratic Foreign Policy Making," *American Behavioral Scientist* 21 (September–October): 87–110.

Calvocoressi, Peter, Guy Wint, and John Pritchard. (1989) *Total War: The Causes and Courses of the Second World War*, 2nd ed. New York: Pantheon.

Carment, David. (1993) "The International Dimensions of Ethnic Conflict," *Journal of Peace Research* 30 (May): 137–50.

Carothers, Thomas. (1997) "Democracy without Illusions," *Foreign Affairs* 76 (January/February): 85–99.

Carpenter, Ted Galen. (1991) "The New World Disorder," *Foreign Policy* 84 (Fall): 24–39.

Carr, E. H. (1939) *The Twenty-Years' Crisis, 1919–1939*. London: Macmillan.

Carter, Ashton B. (1990–1991) "Chairman's Note," *International Security* 15 (Winter): 3–4.

Cashman, Greg. (1993) *What Causes War? An Introduction to Theories of International Conflict*. New York: Lexington Books.

Caspary, William R. (1993) "New Psychoanalytic Perspectives on the Causes of War," *Political Psychology* 14 (September): 417–46.

Cederman, Lars-Erik. (1997) *Emergent Actors in World Politics: How States and Nations Develop and Dissolve*. Princeton, N.J.: Princeton University Press.

Cerny, Philip G. (1994) "The Dynamics of Financial Globalization: Technology, Market Structure, and Policy Response," *Policy Sciences* 287 (No. 4): 319–42.

Chaliand, Gérald, and Jean-Pierre Rageau. (1993) *Strategic Atlas*, 3rd ed. New York: Harper Perennial.

Chan, Steve. (1997) "In Search of Democratic Peace: Problems and Promise," *Mershon International Studies Review* 41 (May): 59–91.

———. (1987) "Military Expenditures and Economic Performance," pp. 29–37 in U.S. Arms Control and Disarmament Agency, *World Military Expenditures and Arms Transfers 1986*. Washington, D.C.: U.S. Government Printing Office.

———. (1984) "Mirror, Mirror on the Wall . . .: Are the Free Countries More Pacific?" *Journal of Conflict Resolution* 28 (December): 617–48.

Chatterjee, Partha. (1993) *The Nation and Its Fragments*. Princeton, N.J.: Princeton University Press.

Chubin, Shahram. (1998) "Southern Perspectives on World Order," pp. 208–20 in Charles W. Kegley, Jr. and Eugene R. Wittkopf (eds.), *The Global Agenda*, 5th ed. New York: McGraw-Hill.

Cimbala, Stephen J. (1997) *The Politics of Warfare: The Great Powers in the Twentieth Century*. University Park: The Penn State University Press.

Clad, James C. (1994) "Slowing the Wave," *Foreign Policy* 95 (Summer): 139–50.

Clancy, Tom, and Russell Seitz. (1991–1992) "Five Minutes Past Midnight—and Welcome to the New Age of Proliferation," *The National Interest* 26 (Winter): 3–17.

Claude, Inis L., Jr. (1989) "The Balance of Power Revisited," *Review of International Studies* 15 (January): 77–85.

———. (1988) *States and the Global System: Politics, Law, and Organization*. New York: St. Martin's Press.

———. (1971) *Swords into Plowshares*, 4th ed. New York: Random House.

———. (1967) *The Changing United Nations*. New York: Random House.

———. (1962) *Power and International Relations*. New York: Random House.

Clausewitz, Karl von. (1976 [1832]) *On War*. Princeton, N.J.: Princeton University Press.

Cobb, Roger, and Charles Elder. (1970) *International Community*. New York: Harcourt, Brace & World.

Cockburn, Andrew. (1995) "A U.S. Military Porkfest Fattens Contractors," *International Herald Tribune* (October 5): 9.

Cohen, Benjamin J. (1996) "Phoenix Risen: The Resurrection of Global Finance," *World Politics* 48 (January): 268–96.

———. (1973) *The Question of Imperialism*. New York: Basic Books.

Cohen, Eliot A. (1998) "A Revolution in Warfare: The Changing Face of Force," pp. 34–46 in Charles W. Kegley, Jr. and Eugene R. Wittkopf (eds.), *The Global Agenda*, 5th ed. New York: McGraw-Hill.

———. (1995) "The Future of Military Power: The Continuing Utility of Force," pp. 35–43 in Charles W. Kegley, Jr. and Eugene R. Wittkopf (eds.), *The Global Agenda*, 4th ed. New York: McGraw-Hill.

Cohen, Joel E. (1995) *How Many People Can the Earth Support?* New York: Norton.

Collins, John M. (1994) *Military Preparedness: Principles Compared with U.S. Practices*. Washington, D.C.: Congressional Research Service.

Commager, Henry Steele. (1983) "Misconceptions Governing American Foreign Policy," pp. 510–17 in Charles W. Kegley, Jr. and Eugene R. Wittkopf (eds.), *Perspectives on American Foreign Policy*. New York: St. Martin's Press.

Commission on Transnational Corporations. (1991) "Recent Developments Related to Transnational Corporations and International Economic Relations," U.N. Doc. E/E.10/1991/2, United Nations Economic and Social Council.

Connelly, Matthew, and Paul Kennedy. (1994) "Must It Be the Rest against the West?" *Atlantic Monthly* 274 (December): 61–84.

Coplin, William D. (1971) *Introduction to International Politics*. Chicago: Markham.

———. (1966) *The Functions of International Law*. Chicago: Rand McNally.

———. (1965) "International Law and Assumptions about the State System," *World Politics* 17 (July): 615–34.

Cortwright, David, and George A. Lopez. (1995) "The Sanctions Era: An Alternative to Military Intervention," *The Fletcher Forum of World Affairs* 19 (May): 65–85.

Coser, Lewis. (1956) *The Functions of Social Conflict*. London: Routledge & Kegan Paul.

Craig, Gordon A., and Alexander L. George. (1990) *Force and Statecraft*, 2nd ed. New York: Oxford University Press.

Crenshaw, Martha. (1990) "Is International Terrorism Primarily State-Sponsored?" pp. 163–69 in Charles W. Kegley, Jr. (ed.), *International Terrorism: Characteristics, Causes, Controls*. New York: St. Martin's Press.

Crook, Clive. (1997) "The Future of the State," *Economist* 344 (September 20): 5–20.

Crossette, Barbara. (1997) "Vying to Forge a World Criminal Court," *International Herald Tribune* (August 19): 1, 6.

———. (1995) "The Second Sex in the Third World," *New York Times* (September 10): E1, E3.

Culpitt, Richard T., Rodney L. Whitlock, and Lynn Williams Whitlock. (1996) "The [Im]mortality of International Governmental Organizations," *International Interactions* 21 (No. 4): 389–404.

Curtis, Bronwyn. (1998) "What Asia Could Learn from Europe," *New York Times* (January 25): A12.

D'Amato, Anthony. (1982) "What `Counts' as Law?" pp. 83–107 in Nicholas Greenwood Onuf (ed.), *Law-Making in the Global Community*. Durham, N.C.: Carolina Academic Press.

Daly, Herman E. (1993) "The Perils of Free Trade," *Scientific American* 269 (November): 50–57.

Daly, Herman E., and John B. Cobb, Jr. (1989) *For the Common Good*. Boston: Beacon Press.

Davidson, Keay. (1991) "Slashing U.S. Nuclear Arsenal Now Thinkable," *Sunday Advocate* (Baton Rouge, La.) (November 10): E1.

Davies, Norman. (1996) *Europe*. New York: Oxford University Press.

Davis, Bob. (1994) "Global Paradox: Growth of Trade Binds Nations but It Can Also Spur Separatism," *Wall Street Journal* (June 20): A1, A10.

Deger, Saadet, and Ron Smith. (1983) "Military Expansion and Growth in Less Developed Countries," *Journal of Conflict Resolution* 27 (June): 335–53.

Dehio, Ludwig. (1962) *The Precarious Balance*. New York: Knopf.

Demko, George J., and William B. Wood. (1994) *Reordering the World: Geopolitical Perspectives on the 21st Century*. Boulder, Colo.: Westview.

Dentzer, Susan. (1993) "Meet the New Economic Bogymen," *U.S. News and World Report* (October 18): 67.

Der Derian, James. (ed.). (1995) *International Theory: Critical Investigations*. New York: New York University Press.

DeRivera, Joseph H. (1968) *The Psychological Dimension of Foreign Policy*. Columbus, Ohio: Merrill.

Destler, I. M. (1995) *American Trade Politics*, 3rd ed. Washington, D.C.: Institute for International Economics.

de Tocqueville, Alexis. (1969 [1835]) *Democracy in America*. New York: Doubleday.

Deutsch, Karl W., et al. (1999) *Backgrounds to Community*. Columbia: University of South Carolina Press.

———. (1974) *Politics and Government*. Boston: Houghton Mifflin.

———. (1957) *Political Community and the North Atlantic Area.* Princeton, N.J.: Princeton University Press.

———. (1953) "The Growth of Nations: Some Recurrent Patterns in Political and Social Integration," *World Politics* 5 (October): 168–95.

Deutsch, Karl W., and J. David Singer. (1964) "Multipolar Power Systems and International Stability," *World Politics* 16 (April): 390–406.

Dionne, E. J., Jr. (1998) "Modest Success in Bosnia for 'Clinton Doctrine'," *International Herald Tribune* (January 1): 9.

DiRenzo, Gordon J. (ed.). (1974) *Personality and Politics.* Garden City, N.Y.: Doubleday-Anchor.

Diwan, Ishac, and Ana Revenga. (1995) "Wages, Inequality, and International Integration," *Finance & Development* 32 (September): 7–9.

Dixon, William J. (1994) "Democracy and the Peaceful Settlement of International Conflict," *American Political Science Review* 88 (March): 14–32.

Dobbs, Michael. (1991) "Disaster, Nuclear and Bureaucratic," *Washington Post National Weekly Edition* 8 (May 6–12): 10–11.

Doremus, Paul N., William W. Keller, Louis W. Pauly, and Simon Reich. (1998) *The Myth of Global Corporation.* Princeton, N.J.: Princeton University Press.

Dorraj, Manochehr. (1995) "Introduction: The Changing Context of Third World Political Economy," pp. 1–13 in Manochehr Dorraj (ed.), *The Changing Political Economy of the Third World.* Boulder, Colo.: Lynne Rienner.

Dos Santos, Theotonio. (1970) "The Structure of Dependence," *American Economic Review* 60 (May): 231–36.

Downs, George W. (ed.). (1994) *Collective Security beyond the Cold War.* Ann Arbor: University of Michigan Press.

Doyle, Michael W. (1995) "Liberalism and World Politics Revisited," pp. 83–106 in Charles W. Kegley, Jr. (ed.), *Controversies in International Relations Theory: Realism and the Neoliberal Challenge.* New York: St. Martin's Press.

Doyle, Michael W., and G. John Ikenberry (eds.). (1997) *New Thinking in International Relations Theory.* Boulder, Colo.: Westview.

Drozdiak, William. (1997) "Down with Yankee Dominance," *Washington Post National Weekly Edition* 15 (November 24): 15.

Drucker, Peter F. (1997) "The Global Economy and the Nation-State," *Foreign Affairs* 76 (October): 159–71.

———. (1994) "Trade Lessons from the World Economy," *Foreign Affairs* 73 (January/February): 99–108.

Dulles, John Foster. (1939) *War, Peace, and Change.* New York: Harper.

Durbin, Andrea C. (1995) "Trade and the Environment," *Environment* 37 (September): 16–20, 37–41.

Durning, Alan Thein. (1993) "Supporting Indigenous Peoples," pp. 80–100 in Lester R. Brown et al., *State of the World 1993.* New York: Norton.

———. (1991) "Asking How Much Is Enough," pp. 153–69 in Lester R. Brown et al., *State of the World 1991.* New York: Norton.

Dyson, Freeman. (1997) *Imagined Worlds.* Cambridge, Mass.: Harvard University Press.

Easton, David. (1969) "The New Revolution in Political Science," *American Political Science Review* 63 (December): 1051–61.

Easton, Stewart C. (1964) *The Rise and Fall of Western Colonialism.* New York: Praeger.

Eberstadt, Nicholas. (1995) "Population, Food, and Income: Global Trends in the Twentieth Century," pp. 7–47 in Ronald Bailey (ed.), *The True State of the Planet.* New York: Free Press.

———. (1991) "Population Change and National Security," *Foreign Affairs* 70 (Summer): 115–31.

Economic Report of the President. (1994) Washington, D.C.: Government Printing Office.

The Economist. (1998) "The Institutional Pillars of Global Order: The Nation-State Is Dead; Long Live the Nation-State," pp. 232–40 in Charles W. Kegley, Jr. and Eugene R. Wittkopf (eds.), *The Global Agenda*, 5th ed. New York: McGraw-Hill.

Edwards, Jim. (1997) "Center of the Action," *American* 48 (Winter): 14–17.

Edwards, Stephen R. (1995) "Conserving Biodiversity: Resources for Our Future," pp. 212–65 in Ronald Bailey (ed.), *The True State of the Planet.* New York: Free Press.

Ehrlich, Paul. (1968) *The Population Bomb.* New York: Ballantine.

Eichengreen, Barry. (1996) *Globalizing Capital.* Princeton, N.J.: Princeton University Press.

Elliott, Kimberly Ann. (1993) "Sanctions: A Look at the Record," *Bulletin of the Atomic Scientists* 49 (November): 32–35.

Emerson, Sarah A. (1997) "Resource Plenty: Why Fears of an Oil Crisis Are Misinformed," *Harvard International Review* 19 (Summer): 12–15, 64.

Emmanuel, Arghiri. (1972) *Unequal Exchange: An Essay on the Imperialism of Trade.* New York: Monthly Review Press.

Enloe, Cynthia. (1993) *The Morning After: Sexual Politics at the End of the Cold War.* Berkeley: University of California Press.

"Environmental Intelligence." (1994) *World Watch* 7 (November/December): 6–8.

Epstein, William. (1995) "NPT Wrap-Up: Indefinite Extension—With Increased Accountability," *Bulletin of Atomic Scientists* 51 (July/August): 27–30.

Erikson, Kai. (1994) "Out of Sight, Out of Our Minds," *New York Times Magazine* (March 6): 36–49, 63.

Etzioni, Amital. (1968) "Toward a Sociological Theory of Peace," pp. 403–28 in Leon Bramson and George W. Goethals (eds.), *War.* New York: Basic Books.

European Commission Delegation to the United States. (1994) *The European Union: A Guide.* Washington, D.C.: The European Commission Delegation to the United States.

Evans, Gareth. (1995) "A Struggling UN Must Now Appreciate the Art of the Possible," *International Herald Tribune* (October 7–8): 8.

Evans, Tony. (1997) *What a Way to Live!* Dallas, Tex.: Word Publishing.

Falk, Richard A. (1993) "Sovereignty," pp. 851–54 in Joel Krieger (ed.), *The Oxford Companion to Politics of the World.* New York: Oxford University Press.

———. (1992) *Explorations at the Edge of Time: The Prospects for World Order.* Philadelphia: Temple University Press.

———. (1970) *The Status of Law in International Society.* Princeton, N.J.: Princeton University Press.

———. (1965) "World Law and Human Conflict," pp. 227–49 in Elton B. McNeil (ed.), *The Nature of Human Conflict.* Englewood Cliffs, N.J.: Prentice Hall.

———. (1964) *The Role of Domestic Courts in the International Legal Order.* Syracuse, N.Y.: Syracuse University Press.

Falkenheim, Peggy L. (1987) "Post-Afghanistan Sanctions," pp. 105–30 in David Leyton-Brown (ed.), *The Utility of International Economic Sanctions.* New York: St. Martin's Press.

FAO Yearbook: Production 1994. (1995) Rome: Food and Agriculture Organization of the United Nations.

FAO Yearbook: Production 1990. (1991) Rome: Food and Agriculture Organization of the United Nations.

Fedarko, Kevin. (1995) "Louder Than Words," *Time* (September 11): 49–59.

Ferencz, Benjamin B., and Ken Keyes, Jr. (1991) *PlanetHood.* Coos Bay, Ore.: Love Line Books.

Festinger, Leon. (1957) *A Theory of Cognitive Dissonance.* Evanston, Ill.: Row, Peterson.

Fetter, Steve. (1991) "Ballistic Missiles and Weapons of Mass Destruction: What Is the Threat? What Should Be Done?" *International Security* 16 (Summer): 5–42.

Fieldhouse, D. K. (1973) *Economics and Empire, 1830–1914.* Ithaca, N.Y.: Cornell University Press.

Flavin, Christopher. (1992) "Building a Bridge to Sustainable Energy," pp. 27–45 in Lester R. Brown et al., *State of the World 1992.* New York: Norton.

Flavin, Christopher, and Odil Tunali. (1995) "Getting Warmer: Looking for a Way Out of the Climate Impasse," *World Watch* 18 (March/April): 10–19.

Føland, Tor Egil. (1993) "The History of Economic Warfare: International Law, Effectiveness, Strategies," *Journal of Peace Research* 30 (May): 151–62.

Forsythe, David. (1997) "The International Court of Justice at Fifty," pp. 385–405 in A. S. Miller et al. (eds.), *The International Court of Justice.* Amsterdam: Klumer Law International.

Francis, David R. (1997) "Welcome Mat Now Offered Foreign Firms," *Christian Science Monitor* 88 (May 28): 1, 8–9.

Francis, Emerich K. (1976) *Interethnic Relations.* New York: Elsevier.

Franck, Thomas M. (1994) "The Emerging Democratic Entitlement," pp. 367–73 in Anthony D'Amato (ed.), *International Law Anthology.* Cincinnati, Ohio: Anderson.

Frank, Andre Gunder. (1969) *Latin America: Underdevelopment or Revolution.* New York: Monthly Review Press.

Frankel, Glenn. (1987) "Weapons: The Global Commodity," *Washington Post National Weekly Edition* 4 (January 12): 6–7.

Frankel, Jeffrey A. (1997) *Regional Trading Blocs in the World Economic System.* Washington, D.C.: Institute for International Economics.

Freedom House. (1998) *Freedom in the World: An Annual Survey of Political Rights and Civil Liberties.* Lanham, Md.: University Press of America.

Freeman, Orville L. (1990) "Meeting the Needs of the Coming Decade: Agriculture vs. the Environment," *Futurist* 24 (November–December): 15–20.

French, Hilary F. (1994) "Can the Environment Survive Industrial Demands?" *USA Today* 122 (January): 66–69.

Freud, Sigmund. (1968) "Why War," pp. 71–80 in Leon Bramson and George W. Goethals (eds.), *War.* New York: Basic Books.

Fried, John H. E. (1971) "International Law—Neither Orphan nor Harlot, Neither Jailer nor Never-Never Land," pp. 124–76 in Karl W. Deutsch and Stanley Hoffmann (eds.), *The Relevance of International Law.* Garden City, N.Y.: Doubleday-Anchor.

Friedheim, Robert L. (1965) "The 'Satisfied' and 'Dissatisfied' States Negotiate International Law," *World Politics* 18 (October): 20–41.

Friedman, Thomas L. (1996) "Answers Needed to Globalization Dissent," *Houston Chronicle* (February 8): 30.

———. (1993) "Friends Like Russia Make Diplomacy a Mess," *New York Times* (March 28): E5.

Fry, Earl H., Stan A. Taylor, and Robert S. Wood. (1994) *America the Vincible.* Englewood Cliffs, N.J.: Prentice Hall.

Fukuyama, Francis. (1994) "The Ambiguity of National Interest," pp. 10–23 in Stephen Sestanovich (ed.), *Rethinking Russia's National Interests.* Washington, D.C.: Center for Strategic and International Studies.

———. (1992a) "The Beginning of Foreign Policy," *The New Republic* 207 (August 17 and 24): 24–32.

———. (1992b) *The End of History and the Last Man.* New York: Free Press.

———. (1989) "The End of History?" *The National Interest* 16 (Summer): 3–16.

Fuller, Graham E. (1995) "The Next Ideology," *Foreign Policy* 98 (Spring): 145–58.

———. (1991–1992) "The Breaking of Nations—and the Threat to Ours," *The National Interest* 26 (Winter): 14–21.

Gaddis, John Lewis. (1997) *We Now Know: Rethinking Cold War History.* New York: Oxford University Press.

———. (1991) "Great Illusions, the Long Peace, and the Future of the International System," pp. 25–55 in Charles W. Kegley, Jr. (ed.), *The Long Postwar Peace.* New York: HarperCollins.

———. (1990) "Coping with Victory," *Atlantic Monthly* 265 (May): 49–60.

———. (1983) "Containment: Its Past and Future," pp. 16–31 in Charles W. Kegley, Jr. and Eugene R. Wittkopf (eds.), *Perspectives on American Foreign Policy.* New York: St. Martin's Press.

Galtung, Johan. (1969) "Violence, Peace, and Peace Research," *Journal of Peace Research* 6 (No. 3): 167–91.

Gardels, Nathan. (1991) "Two Concepts of Nationalism," *New York Review of Books* 38 (November 21): 19–23.

Gardner, Lloyd C. (1970) *Architects of Illusion.* Chicago: Quadrangle.

Garrett, Laurie. (1998) "Runaway Diseases," *Foreign Affairs* 77 (January/February): 139–42.

Gelb, Leslie H. (1993) "Tailoring a U.S. Role at the U.N.," *International Herald Tribune* (January 2–3): 4.

———. (1979) "The Future of Arms Control: A Glass Half Full," *Foreign Policy* 36 (Fall): 21–32.

Gelb, Leslie H., and Morton H. Halperin. (1973) "The Ten Commandments of the Foreign Affairs Bureaucracy," pp. 250–59 in Steven L. Spiegel (ed.), *At Issue.* New York: St. Martin's Press.

Gelber, Harry. (1998) *Sovereignty Through Interdependence.* Cambridge, Mass.: Kluwer Law International.

George, Alexander L. (1992) *Forceful Persuasion: Coercive Diplomacy as an Alternative to War.* Washington, D.C.: United States Institute of Peace.

———. (1986) "U.S.–Soviet Global Rivalry: Norms of Competition," *Journal of Peace Research* 23 (September): 247–62.

———. (1972) "The Case for Multiple Advocacy in Making Foreign Policy," *American Political Science Review* 66 (September): 751–85.

German, F. Clifford. (1960) "A Tentative Evaluation of World Power," *Journal of Conflict Resolution* 4 (March): 138–44.

Gill, Stephen. (1993a) "Group of 7," pp. 369–70 in Joel Krieger (ed.), *The Oxford Companion to Politics of the World.* New York: Oxford University Press.

———. (1993b) "Hegemony," pp. 384–86 in Joel Krieger (ed.), *The Oxford Companion to Politics of the World.* New York: Oxford University Press.

Gilpin, Robert. (1998) "Three Ideologies of Political Economy," pp. 277–95 in Charles W. Kegley, Jr. and Eugene R. Wittkopf (eds.), *The Global Agenda*, 5th ed. New York: McGraw-Hill.

———. (1987) *The Political Economy of International Relations.* Princeton, N.J: Princeton University Press.

———. (1985) "The Politics of Transnational Economic Relations," pp. 171–94 in Ray Maghroori and Bennett Ramberg (eds.), *Globalism versus Realism: International Relations' Third Debate.* Boulder, Colo.: Westview.

———. (1981) *War and Change in World Politics.* Cambridge, Eng.: Cambridge University Press.

———. (1975) *U.S. Power and the Multinational Corporation.* New York: Basic Books.

Glahn, Gerhard von. (1996) *Law among Nations*, 7th ed. Boston: Allyn & Bacon.

Gleditsch, Nils Petter. (1995) "35 Major Wars?" *Journal of Conflict Resolution* 39 (September): 584–87.

Gochman, Charles S., and Zeev Maoz. (1984) "Militarized Interstate Disputes, 1816–1976: Procedures, Patterns, and Insights," *Journal of Conflict Resolution* 28 (December): 585–616.

Goldgeier, James M., and Michael McFaul. (1992) "A Tale of Two Worlds: Core and Periphery in the Post-Cold War Era," *International Organization* 46 (Spring): 467–91.

Goldstein, Joshua S. (1988) *Long Cycles: Prosperity and War in the Modern Age.* New Haven, Conn.: Yale University Press.

Goldstein, Morris. (1995) *The Exchange Rate System and the IMF: A Modest Agenda.* Washington, D.C.: Institute for International Economics.

Gordon, Michael R. (1993b) "U.S. Seeking to Ease 1972 Treaty Limits on Missile Defenses," *New York Times* (December 3): A7.

Goshko, John M. (1996) "UN Leader Dangles a Carrot to U.S. over Dues," *International Herald Tribune* (February 8): 6.

Gottlieb, Gidon. (1982) "Global Bargaining: The Legal and Diplomatic Framework," pp. 109–30 in Nicholas Greenwood Onuf (ed.), *Law-Making in the Global Community.* Durham, N.C.: Carolina Academic Press.

Graham, Bradley. (1995) "Revolutionary Warfare: New Technologies Are Transforming the U.S. Military," *Washington Post National Weekly Edition* 12 (March 6–12): 6–7.

Graham, Edward M., and Paul R. Krugman. (1995) *Foreign Direct Investment in the United States.* Washington, D.C.: Institute for International Economics.

Grant, Rebecca, and Kathleen Newland (eds.). (1991) *Gender and International Relations.* Bloomington: Indiana University Press.

Greene, David. (1997) "Economic Scarcity: Forget Geology, Beware Monopoly," *Harvard International Review* 19 (Summer) 16–19, 65.

Greenfield, Meg. (1997) "Back to the Future," *Newsweek* (January 27): 96.

———. (1995) "When the Budget Is Colonized: Cutting a Program Is Like Bombing a Settlement," *Newsweek* (May 22): 78.

Greenstein, Fred I. (1987) *Personality and Politics.* Princeton, N.J.: Princeton University Press.

Grey, Edward. (1925) *Twenty-Five Years, 1892–1916.* New York: Frederick Stokes.

Grieco, Joseph M. (1995) "Anarchy and the Limits of Cooperation: A Realist Critique of the Newest Liberal Institutionalism," pp. 151–71 in Charles W. Kegley, Jr. (ed.), *Controversies in International Relations Theory: Realism and the Neoliberal Challenge.* New York: St. Martin's Press.

Grimmett, Richard F. (1997) *Conventional Arms Transfers to Developing Nations, 1989–1996.* Washington, D.C.: Congressional Research Office.

———. (1995) *Conventional Arms Transfers to Developing Nations 1987–1994.* Washington, D.C.: Congressional Research Service, U.S. Library of Congress.

Guéhenno, Jean-Marie. (1995) *The End of the Nation-State.* Minneapolis, Minn.: University of Minnesota Press.

Gulick, Edward Vose. (1955) *Europe's Classical Balance of Power.* Ithaca, N.Y.: Cornell University Press.

Gurney, Kevin Robert. (1996) "Saving the Ozone Layer Faster," *Technology Review* 99 (January): 58–59.

Gurr, Ted Robert. (1998) "Communal Conflicts and Global Security," pp. 197–207 in Charles W. Kegley, Jr. and Eugene R. Wittkopf (eds.), *The Global Agenda*, 5th ed. New York: McGraw-Hill.

———. (1997) "The Ethnic Challenge to International Security," *Futures Research Quarterly* 13 (Spring): 11–23.

———. (1994) "Peoples against States: Ethnopolitical Conflict and the Changing World System," *International Studies Quarterly* 38 (September): 347–77.

———. (1993) *Minorities at Risk: A Global View of Ethnopolitical Conflicts.* Washington, D.C.: United States Institute of Peace.

———. (1990) "Ethnic Warfare and the Changing Priorities of Global Security," *Mediterranean Quarterly* 1 (Winter): 82–98.

———. (1970) *Why Men Rebel.* Princeton, N.J.: Princeton University Press.

Gwartney, James D., Robert Lawson, and Walter Block. (1996) *Economic Freedom of the World, 1975–1995.* Vancouver: Fraser Institute.

Haas, Ernst B. (1986) *Why We Still Need the United Nations: The Collective Management of International Conflict, 1945–1984.* Berkeley: Institute of International Studies, University of California.

Haas, Ernst B., and Allen S. Whiting. (1956) *Dynamics of International Relations.* New York: McGraw-Hill.

Haas, Peter M., Robert O. Keohane, and Marc A. Levy (eds.). (1993) *Institutions for the Earth: Sources of Effective International Environmental Protection.* Cambridge, Mass.: MIT Press.

Haass, Richard N. (1997) "Sanctioning Madness," *Foreign Affairs* 76 (December): 74–85.

Haffa, Robert P., Jr. (1992) "The Future of Conventional Deterrence," pp. 5–30 in Gary L. Guertner, Robert Haffa, Jr., and George Quester, *Conventional Forces and the Future of Deterrence.* Carlisle Barracks, Penn.: U.S. Army War College.

Hagan, Joe D. (1993) *Political Opposition and Foreign Policy in Comparative Perspective.* Boulder, Colo.: Lynne Rienner.

Haggard, Stephan, and Beth A. Simmons. (1987) "Theories of International Regimes," *International Organization* 41 (Summer): 491–517.

Hall, John A. (1993) "Liberalism," pp. 538–42 in Joel Krieger (ed.), *The Oxford Companion to Politics of the World.* Oxford, Eng.: Oxford University Press.

Hallenbeck, Ralph A., and David E. Shaver (eds.). (1991) *On Disarmament.* New York: Praeger.

Hamilton, Kimberly A. (1994) "The HIV and AIDS Pandemic as a Foreign Policy Concern," *Washington Quarterly* 17 (Winter): 201–15.

Hammond, Grant T. (1996) "The Difficult Pursuit of Peace," *USA Today* 125. (November): 13.

Handbook of International Economic Statistics. (1997) Landley, Va.: U.S. Central Intelligence Agency.

———. (1996) Landley, Va.: U.S. Central Intelligence Agency.

Hardin, Garrett. (1993) *Living within Limits*. New York: Oxford University Press.

———. (1968) "The Tragedy of the Commons," *Science* 162 (December): 1243–48.

Harknett, Richard J. (1994) "The Logic of Conventional Deterrence and the End of the Cold War," *Security Studies* 4 (Autumn): 86–114.

Harries, Owen. (1995) "Realism in a New Era," *Quadrant* 39 (April): 11–18.

Harrison, Selig S. (1993) "Japan's Second Thoughts about Nuclear Weapons: With Its Neighbors Armed to the Teeth, Will Tokyo Join the Club?" *Washington Post National Weekly Edition* 11 (November 8–14): 23–24.

Hassner, Pierre. (1968) "The Nation–State in the Nuclear Age," *Survey* 67 (April): 3–27.

Heilbroner, Robert L. (1991) *An Inquiry into the Human Prospect: Looked at Again for the 1990s*. New York: Norton.

Helman, Udi. (1995) "Sustainable Development: Strategies for Reconciling Environment and Economy in the Developing World," *Washington Quarterly* 18 (Autumn): 189–207.

Helprin, Mark. (1995) "What to Do about Terrorism, Really," *Wall Street Journal* (May 10): A14.

Henkin, Louis. (1991) "The Use of Force: Law and U.S. Policy," pp. 37–69 in Stanley Hoffmann et al. (eds.), *Right vs. Might: International Law and the Use of Force*, 2nd ed. New York: Council on Foreign Relations.

Heredia, Blanca. (1997) "Prosper or Perish: Development in the Age of Global Capital," *Current History* 96 (November): 383–88.

Hermann, Charles F. (1988) "New Foreign Policy Problems and Old Bureaucratic Organizations," pp. 248–65 in Charles W. Kegley, Jr. and Eugene R. Wittkopf (eds.), *The Domestic Sources of American Foreign Policy*. New York: St. Martin's Press.

———. (1972) "Some Issues in the Study of International Crisis," pp. 3–17 in Charles F. Hermann (ed.), *International Crises*. New York: Free Press.

Hermann, Charles F., Charles W. Kegley, Jr., and James N. Rosenau (eds.). (1987) *New Directions in the Study of Foreign Policy*. Boston: Allen & Unwin.

Hermann, Margaret G. (1988) "The Role of Leaders and Leadership in the Making of American Foreign Policy," pp. 266–84 in Charles W. Kegley, Jr., and Eugene R. Wittkopf (eds.), *The Domestic Sources of American Foreign Policy*. New York: St. Martin's Press.

———. (1976) "When Leader Personality Will Affect Foreign Policy: Some Propositions," pp. 326–33 in James N. Rosenau (ed.), *In Search of Global Patterns*. New York: Free Press.

Herz, John H. (1951) *Political Realism and Political Idealism*. Chicago: University of Chicago Press.

Hiatt, Fred. (1997) "Globalization: Real Benefits, but Also Real Costs for Many," *International Herald Tribune* (June 12): 8.

Hiatt, Fred, and Margaret Shapiro. (1995) "Russia Recovers from a Nervous Breakdown," *Washington Post National Weekly Edition* 12 (July 31–August 6): 23–24.

Higgins, Benjamin, and Jean Downing Higgins. (1979) *Economic Development of a Small Planet*. New York: Norton.

Higgins, Rosalyn. (1994) *Problems and Process: International Law and How We Use It*. Oxford, Eng.: Oxford University Press.

Hilsman, Roger. (1967) *To Move a Nation*. New York: Doubleday.

Hoagland, Jim. (1996) "Yes, Sanctions Can Be Effective, But You Have to Work at It," *International Herald Tribune* (February 8): 8.

———. (1993a) "A Breakthrough for Clinton Too," *Washington Post National Weekly Edition* 10 (September 20–26): 29.

———. (1993b) "Economic Sanctions Sometimes Do More Harm Than Good," *The State* (Columbia, S.C.) (November 11): A12.

Hoebel, E. Adamson. (1961) *The Law of Primitive Man*. Cambridge, Mass.: Harvard University Press.

Hoffmann, Stanley. (1992) "To the Editors," *The New York Review of Books* 40 (June 24): 59.

———. (1971) "International Law and the Control of Force," pp. 34–66 in Karl W. Deutsch and Stanley Hoffmann (eds.), *The Relevance of International Law*. Garden City, N.Y.: Doubleday-Anchor.

———. (1961) "International Systems and International Law," pp. 205–37 in Klaus Knorr and Sidney Verba (eds.), *The International System*. Princeton, N.J.: Princeton University Press.

Hollingsworth, J. Rogers, and Robert Boyer (eds.). (1997) *Contemporary Capitalism: The Embeddedness of Institutions*. New York: Cambridge University Press.

Holloway, David. (1983) *The Soviet Union and the Arms Race*. New Haven, Conn.: Yale University Press.

Holsti, Kalevi J. (1996) *The State, War, and the State of War*. New York: Cambridge University Press.

———. (1995) "War, Peace, and the State of the State," *International Political Science Review* 16 (October): 319–39.

———. (1992) *International Politics: A Framework for Analysis*, 6th ed. Englewood Cliffs, N.J.: Prentice Hall.

———. (1991) *Peace and War: Armed Conflicts and International Order, 1648–1989*. Cambridge, Eng.: Cambridge University Press.

———. (1988) *International Politics: A Framework for Analysis*, 5th ed. Englewood Cliffs, N.J.: Prentice Hall.

Holsti, Ole R. (1998) "Models of International Relations: Realist and Neoliberal Perspectives on Conflict and Cooperation," pp. 131–44 in Charles W. Kegley, Jr. and Eugene R. Wittkopf (eds.), *The Global Agenda*, 5th ed. New York: McGraw-Hill.

———. (1995) "Theories of International Relations and Foreign Policy: Realism and Its Challengers," pp. 35–65 in Charles W. Kegley, Jr. (ed.), *Controversies in International Relations Theory: Realism and the Neoliberal Challenge*. New York: St. Martin's.

———. (1989) "Crisis Decision Making," pp. 8–84 in Philip E. Tetlock et al. (eds.), *Behavior, Society, and Nuclear War*. N.Y.: Oxford University Press.

Homer-Dixon, Thomas F. (1998) "Environmental Scarcities and Violent Conflict—Global Implications," pp. 465–72 in Charles W. Kegley, Jr. and Eugene R. Wittkopf (eds.), *The Global Agenda*, 5th ed. New York: McGraw-Hill.

House, Karen Elliot. (1989) "As Power Is Dispersed among Nations, Need for Leadership Grows," *Wall Street Journal* (February 21): A1, A10.

Howard, Michael E. (1983) *The Causes of War*. Cambridge, Mass.: Harvard University Press.

———. (1978) *War and the Liberal Conscience*. New York: Oxford University Press.

Howell, Llewellyn D. (1995) "Economic Sanctions as Weapons," *USA Today* 124 (July): 37.

Hufbauer, Gary Clyde. (1994) "The Futility of Sanctions," *Wall Street Journal* (June 1): A14.

Hufbauer, Gary Clyde, Jeffrey J. Schott, and Kimberly Ann Elliott. (1990) *Economic Sanctions Reconsidered: History and Current Policy*, 2nd ed. Washington, D.C.: Institute for International Economics.

Hughes, Barry B. (1997) *Continuity and Change in World Politics*, 3rd ed. Upper Saddle River, N.J.: Prentice Hall.

Hughes, Emmet John. (1972) *The Living Presidency*. New York: Coward, McGann, and Geoghegan.

Hughes, John. (1997) "Democracy Makes Gains, but Too Many Countries Still Not Free," *Christian Science Monitor* 89 (May 7): 19.

Huntington, Samuel P. (1996) *The Clash of Civilizations and the Remaking of World Order*. New York: Simon & Schuster.

———. (1993) "The Clash of Civilizations?" *Foreign Affairs* 72 (Summer): 22–49.

———. (1991a) "America's Changing Strategic Interests," *Survival* 33 (January/February): 3–17.

———. (1991b) *The Third Wave: Democratization in the Late Twentieth Century*. Norman: University of Oklahoma Press.

———. (1989) "No Exit: The Errors of Declinism," *The National Interest* 17 (Fall): 3–10.

Hurwitz, Jon, and Mark Peffley. (1987) "How Are Foreign Policy Attitudes Structured? A Hierarchical Model," *American Political Science Review* 81 (December): 1099–1120.

Ikenberry, G. John. (1993) "Salvaging the G-7," *Foreign Affairs* 72 (Spring): 132–39.

Iklé, Fred Charles. (1991–1992) "Comrades in Arms," *The National Interest* 26 (Winter): 22–32.

International Monetary Fund [IMF]. (1997) *World Economic Outlook May 1997*. Washington, D.C.: International Monetary Fund.

Isaak, Robert A. (1995) *Managing World Economic Change: International Political Economy*, 2nd ed. Englewood Cliffs, N.J.: Prentice Hall.

———. (1975) *Individuals and World Politics*. North Scituate, Mass.: Duxbury.

Jackson, John H. (1994) "Managing the Trading System: The World Trade Organization and the Post–Uruguay Round GATT Agenda," pp. 131–51 in Peter B. Kenen (ed.), *Managing the World Economy: Fifty Years after Bretton Woods*. Washington, D.C.: Institute for International Economics.

Jacobson, Harold K. (1984) *Networks of Interdependence: International Organizations and the Global Political System*. New York: Knopf.

Jaggers, Keith, and Ted Robert Gurr. (1995) "Transitions to Democracy: Tracking Democracy's Third Wave," *Journal of Peace Research* 32 (November): 469–82.

Jakobson, Max. (1991) "Filling the World's Most Impossible Job," *World Monitor* 4 (August): 25–33.

James, Barry. (1995) "Religious Fanaticism Fuels Terrorism," *International Herald Tribune* (October 31): 6.

James, Patrick. (1993) "Neorealism as a Research Enterprise: Toward Elaborated Structural Realism," *International Political Science Review* 14 (no. 2): 123–48.

Janis, Irving. (1982) *Groupthink: Psychological Studies of Policy Decisions and Fiascoes*, 2nd ed. Boston: Houghton Mifflin.

Jenkins, Simon. (1995) "Dresden: Time to Say We're Sorry," *Wall Street Journal* (February 14): A22.

Jensen, Lloyd. (1982) *Explaining Foreign Policy*. Englewood Cliffs, N.J.: Prentice Hall.

Jervis, Robert. (1992) "A Usable Past for the Future," pp. 257–68 in Michael J. Hogan (ed.), *The End of the Cold War*. New York: Cambridge University Press.

———. (1991–1992) "The Future of World Politics: Will It Resemble the Past?" *International Security* 16 (Winter): 39–73.

———. (1991) "Will the New World Be Better?" pp. 7–19 in Robert Jervis and Seweryn Bialer (eds.), *Soviet–American Relations after the Cold War*. Durham, N.C.: Duke University Press.

———. (1982) "Security Regimes," *International Organization* 16 (Spring): 357–78.

———. (1976) *Perception and Misperception in World Politics*. Princeton, N.J.: Princeton University Press.

Joffe, Josef. (1990) "Entangled Forever," *The National Interest* 21 (Fall): 35–40.

———. (1985) "The Foreign Policy of the Federal Republic of Germany," pp. 72–113 in Roy C. Macridis (ed.), *Foreign Policy in World Politics*, 6th ed. Englewood Cliffs, N.J.: Prentice Hall.

Johansen, Robert C. (1995) "Swords into Plowshares: Can Fewer Arms Yield More Security?" pp. 253–79 in Charles W. Kegley, Jr. (ed.), *Controversies in International Relations Theory: Realism and the Neoliberal Challenge*. New York: St. Martin's.

———. (1991) "Do Preparations for War Increase or Decrease International Security?" pp. 224–44 in Charles W. Kegley, Jr. (ed.), *The Long Postwar Peace*. New York: HarperCollins.

Jones, Dorothy V. (1991) *Code of Peace: Ethics and Security in the World of the Warlord States*. Chicago: University of Chicago Press.

Joyner, Christopher C. (1998) "The Reality and Relevance of International Law in the 21st Century," pp. 252–65 in Charles W. Kegley, Jr. and Eugene R. Wittkopf (eds.), *The Global Agenda*, 5th ed. New York: McGraw-Hill.

———. (1995) "Collective Sanctions as Peaceful Coercion," pp. 241–70 in *The Australian Yearbook of International Law 1995*. Canberra: Australian National University.

Juergensmeyer, Mark. (1993) *The New Cold War? Religious Nationalism Confronts the Secular State*. Berkeley: University of California Press.

Kagan, Donald. (1995) *On the Origins of War and the Preservation of Peace*. New York: Doubleday.

Kaiser, David. (1990) *Politics and War: European Conflict from Philip II to Hitler*. Cambridge, Mass.: Harvard University Press.

Kane, Hal. (1995a) *The Hour of Departure: Forces That Create Refugees and Migrants*. Washington, D.C.: Worldwatch Institute.

———. (1995b) "Wars Reach a Plateau," pp. 110–11, 165 in Linda Starke (ed.), *Vital Signs 1995*. New York: Norton.

Kaplan, Morton A. (1957) *System and Process in International Politics*. New York: Wiley.

Kaplan, Morton A., and Nicholas DeB. Katzenbach. (1961) *The Political Foundations of International Law*. New York: Wiley.

Kaplan, Robert. (1994) "The Coming Anarchy," *Atlantic Monthly* 273 (February): 44–76.

Kaplan, Stephen S. (1981) *Diplomacy of Power*. Washington, D.C.: Brookings Institution.

Kapstein, Ethan Barnaby. (1991–1992) "We Are Us: The Myth of the Multinational," *The National Interest* 26 (Winter): 55–62.

Karatnycky, Adrian. (1997) "Skeptical about Democracy? Look at the Record," *International Herald Tribune* (December 30): 8.

Karatnycky, Adrian, and Jessica Cashdan. (1997) "Liberty's Ebb and Flow," *Christian Science Monitor* 89 (May 9): 18–19.

Keeley, Lawrence. (1996) *War Before Civilization*. New York: Oxford University Press.

Keeny, Spurgeon M., Jr. (1993) "Arms Control during the Transition to the Post-Soviet World," pp. 175–97 in Joseph Kruzel (ed.), *American Defense Annual*, 8th ed. New York: Lexington Books.

Keeny, Spurgeon M., Jr., and Wolfgang K. H. Panofsky. (1981) "MAD vs. NUTS: Can Doctrine or Weaponry Remedy the Mutual Hostage Relationship of the Superpowers?" *Foreign Affairs* 60 (Winter): 287–304.

Kegley, Charles W., Jr. (ed.). (1995) *Controversies in International Relations Theory: Realism and the Neoliberal Challenge.* New York: St. Martin's Press.

———. (1993) "The Neoidealist Moment in International Studies? Realist Myths and the New International Realities," *International Studies Quarterly* 37 (June): 131–46.

Kegley, Charles W., Jr., and Margaret G. Hermann. (1997) "Putting Military Intervention into the Democratic Peace: A Research Note," *Comparative Political Studies* 30 (February): 78–107

———. (1996) "How Democracies Use Intervention: A Neglected Dimension in Studies of the Democratic Peace," *Journal of Peace Research* 33 (August): 309–20.

Kegley, Charles W., Jr., and Gregory A. Raymond. (1999) *How Nations Make Peace.* New York: St. Martin's/Worth.

———. (1994) *A Multipolar Peace? Great-Power Politics in the Twenty-First Century.* New York: St. Martin's Press.

———. (1990) *When Trust Breaks Down: Alliance Norms and World Politics.* Columbia: University of South Carolina Press.

Kegley, Charles W., Jr., Gregory A. Raymond, and Margaret G. Hermann. (1998) "The Rise and Fall of the Nonintervention Norm: Some Correlates and Potential Consequences," *The Fletcher Forum of World Affairs* 22 (Winter/Spring): 81–101.

Kegley, Charles W., Jr., and Eugene R. Wittkopf. (1996) *American Foreign Policy: Pattern and Process,* 5th ed. New York: St. Martin's Press.

Kelman, Herbert C. (1965) *International Behavior: A Social-Psychological Analysis.* New York: Holt, Rinehart & Winston.

Kelsen, Hans. (1945) *General Theory of Law and State.* Cambridge, Mass.: Harvard University Press.

Kennan, George F. (1984a) *The Fateful Alliance: France, Russia, and the Coming of the First World War.* New York: Pantheon.

———. (1984b) "Soviet–American Relations: The Politics of Discord and Collaboration," pp. 107–20 in Charles W. Kegley, Jr. and Eugene R. Wittkopf (eds.), *The Global Agenda.* New York: Random House.

———. (1982) *The Nuclear Delusion.* New York: Pantheon.

———. (1976) "The United States and the Soviet Union, 1917–1976," *Foreign Affairs* 54 (July): 670–90.

———. (1967) *Memoirs.* Boston: Little, Brown.

———. (1954) *Realities of American Foreign Policy.* Princeton, N.J.: Princeton University Press.

———. (1951) *American Diplomacy, 1900–1950.* New York: New American Library.

——— ["X"]. (1947) "The Sources of Soviet Conduct," *Foreign Affairs* 25 (July): 566–82.

Kennedy, Paul. (1994) "Overpopulation Tilts the Planet," *New Perspectives Quarterly* 11 (Fall): 4–6.

———. (1993) *Preparing for the Twenty-First Century.* New York: Random House.

———. (1992) "A Declining Empire Goes to War," pp. 344–46 in Charles W. Kegley Jr. and Eugene R. Wittkopf (eds.), *The Future of American Foreign Policy.* New York: St. Martin's Press.

———. (1987) *The Rise and Fall of the Great Powers.* New York: Random House.

Keohane, Robert O. (1989) "International Relations Theory: Contributions from a Feminist Standpoint," *Millennium* 18 (Summer): 245–53.

———. (ed.). (1986a) *Neorealism and Its Critics.* New York: Columbia University Press.

———. (1986b) "Realism, Neorealism and the Study of World Politics," pp. 1–26 in Robert O. Keohane (ed.), *Neorealism and Its Critics.* New York: Columbia University Press.

———. (1984) *After Hegemony: Cooperation and Discord in the World Political Economy.* Princeton, N.J.: Princeton University Press.

———. (1983) "Theory of World Politics: Structural Realism and Beyond," pp. 503–40 in Ada Finifter (ed.), *Political Science: The State of the Discipline.* Washington, D.C.: American Political Science Association.

Keohane, Robert O., and Stanley Hoffmann. (1991) "Institutional Change in Europe in the 1980s," pp. 1–39 in Robert O. Keohane and Stanley Hoffmann (eds.), *The New European Community: Decisionmaking and Institutional Change.* Boulder, Colo.: Westview.

Keohane, Robert O., and Joseph S. Nye, Jr. (1989) *Power and Interdependence,* 2nd ed. Glenview, Ill.: Scott, Foresman/Little, Brown.

———. (1988) "Complex Interdependence, Transnational Relations, and Realism: Alternative Perspectives on World Politics," pp. 257–71 in Charles W. Kegley, Jr. and Eugene R. Wittkopf (eds.), *The Global Agenda,* 2nd ed. New York: Random House.

———. (1977) *Power and Interdependence.* Boston: Little, Brown.

Khripunov, Igor. (1997) "Have Guns Will Travel," *Bulletin of the Atomic Scientists* 53 (May–June): 47–51.

Kidder, Rushworth, M. (1990) "Why Modern Terrorism?" pp. 135–38 in Charles W. Kegley, Jr. (ed.), *International Terrorism: Characteristics, Causes, Controls.* New York: St. Martin's Press.

Kidron, Michael, and Ronald Segal. (1995) *The State of the World Atlas,* new rev. 5th ed. London: Penguin Reference.

Kim, Samuel S. (1991) "The United Nations, Lawmaking and World Order," pp. 109–24 in Richard A. Falk, Samuel S. Kim, and Saul H. Mendlovitz (eds.), *The United Nations and a Just World Order.* Boulder, Colo.: Westview.

Kindleberger, Charles P. (1973) *The World in Depression, 1929–1939.* Berkeley: University of California Press.

Kinnas, J. N. (1997) "Global Challenges and Multilateral Diplomacy," pp. 23–48 in Ludwik Dembinski (ed.), *International Geneva Yearbook.* Berne, Switzerland: Peter Lang.

Kinsella, Kevin G. (1994) "An Aging World Population," *World Health* 47 (July–August): 6.

Kirschten, Dick. (1994) "No Refuge," *National Journal* (September 10): 2068–73.

Kissinger, Henry A. (1997) "A World We Have Not Known," *Newsweek* (January 27): 74–81.

———. (1994) *Diplomacy.* New York: Simon & Schuster.

———. (1992) "Balance of Power Sustained," pp. 238–48 in Graham Allison and Gregory F. Treverton (eds.), *Rethinking America's Security: Beyond Cold War to New World Order.* New York: Norton.

———. (1979) *White House Years.* Boston: Little, Brown.

———. (1969) "Domestic Structure and Foreign Policy," pp. 261–75 in James N. Rosenau (ed.), *International Politics and Foreign Policy.* New York: Free Press.

———. (1994) "Adding Fuel to the Fires: The Conventional Arms Trade in the 1990s," pp. 134–54 in Michael T. Klare and Daniel C. Thomas (eds.), *World Security.* New York: St. Martin's Press.

———. (1993) "The Next Great Arms Race," *Foreign Affairs* 72 (Summer): 136–52.

———. (1990a) "An Arms Control Agenda for the Third World," *Arms Control Today* 20 (April 1990): 8–12.

———. (1990b) "Wars in the 1990s: Growing Firepower in the Third World," *Bulletin of Atomic Scientists* 46 (May): 9–13.

———. (1988) "Low-Intensity Conflict," *Christianity and Crisis* 48 (February 1): 11–14.

———. (1987) "The Arms Trade: Changing Patterns in the 1980s," *Third World Quarterly* 9 (October): 1257–81.

———. (1985) "Leaping the Firebreak," pp. 168–73 in Charles W. Kegley, Jr. and Eugene R. Wittkopf (eds.), *The Nuclear Reader: Strategy, Weapons, War*. New York: St. Martin's Press.

Klare, Michael T., and Daniel C. Thomas (eds.). (1991) *World Security: Trends and Challenges at Century's End*. New York: St. Martin's Press.

Kluckhohn, Clyde. (1944) "Anthropological Research and World Peace," pp. 143–52 in L. Bryson, Laurence Finkelstein, and Robert MacIver (eds.), *Approaches to World Peace*. New York: Conference on Science, Philosophy, and Religion.

Knickerbocker, Brad. (1994) "Report on Environment Paints Sober Picture of World's Future," *The Christian Science Monitor* 87 (March 23): 7.

Knorr, Klaus. (1977) "International Economic Leverage and Its Uses," pp. 99–126 in Klaus Knorr and Frank N. Trager (eds.), *Economic Issues and National Security*. Lawrence: Regents Press of Kansas.

———. (1975) *The Power of Nations*. New York: Basic Books.

Knorr, Klaus, and James N. Rosenau (eds.). (1969) *Contending Approaches to International Politics*. Princeton, N.J.: Princeton University Press.

Knorr, Klaus, and Sidney Verba (eds.). (1961) *The International System*. Princeton, N.J.: Princeton University Press.

Kober, Stanley. (1990) "Idealpolitik," *Foreign Policy* 79 (Summer): 3–24.

Kobrin, Stephen J. (1997) "Electronic Cash and the End of National Markets," *Foreign Policy* 107 (Summer): 65–77.

Kohn, Hans. (1944) *The Meaning of Nationalism*. New York: Macmillan.

Kokoski, Richard. (1994) "Non-Lethal Weapons: A Case Study of New Technology Developments," pp. 367–88 in the Stockholm International Peace Research Institute, *SIPRI Yearbook 1994*. New York: Oxford University Press.

Korany, Bahgat. (1986) *How Foreign Policy Decisions Are Made in the Third World*. Boulder, Colo.: Westview.

Korb, Lawrence J. (1995a) "The Indefensible Defense Budget," *Washington Post National Weekly Edition* 12 (July 17–23): 19.

———. (1995b) "Our Overstuffed Armed Forces," *Foreign Affairs* 74 (November/December): 23–34.

Koretz, Gene. (1996) "Fewer Guns, More Butter," *Business Week* (July 1): 22.

Korten, David. (1995) *When Corporations Rule the World*. West Hartford, Conn.: Berrett–Koehler.

Krasner, Stephen D. (1993) "International Political Economy," pp. 453–55 in Joel Krieger (ed.), *The Oxford Companion to Politics of the World*. New York: Oxford University Press.

———. (1979) "The Tokyo Round: Particularistic Interests and Prospects for Stability in the Global Trading System," *International Studies Quarterly* 23 (December): 491–531.

Krauthammer, Charles. (1991) "The Unipolar Moment," *Foreign Affairs* 70 (no. 1): 23–33.

Kristof, Nicholas D. (1993) "The Rise of China," *Foreign Affairs* 72 (November/December): 59–74.

Kruzel, Joseph. (1993) "American Security Policy in a New World Order," pp. 1–23 in Joseph Kruzel (ed.), *American Defense Annual*, 8th ed. New York: Lexington Books.

———. (1991) "Arms Control, Disarmament, and the Stability of the Postwar Era," pp. 247–69 in Charles W. Kegley, Jr. (ed.), *The Long Postwar Peace*. New York: HarperCollins.

Kugler, Jacek. (1993) "War," pp. 962–66 in Joel Krieger (ed.), *The Oxford Companion to Politics of the World*. New York: Oxford University Press.

Kugler, Jacek, and Douglas Lemke (eds.). (1996) *Parity and War*. Ann Arbor: University of Michigan Press.

Kunz, Josef L. (1960) "Sanctions in International Law," *American Journal of International Law* 54 (April): 324–47.

Lake, David A. (1992) "Powerful Pacifists: Democratic States and War," *American Political Science Review* 86 (March): 24–37.

Langer, William L. (1962) "Farewell to Empire," *Foreign Affairs* 41 (October): 115–30.

Laqueur, Walter. (1998) "Postmodern Terrorism," pp. 89–98 in Charles W. Kegley, Jr. and Eugene R. Wittkopf (eds.), *The Global Agenda*, 5th ed. New York: McGraw-Hill.

———. (1986) "Reflections on Terrorism," *Foreign Affairs* 65 (Fall): 86–100.

Larson, Deborah Welch. (1997) *Anatomy of Mistrust: U.S.–Soviet Relations During the Cold War*. Ithaca, N.Y.: Cornell University Press.

Laurenti, Jeffrey. (1995) *National Taxpayers, International Organizations*. New York: United Nations Association of the United States.

Lebow, Richard Ned. (1996) *The Art of Bargaining*. Baltimore: The Johns Hopkins University Press.

———. (1981) *Between Peace and War: The Nature of International Crisis*. Baltimore: The Johns Hopkins University Press.

Lebow, Richard Ned, and Janice Gross Stein. (1994) *We All Lost the Cold War*. Princeton, N.J.: Princeton University Press.

Lee, Rensselaer W., III. (1995) "Global Reach: The Threat of International Drug Trafficking," *Current History* 94 (May): 207–11.

Leventhal, Paul L. (1992) "Plugging the Leaks in Nuclear Export Controls: Why Bother?" *Orbis* 36 (Spring): 167–80.

Levi, Isaac. (1990) *Hard Choices: Decision Making under Unresolved Conflict*. New York: Cambridge University Press.

Levy, Jack S. (1999) *Power, Politics, and Perception: Essays on the Causes of War*. Columbia: University of South Carolina Press.

———. (1998) "Towards a New Millennium: Structural Perspectives on the Causes of War," pp. 47–57 in Charles W. Kegley, Jr. and Eugene R. Wittkopf (eds.), *The Global Agenda*, 5th ed. New York: McGraw-Hill.

———. (1992) "An Introduction to Prospect Theory," *Political Psychology* 13 (June): 171–86.

———. (1991) "Long Cycles, Hegemonic Transitions, and the Long Peace," pp. 147–76 in Charles W. Kegley, Jr. (ed.), *The Long Postwar Peace*. New York: HarperCollins.

———. (1990–1991) "Preferences, Constraints, and Choices in July 1914," *International Security* 15 (Winter): 151–86.

———. (1989a) "The Causes of War: A Review of Theories and Evidence," pp. 209–333 in Philip E. Tetlock, Jo L. Husbands, Robert Jervis, Paul C. Stern, and Charles Tilly (eds.), *Behavior, Society, and Nuclear War*. New York: Oxford University Press.

———. (1989b) "The Diversionary Theory of War: A Critique," pp. 259–88 in Manus I. Midlarsky (ed.), *Handbook of War Studies*. Boston: Unwin Hyman.

Levy, Marc A. (1995) "Is the Environment a National Security Issue?" *International Security* 20 (Fall): 35–62.

Lewis, George, and Theodore Postol. (1997) "Portrait of a Bad Idea," *Bulletin of the Atomic Scientists* 53 (July/August): 18–24.

Lewontin, R. C., Steven Rose, and Leon J. Kamin. (1984) *Not in Our Genes: Biology, Ideology, and Human Nature.* New York: Pantheon.

Leyton-Brown, David. (1987) "Introduction," pp. 1–4 in David Leyton-Brown (ed.), *The Utility of International Economic Sanctions.* New York: St. Martin's Press.

Licklider, Roy. (1995) "The Consequences of Negotiated Settlements in Civil Wars, 1945–1993," *American Political Science Review* 89 (September): 681–90.

Lifton, Robert Jay, and Richard Falk. (1982) *Indefensible Weapons: The Political and Psychological Case against Nuclearism.* New York: Basic Books.

Lind, Michael. (1993) "Of Arms and the Woman," *New Republic* 209 (November 15): 36–38.

Lindblom, Charles E. (1979) "Still Muddling, Not Yet Through," *Public Administration Review* 39 (November/December): 517–26.

Linden, Eugene. (1996) "The Exploding Cities of the Developing World," *Foreign Affairs* 75 (January/February): 52–65.

Lindsay, James M. (1986) "Trade Sanctions as Policy Instruments: A Re–examination," *International Studies Quarterly* 30 (June): 153–73.

Lipow, Jonathan. (1990) "Defense, Growth, and Disarmament: A Further Look," *Jerusalem Journal of International Relations* 12 (June): 49–59.

Liska, George. (1968) *Alliances and the Third World.* Baltimore: Johns Hopkins University Press.

———. (1962) *Nations in Alliance: The Limits of Interdependence.* Baltimore: Johns Hopkins University Press.

Lissitzyn, Oliver J. (1963) "International Law in a Divided World," *International Conciliation* 542 (March): 3–69.

Little, David. (1993) "The Recovery of Liberalism," *Ethics and International Affairs* 7: 171–201.

Lopez, George A., and David Cortright. (1995) "Economic Sanctions in Contemporary Global Relations," pp. 3–16 in David Cortright and George A. Lopez (eds.), *Economic Sanctions.* Boulder, Colo.: Westview.

———. (1993) "Sanctions: Do They Work?" *Bulletin of the Atomic Scientists* 49 (November): 14–15.

Lopez, George A., Jackie G. Smith, and Ron Pagnucco. (1995) "The Global Tide," *Bulletin of the Atomic Scientists* 51 (July/August): 33–39.

Lorenz, Konrad. (1963) *On Aggression.* New York: Harcourt, Brace & World.

Low, Patrick. (1993) *Trading Free: The GATT and U.S. Trade Policy.* New York: Twentieth Century Fund Press.

Lundestad, Geir. (1994) *The Fall of the Great Powers.* Oslo: Scandinavian University Press.

Lutz, Wolfgang. (1994) "The Future of World Population," *Population Bulletin* 49 (June): 1–47.

Mack, Andrew. (1996) "Allow the Idea of Nuclear Disarmament a Hearing," *International Herald Tribune* (January 26): 8.

Mackinder, Sir Halford. (1919) *Democratic Ideals and Reality.* New York: Henry A. Holt.

Mahan, Alfred Thayer. (1890) *The Influence of Sea Power in History.* Boston: Little, Brown.

Majeed, Akhtar. (1991) "Has the War System Really Become Obsolete?" *Bulletin of Peace Proposals* 22 (December): 419–25.

Malkin, Lawrence. (1995) "Two New York Banks Join to Become Largest in U.S.," *International Herald Tribune* (August 19): 1, 8.

Mann, Jonathan M., and Daniel J. M. Tarantola. (1995) "Preventive Medicine: A Broader Approach to the AIDS Crisis," *Harvard International Review* 17 (Fall): 46–49, 87.

Mansfield, Edward D., and Jack Snyder. (1995) "Democratization and the Danger of War," *International Security* 20 (Summer): 5–38.

Marantz, Paul. (1987) "Economic Sanctions in the Polish Crisis," pp. 131–46 in David Leyton-Brown (ed.), *The Utility of International Economic Sanctions.* New York: St. Martin's Press.

Marin-Bosch, Miguel. (1998) "Europe's Nuclear Family," *Bulletin of the Atomic Scientists* 54 (January/February): 35–37.

Markusen, Ann, Peter Hall, Scott Campbell, and Sabina Dietrick. (1991) *The Rise of the Gunbelt: The Military Remapping of America.* New York: Oxford University Press.

Marshall, Ray. (1995) "The Global Jobs Crisis," *Foreign Policy* 100 (Fall): 50–68.

Mastanduno, Michael. (1991) "Do Relative Gains Matter? America's Response to Japanese Industrial Policy," *International Security* 16 (Summer): 73–113.

Masters, Roger D. (1969) "World Politics as a Primitive Political System," pp. 104–18 in James N. Rosenau (ed.), *International Politics and Foreign Policy.* New York: Free Press.

Mathews, Jessica T. (1997) "Power Shift: The Rise of Global Civil Society," *Foreign Affairs* 76 (January/February): 50–66.

———. (1996) "Global Warming: No Longer in Doubt," *Washington Post National Weekly Edition* 13 (January 1–7): 29.

———. (1991) "Iraq's Nuclear Warning," *Washington Post National Weekly Edition* 9 (July 22–28): 19.

———. (1989) "Redefining Security," *Foreign Affairs* 68 (Spring): 162–77.

May, Ernest R., and Philip D. Zelikow (eds.). (1997) *The Kennedy Tapes: Inside the White House during the Cuban Missile Crisis.* Cambridge, Mass.: Harvard University Press.

McGowan, Patrick J. (1981) "Imperialism in World-System Perspective," *International Studies Quarterly* 25 (March): 43–68.

McGranahan, Donald. (1995) "Measurement of Development," *International Social Science Journal* 143 (March): 39–59.

McKibben, Bill. (1998) "The Fortune of Population," *Atlantic Monthly* 286 (May): 55–78.

Mead, Margaret. (1968) "Warfare Is Only an Invention—Not a Biological Necessity," pp. 270–74 in Leon Bramson and George W. Goethals (eds.), *War.* New York: Basic Books.

Mead, Walter Russell. (1995) "Forward to the Past," *New York Times Magazine* (June 4): 48–49.

Meadows, Donella H. (1993) "Seeing the Population Issue Whole," *The World & I* 8 (June): 396–409.

Meadows, Donella H., Dennis L. Meadows, Jørgen Randers, and William W. Behrens III. (1974) *The Limits to Growth.* New York: New American Library.

Mearsheimer, John J. (1990) "Back to the Future: Instability in Europe after the Cold War," *International Security* 15 (Summer): 5–56.

Melanson, Richard A. (1983) *Writing History and Making Policy: The Cold War, Vietnam, and Revisionism.* Lanham, Md.: University Press of America.

Metz, Steven, and James Kievit. (1995) *Strategy and the Revolution in Military Affairs.* Carlisle Barracks, Penn.: U.S. Army War College.

Michaels, Marguerite. (1993) "Blue-Helmet Blues," *Time* (November 15): 66–67.

Midlarsky, Manus I. (1988) *The Onset of World War.* Boston: Unwin Hyman.

Miller, Marian A. L. (1995) *The Third World in Global Environmental Politics.* Boulder, Colo.: Lynne Rienner.

Mills, C. Wright. (1956) *The Power Elite.* New York: Oxford University Press.

Mitrany, David. (1966) *A Working Peace System.* Chicago: Quadrangle.

Mittelman, James H. (ed.). (1997) *Globalization: Critical Reflections.* Boulder, Colo.: Lynne Rienner.

Modelski, George (ed.). (1987a) *Exploring Long Cycles.* Boulder, Colo.: Lynne Rienner.

———. (1987b) "The Study of Long Cycles," pp. 1–15 in George Modelski (ed.), *Exploring Long Cycles.* Boulder, Colo.: Lynne Rienner.

———. (1978) "The Long Cycle of Global Politics and the Nation-State," *Comparative Studies in Society and History* 20 (April): 214–35.

———. (1964) "The International Relations of Internal War," pp. 14–44 in James N. Rosenau (ed.), *International Aspects of Civil Strife.* Princeton, N.J.: Princeton University Press.

Modelski, George, and William R. Thompson. (1996) *Leading Sectors and World Powers.* Columbia: University of South Carolina Press.

———. (1989) "Long Cycles and Global War," pp. 23–54 in Manus I. Midlarsky (ed.), *Handbook of War Studies.* Boston: Unwin Hyman.

Moffett, George D. (1994) *Critical Masses: The Global Population Challenge.* New York: Viking.

Moisy, Claude. (1997) "Myths of the Global Information Village," *Foreign Policy* 107 (Summer): 78–87.

Møller, Bjørn. (1992) *Common Security and Nonoffensive Defense: A Neorealist Perspective.* Boulder, Colo.: Lynne Rienner.

Moon, Bruce E., and William J. Dixon. (1992) "Basic Needs and Growth–Welfare Trade-offs," *International Studies Quarterly* 36 (June): 191–212.

———. (1985) "Politics, the State, and Basic Human Needs: A Cross-National Study," *American Journal of Political Science* 29 (November): 661–94.

Moore, Mike. (1995) "Midnight Never Came," *Bulletin of the Atomic Scientists* 51 (November/December): 16–27.

Moran, Theodore H. (1991) "International Economics and U.S. Security," *Foreign Affairs* 69 (Winter): 74–90.

Moravcsik, Andrew. (1997) "Taking Preferences Seriously: A Liberal Theory of International Politics," *International Organization* 51 (Autumn): 513–53.

Morgan, T. Clifton, and Kenneth N. Bickers. (1992) "Domestic Discontent and the External Use of Force," *Journal of Conflict Resolution* 36 (March): 25–52.

Morgan, T. Clifton, and Sally Howard Campbell. (1991) "Domestic Structure, Decisional Constraints and War," *Journal of Conflict Resolution* 35 (June): 187–211.

Morgan, T. Clifton, and Valerie L. Schwebach. (1992) "Take Two Democracies and Call Me in the Morning: A Prescription for Peace?" *International Interactions* 17 (no. 4): 305–20.

Morgenthau, Hans J. (1985) *Politics among Nations,* 6th ed. Revised by Kenneth W. Thompson. New York: Knopf.

———. (1983) "Defining the National Interest—Again," pp. 32–39 in Charles W. Kegley, Jr. and Eugene R. Wittkopf (eds.), *Perspectives on American Foreign Policy.* New York: St. Martin's Press.

———. (1959) "Alliances in Theory and Practice," pp. 184–212 in Arnold Wolfers (ed.), *Alliance Policy in the Cold War.* Baltimore: The Johns Hopkins University Press.

———. (1948) *Politics among Nations.* New York: Knopf.

Morley, Samuel A. (1994) *Poverty and Inequality in Latin America: Past Evidence, Future Prospects.* Washington, D.C.: Overseas Development Council.

Morris, Desmond. (1969) *The Human Zoo.* New York: Dell.

Mowlana, Hamid. (1995) "The Communications Paradox," *Bulletin of the Atomic Scientists* 51 (July): 40.

———. (1983) "Needed: A New World Information Order," *USA Today* 112 (September): 42–44.

Mueller, John. (1989) *Retreat from Doomsday: The Obsolescence of Major War.* New York: Basic Books.

Mulhollin, Gary. (1994) "The Business of Defense Is Defending Business," *Washington Post National Weekly Edition* 11 (February 14–20): 23.

Nardin, Terry. (1983) *Law, Morality, and the Relations of States.* Princeton, N.J.: Princeton University Press.

Nardin, Terry, and David R. Mapel (eds.). (1992) *Traditions of International Ethics.* New York: Cambridge University Press.

Nathan, James A. (1997) "Can Economic Sanctions Succeed as Foreign Policy?" *USA Today* 126 (September): 37.

Neier, Aryeh. (1995) "War Crime Doesn't Pay," *Washington Post* (July 30): C2.

Nelson, Stephan D. (1974) "Nature/Nurture Revisited: A Review of the Biological Bases of Conflict," *Journal of Conflict Resolution* 18 (June): 285–335.

Neuman, Johanna. (1995–1996) "The Media's Impact on International Affairs, Then and Now," *The National Interest* 16 (Winter): 109–23.

Neumann, Iver B., and Ole Waever (eds.). (1997) *The Future of International Relations: Masters in the Making?* London: Routledge.

Newark, John W. (1995) "Foreign Aid in the 1990s: The New Realities," pp. 223–44 in Manochehr Dorraj (ed.), *The Changing Political Economy of the Third World.* Boulder, Colo.: Lynne Rienner.

Newland, Kathleen. (1994) "Refugees: The Rising Flood," *World Watch* 7 (May/June): 10–20.

Nicholson, Michael. (1992) *Rationality and the Analysis of International Conflict.* Cambridge, Eng.: Cambridge University Press.

Niebuhr, Reinhold. (1947) *Moral Man and Immoral Society.* New York: Scribner's.

Nietschmann, Bernard. (1991) "Third World War: The Global Conflict over the Rights of Indigenous Nations," pp. 172–76 in Robert M. Jackson (ed.), *Global Issues 91/92.* Guilford, Conn.: Dushkin.

———. (1982) *The Arms Race: The Political Economy of Military Growth.* New York: Praeger.

Nnoli, Okwudiba. (1993) "Ethnicity," pp. 280–84 in Joel Krieger (ed.), *The Oxford Companion to Politics of the World.* New York: Oxford University Press.

Nye, Joseph S., Jr. (1998) "The Changing Nature of World Power," pp. 108–20 in Charles W. Kegley, Jr. and Eugene R. Wittkopf (eds.), *The Global Agenda,* 5th ed. New York: McGraw-Hill.

———. (1990) *Bound to Lead: The Changing Nature of American Power.* New York: Basic Books.

———. (1988) "Neorealism and Neoliberalism," *World Politics* 40 (January): 235–51.

———. (1987) "Nuclear Learning and U.S.–Soviet Security Regimes," *International Organization* 41 (Summer): 371–402.

Nye, Joseph S., and William A. Owens. (1996) "America's Information Edge," *Foreign Affairs* 75 (March/April): 20–36.

Oberdorfer, Don. (1991) *The Turn: From the Cold War to a New Era.* New York: Poseidon.

O'Brien, Conor Cruise. (1993) "The Wrath of Ages," *Foreign Affairs* 72 (November/December): 142–49.

———. (1977) "Liberty and Terrorism," *International Security* 2 (Fall): 56–67.

O'Brien, Richard. (1992) *Global Financial Integration: The End of Geography.* New York: Council on Foreign Relations Press.

Olson, Mancur. (1971) "Rapid Growth as a Destabilizing Force," pp. 215–27 in James C. Davies (ed.), *When Men Revolt and Why.* New York: Free Press.

Onuf, Nicholas Greenwood. (1989) *World of Our Making: Rules and Rule in Social Theory and International Relations.* Columbia: University of South Carolina Press.

———. (1982) "Global Law-Making and Legal Thought," pp. 1–82 in Nicholas Greenwood Onuf (ed.), *Law-Making in the Global Community.* Durham, N.C.: Carolina Academic Press.

Organski, A. F. K. (1968) *World Politics.* New York: Knopf.

Organski, A. F. K., and Jacek Kugler. (1980) *The War Ledger.* Chicago: University of Chicago Press.

Osgood, Robert E. (1968) *Alliances and American Foreign Policy.* Baltimore: Johns Hopkins University Press.

Ostrom, Charles W., and Brian L. Job. (1986) "The President and the Use of Force," *American Political Science Review* 80 (June): 554–66.

Packenham, Robert. (1992) *The Dependency Movement: Scholarship and Politics in Dependency Studies.* Cambridge, Mass.: Harvard University Press.

Paddock, William, and Paul Paddock. (1967) *Famine—1975!* Boston: Little, Brown.

Paget, Karen M. (1995) "Can't Touch This? The Pentagon's Budget Fortress," *The American Prospect* 23 (Fall): 37–43.

Parry, Clive. (1968) "The Function of Law in the International Community," pp. 1–54 in Max Sorensen (ed.), *Manual of Public International Law.* New York: St. Martin's Press.

Passel, Jeffrey S., and Michael Fix. (1994) "Myths about Immigrants," *Foreign Policy* 95 (Summer): 151–60.

Payne, James E., and Anandi P. Sahu (eds.). (1993) *Defense Spending and Economic Growth.* Boulder, Colo.: Westview.

Pear, Robert. (1997) "AIDS' Numbers Make a Giant Leap," *International Herald Journal* (November 27): 1, 6.

Pearson, Frederic S., Robert A. Baumann, and Jeffrey J. Pickering. (1991) "International Military Intervention: Global and Regional Redefinitions of Realpolitik." Paper presented at the Annual Meeting of the American Political Science Association, Washington, D.C., August 29–September 1.

Peirce, Neal R. (1997) "Does the Nation-State Have a Future?" *International Herald Tribune* (April 4): 9.

Peterson, Erik. (1998) "Looming Collision of Capitalisms?" pp. 296–307 in Charles W. Kegley, Jr. and Eugene R. Wittkopf (eds.), *The Global Agenda,* 5th ed. New York: McGraw-Hill.

Peterson, V. Spike, and Anne Sisson Runyan. (1993) *Global Gender Issues.* Boulder, Colo.: Westview.

Pfaff, William. (1996) "Seeking a Broader Vision of Economic Society," *International Herald Tribune* (February 3–4): 6.

Philips, Rosemarie, and Stuart K. Tucker. (1991) *U.S. Foreign Policy and Developing Countries: Discourse and Data 1991.* Washington, D.C.: Overseas Development Council.

Phillips, David. (1993) "Dolphins and GATT," pp. 133–38 in Ralph Nader (ed.), *The Case Against Free Trade.* San Francisco: Earth Island Press.

Pierre, Andrew J. (1984) "The Politics of International Terrorism," pp. 84–92 in Charles W. Kegley, Jr. and Eugene R. Wittkopf (eds.), *The Global Agenda.* New York: Random House.

Pipes, Richard. (1977) "Why the Soviet Union Thinks It Could Fight and Win a Nuclear War," *Commentary* 26 (July): 21–34.

Pirages, Dennis. (1998) "An Ecological Approach to International Relations," pp. 387–94 in Charles W. Kegley, Jr. and Eugene R. Wittkopf (eds.), *The Global Agenda,* 5th ed. New York: McGraw-Hill.

Population Reference Bureau. (1995) *1995 World Population Data Sheet.* Washington, D.C.: Population Reference Bureau.

———. (1981) *World Population: Toward the Next Century.* Washington, D.C.: Population Reference Bureau.

Porter, Bruce D. (1994) *War and the Rise of the State.* New York: Free Press.

Porter, Gareth. (1995) "Environmental Security as a National Security Issue," *Current History* 94 (May): 218–22.

Porter, Gareth, and Janet Welsh Brown. (1996) *Global Environmental Politics,* 2nd ed. Boulder, Colo.: Westview.

Postel, Sandra. (1994) "Carrying Capacity: Earth's Bottom Line," pp. 39–55 in Lester R. Brown et al., *State of the World 1994.* New York: Norton.

Potter, William C. (1992) "The New Nuclear Suppliers," *Orbis* 46 (Spring): 199–210.

Pound, Edward T., and Jihan El-Tahri. (1994) "Sanctions: The Pluses and Minus," *U.S. News & World Report* (October 31): 58–71.

Powers, Thomas. (1994) "Downwinders: Some Casualities of the Nuclear Age," *Atlantic Monthly* 273 (March): 119–24.

Puchala, Donald J. (1994) "Some World Order Options for Our Time," *Peace Forum* 11 (November): 17–30.

Putnam, Robert D. (1988) "Diplomacy and Domestic Politics: The Logic of Two-Level Games," *International Organization* 42 (Summer): 427–60.

Quester, George. (1992) "Conventional Deterrence: The Past as Prologue," pp. 31–51 in Gary L. Guertner, Robert Haffa, Jr., and George Quester, *Conventional Forces and the Future of Deterrence.* Carlisle Barracks, Penn.: U.S. Army War College.

Quinn, Dennis. (1997) "The Correlates of Change in International Financial Regulation," *American Political Science Review* 91 (September): 531–51.

Rapkin, David, and William Thompson, with Jon A. Christopherson. (1989) "Bipolarity and Bipolarization in the Cold War Era," *Journal of Conflict Resolution* 23 (June): 261–95.

Ratner, Stephen A. (1997) *The New UN Peacekeeping: Building Peace in Lands of Conflict After the Cold War.* New York: St. Martin's Press.

Ray, James Lee. (1995) *Democracy and International Conflict: An Evaluation of the Democratic Peace Proposition.* Columbia: University of South Carolina Press.

Raymond, Gregory A. (1994) "Democracies, Disputes, and Third-Party Intermediaries," *Journal of Conflict Resolution* 38 (March): 24–42.

Reardon, Betty. (1985) *Sexism and the War System.* New York: Teachers College Press.

Regan, Patrick M. (1994) *Organizing Societies for War: The Process and Consequences of Societal Militarization*. Westport, Conn.: Praeger.

Reich, Robert. (1990) "Who Is Us?" *Harvard Business Review* 68 (January–February): 53–64.

Reinicke, Wolfgang H. (1997) "Global Public Policy," *Foreign Affairs* 76 (November/December): 127–38.

Reno, Robert. (1993) "Defense Conversion Bombs Out," *The State* (Columbia, S.C.) (April 2): A15.

Repetto, Robert, and Jonathan Lash. (1997) "Planetary Roulette: Gambling with the Climate," *Foreign Policy* 108 (Fall): 84–98.

Richardson, Lewis F. (1960a) *Arms and Insecurity*. Pittsburgh: Boxwood Press.

———. (1960b) *Statistics of Deadly Quarrels*. Chicago: Quadrangle.

Richardson, Michael. (1995) "Fears of a Militarily Resurgent Japan," *International Herald Journal Tribune* (August 15): 1, 7.

Richardson, Neil R. (1995) "International Trade as a Force for Peace," pp. 281–93 in Charles W. Kegley, Jr. (ed.), *Controversies in International Relations Theory*. New York: St. Martin's Press.

Riddell-Dixon, Elizabeth. (1995) "Social Movements and the United Nations," *International Social Science Journal* 144 (June): 289–303.

Ridley, Matt. (1998) *The Origins of Virtue: Human Instincts and the Evolution of Cooperation*. New York: Viking.

Riggs, Robert E., and Jack C. Plano. (1994) *The United Nations: International Organization and World Politics*, 2nd ed. Belmont, Calif.: Wadsworth.

Riker, William H. (1962) *The Theory of Political Coalitions*. New Haven, Conn.: Yale University Press.

Roca, Sergio. (1987) "Economic Sanctions against Cuba," pp. 87–104 in David Leyton-Brown (ed.), *The Utility of International Economic Sanctions*. New York: St. Martin's Press.

Rodrik, Dani. (1997a) *Has Globalization Gone Too Far?* Washington, D.C.: Institute for International Economics.

———. (1997b) "Sense and Nonsense in the Globalization Debate," *Foreign Policy* 107 (Summer): 19–37.

Rosati, Jerel A., Joe D. Hagan, and Martin W. Sampson III (eds.). (1994) *Foreign Policy Restructuring: How Governments Respond to Global Change*. Columbia: University of South Carolina Press.

Rosecrance, Richard. (1997) "Economics and National Security: The Evolutionary Process," pp. 209–38 in Richard Shultz, Roy Godson, and George Quester (eds.), *Security Studies for the Twenty-First Century*. New York: Brassey's.

Rosen, Steven J. (ed.). (1973) *Testing the Theory of the Military-Industrial Complex*. Lexington, Mass.: Heath.

Rosenau, James N. (1998) "Disorder and Order in a Turbulent World: The Evolution of Globalized Space," pp. 145–69 in Charles W. Kegley, Jr. and Eugene R. Wittkopf (eds.), *The Global Agenda*, 5th ed. New York: McGraw-Hill.

———. (1997) *Along the Domestic-Foreign Frontier: Exploring Governance in a Turbulent World*. Cambridge, Eng.: Cambridge University Press.

———. (1995) "Security in a Turbulent World," *Current History* 94 (May): 193–200.

———. (1990) *Turbulence in World Politics: A Theory of Change and Continuity*. Princeton, N.J.: Princeton University Press.

———. (1980) *The Scientific Study of Foreign Policy*. New York: Nichols.

Rosenau, Pauline Marie. (1992) *Post-Modernism and the Social Sciences*. Princeton, N.J.: Princeton University Press.

Rosenberg, Shawn W. (1988) *Reason, Ideology and Politics*. Princeton, N.J.: Princeton University Press.

Rosenthal, Joel H. (1991) *Righteous Realists*. Baton Rouge: Louisiana State University Press.

Ross, Philip E. (1997) "The End of Infantry?" *Forbes* 160 (July 7): 182–85.

Rostow, W. W. (1960) *The Stages of Economic Growth*. Cambridge, Eng.: Cambridge University Press.

Rothgeb, John M., Jr. (1993) *Defining Power: Influence and Force in the Contemporary International System*. New York: St. Martin's Press.

Ruggie, John Gerald. (1993) "Wandering in the Void: Charting the U.N.'s New Strategic Role," *Foreign Affairs* 72 (November/December): 27–31.

———. (1983) "Continuity and Transformation in the World Polity: Toward a Neorealist Synthesis," *World Politics* 35 (January): 261–85.

Rummel, Rudolph J. (1994) *Death by Government*. New Brunswick, N.J.: Transaction Books.

———. (1983) "Libertarianism and International Violence," *Journal of Conflict Resolution* 27 (March): 27–71.

Rupert, James. (1995) "The Cloud over Chernobyl," *Washington Post National Weekly Edition* 12 (June 26–July 2): 6–7.

Rusi, Alpo. (1997) *Dangerous Peace*. Boulder, Colo.: Westview.

Russett, Bruce. (1998) "A Community of Peace: Democracy, Interdependence, and International Organization," pp. 241–51 in Charles W. Kegley, Jr. and Eugene R. Wittkopf (eds.), *The Global Agenda*, 5th ed. New York: McGraw-Hill.

———. (1995) "The Democratic Peace: 'And Yet It Moves'," *International Security* 19 (Spring): 164–75.

———. (1993) *Grasping the Democratic Peace: Principles for a Post–Cold War World*. Princeton, N.J.: Princeton University Press.

———. (1982) "Defense Expenditures and National Well-Being," *American Political Science Review* 76 (December): 767–77.

Russett, Bruce, and Harvey Starr. (1996) *World Politics: The Menu for Choice*, 5th ed. New York: Freeman.

Russett, Bruce, and James S. Sutterlin. (1991) "The U.N. in a New World Order," *Foreign Affairs* 70 (Spring): 69–83.

Sachs, Aaron. (1996) "Upholding Human Rights and Environmental Justice," pp. 133–51 in Lester R. Brown et al. (eds.), *State of the World 1996*. New York: Norton.

Sachs, Jeffrey. (1997) "The Limits of Convergence," *The Economist* 343 (June 14): 19–22.

———. (1989) "Making the Brady Plan Work," *Foreign Affairs* 68 (Summer): 87–104.

Sagan, Carl. (1989) "Understanding Growth Rates: The Secret of the Persian Chessboard," *Parade* (February 14): 14.

———. (1988) "The Common Enemy," *Parade* (February 7): 4–7.

Sagan, Carl, and Richard Turco. (1993) "Nuclear Winter in the Post–Cold War Era," *Journal of Peace Research* 30 (November): 369–73.

Sagan, Scott D. (1993) *The Limits of Safety: Organizations, Accidents, and Nuclear Weapons*. Princeton, N.J.: Princeton University Press.

Sandel, Michael J. (1996) "America's Search for a New Public Philosophy," *Atlantic Monthly* 277 (March): 57–74.

Sandler, Todd, and Keith Hartley. (1995) *The Economics of Defense*. New York: Cambridge University Press.

Scarborough, Grace E. Iusi, and Bruce Bueno de Mesquita. (1988) "Threat and Alignment," *International Interactions* 14 (No. 1): 85–93.

596

Schelling, Thomas C. (1978) *Micromotives and Macrobehavior.* New York: Norton.

———. (1966) *Arms and Influence.* New Haven, Conn.: Yale University Press.

Schlagheck, Donna M. (1990) "Superpowers, Foreign Policy, and Terrorism," pp. 170–97 in Charles W. Kegley, Jr. (ed.), *International Terrorism.* New York: St. Martin's Press.

Schlesinger, Arthur, Jr. (1997) "Has Democracy a Future?" *Foreign Affairs* 76 (September/October): 2–12.

———. (1986) *The Cycles of American History.* Boston: Houghton Mifflin.

———. (1983) "Pretension in the Presidential Pulpit," *Wall Street Journal* (March 17): 26.

Schneider, Barry R., and Lawrence E. Grinter (eds.). (1995) *Battlefield of the Future: 21st Century Warfare Issues.* Maxwell Air Force Base, Ala.: Air War College.

Schott, Jeffrey J. (1996) *WTO 2000: Setting the Course for the World Trading System.* Washington, D.C.: Institute for Internal Economics.

Schwab, Klaus, and Claude Smadja. (1996) "Start Taking the Backlash Against Globalization Seriously," *International Herald Tribune* (February 1): 1, 8.

Schwartz, Regina M. (1997) *The Curse of Cain: The Violent Legacy of Monotheism.* Chicago, Ill.: University of Chicago Press.

Schweller, Randall L. (1992) "Domestic Structure and Preventive War," *World Politics* 44 (January): 235–69.

Seager, Joni. (1995) *The New State of the Earth Atlas.* New York: Touchstone.

Sebenius, James K. (1991) "Designing Negotiations toward a New Regime: The Case of Global Warming," *International Security* 15 (Spring): 110–48.

Sedjo, Robert A. (1995) "Forests: Conflicting Signals," pp. 177–209 in Ronald Bailey (ed.), *The True State of the Planet.* New York: Free Press.

Sen, Amartya. (1994) "Population: Delusion and Reality," *New York Review of Books* 41 (September 22): 62–71.

Shannon, Thomas Richard. (1989) *An Introduction to the World-System Perspective.* Boulder, Colo.: Westview.

Shaw, Timothy M. (1994) "Beyond Any New World Order: The South in the 21st Century," *Third World Quarterly* 15 (March): 139–46.

Sheehan, Michael. (1996) "A Regional Perspective on the Globalization Process," *Korean Journal of Defense Analysis* 8 (Winter): 53–74.

Shenon, Philip. (1996) "AIDS Epidemic, Late to Arrive, Now Explodes in Populous Asia," *New York Times* (January 21): 1, 8.

Shultz, Richard, Roy Godson, and George Quester (eds.). (1997) *Security Studies for the 21st Century.* New York: Brassey's.

Shultz, Richard H., Jr., and William J. Olson. (1994) *Ethnic and Religious Conflict: Emerging Threat to U.S. Security.* Washington, D.C.: National Strategy Information Center.

Siegel, Martin J. (1983) "Survival," *USA Today* 112 (August): 1–2.

Simmel, Georg. (1956) *Conflict.* Glencoe, Ill.: Free Press.

Simon, Herbert A. (1982) *Models of Bounded Rationality.* Cambridge, Mass.: MIT Press.

———. (1957) *Models of Man.* New York: Wiley.

Simon, Julian L., and Aaron Wildavsky. (1984) "On Species Loss, the Absence of Data, and Risks to Humanity," in Julian L. Simon and Herman Kahn (eds.), *The Resourceful Earth: A Response to Global 2000.* Oxford, Eng.: Blackwell.

Singer, Hans W., and Javed A. Ansari. (1988) *Rich and Poor Countries,* 4th ed. London: Unwin Hyman.

Singer, J. David. (1991) "Peace in the Global System: Displacement, Interregnum, or Transformation?" pp. 56–84 in Charles W. Kegley, Jr. (ed.), *The Long Postwar Peace.* New York: HarperCollins.

———. (1981) "Accounting for International War: The State of the Discipline," *Journal of Peace Research* 18 (No. 1): 1–18.

———. (ed.). (1968) *Quantitative International Politics.* New York: Free Press.

———. (1961) "The Level-of-Analysis Problem in International Relations," pp. 77–92 in Klaus Knorr and Sidney Verba (eds.), *The International System.* Princeton, N.J.: Princeton University Press.

———. (1960) "Theorizing about Theory in International Politics," *Journal of Conflict Resolution* 4 (December): 431–42.

Singer, J. David, and Melvin Small. (1974) "Foreign Policy Indicators," *Policy Sciences* 5 (September): 271–96.

———. (1968) "Alliance Aggregation and the Onset of War, 1815–1945," pp. 247–85 in J. David Singer (ed.), *Quantitative International Politics.* New York: Free Press.

Singer, Max, and Aaron Wildavsky. (1993) *The Real World Order: Zones of Peace/Zones of Turmoil.* Chatham, N.J.: Chatham House.

Sivard, Ruth Leger. (1996) *World Military and Social Expenditures 1996.* Washington, D.C.: World Priorities.

———. (1993) *World Military and Social Expenditures 1993.* Washington, D.C.: World Priorities.

———. (1991) *World Military and Social Expenditures 1991.* Washington, D.C.: World Priorities.

———. (1982) *World Military and Social Expenditures 1982.* Leesburg, Va.: World Priorities.

———. (1979) *World Military and Social Expenditures 1979.* Leesburg, Va.: World Priorities.

Siverson, Randolph M., and Julian Emmons. (1991) "Democratic Political Systems and Alliance Choices," *Journal of Conflict Resolution* 35 (June): 285–306.

Sjolander, Claire Turenne, and Wayne S. Cox (eds.). (1994) *Beyond Positivism: Critical Reflections on International Relations.* Boulder, Colo.: Lynne Rienner.

Skjelsbaek, Kjell. (1991) "The U.S. Secretary-General and the Mediation of International Disputes," *Journal of Peace Research* 28 (February): 99–115.

Sklair, Leslie. (1991) *Sociology of the Global System.* Baltimore: Johns Hopkins University Press.

Slater, Jerome, and David Goldfischer. (1988) "Can SDI Provide a Defense?" pp. 74–86 in Charles W. Kegley, Jr. and Eugene R. Wittkopf (eds.), *The Global Agenda,* 2nd ed. New York: Random House.

Slaughter, Anne-Marie. (1997) "The Real New World Order," *Foreign Affairs* 76 (September–October): 183–97.

Small, Melvin, and J. David Singer. (1982) *Resort to Arms: International and Civil Wars, 1816–1980.* Beverly Hills, Calif.: Sage.

———. (1976) "The War-Proneness of Democratic Regimes, 1816–1965," *Jerusalem Journal of International Relations* 1 (March): 50–69.

———. (1972) "Patterns in International Warfare, 1816–1965," pp. 121–31 in James F. Short, Jr. and Marvin E. Wolfgang (eds.), *Collective Violence.* Chicago: Aldine-Atherton.

Smith, Dan. (1997) *The State of War and Peace Atlas,* 3rd ed. New York: Penguin.

Smith, Ron P., and George Georgiou. (1983) "Assessing the Effect of Military Expenditures on OECD Economies: A Survey," *Arms Control* 4 (May): 3–15.

597

Smith, Steve. (1997) "Bridging the Gap: Social Constructivism," pp. 183–87 in John Baylis and Steve Smith (eds.), *The Globalization of World Politics*. New York: Oxford University Press.

Smith, Steve, and Michael Clarke. (1985) *Foreign Policy Implementation*. London: Allen & Unwin.

Snidal, Duncan. (1993) "Relative Gains and the Pattern of International Cooperation," pp. 181–207 in David A. Baldwin (ed.), *Neorealism and Neoliberalism: The Contemporary Debate*. New York: Columbia University Press.

Snider, Lewis W. (1991) "Guns, Debt, and Politics: New Variations on an Old Theme," *Armed Forces and Society* 17 (Winter): 167–90.

Snyder, Glenn H. (1991) "Alliance Threats: A Neorealist First Cut," pp. 83–103 in Robert L. Rothstein (ed.), *The Evolution of Theory in International Relations*. Columbia: University of South Carolina Press.

———. (1984) "The Security Dilemma in Alliance Politics," *World Politics* 36 (July): 461–95.

Snyder, Glenn H., and Paul Diesing. (1977) *Conflict among Nations: Bargaining, Decision-Making, and System Structure in International Crisis*. Princeton, N.J.: Princeton University Press.

Snyder, Jack. (1993) "The New Nationalism: Realist Interpretations and Beyond," pp. 179–200 in Richard Rosecrance and Anthony A. Stein (eds.), *The Domestic Bases of Grand Strategy*. Ithaca, N.Y.: Cornell University Press.

———. (1991) *Myths of Empire: Domestic Politics and International Ambition*. Ithaca, N.Y.: Cornell University Press.

Sobel, Andrew C. (1994) *Domestic Choices, International Markets: Dismantling National Barriers and Liberalizing Securities Markets*. Ann Arbor, Mich.: University of Michigan Press.

Sollenberg, Margareta, and Peter Wallensteen. (1998) "Major Armed Conflicts," forthcoming in Stockholm International Peace Research Institute, *SIPRI Yearbook 1998*. New York: Oxford University Press.

Somit, Albert. (1990) "Humans, Chimps, and Bonobos: The Biological Bases of Aggression, War, and Peacemaking," *Journal of Conflict Resolution* 34 (September): 553–82.

Sørensen, Georg. (1995) "Four Futures," *Bulletin of the Atomic Scientists* 51 (July/August): 69–72.

Sorensen, Theodore C. (1963) *Decision Making in the White House*. New York: Columbia University Press.

Sorokin, Pitirim A. (1937) *Social and Cultural Dynamics*. New York: American Book.

Soroos, Marvin S. (1998) "The Tragedy of the Commons in Global Perspective," pp. 422–35 in Charles W. Kegley, Jr. and Eugene R. Wittkopf (eds.), *The Global Agenda*, 5th ed. New York: McGraw-Hill.

———. (1986) *Beyond Sovereignty: The Challenge of Global Policy*. Columbia: University of South Carolina Press.

Spanier, John. (1975) *Games Nations Play*, 2nd ed. New York: Praeger.

Spector, Leonard S., and Mark G. McDonough with Evan S. Medeiros. (1995) *Tracking Nuclear Proliferation*. Washington, D.C.: Carnegie Endowment for International Peace.

Spero, Joan E., and Jeffrey A. Hart. (1997) *The Politics of International Economic Relations*, 5th ed. New York: St. Martin's Press.

Spykman, Nicholas. (1944) *Geography of Peace*. New York: Harcourt Brace.

Stanley Foundation. (1993) *The UN Role in Intervention*. Muscatine, Iowa: The Stanley Foundation.

The State of the World's Children 1995. (1995). New York: Oxford University Press.

The State of the World Population 1995. (1995). New York: United Nations Population Fund.

The State of the World Population 1994. (1994). New York: United Nations Population Fund.

Stein, Janice Gross. (1993) "Reassurance in International Conflict Management," pp. 77–97 in Demetrios Caraly and Cerentha Harris (eds.), *New World Politics*. New York: Academy of Political Science.

Stein, Janice Gross, and Louis W. Pauly. (1993) *Choosing to Cooperate: How States Avoid Loss*. Baltimore: The Johns Hopkins University Press.

Steinbruner, John D. (1995) "Reluctant Strategic Realignment: The Need for a New View of National Security," *Brookings Review* 13 (Winter): 4–9.

Stengal, Richard. (1995) "Brink of Armageddon," *Time* (August 21): 44–46.

Sterling, Claire. (1994) *Thieves' World: The Threat of the New Global Network of Organized Crime*. New York: Simon & Schuster.

Stevens, William K. (1997) "Five Years after Rio Summit, Old Ways Still Dominate," *International Herald Tribune* (June 18): 4.

Stevenson, Richard W. (1997) "The Cost of 'Fast-Track' Seback," *International Herald Tribune* (November 11): 3.

Stockholm International Peace Research Institute (SIPRI). (1997) *SIPRI Yearbook 1997*. New York: Oxford University Press.

Strang, David. (1991) "Global Patterns of Decolonization, 1500–1987," *International Studies Quarterly* 35 (December): 429–545.

———. (1990) "From Dependence to Sovereignty: An Event History Analysis of Decolonization 1870–1987," *American Sociological Review* 55 (December): 846–60.

Strange, Susan. (1996) *The Retreat of the State*. Cambridge, Eng.: Cambridge University Press.

———. (1982) "Cave! Hic Dragones: A Critique of Regime Analysis," *International Organization* 36 (Spring): 479–96.

Sumner, William Graham. (1968) "War," pp. 205–28 in Leon Bramson and George W. Goethals (eds.), *War*. New York: Basic Books.

Talbott, Strobe. (1990) "Rethinking the Red Menace," *Time* (January 1): 66–72.

Taylor, Peter J. (ed.). (1990) *World Government*. New York: Oxford University Press.

Tefft, Sheila. (1995) "Rush to Burn Coal Turns China into Asia's Polluter," *Christian Science Monitor* (September 30): 1, 8.

Thompson, Kenneth W. (1960) *Political Realism and the Crisis of World Politics*. Princeton, N.J.: Princeton University Press.

———. (1953) "Collective Security Reexamined," *American Political Science Review* 47 (September): 753–72.

Thompson, William R. (1988) *On Global War: Historical-Structural Approaches to World Politics*. Columbia: University of South Carolina Press.

Thurow, Lester C. (1998) "The American Economy in the Next Century," *Harvard International Review* 20 (Winter): 54–59.

———. (1992) *Head to Head: Coming Economic Battles among Japan, Europe, and America*. New York: William Morrow.

Tickner, J. Ann. (1997) "You Just Don't Understand: Troubled Engagements between Feminists and IR Theorists," *International Studies Quarterly* 41 (December): 611–32.

———. (1992) *Gender in International Relations: Feminist Perspectives on Achieving Global Security*. New York: Columbia University Press.

Tilford, Earl H., Jr. (1995) *The Revolution in Military Affairs: Prospects and Cautions*. Carlisle Barracks, Penn.: U.S. Army War College.

Tillema, Herbert K. (1998) *Overt Military Intervention in the Cold War Era*. Columbia, S.C.: University of South Carolina Press.

———. (1994) "Cold War Alliance and Overt Military Intervention, 1945–1991," *International Interactions* 20 (No. 3): 249–78.

———. (1989) "Foreign Overt Military Intervention in the Nuclear Age," *Journal of Peace Research* 26 (May): 179–95.

Tillema, Herbert K., and John R. Van Wingen. (1982) "Law and Power in Military Intervention: Major States after World War II," *International Studies Quarterly* 26 (June): 220–50.

Timmerman, Kenneth. (1991) *The Death Lobby: How the West Armed Iraq*. Boston: Houghton Mifflin.

Todaro, Michael P. (1994) *Economic Development in the Third World*, 5th ed. New York: Longman.

Toffler, Alvin, and Heidi Toffler. (1993) *War and Anti-War: Survival at the Dawn of the Twenty-First Century*. New York: Little, Brown.

Toynbee, Arnold J. (1954) *A Study of History*. London: Oxford University Press.

Trachtenberg, Marc. (1990–1991) "The Meaning of Mobilization in 1914," *International Security* 15 (Winter): 120–50.

Triffin, Robert. (1978–1979) "The International Role and Fate of the Dollar," *Foreign Affairs* 57 (Winter): 269–86.

Tuchman, Barbara. (1962) *The Guns of August*. New York: Dell.

Tucker, Robert C., and David C. Hendrickson. (1990) *Empire of Liberty*. New York: Oxford University Press.

Ullman, Richard. (1983) "Refining Security," *International Security* 8 (Summer): 129–53.

United Nations. (1995) *World Population Prospects: The 1994 Revision*. New York: United Nations.

———. (1994a) *The Sex and Age Distribution of the World Populations: The 1994 Revision*. New York: United Nations.

———. (1994b) *World Social Situation in the 1990s*. New York: United Nations.

———. (1991) *World Economic Survey 1991*. (1991) New York: United Nations.

United Nations Development Programme (UNDP). (1997) *Human Development Report 1997*. New York: Oxford University Press.

———. (1995) *Human Development Report 1995*. New York: Oxford University Press.

———. (1994) *Human Development Report 1994*. New York: Oxford University Press.

———. (1993) *Human Development Report 1993*. New York: Oxford University Press.

———. (1991) *Human Development Report 1991*. New York: Oxford University Press.

United Nations Programme on Transnational Corporations. (1993) "World Investment Report 1993," *Transnational Corporations* 2 (August): 99–123.

U.S. Arms Control and Disarmament Agency [ACDA]. (1997) *World Military Expenditures and Arms Transfers 1995*. Washington, D.C.: U.S. Government Printing Office.

———. (1995) *World Military Expenditures and Arms Transfers 1993–1994*. Washington, D.C.: U.S. Government Printing Office.

U.S. CIA. (1997) *Handbook of International Economic Statistics*. Washington, D.C.: Government Printing Office.

U.S. Commission on Integrated Long-Term Strategy. (1988) *Discriminate Deterrence*. Washington, D.C.: U.S. Government Printing Office.

U.S. Department of State. (1998) *Patterns of Global Terrorism 1998*. Washington, D.C.: U.S. Department of State.

———. (1996) *Patterns of Global Terrorism 1996*. Washington, D.C.: U.S. Department of State.

———. (1995) *Patterns of Global Terrorism 1995*. Washington, D.C.: U.S. Department of State.

———. (1993) *State 2000: A New Model for Managing Foreign Affairs*. Washington, D.C.: Office of Management Task Force, U.S. Department of State.

———. (1991) *Patterns of Global Terrorism 1990*. Washington, D.C.: U.S. Department of State.

———. (1983) *Security and Arms Control: The Search for a More Stable Peace*. Washington, D.C.: U.S. Government Printing Office.

U.S. Office of Technology Assessment. (1981) *Technology and Soviet Energy Availability*. Washington, D.C.: U.S. Government Printing Office.

Urquhart, Brian. (1994) "Who Can Police the World?" *New York Review of Books* 41 (May 12): 29–33.

van de Kaa, Dirk J. (1987) "Europe's Second Demographic Transition," *Population Bulletin* 42 (No. 1). Washington, D.C.: Population Reference Bureau.

Van Evera, Stephen. (1994) "Hypotheses on Nationalism and War," *International Security* 18 (Spring): 5–39.

———. (1990–1991) "Primed for Peace: Europe after the Cold War," *International Security* 15 (Winter): 7–57.

Vasquez, John A. (1997) "The Realist Paradigm and Degenerative versus Progressive Research Programs," *American Political Science Review* 91 (December): 899–912.

———. (1993) *The War Puzzle*. Cambridge, Eng.: Cambridge University Press.

———. (1991) "The Deterrence Myth: Nuclear Weapons and the Prevention of Nuclear War," pp. 205–23 in Charles W. Kegley, Jr. (ed.), *The Long Postwar Peace*. New York: HarperCollins.

Väyrynen, Raimo. (1992) *Military Industrialization and Economic Development*. Aldershot, Eng.: Dartmouth.

Verba, Sidney. (1969) "Assumptions of Rationality and Non-Rationality in Models of the International System," pp. 217–31 in James N. Rosenau (ed.), *International Politics and Foreign Policy*. New York: Free Press.

Vernon, Raymond. (1971) *Sovereignty at Bay*. New York: Basic Books.

Vital Signs 1997. (1997) Lester R. Brown, Michael Renner, and Christopher Flavin, et al., eds. New York: W. W. Norton.

Walker, Martin. (1995a) "The Next American Internationalism," *World Policy Journal* 12 (Summer): 52–54.

———. (1995b) "Overstretching Teutonia: Making the Best of the Fourth Reich," *World Policy Journal* 12 (Spring): 1–18.

Walker, R. B. J. (1993) *Inside/Outside: International Relations as Political Theory*. Cambridge, Eng.: Cambridge University Press.

Walker, William O. (1991) "Decision-Making Theory and Narcotic Foreign Policy: Implications for Historical Analysis," *Diplomatic History* 15 (Winter): 31–45.

Wallace, Brian. (1978) "True Grit South of the Border," *Osceola* (January 13): 15–16.

Wallensteen, Peter, and Margareta Sollenberg. (1997) "Armed Conflicts, Conflict Termination and Peace Agreements, 1989–96," *Journal of Peace Research* 34 (May): 339–58.

———. (1995) "After the Cold War: Emerging Patterns of Armed Conflict 1989–94," *Journal of Peace Research* 32 (August): 345–60.

Waller, Douglas. (1995) "Onward Cyber Soldiers," *Time* (August 21): 40–46.

Wallerstein, Immanuel. (1988) *The Modern World-System III: The Second Era of Great Expansion of the Capitalist World-System, 1730–1840.* San Diego: Academic Press.

———. (1980) *The Modern World-System II.* New York: Academic Press.

———. (1974a) *The Modern World-System: Capitalist Agriculture and the Origins of the European World-Economy in the Sixteenth Century.* New York: Academic Press.

———. (1974b) "The Rise and Future Demise of the World Capitalist System: Concepts for Comparative Analysis," *Comparative Studies in Society and History* 16 (September): 387–415.

Walter, Barbara F. (1997) "The Critical Barrier to Civil War Settlement," *International Organization* 51 (Summer): 335–64.

Walters, Robert S., and David H. Blake. (1992) *The Politics of Global Economic Relations,* 4th ed. Englewood Cliffs, N.J.: Prentice Hall.

Waltz, Kenneth N. (1995) "Realist Thought and Neorealist Theory," pp. 67–83 in Charles W. Kegley, Jr. (ed.), *Controversies in International Relations Theory: Realism and the Neoliberal Challenge.* New York: St. Martin's Press.

———. (1993) "The Emerging Structure of International Politics," *International Security* 18 (Fall): 44–79.

———. (1979) *Theory of International Politics.* Reading, Mass.: Addison-Wesley.

———. (1964) "The Stability of a Bipolar World," *Daedalus* 93 (Summer): 881–909.

———. (1954) *Man, the State, and War.* New York: Columbia University Press.

Ward, Michael D., David R. Davis, and Corey L. Lofdahl. (1995) "A Century of Tradeoffs: Defense and Growth in Japan and the United States," *International Studies Quarterly* 39 (March): 27–50.

Warrick, Joby. (1998) "Turning Cool Toward the Kyoto Accords," *Washington Post National Weekly* 15 (February 23): 31.

———. (1997) "How Warm Will It Get?" *Washington Post National Weekly Edition* 14 (December 1): 6–7.

Watson, Douglas. (1997) "Indigenous Peoples and the Global Economy," *Current History* 96 (November): 389–91.

Weart, Spencer R. (1994) "Peace among Democratic and Oligarchic Republics," *Journal of Peace Research* 31 (August): 299–316.

Weinberg, Gerhard L. (1994) *A World at Arms: A Global History of World War II.* Cambridge, Eng.: Cambridge University Press.

Weiner, Myron. (1995) *The Global Migration Crisis: Challenges to States and Human Rights.* New York: HarperCollins.

Wendt, Alexander. (1992) "Anarchy Is What States Make of It: The Social Construction of Power Politics." *International Organization* 46 (Spring): 395–424.

Wendzel, Robert L. (1980) *International Relations: A Policymaker Focus.* New York: Wiley.

White, Donald W. (1998) "Mutable Destiny: The End of the American Century?" *Harvard International Review* 20 (Winter): 42–47.

White, Ralph K. (1990) "Why Aggressors Lose," *Political Psychology* 11 (June): 227–42.

White, Robert M. (1998) "Climate Science and National Interests: Coping with Global Climate Change," pp. 430–37 in Charles W. Kegley, Jr. and Eugene R. Wittkopf (eds.), *The Global Agenda,* 5th ed. New York: McGraw-Hill.

Whiting, Allen S. (1985) "Foreign Policy of China," pp. 246–90 in Roy C. Macridis (ed.), *Foreign Policy in World Politics,* 6th ed. Englewood Cliffs, N.J.: Prentice Hall.

Wilmer, Franke. (1993) *The Indigenous Voice in World Politics: Since Time Immemorial.* Newbury Park, Calif.: Sage.

Wilson, James Q. (1993) *The Moral Sense.* New York: Free Press.

"Wireless Phones Ring Off the Hook." (1995). *Christian Science Monitor* (May 31): 1, 7.

Wise, Michael Z. (1993) "Reparations," *Atlantic Monthly* 272 (October): 32–35.

Wittkopf, Eugene R. (1990) *Faces of Internationalism: Public Opinion and American Foreign Policy.* Durham, N.C.: Duke University Press.

Wolfers, Arnold. (1962) *Discord and Collaboration.* Baltimore: Johns Hopkins University Press.

Woods, Alan. (1989) *Development and the National Interest: U.S. Economic Assistance into the 21st Century.* Washington, D.C.: Agency for International Development.

Woodward, Bob. (1991) *The Commanders.* New York: Simon & Schuster.

Woodward, Bob, and Rick Atkinson. (1990) "Launching Operation Desert Shield," *Washington Post National Weekly Edition* 7 (September 3–9): 8–9.

The World Bank Atlas 1996. (1995). Washington, D.C.: World Bank.

World Bank. (1997) *World Development Report 1997.* New York: Oxford University Press.

———. (1996) *World Debt Tables 1996,* Vol. 1. Washington, D.C.: World Bank.

———. (1995a) *Global Economic Prospects and the Developing Countries 1995.* Washington, D.C.: World Bank.

———. (1995b) *Monitoring Environmental Progress.* Washington, D.C.: World Bank.

World Development Report 1997. (1997) New York: Oxford University Press.

World Development Report 1995. (1995) New York: Oxford University Press.

World Development Report 1992. (1992) New York: Oxford University Press.

World Economic and Social Survey 1995. (1995). New York: United Nations.

World Factbook 1997. (1997) Washington, D.C.: U.S. Central Intelligence Agency.

World Health Report 1995. (1995). Geneva: World Health Organization.

World Investment Report 1995. (1995). New York: United Nations.

World Investment Report 1994. (1994). New York: United Nations.

World Refugee Survey 1995. (1995). Washington, D.C.: U.S. Committee for Refugees.

World Resources Institute. (1994) *World Resources 1994–95.* New York: Oxford University Press.

Wright, Quincy. (1953) "The Outlawry of War and the Law of War," *American Journal of International Law* 47 (July): 365–76.

———. (1942) *A Study of War.* Chicago: University of Chicago Press.

Wurst, Jim. (1996) "Inching Toward a Ban," *Bulletin of the Atomic Scientists* 52 (March/April): 10–12.

Yearbook of International Organizations, 1996/97. (1997) Vols.1 and 2. Munich: K.G. Sauer.

Yoder, Edwin M., Jr. (1991) "Isolationists Would Put America on a Dangerous Course," *The State* (Columbia, S.C.) (December 14): A10.

Young, John E. (1991) "Reducing Waste, Saving Materials," pp. 39–55 in Lester R. Brown et al., *State of the World 1991*. New York: Norton.

Young, Oran R. (1995) "System and Society in World Affairs: Implications for International Organizations," *International Social Science Journal* 144 (June): 197–212.

Zacher, Mark W. (1987) "Trade Gaps, Analytical Gaps: Regime Analysis and International Commodity Regulation," *International Organization* 41 (Spring): 173–202.

Zacher, Mark W., and Richard A. Matthew. (1995) "Liberal International Theory: Common Threads, Divergent Strands," pp. 107–49 in Charles W. Kegley, Jr. (ed.), *Controversies in International Relations Theory: Realism and the Neoliberal Challenge*. New York: St. Martin's Press.

Zagare, Frank C. (1990) "Rationality and Deterrence," *World Politics* 42 (January): 238–60.

Zakaria, Fareed. (1992–1993) "Is Realism Finished?" *The National Interest* 30 (Winter): 21–32.

Zelikow, Philip. (1987) "The United States and the Use of Force: A Historical Summary," pp. 31–81 in George K. Osburn et al. (eds.), *Democracy, Strategy, and Vietnam*. Lexington, Mass.: Lexington Books.

Ziegler, David. (1995) Review of *World Politics and the Evolution of War* by John Weltman, *American Political Science Review* 89 (September): 813–14.

Zimmerman, Tim. (1996) "CIA Study: Why Do Countries Fall Apart?" *U.S. News & World Report* 120 (February 12): 46.

———. (1994) "Arms Merchant to the World," *U.S. News & World Report* (April 4): 37.

Zinnes, Dina A., and Jonathan Wilkenfeld. (1971) "An Analysis of Foreign Conflict Behavior of Nations," pp. 167–213 in Wolfram F. Handieder (ed.), *Comparative Foreign Policy*. New York: McKay.

Acknowledgments

Acknowledgments *(continued from copyright page)*

Map 1.4: World View Time. Source: Copyright © World View Time, Inc., 1989. Reprinted by permission of World View Time, Inc., P.O. Box 266, Brockville, Ontario, Canada K6V5V5.

Map 2.1: Regimes and the Transnational Management of Global Problems: Acid Rain. Source: Adapted from Seager (1995), *The New State of the Earth Atlas* (New York: Touchstone), 48–49.

Focus 3.1: Democracies in Foreign Affairs: A U.S. Policymaker's Characterization. Source: Excerpt from George F. Kennan, *American Diplomacy 1900–1950* (1951: New American Library), p. 59. Reprinted by permission of the University of Chicago Press.

Map 4.1: Territorial Changes in Europe following World War I. Source: *Strategic Atlas, Comparative Geopolitics of the World's Powers*, third edition by Gérard Chaliand and Jean-Pierre Rageau. Copyright © 1993 by Gérard Chaliand and Jean-Pierre Rageau. Reprinted by permission of HarperCollins Publishers, Inc.

Map 4.2: Territorial Changes in Europe following World War II. Source: Europe 1938 is based on Map 5.3 from Charles W. Kegley, Jr. and Gregory A. Raymond (1944a: 118); Europe 1945 is from *Strategic Atlas, Comparative Geopolitics of the World's Powers*, third edition by Gérard Chaliand and Jean-Pierre Rageau. Copyright © 1993 by Gérard Chaliand and Jean-Pierre Rageau. Reprinted by permission of HarperCollins Publishers, Inc.

Figure 4.1: U.S.–Soviet Relations during the Cold War, 1948–1991. Source: Adapted from Edward E. Azar's Conflict and Peace Data Bank (COPDAB), with data based on Edward E. Azar and Thomas J. Sloan (1973). Data for 1966–1991 are derived from the World Interaction Survey (WEIS), as compiled and scaled by Professor Rodney G. Tomlinson.

Map 4.3: Emerging Centers of Power in a New International Hierarchy. Source: United States Central Intelligence Agency (1994:22).

Figure 5.1: Differences in the Global North and South. Source: Population Reference Bureau, McEvedy and Jones. Data presented in *World Bank Atlas, 1995*.

Map 5.2: Groups of Economies: The Geographic Distribution of GNP per Capita 1995. Source: *World Development Report 1995*, pp. 158–159. World Bank, Washington, D.C.

Focus 5.1: Measuring Living Standards: GNP per Capita versus Purchasing Power Parity. Source: *1995 World Population Data Sheet*. Population Reference Bureau.

Focus 5.2: Measuring Development: GNP per Capita versus Human Development. Source: United Nations Development Programme (UNDP), *Human Development Report 1995*. Reprinted by permission of the United Nations Bureau of External Relations.

Focus 5.3: A Balance Sheet on Human Development in the Global South. Source: Extracted and adapted from the United Nations Development Programme, *Human Development Report 1995*. Reprinted by permission of the United Nations Bureau of External Relations.

Table 5.1: Level of Human Development and Related Economic Attributes (selected countries). Source: Adapted from the United Nations Development Programme, *Human Development Report 1995*. Reprinted by permission of the United Nations Bureau of External Relations.

Focus 6.1: The Politics of UN Membership: The Case of Taiwan. Source: *The Economist* (December 10, 1994: 16). Copyright © 1994 The Economist Newspaper Group, Inc. Reprinted with permission. Further reproduction prohibited.

Figure 6.1: The Number of States, IGOs, and NGOs since 1990. Note: Figures for states are based on the Correlates of War (COW) project at the University of Michigan under the direction of J. David Singer. Source: States, Polity III data (Jaggers and Gurr, 1995); IGOs and Ngos, *Yearbook of International Organizations, 1993/1994* (1993: 1699), and moving averages from selected prior volumes. Reprinted with permission of the Union of International Associations, Belgium.

Figure 6.2: The Changing Membership of the United Nations, 1946–1998. Source: United Nations, using classifications of regions of the U.S. Department of State (1985: 18).

Figure 6.4: The UN at Fifty: A Look at Its First Half-Century. Source: *New York Times* (October 22, 1995: 8). Copyright © 1995 by The New York Times Company. Reprinted by permission.

Figure 6.5: The Structure of the European Union. Source: Adapted from the European Commission to the United States, 1995.

Figure 6.6: The Co-Decision Procedure for the European Union. Source: The European Commission Delegation to the United States (1994:10 11).

Figure 6.7: The Cross-Crossing Memberships of Europe's Primary International Institutions, 1998. Source: *NATO Review* 43 (November 1995).

Focus 7.2: Where the Creed Is Greed: The Threat of the Global Network of Organized Crime. Source: Richard H. Schultz, National Strategy Information Agency. Reprinted by permission.

Page 202: Excerpt from *Global Dreams: Imperial Corporations and the New World Order* by Richard J. Barnet and John J. Cavanagh. Copyright © 1994 by Richard J. Barnet and John J. Cavanagh. Simon & Schuster, Inc.

Page 202: Excerpt from The Commission on Transnational Corporations, 1991. Source: The Commission on Transnational Corporations, 1991: 33.

Map 7.1: The World's Great Cultural Domains. Source: *Strategic Atlas, Comparative Geopolitics of the World's Powers*, third edition by Gérard Chaliand and Jean-Pierre Rageau. Copyright © 1993 by Gérard Chaliand and Jean-Pierre Rageau. Reprinted by permission of HarperCollins Publishers, Inc.

Map 7.2: The Geographic Concentration of the World's Principal Religions. Source: *Concise Earth Atlas* (1994: 11). Bo Gramfors and Siu Eklund, Maps International AB. Reprinted by permission.

Figure 7.1: Ethnopolitical Groups Involved in Serious Conflicts since 1945. Source: *Minorities at Risk: A Global View of Ethnopolitical Conflicts*. Ted Robert Gurr (1993). United States Institute of Peace: Washington, D.C.

Map 7.3: Caesar and God: State Support for Particular Religions in a Pluralistic World Community. Source: Adapted from *State of the World Atlas*, New Edition, by Michael Kidron and Ronald Segal. Copyright © 1995 by Michael Kidron and Ronald Segal, text. Copyright © 1995 by Myriad Editions Limited, maps and graphics. Used by permission of Viking Penguin, a division of Penguin Books USA Inc., and Myriad Editions Limited: London, England.

Focus 8.1: Comparative Advantage and the Gains from Trade. Source: Adapted from Daniel Rosen, "The Basics of Foreign Trade and Exchange" (New York: Federal Reserve Bank of New York, 1987).

Figure 8.4: The Decline of Tariffs in the Industrialized Countries, 1940 Projected to 2000. Source: Office of the U.S. Trade Representative and the Center for International Economics as upgraded by *Time* (December 27, 1993: 16).

Focus 9.2: The Internet: Cyberspace Pros and Cons. Source: Excerpt from "The Internet Elite" pp. 44–45 in *Bulletin of the Atomic Scientists* 51 (July/August 1995). Copyright © 1995 by the Educational Foundation for Nuclear Science, 6042 South Kimbark Avenue, Chicago, Illinois, 60637, USA. A one-year subscription is $36.00 Reprinted by permission.

Figure 9.2: Growth of World Output and Trade, 1981–1996. Source: *World Economic and Social Survey 1995*: 35. Copyright © United Nations. All United Nations rights reserved.

Figure 9.3: The Global South in World Trade. Source: *Global Economic Prospects and the Developing Countries, 1995* (Washington: D.C. The World Bank, 1995: 58).

Map 9.1: Uneven Spread: Global Connections to the Internet. Source: Adapted from *Time* (1995), 81.

Focus 10.2: The "Graying" of Nations. Source: Kevin G. Kinsella, "An Aging World Population." from *World Health* (July-August 1994), the magazine of the World Health Organization. Reprinted with permission.

Focus 11.1: National Security and Environmental Security: Competing or Complementary? Source: Excerpt from pp. 218–220 from *Current History*. Reprinted by permission.

Focus 11.2: The Making of an Ecological Disaster: The Aral Sea. Source: Excerpt from p. 38 in *World Development Report 1992*.

Focus 11.4: Free Trade and Sustainable Development: An Oxymoron? Source: excerpt from p. 67 in *World Development Report 1992*.

Figure 11.1: World Oil Demand, 1994 and 2010. Source: Adapted from *World Economic and Social Survey 1995* (New York: United Nations, 1995: 168).

Figure 11.2: Crude Oil Prices since 1861. Source: *BP Statistical Review of World Energy* (1995): 12.

Figure 11.3: Ratio of Fossil-Fuel Reserves to Production. Source: *BP Statistical Review of World Energy* (1995): 36.

Map 11.1: Forests and Rainforests. Source: Pulp and Paper International, 600 Harrison Street, San Francisco, CA. 94107.

Figure 12.2: The Percentage of the World's Governments That Are Fully "Free" Democracies. Source: Herman, Kegley, and Raymond (1995), based on Polity III data (Jaggers and Gurr, 1995).

Figure 12.3: The Long Cycle of Global Leadership and Global War, 1492–2000. Source: Adapted from George Modelski (1987a: 6).

Figure 12.4: International Terrorist Incidents, 1968–1997. Source: Office of the Coordination of Counterterrorism, U.S. Department of State.

Figure 13.1: The World's Twenty Leading Military Spenders and Armed Forces, 1995. Source: U.S. Arms Control and Disarmament Agency (1995: 4).

Figure 13.2: The Ebb and Flow of World Military Expenditures, 1961–1995. Source: U.S. Arms Control and Disarmament Agency (1995: 1).

Map 13.1: Nuclear Nations and the States Likely to Join the Nuclear Club. Source: Projections based on predictions provided by the Arms Control Association, March 1996.

Table 13.1: The Power Potential of the Great Powers: The Top Ten Ranked by Five Measures. Source: Territory, *World Bank Atlas* (1995); population and GDP, U.S. CIA (1995: 32–33, 24–25); scientists, Hughes (1994: 82).

Table 13.2: The Relative Burden, or Economic Costs to the Average Citizen, of States' Military Expenditures, 1995. Source: U.S. ACDA (1995: 25).

Focus 13.3: Redefining "Security" in the New World Order. Source: Excerpt from *World Security* by Michael T. Klare and Daniel C. Thomas, editors. Copyright © 1991 by Michael T. Klare and Daniel C. Thomas. Reprinted with permission of St. Martin's Press, Inc.

Page 438: Excerpts from pp. 247–269 in *The Long Postwar Peace* by Charles W. Kegley, Jr. Copyright © 1990 by Charles W. Kegley, Jr. Reprinted by permission of HarperCollins Publishers, Inc.

Figure 14.1: The Changing Strategic Balance, 1990, 1997, and 2003. Source: Adapted from the Stockholm International Peace Research Institute (SIPRI): *SIPRI Yearbook 1995*.

Figure 14.3: International Tension since World War I: The Annual Frequency of International Crises, 1918–2000. Source: *Crises in World Politics: Theory and Reality* by Michael Brecher. Copyright © 1993 by Michael Brecher. (Oxford, England: Pergamon).

Map 14.1: Vulnerable Single-Commodity-Dependent Economies. Source: *Handbook of International Economic Statistics 1995* (Washington, D.C.: Central Intelligence Agency, 1995), pp. 130-131.

Focus 15.2: The Balance of Power: A Precarious and Failed Security System? Source: Excerpt from *Review of International Studies* 15 (January 1989): 77–85. Reprinted with permission.

Table 15.2: Major Multilateral Arms Control Treaties since 1945. Source: Adapted from R. Ferm, "Arms Control and Disarmament Agreements." Stockholm International Peace Research Institute, SIPRI Yearbook 1995: Armaments, Disarmament, and International Security (Oxford University Press: Oxford, 1995), Annexe A, pp. 839–871. Reprinted by permission.

Figure 15.1: Countdown to Strategic Parity: The Negotiated End of the U.S.–Russian Arms Race. Source: Robert S. Norris and William M. Arkin, "Estimated U.S. and Soviet/Russian Nuclear Stockpiles, 1945–1994" *Bulletin of Atomic Scientists* (November/December 1994). See Worldwatch publication *Vital Signs 1995* for further information. Reprinted by permission.

Figure 16.1: The Legal Prohibition of War of Aggression since 1815. Source: Transnational Rules Indicators Project (TRIP) from *When Trust Breaks Down: Alliance Norms and World Politics* by Charles W. Kegley, Jr. and Gregory A. Raymond. Copyright © 1990 by Charles W. Kegley, Jr. and Gregory A. Raymond. The University of South Carolina Press. Reprinted by permission.

Figure 16.2: The Changing Status of the Nonintervention Rule in International Law since 1820. Source: As measured in "The Decay of the Nonintervention Principle" paper presented at the Joint Conference of the Japan Association of International Relations (JAIR) and the International Studies Association (ISA), Tokyo (September 20, 1995). Margaret G. Hermann and Charles W. Kegley Jr., and Gregory A. Raymond. Reprinted by permission.

Map 16.1: The Legal Battle over East Timor. Source: Adapted from "East Timor" map by Dave Herring. *Christian Science Monitor* (February 1, 1995), p. 7. Copyright © The Christian Science Monitor. Reprinted by permission.

Map 16.2: UN Peace Missions since 1948. Source: United Nations.

Photo Credits

Chapter 1: Page 4: Eric Bouvet/Gamma Liaison; 11: I. Uimonen/Sygma; 17: NASA.

Chapter 2: Page 25: The Granger Collection, N.Y.; Corbis/Bettmann; 28: Scala/Art Resource, N.Y.; Bridgeman/Art Resource, N.Y.

Chapter 3: Page 49: Orban/Sygma; 57: Barbara Kinney/The White House; 63: UPI/Corbis/Bettmann; 70: AP/Wide World.

Chapter 4: Page 76: Robert Harbison/The Christian Science Monitor; 84: Topham/Image Works; 94: Biber/Sipa.

Chapter 5: Page 110: Rene Burri/Magnum; 113: Corbis/Bettmann; 121: J.P. Laffont/Sygma; 125: Tim Holt/Photo Researchers; 136: Les Stone/Sygma.

Chapter 6: Page 150: UPI/Corbis/Bettmann; 161: Figaro Magazine/Gamma Liaison.

Chapter 7: Page 178: Tannenbaum/Sygma; 183: Seamus Conlan, F.S.P./Gamma Liaison; 188: P. Aventurier/Gamma Liaison; 201: Bob Nickelsberg/Time Magazine.

Chapter 8: Page 217: Culver Pictures; 233: Frederic J.Brown/AFP; Eric Feferberg/AFP; 238: Kurita, Murayama/Gamma Liaison; 242: Jeffrey Aaronson/Network Aspen.

Chapter 9: Page 249: Sally Wiener Grotta/The Stock Market; 264: P.F. Bentley/Black Star; Frank Fournier/Contact; 268: Jeffrey Aaronson/Network Aspen; 272: Ira Wyman/Sygma.

Chapter 10: Page 291: Mariella Furrer/Saba; 299: Robert Harbison/Christian Science Monitor; 307: AP/Wide World.

Chapter 11: Page 316: Ray Ellis/Photo Researchers; Steve Vidler/Leo de Wys; 329: Daniel Beltra/Greenpeace; 336: Wesley Bocxe/Photo Researchers.

Chapter 12: Page 349: Sygma; 355: Noel Quidu/Gama Liaison; 371: A. Yagobzadeh/Sipa; 378: Reuters/Flash '90/Archive Photos.

Chapter 13: Page 392: Scott Peterson/Gamma Liaison; 395: Lockheed Martin; 398: AP/Wide World; 412: U.S. Air Force; 418: China Features/Sygma.

Chapter 14: Page 430: Copyright © NASM/Sygma; 431: Bernard Hermann/Gamma Liaison; 445: AP/Wide World; 447: AP/Wide World; 452: AP/Wide World; 458 © 1996 Charles Crowell/Black Star.

Chapter 15: Page 466: The Granger Collection, NY; 476: Reuters/Archive Photos; 480: Reuters/Archive Photos; 485: H. Ardvisson/Un Photo.

Chapter 16: Page 505: Erich Lessing/Art Resource, NY; 517: AFP Photo; 529: Reuters/Peter Morgan/Archive Photos; 533: Reuters/Archive Photos.

Chapter 17: Page 551: AP/Wide World; 552: AFP/Corbis/Bettmann; 559: NASA.

Index

Note: Glossary terms appear in boldfaced type. Boldfaced page numbers indicate pages where definitions appear. Page numbers followed by italicized letters *f, m,* and *t* indicate figures, maps, and tables, respectively.

607